Part II: Using the Inquiry Process

Part III: Developing Projects

Photo Credits

Shutterstock: iv, v, vii, ix, x, xii, xv, 7, 14, 18, 27, 33, 34, 40, 42, 43, 49, 51, 55, 58, 60, 62, 65, 69, 72, 73, 77, 78, 81, 91, 93, 100, 105, 107, 116, 119, 122, 128, 131, 144, 147, 155, 160, 163, 167, 168, 169, 171, 172, 173, 175, 177, 180, 182, 185, 192, 193, 197, 199, 201, 205, 216, 218, 222, 224, 225, 234, 241, 244, 247, 251, 252, 255, 256, 273, 274, 279, 281, 282, 283, 286, 288, 292, 295, 297, 299, 302, 305, 317, 321, 329, 337, 339, 340, 342, 345, 348, 357, 362, 367, 373, 379, 382, 383, 385, 386, 389, 400, 401, 406, 408, 410, 416, 419, 422, 425, 427, 428, 433, 434, 435, 436, 437, 438, 439, 440, 441, 442, 446, 447, 448, 449, 450, 451, 452, 455, 456, 459, 460, 461, 462, 463, 464, 465, 469, 470, 471, 472, 473, 474, 475, 478, 479, 480, 481, 482, 489, 484, 494, 495, 497, 509, 510, 511, 513, 514, 518, 519, 520, 521, 522, 523, 524, 529, 530, 531, 534, 535, 536, 537, 539, 540, 542, 543, 544, 545, 551, 552, 553, 555, 557, 558, 559, 560, 561, 565, 566, 567, 571, 572, 573, 575, 576, 577, 579, 581, 582, 583, 585, 586, 587, 591, 592, 593, 595, 596, 597, 601, 605

Wikimedia: 5, 14, 36, 219, 223, 225, 234, 270, 412, 464, 465, 499, 501, 513, 516, 553

Flickr: 516, 517, 535, 577, 587

Liter of Light: 52

Why *Inquire?*

What do artists, engineers, scientists, doctors, and students like you have in common? All of you have to ask questions, conduct research, communicate, and collaborate to do your best work. In fact, skills like these are at the core of real learning.

A Handbook for 21st Century Skills

Inquire will help you learn about and practice all of the key learning skills. Here are the main skills covered in the first part of the book:

- Critical and creative thinking
- Collaborating and communicating
- Problem solving and building arguments
- Understanding and using media
- Studying and taking tests

A Handbook for Inquiry and Projects

Inquire also helps you use the inquiry process to solve problems and develop great projects. Here are some of the inquiry-based skills and projects covered in the next two parts of the book:

- Asking questions and planning research
- Creating and presenting projects
- Developing writing and Web projects
- Building audio-visual and graphic projects
- Preparing community and performing projects

A Handbook for All of Your Classes

You can use *Inquire* in all of your classes, in your extracurricular activities, and in life itself. *Inquire* will help you succeed right now and prepare you to learn and succeed for years to come!

Part I:
Building 21st Century Skills

Part I: Building 21st Century Skills

This section covers all of the important 21st century skills—and more. If you follow the strategies in each chapter, you will become a better thinker and learner now and for years to come. These skills will also help you use the inquiry process and create great projects in Parts II and III.

Chapters in This Section

Chapter 1
Overview of 21st Century Skills

Imagine for a moment what life was like just 10 years ago. There was no Facebook. No Twitter. No YouTube, GPS, smartphones, texting. Now imagine what life will be like 10 years from now. It's almost impossible to do. New innovations and events may completely change your world. How can you be ready?

You can begin by learning the 21st century skills discussed in general in this chapter and more thoroughly later on. You can sharpen your critical thinking, improve your creative thinking, hone your communication skills, become a problem solver, and much more.

That's what this book is meant to do—help you prepare for and thrive in a future you can't even imagine.

You will learn . . .

- Your Brain: A User's Guide
- Critical and Creative Thinking
- Communicating and Collaborating
- Building Arguments
- Literacy Skills
- 21st Century Skills in Context

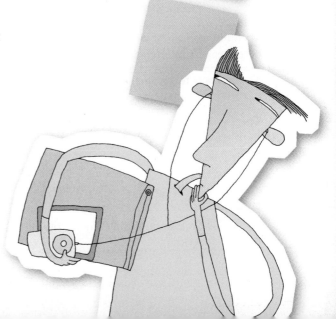

Your Brain: A User's Guide

Learning 21st century skills means fine-tuning your brain. Let's begin by examining a few myths and facts about the brain.

Brain Myths and Facts

Your brain weighs only three pounds but requires 20 percent of the energy your body uses. That makes it the highest-maintenance organ in your body. The cost is worth it. Your brain is more powerful than a supercomputer. The facts about your brain are more amazing than the myths:

Myths	Facts
I use only 10 percent of my brain.	You use all of your brain, just at different times.
My left hemisphere is logical, and my right hemisphere is creative.	Your left brain controls the right half of your body, and your right brain controls the left half; but logic and creativity stem from both hemispheres.
I have a set number of neurons, and they never grow back.	Your brain is constantly growing new neurons and making new connections. You can change your IQ, up or down.
Modern technology makes me less smart.	Modern technology does rewire the way your brain works, but thoughtful use of technology can actually make you smarter.
My brain works best under pressure.	Excess pressure reduces performance. Your brain needs nourishment, sleep, safety, and social connection to work best.
My brain works best without other people's interference.	Human brains are social. Your brain wants to connect with others.
The best way to get smart is to do brainteasers.	The best way to get smart is to use your brain to do things you want to do.
There is no such thing as a sixth sense.	There are more than five senses. Proprioception tells you where your body is in space. Nociception is the perception of pain. You have other senses, too, including a sense of balance.

Your Turn Go to thoughtfullearning.com/h4 to find links to articles about these and other brain facts.

Understanding the Parts and Functions

Let's take a quick look at the brain's parts and what they do for you. At any given time, many areas of your brain are firing. Consider this example: You walk into class (cerebellum and parietal lobe), see your friend (occipital lobe), wave (cerebellum), say "hi" and smile (temporal lobe, cerebellum, and endocrine glands), and make a joke about a movie you both saw (frontal and temporal lobes and endocrine glands). And you haven't even sat down yet.

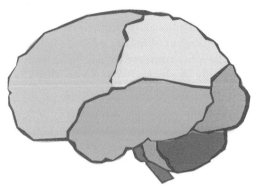

Occipital Lobe Sight

Parietal Lobe Sensory Integration; Proprioception

Temporal Lobe Hearing; Language; Long-Term Memory

Endocrine Glands Autonomic Regulation and Emotion

Cerebellum Motor Function; Muscle Memory

Frontal Lobe Logic; Planning; Decision Making; Short-Term Memory

Medulla Oblongata Circulation and Respiration; Involuntary Function

Understanding the Types of Thinking

Your brain processes many different types of information, each of which requires a specific kind of thinking:

- **Sensations** provide information from the senses.
- **Perceptions** are your thoughts about what you are sensing.
- **Memories** are experiences and ideas you have gathered.
- **Emotions** are states that shape your behavior and connect you to others.
- **Executive functions** are conscious actions, such as decision making, planning, and problem solving.
- **Motor functions** are muscle movements.
- **Mechanical functions** are unconscious actions.

Your Turn

1. Which type of thinking is dominant when you play a sport? When you read a novel? When you hang out with friends?

2. Which of the myths or facts about the brain was most surprising to you? Imagine that you wanted to increase your IQ by 10 points. What would you do? Why?

3. When you learn something new, your brain grows new neural connections. That's why learning works best when it happens over time rather than all at once. What does this fact tell you about cramming for tests or reading a novel in a single evening?

Critical and Creative Thinking

Everyone needs to think critically and creatively, just as everyone needs to breathe in and breathe out. These two key thinking patterns work together in most activities you do.

Critical Thinking

Critical thinking is focused, careful, and intentional. It's sometimes called *convergent thinking* because your thoughts converge on a topic as you study it closely. When you think critically, you do the following:

Identify	Analyze
Reason	Classify
Diagram	Evaluate
Measure	Critique
Assess	Implement
Organize	Choose

Creative Thinking

Creative thinking is expansive, prolific, and original. It's sometimes called *divergent thinking* because creative thoughts often reach out into the unknown. When you think creatively, you do the following:

Wonder	Prototype
Imagine	Create
Brainstorm	Innovate
Connect	Renovate
Revolutionize	Improvise
Invent	Improve

Problem Solving: Problem solving involves a series of steps that move back and forth between critical and creative thinking. Though no two problems are ever solved in exactly the same way, here's a general map of problem solving.

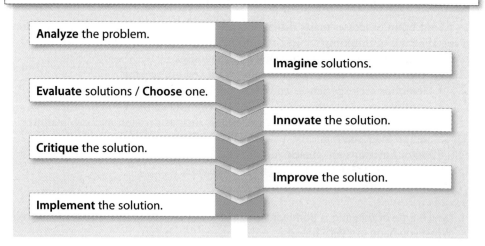

Analyze the problem.

Imagine solutions.

Evaluate solutions / **Choose** one.

Innovate the solution.

Critique the solution.

Improve the solution.

Implement the solution.

Your Turn Think of another activity that requires problem solving, such as setting up your school schedule or designing a homecoming float. Create your own map like the one above to lay out your path through critical and creative thinking to complete this problem-solving task.

Communicating

Your brain needs other brains. Human beings invented language so that they could share ideas with each other. Listening, speaking, writing, and reading all play a role as your brain communicates with others.

Every communication situation has five basic parts: sender, message, medium, receiver, and context. Whether you're writing a blog post, speaking to your friend's parents, or listening to a physics lecture, these five parts are influencing the situation.

The Communication Situation

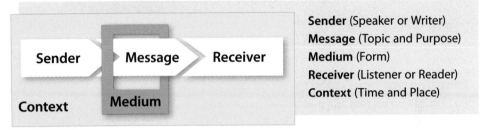

Sender (Speaker or Writer)
Message (Topic and Purpose)
Medium (Form)
Receiver (Listener or Reader)
Context (Time and Place)

Your Turn Think about a recent communication situation you experienced. Identify each of the five parts. Was the communication successful or unsuccessful? What challenges did you face or could you have faced in the situation?

Collaborating

Working with others goes beyond communication. You need to connect with others, develop trust, conduct meetings, brainstorm ideas, set common goals, plan work, make decisions, delegate duties, cooperate, resolve conflicts, and present your work. These abilities are key to your success in school, in the workplace, and in life. In this photo, students work together on a book drive for children in Ghana.

Clive Chilvers / Shutterstock.com

Your Turn Write down a big problem in your school or community. Perhaps the school is facing budget cuts, or some students are getting bullied, or the community has a lot of homeless people. These problems may feel too big for you to solve on your own, but what would happen if you worked with others? List people you could work with. Then write a paragraph reflecting on ways that you could collaborate to solve the problem you identified.

Building Arguments

Arguing with your friends is one thing, but do you know how to build a logical argument? In this book you'll discover how to use premises and inferences to reach conclusions, marshal evidence for your position, and ethically persuade the reader. Here is a quick overview of the types of arguments you will learn about.

Deductive arguments reason from a general premise to a specific case.	**Inductive arguments** reason from a specific case to a general conclusion.

General Rule		Specific Case	Specific Case		General Rule

Persuasive arguments appeal to readers' needs.
Ethical persuasion fairly addresses needs like those below:
- Physiological needs
- Safety
- Love and belonging
- Esteem
- Self-actualization

Avoiding Logical Fallacies

Of course, not all persuasion is ethical. You'll learn to recognize the logical fallacies that are commonly used by individuals, organizations, and campaigns to influence your thinking. Recognizing these fallacies will help you think critically about the information you receive. Here are a few of the fallacies that you will learn about.

Logical Fallacies

Ad hoc reasoning	False cause	Red herring
Ad hominem	False continuum	Reductio ad absurdum
Ad ignorantiam	False dichotomy	Slippery slope
Authority argument	Genetic fallacy	Straw man
Begging the question	Incredulity argument	Tautology
Correlation as causation	Inconsistent criteria	Tu quoque
False analogy	Non sequitur	
	No true Scotsman	

Your Turn

1. Deductive arguments use a general rule to determine a specific case, while inductive arguments start with a specific case to determine a general rule. Why are both kinds of reasoning valuable?

2. Think of commercials you have recently seen. What needs of the receiver do they target? Do the commercials fairly or unfairly appeal to those needs?

3. Watch a debate on television or in person. Do the participants use logical appeals, emotional appeals, or both? What errors in logic do you notice?

Literacy Skills

You live in the information age, which means that you consume and produce information at a faster rate than any generation before.

Information, Media, and Technology Literacy

Information literacy begins with understanding the many forms that information takes. Information comes in pictures, diagrams, PSAs, Web pages, billboards, bank statements, train schedules—anything that people create to communicate. The communication situation is the key that can unlock these media and help you understand the message.

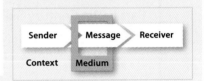

- **Sender:** Who created this message? Is the sender one person, a group, unknown? What authority does the sender have?

- **Message:** What is the subject? The main point? The purpose? What ideas support the main point? Is the message reliable?

- **Medium:** What medium is used? How public is it? What strengths does the medium have? What weaknesses?

- **Receiver:** Who is reading, hearing, or viewing this message? Is the receiver one person, a group, unknown? How will the receiver feel about the message? What should the receiver do with the message?

- **Context:** In what place and time was the message created? In what place and time will it be received? What came before? What should come after?

Financial Literacy

You may already have a job, or you may be searching for one. Jobs involve a set of challenges and responsibilities. You need to acquire these skills:

- ☑ **Fiscal responsibility**
- ☑ **Career planning**
- ☑ **Money management**
- ☑ **Credit and debt management**
- ☑ **Risk management**
- ☑ **Saving and investing**

Your Turn

1. Think about a message you recently received. Use the questions above to analyze each part of the communication situation.

2. What medium do you prefer for casual messages: talking face to face, texting, phoning, using social media? Why do you prefer this medium?

3. What career are you aiming for? Look online to find the starting yearly wage for that job. Divide that number by 12. Where do you want to live? Look online to find average monthly prices for apartments. How much money will be left after you've paid your rent? Consider how far that money will stretch to cover your other expenses.

21st Century Skills in Context

The best way to practice critical thinking is to have something to think critically about, and the best way to practice creative thinking is to create something. You'll get plenty of practice with these and the other 21st century skills in Part I of this handbook. These skills are then used in every step of the inquiry process (Part II), which in turn is used in every project in Part III. The following graphic shows how all of this important information fits together for a dynamic learning experience.

Part I: 21st Century Skills
- Critical thinking
- Creative thinking
- Problem solving
- Communicating
- Collaborating
- Building arguments
- Information literacy
- Media literacy
- Technology literacy
- Financial literacy

Part II: Inquiry Process
- Questioning
- Planning
- Researching
- Creating
- Improving
- Presenting

Part III: Projects
- Writing
- Graphing
- Web developing
- Audio-visual
- Design
- Performing
- Community

Across the Curriculum

Life Skills

In addition to the learning and literacy skills we've discussed so far, the Partnership for 21st Century Skills lists life skills that everyone needs to succeed. Using the inquiry process to complete a project is a natural training ground for developing life skills:

- ☑ Flexibility and adaptability
- ☑ Initiative and self-direction
- ☑ Social and cross-cultural skills
- ☑ Productivity and accountability
- ☑ Leadership and responsibility

Your Turn Which of the 21st century skills is your strongest right now? Which do you most need to improve? How will improving this skill help you in school and in the workplace?

Chapter 2
Critical Thinking

The word *critical* stems from the Greek root *kritikos,* which means "the ability to discern or judge." That definition points directly to the critical thinking necessary for making decisions and taking action. Such thinking is focused and purposeful. It evaluates ideas using *criteria*, another word from the same Greek root. It faces down *crises* (decision points) and makes tough choices. Critical thinking is pointed and practical—focused, rational, and dispassionate.

This chapter will help you sharpen your critical-thinking skills, reaching to ever deeper levels of thought.

You will learn . . .
- Critical Thinking and the Inquiry Process
- Critical-Thinking Strategies
- Remembering
- Understanding
- Applying
- Analyzing
- Evaluating
- Creating

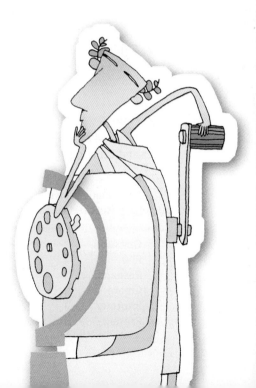

Critical Thinking and the Inquiry Process

Critical thinking enables you to delve deeply into a topic, separating its parts to examine them. It helps you sort through possibilities, deciding what to keep and what to throw away. While creative thinking broadens your focus, critical thinking narrows and sharpens it. Seeking an ever finer focus, critical thinking is *convergent*. Critical thinking is important to each step of the inquiry process, as shown in the text and chart below.

Critical Thinking   Inquiry Process

Connect
Connect with a topic by activating your prior knowledge, asking initial questions, getting a sense of the whole, and considering its importance.

Question

Commit
Commit your time, energy, and other resources to learn about the topic. Decide how to proceed.

Plan

Read
Read to learn, listen to learn, expand your vocabulary, examine ideas, gather information, assess its reliability, and organize your research.

Research

Express
Express what you have learned, defining, describing, interpreting, inferring, analyzing, arguing, and concluding.

Create

Evaluate
Evaluate what you have created. Check your logic and conclusions, resolve ambiguities, entertain alternatives, and reconstruct meaning.

Improve

Share
Share what you have learned with others, teaching and debating.

Present

Your Turn Examine your own critical thinking during the inquiry process. Rate it from 1 (struggle) to 6 (succeed) at each step. The strategies in this chapter will help you improve.

	(Struggle) ⟶ (Succeed)					
Question	1	2	3	4	5	6
Plan	1	2	3	4	5	6
Research	1	2	3	4	5	6
Create	1	2	3	4	5	6
Improve	1	2	3	4	5	6
Present	1	2	3	4	5	6

Critical-Thinking Strategies

Critical thinking is precise, engaging with material in a thorough way. Researcher Benjamin Bloom developed the following list of thinking skills that progress from surface to deeper levels of thought. On the pages that follow, you will learn the specific strategies listed below for each level of thinking.

Critical-Thinking Strategies	Bloom's Revised Taxonomy
■ Pattern finding ■ Mnemonics	**Remembering** Remembering is recalling information.
■ Sequencing ■ Classifying ■ Comparing and contrasting ■ Tracing causes and effects	**Understanding** Understanding is knowing what the information means.
■ Creating instructions ■ Creating algorithms	**Applying** Applying is putting the information to use.
■ Identifying variables ■ Designing experiments	**Analyzing** Analyzing is looking at the parts of something and figuring out how they fit together.
■ Building rubrics ■ Using rubrics	**Evaluating** Evaluating is determining the value or worth of something.
■ Using inquiry to create ■ Using engineering design ■ Thinking computationally	**Creating** Creating is putting ideas together in new ways to make something.

Your Turn Which of the critical thinking strategies above have you used in the past? Which strategies are new to you? What other critical thinking strategies have you learned in math, science, social studies, and English?

Remembering

One of the best ways to remember an idea is to connect it either to something you already know or to another important concept. Our brains like to hold on to grouped ideas rather than to individual ideas. These pages provide strategies for doing so.

Pattern Finding

Our brains are pattern-finding organs. A pattern is a form, model, shape, design, or configuration. When you see a pattern, you can fit individual pieces of information into a larger structure and thereby remember the information. For example, once you recognize this logarithmic spiral pattern, you'll see it in many places.

Logarithmic Spiral Pattern

Your Turn How are spirals used in language? Do you sometimes circle around bad news before you tell it? Do some stories circle around a central idea before reaching it? Try to find more examples of spirals in each class you have throughout the day.

Mnemonics: Pattern Making

Mnemonics are other memory techniques that create associations in your mind. The more places information is stored, the easier it is to find again. You can use ready-made mnemonics or devise your own.

Acronyms

are words made up of the first letters in a set of other words.

HOMES
Huron, **O**ntario, **M**ichigan, **E**rie, **S**uperior

Acrostics

are amusing sentences made up of words that begin with the first letters in a set of other words.

Dear King Philip Came Over For Good Spaghetti.
Domain, **K**ingdom, **P**hylum, **C**lass, **O**rder, **F**amily, **G**enus, **S**pecies

Chaining

connects words so that one item triggers the thought of the next, and so on.

James won, and Charles won. Then the Cromwells won—then Charles too, and James too. Mary, too? William, on his third try, threw up his 'ands.
James I, Charles I, Oliver Cromwell, Richard Cromwell, Charles II, James II, Mary II, William III, Anne

Numerical

sentences use words that have the same number of letters as a number you want to remember.

How I wish I could enumerate pi easily, since all these horrible mnemonics prevent recalling any of pi's sequence more simply.
3.14159265358979323846

Rhymes

help you associate a sound with a specific word or idea.

Righty tighty; lefty loosey.
(Direction to turn bolts or lids)

Stories

use a brief narrative to trigger memory.

Pa separated the children.
(Remembering that "separate" is spelled with "pa" instead of "pe" in the center)
In fourteen hundred and ninety-two, Columbus sailed the ocean blue.
(Remembering the date 1492)

Word play

uses parts of a word to remember its meaning or spelling.

*Stala**ctites** cling **tight** to the ceiling. Stala**gmites** **might** reach the ceiling.*
lo-d-hi minus hi-d-lo all over lo squared

$$\frac{d}{dx}\frac{hi}{lo} = \frac{lo \cdot hi' - hi \cdot lo'}{lo^2}$$

Your Turn Go to thoughtfullearning.com/h15 to find links to mnemonic devices and generators.

Understanding

Understanding goes beyond simply remembering information. Understanding is knowing what something means, why it is important, and how it fits in with other ideas. Graphic organizers can help you understand a topic.

Sequencing

Sequencing information means putting it in time order, from first to last. A numbered list or time line can help you sequence details.

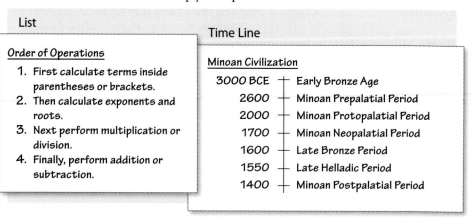

List

Order of Operations
1. First calculate terms inside parentheses or brackets.
2. Then calculate exponents and roots.
3. Next perform multiplication or division.
4. Finally, perform addition or subtraction.

Time Line

Minoan Civilization

3000 BCE	Early Bronze Age
2600	Minoan Prepalatial Period
2000	Minoan Protopalatial Period
1700	Minoan Neopalatial Period
1600	Late Bronze Period
1550	Late Helladic Period
1400	Minoan Postpalatial Period

Your Turn Think of a process or period you are studying. Create a list or a time line that puts details in the proper sequence.

Classifying

Classifying information means sorting it into groups or categories. A given category includes items that share a specific property or feature. For example, your class could be grouped according to gender, hair color, length of first names, favorite type of music, and so on. A table can help you sort categories.

Types of Fruit					
Berry	Gourd	Aggregate	Citric	Multiple	Accessory
Cranberry	Cucumber	Boysenberry	Grapefruit	Fig	Apple
Chili	Melon	Blackberry	Lemon	Mulberry	Strawberry
Currant	Pumpkin	Raspberry	Lime	Pineapple	
Grape			Orange		
Tomato					

Your Turn Think of a broad topic that can be sorted into groups or categories. Create a table like the one above to list your topic, categories, and examples.

Comparing and Contrasting

Comparing means finding the similarities between two things. Contrasting means finding the differences between them. Comparing and contrasting helps you understand both topics better. You can compare two subjects using a similarities/differences chart or a Venn diagram.

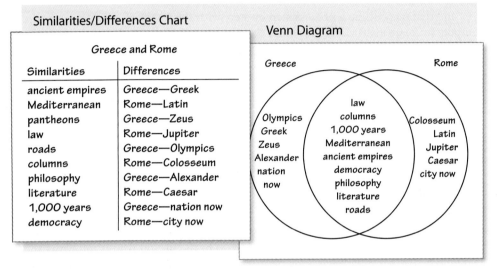

Similarities/Differences Chart

Greece and Rome

Similarities	Differences
ancient empires	Greece—Greek
Mediterranean	Rome—Latin
pantheons	Greece—Zeus
law	Rome—Jupiter
roads	Greece—Olympics
columns	Rome—Colosseum
philosophy	Greece—Alexander
literature	Rome—Caesar
1,000 years	Greece—nation now
democracy	Rome—city now

Venn Diagram

Greece — Rome

Olympics, Greek, Zeus, Alexander, nation now

law, columns, 1,000 years, Mediterranean, ancient empires, democracy, philosophy, literature, roads

Colosseum, Latin, Jupiter, Caesar, city now

Your Turn Choose two topics that you are currently studying and that display a number of similarities and differences. Compare and contrast the topics.

Tracing Causes and Effects

One way to thoroughly understand an event or situation is to trace its causes and effects. A cause-effect chart like the one below can help you explore a phenomenon. Write the name of the phenomenon in the central circle. On the left, write causes. On the right, write effects.

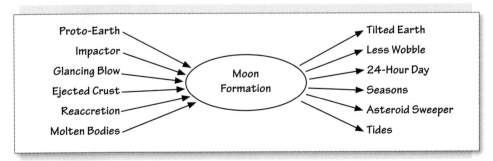

Proto-Earth, Impactor, Glancing Blow, Ejected Crust, Reaccretion, Molten Bodies → Moon Formation → Tilted Earth, Less Wobble, 24-Hour Day, Seasons, Asteroid Sweeper, Tides

Your Turn Create a cause-effect chart to better understand a phenomenon you are studying.

Applying

When you apply an idea, you put it to use for a specific purpose. You might create instructions for a person to follow or an algorithm for a computer to use.

Creating Instructions

Instructions outline a process step by step, with the intent of creating a specific output. To create instructions, sequence the steps in time order, and express each step using a command verb. For example, here is a simple set of instructions for making a peanut butter and jelly sandwich:

Sandwich-Making Instructions

1. Get bread, peanut butter, jelly, and a knife.
2. Spread peanut butter on one side of one slice of bread.
3. Spread jelly on one side of the other slice of bread.
4. Put the bread sides with peanut butter and jelly together.
5. Enjoy.

Most people who can read English would be able to follow these instructions, but they actually leave some problem solving up to the person who is following the directions. For example, what does "get" mean? From where? And given that bread, peanut butter, and jelly are usually packaged, the instructions assume that you'll think to open the packaging and remove two slices of bread before you start spreading. What if the bread isn't sliced? And what does it mean to enjoy?

These may seem like minor problems to you, but they would be insurmountable for a robot that knew only the following commands:

Sandwich-Making Commands

- **Clamp:** Close left or right hand.
- **Unclamp:** Open left or right hand.
- **Lift:** Raise left or right hand.
- **Lower:** Drop left or right hand.
- **Pull:** Draw item nearer.
- **Push:** Move item farther.
- **Twist:** Turn left or right hand clockwise or counterclockwise.
- **Spread:** Smear material on indicated object.

Creating an Algorithm

An algorithm is a step-by-step problem-solving procedure. A sandwich-making algorithm for the robot would have to spell out every step. The flowchart below is an algorithm that directs the robot to open the bread sack.

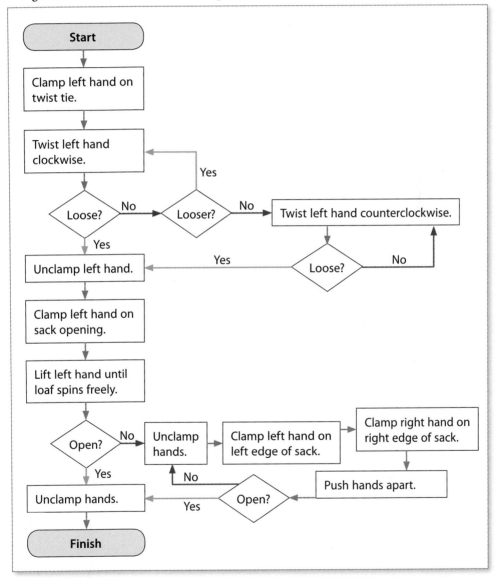

Your Turn Create a flowchart like the one above, expressing the algorithm for getting the robot to remove the lids from the jars of peanut butter and jelly. (Go to thoughtfullearning.com/h19 for flowcharting software.)

Analyzing

When you analyze something, you study it closely, taking it apart and recognizing the way that the different parts work together. Analysis deepens understanding, giving you a thorough grasp of a topic.

Identifying Constants and Variables

In math and science, you've probably learned about constants and variables.

Constants	Variables
Constants are values that do not change (remain constant).	Variables are values that do change (vary).

Formula for Calculating the Circumference of a Circle: $c = 2\pi r$

Constants:	Variables:
2 and π	c (circumference) and r (radius)

Beyond math and science, constants and variables apply in all situations. For example, if you tell one of your favorite jokes and no one laughs, you'll wonder why and naturally start to identify constants and variables:

Constants:	Variables:
"I used the exact same words I used last time."	"The audience is different. The context is different. My timing may have been off. Maybe I should have added a facial expression or a gesture."

Your Turn **English Language Arts:** Find a poem that you are interested in. Choose one word to replace in each line. How do the replacement words (variables) affect the meaning of the other words (constants)? Do the replacements enhance or detract from the overall meaning?

Social Studies: Think about a governmental action that failed to have its intended effect (e.g., the Bay of Pigs invasion). Identify the constants—factors that were the same in previously successful actions. Identify the variables—factors that were different this time. Which variables most likely caused the failure?

Science: Consider a phenomenon you are studying in a science class. What are the constants in the phenomenon? What are the variables? How might you test to discover the effects of different variables?

Everyday Life: When you have trouble with a piece of technology—a TV remote, a computer program, a cell phone—list the factors that have not changed and those that have. Narrow the list of variables to find the cause of the problem. Then fix it.

Isolating Variables

Once you have identified constants and variables, you need to isolate the variables. You may be familiar with isolating variables in math:

$7x + 3 = 6x + 6$ *(Original equation)*		
$7x + 3 - 3 = 6x + 6 - 3$ (Subtract 3 from both sides.)	$7x = 6x + 3$ (Resulting equation)	$7x - 6x = 6x - 6x + 3$ (Subtract 6x from both sides.)
$x = 3$ *(Isolated variable)*		

In science, isolating variables is the key to experimental design. After listing all the possible variables for a given phenomenon, you select and test for the effect of one variable. You can start by completing a cause-effect chart:

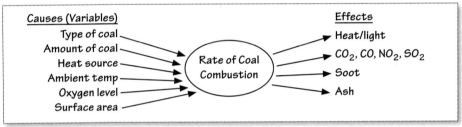

Causes (Variables)
- Type of coal
- Amount of coal
- Heat source
- Ambient temp
- Oxygen level
- Surface area

Rate of Coal Combustion

Effects
- Heat/light
- CO_2, CO, NO_2, SO_2
- Soot
- Ash

Your Turn Select a science topic that interests you and create a cause-effect chart like the one above.

Designing Experiments

To design an experiment, you must decide which variable you will test, and then control the other variables by turning them into constants. This experiment tests how surface area affects coal combustion by controlling other variables listed above.

> **Problem:** How does the surface area of coal affect its rate of combustion?
>
> **Hypothesis:** Combustion rate is directly correlated to surface area.
>
> **Materials:** 4 gas burners, high-temperature thermometer, 4 metal frames, charcoal briquettes, paper, pencil, safety goggles, gloves
>
> **Method:** The 4 gas burners are ignited and adjusted to produce 1-centimeter flames. Each flame is measured to determine temperature, and the burners are adjusted to provide identical heat. A metal frame to hold the coal is situated 1 centimeter above each flame. Flame A burns a single charcoal briquette; flame B, a briquette broken in 2; flame C, a briquette broken in 4; flame D, crushed charcoal. Each charcoal sample is placed simultaneously, and the combustion rates are timed.

Your Turn Design an experiment for the science topic you selected above. Control all the variables except the one you are testing.

Evaluating

When you evaluate something, you determine its value or worth. To do so, you judge the thing using a set of desired qualities.

Building Basic Rubrics

A rubric lists the qualities you desire and provides a scale for rating each. The basic rubric below works for any project. Simply write your project goal in the top left box and answer the 5 W's and H in each box below (objectives). Then evaluate, rate, and score the goal and objectives in the final three columns.

Basic Rubric for Global Crises Project

	Goal	Evaluation	Rating	Score
Goal	Create a public service announcement (P.S.A.) about the problem of child warriors.	We created a powerful P.S.A. with strong narration and images.	Beat Met Didn't 60 (40) 20	40
	Objectives	Stephen and I did most of the work. We had some trouble with teamwork.	Beat Met Didn't 10 6 (2)	2
Who?	**1.** I will work on this with the other three students at my table.			
What?	**2.** We will research child warriors and find resources to create a P.S.A.	We found creative photos and composed our own music.	Beat Met Didn't (10) 6 2	10
Where?	**3.** We'll work in class, in the library, and in the media center.	We worked at home, in the library, and in the media center.	Beat Met Didn't (10) 6 2	10
When?	**4.** The P.S.A. needs to be ready to present on 1/24.	We got our P.S.A. done the night before the deadline, so we're in good shape!	Beat Met Didn't 10 (6) 2	6
Why?	**5.** We want viewers to help end the use of children in wars.	Our P.S.A. is pretty convincing.	Beat Met Didn't 10 (6) 2	6
How?	**6.** We'll use the equipment in the media center.	We used the media center as well as our home computers.	Beat Met Didn't (10) 6 2	10
			Total:	84

Your Turn Create a rubric for a project. Write a goal in the top left box, answer the 5 W's and H, and evaluate and rate each. (Go to thoughtfullearning.com/h22 for a template.)

Building Advanced Rubrics

You can create a more advanced rubric by listing each desired quality or trait in the first column and indicating what each rating and overall score means.

Advanced Rubric for Global Crises Project

Trait	4 (Excellent)	3 (Good)	2 (Fair)	1 (Poor)
Persuasiveness	The P.S.A. moves the viewer emotionally.	The P.S.A. connects with the viewer.	The P.S.A. is watchable.	The P.S.A. is ineffective.
Main point	The main point is clear and powerful.	The main point is clear.	The P.S.A. has a main point.	The P.S.A. lacks a main point.
Support	Many strong details support the main point.	Details support the main point.	The P.S.A. includes some support.	Details are needed to support the main point.
Documentation	All materials are free of copyright infringement and are documented.	All materials are free of copyright infringement, and most are documented.	Some materials are free of copyright infringement and are documented.	Materials are not free of copyright infringement and are not documented.
Production values	Narration, images, and music are stunning.	Narration, images, and music work.	Narration, images, and music are okay.	Technical aspects are ineffective.

20	15	10	5	<5
Excellent	Good	Fair	Poor	Incomplete

Your Turn Choose a project to evaluate. Create a rubric like the one above. List key traits and define each level of performance. (Get a template at thoughtfullearning.com/h23.)

Using Rubrics

Rubrics have numerous uses throughout the inquiry process.

- **Planning:** Rubrics define your goal and indicate what success will look like.
- **Improving:** Rubrics help you assess and improve your completed work.
- **Presenting:** Rubrics keep you on track and assist in your final assessment.

Your Turn Use one of the rubrics you created on these two pages to plan, improve, or present a project.

Creating

Creating brings together all the other levels of thinking. As the definitive step in the inquiry process, creating allows you to express what you have learned.

Using Inquiry to Create

Different disciplines follow different versions of the inquiry process. Here are six specific versions, meant to accomplish different tasks.

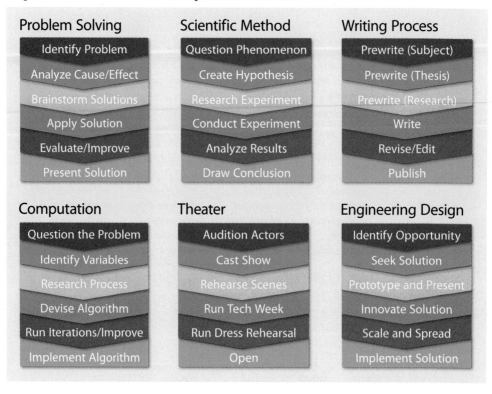

Problem Solving
- Identify Problem
- Analyze Cause/Effect
- Brainstorm Solutions
- Apply Solution
- Evaluate/Improve
- Present Solution

Scientific Method
- Question Phenomenon
- Create Hypothesis
- Research Experiment
- Conduct Experiment
- Analyze Results
- Draw Conclusion

Writing Process
- Prewrite (Subject)
- Prewrite (Thesis)
- Prewrite (Research)
- Write
- Revise/Edit
- Publish

Computation
- Question the Problem
- Identify Variables
- Research Process
- Devise Algorithm
- Run Iterations/Improve
- Implement Algorithm

Theater
- Audition Actors
- Cast Show
- Rehearse Scenes
- Run Tech Week
- Run Dress Rehearsal
- Open

Engineering Design
- Identify Opportunity
- Seek Solution
- Prototype and Present
- Innovate Solution
- Scale and Spread
- Implement Solution

Consider how the inquiry process can be used to create the essentials listed here:

- food
- communication
- agriculture
- money
- clothing
- entertainment
- medicine
- government
- shelter
- recreation
- literature
- science
- family
- tradition
- art
- careers
- community
- tools
- music
- goals
- education
- machines
- mythology
- transportation

Your Turn Think of something that you know how to create—a painting, an equation, a club, a homemade pizza. What process do you use? How is your process similar to or different from the processes charted above?

Using Engineering Design

The engineering-design process has produced the computer revolution and the information age. Mastering this process can give you a key to the future. Here is one version of this powerful process.

Critical Thinking

Inquiry Process

See the Problem
Engineers see problems as opportunities. When something is inefficient, inconvenient, or unrealized, engineers see ways to innovate solutions.

Identify Opportunity

Brainstorm a Solution
Engineers brainstorm solutions, sometimes focusing on specific problems and sometimes seeking approaches that completely overthrow conventional wisdom.

Seek Solutions

Prototype
After choosing a solution, engineers prototype it. They try it on a small scale, in drawings and wire frames. Then they present their idea to key stakeholders (decision makers who are invested in solving the problem).

Prototype and Present

Build
Once a prototype is okayed, engineers build the full-scale version of their solution. They test their design, making improvements along the way.

Innovate Solution

Review
The full-size solution goes through another review period with stakeholders, and engineers make more changes. Then they work out ways to replicate the solution and market it to those who need it.

Scale and Spread

Implement
Once the solution is ready, engineers implement it, whether in one place or many. A time line of the last decade would show how many new, life-changing technologies have been implemented.

Implement Solution

Your Turn Practice engineering-design thinking. Start by identifying some design opportunities in your school, community, or home. Note inefficiencies, inconveniences, and unrealized possibilities. Select a problem that you would like to tackle, and then follow the steps above to design a solution.

Thinking Computationally

Obviously, computational thinking has given us our modern computer age. When you identify a series of discrete commands to accomplish a task, you are thinking computationally. This kind of thinking takes many forms:

1. **Instructions:** Any set of instructions, from directions for hooking up a new computer to recipes for making bread (or steel), require computational thinking. The instruction writer devises a set of discrete steps, and when they are followed, the steps lead to a specific result.

2. **Computer programs:** When someone programs a computer to carry out a task, he or she gives a set of commands to the computer. Those commands may be expressed in a number of different forms:
   - **Natural language:** A program can be explained in a particular human language, but such language is imprecise. Most computers cannot decipher natural language.
   - **Pseudo code:** This format follows the conventions of computer code but is still meant for human readers rather than computers.
   - **Flowchart:** This visual expression of an algorithm provides greater precision than natural language or pseudo code, noting actions, decision points, and flow.
   - **Programming languages:** These languages are a halfway point between natural human languages and the binary code of computers.
   - **Binary code:** This is the "natural language" of computers, a series of 0's and 1's representing on and off states. At some level, programming languages are rendered in binary code, but few people are able to read and compose binary code.

3. **Mathematical expressions:** All math formulas are types of algorithms, giving a specific set of commands, constants, and variables. So when you learn algebra, you are learning an ancient form of computational thinking. In fact, you are functioning as the computer, carrying out the commands inherent in +, −, ÷, and ×.

$$x = \frac{-b \pm \sqrt{b^2 - 4ac}}{2a}$$

Your Turn Which type of computational thinking are you most familiar with? Which type are you least familiar with? How can learning to write a clear set of instructions help you learn to write computer code? How can understanding mathematical computation help you write computer code?

Critical-Thinking Activities

The activities listed below will help you work on your critical-thinking skills and become a more thoughtful learner.

Pattern Finding

You've already sought out spiral patterns in each of your classes. The activity below will help you explore two other patterns across the curriculum.

Your Turn Look at the two illustrations below. One shows bilateral symmetry—a line down the middle divides the form into similar halves. The other shows radial symmetry—any line through the midpoint reveals similar halves. Find an example of each kind of symmetry in your current science, math, English, and social studies classes. Why does each type occur?

Bilateral Symmetry   Radial Symmetry

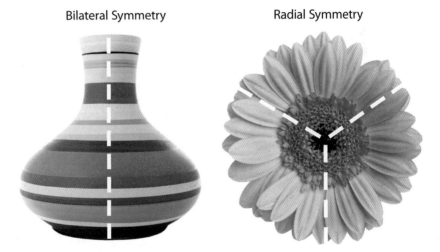

Causes and Effects

Human beings live in time. What came before impacts what is happening now, which in turn will affect what happens in the future. Considering these causes and effects connects you to your past and to your future.

Your Turn What kind of day are you having? What factors caused this day? Create a cause-effect chart about your day. What causes could you change to have a better day tomorrow? See the example at the right.

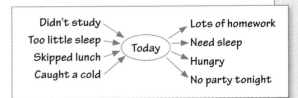

Identifying and Isolating Variables

The kind of cause-effect analysis you did on the previous page about your day can also help you think about your day's constants and variables.

Your Turn Think about your day. List its constants and its variables. Choose one variable to isolate; then indicate how you would turn all the other variables into constants. Use the following example:

Constants	Variables	Constants
Walk to and from school	Weather ——————→	Keep umbrella in locker
School schedule	Homework load	
Cereal for breakfast	Hot lunch ——————→	Bring sack lunch
Hanging with Jon	"Drama" with friends ——→	Don't get involved
Hungry by 6:00 p.m.	Dinner (uncertain) ———→	Make dinner myself

Creating Algorithms

On page 19, you created a flowchart algorithm involving a robot and a peanut butter and jelly sandwich. Here's another chance to practice computational thinking.

Your Turn Imagine you have a robot that understands the commands below. Create a flowchart algorithm that directs the robot to high-five you and then give you a fist bump.

- **Clamp:** Close left or right hand.
- **Unclamp:** Open left or right hand.
- **Lift:** Raise left or right hand.
- **Lower:** Drop left or right hand.
- **Pull:** Draw item nearer.
- **Push:** Move item farther.
- **Twist:** Turn left or right hand clockwise or counterclockwise.

Rubrics for Life

By setting goals and listing objectives for achieving those goals, you can effect positive changes in your life.

Your Turn Write out your number one goal in life as a single sentence. Answer the 5 W's and H about the goal. Plug your goal and objectives into a basic rubric sheet (thoughtfullearning.com/h28). Evaluate your progress so far and consider what you must still do to reach your goal.

Chapter 3
Creative Thinking

Look around you. The most amazing innovations are popping up everywhere. And who has developed these fantastic inventions? People who think creatively . . . people very much like you.

Creative thinking is not magic. Anyone who has an idea to grow or a problem to solve thinks creatively. You can improve your creative thinking, too, by learning the strategies discussed in this chapter. So get ready to think your way into all kinds of unique ideas and solutions.

You will learn . . .

- Creative Thinking and the Inquiry Process
- Creative-Thinking Strategies
- Remembering
- Understanding
- Applying
- Analyzing
- Evaluating
- Creating

Creative Thinking and the Inquiry Process

Creative thinking seeks possibilities. It reaches from the known to the unknown to find innovative solutions. While critical thinking narrows your focus, creative thinking broadens it by breaking down barriers and challenging assumptions. Creativity uses divergent thinking to look for many unique answers. Creative thinking is critical to the inquiry process. The chart below indicates creativity's role during each step.

Creative Thinking   Inquiry Process

Consider   **Question**
Consider your situation. What question must you
answer? What problem must you solve? Start playing
around with ideas, materials, and objects.

Brainstorm   **Plan**
Make sketches, write thoughts, discuss ideas, set goals,
brainstorm possibilities. Select the most promising ones.

Work with Ideas   **Research**
Continue to work with your ideas, but take breaks to
let them incubate. Inspiration often arrives through
subconscious thought.

Use Inspiration   **Create**
Use your inspiration. Innovate by writing, graphing,
building, recording, designing, performing, organizing.

Put It Aside   **Improve**
Put your creation aside for a while. Then return to
evaluate it. Get others' opinions also. Finally, make
improvements.

Introduce   **Present**
After improving and polishing your work, introduce it
to the world.

Your Turn Think about a recent project you completed and evaluate your creative thinking. For each step in the inquiry process, rate your thinking from 1 (struggle) to 6 (succeed). The strategies in this chapter will help you improve in each area.

(Struggle) ————————▶ (Succeed)

Question	1 . . . . . 2 . . . . . 3 . . . . . .4 . . . . . .5 6
Plan	1 . . . . . 2 . . . . . 3 . . . . . .4 . . . . . .5 6
Research	1 . . . . . 2 . . . . . 3 . . . . . .4 . . . . . .5 6
Create	1 . . . . . 2 . . . . . 3 . . . . . .4 . . . . . .5 6
Improve	1 . . . . . 2 . . . . . 3 . . . . . .4 . . . . . .5 6
Present	1 . . . . . 2 . . . . . 3 . . . . . .4 . . . . . .5 6

Creative-Thinking Strategies

In addition to shaping each stage of the inquiry process, creative thinking can help you dig more deeply into any topic. Researcher Benjamin Bloom developed the following list of thinking skills that progress from surface to deeper levels of thought.

Creative-Thinking Strategies	Bloom's Revised Taxonomy
■ Brainstorming ■ Visualization	**Remembering** Remembering is recalling information.
■ Metaphorical thinking ■ Conceptual blending ■ Using forced connections ■ Perspective shifting	**Understanding** Understanding is knowing what the information means.
■ Square-pegging ■ Modeling ■ Role-playing ■ Using manipulative verbs	**Applying** Applying is putting the information to use.
■ Using Socratic questions ■ Counterfactual thinking ■ Provocative thinking ■ Reversal thinking	**Analyzing** Analyzing is looking at the parts of something and figuring out how they fit together.
■ Trait evaluation ■ SCAMPER evaluation	**Evaluating** Evaluating is determining the value or worth of something.
■ Setting a goal ■ Identifying objectives ■ Defining tasks, scheduling ■ Defining team and tools	**Creating** Creating is putting ideas together in new ways to make something.

Your Turn How do you spark your creativity? What creative-thinking strategies do you use? Which thinking skills above do your strategies fit with or match?

Remembering

Creative techniques can help you generate ideas as well as remember them later.

Brainstorming

Brainstorming is the process of rapidly listing as many ideas as you can about a topic or question. You can brainstorm on your own or in a group, but don't judge the ideas. Just keep writing them in a cluster or a list until you can't think of any more.

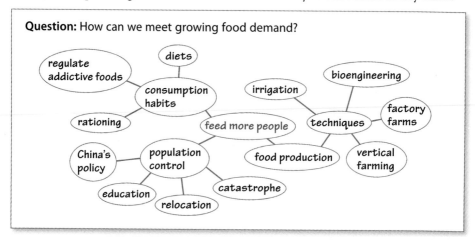

Once you've finished the initial brainstorming, select one of the ideas and use it to start a new cluster. By repeating this process, you make deeper creative connections.

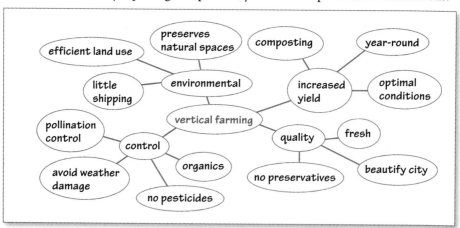

Your Turn Brainstorm ideas about a topic that your instructor supplies, or use this topic: How can we reduce bullying? Then choose one of your initial ideas and continue brainstorming to make creative connections and delve more deeply into the topic.

Visualization

One way to remember an abstract concept or a difficult word is to create a visual version of it. To visualize a concept, follow these steps:

1. **List the information you want to remember.**

   Your "radius" is the forearm bone that rotates.

   Your "ulna" is the forearm bone connected at the elbow.

   Your "humerus" is the large upper arm bone.

2. **Associate the tough words with easy words that sound similar.**

   Radius sounds like "radios."

   Ulna sounds like "all know."

   Humerus sounds like "humorous."

3. **Create a sentence that connects the three words.**

   We "all know" the "humorous" D.J. on our "radios."

4. **Visualize the sentence and imagine the tough words on the image. Practice the words while picturing the image.**

Ulna
Radius
Humerus

Visualization works for four reasons:
1. Visual, concrete ideas are easier to remember than abstract ideas.
2. Playful and silly ideas are easier to remember than serious ideas.
3. Creating a story causes you to repeat the material you are trying to learn.
4. Creating a visualization focuses your thoughts on the topic.

Your Turn Think of a difficult term or list of terms that you are dealing with in a class. Create a visualization for the term or terms, following the process above.

Understanding

When you understand an idea, you know what it means, why it is important, and how it fits with other ideas. Creative thinking can help you understand an idea by connecting it to others.

Metaphorical Thinking

Metaphorical thinking connects two different ideas to show how they are similar. One way to learn something new is to associate it with something you already know. The fit will not be exact, but that mismatch creates the possibility to discover new connections. Here are four types of metaphorical thinking:

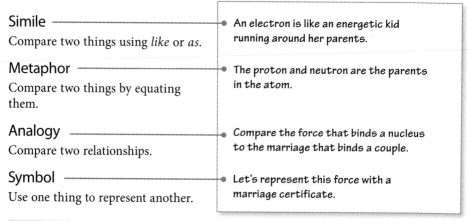

Simile — An electron is like an energetic kid running around her parents.
Compare two things using *like* or *as*.

Metaphor — The proton and neutron are the parents in the atom.
Compare two things by equating them.

Analogy — Compare the force that binds a nucleus to the marriage that binds a couple.
Compare two relationships.

Symbol — Let's represent this force with a marriage certificate.
Use one thing to represent another.

Your Turn Choose a topic that you are currently studying. Then associate that topic with familiar ideas, creating a simile, a metaphor, an analogy, and a symbol.

Conceptual Blending

Conceptual blending, which connects two unrelated systems or organizations, is another type of metaphorical thinking. Create conceptual blends by forcing two concepts together and trying to work out the conflicts between them.

- How could **classrooms** become more like **playgrounds**?
- How could a **cruise ship** become a **sovereign nation**?
- How might **computers** become more like **clothing**?
- How could the **Internet** become a **person**?
- How can a **scientist** think like a **musician**?
- What would a **portrait** of the **general theory of relativity** look like?

Your Turn Choose something you are currently studying—a concept, an organization, an idea— and then think of something entirely different. Construct a question creating a conceptual blend. Then answer the question as creatively as you can.

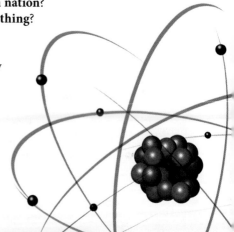

Forced Connections

Creative thinking discovers connections that no one else has noticed. You can force connections by writing down two dissimilar things and writing as many connections as you can between them.

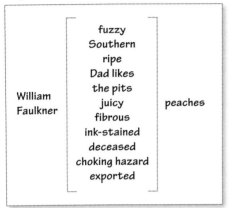
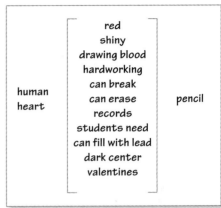

Creating forced connections between two subjects deepens your understanding of each subject.

Your Turn Select a topic you are currently studying. Choose something else completely unrelated to it. Write down the two topics and list as many connections as you can between them.

Perspective Shifting

Creative thinking discovers unique ways to look at something. Start by identifying your perspective, from very broad to very specific. Then change one or more aspects of the perspective and think about the topic again.

I am (a/an) . . .	What if I were (a/an) . . .
living creature	ghost
vertebrate	vertebrate
human being	human being
male	male
American	Paleo-Indian
living in the 21st century	living in the 21st century
monolingual	monolingual
Hoosier	Great Plains native
high school junior	elderly

Specific

By intentionally shifting out of your typical perspective, you can discover all-new ways of thinking.

Your Turn Write "I am (a/an) . . ." and list key traits about yourself, from broad to specific. Then write "What if I were (a/an) . . ." and change some of the things on your list. Then think about a topic from your new perspective.

Applying

Applying something means putting it to work in a specific situation. By creatively applying an idea, you can discover new possibilities and solutions.

Square-Pegging

You've heard the expression of putting a square peg in a round hole. Usually, that solution is not preferred; but by forcing something to be used in a novel way, you can come up with many new ideas. Create a square-peg question by using the following formula. Then answer the questions in as many ways as you can.

How can _____ _____ ?
           (your topic)   (do something it was not intended to do)

How can a rowboat win an election?
- Take the political race to a desert island.
- Let your candidate use the boat to reenact Washington crossing the Potomac.
- Use the boat to ferry in disenfranchised voters.
- Use the boat to bring absentee ballots to voters.
- Show that the boat is smarter than other candidates.
- Make the rowboat a symbol—saved from the sinking ship.

Your Turn Create a square-peg question of your own. Ask how your topic can do something it was not intended to do. Answer the question in as many ways as you can.

Modeling

Modeling an idea means expressing it in a conceptual form. You can model something by sketching it, molding it from clay, building a prototype or scale model, graphing it, creating an equation, or expressing it in some other form. The image to the right shows a working scale model of a medieval trebuchet.

Your Turn Think of an idea that you would like to model. Express the idea by sketching it, molding it, building it, graphing it, or creating some other conceptual form.

By Ron L. Toms (http://www.Trebuchet.com) [GFDL (http://www.gnu.org/copyleft/fdl.html) or CC-BY-3.0 (http://creativecommons.org/licenses/by/3.0)], via Wikimedia Commons

Role-Playing

Role-playing means acting out a situation, usually with someone else. It allows you to move creatively in space and to collaborate with others through words, gestures, expressions, and actions. Role-playing can take many forms, but the following prompts work well to put your knowledge of a topic to work.

Game Show: Choose a host of a game show and have the person quiz participants on their knowledge of a subject.	**Interview:** Choose an interviewer and an interviewee and have them carry on a conversation about a topic.	**Press Conference:** Provide a news topic to three reporters and have an "expert" answer their questions about it.
Debate: Assign three or more people to take on different points of view and debate a topic.	**Party:** Assign roles to three party guests and ask a party host to guess the role of each guest.	**Scenario:** Ask a group to act out a scenario about a situation set in a specific place and time.

Your Turn Think of a topic that you are currently studying. Choose one of the role-playing approaches above and act out a scene with other students.

Using Manipulative Verbs

Manipulative verbs are imperative (or command) verbs. You can use them to apply actions to an object or an idea to change or improve it. Here is a list of example manipulative verbs:

accelerate	brand	deflate	reverse
accessorize	break	divide	shrink
amplify	elevate	inflate	simplify
automate	freeze	melt	stretch
bend	decelerate	multiply	twist

Example Manipulation

Topic: Benedict Arnold's plot to turn West Point over to the British

Manipulative verb: Accelerate

Questions: What if Arnold's betrayal had happened earlier? What if it had involved more officers? What if it had been successful?

Manipulative verb: Twist

Questions: Did the Tories consider Arnold a true patriot? Did George III? Was Arnold's betrayal justified? Is treason ever heroic?

Your Turn Choose a topic you are currently studying. Then pick one of the manipulative verbs above (or some other command verb). Ask questions that apply the action of the verb to your topic. Look for answers.

Analyzing

Analyzing requires you to disassemble a topic, examine its parts, and explore their connections. Certain creative thinking strategies can strengthen such analysis.

Using Socratic Questions

The philosopher Socrates taught not by lecturing but by engaging students in conversation that made them think. You can use his questions to analyze ideas.

Clarification — How could we summarize this point?
What's another way of saying that?

Assumption — What are the assumptions underlying this idea?
Are any of these assumptions unwarranted?

Reason — What causes this situation to occur?
What is this situation like, and how?

Perspective — What would the opposition say about this idea?
What counterarguments can we come up with?

Consequence — What will result from this assumption?
How can this idea be applied in a new way?

Recursion — Why are we asking this question?
How does this question apply to the situation at hand?

Your Turn Freewrite about a topic that you are currently studying. When you run out of ideas, apply one or more of the Socratic questions to your topic and continue freewriting.

Counterfactual Thinking

Counterfactual thinking means asking "what if" questions. Einstein used counterfactual questions like those below to arrive at his factual theory of relativity:

Einstein's Counterfactual Questions
- What would it be like to ride on a photon (a particle of light)?
- What would it be like to ride in an elevator in free fall?
- What if space and time were one thing?
- What if matter and energy were one thing?

Your Turn Choose a topic you are currently studying and write four counterfactual questions about it. Select one question and begin freewriting.

Provocative Thinking

Provocative thinking takes a step beyond counterfactual thinking by intentionally attacking assumptions. To apply this kind of thinking, first list your basic assumptions about a situation. Then ask questions that overturn the assumptions, as in the following example about cell phones:

Assumptions	Provocative Questions
Cell phones should be designed to match the needs of most users.	How can we design a cell phone for people who don't want one?
Cell phones should fit comfortably in a pocket and be easy to hold.	What if you couldn't hold your cell phone? What if you wore just a receiver and its features were in the "cloud"?
People want multimedia on their phones.	How would a text-only cell phone work?
Everyone wants his or her own cell phone.	How could we rent cell phones by the day?
Teachers think cell phones are distracting to students.	How can we make cell phones central to education?

Your Turn Choose a topic that you are currently studying. Write down as many assumptions as you can about the topic. Then create a provocative question for each assumption.

Reverse Thinking

Reverse thinking turns a situation on its head. Imagine that the effects are the causes, the problem is the solution, the opposite position is valid, and so on. Reverse thinking can break through conventional barriers to new ideas.

Conventional Wisdom	Reverse Thinking
A group should learn about a topic from the most knowledgeable person.	The person who is most knowledgeable about a topic should learn from the group.
Wikipedia demonstrates why people should trust experts instead of consensus thinking.	Wikipedia demonstrates why people should trust consensus thinking instead of experts.
The world needs more brilliant specialists to further their fields.	The world needs more brilliant generalists to connect multiple fields.
The best scientists think critically.	The best scientists think creatively.

Your Turn Choose a topic that you are currently studying. Write down the conventional wisdom about the topic. Then create a reverse-thinking statement for each conventional thought.

Evaluating

Evaluating means determining the value or worth of something. Whenever you evaluate something, you compare it to a standard or a set of attributes. The following creative strategies can help you evaluate any topic.

Trait Evaluation

A trait is simply a feature of something. You can do a trait analysis by first listing the traits of something in one column of a chart, evaluating each trait in a second column, and listing suggested improvements in a third column. The following chart evaluates a standard screwdriver.

Trait	Evaluation	Improvements
It drives screws.	It drives standard screws well, but it cannot handle Phillips-, hex-, or square-head screws.	We could fit the end with a removable tip so different types of bits could be used.
It is durable.	This screwdriver holds up well for most household tasks.	N.A.
It reaches hard-to-reach screws.	This screwdriver is long and thin, so it can reach into tight spots.	We could provide some angled or extra long bits.
It is easy to grip.	The grip is nonslip, but it is narrow, which makes it difficult to provide torque.	A wider grip would make the screwdriver easier to use, as long as it doesn't make it significantly heavier.
It is inexpensive.	This screwdriver is cheap, which is one of its chief virtues. If we add other features, we have to avoid increasing the cost too much.	N.A.
It is attractive.	The two-tone design is pleasant, though a bit dated.	Providing different color options might help.

Your Turn Select a topic you are studying and create a trait evaluation chart about it. List traits in the first column, evaluations in the second column, and improvements in the third.

SCAMPER Evaluation

A researcher named Bob Eberle created a set of questions that you can use to evaluate and improve an idea. The first letter in each category spells out **SCAMPER:**

Substitute ———
What alternatives can I discover?
Who else could be involved with this issue?
What other ideas, approaches, or materials would be useful?
What new goals should we focus on?

Combine ———
How can this be combined with something else?
How would this work if it were more like that?
How can this be used in a new context?
How can this idea connect to other people?

Adapt ———
What changes would improve this?
How could this be modified to better fit the situation?
What traits could be adjusted to improve this?
How can this become more desirable?

Magnify ———
How can this be made bigger or more powerful?
How can I improve performance or efficiency?
How can I make this faster?
How can I make this more impressive?

Put to
  Other Uses ———
What other uses does this have?
Who else could use this?
Where else could this be applied?
What other problem could this solve?

Eliminate ———
What would simplify this?
What would streamline it?
How can I make this less costly?
What would make this more subtle?

Rearrange ———
What other sequence could work for this?
How could I turn this completely around?
What other part of the issue might be more important?
Could this happen at a different time or in a different place?

Your Turn Choose a concept from one of your classes. Select one question from each of the SCAMPER categories and apply it to the concept. Be creative with your answers. If a question doesn't seem to suit your topic exactly, revise it so it works.

Creating

Creating is the deepest form of thinking on Bloom's taxonomy. It results from and calls upon all the other levels. Creation takes many forms, including the following:

acting	dramatizing	gaming	performing
arranging	drawing	graphing	playing
building	educating	innovating	recording
composing	engineering	modeling	reporting
dancing	experimenting	nurturing	sculpting
designing	exploring	organizing	singing
developing	founding	painting	writing

Often, creators combine several of these forms into one project and collaborate with others.

In Focus

Steven Spielberg has created dozens of films, including *Jaws, Schindler's List,* and *War Horse.* He draws inspiration for his films from other creators, such as musicians and artists. Spielberg has an impressive collection of the artist Norman Rockwell's work, including one painting of a boy staring in terror over the edge of the high dive. Spielberg says, "Every time I'm ready to make a movie, every time I'm ready to commit to direct a movie, that's me. That's the feeling in my gut, before I say 'yes' to a picture, because every movie is like looking off a three-meter diving board, every one." The moral of the story is that creating might seem frightening and messy, even for a seasoned pro like Spielberg, but the best way to create, perhaps, is to just dive in.

Neftali / Shutterstock.com

Projects

In the third part of this book, you'll find chapters that contain many different kinds of projects: writing, graphing, Web developing, audio-visual, design, performing, and community projects. Though you may create a number of these projects on your own, you will likely work with a group on multipart projects as well. Here's a high-level plan for an example multipart project.

Global-Crisis Documentary

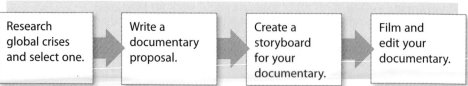

Research global crises and select one. → Write a documentary proposal. → Create a storyboard for your documentary. → Film and edit your documentary.

Your Turn Turn to the project section of this book on pages 429–606 and consider the many project types. Which projects are you most interested in doing? Why?

Setting a Goal

You may begin creating by simply experimenting. That's fine. But you can also start with a specific goal in mind. Your goal may be as simple as "write a great song" or as complex as "come up with an equation that extends the Schwarzschild solution within massive nonrotating bodies." Use the following formula to write a clear goal statement:

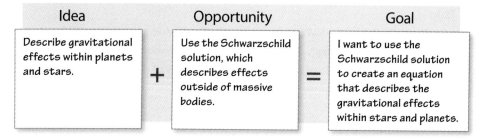

Idea		Opportunity		Goal
Describe gravitational effects within planets and stars.	**+**	Use the Schwarzschild solution, which describes effects outside of massive bodies.	**=**	I want to use the Schwarzschild solution to create an equation that describes the gravitational effects within stars and planets.

Your Turn Choose something to create. It can be anything from a school assignment to a cure for cancer. Use the formula above to write a goal statement.

Identifying Objectives

Once you have a goal in mind, you'll need to carefully consider how to reach it. Answering the 5 W's and H will help you write objectives.

Who?	I will work with my physics teacher and the equation of Karl Schwarzschild.
What?	I will create a new equation.
Where?	The work will happen in physics class and at home.
When?	I should be done in two weeks.
Why?	I want to understand the Schwarzschild metric and create and test my own equation.
How?	I'll create the equation by studying the metric, learning all its parts, and manipulating them to describe gravity in planets.

Your Turn Using the goal you wrote above, answer the 5 W's and H about it in complete sentences. Each of your answers will become an objective.

Defining Tasks and Scheduling Time

After setting a goal, you need to figure out how to reach it. Usually, you can't get there in one giant leap, but you can get there by taking small steps. Make a list of the steps or tasks you must complete to reach your goal. Then, next to each task, indicate when the task should be done.

Tasks	Time
1. Study the Schwarzschild metric.	Mon. and Tue./Nov. 5&6
2. Decide which terms apply within massive objects.	Wed./Nov. 7
3. Manipulate the metric to calculate inward.	Wed. and Thu./Nov. 7&8
4. Test the new equation.	Fri./Nov. 9
5. Produce data tables for stars and planets.	Mon. and Tue./Nov. 12&13
6. Present equation and tables to Mrs. Smith.	Wed./Nov. 14
7. Revise equation as needed.	Thu./Nov. 15
8. Submit to astrophysics forums.	Fri./Nov. 16

Your Turn Make a list of tasks and completion times for the goal you established on the previous page.

Defining Team and Tools

After establishing your tasks within a time frame, consider the team and tools you'll need to do the job. Freewrite about them, and then make a list of team members and tools.

I'll be the main one doing the conversion using my graphing calculator and computer. Mrs. Smith will help me check my work, but I need someone else to help with some of the calculations. John is great with math, so I'll ask him for help. The people on the astrophysics forums will be able to help, too. I've got the Schwarzschild metric, but I need reliable data for the sun and all of the planets.

Team	Tools
Me	Schwarzschild metric
John	Graphing calculator
Astrophysics forum	Computer
Mrs. Smith	NASA Web site

Your Turn Freewrite about the team and tools you will need to reach your goal. Then make a list of team members and tools. Next, decide if you would like to continue your work by completing the project you have planned.

Creative-Thinking Activities

The activities below and on the next page will help you practice your creative-thinking skills.

Developing a Creative Mindset

Creative thinking requires a certain mindset characterized by these qualities:

- **Curiosity:** Open yourself to possibilities. Wonder about your world, about how things work and what is going on.
- **Passion:** Pursue what you love. Seek it unapologetically. Make choices to develop ideas unique to your interests.
- **Productivity:** Create in quantity. Make more than you need and select the best to pass along.
- **Courage:** Overcome obstacles. Work persistently. Take time away when you need to, but then come back.

Your Turn Rate yourself for each of the parts of a creative mindset. Then consider one thing you could do to improve each rating.

	(Less) ————————————➤ (More)
Curiosity	1 . . . .2 . . . . 3 . . . . 4 . . . .5 6
Passion	1 . . . .2 . . . . 3 . . . . 4 . . . .5 6
Productivity	1 . . . .2 . . . . 3 . . . . 4 . . . .5 6
Courage	1 . . . .2 . . . . 3 . . . . 4 . . . .5 6

Abundance and Novelty

Creative thinking does not focus on one answer, but on many answers. It doesn't focus on the right answer, but on unique answers. Creative thinking produces many new ideas, and the following activities will help you create some of your own.

Your Turn **Rock on.** List as many original uses for a rock as you can. Go beyond building materials, paperweights, and bookends. Afterward, compare your list with a classmate's. Cross out any common answers. How many unique ideas did the two of you devise?

Use it or lose it. Select an object you are currently using or studying. Write as many original uses for the object as you can think of. Compare your list with a classmate's, crossing out common answers. How many unique ideas did the two of you devise?

Corporate clip climber. Imagine that you want to land your dream job and must use a paperclip to do so. Write as many ways as possible to use the paperclip to land this job.

Tiny turning points. Choose one of the classes you are taking now. Within that subject, think of the smallest object that has made the biggest difference (for example, in American history, the pen that signed the *Emancipation Proclamation*). Make a class list of original answers.

Alarming Innovation

Creative thinking makes unusual connections and uses materials in new ways. Creativity is key to innovation. The following activity will help you innovate.

Your Turn Imagine that you want to create an alarm system to let you know if someone walks past your desk. Look at the things on the desk or table in front of you. Use these things (paper, pens, books, etc.) in a creative way to make an alarm system that will alert you if someone walks past your desk. Compare your solution with another student's.

What's the Value?

Creative thinking helps you discover possibilities for improving or changing things that you had taken for granted. This activity will help you find new possibilities.

Your Turn **Take a seat.** Consider the chair or bench you are sitting on. What is good about it? What is not so good? Do a trait evaluation of the seat, listing its attributes in the first column, evaluating each attribute in the second column, and writing improvements in the third column. Use a chart like the one here.

Trait	Evaluation	Improvements

Your Turn **Evaluate a subject.** Select a person, place, thing, or idea you have been learning about. Do a trait evaluation of this topic.

Manipulative Creativity

Creativity can transform a topic. It considers not only what the topic is, but also what it could become. Manipulative verbs help you to create such transformations.

accelerate	brand	deflate	reverse
accessorize	break	divide	shrink
amplify	elevate	inflate	simplify
automate	freeze	melt	stretch
bend	decelerate	multiply	twist

Your Turn **Seat strategies.** Select one of the manipulative verbs above and apply it to the chair or bench you are sitting on. List as many transformations as you can imagine.

Subject strategies. Select a person, place, thing, or idea you have been studying. Apply one of the manipulative verbs to your selection, and list as many transformations as you can imagine.

Chapter 4
Problem Solving

You've probably heard that to a hammer, every problem looks like a nail. That's because a hammer has just two strategies for solving problems—pound it in or pry it out.

Our world has many problems that can't be solved by these two strategies. In fact, most real problems are complex and require individualized solutions. The problem-solving process requires that you engage the problem, analyze it carefully, and then work toward the best solution.

If you learn the skills taught in this chapter, you'll be able to master just about any problem that comes your way.

You will learn . . .

- Understanding Problem Solving
- Problem Solving in Action
- Problem Solving as Inquiry
- Scientific Inquiry
- Mathematical Inquiry
- Historical Inquiry
- Language Inquiry

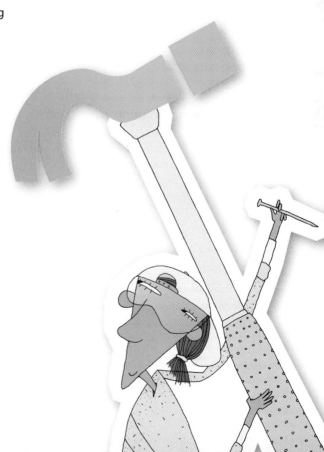

Understanding Problem Solving

Problem solving requires both critical and creative thinking. The diagram below shows how you move through the stages of problem solving.

Critical Thinking

Creative Thinking

Analyze the Problem

To solve a problem, you must analyze it, investigating all aspects of it, especially its causes and effects. (See page 49 for an example.)

Imagine Solutions

Next, imagine as many ways as you can to solve the problem. Don't hold back. Think rapidly to gather all the possible solutions. (See page 50.)

Plan a Solution

After gathering possible solutions, you must choose the best one for the situation. Then plan how to implement your solution, considering your goal, the tasks, time, tools, and team involved. (See page 50.)

Create the Solution

Once you have a plan, you need to dive in and create the solution. Be ready for surprises and setbacks, and don't get sidetracked. (See page 51.)

Evaluate the Solution

When the solution is complete, you need to evaluate it. Check it against your plan and rate the quality of each part. Consider how to strengthen the solution. (See page 51.)

Make Improvements

After evaluating the solution, you should work to improve it. A set of activities and questions will guide your work. (See page 52.)

Implement the Solution

Once the solution is ready to apply, you should put it to work and solve the problem. (See page 52.)

Your Turn Think of a problem in your school or community. How could you use the problem-solving process above to fix the problem? Whom would you involve in your solution?

Problem Solving in **Action**

The following pages explain the problem-solving process using an example that began with students at the Massachusetts Institute of Technology. Their solution to a real-world problem is now making a huge difference for many of the world's poor.

Analyze the Problem

The first step in the problem-solving process is to understand and analyze the problem. Use one or more of the thinking techniques that you learned in chapters 2 and 3 of this book:

Critical-Thinking Strategies	Creative-Thinking Strategies
▪ Sequencing	▪ Metaphorical Thinking
▪ Classifying	▪ Conceptual Blending
▪ Comparing and Contrasting	▪ Forced Connections
▪ Tracing Causes and Effects	▪ Perspective Shifting
▪ Identifying Constants and Variables	▪ Using Socratic Questions
▪ Isolating Variables	▪ Counterfactual Thinking
	▪ Provocative Thinking
	▪ Reverse Thinking

Real-World Example

Around the world, millions of people live in slums, in shacks that are so tightly crammed that no light can enter the living spaces. For most of these homes, electricity and fuel for fires is unavailable. Millions of people spend their days and nights in darkness. A group of MIT students decided to do something about the situation. They began by analyzing the problem.

Tracing Causes and Effects

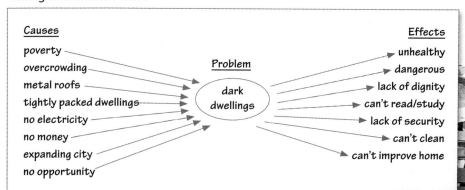

Causes
- poverty
- overcrowding
- metal roofs
- tightly packed dwellings
- no electricity
- no money
- expanding city
- no opportunity

Problem
- dark dwellings

Effects
- unhealthy
- dangerous
- lack of dignity
- can't read/study
- lack of security
- can't clean
- can't improve home

Your Turn Consider the problem you identified on the previous page or choose another. Analyze the problem by considering its causes and effects.

Imagine and Plan Solutions

After thoroughly analyzing a problem, you need to brainstorm and plan solutions. Use one or more of the thinking strategies you learned in chapters 2 and 3:

Critical-Thinking Strategies	Creative-Thinking Strategies
▪ Pattern Finding ▪ Creating Instructions ▪ Creating Algorithms ▪ Designing Experiments	▪ Brainstorming ▪ Square Pegging ▪ Modeling ▪ Role-Playing ▪ Using Manipulative Verbs

Real-World Brainstorming

After thoroughly analyzing the causes and effects of the dark dwellings of the world's poor, the MIT students started brainstorming solutions. One way to do this is to create a cluster, writing down as many ideas as possible without judging them.

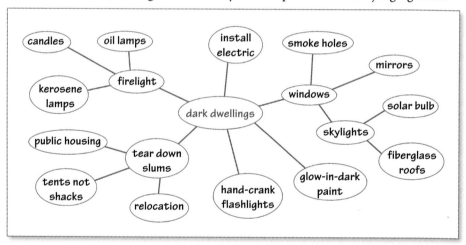

Your Turn Brainstorm solutions to the problem you analyzed on the previous page. If possible, work with another student or a group to produce many solution ideas.

Real-World Planning

The students at MIT decided to work on an inexpensive solar light bulb made from readily available materials. They designed and prototyped their ideas, testing to find the best solution.

Your Turn Select a solution from the ideas you generated above and plan how you could create the solution.

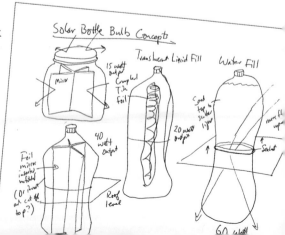

Create and Evaluate the Solution

Once you have planned a solution, you need to launch into creating and evaluating the solution. Use one or more of the strategies that you learned in chapters 2 and 3.

Critical-Thinking Strategies	Creative-Thinking Strategies
■ Problem Solving	■ Setting Goals
■ Scientific Method	■ Listing Tasks
■ Engineering-Design	■ Scheduling Time
■ Writing Process	■ Gathering Teams and Tools
■ Computational Thinking	■ Trait Evaluation
■ Using Rubrics	■ SCAMPER Evaluation

Real-World Creating

After the MIT students tested many possible designs, they settled on a simple structure built from a discarded liter soda bottle, water, chlorine, and a piece of flashing (sheet metal).

Real-World Evaluating

The bulb inventions worked well, but there is always room for improvement. A trait evaluation can pinpoint ways in which the design is working well and ways in which it could work better.

Trait Evaluation: Solar Bottle Bulbs

Trait	Evaluation	Improvements
Light production	Most liter bulbs transfer as much sunlight as a 60-watt bulb, though bleach-scoring of plastic can reduce glow.	Experiment to find the optimal amount of bleach to keep water and plastic clear.
Expense	The liter bottles are free. The sealant and some types of flashing are the main expense.	Investigate most durable but least expensive flashings and sealants. Get donations?
Ease of installation	Many roofs are made of corrugated metal, so we need a way to cut the metal.	Let's work on a low-tech metal-cutting technique.

Your Turn Imagine that you have applied your solution. Perform a trait evaluation to decide on improvements.

BLEACH

Improve and Implement the Solution

After evaluating the solution, it's time to make changes that improve it and then to implement the solution in its real-world context. Use one or more of these strategies from chapters 2 and 3.

Critical-Thinking Strategies	Creative-Thinking Strategies
▪ Creating Instructions ▪ Creating an Algorithm ▪ Using Engineering Design ▪ Thinking Computationally	▪ Setting a Goal ▪ Identifying Objectives ▪ Defining Tasks and Time ▪ Defining Tools and Teams

Real-World Improving and Implementing

The team found the exact right amount of bleach to use to keep the bottle lights shining for years. They also discovered that some plastic bottles crumpled too easily or didn't hold up to the weather. They made many adjustments to increase the light yield, decrease the expense, make implementation easier, and maximize the longevity of the design. In addition to making physical improvements in their design, the students partnered with an organization called "Isang Litrong Liwanag," which is Filipino for "A Liter of Light." (Go to aliteroflight.org to learn how you can help.)

Your Turn Go to aliteroflight.org to see how this organization is taking the ideas of students and turning them into real change in the world.

Problem Solving as Inquiry

Over the last few pages, you've walked through the problem-solving process. Problem solving is actually a version of the inquiry process. The two processes are charted side by side here to illustrate the comparison.

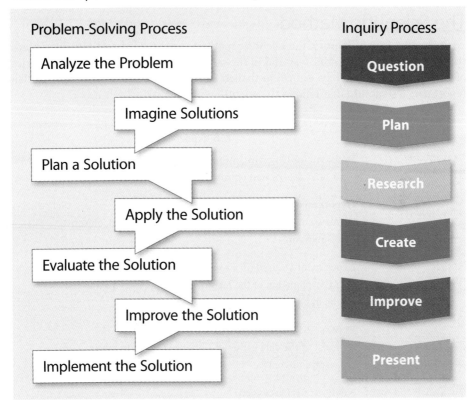

Problem-Solving Process

- Analyze the Problem
- Imagine Solutions
- Plan a Solution
- Apply the Solution
- Evaluate the Solution
- Improve the Solution
- Implement the Solution

Inquiry Process

- Question
- Plan
- Research
- Create
- Improve
- Present

On the next pages, you will see how the inquiry process takes a number of different forms in science, math, social studies, and language arts.

Your Turn **Problem Solving in History:** Choose a historical catastrophe such as the Black Plague, World War I, or the Great Chicago Fire. What causes led to the catastrophe? What effects resulted? If you had a time machine, could you avert the catastrophe? How?

Problem Solving in Science: Think of a modern problem that science could solve, for example, pandemics, increasing energy needs, or protection from Earth impactors. Use the process above to sketch out a possible scientific solution.

Everyday Problem Solving: Think about your daily activities—getting ready for school, taking on a new assignment, trying out for a team or a play. How many of these processes require inquiry and problem solving?

Scientific Inquiry

Science is all about inquiry—questioning phenomena and searching for answers. Over thousands of years, scientists have developed a general method for seeking answers.

The Scientific Method

Like all forms of inquiry, the scientific method is not a hard-and-fast set of steps that always occur in the same way and in the same order. Still, the method has a series of widely agreed upon steps, shown to the left of the outline below. The standard lab report uses a structure that follows the scientific method.

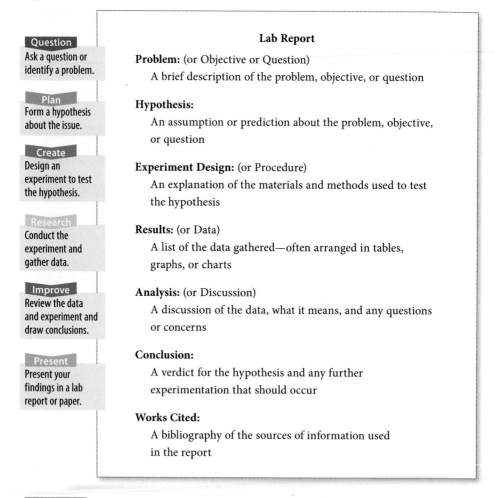

Question
Ask a question or identify a problem.

Plan
Form a hypothesis about the issue.

Create
Design an experiment to test the hypothesis.

Research
Conduct the experiment and gather data.

Improve
Review the data and experiment and draw conclusions.

Present
Present your findings in a lab report or paper.

Lab Report

Problem: (or Objective or Question)
A brief description of the problem, objective, or question

Hypothesis:
An assumption or prediction about the problem, objective, or question

Experiment Design: (or Procedure)
An explanation of the materials and methods used to test the hypothesis

Results: (or Data)
A list of the data gathered—often arranged in tables, graphs, or charts

Analysis: (or Discussion)
A discussion of the data, what it means, and any questions or concerns

Conclusion:
A verdict for the hypothesis and any further experimentation that should occur

Works Cited:
A bibliography of the sources of information used in the report

Your Turn Reflect on a science experiment that you have conducted. What was the main question or problem? What did you discover? How is science a specialized form of inquiry?

Designing Experiments

The scientific method and the lab-report form give you the basic structure for designing an experiment:

1. **Identify a question or problem.** Often your science teacher will provide the question or problem, but professional scientists come up with their own questions. You can identify a question by noticing patterns and identifying problems in the world around you.

   The sun is so blazing hot today. I feel like I'm frying. What would it take to make a solar stove that could actually cook food?

2. **Create a hypothesis.** Make a prediction about the question or problem you have identified. State your hypothesis as a fact with measurable variables.

   Hypothesis: Using tin foil on a parabolic curve, I could concentrate enough sunlight to heat a hot dog to 190 degrees F.

3. **Identifying variables.** Think about the hypothesis and the variables that you want to test. Decide how to test them.

   Variables: Size of reflector, cooking temperature, cooking time

   Test for reflector size: Use 1-foot, 1½-foot and 2-foot reflectors.

   Test for temperature: Use meat thermometers.

   Test for cooking time: Use watch with second hand.

4. **Identify variables to control.** Think about other variables that could affect the outcome. Then devise ways to control these variables.

   Variables: Ambient temperature, wind

   Controls: Require 80–85 degrees F ambient temperature, < 5 m.p.h. wind

5. **Summarize the experiment.** Write the process you will follow.

   Design: I will create a set of solar cookers using parabolic curves covered in tin foil. Each curve will be 6 inches wide, but I will test these at 1-foot, 1½-foot, and 2-foot lengths. For each reflector, I will test the time it takes for a hot dog to reach 190 degrees F.

Your Turn Think of interesting phenomena in the world around you: the movement of shadows, the formation of snow drifts, the erosion of soil, or some other pattern. Then follow steps 1 to 5 above to design your own experiment. If your instructor approves your design, carry out the experiment and report the results.

Deductive Reasoning

The experiment design on the previous page uses a deductive pattern of thinking. It begins with a general question and works toward specific observations. Here's a lab report that also uses deductive reasoning:

Osmosis in Chicken Eggs

Abstract:
This lab experiment tests osmosis in chicken eggs, specifically focusing on the effect of water concentration inside and outside the eggs.

Deduction begins with a general observation, a problem, and a hypothesis.

Problem:
How does water content inside and outside an egg affect osmosis?

Hypothesis:
Higher water concentration inside an egg will cause osmosis outward, and higher concentration outside will cause osmosis inward.

An experimental design allows scientists to test the hypothesis through a step-by-step procedure.

Experiment Design:
1. Using four eggs, measure the length, width, and mass of each.
2. Place one egg in each of four beakers. Add solution as follows:
   A. Distilled water (100 percent H_2O)
   B. Salt water (98 percent H_2O)
   C. Isopropyl alcohol (30 percent H_2O)
   D. Corn syrup (5 percent H_2O)
3. After two days, measure the length, width, and mass of each egg.

Specific results appear in a table.

Results:

Egg	Width Before	Width After	Length Before	Length After	Mass Before	Mass After
A. Water	41 mm	43 mm	54 mm	57 mm	52 g	62 g
B. Salt water	44 mm	41 mm	56 mm	53 mm	54 g	49 g
C. Isopropyl alcohol	46 mm	42 mm	57 mm	55 mm	55 g	45 g
D. Corn syrup	42 mm	38 mm	55 mm	52 mm	52 g	43 g

Analysis reveals patterns in the data.

Analysis: (or Discussion)
The egg in distilled water gained width, height, and mass. All of the other eggs lost in each category. The solutions with the lowest amount of water show the greatest reduction in the size and mass of the egg.

The conclusion applies the general hypothesis to the specific data.

Conclusion:
Water moved from greater concentrations to lesser concentrations, thus swelling or dehydrating the egg.

Your Turn Discuss with a partner how lab reports exhibit a deductive structure (see also page 97).

Inductive Reasoning

Scientists also work inductively, beginning with a mountain of data and sifting through it to discover patterns and processes. The table below from NASA shows near-Earth objects, indicating date, distance from Earth, size, and relative velocity.

Inductive reasoning begins with specific data, such as this information about near-Earth objects.

Inductive reasoning looks for patterns: objects that are close, those that are large, and those that are fast.

Inductive reasoning makes connections: Some objects appear in two categories.

General conclusions result: Objects sharing two or more of these traits are concerning due to chance of hitting Earth and energy imparted by hitting.

Near-Earth Objects, Jan 25–April 19, 2012

Object	Nearest Date	Miss (Lunar Distances)	Diameter Range	Relative Velocity (km/s)
Near-Earth Objects (<10 Lunar Distances Miss)				
(2012 BW13)	Jan-26	1.7	9.8 m–22 m	11.80
(2012 BD14)	Jan-30	5.8	12 m–27 m	7.18
(2011 CP4)	Feb-23	9.1	160 m–350 m	30.47
(2008 EJ85)	Mar-06	9.1	27 m–60 m	6.52
(2007 HV4)	Apr-19	4.8	4.9 m–11 m	8.98
Near-Earth Objects (>1 km in Diameter)				
7341 (1991 VK)	Jan-25	25.3	1.2 km–2.7 km	8.73
433 Eros	Jan-31	69.5	17 km	5.95
(2006 AL8)	Feb-01	40.9	580 m–1.3 km	36.73
(2008 QY)	Feb-14	59.6	520 m–1.2 km	22.29
(2009 AV)	Feb-16	44.9	710 m–1.6 km	24.01
162421 (2000 ET70)	Feb-19	17.7	630 m–1.4 km	11.54
(2008 WZ13)	Feb-21	57.2	520 m–1.2 km	10.49
(2011 UU106)	Mar-11	67.6	500 m–1.1 km	8.81
192642 (1999 RD32)	Mar-14	57.9	1.4 km–3.2 km	18.80
(2011 YU62)	Mar-16	73.4	830 m–1.8 km	17.85
(2009 WD106)	Apr-15	75.0	500 m–1.1 km	25.20
297274 (1996)	Apr-18	67.2	1.0 km–2.2 km	19.26
Near-Earth Objects (>20 km/s Relative Velocity)				
(2006 CJ)	Feb-01	17.6	250 m–560 m	21.89
(2006 AL8)	Feb-01	40.9	580 m–1.3 km	36.73
(2008 QY)	Feb-14	59.6	520 m–1.2 km	22.29
(2009 AV)	Feb-16	44.9	710 m–1.6 km	24.01
(2011 CP4)	Feb-23	9.1	160 m–350 m	30.47
(2008 GD)	Mar-30	65.6	300 m–670 m	32.35
(2004 FG11)	Apr-10	22.3	170 m–390 m	25.09
(2009 WD106)	Apr-15	75.0	500 m–1.1 km	25.20

Your Turn Investigate the chart above. Do you notice any other interesting patterns? Can you draw any conclusions from what you see?

Mathematical Inquiry

If you think math is mainly about getting the same answer that someone else has already figured out, you are missing the wonder of it. Math is a language that can explain the world for you, and you can use mathematical inquiry in life.

Begin Your Inquiry

Imagine, for instance, that you are stuck in traffic on a freeway. Rather than just sitting there and getting angry, you could do a little mathematical inquiry.

Question
Ask a question or identify a problem.

Plan
Identify variables and constants.

Why are we suddenly creeping along? A minute ago, it was free flow, and now it's stop and go. What's up with that?

What's changed? It's been raining the whole time. We haven't lost a lane. There's no accident. Sure, people have been merging, but people have also been exiting. I wonder if more people are merging than exiting?

Research Your Inquiry

You decide to find out whether your hunch about more people merging is true. At home, watching a traffic camera, you count the number of vehicles that enter in one minute and the number that exit in one minute. You find that 39 vehicles enter while 27 exit, and now traffic has stopped. So the problem seems to be too many vehicles sharing the road.

Exit 36: Entering: 12
          Exiting: 11
Exit 37: Entering: 19
          Exiting: 0 (no exit)
Exit 38: Entering: 8
          Exiting: 16
Totals: Entering: 39
          Exiting: 27

Research
Design a formula to explain the phenomenon.

How many is too many? What's the tipping point? You look to the lanes of oncoming traffic and see that they are moving pretty well. You could compare the density of vehicles there to the density in the traffic where you were stuck.

You discover that, in an eighth-mile stretch of road, each lane on your side has an average of 19 vehicles, while the other side has an average of 9. In subsequent samples, you find that the other side can get up to 15 vehicles in an eighth-mile stretch of lane and still flow. At 17, they slow. And at 19, they stop, like you.

Create and Improve Your Inquiry

Next, you devise a formula to explain the density of vehicles at which free flow ceases. You simplify the formula to account for flow over a mile of roadway (more than you could count).

Free-Flow Traffic Formula

If F is free-flow density, then . . .

F < 17 vehicles per lane/eighth mile

F < 136 vehicles per lane/mile

(the < means less than)

Create
Run data through the formula to get results.

Can I find more than 17 vehicles in a lane that is still flowing?
As you test your formula, you discover that it seems to be true, with a plus-or-minus-1 error rate. At least it seems true for *this* roadway under *these* conditions with *these* drivers.

Improve
Check results against observations and adjust formula.

You want to see if your traffic formula holds up in other situations. Online, you find the information below:

Free-Flow Traffic Formula

If F is free-flow density, then . . .

F < 22 vehicles per lane/eighth mile

F < 180 vehicles per lane/mile

Present Your Inquiry

Your calculation was off by 44 vehicles! Even with your error rate, you didn't expect a 44-vehicle difference. If math were all about getting the same exact answer as someone already got, you might be feeling pretty bad right now. But mathematicians in the real world don't have answer keys. They are playing with numbers. If their results are different, they try to figure out the reason for the difference. Then you remember: It was raining that day. People slow down in the rain. And that's only one of the possible factors that could have caused your variant observation.

Present
Present your formula for others to use.

Finally, you go online to a math forum and post your observations and flow-rate formula, asking for comments. There you find other interesting formulas and charts that other people have posted.

Your Turn **School Traffic:** You probably encounter "traffic jams" every day in school: hallways, entrances, exits, the cafeteria, the gym, the auditorium. Use a similar math inquiry process to come up with a flow-rate formula for traffic in these places. After you establish your formula, compare it to those of other classmates. Discuss any differences and variables that you notice.

Patterns of Flow: Think of other things that flow: liquids, gasses, people, particles, ideas, videos, emotions. In your current class, make a list of "Things That Flow." Choose one idea from your list and explore it using a similar mathematical inquiry process.

Mathematical Estimating

As you saw on previous pages, mathematical inquiry often involves estimating. When you don't have the time or means to count or measure something exactly, you need to be able to make an educated guess that is close enough.

Your car has a 21-gallon tank that is 1/8 full, it gets 23 miles per gallon, and the next gas exit is 39 miles down the road—do you exit now?	*An eighth of 21 gallons is more than 2 gallons, and 2 gallons times 23 miles per gallon is more than 39 miles, so I can keep driving.*

If you don't estimate well, you may run out of gas, order too little pizza, pay too much at the register, or report ridiculous statistics. Estimation is a key math skill.

Estimating Techniques

The best way to become skilled at estimating is to practice. Here are some specific strategies that work well.

■ **Focus on the first digit and round the rest.**	4,683 + 7,336 is about 12,000.
■ **Round to the multiplication table.**	183 ÷ 58 is about 3 (183 ÷ 58 is like 180 ÷ 60, or 18 ÷ 6)
■ **Round fractions, decimals, and percents.**	0.92 × 5/9 is about 0.5 (0.92 is almost 1 and 5/9 is a little over half)
■ **Group numbers to round them.**	44 + 95 + 63 is about 200 (44 and 63 are about 100, and so is 95)
■ **Average similar numbers.**	723 + 695 + 733 + 701 + 692 is about 3,500 (700 × 5)
■ **Check zeros.** When multiplying, keep all zeroes. When dividing, subtract them.	7,000 × 2,000 is 14,000,000 (not 14,000) 7,000 ÷ 2,000 is 3.5 (not 3,500)
■ **Estimate one part, count all parts, and multiply.**	9 in² ▷ about 54 in²

Your Turn Estimate the number of jellybeans in the jar to the right. Indicate how you came up with your estimate. Compare your answer with a classmate's.

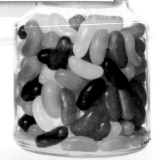

Mathematical Problem Solving

Think of word problems as verbal versions of the real-world problems you've solved before. Use the inquiry process you are familiar with, but apply it to the given question and problem.

> **Word Problem:** A man has three sons—Eli, Aidan, and Gabe—and the younger two have cats, Merlin and Gato. Eli is two years older than Aidan, and Aidan is twice the age of Gabe. Gabe is the same age as Merlin. The boys' ages add up to 17. How old is each boy?

Question
Ask a question or identify a problem.

What is the age of each boy? Eli (E) is two years older than Aidan, and Aidan (A) is twice the age of Gabe (G). The boy's ages add up to 17. (It doesn't tell how old Merlin is, so it doesn't matter that Gabe is the same age.)

$$E = A + 2$$
$$A = 2G$$
$$G = ?$$

Plan
Identify variables and constants. (Get rid of unimportant information.)

Research
Run calculations through the formula to get results.

What age is each boy?
$$E + A + G = 17$$
If A = 2G, then
$$E + 2G + G = 17$$
If E = A + 2 and A = 2G, then E = 2G + 2, and
$$2G + 2 + 2G + G = 17$$

Create
Design a formula to explain the phenomenon.

Isolate the variable. (Add the G's.)
$$2G + 2 + 2G + G = 17$$
$$5G + 2 = 17$$
$$5G + 2 - 2 = 17 - 2$$
$$5G = 15$$
$$5G/5 = 15/5$$
$$G = 3$$

Improve
Check results against observations and make adjustments.

Use the numbers in the original equations.
$$G = 3$$
$A = 2G$ so $A = 6$ (Aidan is twice Gabe's age)
$E = A + 2$ so $E = 8$ (Eli is two years older)
$$8 + 6 + 3 = 17$$

Present
Present your results.

Give the result. Eli is 8, Aidan is 6, and Gabe is 3.

Historical Inquiry

Problem solving in history goes well beyond your textbook. Instead of memorizing names and dates from a secondary source, you can engage history firsthand by going to primary sources. You follow the same basic process you've learned:

Question
Ask a question or identify a problem.

What are the historic roots of the modern computer? Who invented the first computer? Where did the idea come from? What previous technology was included?

Plan
Decide how you will find out about the question or problem. Create a hypothesis.

1. **Engage tertiary sources** to find initial answers, including textbooks and Web sites.
2. **Find secondary sources** to understand what others have said, reading scholarly books and journal articles.
3. **Find primary sources** to understand the issue firsthand, conducting interviews and attending museums.

Research
Conduct research, focusing on primary sources.

Tertiary sources reveal that Konrad Zuse created the first programmable computer in 1936.

Secondary sources reveal that computers stored data using perforated paper like player pianos.

Primary sources let you study your grandmother's player piano and rolls to understand how data is stored.

Create
Synthesize your findings in a form to share.

One critical piece of pre-computer technology arrived in 1801, when Joseph Marie Jacquard invented a mechanical loom that used a series of punched cards to program a textile pattern.

Improve
Improve your work so it clearly expresses what you found.

This history shows just the most recent resurgence of computer technology. The Antikythera mechanism is a computer from the first or second century B.C.E. that calculated the position of planets and stars. A reconstruction at the Children's Museum of Manhattan shows its precision.

Present
Share your findings in the appropriate form.

We tend to think of computers as modern innovations, but they have been with us at least 2,000 years, and the technology that went into modern computers began in looms and player pianos.

Your Turn Solve a problem in history. Ask questions and identify problems. Plan how you will find answers to your questions, and delve into research. Follow the rest of the steps above to put your findings in a form that you can share.

Inquiry into Society

You don't have to limit your inquiry to solving problems of the past. The present and future offer plenty of problems to examine. Use inquiry to identify those problems and come up with solutions, much as the Liter of Light project has done (see pages 49–52). The following report focuses on solutions to a terrible problem—genocide.

Ancient Crime, New Solutions

Genocide is as old as the world itself, though the word is shockingly new. In 1944, when the Allies began to discover the depravities occurring in Nazi concentration camps, the Polish-Jewish legal scholar Raphael Lemkin coined the term *genocide*. The word combines the Greek word for "race" with the Latin word for "kill" ("Genocide"). Four years later, the United Nations created a convention to prevent and punish genocide. The definition of *genocide*, however, was problematic because it referred to the intent to kill "wholly or in part" a group based upon race, ethnicity, nationality, or religion—a definition perpetrators have twisted to their own ends (Carlson).

Definitions and rulings, however, did not stop genocides in Cambodia and Rwanda. In response to these tragedies, Gregory Stanton of Genocide Watch established eight stages of genocide, outlining the actions that the international community should take to prevent genocide:

Stage	Problem	Solution
1. Classification	A population is divided.	Develop institutions to transcend divisions.
2. Symbolization	Outcasts become associated with hate symbols and speech.	Outlaw hate symbols and hate speech.
3. Dehumanization	Outcasts are compared to vermin and disease.	International leaders should condemn this and freeze assets of perpetrators.
4. Organization	Perpetrators train and arm militias.	The U.N. should sanction governments.
5. Polarization	Hate propaganda is broadcast.	The U.N. should launch human-rights interventions.
6. Preparation	Victims are separated from the populace.	The U.N. should declare a genocide emergency.
7. Extermination	Victims are murdered.	Armed intervention must be launched.
8. Denial	Perpetrators deny wrongdoing.	International tribunals must act.

Your Turn Select a modern problem and investigate possible solutions.

Language Inquiry

As you have seen, the problem-solving process applies in science, math, and social studies. These two pages will show how to apply problem solving in language arts.

The Reading Process

Imagine that you need to read and understand a letter written in 1865. Where do you begin? The reading process gives you a problem-solving approach for extracting meaning from a text.

Question

Question the work, its author, and your expectations.

Plan

Research

Scan the work, looking at formal structures.

Create

Read the work carefully, marking it as you go.

Improve

Review the text and formal structures, reminding yourself of main points.

Present

Discuss the text with another reader to cement its ideas in your mind.

Dayton, Ohio, August 7, 1865

To My Old Master, Colonel P. H. Anderson, Big Spring, Tennessee

Sir: I got your letter, and was glad to find that you had not forgotten Jourdon, and that you wanted me to come back and live with you again, promising to do better for me than anybody else can. I have often felt uneasy about you. I thought the Yankees would have hung you long before this, for harboring Rebs they found at your house. I suppose they never heard about your going to Colonel Martin's to kill the Union soldier that was left by his company in their stable. Although you shot at me twice before I left you, I did not want to hear of your being hurt, and am glad you are still living. . . .

I want to know particularly what the good chance is you propose to give me. I am doing tolerably well here. I get twenty-five dollars a month, with victuals and clothing; have a comfortable home for Mandy,—the folks call her Mrs. Anderson,—and the children—Milly, Jane, and Grundy—go to school and are learning well. The teacher says Grundy has a head for a preacher. They go to Sunday school, and Mandy and me attend church regularly. We are kindly treated. Sometimes we overhear others saying, "Them colored people were slaves" down in Tennessee. The children feel hurt when they hear such remarks; but I tell them it was no disgrace in Tennessee to belong to Colonel Anderson. . . .

As to my freedom, which you say I can have, there is nothing to be gained on that score, as I got my free papers in 1864 from the Provost-Marshal-General of the Department of Nashville. Mandy says she would be afraid to go back without some proof that you were disposed to treat us justly and kindly; and we have concluded to test your sincerity by asking you to send us our wages for the time we served you. This will make us forget and forgive old scores, and rely on your justice and friendship in the future. I served you faithfully for thirty-two years, and Mandy twenty years. At twenty-five dollars a month for me, and two dollars a week for Mandy, our earnings would amount to eleven thousand six hundred and eighty dollars. Add to this the interest for the time our wages have been kept back, and deduct what you paid for our clothing, and three doctor's visits to me, and pulling a tooth for Mandy, and the balance will show what we are in justice entitled to. Please send the money by Adams's Express, in care of V. Winters, Esq., Dayton, Ohio. If you fail to pay us for faithful labors in the past, we can have little faith in your promises in the future. We trust the good Maker has opened your eyes to the wrongs which you and your fathers have done to me and my fathers, in making us toil for you for generations without recompense. Here I draw my wages every Saturday night; but in Tennessee there was never any pay-day for the negroes any more than for the horses and cows. Surely there will be a day of reckoning for those who defraud the laborer of his hire. . . .

Say howdy to George Carter, and thank him for taking the pistol from you when you were shooting at me.

From your old servant, Jourdon Anderson

The Writing Process

The writing process also solves a problem—how to go from a blank page to an effective piece of writing. This process is another unique form of inquiry (steps outlined on the left). The example writing is a response to the letter "To My Old Master."

Question
Question the communication situation.

Plan
State your thesis and plan your research.

Research
Gather and organize the information you need to write.

Create
Write a first draft, creating a beginning, middle, and ending.

Improve
Revise and edit your drafts.

Present
Publish your work.

Sender: Jourdon Anderson, a former slave
Subject: A letter refusing work from his one-time master
Purpose: To point out the evils of slavery in a surprising way
Receiver: The master, who wrote to request the man's return

Thesis: Jourdon Anderson powerfully demonstrates his humanity through a letter that is matter-of-fact on the surface but angry and earnest beneath.

Understatement: Throughout, Jourdon states horrible situations in mild language, creating a powerful contrast:

- "Although you shot at me twice before I left you, I did not want to hear of your being hurt."
- "The children feel hurt when they hear such remarks; but I tell them it was no disgrace in Tennessee to belong to Colonel Anderson."
- "At twenty-five dollars a month for me, and two dollars a week for Mandy, our earnings would amount to eleven thousand six hundred and eighty dollars."
- "Say howdy to George Carter, and thank him for taking the pistol from you when you were shooting at me."

Beginning: Jourdon Anderson had faithfully served his master for 32 years before he and his family were emancipated. Then Jourdon received a letter from his former master, asking him to return. Jourdon's reply powerfully demonstrates his humanity in a letter that is matter-of-fact on the surface but deadly earnest beneath.

Revise and edit: I need to provide more quotations. The letter is powerful.

AlphaRom77   22h
Black History Month Must-Read: Letter to My Old Master
ow.ly/8Ob0z Brilliant! #sschat #edchat #inquiry

Expand

Your Turn Use the reading process to absorb and understand "To My Former Master" and the writing process to create your own response.

Problem-Solving Activities

The following activities will help you work through the problem-solving process in your own life.

Pick a Problem and Analyze It

Think about the "pain points" you experience at school, at home, on the job, or in the community. What problems do you face? Which would you most like to solve?

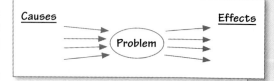

To solve a problem, you need to thoroughly understand its causes and effects.

Your Turn List problems you face in the four locations indicated above. Select one problem that you would like to solve. Create a cause-effect chart about the problem you identified. Write the problem in the center circle, causes to the left, and effects to the right.

Brainstorm Solutions

Once you fully understand the causes and effects of a problem, you can brainstorm ways to eliminate the causes, the effects, or both.

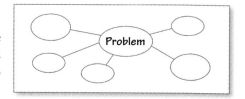

Your Turn Use a list or cluster to brainstorm solutions to the problem that you analyzed above.

Evaluate Solutions

After you have listed many possible solutions, you must decide which solution will work best and why.

Your Turn Choose one of the solutions you have thought of and would like to pursue. Fill in a trait-evaluation chart for your solution (see page 51). In the first column, list traits that your solution should have—ways it should fix the problem. In the center column, evaluate each trait. And in the final column, write possible improvements.

Trait	Evaluation	Improvements

Chapter 5
Communicating

So far in this book, you've focused on thinking—the ways in which you explore, develop, and compose ideas. Communicating takes thinking to the next level. If thinking is composing, communicating is the concert. The ideas are no longer confined to your own head. You "play" them for someone else, who listens, thinks, and responds with new ideas—and maybe even cheers.

Communicating is a back-and-forth process that involves speaking and listening. When you speak, you are the performer, and when you listen, you are the audience. Then the roles reverse. To communicate well, you need to speak and listen effectively in a variety of situations. This chapter will show you how.

You will learn . . .

- Understanding the Communication Situation
- Listening Actively
- Reading Faces and Body Language
- Speaking
- Speaking One-on-One
- Speaking in a Group
- Speaking to an Audience
- Overcoming Stage Fright
- Listening and Speaking Terms

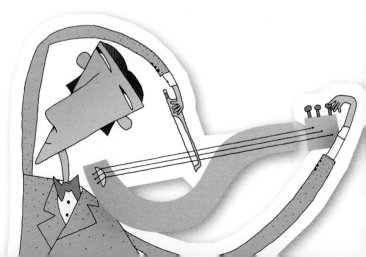

Understanding the Communication Situation

Effective, clear communication requires that you first examine the situation. Every communication situation has five basic components.

The Communication Situation

1. **Sender:** The creator of the message (speaker, writer, director, designer, marketer)
2. **Message:** The subject and purpose (inform, persuade, entertain)
3. **Medium:** The way the message is expressed (speech, email, ad, video, painting)
4. **Receiver:** The audience of the message (listener, reader, viewer)
5. **Context:** The place and time of the message (history, hurdles, opportunities)

Sender ▷ Message ▷ Receiver

Context   Medium

Medium

Communication uses many media. This chapter focuses on the listener/speaker form, though later chapters will focus on written forms (reader/writer). Part 3 of this book includes other forms of communication, from videos to models to experiments to clubs. Media fall on a continuum from quick and casual to deliberate and formal.

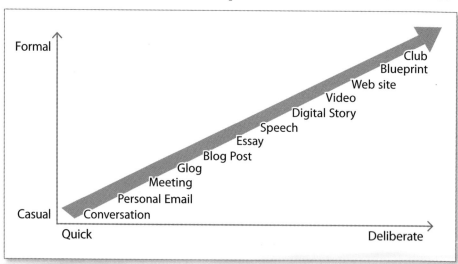

Your Turn Think of one of your recent communication situations. Where would it fall on this graph?

Listening Actively

Hearing involves the ears. Listening involves the mind. Earlier, we looked at the different levels of thinking, which also apply to listening. Below, you will see that as thinking becomes deeper, listening becomes more active.

Levels of Thinking	Levels of Listening
Remembering	■ Hearing the message. ■ Repeating the message.
Understanding	■ Knowing the 5 W's and H of the message. ■ Paraphrasing the message correctly. ■ Reflecting on the meaning.
Applying	■ Contextualizing the message. ■ Inferring from the message. ■ Connecting the message to other ideas.
Analyzing	■ Identifying the main point. ■ Recognizing the support for the main point. ■ Questioning the purpose of the message.
Evaluating	■ Testing the reliability of the message. ■ Noting the effectiveness of the message. ■ Suggesting ways the message could be improved.
Creating	■ Combining the ideas with others. ■ Generating questions and comments. ■ Composing a response to the message.

Deeper (downward arrow at left)   *More Active* (downward arrow at right)

In the chart above, note that each level of listening ends with a response option. For example, at the shallowest level, you might show that you are listening simply by repeating the message back to the person. At a deeper level, you would reflect on the meaning. You might also connect the message to other ideas, question its purpose, or suggest improvements. The depth of conversation relates directly to the depth of thinking and level of listening that you apply.

Your Turn With a partner, begin a conversation by completing the following sentence: "The most interesting thing I learned today was . . ." The partner then responds at the "remembering" level of listening, following one of the bulleted points there. You reply by explaining more about the interesting thing that you learned, and the partner responds at the "understanding" level. Keep the conversation going to the deepest levels of thinking and the most active levels of listening. Discuss the difference in responses at various levels. Then switch roles and repeat.

Listening to Words

Listening begins as we receive the words that come to us. We hear them with our ears, and our brains turn the sounds into sentences and extract their meaning. This page focuses on the parts of a message that you should think about when listening.

1. **Subject:** The subject is what the person is talking about. A subject can be broad (school spirit) or narrow (the first song the band will play at this afternoon's pep rally).

2. **Main point:** The main point sums up the specific focus about the subject. It condenses what the person is saying. Listen for this point and be ready to repeat and remember it.

3. **Support:** The speaker will support the main point by providing details—reasons, statistics, anecdotes, and so on. Listen to the support, but don't let it eclipse the main point.

4. **Purpose:** The speaker is talking for a reason, even if the reason is not mentioned. Try to decide why the person is speaking. Think about what the person wants you to do with the information.

5. **Implication:** Often, what is left unsaid is more important than what is said. Think about what the message means in its larger context. What is the speaker implying? What can you infer?

6. **Outcome:** The outcome of the message could be simply that you understand something new. The outcome might also require you to reply, agree or disagree, or take action. Decide how (and whether) to respond to what has been said.

Your Turn **Social Studies:** Find a video of a famous speech and listen to it. Then write down the subject, main point, support, purpose, implications, and outcome of the speech.

Science: Search online for a scientific news conference in which a discovery is presented. Listen. Write down the subject, main point, support, purpose, implications, and outcome.

Math: Think about your most recent math lecture. Write down the subject, main point, support, purpose, implications, and outcome of the lecture.

English: Search online to find famous soliloquies (solo speeches) from plays. Choose one. Write down the subject, main point, support, purpose, implications, and outcome of the soliloquy.

Home: Listen to a conversation at home, whether at the dinner table, in front of the TV, or on the front stoop. Think about the subject, main point, support, purpose, implication, and outcome.

Listening to Voice

Voice reveals a speaker's connection to each part of the communication situation. As you listen to a speaker, think about what his or her voice is telling you.

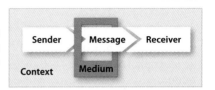

Sender → Message → Receiver

Context   Medium

Sender:
Voice reveals the speaker's identity (who he or she is), personality (bubbly, quiet, gruff), and position (teacher, entertainer, cop). It reveals the person's gender and age and how the person is feeling. Consider the examples to the right.

> "Um, Mrs. Willis? I, uh, well . . . my homework's at home."

> "It is, is it? That would be the second time this week, Mr. Jones."

Message:
Voice reveals the speaker's opinion of the subject (lighthearted, grave, flippant, confused, worried). Voice also reveals what the person's purpose is for sharing this message (consoling, joking, cajoling, informing).

> "Huh, yeah, and second time my dog ate it. Need a new dog."

> "You won't be laughing when you see your grade for this class."

Medium:
Voice reveals how capable the speaker is with the communication medium. In spoken language, voice shows if the person feels confident or not and what level of proficiency the person has.

> "I, uh. Yeah. Both of 'em. Sure. I gotta do both assignments."

> "That's what you've got to do."

Receiver:
Voice reveals the speaker's relationship to the audience (formal, congenial, combative, businesslike). Voice also shows the relative position of the speaker (superior, equal, subordinate).

> "I'll make it up. I swear. I'll turn it in tomorrow and do extra credit."

> "You'll turn in this assignment and the last one as well."

Context:
Voice reveals the speaker's perception of the situation that surrounds the message. It tells how the person thinks the message fits in with other messages and circumstances.

> "I promise. I know I promised before, but this time I mean it."

> "Good. I've threatened before, and this time I mean it, too."

Your Turn Listen to a conversation in a movie, or read a conversation in a novel or short story. Choose one of the people in the conversation and indicate what the person's voice tells about all aspects of the communication situation.

Reading Faces

A recent study of South American primates discovered that the more solitary a species is, the more elaborate the facial markings are. The more social a species, the more plain the faces. That's because plain faces more easily form expressions that communicate emotion. Human faces are plainer and more expressive than monkey faces. As you listen, make sure to read the facial expressions of the speaker.

Your Turn Identify the emotion behind the facial expression above. Compare your answers with a partner's. Discuss any differences, and indicate the facial evidence for the emotion you identified.

Reading Body Language

As with facial expressions, body language also communicates. In fact, our faces and bodies tend to be honest about our feelings even when our words are not. That's because, as infants, we expressed ourselves physically long before we did verbally.

Your Turn For each picture above, indicate what the body language is expressing. Compare your answers with a partner's and discuss any differences. Indicate what posture cues support your response.

Speaking

Much of human communication is spoken—whether during a friendly conversation, a news broadcast, a lecture, or a negotiation over the price of a car. The way that you speak depends on the communication situation. For example, if you get pulled over by a police officer, you will speak differently than if you are talking to a friend at your locker. Each situation calls for a specific level of formality.

Formality

Formality relates to all aspects of the communication situation. The chart below discusses levels of formality and tells the kind of situation each level fits:

Informal

Relaxed language with slang, contractions, humor, personal pronouns, and fragments.

▶ Use for routine messages delivered face-to-face with friends.

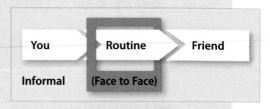

Semiformal

Language with some contractions and personal pronouns, occasional humor.

▶ Use for important messages to strangers; for example, on the phone.

Formal

Correct, serious language using complete sentences and avoiding slang.

▶ Use for serious messages to authorities or groups and in other formal contexts.

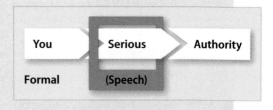

Your Turn Think about situations in which you speak. Write down an informal speaking situation, a semiformal one, and a formal one. Then, for each situation, write an example sentence that uses the appropriate level of formality.

Example:

Formal: An award speech—"I would like to thank Principal Parker, the staff, the awards committee, and the students of BHS for selecting me for this honor."

Speaking One-on-One

Many one-on-one conversations require a formal speaking style—for example, meeting with a guidance counselor, interviewing someone, or talking to a college admissions director. Follow these tips for formal one-on-one conversations:

Before . . .

☑ **Analyze the situation.** Think about whether you are representing yourself or a group (like the school newspaper or the student council). Think about the subject, your reason for discussing it, and the context.

☑ **Learn about the audience.** Find out what the person knows and needs to know about the topic. Think about what the person wants to get out of the conversation. Learn how to correctly pronounce the person's name and which courtesy title to use (Mr., Mrs., Ms., Dr., Coach).

During . . .

☑ **Greet the person.** Introduce yourself, shake the person's hand, and thank the person for speaking with you.

☑ **Be polite and respectful.** Use *please* and *thank you* and show that you appreciate the person's time.

☑ **Make eye contact.** Give the other person your full attention and smile. Keep your facial expressions open and interested.

☑ **Use appropriate body language.** Stand or sit with upright posture. Nod your head to show that you are paying attention. Use gestures when appropriate.

☑ **Speak clearly and calmly.** Use formal language and pronounce words carefully. Avoid slang and other informal constructions.

☑ **Focus your conversation.** Stay on topic and remember your reason for speaking with the person. Avoid straying into other issues.

☑ **Thank the person.** End the conversation by telling how much you appreciated the opportunity. Shake the person's hand once again.

After . . .

☑ **Reflect on the conversation.** Review the main points of the conversation and write down any part that you will need to remember.

☑ **Follow up, if appropriate.** You can send an email thanking the person again, or you can send a message requesting any clarification you need.

Your Turn Think about appropriate formality for speaking with a friend or a counselor. Create a chart of informal and formal phrasing.

Informal	Formal
Hey, how goes it?	Good afternoon, Mr. Daniels.

Speaking in a Group

In school and in the workplace, you'll often be asked to participate in small-group discussions. Follow these tips to get the most out of these communication situations.

Before . . .

- ☑ **Analyze the situation.** Think about what the group is trying to accomplish, what you will discuss, and where the conversation will take place.

- ☑ **Think about the group members.** Make sure you know everyone's name. Consider what the other members want from the group.

During . . .

- ☑ **Engage in the conversation.** Speak and listen, make eye contact, and stand or sit in an upright posture that shows your interest. Avoid slouching and nervous tapping.

- ☑ **Start sentences with "I" instead of "You."** In this way, you avoid sounding accusatory and signal that you are speaking for yourself.

- ☑ **Take turns.** Don't dominate the conversation, but don't remain silent either. If you see that someone hasn't gotten a chance to speak, prompt the person: "Jana, what do you think of this idea?"

- ☑ **Be polite.** Make sure that everyone feels welcome and safe to contribute. Recognize when someone has a good suggestion. Apologize when needed.

- ☑ **Focus on ideas, not on personalities.** Direct comments and questions to the issue you are discussing rather than to the people involved in the conversation.

- ☑ **Stay on task.** If the conversation veers off topic, gently bring the group back to the issue at hand: "Let's set that issue aside until we make a decision about which approach we're going to use."

- ☑ **Facilitate the conversation.** Keep the group moving forward by nudging the conversation along: "It sounds like everybody agrees with this suggestion—is that true? All right, so what next steps should we take?"

After . . .

- ☑ **Review the discussion.** Write down decisions made and major topics discussed. Think about whether the group completed all the work it needed to do.

Your Turn Think about a recent group discussion you have had. How did it go? Which of the tips above were evident in the discussion? Which tips could have improved the conversation?

Speaking to an Audience

In school and out, you will occasionally need to speak to a large group. Careful preparation will equip you for success. Follow these tips for giving a speech.

Before . . .

☑ **Analyze the situation.** Think about the message you want to deliver. What is the main point? What support do you need? Consider the place where you will deliver your speech and the audience who will be listening.

☑ **Know your topic.** Carefully research your topic and gather the information you need to present.

☑ **Prepare your speech.** Write out your speech word for word if you wish, or prepare note cards to help you remember what you want to say.

☑ **Prepare visuals.** Create a slide show to accompany your speech, or provide other visuals to get your point across.

☑ **Practice.** Videotape yourself and watch your delivery. Make your presentation in front of family or friends and use their suggestions to improve your delivery.

During . . .

☑ **Stand tall and look out just above the audience.** Don't slouch, and remember to make eye contact occasionally.

☑ **Speak loudly and slowly.** Project your voice to the back of the room. Pronounce words clearly.

☑ **Eliminate _ums_ and _uhs_.** Speak without distracting hedging sounds.

☑ **Use visuals.** Present visuals that get your point across.

☑ **Engage the audience.** Consider asking one or more audience members to come up and get involved with a demonstration or an activity.

☑ **Videotape the presentation.**

After . . .

☑ **Reflect on the presentation.** Watch the video if you have one. Think about what parts went well and what parts did not.

☑ **Consider ways to improve.** Think about what you will do differently in your next presentation.

Your Turn Think about a speech you have given or one you may give in the future. Which of the tips above is most important to you? Which do you already do naturally?

Parts of a Speech

Every speech needs to have a beginning, a middle, and an ending. You can write out the whole speech as a manuscript, or you can use note cards like those below.

The **first card** includes the complete introduction.

Introduction (show first slide)   1

In every one of our cells, we have two types of DNA. Most people are aware of the DNA in a cell's nucleus, but they may not know of the mitochondrial DNA inherited from the mother alone, which is used to trace matrilineal descent.

Mitochondria provide power to cells by converting the chemical energy of food into adenosine triphosphate—a form cells can use.

Mitochondrion

Inner boundary membrane
Intermembrane compartment
Matrix
Outer boundary membrane
Cristae

The **middle cards** list main points.

Endosymbiotic Theory

- Mitochondria as prokaryotic bacteria
- Eukaryotic cells engulfed early on
- Mitochondria in all animal and plant cells

Chloroplasts and Plants   3

- Chloroplasts conduct photosynthesis
- Came from cyanobacteria
- Similar endosymbiotic event
- All photosynthesizers have them

nucleus
vacuole
vacuole
mitochondrions
cell wall
cytoplasm
chloroplasts
ribosomes

The **final card** includes the complete closing.

Closing (show last slide)

The simple cell is anything but simple. In plant cells, two separate endosymbiotic events have led to the inclusion of mitochondria and chloroplasts. In our own cells, the presence of two types of DNA demonstrates our connection to very early bacterial forms. They live on within us, providing energy for everything we do.

Overcoming Stage Fright

Many people are afraid to speak in public, and even seasoned speakers get nervous before a big presentation. The nervousness comes from adrenaline—your body recognizes a threat and wants to trigger the "fight or flight" response. Instead of fleeing, use the energy to step up boldly and deliver your speech. Here are some tips.

1. **Know your topic.**
   Be sure to thoroughly explore the issue you will be presenting. If you know more than you have time to present, you'll be able to respond well to questions.

2. **Practice, practice, practice.**
   Go over your presentation many times, sometimes by yourself and sometimes with an audience. Record the presentation and watch it, making improvements.

3. **Get into a wholesome mental space.**
   Get a good night's sleep the day before your presentation. Exercise, shower, eat, and wear comfortable clothing. When you begin, take a deep breath and relax.

4. **Dive in.**
   Start your presentation, speaking loudly and confidently. Giving a speech is like jumping into a cold pool. It's a shock at first, but once you're in, you'll feel much better.

5. **Focus your energy.**
   As you give your presentation, show your enthusiasm for the topic and draw in the crowd.

6. **Connect to the audience.**
   Make eye contact when possible. If appropriate, you might even refer to one or more people you know. By "breaking the fourth wall" (connecting with the audience), you won't feel so alone up there.

7. **Use visuals.**
   Show your audience, don't just tell them. The more senses you enlist, the more engaging your presentation will be.

8. **Bring moral support.**
   Ask a friend or family member to attend the speech and sit where you can see him or her. You'll feel safer, and you'll have someone to help if you run into a problem.

9. **Learn from the pros.**
   Watch excellent speakers give presentations. Observe their tricks for connecting and communicating. Emulate them.

Your Turn With a partner, discuss the tips above. Which have you used in the past? What other tricks do you use to overcome stage fright? Choose one new strategy to use the next time you give a speech.

Listening and Speaking Glossary

The following terms relate to aspects of speaking and listening.

Allusion: Reference to something, often to explain or demonstrate a point

Analogy: Describing an unfamiliar concept by comparing it to a familiar one

Anecdote: A brief story that demonstrates a point

Antithesis: The opposite of a specific idea

Audience: The person or people who receive a message

Body language: What your posture, gestures, and movements tell the audience

Cadence: The rhythm or flow of a speech

Coherence: The quality of ideas that hold together and make sense

Communication situation: The sender, message, medium, receiver, and context of communication

Conciseness: Packing the most meaning into the fewest words

Context: The time and place in which a message is created or received

Definition: The meaning of a word or idea, often with examples

Demonstration: Showing how to do something or how something works

Diction: Level of language; see *formality*

Emphasis: Imparting special attention or stress on specific words or phrases

Energy: Engagement of the speaker, connecting to the audience and topic

Enunciation: The clear pronunciation of words and phrases

Exposition: A speech that informs, explaining something to the audience

Facial expression: What your facial features tell the audience

Filters: The way in which a sender codes a message and a receiver decodes a message

Formality: The level of language (or diction), from informal to formal

Gesture: Motion used to emphasize a point

Hyperbole: Exaggeration; overstatement

Inflection: The rise and fall in the pitch of a voice

Irony: When an action intended to have one consequence has the opposite

Message: The main point and supporting details, provided for a purpose

Metaphor: Comparing two things by equating them

Monotone: One tone—a dull voice that shows no interest

Narration: A speech that tells a story

Overstatement: Exaggerated language, usually for comedic effect

Pace: The speed or movement in a speech

Personification: Ascribing human traits to something not human

Persuasion: A speech meant to convince listeners of something

Pitch: The high, middle, or low tones of a voice

Projection: Speaking loudly and clearly

Prop: An object used to demonstrate a point

Purpose: The reason for communicating—to inform, persuade, entertain

Receiver: The person who gets the message from the sender

Sarcasm: Saying the opposite of what you mean

Script: The written copy of a speech

Sender: The creator of the message

Simile: Comparing two things using *like* or *as*

Slide show: A series of visuals projected onto a screen to help viewers follow along with the presentation

Soliloquy: A solo speech given by a single character in a play

Stage fright: The nervousness a speaker feels before and during a speech

Theme: A general concept or statement about life

Thesis: The main point of a specific message

Tone: The feeling or attitude the speaker has toward the topic

Understatement: Using minimal language for something huge, usually for comedic effect

Visuals: Elements such as a slide show, a picture, or a prop that makes a point visually

Your Turn Select five terms above that are new to you. Write down the terms and their definitions. Then search for an example of each from famous speeches. (Go to thoughtfullearning.com/h80 to find links to famous speeches.)

Communication Activities

The activities on this and the next page practice the speaking and listening skills you have learned in this chapter.

Telephone Variations

You probably remember the childhood game "telephone," in which you pass a message down a chain of people to discover how it changes. The variations in this game, given below, will help you explore how communication can break down.

Your Turn Form a group of five or more people. Play telephone by having the first person whisper a message to the second, who whispers it to the next, and so on. The last person repeats the message aloud. Try these variations:

1. Have each person write down the message before repeating it. Afterward, track where changes happened as the message was passed along. Discuss reasons for changes.
2. Play the game in a loud setting, such as the gym or the cafeteria. Compare the resulting final message with the one in the original version of the game.
3. Include one nonsense word in the original message (for example, "glimbot" or "gripshun"). Trace it to see how it changes and how other words change.

Active Listeners

As you have seen, active listeners use their brains as well as their ears. The following activity will help you listen more actively.

Your Turn After a lecture or presentation, perform one or more of the following to deepen your thinking.
- List the 5 W's and H (*who, what, where, when, why,* and *how*) about the lecture.
- Paraphrase the main point of the lecture.
- Find one idea in the lecture that relates to an idea you are learning about in another class.
- Write at least one idea you can infer from the lecture.
- Ask yourself why this information is important and answer the question.
- Evaluate the support for the main point, indicating why it is or isn't reliable.
- Evaluate the effectiveness of the lecture in conveying the main point.
- Compose a response to the lecture, indicating what you still wonder about the topic.

Introductions

The whole of the communication situation is present in an introduction between two people.

Your Turn Introduce yourself to a classmate, telling who you are and why you are introducing yourself. Have the person reply, saying who he or she is. Afterward, analyze the communication situation by defining the sender, message, medium, receiver, and context of each introduction.

Situational Speaking

As you have seen, different speaking situations require different levels of formality. The following activity helps you explore different levels of formality.

Your Turn Act out the following scenes with a partner. Continue acting for about a minute before shifting scenes. Change your formality level as you go.

1. A teenager (partner 1) talks to a police officer (partner 2)
2. A restaurant server (partner 1) talks to a patron (partner 2)
3. The president of the United States (partner 1) talks to a bodyguard (partner 2)
4. A patient (partner 1) talks to a surgeon (partner 2)
5. A scientist (partner 1) talks to another scientist (partner 2)

Conversation Chart

A conversation chart is a record not only of what is said, but also of what is implied and communicated in nonverbal ways.

Your Turn Listen to a brief conversation in a movie. Create a conversation map by filling in the spaces of a chart like the one below. Quickly summarize what each person says and implies without saying it, and record any facial expressions or body language involved.

Conversation Chart

Speaker	What Is Said	What Is Implied	Expression	Body Language
Paul	Have you seen my favorite tie?	Did you move it?	Eyebrows arched	Questioning
Anne	No.	Am I the keeper of your ties?	Face blank	Small head shake
Paul	It was in my closet yesterday—	You must have moved it.	Thinking	Staring in closet
Anne	Did you check on the floor?	It's probably still in your closet.	Matter-of-fact	Arms crossed
Paul	Was someone in my closet?	I think you know where it is.	Eyebrows scrunched	Hands on hips
Anne	Yep. I'm raising a goat in your closet. It ate your tie.	You're being ridiculous.	Laughing	Confronting
Paul	Oh, here it is, on the floor.	Never mind. I found it.	Smiling sheepishly	Shrugging
Anne	I'd better talk to that goat. Slacker.	Look harder before accusing me.	Shaking head	Walking away

Chapter 6
Collaborating

When you communicate with others, you think together. When you collaborate, you work together—each doing your part and bringing something unique to the project.

Look around you. Most things you see are the result of collaboration. Every building, every computer, every meal, every class—all of it requires the collaboration of dozens or hundreds of people, sharing the work to accomplish a big job.

This chapter focuses on how people work together to achieve a common goal.

You will learn . . .

- Understanding Collaboration
- Using Strategies in Groups
- Understanding the Situation
- Brainstorming Ideas
- Making Decisions and Resolving Conflicts
- Planning and Delegating
- Conducting Formal Meetings
- Collaborating Online

Understanding Collaboration

Collaboration is fundamentally problem solving in a group. Instead of one person tackling a problem, the group takes on the work of finding a solution. Collaboration involves critical and creative thinking as well as communication.

Problem-Solving Process

This chapter outlines the ways in which groups solve problems. Beginning with a discussion of leadership as well as the dynamic roles that other group members play, these pages will take you through the problem-solving process:

- Analyzing the situation
- Imagining ideas
- Making decisions and resolving conflicts
- Planning and delegating
- Monitoring progress

The workhorse of collaboration is the group meeting. While many meetings are informal in nature, others are more tightly structured. The end of the chapter provides a quick overview of *Robert's Rules of Order* and explains how to take meeting minutes.

Respect, Trust, and Goal Setting

For any group to collaborate effectively, members must respect and trust each other as well as share common goals.

- **Respect** creates an atmosphere in which all group members can contribute. Without respect, the group will disintegrate before it even gets started. But respect alone is not enough to ensure true collaboration.
- **Trust** is the belief that other group members will do the tasks they have agreed to do, on time and in a way that benefits the whole effort. Without trust, some group members will try to do everything, while others will feel excluded. Trust makes true collaboration possible.
- **Goal setting** establishes a direction for the group. Without a common goal, the group's effort will at best be fragmented, and at worst self-destructive. Once group members respect each other, trust each other, and have common goals, barriers to achievement drop away.

Your Turn Think of a group with which you have collaborated. How successful has it been? On a scale of 1 (none) to 5 (total), rate the three key attributes of the group: respect, trust, and goal setting. How did the presence or absence of these attributes impact the group's effectiveness? Discuss your answers with a classmate.

Using Strategies in Groups

Every group has its own dynamic—the chemistry of different personalities in different situations. This page outlines strategies for different groups and situations.

Leadership Strategies

Leaders respond dynamically to the situation around them. At times, leaders must act decisively. At other times, they must create a space for others to act, or they must work hand in hand with other leaders. They use these three strategies:

Directing

In many cases, leaders take charge, lay out a plan, assign duties, and keep the group moving. They enlist the help of others but set the direction and make the final decisions.

"Innovation distinguishes between a leader and a follower."
—Steve Jobs

Facilitating

At other times, leaders create a space that allows others to contribute their ideas, talents, and energies to set the direction. Facilitating creates consensus in decision making.

"I've got to follow them— I am their leader."
—Alexandre Rollin

Collaborating

When a group has several leaders, they work hand in hand. Collaborating requires every group member to exercise leadership and to negotiate with others.

"Leaders don't create followers; they create more leaders."
—Tom Peters

Your Turn Think of a group you have been part of. What leadership strategies do you notice in the group? What factors in the group make these strategies work well or not work well?

Group Member Strategies

Group members also respond dynamically, using the following strategies:

- **Diagnosing** occurs when you recognize problems and point to causes.
- **Energizing** gets the group excited about the tasks at hand.
- **Focusing** means pointing the group in the right direction.
- **Harmonizing** reduces friction between group members.
- **Inquiring** means asking critical questions to spur the group's thinking.
- **Timekeeping** means keeping the group on schedule.
- **Testing** probes ideas to make sure they are realistic.

Your Turn Think about recent groups you have been part of. Which of these strategies have you used? Explain. Compare your answers with a classmate's. What differences are there?

Understanding the Situation

The collaboration situation resembles an individual communication situation, but it involves more people.

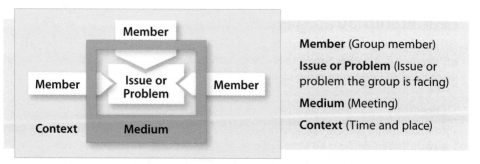

Member (Group member)

Issue or Problem (Issue or problem the group is facing)

Medium (Meeting)

Context (Time and place)

Your Turn Think of a group with which you have recently collaborated. Plot the situation by drawing a diagram like the one above. Name the members, fill in the issue or problem, and list the time and place of the collaboration (context).

Answering the 5 W's and H

Whenever a group gathers, the members must focus on the issue or problem facing the group. Reviewing the 5 W's and H will provide this focus.

> Who? Tasha, Sammi, Greg, Latrisha, Dave, and myself
> What? Need to create a bridge design that will hold a 10-pound weight
> Where? In physics class
> When? Over the next two class periods
> Why? To understand loads and weight distribution
> How? Using Popsicle sticks and wood glue

If a group has met before or meets regularly, discussing "old business" and "new business" will serve to focus the group members.

- **Old business** refers to decisions made and actions taken during the previous meeting. Group members must not only acknowledge these issues but also monitor whether the requested actions have taken place.
- **New business** refers to any new issues or problems that the group faces. The new business of the current meeting will become the old business of the next.

Your Turn Answer the 5 W's and H (*who, what, where, when, why,* and *how*) about a group that you either worked with or will be working with. If you are currently in the group, review one of your meetings. List the old business that was discussed and the new business you took on.

Brainstorming Ideas

Once the group understands the problem it is facing, group members must generate ideas for solving the problem. The brainstorming process usually results in a lengthy list of ideas and possible solutions. Follow these tips.

Brainstorming Tips

1. **Identify the problem or issue.** Clearly define the situation you are addressing, remembering that how you state the problem will limit or affect the solutions you'll think of. In the box to the right, the problem of an underfunded music program is defined in three different ways. Each definition suggests a different type of solution.

2. **Ask group members to offer suggestions to solve the problem.** At this point, the quantity of ideas is more important than the quality. You'll have time to sort through suggestions later. By encouraging all ideas, you let group members know they will not be harshly judged for suggestions that are impractical, exorbitant, or counterproductive.

3. **Choose a recorder.** This person writes down all suggestions in a list or cluster, perhaps on a white board or flip pad. The recorder does not pause to criticize suggestions but instead includes every suggestion that is offered in an honest attempt to solve the problem. Doing so keeps the ideas coming and avoids shutting off the flow.

4. **Select promising ideas.** Next, the group selects a few promising possibilities to explore. Then the process begins again, brainstorming with each selected possibility.

5. **Pro-con evaluation.** For each possibility, the group lists its pros (the good things about it) and its cons (the bad things about it).

6. **Choosing ideas to develop.** After evaluating the pros and cons of each idea, the group selects an idea to move forward with.

Problem:
Budget cuts to music

Problem:
Reducing program costs

Problem:
Additional funding

Music booster club
Special referendum
Fund-raiser
Corporate sponsors
Budget increase
Hiring out musicians
Participation fees
Combining bands
Combining choirs
Tougher entry criteria

Corporate sponsors
Feature company name
Perform at corp. events
Create sponsor wall

Pro	Con
Community	Tacky
Money	Sell out
Performance	Admin

Your Turn Select an issue or problem that you could address by collaborating with a group. With classmates, follow the steps above to brainstorm ideas.

Making Decisions

The way that a group makes decisions depends on the situation. Sometimes the leader will decide for the group, while at other times, the group collaboratively negotiates a solution. The group might also vote, doing whatever the majority decides. Formal meetings use the following process to vote on decisions:

- **Making a motion:** One of the group members presents a decision for the group to consider: "I move that we proceed with the mascot change to the Eagles."
- **Seconding the motion:** Another group member shows support for the motion, indicating the matter should come to a vote: "I second the motion."
- **All in favor/all opposed:** The leader of the meeting then calls for a vote with an "aye" (yes) or "nay" (no), a show of hands, or some other method.
- **Motion passed/motion defeated:** The leader indicates whether the votes were sufficient or insufficient to pass the motion. Some groups use a simple majority, and others require a unanimous vote.

Your Turn What meetings have you attended that used this procedure? How does it help groups come to decisions?

Resolving Conflicts

Conflicts often arise because of a simple misunderstanding. If you have a disagreement with another group member, try the following listening exercise:

Listening Strategy

1. The first person gets one to two minutes to calmly explain his or her point of view and to list the reasons why his or her suggested course of action would be best.
2. The second person then paraphrases the first person's thoughts aloud, starting with "I hear you saying . . ." and ending with "Am I understanding you correctly?"
3. If the answer is "no," the first person has another 30 to 60 seconds to clarify his or her position.
4. Once the first person is heard and understood, the process is repeated, with the second person getting one to two minutes to explain his or her point of view.
5. Both sides should then work to find a cooperative solution. They might choose portions of each person's plan to create a compromise.
6. If the sides cannot reach a compromise, they should ask a third party, such as a teacher or guidance counselor, to mediate and help resolve the conflict.

Your Turn Think of a recent situation in which you and another person disagreed. Write a reflection about how the strategy above would have worked to resolve the conflict.

Planning

A plan lays out the specific steps for accomplishing a goal. On pages 355–362 of this book, you'll find a whole chapter on planning. The following list summarizes the process:

1. **Define a goal.** In one or two sentences, describe what you plan to do.
2. **Write objectives.** Flesh out your goal by answering the 5 W's and H about it.
3. **List tasks.** Write down the tasks that need to be accomplished to reach the goal.
4. **Schedule time.** Assign a completion date to each task.
5. **Outline the team.** Decide who will take on the various tasks.
6. **List tools.** Write down the equipment, materials, information, and resources you need to reach the goal.

Your Turn Create a career plan. Start by defining your goal—the career that you want. Write objectives by answering the 5 W's and H about the goal. Then list tasks, time, team, and tools necessary to reach your goal. (To download a planning sheet, go to thoughtfullearning.com/h89.)

Delegating

Leaders must learn to delegate—asking others to take on part of the job. If leaders do not delegate, they end up having to do everything themselves. Failing to delegate also prevents others from contributing. When a group works collaboratively, however, delegation comes easily. The whole group can see what needs to be done, and the leader can ask each member to take on part of the work necessary to reach the goal. Each person's contribution should be recorded and a completion date assigned.

Your Turn Using your career plan from above, think about who could help you and how. Decide on specific tasks within a specific time frame. Finally, ask the person for help.

Monitoring Progress

Of course, delegating responsibility doesn't work if people don't follow through. When a group meets, it should review the list of tasks that have been delegated, asking each person to report on his or her progress. The group can decide at that point what to do about tasks that have fallen behind schedule.

Your Turn Think of a group assignment you have. Use the approach on this page to plan the project. (Download a planning sheet at thoughtfullearning.com/h89.) Delegate work, recording who is doing what in what time frame. Monitor everyone's progress.

Conducting Formal Meetings

Formal meetings often follow *Robert's Rules of Order,* which describes parliamentary procedure. The summary below will work for most meetings, but if you need the full set of rules, find the newly revised edition in your school library.

Summary of *Robert's Rules*

1. **Agenda and committee reports:** The meeting agenda and any committee reports are mere suggestions, used as the chair deems appropriate.

2. **Powers of the chair:** The chair can open and close meetings, recognize speakers and give them the floor (the right to speak), and call for votes.

3. **Gaining the floor:** Members must be recognized by the chair before they have the floor.

4. **Making remarks:** Members must address remarks to the chair, and remarks must be courteous, without reference to personalities or motives.

5. **Making motions:** Members can make motions, indicating decisions they want the general body to vote on.

6. **Seconding motions:** Another member must second a motion to bring it to a vote.

7. **Changing, amending, or withdrawing one's own motions:** Before the chair calls the motion for a vote, members can change, amend, or withdraw their own motions. If the motion is changed, the member who seconded the motion can remove the second.

8. **Changing or amending another's motion:** Before the chair calls the original motion for a vote, members can make a motion to change or amend the motion of another member. Such a motion to change has to be seconded and approved by the group.

9. **Voting on motions:** The chair calls for a vote on a motion that has been made, seconded, and discussed. The motion as stated by the chair is called the "immediate pending question."

10. **Passing motions:** A motion passes if it receives a simple majority—more than half of the votes.

11. **Adjourning:** As with any other decision, the motion to adjourn must be made, seconded, and voted upon by the group.

Your Turn Review the rules above. The next time you have a group meeting, follow *Robert's Rules.* Appoint a chair (the leader) who will open the meeting, recognize members and motions, and call for votes. How does this approach help or hamper group discussion?

Creating a Meeting Agenda

An agenda is a list of activities anticipated for a specific meeting. Agendas take different forms, depending on the meeting. The following agenda is for a student council meeting.

Heading
The group, date, and time are indicated.

Items of Business
Action items for the meeting are listed.

Reports
Additional information appears in separate reports.

> **WINKLER STUDENT COUNCIL**
> **TUESDAY, FEBRUARY 7, 2012, 7:30 A.M.**
>
> **AGENDA**
>
> 1. **CALL TO ORDER:** Stephani Nealy, Chair
> 2. **APPROVAL OF MINUTES**
> 3. **COMMITTEE REPORTS**
>   - Service: NO MEETING
>   - Fund-Raising: SEE REPORT
> 4. **OLD BUSINESS**
>   - Needy Family Drive
>   - Long-Range Planning Committee
> 5. **NEW BUSINESS**
>   - Prom Planning
>   - National Honor Society Induction
> 6. **ADJOURNMENT**

Taking Meeting Minutes

The minutes of a meeting parallel the agenda of the meeting, indicating what happened, what decisions were made, and who did what. The following meeting minutes show the first few items from the meeting above.

Heading
The group, date, and time are indicated.

Attendance
The roll is called.

Actions
Motions, seconds, and votes are noted.

Reports
Reports are summarized.

> **WINKLER STUDENT COUNCIL**
> **TUESDAY, FEBRUARY 7, 2012, 7:30 A.M.**
>
> **MINUTES**
>
> 1. **CALL TO ORDER:** Stephani Nealy called the meeting to order. In attendance: Leslie Avery, Jen Davidson, Tara Jenkins, Darla Lindell, Stephani Nealy, Carl Reichstadt, Rob Taylor
> 2. **APPROVAL OF MINUTES:** The council reviewed the January 31 minutes. Carl Reichstadt moved for approval; Darla Lindell seconded. Minutes were approved as submitted.
> 3. **COMMITTEE REPORTS**
>   - Service: NO MEETING
>   - Fund-Raising: Tara Jenkins reported that the fund-raiser is going well, with over $200 gathered so far and five school days remaining.

Collaborating Online

Our present-day connectedness means that you can collaborate with people that you have never met in person. These two pages provide tips for safely working with others on the Internet.

Collaboration Opportunities

Because the Internet makes information and ideas easy to share, online collaboration allows you to present your work, comment on others' work, and even create something together. Here are common types of online collaboration.

Wikis are Web pages that provide a common space for creating, editing, and saving text and other media. Many users can log on to the wiki and make changes to the content there.

Blogs are "Web logs"—online journals or information sites. Unlike a wiki, a personal blog has one person or one narrowly defined group as the creator of content. However, you can get involved by leaving comments after blog posts or the comments of other readers. You might even get into a conversation with the person who wrote the original post.

Social media such as Facebook and Twitter can connect you with people who have similar interests. You'll find links to articles, videos, and other interesting media, and you can use social media to crowd-source answers to questions that you have.

Chat services let you write in real time to one or more persons, creating a kind of digital conversation.

Email lets you quickly and reliably communicate with others. It can carry links, files, pictures, videos, and other media as well. Email has taken the place of business letters for most official correspondence.

VOIP (Voice Over Internet Protocol) allows you to make a video phone call to people around the world. VOIP also allows you to send files, share screens, and basically carry on a meeting with those on the other end. Some VOIP services charge a fee, but others are free.

Forums, or message boards, offer opportunities to discuss topics with others who are interested in the same issues. You'll find forums on everything from astrophysics to popular entertainers. Ask questions—or answer them—and join the discussion.

Your Turn What is your favorite way to collaborate with others online? What way have you not yet tried but would like to? Discuss your answers with a partner.

Using Netiquette

Netiquette is the etiquette of the Internet—the behaviors considered acceptable and unacceptable on the World Wide Web. Follow these tips to ensure that you work well with others online.

Respect yourself. Know that the Internet is written in permanent ink. Whatever you post there will be available somewhere for the rest of time. For that reason, represent yourself well. Avoid posting photos or comments that you will regret. Connect with those that you trust.

Respect others. Remember that there are real people at the other end of your message. Just as you would not insult or hurt someone sitting across the table from you, don't insult or hurt people in an online setting.

Respect privacy. Don't reveal anyone's private information. Don't post pictures that you would not want a potential employer to see, and don't post such pictures of others.

Respect cultural differences. When you go online, you'll bump into people from India to South Africa to Finland. Recognize that different cultures have different ideas about what is acceptable. Be respectful of diverse histories, religions, and customs.

Know the ground rules. When collaborating with others online, be aware of what you can change and what you need permission to change in someone else's work. Make sure that you and others agree about how to proceed.

Cite sources. If you get ideas or information from a specific location, make sure to refer to the source and link to it. In the same way, those who get information from a page that you create should give you credit.

Interact. If you read an article that you like, leave a comment letting the person know. If you have a question about a blog post, respectfully ask the question. People want to hear from you and converse with you.

Your Turn Review the netiquette rules above. Which do you think is most important to remember? Why? What other rules of netiquette would you add to the list? Why?

Collaboration Activities

Respect for All

This chapter began by underlining the importance of respect in collaborative relationships and ended by underlining the importance of respect in online collaboration. This activity will help you focus on respect.

Your Turn Complete the following sentence in as many ways as you can. "To me, respect means . . ." Compare your answers with those of a classmate. What answers do you have in common? Discuss your unique answers.

Directing, Facilitating, and Collaborating

On page 81, you learned about three different leadership strategies. This activity will help you identify situations when you would use each strategy.

Your Turn Create a chart like the one to the right, with a column for each of the three leadership strategies. In each column, list a situation in which you should use that strategy. Compare your chart with a classmate's.

Directing	Facilitating	Collaborating
Giving speech	Camp counselor	Garage band
Running snack shop	Scouting	Volleyball

Analyze a Group Situation

When a group begins working together, the first step is to analyze the collaboration situation. This exercise will help you practice.

Your Turn Think about a group that you have recently been involved with or one that you will soon be involved with. Answer the 5 W's and H about the collaboration situation.

Resolving Conflict

You've learned about a listening strategy for resolving conflict. This activity will help you reflect on your own experience with conflict resolution.

Your Turn Think of a conflict you recently had with someone. Then answer the following questions:
- Was the conflict the result of a misunderstanding?
- Did you try the listening exercise outlined on page 88? If so, were you able to come to an agreement? If not, how do you think the exercise might have helped resolve the conflict?
- How does speaking from the other person's point of view help you to understand where he or she is coming from?
- How does listening to the other person express your point of view help you to feel better understood?

Chapter 7
Building Arguments

You exist. This may come as no surprise to you, especially as you look in a mirror. But during the Enlightenment, thinkers wanted to establish a completely rational basis for all knowledge. The French philosopher René Descartes gave them a strong starting point by coming up with one of the most concise and compelling arguments ever stated: "I think, therefore I am." So mirrors aside, because you think, you exist.

This chapter shows you how to use your thinking ability to build strong, logical arguments. You'll also learn about logical fallacies that you have encountered repeatedly in political speeches and advertising. You'll learn to recognize these flaws in other people's arguments and to avoid such errors in your own thinking.

You will learn . . .

- Understanding Logic
- Using Deductive and Inductive Arguments
- Understanding the Basic Elements
- Creating Mathematical Proofs
- Building Strong Arguments
- Avoiding Logical Fallacies

Understanding Logic

Logic is the careful thought that guides an argument. It comes from the Latin root *logos*, which means "word." In its most basic form, then, logic refers to the way that words connect to make meaning. Here are three basic ways that words carry meaning:

- **Definitions:** Every word has a definition, which is the starting point for making meaning. Often, a word will have multiple definitions, and the true meaning must be derived from the way it is used.

  manipulate: (1) to change with the hands, (2) to handle skillfully, (3) to modify in an unfair or deceitful way

- **Syntax:** The syntax is the way that words are arranged or used. A word's meaning becomes apparent by whether it is used as a subject, a verb, an object, or a modifier. In the phrase "manipulate feelings," meaning is determined by the words' use.

  manipulate feelings: to unfairly or deceitfully modify a person's emotions

- **Semantics:** Semantics refers to the larger-scale meaning of language. A complete sentence offers you the basic semantic structure, or claim. Paragraphs, essays, and books extend the semantic structures to larger and larger forms.

  Negative political ads manipulate voters' feelings so that they vote against rather than for a candidate.

Your Turn Open one of your textbooks and point randomly to a word. Define the word. Then consider the words next to the one you chose. Does the syntax change your definition? Finally, consider the whole sentence. What does it mean semantically? Write the sentence in your own words.

Separating Fact from Opinion

At a very basic level, you need to understand the difference between a fact and an opinion. Often your argument will start with an opinion, but all arguments must contain plenty of factual evidence.

- **Facts** are statements that can be objectively proven based on evidence.

  John F. Kennedy was the 35th president of the United States.

- **Opinions** are personally held beliefs that cannot be objectively proven.

  John F. Kennedy was the most important president of the 20th century.

Your Turn Write a factual statement about the current president of the United States. Write an opinion statement about the current president. Compare your statements with a classmate's and discuss what makes each a fact or an opinion.

Using Deductive and Inductive Arguments

Arguments come in two basic varieties: deductive and inductive. A deductive argument moves from a general statement to a specific case, while an inductive argument moves from specific cases to a general statement.

Deductive Arguments

A deductive argument guarantees its conclusion by starting with a general principle and ending with a specific case. If the general principle is true and the logic of the argument does not have flaws, the conclusion must be true.

The strength of deductive arguments is that they guarantee their conclusions. The weakness is that they apply known principles to specific conclusions but do not discover new principles. A brief deductive argument, reduced to its basics such as this one, is called a syllogism.

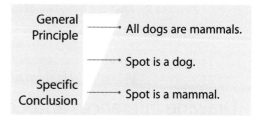

General Principle ———→ All dogs are mammals.

———→ Spot is a dog.

Specific Conclusion ———→ Spot is a mammal.

> **Your Turn** Construct a deductive argument by starting with a general principle or statement. Add an observation that relates to it. Then reach a specific conclusion. Is the conclusion true?

Inductive Arguments

An inductive argument does not guarantee its conclusion because it starts with specific cases and arrives at a general principle. It creates a hypothesis that may be supported by the specific facts, but may also prove to be false.

Though it is true that Spot, Rover, and Fido have four legs and that all of them are dogs, it is not true that all dogs have four legs. (Some have three or fewer.) So the general principle is a hypothesis based on evidence, but one that must be proved or disproved through testing.

Specific Case ———→ Spot has four legs.

———→ Rover has four legs.

———→ Fido has four legs.

———→ Spot, Rover, and Fido are dogs.

General Principle ———→ All dogs have four legs.

> **Your Turn** Use the following pattern to construct an inductive argument. Is the conclusion true?

_____(First specific case)_____	has _____	(specific feature)_____ .
_____(Second specific case)_____	has _____	(same specific feature)____ .
_____(Third specific case)_____	has _____	(same specific feature)____ .
_____(First, second, third)_____	are _____	(category of group)_____ .
All _____(category of group)s_____	have _____	(same specific feature)____ .

Understanding the Basic Elements

Arguments consist of three basic elements: premises, inferences, and conclusions.

Using Premises

Premises are statements assumed to be true and presented as evidence in support of a claim. The argument does not try to prove the truth of a premise but just takes it to be true:

> **Premise 1:** Every graduate of Jackson College has a degree.
>
> **Premise 2:** Anya is a graduate of Jackson College.
>
> **Conclusion:** Anya has a degree.

The two premises above are assumed to be true. The argument does not try to prove the premises but rather uses them to draw its conclusion or claim.

Drawing Inferences and Conclusions

An inference is a statement that is derived from previous statements—whether premises or other inferences. The truth of an inference is based on both the truth of the previous statements and on the way the inference is derived.

> Anya has a degree.
>
> **Premise 1:** Anya has a degree in engineering.
>
> **Premise 2:** Engineers have to pass calculus.
>
> **Inference:** Anya has passed calculus.

The inference that Anya has passed calculus is based on premises 1 and 2. If Anya has an engineering degree and all engineers have to pass calculus, Anya must have passed calculus.

> Anya has passed calculus.
>
> **Conclusion:** Anya understands calculus.

A conclusion is simply the final inference, derived from previous statements. Here, the concluding inference is that if Anya has passed calculus, she must understand it. A conclusion can become a premise in a new argument.

Your Turn Create your own argument. Begin with this premise: "I am a student." Add at least one more premise. Then derive at least one inference from the premises. Reach a conclusion derived from a premise and an inference. Afterward, test the truth of your argument.

Understanding Logical Rules

Classical logic has created a set of rules for indicating a statement's truth.

Three Classic Laws of Thought

The Greek philosopher Aristotle determined the following three rules of logic:

1. **Law of identity (the most elemental law):** P is P.
   - Paul is Paul.
2. **Law of noncontradiction:** If P is Q, then it is false that P is not Q.
   - If Paul is an editor, it is false that Paul is not an editor.
3. **Law of excluded middle:** Either P is Q or P is not Q—there is no middle possibility.
   - Either Paul is an editor, or Paul is not an editor. There is no other possibility.

Four Basic Propositions

To put ideas into categories, Aristotle came up with four basic propositions. (Proposition refers to the content or meaning of a sentence.) Propositions that are diagonal contradict each other, as do the top two propositions.

1. **Universal affirmative:** Every P is Q.
   - Every kangaroo is a marsupial.
2. **Universal negative:** No P is Q.
   - No kangaroo is a marsupial.
3. **Particular affirmative:** Some P is Q.
   - Some kangaroos are marsupials.
4. **Particular negative:** Some P is not Q.
   - Some kangaroos are not marsupials.

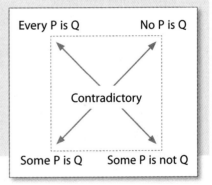

Every P is Q   No P is Q

Contradictory

Some P is Q   Some P is not Q

Three Function Words

Two thousand years after Aristotle, George Boole came up with a system for testing the truth of a claim using three basic words.

1. **And:** P and Q (Both must be true for the statement to be true.)
   - Sarah and Janelle are astronomers.
2. **Or:** P or Q (One must be true for the statement to be true.)
   - Sarah or Janelle is an astronomer.
3. **Not:** P not Q (P must be true for the statement to be true.)
   - Sarah, not Janelle, is an astronomer.

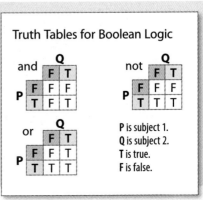

Truth Tables for Boolean Logic

and	Q	
	F	T
P F	F	F
T	F	T

not	Q	
	F	T
P F	F	F
T	T	T

or	Q	
	F	T
P F	F	T
T	T	T

P is subject 1.
Q is subject 2.
T is true.
F is false.

Nine Inference Rules

In addition to rules about the truth or falsity of a statement, classical logic includes a set of rules for making inferences and conclusions. As you develop your logical arguments, use the rules below to make inferences.

1. **Modus Ponens**
   (The way that affirms)
   If P then Q. ▶ P. ▶ Therefore Q.

   - If Sue is here, then Ty is here.
   - Sue is here.
   - Therefore Ty is here.

2. **Modus Tollens**
   (The way that denies)
   If P then Q. ▶ Not Q. ▶
   Therefore Not P.

   - If Bob agrees, then Teri agrees.
   - Teri does not agree.
   - Therefore Bob does not agree.

3. **Hypothetical Syllogism**
   If P then Q. ▶ If Q then R. ▶ P. ▶
   Therefore R.

   - If I laugh, then Duke barks.
   - If Duke barks, then Polly squawks.
   - I laugh.
   - Therefore Polly squawks.

4. **Disjunctive Syllogism**
   Either P or Q. ▶ Not P. ▶
   Therefore Q.

   - Either you win or I win.
   - I do not win.
   - Therefore you win.

5. **Constructive Dilemma**
   If P then Q, and if R then S. ▶
   P or R. ▶ Therefore Q or S.

   - If I go, he goes; and if she goes, they go.
   - I go, or she goes.
   - Therefore he goes, or they go.

6. **Destructive Dilemma**
   If P then Q, and if R then S. ▶
   Not P and Not R. ▶
   Therefore Not Q and Not S.

   - If I go, he goes; and if you go, they go.
   - I do not go, and you do not go.
   - Therefore he does not go, and they do not go.

7. **Simplification**
   P and Q. ▶ Therefore P.

   - Spot is a dog and Rex is a dog.
   - Therefore Spot is a dog.

8. **Conjunction**
   P. ▶ Q. ▶ Therefore P and Q.

   - Spot stinks.
   - Rex stinks.
   - Therefore Spot stinks and Rex stinks.

9. **Addition**
   P. ▶ Therefore P or Q.

   - Spot stinks.
   - Therefore Spot stinks or Rex stinks.

Your Turn Write your own examples for the inference patterns on this page. What does this activity teach you about logical inferences for arguments?

Creating Mathematical Proofs

A geometric proof works very much like the arguments you have been studying so far. A proof begins with a set of givens—things that are known, including information provided within a graphic. The proof then asks you to prove a specific conclusion. Use a two-column approach. In the first column, write a series of statements—premises (givens), inferences, and conclusions. In the second column, indicate the reason for each statement. Here's an example.

Given: AB || DC and AD || BC
(lines AB and DC are parallel; lines AD and BC are parallel)

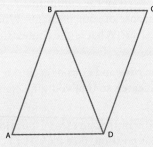

Prove: ∠BAD = ∠BCD
(angles BAD and BCD are equal)

Statements	Reasons
1. AB || DC	Given
2. ∠ABD = ∠BDC	Alternate interior angles are equal.
3. AD || BC	Given
4. ∠ADB = ∠DBC	Alternate interior angles are equal.
5. ∠ADB + ∠ABD + ∠BAD = 180	Angles of triangle = 180.
6. ∠BDC + ∠DBC + ∠BCD = 180	Angles of triangle = 180.
7. ∠ADB + ∠ABD + ∠BAD = ∠BDC + ∠DBC + ∠BCD	Substitution of equivalent amounts.
8. ∠BAD = ∠BCD	Substitution of equivalent amounts.

Discussion: The student recognized that line BD was crossing parallel lines AB and DC as well as parallel lines AD and BC. The student also knew that a line that crosses parallel lines makes the same acute angle with one line as with the other. That one rule applied twice showed that triangle ABD had two of the same angles as triangle BCD. Since all angles of a triangle add up to 180, the student could prove that the final angles were equal—that ∠BAD = ∠BCD.

Your Turn Which of the statements in the argument above are premises? Which are inferences? Which is a conclusion? Is this proof deductive or inductive? Does it guarantee its conclusion?

Math and Language Arts: Respond to each prompt:

1. Write a mathematical symbol that means "and."
2. Write a mathematical symbol that means "is."
3. Write the following as a mathematical statement: *Jason and Jana are a couple.*
4. How are sentences with linking verbs like equations?

Building Strong Arguments

For essays, speeches, debates, meetings, or intense discussions, you may need to organize your thoughts and defend them against people who might not agree with you. To do your best in these situations, follow the process outlined in the next few pages. Remember that arguments stem from a claim or position supported by compelling evidence—evidence that persuades the reader or listener to accept a point of view.

The Seven C's of Building an Argument

When you need to build an argument, use the seven C's to develop and support a position about a specific topic:

1. **Consider the situation.** Think of all aspects of the communication situation What are the subject and purpose of your message? What medium will you use? Who is the receiver? What is the context? (See the next page.)

2. **Clarify your thinking.** Think about the pros and cons of each side of the issue, and do some preliminary research so that you understand the subject well. (See the next page.)

3. **Construct a claim.** Write a single statement that gives your position and the main reason that you hold that position. (See page 104.)

4. **Collect evidence.** Research the issue in depth, using primary, secondary, and tertiary sources. Investigate to make sure your claim holds up, and change it if it doesn't. Gather a variety of key evidence to support your claim. (See page 104.)

5. **Consider key objections.** Think about other viewpoints related to the argument. What reasons could people cite to support opposing positions? What major problems could they see with your argument? Decide how you will answer those objections— by countering them (saying why they are unimportant) or by conceding them (saying they are important but can be overcome). (See page 105.)

6. **Craft your argument.** Use your claim statement and the evidence you have gathered to argue persuasively for your position. Appeal to the needs of your reader, and answer any key objections. (See page 106.)

7. **Confirm your main point.** Wrap up your argument by stating your claim in a new way, connecting it to real life and to the future.

Your Turn Which step in the process outlined above corresponds to the questioning phase of the inquiry process? Which steps correspond to planning? Which steps relate to research? In what ways does building an argument require the inquiry process?

1. Consider the situation.

Before you can build a strong argument, you need to analyze the communication situation. Ask yourself the following questions:

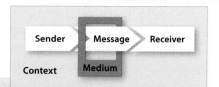

- As sender, what role do I have?
- What subject is my message about?
- What purpose do I have?
- What medium am I using?

- Who is the receiver? How can I convince that person?
- What is the context? When and where will the message arrive?

Sender:	I'm writing less as a high school student and more as a concerned American citizen.
Message Subject:	I'm writing about the national debt.
Message Purpose:	I'm calling for spending cuts and tax increases to address the debt.
Medium:	This should be a letter to the editor, so it can reach a general audience.
Receiver:	My audience is all Americans who are worried about federal fiscal responsibility.
Context:	This message will appear in a newspaper locally, and it could be picked up by a wire service to appear in national papers.

Your Turn Think of the topics you are studying in your classes. Which topic do you feel most strongly about? What position would you most like to argue for? Analyze your communication situation by answering the questions above.

2. Clarify your thinking.

Before you can convince others, you must be clear in your own mind about your position. What are you trying to prove? Why do you feel the way you do? What kind of proof do you have? In addition, you should consider both sides of the issue. To do this, set up a pro-con chart like the one shown here:

Pro	Con
Reducing the national debt . . .	Reducing the national debt . . .
• is the right choice for the future.	• may slow the economy.
• requires us to live within our means.	• requires bipartisan support.
• improves our country's credit scores.	• requires tax increases.
• sets an example for other nations regarding fiscal responsibility.	• requires cuts to spending.
• creates a sustainable budget.	• impacts those receiving entitlements.
	• impacts the military.

Your Turn Create a pro-con chart, arguing for and against your position. Thoroughly explore both pros and cons. You will need to understand all perspectives to make a convincing case.

3. Constructing a Claim

After you have thoroughly investigated an issue, you are ready to construct a claim about it. Arguments develop three types of claims:

1. **A truth claim** indicates that you believe something is or is not true.	The national debt threatens the future of our nation.
2. **A value claim** indicates the worth that you assign to something.	A balanced budget would be the best gift we can give our children.
3. **A policy claim** says what you think should or should not be done.	The federal government must cut spending to reduce the national debt.

To formulate a claim, name your subject and express the truth, value, or policy you want to promote.

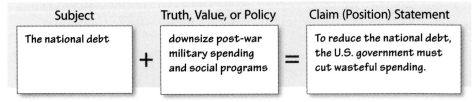

Subject		Truth, Value, or Policy		Claim (Position) Statement
The national debt	**+**	downsize post-war military spending and social programs	**=**	To reduce the national debt, the U.S. government must cut wasteful spending.

4. Collecting Evidence

After stating a claim, you must support it. Different types of details provide different types of support:

■ **Facts and statistics** connect your claim to specific realities.	Each taxpayer's portion of the U.S. national debt is over $140,000.
■ **Reasons and results** show the causes and effects of a situation.	The debt-ceiling debacle of 2011 caused the U.S. credit rating to slip.
■ **Examples and anecdotes** show how the claim works.	A person who makes $46,000 can't spend $71,000—but the government does.
■ **Quotations and reflections** get at the feelings of the audience.	"We must not let our rulers load us with perpetual debt," said Thomas Jefferson.

Your Turn (1) Use the formula above to construct a truth, a value, and a policy claim about a subject you feel strongly about. (2) Choose one of your claims and research it. Write down one of each of the four types of supporting details listed in the chart above.

5. Considering Key Objections

Any debatable issue has at least two, and often many, points of view. When you build an argument, you need to consider alternate positions. Just as you have gathered support for your position, those with other perspectives will have gathered objections. Start by identifying them.

Objection 1:	The debt matches our gross domestic product, which means that the debt has not yet reached an unmanageable size.
Objection 2:	The boom of the '90s balanced the federal budget, and the next boom will balance this budget.
Objection 3:	The time to cut government spending is not during a recession but during a boom.

Your Turn Reverse your thinking. Imagine that you strongly oppose the claim you made and researched on the previous pages. List at least three serious objections to your previous position.

Answering Objections

Ignoring the objections to your argument weakens rather than strengthens it. You need to face objections head-on. The following strategies have been applied to each of the example objections above.

■ **Rebut the objection.**	If our gross domestic product goes down, our debt goes up as we try to stimulate the economy. Allowable debt can't be based solely on GDP.
■ **Recognize part of the objection but overcome the rest.**	It is true that the boom of the '90s resulted in a balanced budget, but a balanced budget fixes only that year's deficit, not the compounded national debt.
■ **Concede the objection and move on.**	Yes, during a recession, government spending is needed to get the economy moving again. Now that the recession is over, we need to reduce spending.

Your Turn Answer each of the objections to your own claim that you listed in the previous "Your Turn" activity. Either rebut the objection, recognize part of it but overcome the rest, or concede and move on.

6. Crafting Your Argument

How you structure your argument depends a great deal on how receptive or resistant your audience is. For a receptive audience, you can provide support up front and rebuttal of objections near the end. For opposed audiences, you may want to start with rebuttals.

Receptive	Skeptical	Resistant	Opposed
Position	**Position**	**Position**	**Position**
Support	**Support**	**Rebuttal**	**Rebuttal**
Support	**Rebuttal**	**Support**	**Rebuttal**
Support	**Support**	**Rebuttal**	**Rebuttal**
Rebuttal	**Rebuttal**	**Support**	**Support**
Position	**Position**	**Position**	**Position**

Your Turn Think about the audience for the position (claim) you chose to work with on pages 103-104. How receptive or resistant are they? Which of the structures above would you use to craft your argument? Or would you use a different structure? Explain your answer.

Using Persuasive Appeals

Classical rhetoric, or the art of persuasion, prescribes three ways to appeal to your audience:

1. **Appeal to ethos**—demonstrate that you are an ethical and trustworthy source.
2. **Appeal to logos**—use logic to argue for your position.
3. **Appeal to pathos**—move the person emotionally to connect with your position.

The most persuasive arguments may use all three types of appeals—but always responsibly. Each of these appeals can be abused, as you will see in the section on logical fallacies (pages 108–112).

Your Turn You've learned about using logic (logos) to connect with the reader. Now consider what your audience wants or needs in order to make an emotional connection (pathos). How does your position help them get what they need, want, or expect?

7. Confirming Your Main Point

Complete your argument by stating your main point in a new way and connecting it to the future. Leave your audience with a strong final thought.

Using Socratic Questions to Examine Arguments

You've learned how to build a compelling argument. There's also a technique for examining arguments and deepening thinking.

The Greek philosopher Socrates examined arguments through questions, pushing students to use logic to deduce answers. Socratic questions are especially useful for probing the thinking of opponents in a debate.

Socratic Questions

Clarifying questions ask the person to restate an idea in a new way.
- Could you please rephrase that statement?
- How would you summarize your position?
- Are you saying that _____?

Assumption questions explore the person's underlying ideas.
- What are the assumptions underlying that statement?
- Is that statement based on the belief that _____?
- Could you explain how/why _____?

Reasoning questions get at the logic the person is using.
- Can you demonstrate how this premise is true?
- What evidence supports this claim?
- Are you implying/concluding that _____?

Perspective questions prompt the person to use a different point of view.
- What analogy could you use to express that idea?
- How would _____ respond to that idea?
- How do you answer the objection that _____?

Consequence questions ask the person to consider what might happen.
- What will result from that position?
- How can we apply that idea in a broader context?
- What is the value of that idea, and why?

Recursive questions return to the original question.
- Why are we asking this question?
- How does this question connect to the situation?
- How can we reframe this question?

Your Turn With a partner, discuss a current issue that you are studying in class. Use Socratic questions occasionally to deepen the discussion. Which questions were most helpful? Which were least helpful? Why?

Avoiding Logical Fallacies

Logic can go wrong in many ways. We've talked about building logical arguments. Now let's consider how to avoid building illogical ones. The logical fallacies below can slip into your own and others' arguments. Learn to identify them.

Distortions in Logic

Ad hoc reasoning refers to making up dismissive excuses rather than truly engaging an idea. (The Latin words *ad hoc* mean "for this"—signifying "in this situation" or "making due with whatever is available.")

- Librarians argue that the plight of libraries should concern all citizens, but maybe they should listen to their own advice and "shhhhhh!"
  (Instead of engaging the claim, the response dismisses its importance.)

Ambiguity refers to a statement that can be taken two different ways.

- You can never have too much water in a nuclear power plant.
  (Does this mean we need to minimize or maximize the amount of water?)

Bare assertions deny an opposing position by saying "that's just the way it is."

- There will always be poor people, so there's no point in helping them.
  (This claim dismisses opposition by saying poverty is just a fact of life.)

Broad generalizations take some cases and apply them to every case. A similar fallacy is the **hasty conclusion,** which leaps over intervening steps of logic.

- The news is full of cases of husbands abusing wives. All domestic violence is committed by men.
  (This claim generalizes from some spousal abuse to all domestic violence.)

Circular reasoning uses its own premise for a conclusion. By starting with the conclusion, the argument has not actually proven anything. (This form is also called a **tautology,** which is Greek for "the same words.")

- During war, Republican presidents lead better than Democrats. When the United States faces a war, it should elect a Republican. That shows that Republicans make better wartime presidents.
  (In place of an argument, the same assertion is made three times.)

Complex questions phrase an idea in a way that makes it impossible to counter.

- When will your party stop destroying the country?
  (To answer the question would be to admit to destroying the country.)

Correlation as causation wrongly asserts that because two things happen at the same time, they have a cause-effect relationship.

- President Bush was reading to schoolchildren when the attacks of 9/11 took place. If he had been in Washington, the nation would have been safe.
  (This statement incorrectly assumes that the president's location caused the 9/11 attacks.)

False analogies compare situations to other situations that are not truly similar.

- The presidential race is just like voting for the homecoming king; in the end, the winner gets a lot of credit but very little power.
  (This analogy does not accurately represent the process, in which the winner becomes arguably the most powerful person in the world.)

False causes incorrectly identify the reason that something has happened.

- Every time the economy worsens, the Fed lowers interest rates. If the Fed just kept rates high, the economy would be fine.
  (This claim swaps the cause and the effect. The worsening economy causes the Fed to lower interest rates, not the other way around.)

False continuum refers to the idea that two things that are on the same spectrum are actually the same thing.

- What is the difference between someone who constantly criticizes the government and someone committing treason? There is no difference.
  (This claim ignores the difference between free speech and treason.)

False dichotomies simplify a complex situation into two extreme choices. This fallacy is also called **either/or thinking**.

- Either we renew NASA's funding at its former levels or the whole agency shuts down.
  (The agency can function on a reduced budget without shutting down.)

Genetic fallacies assume that the origin of something is analogous to its current significance.

- The Democratic Party stems from the Democratic-Republican Party of Jefferson in the early 1800s. As a result, Democrats are really Republicans.
  (This statement ignores the long evolution of both parties.)

Inconsistent criteria occur when what is required in one case is not required in another.

- Your candidate won't back down because he is obstinate. Mine won't back down because he is determined.
  (Both candidates won't back down, so both should get the same praise or blame.)

Non sequitur comes from the Latin phrase for "does not follow."

- My candidate has less than 6 percent body fat. If he can trim his own fat, he can trim government fat.
  (This statement does not follow. A person's body fat percentage does not relate to his or her ability to balance governmental budgets.)

Your Turn Find a political debate online and listen to it. Write down as many examples as you can of the fallacies on these two pages.

No true Scotsman refers to discounting a counterexample rather than adjusting faulty criteria. It comes from a famous exchange:

- All Scotsmen are brave.
  What about Andrew? He's a coward, and he's a Scotsman.
  Then Andrew is no true Scotsman, for all Scotsmen are brave.
  (Instead of changing the false assumption that all Scotsmen are brave, the person discounts the counterexample of cowardly Andrew.)

Obfuscation uses confusing wording in order to prevent arguments.

- It behooves all of us to ameliorate deleterious detriments.
  (This statement means "We should get rid of harmful influences," an idea so obvious that it really doesn't need to be stated.)

Oversimplification involves stating a complex situation in simplistic terms.

- To remove the national debt, the U.S. government can just print however many dollars it needs.
  (This oversimplification ignores the fact that such an act would catastrophically devalue the dollar.)

Reductio ad absurdum, Latin for "reduce to absurdity," breaks something down into such small pieces that it no longer makes any sense.

- If we allow employees choice about when they work, some will decide to work every other minute.
  (This statement applies a reasonable principle to absurd specificity.)

Slanted language uses unfair terms that skew the discussion.

- Politicians are crooks, and we can't allow crooks to make laws.
  (The language in this statement allows for no reasonable discussion.)

Slippery slope reasoning says that one small change will lead to an unavoidable cascade of terrible consequences. People who use this fallacy may even use the phrase "slippery slope" in their argument.

- If we grant legal status to illegal immigrants, we'll have to pardon all illegal activity.
  (Immigration reform does not require pardoning all illegal activity.)

Straw man reasoning creates a "dummy" argument for an opposing view and refutes it rather than dealing with the true argument of the opposition.

- My political rival wants to destroy the country and put everyone in prison. I disagree. I think we should save the country and put everyone to work.
  (That a politician wants to destroy the country is a dummy argument.)

Your Turn Pick four of the fallacies on this page and write your own examples. Share your answers with a partner and discuss the faulty logic in each.

Misusing Evidence

Appeals to hypocrisy say that one's own guilt can be forgiven because of someone else's guilt. The Latin term for this fallacy is *tu quoque*—literally "you, too!"

- The previous administration spent well beyond the country's means, so this administration can do the same thing.
  (Someone else's bad behavior doesn't justify one's own bad behavior.)

Appeals to ignorance say that something is false because no one has proved it, or that something is true because no one has disproved it.

- Scientists have yet to find life beyond our planet, which proves that life does not exist elsewhere in the universe.
  (Absence of evidence is not evidence of absence.)

Appeals to pity beg the audience to not make the arguer suffer.

- I've worked hard on this proposal, so you have to accept it.
  (A proposal should be accepted on its own merits, not due to hard work.)

Appeals to popular sentiment try to sell an idea by connecting it to something that is beloved.

- For your grandma's sake, buy Grandma Smith's All-American Peanut Butter.
  (A sentimental name doesn't make peanut butter worth buying.)

Arguments from authority use someone's position to indicate that something is worthy or unworthy. Often, this appeal uses paid celebrities who actually know little about the issue or product.

- On my doctor show, I often prescribe Buffervyl, the all-star pain reliever.
  (An actor who plays a doctor is not a medical authority.)

Arguments from consequence indicate that something must be true because if it were not, terrible things would result. Ignoring a threat does not remove it.

- The world's nuclear arsenal must be secure because a rogue nuke would be too horrible to imagine.
  (The horror of the idea does not preclude its possibility.)

Arguments from incredulity state that something can't be true because it is hard to believe.

- The idea that a subatomic particle can be in two places at once is silly.
  (Actually, quantum physicists have proven this idea.)

Attacks against the person criticize the individual rather than the person's ideas. The Latin term for this is *ad hominem*, "to the person."

- We can't agree on Senator Smith's proposed tax cuts, but we can agree that he needs to get a haircut.
  (This ad hominem attack diverts attention from the real issue: taxes.)

Bandwagoning argues for something because many other people like it.

- All of your neighbors get the *Times,* and you should, too.
  (A stronger argument would focus on the value of the paper.)

Half-truths distort the issue by telling only part of the story.

- Every year, thousands of Americans are injured by power tools, so it is time to ban their use.
  (The thousands who are injured are a tiny fraction of the millions who use power tools safely and who rely on them to make a living.)

Hypothesis contrary to fact forms an argument on the basis of something that didn't happen. This fallacy is also called "if only" thinking.

- If only my candidate had won, the economy would be fixed by now.
  (There is no way to prove or disprove what would have happened if the other candidate had won, so the argument is meaningless.)

Impressing with numbers uses statistics to baffle the audience and into agreeing.

- A full 64 percent of the 25 percent of Americans who favor an 80-20 split of public/private land in Alaska live at the 70th parallel.
  (The use of numbers baffles the audience into acceptance.)

Misuse of humor uses a joke to cover up a serious issue.

- One way to end world hunger would be to require everyone in the world to watch this documentary: They'll lose their appetite forever.
  (World hunger is a serious problem that shouldn't be dismissed with a joke.)

Red herrings distract the audience by using something emotionally charged. This fallacy gets its name from an attempt to throw off scent hounds by dragging a smelly fish across one's path.

- The use of child soldiers in many conflicts across the globe is terrible, but not as terrible as seeing a person consumed by the Ebola virus.
  (The Ebola virus, a separate problem, should not be used to distract from the abhorrent use of child soldiers.)

Threatening is saying that one should accept an argument "or else."

- Before you sign that petition, think about the consequences for your family.
  (Threats are never an acceptable form of persuasion.)

Your Turn Watch commercials on television or on the Internet and write down two examples of the misuse of evidence on pages 111–112.

Argumentation Activities

Fact or Opinion?

This chapter has focused on the use of facts and opinions to build arguments. Recognizing the difference between fact and opinion is key.

Your Turn Select an article on the editorial page of a newspaper. Read the article, underlining facts and circling opinions. How much of the article is factual? How much is opinion based? How does this combination affect your perception of the article?

Deductive and Inductive Arguments

Deductive arguments guarantee their solutions by beginning with a general premise and ending with a specific conclusion. Inductive arguments create hypotheses by beginning with specific premises and deriving a general conclusion.

Your Turn Use the general premise as a starting point to create a deductive argument. Use the specific premise to create an inductive argument. Compare your arguments with those of a classmate.

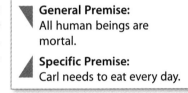

General Premise:
All human beings are mortal.

Specific Premise:
Carl needs to eat every day.

Four Basic Propositions

On page 99, you learned about four basic propositions—the universal affirmative, the universal negative, the particular affirmative, and the particular negative. The following activity will help you think through these propositions.

Your Turn For each position, write your own example by replacing P and Q. Then answer the questions below.

- **Universal affirmative:** Every P is Q.
- **Universal negative:** No P is Q.
- **Particular affirmative:** Some P is Q.
- **Particular negative:** Some P is not Q.

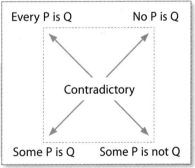

Every P is Q   No P is Q

Contradictory

Some P is Q   Some P is not Q

1. If the universal affirmative is true, what other proposition is also true?
2. If the universal negative is true, what other proposition is also true?
3. If the universal affirmative is true, what other propositions must be false?
4. If the universal negative is true, what other propositions must be false?

Rules of Inference

On page 100, you learned about nine rules of inference. This activity will help you review four of those rules.

Your Turn For each of the following rules of inference, write your own example by replacing P, Q, and R.

1. **Modus Ponens** (The way that affirms)
   If P then Q. ▶ *P.* ▶ *Therefore Q.*

2. **Modus Tollens** (The way that denies)
   If P then Q. ▶ *Not Q.* ▶ *Therefore Not P.*

3. **Hypothetical Syllogism**
   If P then Q. ▶ *If Q then R.* ▶ *P.* ▶ *Therefore R.*

4. **Disjunctive Syllogism**
   Either P or Q. ▶ *Not P.* ▶ *Therefore Q.*

Avoiding Logical Fallacies

Pages 108-112 provide examples of common logical fallacies. The activity below will help you practice them.

Your Turn Write your own example of each logical fallacy below.

1. **Bare assertions** deny any opposing position by saying "that's just the way it is."
2. **Complex questions** phrase an idea in a way that makes it impossible to counter.
3. **Correlation as causation** wrongly asserts that because two things happen at the same time, they have a cause-effect relationship.
4. **False analogies** compare situations to other situations that are not truly similar.
5. **False dichotomies** simplify a complex situation into two extreme choices. This fallacy is also called **either/or thinking.**
6. **Appeals to ignorance** say that something is false because no one has proved it, or that something is true because no one has disproved it.
7. **Attacks against the person** criticize the individual rather than the person's ideas. The Latin term for this is *ad hominem,* "to the person."

Chapter 8

Succeeding in School and College

You've likely heard all kinds of good reasons for succeeding in school, but here's one that covers them all: It's like money in the bank. The hard work you do now will eventually pay the dividends of self-confidence and initiative. With those you can pursue a higher education, find a career, be a responsible community member, and much more.

Learning and practicing the skills discussed in this chapter will help you obtain an education, one of your most valuable possessions.

You will learn . . .

- Developing Good Habits
- Setting Goals
- Managing Time
- Completing Assignments
- Managing Stress
- Searching for Colleges
- Applying to Colleges
- Applying for Financial Aid

Developing Good Habits

Your brain is very practical. Its first job is to keep you alive. Its second job is to keep you connected to other people, which is part of staying alive. Its third job is to learn things. Not surprisingly, your brain mostly wants to learn things that connect you to other people and keep you alive. To be ready to learn, you must be healthy, happy, and socially connected. Developing the following 10 critical habits will ensure that you are ready to learn.

Learning

Connected

Alive

10 Critical Habits for Learning

1. **Sleep.** Get eight hours of sleep whenever possible.
2. **Eat.** Have a balanced breakfast each morning.
3. **Move.** Exercise your body to increase blood circulation to your brain.
4. **Connect.** Share what you learn with friends and family.
5. **Relax.** Find a way to feel safe and comfortable so that you can learn.
6. **Work.** Set goals, and work to achieve them.
7. **Wonder.** Nurture curiosity, which is a key to learning.
8. **Discover.** Seek answers and put new ideas together.
9. **Create.** Bring new ideas and inventions into the world.
10. **Share.** Apply your ideas to make a difference in the world.

Your Turn Rate how often you practice the 10 critical habits for learning, from 1 (rarely) to 5 (always). Then choose two habits that need more attention, and tell how you will improve each.

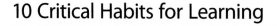

	(Rarely) ⟶ (Always)
1. **Sleep**	1 . . . . . . 2 . . . . . 3 . . . . . 4 5
2. **Eat**	1 . . . . . . 2 . . . . . 3 . . . . . 4 5
3. **Move**	1 . . . . . . 2 . . . . . 3 . . . . . 4 5
4. **Connect**	1 . . . . . . 2 . . . . . 3 . . . . . 4 5
5. **Relax**	1 . . . . . . 2 . . . . . 3 . . . . . 4 5
6. **Work**	1 . . . . . . 2 . . . . . 3 . . . . . 4 5
7. **Wonder**	1 . . . . . . 2 . . . . . 3 . . . . . 4 5
8. **Discover**	1 . . . . . . 2 . . . . . 3 . . . . . 4 5
9. **Create**	1 . . . . . . 2 . . . . . 3 . . . . . 4 5
10. **Share**	1 . . . . . . 2 . . . . . 3 . . . . . 4 5

Living a Full-Color Life

The visible spectrum of light consists of a range of colors, from violet through red. In the same way, your life should consist of a spectrum of priorities. Living a full-color life means balancing the parts of your life so that things don't become just monotone.

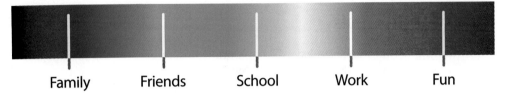

| Family | Friends | School | Work | Fun |

Your Turn How colorful is your life? Do you have a balance of colors, as shown above, or do one or two colors dominate? Would you use the same five labels you see above, or would you replace some with other labels? Create and label a spectrum representing the colors of your own life. How might you improve the balance of colors?

Matching Education to Life Goals

In general, the more education you receive, the farther you can go in your career. Remember, however, that each type of degree takes a number of years to complete. Here is a diagram of different types of degrees, the number of years they take, and some jobs available with those degrees.

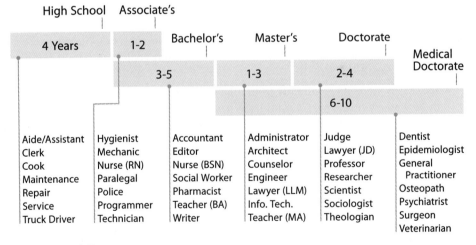

High School	Associate's	Bachelor's	Master's	Doctorate	Medical Doctorate
4 Years	1-2	3-5	1-3	2-4	6-10
Aide/Assistant	Hygienist	Accountant	Administrator	Judge	Dentist
Clerk	Mechanic	Editor	Architect	Lawyer (JD)	Epidemiologist
Cook	Nurse (RN)	Nurse (BSN)	Counselor	Professor	General Practitioner
Maintenance	Paralegal	Social Worker	Engineer	Researcher	Osteopath
Repair	Police	Pharmacist	Lawyer (LLM)	Scientist	Psychiatrist
Service	Programmer	Teacher (BA)	Info. Tech.	Sociologist	Surgeon
Truck Driver	Technician	Writer	Teacher (MA)	Theologian	Veterinarian

The Armed Forces

Another path for training after high school is to enlist in one of the U.S. Armed Forces. Service members receive not only military training but also skills that can lead to civilian occupations and certifications. (See page 506 for an example.)

Your Turn Scan the list of jobs above. Do any match your desired profession? What other jobs can you name for the different education levels? What education do you plan to get in order to get the best job for you?

Setting Goals

Setting goals is a matter of acting on your dreams—reaching for them. Short-term goals help you work toward long-term goals, and they give you confidence to achieve your dreams. (For more on goal setting, see pages 356–357.)

Short-Term Goals

- **Daily:** Every morning, you have the opportunity to set a goal for the day. It can be as matter-of-fact as getting through the day, or as challenging as applying for a job. Setting daily goals keeps you moving forward.
- **Weekly:** At the beginning of the week, consider the challenges ahead. Set a goal to meet each challenge. Think of what you must do to deal with the challenges, and then go about facing them head-on.
- **Yearly:** At the beginning of each school year, think about what you want to accomplish. Imagine yourself excelling in each class and taking on new activities. Then set your goals and move forward.

Long-Term Goals

- **High school:** Take charge of your high school education. Decide what grade-point average you want, and work at it. Take the courses that prepare the way for your goals after high school, whether you'll enter the workforce immediately, go to a trade school, attend college, or pursue a specific profession. Tell your high school counselor about your goals, and then listen to his or her advice.
- **Job:** Many students go directly from high school into the workplace. Even those who continue their educations often have jobs to pay expenses. What job would you like? What qualifications do you need?
- **Higher education:** What are your higher-education goals? What degree do you need to meet your career goal? Where do you want to go to school?
- **Relationships:** What relationship goals do you have? Do you plan to remain single? To date? To marry? To have a family? How do friends fit into your life?
- **Career:** What do you want to accomplish? How do you see yourself serving a company or society in general? What profession do you envision for yourself? What pay do you need?
- **Lifestyle:** Where do you want to live? How much money do you hope to have? What groups do you want to join? How would you characterize a happy life?

Your Turn Write two or three sentences for each category above, explaining your long-term goals.

Managing Time

Just as with short-term goals, you will find a benefit in managing your time on a variety of scales.

Time Scales

- **Hourly time management** means focusing on the work that you are supposed to be doing, avoiding distractions, and making progress. Remember that what you don't finish in class you must finish later as homework.
- **Daily time management** means getting from class to class on time, using your study hall for the most important homework, taking part in extracurricular activities, and perhaps meeting a work schedule. It also means keeping up with classes rather than cramming the night before.
- **Weekly time management** means scheduling your activities; planning time for family, friends, fun, rest; and avoiding overload. Don't overcommit, or agree to take on too many responsibilities. Don't be irresponsible with your time either. You don't want to miss out on the satisfaction of accomplishing your goals.

Pacing for the Long Term

When you are trying to accomplish something that will take a long time, you need to break the work into doable tasks. Divide the amount of time you have by the tasks you must finish. Here are four example goals and plans.

Goal: Read <u>Grapes of Wrath</u> by May 2.
- Read 30 pages a day for two weeks.

Goal: Memorize my lines in the play by March 14.
- Memorize 1 page of lines a day for seven days.

Goal: Write a 50,000-word novel by Christmas.
- Write 5,000 words per week for 10 weeks.

Goal: Run 150 miles by homecoming.
- Run 15 miles per week for 10 weeks.

Your Turn Write down one of your goals and the time you have to accomplish it. Then split the work of attaining the goal into separate tasks. Figure out what you need to accomplish in a day, a week, a month, and so on, to succeed.

Completing Assignments

In school and in the workplace, success depends on your ability to complete assignments. Use the following tips:

1. **Understand the assignment.** Be sure you know what you are supposed to do.
2. **Know the due date.** Check when the assignment must be turned in.
3. **Review the grading process.** Understand how the assignment will be graded. If there is a rubric or other assessment tool, study it.
4. **Find out about help options.** Know whether you can work with a partner, use the Internet, use a calculator, attend a help session, or otherwise get assistance.
5. **Divide your time.** Think about how long the assignment will take and how much time you have to complete it. Decide when you will work on it in order to get it done on time.
6. **Collect the materials and tools you need.** If you are doing the work in different locations, take the materials with you, whether on paper or digitally or both.
7. **Choose a place to work.** Find a spot that is comfortable and free of distractions.
8. **Note any problem areas.** If you have questions or concerns, contact classmates or the teacher.
9. **Welcome the teacher's ideas.** Getting feedback and suggestions on a current project will improve your performance now and on future assignments.

Your Turn Rate your performance in terms of how you complete assignments. Use a scale of 1 (never) to 5 (always). What tips do you need to follow more closely? Choose two of those points and write about how you could improve on each one.

	(Never) ⟶ (Always)
1. **Understand the assignment.**	1 . . . . 2 . . . . 3 . . . . 4 5
2. **Know the due date.**	1 . . . . 2 . . . . 3 . . . . 4 5
3. **Review the grading process.**	1 . . . . 2 . . . . 3 . . . . 4 5
4. **Find out about help options.**	1 . . . . 2 . . . . 3 . . . . 4 5
5. **Divide your time.**	1 . . . . 2 . . . . 3 . . . . 4 5
6. **Collect materials and tools.**	1 . . . . 2 . . . . 3 . . . . 4 5
7. **Choose a place to work.**	1 . . . . 2 . . . . 3 . . . . 4 5
8. **Note any problem areas.**	1 . . . . 2 . . . . 3 . . . . 4 5
9. **Welcome the teacher's ideas.**	1 . . . . 2 . . . . 3 . . . . 4 5

Managing Stress

Human beings experience stress in two ways. Eustress is beneficial stress and stems from focus, hard work, skilled performance, and achievement. Distress is harmful stress and stems from fear, futility, floundering, and frustration. Eustress improves performance, health, and mood, while distress has a negative effect on these. Consider the chart to the right, which measures performance against stress level.

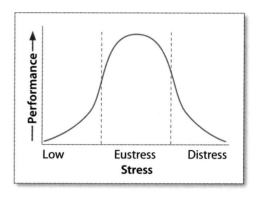

Stress-Management Techniques

When stress overwhelms, you can take action to reduce it. Here are some helpful strategies:

1. **Avoid the problem.** Some stressful situations aren't worth confronting. Step away and get room to think. You might be able to avoid the problem altogether. If you get anxious in crowds, find ways to stay away from them. If you hate being cold, make sure to wear warm clothes.
2. **Care for yourself.** Stress is your body's response to a perceived threat, so many of the best stress-relieving strategies involve caring for your body. Start by taking a deep breath and letting it out slowly. It will calm you. Do other relaxing things, like taking a walk or a bath, watching a show, or talking with friends. Eat right and sleep well.
3. **Face the problem.** Figure out what is causing you to feel stressed and take it on. If you are worried about an assignment, make a plan for completing it, and get to work. If you are concerned about a tryout, practice so that you can do your best.
4. **Get help.** You don't have to face a problem alone. A friend, family member, teacher, coach, or counselor can help you take on the problem. Talk with the person. Discuss strategies for coping. Just sharing the load can reduce the stress you are feeling.
5. **Outlast the problem.** Sometimes, you can neither solve nor evade a problem. But you can outlast it. You're probably tougher than most stressful situations, which do have a way of eventually dissipating.

Your Turn Think about a situation that causes you stress. Is it eustress or distress? If you are experiencing distress, choose two of the above management techniques and follow them. Whenever you feel stress, turn to this page and review the ways for managing it.

Searching for Colleges

You may get a flutter in your heart when you think about finding a college to go to. That's just fine. It's a huge decision with lots of components. When you consider different colleges, think about the following criteria.

- **Type of college:** You can choose from many types of institutions—community colleges, trade and tech schools, specialty colleges, state schools, and private colleges. You can also select online or for-profit colleges.

- **Degrees offered:** Consider the degrees offered by the college. If you want to be a nurse, you need to find a school that offers a nursing degree. If you want to be an engineer or an anthropologist, you need to seek out those programs, and so on.

- **Reputation:** If you are going into a specialized field, such as marine biology, you'll want to graduate from an institution that is recognized as a leader in that field. Consider whether the faculty is renowned in your chosen discipline.

- **Experience:** Some colleges offer huge classes to freshmen and access to professors only at upper levels. Other colleges offer small class sizes taught by professors. Some offer secular campuses, and others offer religious campuses. Some colleges stand in the heart of big cities, and others are surrounded by cornfields. Decide what sort of experience you want.

- **Cost:** The cost of going to college varies widely. Often community colleges offer the same core classes as four-year schools do, at about half the cost. They usually include agreements that allow students to transfer to universities after their first year or two. State schools in one's own state (or a state that has reciprocity) can be more affordable, too. Private schools often cost more but offer strong candidates financial aid packages that make up the difference.

- **Financial aid:** Find out what a college offers in terms of scholarships, student loans, work-study programs, grants, and other types of financial aid. You can also apply for scholarships from philanthropic organizations, churches, charities, and other groups. Some financial aid is based on the student's performance, and some is based on need.

- **Location:** You may want to commute to a nearby college to save on the cost of a room and meals. You may want to attend a faraway college or a college that offers many study-abroad options so that you can gain a completely different cultural experience.

Your Turn Think about the ideal college for you. Would it offer a one-year certificate, a two-year degree, a four-year degree, or an advanced degree? What degree do you most want to get? Would you prefer a large public school or a small private one? Where would it be? Answer these questions and then go online to search for options.

Applying to Colleges

Every college has its own application procedure. Carefully investigate the colleges that interest you and follow their instructions. Here is an overview of common components.

- **Application window:** Find out the earliest date for submitting an application for the coming year, and try to submit on or soon after that date. Also find out the latest date on which applications are accepted and make sure to submit before that date.

- **Application fee:** Most colleges require a nonrefundable application fee, which must be submitted with the application. Although this policy means you ought to apply only to an institution you actually want to attend, it is common to apply to more than one college. This gives you plenty of options to choose from.

- **Application form:** Most colleges want you to complete an application online, either using the college's specific form or the common application, which is used by many colleges. Some colleges still accept paper applications. Don't submit to one school in both formats, however.

- **High school transcript:** Colleges will ask you to send a transcript of your high school years. If you are still in high school, the college will probably also ask you to indicate the classes you have yet to complete. If you are submitting a GED (a high-school equivalency diploma), you'll probably also need to submit a high school transcript to show the classes you completed.

- **SAT/ACT scores:** You may have to submit your ACT and/or SAT test scores as part of your overall application.

- **Letters of recommendation:** You may be asked to submit letters of recommendation along with your application. Ask for letters from teachers, businesspeople, and community leaders who know you and who can speak about your qualifications for the field/discipline that interests you.

- **Entrance essay:** Some colleges ask you to write an essay on a topic they provide. The essay should show your best writing and express a clear main point with strong support. Of course, it must also be error free, so get help with proofreading.

- **Financial aid application:** You'll need to complete a separate application for financial aid. (See page 124.)

- **Housing application:** You'll also need to apply separately for housing on campus. If you are planning to commute or live off campus, you'll need to let the college know that.

Your Turn Go online to view the application process for a college that interests you. Download an application form and study it. Gather the information you would need to complete the form.

Applying for Financial Aid

To apply for financial aid, start by completing the Free Application for Federal Student Aid at the Web site www.fafsa.ed.gov. You can apply starting January 1 of the year the financial aid will apply. (If you apply sooner, you will have to correct your statement once your taxes are complete.) You should apply as soon as you can to increase your chance of getting financial aid, and certainly before March 1, so that you don't miss any school's deadline. Here is the information that you need to have ready:

- ☑ **Social security number and driver's license**
- ☑ **School codes** for the schools you are applying to or attending (go to www. fafsa.ed.gov)
- ☑ **Personal identification number (PIN)** from www.pin.ed.gov
- ☑ **Tax returns and W2 form** for the previous year
- ☑ **Records of untaxed income,** such as welfare checks or veteran's benefits
- ☑ **Information about assets,** such as bank statements and mortgages
- ☑ **The type of aid you want,** such as grants, loans, and work-study opportunities (or all available)
- ☑ **Your dependency status,** indicating whether you are considered a dependent by your parents

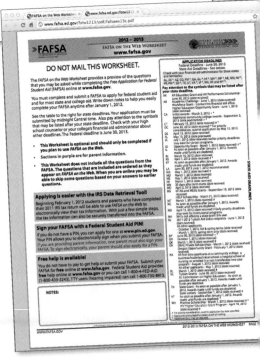

Once you have completed the FAFSA application, the government will send a Student Aid Report (SAR) to you and the schools that you want to attend (allow two to three weeks for online forms and four to six weeks for hard-copy forms). This report indicates what your Expected Family Contribution (EFC) will be. After the schools receive your SAR, they will send you a financial aid package including any federal aid. Some schools may require additional information and forms.

Your Turn Go online to http://www.fafsa. ed.gov/help/ffdef44.htm and download a free FAFSA worksheet. Fill it out to practice applying for financial aid. If you need any help, ask your guidance counselor.

School-Success Activities

Good Habits

School success depends on developing good habits. The following activity will help you think about your habits.

Your Turn Write down the following in a list: 1. Sleep. 2. Eat. 3. Move. 4. Connect. 5. Relax. 6. Work. 7. Wonder. 8. Discover. 9. Create. 10. Share. Next to each item, write the amount of time you spent on each activity yesterday. Which activities did you spend enough time doing? Which do you need to spend more time doing?

Living in Full Color

You will be happiest if you live life in full color rather than monotone. Use the following activity to think about a full-color life.

Your Turn Create a spectrum chart using crayons, pens, or paint, and label each color in the chart with something that is important to you. Compare your chart to another student's. How many important things do you share? How different are you? How does each spectrum represent the full-color life of the person living it?

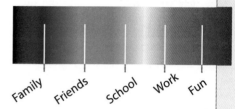

Family   Friends   School   Work   Fun

Setting Long-Term Goals

Setting goals helps you to move forward to accomplish important things in your life and realize your dreams. The activity below will help you set goals.

Your Turn Write a long-term goal for each of the following, using the examples below. Then, for each goal, write one thing you can do right now to move toward that goal.

1. **High school:** I want to graduate with a 3.5 grade point average or better.

2. **Job:** I want to work part-time at a movie theater.

3. **Higher education:** I want to go to a college that has a strong music program.

4. **Relationships:** I want to stay close to my high school friends after high school.

5. **Career:** I want to get a job teaching music.

6. **Lifestyle:** I want to have my own home in a medium-size city.

Eustress and Distress

Eustress improves your performance by motivating, energizing, and focusing you. Distress decreases your performance by reducing your energy, causing worry and pain, and making you want to avoid or escape a situation.

Your Turn List activities that cause you eustress. Then list activities that cause you distress. Beside this second list, write strategies that you can use to reduce your stress. (See the example below.)

Eustress:	Distress:	Reducing Stress:
quiet places	noise	take a deep breath
singing in choir	singing a solo	practice
cleaning my plate	cleaning my room	focus on one task at a time

Thinking About Colleges

Choosing a college is a complex and important process. The following activity will help you think about your options.

Your Turn For each college-related item listed below, write your preference. (See the examples provided.)

1. **Type of college:** I would like to go to a state school but not one that is huge.
2. **Degrees offered:** I need a school that has a strong nursing program.
3. **Reputation:** U.W. Madison has a great pre-med program, but it's too big.
4. **Experience:** I want a smaller-school experience. I want my professors to know me.
5. **Cost:** I can't afford a private school.
6. **Financial aid:** I'm going to need help. I'll need to work while I'm going to school.
7. **Location:** I want something close enough to be able to go home often.

Preparing for Financial Aid

The soaring cost of a higher education means that you ought to explore your options for financial aid. The activity below will help you get started.

Your Turn Go to www.fafsa.ed.gov and find the school codes for colleges that interest you. Then go to www.pin.ed.gov to get a personal identification number. Afterward, go to www.finaid.org/fafsa and watch the "Five-Minute FAFSA Video" to learn more.

Chapter 9

Improving Study Skills

Good habits don't just happen. In the beginning, you must work at them and continue doing them until, finally, you do them automatically. That's when good habits can make a real difference in your life. Brushing your teeth every day, for example, has numerous benefits.

This chapter presents the basic habits of strong learners—taking notes, preparing for tests, and so on. Adopting and continuing to practice these good learning habits can make an important difference in your academic performance.

You will learn . . .

- Taking Classroom Notes
- Using a Learning Log
- Understanding Assessments and Tests
- Improving Test-Taking Skills
- Answering Objective Questions
- Responding to Prompts

Taking Classroom Notes

Almost every day in class, teachers present new information. One helpful way to engage this material and begin to understand it is to take notes. Note taking requires you to translate ideas into your own words and make your own connections. It also provides a record of information you must learn. Here are some note-taking tips.

- **Use an effective format.** For example, you can use a two-column format, writing your main notes in a wide column on the left and questions and comments in a narrow column on the right. (See page 129.)

- **Consider digital options.** You can key notes into a word processing program, or you can keep digital notes using an application such as Evernote or Catch. These programs also make it easy to save links, images, videos, and other media files.

- **Label your notes** with the class name, topic, and date. Also number the pages to keep them in order.

- **Record information** that your teacher writes on the board.

- **Listen for signal words in the lecture,** such as "Notice how . . . ," "Please be aware that . . . ," or "There are three kinds of . . . ."

- **Underline or star key information** so that you can return to it easily.

- **Use numbered lists** for sequentially ordered information. Use bullets or short dashes for lists of nonsequential details.

- **Draw pictures and diagrams** that illustrate the main point.

- **Write down new vocabulary words,** along with definitions. Circle words as a reminder to check the spellings and definitions.

- **Use a personal shorthand.** Focus on recording key words and phrases rather than writing complete sentences.

- **Record references** to further information, such as page numbers in your textbook or useful Web sites.

- **Read your notes later** to review the information and begin learning it. By reviewing your notes in a different place, you send a signal to your brain that you will need to use the material in more than one context.

Your Turn Which of the note-taking tips above do you already practice? Which do you need to adopt or improve upon? Explain your answers in a brief paragraph.

Sample Note Page

For handwritten notes, use a wide column on the left for your main notes and a narrow one on the right for questions, comments, and vocabulary words. If you keep notes digitally, type text and use links, images, comments, and other features.

Label each note page, telling the class and date.

Biology   Feb. 17   16

(Extremophiles)—Means "Loving Extremes"

Underline major topics and subtopics.

A. Types
- Acidophile (low pH)/Alkaliphile (high pH)
- Anaerobic (no O_2)
- Barophile (high pressure)
- Cryophile (super cold)/Psychrophile (cold)
- Endoliths (rock eaters)
- Halophiles (high salt)
- Methanogenic (intestines)
- Thermophile (hot)/
  Hyperthermophile (hugely hot)
- Toxitolerant (poison/radiation)
- Xerophile (no H_2O)

Most end in -phile for "love." Then look at the beginning for clue about meaning.

We need some bacteria to digest our food. Are they extremophiles?

Use numbered, lettered, and bulleted lists to organize details.

B. Where they came from:
- Ancient single cells—(Archaea)
- Date to inhospitable early Earth
- (Hadean)—super-hot period
- Only extreme environments
- Early Earth unstable environment
- No ozone to block ultraviolet
- (Stromatolites) made O_2 atmosphere

Archaea—"old"

Hadean—"Hades Earth"

Stromatolites— "bacteria slime"

Circle new vocabulary words and come back later to write definitions.

C. Some single-cell extremophiles; some multicellular

Draw pictures to help you recall key details.

Yeti Crab
(Totally Hairy)

7 ft. tall
Tube Worms

By hydrothermal vents— super hot, super poisonous, super pressure

Using a Learning Log

Note taking is a good way to initially engage new information. After that, you can deepen your understanding by reflecting on the material and your course work in a learning log (a separate part of your notebook). Here are some tips.

- **Reserve a portion of your notebook** for making reflections about each day's lessons and your work in a particular course.
- **Resolve to write entries on a regular basis,** especially about more difficult information and ideas.
- **Label and date each entry** so that you can track your thinking.
- **Freely explore your thoughts and feelings.** Try writing nonstop for three to five minutes at a time.
- **Spur your thinking with the strategies below** as needed.
- **Read your entries periodically** to see how your thinking has developed and to review key details.

Learning-Log Strategies

Predict —————— Predict what the new ideas will lead to or what you will learn next.

Summarize —————— Summarize what was covered in a lesson or class.

Evaluate —————— Evaluate its importance and meaning.

Ask —————— Ask "what if?" or "why?" about a subject you are studying.

Debate —————— Debate ideas by creating a conversation between you and another person.

Connect —————— Connect an idea to something else you already know.

Argue —————— Argue for or against ideas or beliefs discussed in class.

Your Turn Write a learning-log entry about something you are currently learning. Follow the tips at the top of this page and use one or more of the learning-log strategies to spur your thinking.

Sample Learning-Log Entry

In this entry, a student reflects on a classroom discussion about the biological phenomenon endosymbiosis, connecting the subject to past experience and knowledge.

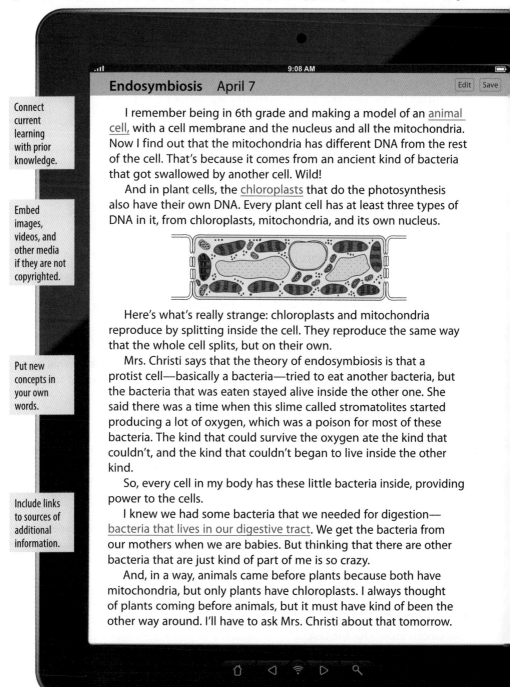

9:08 AM

Endosymbiosis   April 7   Edit Save

Connect current learning with prior knowledge.

I remember being in 6th grade and making a model of an <u>animal cell,</u> with a cell membrane and the nucleus and all the mitochondria. Now I find out that the mitochondria has different DNA from the rest of the cell. That's because it comes from an ancient kind of bacteria that got swallowed by another cell. Wild!

And in plant cells, the <u>chloroplasts</u> that do the photosynthesis also have their own DNA. Every plant cell has at least three types of DNA in it, from chloroplasts, mitochondria, and its own nucleus.

Embed images, videos, and other media if they are not copyrighted.

Here's what's really strange: chloroplasts and mitochondria reproduce by splitting inside the cell. They reproduce the same way that the whole cell splits, but on their own.

Put new concepts in your own words.

Mrs. Christi says that the theory of endosymbiosis is that a protist cell—basically a bacteria—tried to eat another bacteria, but the bacteria that was eaten stayed alive inside the other one. She said there was a time when this slime called stromatolites started producing a lot of oxygen, which was a poison for most of these bacteria. The kind that could survive the oxygen ate the kind that couldn't, and the kind that couldn't began to live inside the other kind.

So, every cell in my body has these little bacteria inside, providing power to the cells.

Include links to sources of additional information.

I knew we had some bacteria that we needed for digestion— <u>bacteria that lives in our digestive tract</u>. We get the bacteria from our mothers when we are babies. But thinking that there are other bacteria that are just kind of part of me is so crazy.

And, in a way, animals came before plants because both have mitochondria, but only plants have chloroplasts. I always thought of plants coming before animals, but it must have kind of been the other way around. I'll have to ask Mrs. Christi about that tomorrow.

Understanding Assessments and Tests

Like it or not, assessments are part of life. In school, they determine your grade. At work, they can determine whether you get hired, certified, and promoted. Consider four different levels of assessment in school.

1. **Self-assessments** allow you to determine how well you are doing with a subject or an idea. You can assess your understanding by reviewing your notes, answering the questions at the end of a textbook chapter, or having friends quiz you on the topic. You also self-assess projects. (See "Evaluating" on pages 416–417.)

2. **Formative assessments** give your instructor feedback. Teachers use observations, discussions, journals, questioning, conferences, and other such techniques for formative assessment. Usually, formative assessments *don't* count toward your grade. They are, instead, a kind of checkup that tells the teacher how well you are learning the material.

3. **Summative assessments** include quizzes, tests, and final exams—the assessments that *do* count toward your grade. They determine your understanding of the material.

4. **High-stakes assessments** include state assessments (which affect funding for your school), exit exams (which indicate whether you graduate), and college entrance exams (like the SAT, ACT, and AP). Many high-stakes assessments use bubble sheets with a multiple-choice format for easy grading, though some include a written component.

Your Turn What types of assessments have you taken so far this week? What types are coming up? For the tests you will be taking, do a quick self-assessment to decide whether you are ready or need to study and prepare further.

Success Criteria

Whenever you are being assessed, it's important to know how your performance will be scored.

- **Rubrics** for a subjective assessment tell what success looks like by listing specific traits of a project and telling what outcome is expected. (See the rubrics on pages 22–23.)
- **Scoring** for an objective test tells how many correct responses are needed for different grades—such as 92 percent and above for an A, 82 to 91 percent for a B, and so on.
- **Weighting** indicates the worth of different parts of a test—such as 50 percent for the objective questions and 50 percent for the essay question.

Your Turn Choose an upcoming test. How will it be scored? Is a rubric involved? Discover the success criteria for the test.

Improving Test-Taking Skills

Make a plan to be a successful test taker. One key is to begin at the top of the list on the facing page. Keep up with self-assessments and refocus your efforts when necessary. Self-assessments help you practice for formative, summative, and high-stakes assessments. Pay attention to the "little" assessments so you can succeed on the "big" ones. Follow these tips. (See also pages 203–216 for help on exams.)

Before the test . . .

☑ **Keep up with your daily work.** Then you'll be ready for surprise inspections, pop quizzes, and other unexpected assessments.

☑ **Know about the test.** Find out what will be covered and whether the test will be multiple choice, true/false, short answer, essay, or a combination.

☑ **Study for the assessment.** Review notes, chapters, and project presentations. Quiz yourself or quiz classmates. Write down questions and key concepts. Paraphrase information aloud.

☑ **Come to the test prepared.** Be rested, bring the right materials, and listen carefully to directions. Preparation reduces test anxiety.

During the test . . .

☑ **Skim the test first.** Get the overall sense of it, and note how much time you have to complete it. Note sections that might require more time.

☑ **Read directions and questions carefully.** Watch for key words such as *always, only, never, all,* which strongly affect the meaning of sentences.

☑ **Answer the questions you are sure of.** Then move on to the more challenging questions.

☑ **Ask the instructor for help.** If anything confuses you about the test, get clarification.

After the test . . .

☑ **Check your answers.** Also check to see that you have answered every question.

☑ **Make sure your name is on the test.** Supply any other required information and turn the test in.

Your Turn Which part of the test-taking process do you do best—before, during, or after? Which part do you most need to improve? Which specific strategies above will you use to improve your test-taking performance? Explore these questions in a learning-log entry.

Answering Objective Questions

Objective questions require specific, correct responses that can be listed in an answer key. These types of questions are easy to grade, testing your surface-level thinking skills—remembering and understanding.

True or False

This type of test provides statements that are either true or false.

- **Read the statement carefully.** If any part is false, the whole statement is false.
- **Watch for key words like** *all, every, always, no,* **and** *never.* Negatives, especially, can change the whole meaning of a sentence.

True	1. In plant cells, chloroplasts provide energy through photosynthesis.
False	2. In animal cells, mitochondria provide energy through photosynthesis.
False	3. Plant cells contain no mitochondria.

Your Turn What word or words could you add to question 1 to make it false? What word or words could you remove from questions 2 and 3 to make them true? Write two of your own true/false questions and have a partner answer them.

Matching

Matching requires you to connect items in one list to items in another.

- **Read the list of terms first.**
- **Scan the list of explanations or definitions next.**
- **Match each term to its correct explanation or definition.**

1. _c_ Prophase	**a.**	Chromosomes split and chromatids move to ends.
2. _e_ Metaphase	**b.**	New cell membranes form in both halves.
3. _a_ Anaphase	**c.**	DNA condenses into chromosomes with two chromatids.
4. _b_ Telophase	**d.**	The cell splits into two cells.
5. _d_ Cytokinesis	**e.**	Chromosomes line up in middle of cell.
6. _f_ Interphase	**f.**	Cell has grown and is ready to divide.

Your Turn Create a matching exercise of your own for a topic you are currently studying. List five or six related terms and then create a list of definitions. Jumble the lists so that the terms and definitions do not match directly across from each other. Give the exercise to a classmate to complete.

Multiple Choice

Multiple-choice questions present a number of possible answers.

- **Read each question carefully.** Determine if you must choose the one right answer, all right answers, or the one answer that does not apply.
- **Read each answer carefully.** Before choosing, look for options such as "All of the above," "None of the above," or "Both A and B."

---

1. Which of the following is not multicellular?
   - **A.** Hydra
   - **B.** Copepod
   - **C.** Paramecium
   - **D.** Volvox
   - **E.** All are multicellular.

2. Which appear in both animal and plant cells?
   - **A.** Endoplasmic reticulum
   - **B.** Golgi apparatus
   - **C.** Lysosome
   - **D.** Both A and B

Your Turn Write two of your own multiple-choice questions about a topic that you are studying. Trade your work with a classmate and answer each other's questions.

Fill in the Blank

Fill-in-the-blank questions require you to enter a specific word in each blank.

- **Use the context of the blank to find the correct answer.**
- **Provide a word for each blank.**
- **Watch for articles.** An *a* indicates that the answer is singular and starts with a consonant. *An* indicates that the answer is singular and starts with a vowel.

The air space in a plant cell is the ____central____ ____vacuole____ . Outside of the cell membrane, a plant cell also has a ____cell____ ____wall____ . The other main feature unique to plant cells are ____chloroplasts____ .

Your Turn You can create fill-in-the-blank questions while reviewing a textbook. Before reading a page, cover boldfaced words in the text using your fingertips or a slip of paper. Read up to the part that is covered and determine what word should come next. Use this technique to quiz yourself in preparation for your next test.

Responding to Prompts

Some assessments include writing prompts. You may be asked to write a short response, a paragraph, or a complete essay. Read the prompt and then analyze it by identifying each part of the communication situation surrounding it.

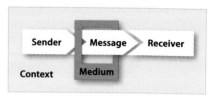

▶ Writing Prompt

Prokaryotic cells and eukaryotic cells are quite different in structure, size, and complexity. In a few short paragraphs, describe the key differences between these types of cells. (20 percent of exam score)

> Prompt Analysis
>
> Sender: **Me**
> Message: **Description of differences between prokaryotic and eukaryotic cells**
> Medium: **A few short paragraphs**
> Receiver: **Mrs. Christi**
> Context: **Essay question worth 20 percent of final exam grade**

Your Turn Read the following writing prompt and analyze it by identifying the five parts of the communication situation. Remember to indicate both the topic and purpose of the message.

A cell reproduces through mitosis, splitting into two cells. The way the main chromosomes end up in identical cells, however, is different from the way the mitochondrial DNA ends up in both cells. Explain in a brief essay how the main DNA and mitochondrial DNA reproduce. (20 percent of exam score)

Purpose Words

A prompt uses purpose words that tell you what you are supposed to do in your response. Watch for these words:

Compare: Show the similarities.
Contrast: Show the differences.
Convince: Change the reader's mind.
Define: Explain the meaning.
Describe: Use details that clarify.

Evaluate: Show the value or worth.
Explain: Show how something works.
Persuade: Convince through reasons.
Prove: Demonstrate with evidence.
Summarize: Give the main point.

Your Turn Find the purpose words in the two prompts above.

Planning and Writing a Response

Usually, you will have a limited amount of time to respond to a writing prompt on an assessment. Use a compacted version of the writing process (see pages 212–215) and these tips:

- **Follow your teacher's directions.** Note how much time you have.

- **Pace yourself.** Determine to spend the first five minutes planning your response and the bulk of your time writing it. Leave 5 to 10 minutes for reviewing your work and checking it for completeness and correctness.

- **Carefully read the prompt.** An otherwise excellent response that is off topic, in the wrong form, or focused on the wrong purpose will score badly.

- **Analyze the prompt.** Do this by identifying the five parts of the communication situation.

- **Create a quick plan.** In response to the prompt, write a thesis statement and list key support on a piece of scrap paper.

- **Write your response.** Include your thesis statement and provide your key support in well-organized paragraphs with topic sentences.

- **Review your writing.** Reread the prompt and any directions to make sure that you have created an on-target response.

> Plant cells and animal cells both have cell membranes, and all organelles within eukaryotic cells are encased in membranes. Write a brief essay that describes the critical functions membranes perform in cells.

> Membranes separate the living thing from its larger environment—even if the larger environment is another living thing.
> - Bringing in food
> - Getting rid of waste
> - Defending against attack
> - Giving the cell structure

Your Turn Practice writing a response to a prompt. Read the prompt below and analyze it by identifying the five parts of the communication situation, as shown on the facing page. Then write a thesis statement and key support. Pace yourself to write a complete response in 45 minutes.

> You've considered both objective questions and writing prompts in this chapter. The two approaches test your thinking in different ways. In an essay, explain the challenges of each type of testing approach.

Sample Response

In the response below, note how the student writer has organized the essay into beginning, middle, and ending paragraphs.

▶ Writing Prompt

Plant cells and animal cells both have cell membranes, and all organelles within eukaryotic cells are encased in membranes. Write a brief essay that describes the critical functions membranes perform in cells.

Response

Beginning paragraph includes a thesis statement.

The biggest organ in our bodies is not the brain. It's our skin. We may not be used to thinking of skin as something particularly important, but it is. It's the dividing line between our bodies and the outer world. <u>On the cellular level, a cell's membrane performs this same function, separating the cell from its larger environment—even if the larger environment is another living thing.</u>

Middle paragraphs focus on key support.

The most important role of the cell membrane is to function as a kind of border patrol. It allows nutrients to enter the cell and provides a way to get waste materials out of the cell. In fact, these functions are so critical that they limit the size a cell can become. Since the surface area of a cell does not increase at the same rate as its volume, eventually a cell reaches a point where its membrane cannot bring in enough food or get rid of enough waste.

Each middle paragraph starts with a topic sentence and includes details.

For single-celled organisms, the cell membrane also helps the cell move through its environment. It may be covered with cilia that flap to move the cell along, or it may have a flagellum extension that moves it along. Amoebas, of course, move along like blobs, with their outer membranes forming pseudopods.

Cell membranes also defend the cell against attack. They prevent alien DNA from entering and make sure that the pH within the cell is correct. Some cell membranes include defensive structures, and some have specific key ports that receive only specific molecules.

Let's not forget the role of cell membranes in reproduction, either. When cells undergo mitosis, the process begins with the dissolving of the nuclear membrane and ends with the fission of the cell into two cell membranes.

Ending paragraph summarizes thesis.

So, though we may be used to ignoring the bag to focus on the groceries inside it, we ought to remember that the cell membrane performs many valuable functions. In fact, its very existence defines what is living and what is not. That's a pretty important role for an often ignored structure.

Study-Skills Activities

Take Note

Note taking is one of the most powerful ways for you to learn information and improve your thinking. This activity will allow you to practice.

Your Turn Read the note-taking tips on page 128. Then, during the next class lecture you attend, take notes using those suggestions. Afterward, reread the tips and decide which two were most helpful to you.

Logging Your Learning

A learning log deepens your thinking, helping you to reflect on your course work and explore new ideas. Use this activity to experiment with learning logs.

Your Turn Choose one of the learning-log strategies below and use it to write a learning-log entry about one of your current classes. Choose another strategy and use it to write an entry for another class. Which strategy worked better for you? Why?

Learning-Log Strategies

Predict ——— Predict what the new ideas will lead to or what you will learn next.

Summarize ——— Summarize what was covered in a lesson or class.

Evaluate ——— Evaluate its importance and meaning.

Ask ——— Ask "what if?" or "why?" about a subject you are studying.

Debate ——— Debate ideas by creating a conversation between you and another person.

Connect ——— Connect an idea to something else you already know.

Argue ——— Argue for or against ideas or beliefs discussed in class.

Self-Assessing

This activity helps you self-assess your test-taking skills.

Your Turn Rate yourself on a scale of 1 (never) to 5 (always) for the following keys to test taking. Which do you most need to improve?
- Keep up with daily work.
- Know about the test.
- Study for the assessment.
- Come to the test prepared.

Understanding Assessment

Think about the assessments you will face soon—project assessments, quizzes, tests, finals, and exit/entrance exams. This activity will help you prepare for them.

Your Turn Choose an upcoming assessment and write down its success criteria (see page 132).
- What **rubric** will be used to assess a project?
- What **information** will be covered on the test?
- What **kinds of questions** will be used?
- How will your performance be **scored?**
- What **weight** will the test or its different parts hold?

Analyzing a Prompt

A writing prompt on an assessment has the same five components as any communication situation. You can use the communication situation to analyze the prompt.

Your Turn Analyze the following writing prompts by identifying the sender, message (including its topic and purpose), medium, receiver, and context of each.

1. Different assessments do different things. Some show how much you are learning. Others help you exit/graduate from a school or enter another school. Decide which type of assessment is most important to you. In an essay, explain the assessment and why it is the most important.

2. Note taking and learning logs give you a way to record and think about what you are learning. Do you take notes? Keep a learning log? In an essay, describe your note-taking and learning-log habits. Tell what changes you could make to improve your work.

3. Developing study skills is called "learning to learn." If you improve your learning skills, you improve your performance in every class. Which study skills do you feel are most important for success in school? Which study skills are critical for learning outside of school? Write an essay that explains your answers.

Planning Your Response

Even though you have a limited amount of time to respond to a writing prompt, you ought to use the first five minutes to make a plan. The following activity will help you do so.

Your Turn Choose one of the prompts above. Consider how you would respond to it. Then make a plan by writing a thesis statement and listing supporting details. Finally, write your essay.

Chapter 10
Reading to Learn

You read casually all the time—when you check Facebook or scan a text from a friend, search for a song on your MP3 player or check your GPS for directions, look at the TV listings, and more. It's like you're wearing a permanent pair of reading glasses.

Reading, in fact, is one of the most common ways to receive information from your environment. It is also a powerful learning tool and the key to success in school. This chapter will help you strengthen this valuable skill.

You will learn . . .

- Reading Actively
- Using Reading Strategies
- Reading Nonfiction
- Nonfiction Glossary
- Reading Fiction
- Fiction Glossary
- Reading Poetry
- Poetry Glossary

Reading Actively

You may think that reading is a passive process, just letting information pour in. But to get the most out of your reading, you must actively engage in it.

Tips for Active Reading

When you read, follow these tips to engage actively with the material.

1. **Question the communication situation.** Whatever you read is a message from a sender. It is presented through a medium, in a context, and to an intended receiver.

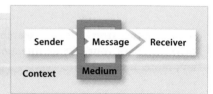

- **Sender:** Who wrote this?
- **Message:** What is the subject? Why might the purpose be?
- **Medium:** How is this message presented? In what way does the medium enhance or detract from the message?
- **Receiver:** Who is supposed to read this? Am I part of the intended audience?
- **Context:** When and where was this written? What was going on then? How does the message fit into today's context? How does it fit with other writings by this author?

2. **Make predictions about the reading.** Before you read, think about what you expect to find out. This will open your mind to the new information. If your expectations are not fulfilled, consider why.
3. **Write while you read.** Jot down names, details, notes, impressions, even drawings. If you own the material, annotate in the margins. (See pages 144-145.) By writing, you engage your kinesthetic sense—involving movement as you process information.
4. **Speak while you read.** Pronounce difficult words. Read aloud any lines that particularly impress you, or things you want to remember. By speaking, you engage your kinesthetic, linguistic, and aural senses, deepening your understanding. The more senses you use, the more deeply you learn.
5. **Discuss what you read.** Tell someone else something interesting about the material. Ask any questions that you have. By discussing what you read, you engage your social mind and help cement your understanding.

Your Turn Before you read the material on the facing page, question the communication situation. Write answers to the questions under number 1 above. Share your answers with a partner.

Using Reading Strategies

Reading with KWL

KWL stands for know, want to know, and learned. The KWL reading strategy prompts you to think about what you already know about a topic and what you want to find out in your reading. Then, after you read, you reflect on what you have learned.

Topic: Terminal Velocity		
Know	**W**ant to know	**L**earned
Terminal velocity is the fastest that an object can fall. I think it's about 200 miles an hour for a person jumping out of a plane. Different weights aren't supposed to fall at different speeds, though.	How can there be different terminal velocities for different objects if they all fall at the same rate?	Terminal velocity is reached when the force of gravity equals the force of drag in the air. If two balls are the same size but weigh different amounts, they fall at the same terminal velocity.

Your Turn Create a three-column chart like the one above. Your topic is SQ3R. In the first column, write what you already know about SQ3R. In the second column, write what you want to know about it. Then read the text below and reflect on what you learned.

Reading with SQ3R

SQ3R is an active-reading strategy that stands for survey, question, read, recite, and review. It helps you get the most meaning out of what you read.

Survey — Look over the text, noting its headings and other boldfaced words, the author, any illustrations, and so on.

Question — Ask questions that you hope to find answers to in the text. This step keeps you focused as you read the material.

Read — Move through the text once quickly to understand the big picture. Then read it again more carefully to catch the details. Take notes and annotate as you go along.

Recite — Speak the main details aloud as you read, engaging more senses to enhance your understanding.

Review — After your reading, look at your notes and annotations and discuss the text with others.

Your Turn Use the SQ3R approach to read the material in one of your next reading assignments in a class of your choice.

Taking Reading Notes

Taking reading notes focuses your attention on the key information in a text while engaging your kinesthetic and visual senses. The notes give you a record of the main points and your thoughts during the reading. Follow these tips:

- **Write down key words and phrases.** Writing complete sentences usually takes too long.
- **Put ideas in your own words.** Paraphrasing helps you to understand and process information.
- **Create shortcuts.** Use symbols where possible.
- **Use dashes, letters, and numbers** to keep your notes organized.
- **Reserve a wide column on the left for your main notes.** Leave a narrow column on the right for questions, comments, and other additions.
- **Consider digital note taking.** Many online services offer note-taking software that you can use to organize, store, and retrieve notes. To learn more about note taking options, see pages 370–371.

The Treaty of Versailles	Feb. 25
Between Germany and Allies—June 28, 1919	
1. War Guilt Clauses	Why so stringent?
• Admit cause of war	
• Give up territory	How are treaties
• Disarm	different now?
• Pay reparations	
2. Reparations: 132 billion Deutsche marks	How were the WWII
• Like $442 billion	treaties different?
• Too much	
• 92 years to pay off	
3. Results:	WWI
• Germany not pacified	↓
• Crushing burden w/Depression	Vers.
• Led to rise of Hitler/WWII	↓
	WWII

Your Turn Use the tips above to take notes about a page from one of your textbooks.

Annotating a Text

If you own a text or have a printout, you can highlight, underline, and make comments on the pages themselves. This helps you to remember the ideas later. Use the tips to the right.

- Write notes in the margins.
- Underline important ideas.
- Circle new vocabulary words.
- Draw lines to connect ideas.
- Use numbers to sort ideas.

Sample Page

The Treaty of Versailles

WWI

In the aftermath of the War to End All Wars, the victorious Entente Powers decided to forge a treaty that, ironically, made World War II inevitable. On June 28, 1919, the Allies concluded the six-month-long Paris Peace conference by signing the Treaty of Versailles. This treaty superseded the armistice that ended hostilities and was an agreement between 32 countries and Germany. The "Big Four" powers behind the treaty were Britain,[1] France,[2] Italy,[3] and the United States.[4] They designed the document to be punitive.

treaty makes war, not peace

seeds of WWII

Articles 231-248 laid out severe conditions that came to be called "War Guilt Clauses." They required Germany to disarm, give up large areas of territory, and pay reparations to specific Allies. Each of these conditions planted a seed for World War II.

- **Disarmament** set strict limits on the number of troops Germany could have and the types of weapons that were forbidden.

territories Hitler invaded first

- **Territory** taken from Germany was annexed by France, Belgium, Poland, and Czechoslovakia; the Rhineland was occupied by the Allies for 15 years; and Austria was forbidden from uniting with Germany.

- **Reparations** took the form of many German resources and goods to be provided to the Allies, as well as large sums of cash, which caused hyperinflation.

German mindset

The humiliation of Germany, as well as the extreme economic hardships suffered under these terms, prepared the way for the rise of National Socialism. Hitler's creation of a huge war machine and use of that machine to invade lost territories were clear reversals of the terms of the Treaty of Versailles. The Allies of World War I became, for the most part, the Allies of World War II. They paid in lives and treasure for the miscalculations of Versailles.

Your Turn Photocopy a page from a textbook, or find a page online. Read and annotate it.

Reading Nonfiction

Nonfiction articles and books offer factual information from every area of human endeavor: science, math, social studies, English, and the arts. News articles tell what is happening in the world, and editorials argue for specific positions. To gain the most from reading nonfiction, read with a plan.

Before . . .

☑ **Analyze the communication situation.** Who is the sender (the author)? What is the message (subject and purpose)? What is the medium? Who is the intended receiver (the reader)? What is the context?

☑ **Understand why you are reading.** What is your purpose?

☑ **Skim the selection.** Pay attention to headings, boldfaced words, graphics, captions, and the beginning and ending paragraphs.

☑ **Predict what you will learn.** Plan to watch for those ideas as you read.

☑ **Note features of the medium.** If you are reading printed material, look for a table of context, an index, a list of figures, and other features that can help you. If you are reading Web material, note links, videos, photo galleries, and other media.

During . . .

☑ **Read actively.** Use a strategy such as KWL or SQ3R. (See page 143.)

☑ **Take notes.** Paraphrase the main points, note new vocabulary words, and ask questions. (See page 144.)

☑ **Annotate the text.** Underline, star, number, and note key points. (See page 145.)

☑ **Read important parts aloud.** This will help you remember them.

After . . .

☑ **Summarize the reading.** Put it into your own words.

☑ **Share your observations.** Talk with a friend, classmate, or family member.

☑ **List any questions that you still have about the material.**

Your Turn Use the tips above to read the article on the facing page, material from a textbook, or an online article. Skim the article, paying attention to its special features. Predict what you will learn. Then read actively. Afterward, write a paragraph that summarizes the piece.

Nonfiction Article

The following nonfiction Web page includes a title, byline, article, and video, as well as links to additional information about the topic.

9:08 AM

The article title sums up the main point.

Secrets of the Brain
By Cristina Reddick

A video provides additional information.

The human brain is an amazing and mysterious organ. It has 100 billion neurons and 100 trillion synapses. Every time a brain learns, it grows new connections. It also routinely prunes old connections to run as efficiently as possible. The brain's tremendous capacity and <u>plasticity</u> makes it more powerful than a supercomputer. In fact, every accomplishment of human civilization including supercomputers is a product of this uniquely brilliant organ.

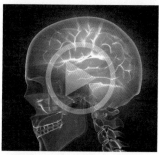

The human brain is strange. It is the size of a 2-liter bottle and the consistency of tofu. Ninety percent of the brain consists of glue-like cells called glia.

A Premium Organ at a Premium Price

Human beings have paid a high price for their huge brains. Childbirth is dangerous because our brains are so large that emerging is a struggle. Babies' skulls aren't even fused yet to allow for growth after birth. While other mammals can walk within hours of birth, humans take many months to do so. While other mammals quickly learn everything they need to know to survive, humans take many years to do so. In the United States, society spends an average of <u>$100,000 per child</u> for K–12 education, and those who go to college may double that amount.

Links lead to other articles and resources.

While those brains are being educated, they're also consuming a huge portion of the body's resources. Human brains require high-protein diets to grow and function. They also

A quotation gives an additional perspective.

> ❝Does the brain control you, or are you controlling the brain? I don't know if I'm in charge of mine.❞
> —Karl Pilkington

require 20 percent of the body's oxygen and a large proportion of the blood sugar. And the brain resides within its own pocket of fluid with a <u>blood barrier</u> that keeps it safe from disease.

Though the brain produces our consciousness, it also requires <u>unconsciousness</u>. The average person will spend 25 years asleep, five of those years dreaming. During that time, the brain sorts information, culls unneeded pathways, and optimizes.

Nonfiction Glossary

Allusion is a reference to an event or story to explain another idea.

Analogy is a comparison of two relationships (for example, *a battery is to current as a heart is to blood*).

Anecdote is a brief story that demonstrates an idea.

Antithesis is something that shows the opposite of an idea or thesis.

Argument refers to a series of statements made to logically prove something.

Author is the person who writes a piece of information.

Autobiography is the story of a person's life told by the person him- or herself.

Balance refers to information that shows both sides of an argument.

Bias refers to information that shows only one side of an argument.

Biography is the story of a person's life told by another person.

Blog is a Web log—a series of articles published on the Internet.

Byline refers to the line of text that identifies the author of an article, usually appearing below the title.

Cause-effect writing explores the reasons something happened and the things that result from it.

Comparison is an analysis of the similarities between two topics.

Connotation refers to what a word suggests, as opposed to the word's direct meaning (denotation).

Contrast is an analysis of the differences between two topics.

Copyright is a law that protects the rights of those who own writing and other intellectual property.

Definition refers to the meaning of a term, often including denotation, connotation, etymology, and examples.

Denotation refers to the literal meaning of a word, as opposed to the associated meanings (connotations).

Description literally means "drawing a line around" something—explaining its key features and its overall identity.

Diction refers to the level of language, from very formal to very informal or slangy.

Editorial is a piece of writing that expresses the opinion of the author.

Editorialize is to express your opinion about a topic; often used as a criticism of supposedly objective reporting.

Epistle is a letter, a term used most often to refer to historical correspondence.

Epitaph is a short piece of prose in honor of a dead person, often on a gravestone.

Epithet is a name given to describe someone, such as "The Hammer" or "Queen of the Nile."

Essay is a form of writing that explores a specific nonfiction topic.

Etymology refers to the origins of a word, often through several languages.

Example refers to a specific case that demonstrates a general idea.

Exposition refers to explanatory writing and also to the beginning of a narrative in which setting, character, and conflict are established.

Evidence refers to facts, statistics, examples, and other supporting details.

Figure of speech refers to a set of literary devices that include *analogy, antithesis, hyperbole, metaphor, metonymy, personification, simile,* and *understatement.*

Hyperbole is exaggeration for effect (for example, *his brain got stuck in the doorway*).

Instructions are a set of commands that tell how to do something.

Intellectual property refers to ideas that are created, sold, and owned, including copyright.

Irony occurs when an action meant to create a specific outcome actually creates the opposite outcome (for example, *my toothbrush knocked out a tooth*).

Journal refers to a series of entries made regularly to record personal observations of a period of life or a specific experience.

Letter to the editor refers to a letter written to a newspaper or periodical and usually published on the op/ed page.

Manuscript is a printed draft of a piece of writing, usually of a longer work.

Masthead refers to a list of staff members published in a newspaper or magazine.

Memoir is a reflection on the meaning of one's accomplishments.

Metaphor is a comparison saying that one thing is another.

Metonymy is using one word to substitute for an associated word (for example, using *bench* to refer to a *judge*).

News refers to current information reported through various media and deemed to be important to readers and other news consumers.

Objective means expressing information in a factual, nonbiased way, without taking a specific perspective.

Op/ed page is the page of a newspaper, usually opposite the editorial page, on which letters to the editor and other nonstaff perspectives are published.

Overstatement is intentionally exaggerating for dramatic effect (for example, *it feels like the surface of the sun in here*).

Oxymoron is a combination of words that sound contradictory (for example, *black light* or *serious fun*).

Paradox refers to a situation or statement that appears to be contradictory (for example, George Orwell's statement *"Ignorance is strength"*).

Periodical refers to information published on a regular basis—such as a newspaper, magazine, or journal.

Personal commentary is a writer's thoughtful reaction to some aspect of life.

Personification gives human traits to a nonhuman thing (for example, *the car groaned and went back to sleep*).

Persuasion refers to writing that is meant to convince the reader to agree with the writer or to take action.

Point-counterpoint is a style of editorial in which two people with opposing positions debate a topic.

Proceedings are the published papers from a professional or academic conference.

Process writing gives instructions for doing something or describes how something works.

Pseudonym refers to a false name that a writer uses (also called a *pen name* or *nom de plume*).

Satire refers to a presentation that makes fun of a topic by imitating it in an absurd way.

Simile is a comparison of two things using *like* or *as*.

Subjective means expressing personal opinion instead of objective fact.

Tone is the quality formed by word choice and ideas, revealing the author's opinion of the topic.

Understatement minimizes by referring in a calm way to something emotionally charged (for example, *when the sun becomes a red giant, picnics will be less enjoyable*).

Reading Fiction

Some of the best written work in any culture is fiction—the great American novel, Shakespeare's plays, and classic movies. Though these works stem from the imagination, they often express the realities of the human condition. Reading fiction is, in part, a search for truth. When you read fiction, follow a plan.

Before . . .
- ☑ **Consider the communication situation.** Analyze each part—who created the work, when and where it was created, and what medium is used.
- ☑ **Find out about the work itself.** What effect has it had? What is the main idea? Why was it written, and why is it important to read?
- ☑ **Skim the work.** Pay attention to any titles, chapters, notes, figures, and other information that tells you about the work. Also note how long it is.
- ☑ **Explore your first thoughts in a notebook or journal.**

During . . .
- ☑ **Read the work once, letting the story unfold.** Experience each event.
- ☑ **Think about the characters.** What do they want? What problems or challenges do the characters face? Which characters do you like and which do you dislike? Why?
- ☑ **Note how the conflict progresses.** How does the writer build suspense? How do you get drawn into the story?
- ☑ **Think about the style of the language.** What tone is used in the story? What figures of speech are used? What symbolism appears in the work?
- ☑ **Explore your thoughts in a notebook or journal.**

After . . .
- ☑ **Consider the climactic moment and its aftermath.** Does the main character succeed or fail? How do events of the story affect you emotionally?
- ☑ **Think about major themes.** What does the story have to say about life? What truths does it point to?
- ☑ **Explore your final thoughts in a notebook or journal.**
- ☑ **Write a formal literary analysis.** Review the story, summarizing it (without spoiling it for others) and tracing the key themes. Indicate whether you recommend reading the work and why.

Your Turn Use the plan above for reading the story excerpt on the facing page. Reflect on the story by writing in your notebook or journal.

Fiction Page

The story excerpt below includes many sensory details. Read through it once for the overall picture, then again to see how the sensory details tell the story.

The title hints at the story's topic.

Reluctant Romeo and Jittery Juliet

Jackson marched up the street toward Tawni's house, the Valentine card clutched in his fingers. Up ahead, her front porch light beamed yellow. He slowed on the sidewalk. He'd have to stand on that porch for the whole block to see, ring the bell, wait, and hope. A car cruised slowly past, the driver rubbernecking.

The story starts from Jackson's point of view.

Jackson turned away and peered at the card in his hand. It was bent. His thumb had pressed a small crater into "Be Mine." He glanced one last time at the glowing porch, then turned toward the street and crossed it, jamming the card into a garbage can waiting in the gutter.

§ § §

A break shifts to Tawni's point of view.

Outside Tawni's window, a garbage can rattled loudly in the street. An old man shouted a threat, and a young man echoed it. Tawni plucked out her earbuds and tiptoed to the window to peek out.

No one was there. Rain began to patter in the lengthening shadows.

Shivering, Tawni drew the sash closed, clicked the lock, and dragged down the fluttering shade. She lay on her bed, listening to the rain.

"Tawni," came a muffled voice outside her window, "I'm getting soaked."

Dialogue moves the story along.

Her breath caught. "Who's there?"

"Jackson."

Another voice—Daddy yelling from the basement: "Who you talking to, Tawni-Girl?"

"Nobody, Daddy. It's just me—singing to my MP3!" Tawni lifted the sash. Jackson gratefully clambered over the sill and spilled, sopping, on the floor. He brought with him the scent of fresh rain and the winds of February. But there was something else: the fragrance of roses?

Tawni gaped. "What did you bring me?"

Jackson looked up awkwardly and raised a dozen red roses, rumpled from his entry. "Um, for you."

Tawni's mouth dropped open. "You? Roses? For me?"

"Yeah," he replied as he climbed to his feet. "And, uh, these, too." He lifted a heart-shaped box.

Despite herself, Tawni laughed a little—not a laugh of derision, but of amazement and delight.

Jackson laughed, too. "Sorry. I'm not good with all the Romeo stuff."

The writer "shows" instead of "tells," using sensory details.

Shaking her head, Tawni took the box of chocolates from him and said, "No, I'd say you're pretty good at it." She lifted a truffle from the heart-shaped box and took a tentative bite. The dark chocolate shell cleaved gently, releasing sweet caramel. In the center was a cashew—salty and rich. She'd never tasted anything so good. "Really good at it."

Fiction Glossary

Allegory is the expression of a truth or generalization using symbols.

Allusion is a reference in a written work to something familiar.

Analogy is the comparison of one thing with another (for example, *his dog served as a confidant*).

Anecdote is a brief story or "slice of life" told to make a point.

Antagonist is the person, group, or force that wars against the protagonist, or the main character, of a story.

Caricature is an exaggerated depiction of a character, emphasizing specific traits absurdly.

Character refers to one of the people in a fictional story—the protagonist, antagonist, or other.

Chorus is a conventional element of classic Greek plays in which a group sings comments about the action onstage.

Climax is the point of greatest tension in a plot, when the protagonist either succeeds or fails.

Comedy refers classically to a story that ends with the redemption of the hero, often with a wedding; it also refers to humorous writing.

Conflict refers to six classic oppositions in literature:
- Person versus self
- Person versus person
- Person versus society
- Person versus nature
- Person versus the supernatural
- Person versus machine

Context refers to the situation surrounding a specific event in a story, or the situation surrounding the composition of the story.

Denouement is the story's resolution following the climax and falling action.

Description refers to the use of sensory details to depict a person, place, or thing in a story.

Dialogue refers to the words that characters in a story speak. Dialogue is usually enclosed in quotation marks.

Epic refers to an ancient form of storytelling including gods and heroes on long, life-changing adventures.

Exposition is the beginning of a story in which the setting and characters are established and the conflict is introduced.

Fable is a story often including talking animals and sharing a specific moral or lesson.

Falling action is what happens in a story immediately following the climax and preceding the denouement.

Farce is a fast-paced comedy centered on absurd situations and exaggerated characters.

Figure of speech refers to a set of literary devices, including *analogy, antithesis, hyperbole, metaphor, metonymy, personification, simile,* and *understatement.*

Flashback is a past event or scene interjected in a story to explain the present.

Flash fiction refers to short stories told in a few paragraphs.

Foreshadowing refers to clues that point to what will soon happen in a story.

Genre refers to the type of story (for example, *mystery, science fiction, historical fiction, Western, romance*).

Hyperbole is exaggeration for effect (for example, *her ego has satellites*).

Imagery refers to the word pictures created by the writer.

Internal dialogue refers to the thoughts of a character—words not enclosed in quotation marks.

Irony occurs when an action produces a result opposite to what was intended (for example, *I studied all night and then slept through the test*).

Metaphor compares two things by equating them (for example, *his face was a leather sack*).

Mood refers to the overall emotional quality of a literary work.

Motif is a recurring thematic element.

Motivation is a character's reason for doing something in a story.

Myth is a story created by a culture to explain how things came to be.

Novel refers to a long, involved story with multiple plotlines and characters.

Novella refers to a short novel with a few plotlines and characters.

Parable is a story that teaches a religious truth or lesson.

Parody is a story that imitates a literary work or style in an exaggerated or absurd way for comic effect.

Plot refers to the following components in a story:
- Exposition
- Rising action
- Climax
- Falling action
- Denouement (resolution)

Point of view indicates who is telling a story:
- **First person:** told by one of the characters
- **Third person:** told by someone outside of the story (**limited** shares the thoughts of one character; **omniscient,** the thoughts of all characters; **objective,** the actions of all characters, but no thoughts)

Protagonist refers to the main character of a story—the hero who struggles with the antagonist.

Quest is a story about a hero who ventures into the world to achieve a goal.

Resolution refers to the denouement, the way the story wraps up.

Rising action is the series of events that present the conflict and increase the suspense, leading up to the climax.

Satire is a story that pokes fun at a situation by exaggerating human faults.

Setting is the time and location of a story.

Short story is a work with a limited set of characters and actions; longer than *flash fiction* but shorter than a *novella*.

Simile is a comparison using *like* or *as*.

Soliloquy is a speech given by a character.

Stereotype is a characterization based on bias rather than on reality.

Story refers to the mix of these elements: setting, characters, plot, conflict, theme.

Stream of consciousness narration follows a character's thoughts exactly in the first person.

Style is an author's unique way of telling a story.

Suspense is the tension created by not knowing how a story will turn out.

Suspension of disbelief is the reader's willing decision to suspend judgment on the believability of the text.

Symbol is something concrete that represents something abstract.

Theme is a life lesson offered through a story; the implied meaning.

Tone is the revelation, through word choice, of the author's feelings about the story.

Tragedy refers classically to a story that ends with the failure of the protagonist, often because of a tragic flaw.

Understatement uses minimal language to describe something maximal (for example, *I woke and wondered where I'd misplaced my right arm*).

Reading Poetry

In his introduction to *The Giant Book of Poetry,* William Roetzheim mentions four meanings in a poem. They are explained here:

- The **denotative** meaning describes what the poem means literally.
- The **connotative** meaning describes the nuances that resonate beyond the poem's literal meaning—what it suggests.
- The **metaphorical** meaning explores the way figures of speech are used in the poem.
- The **symbolic** meaning explores how objects and people represent ideas and things outside of the poem itself.

Before . . .

☑ **Analyze the communication situation.** Who wrote the poem? When? Where? Why? What was the context in which the poem was written? Where did it first appear?

☑ **Focus on the poem itself.** What form does it take? Does it have a regular meter? Does it have a regular rhyme scheme? What are the conventions for this type of poetry?

During . . .

☑ **First, read the poem silently, paying attention to the denotative meaning.** Be patient, read slowly, and reread as necessary.

☑ **Next, read the poem aloud, looking for the connotative meaning.** Let the sounds, the flow and rhythm, the words themselves, resonate.

☑ **Read the poem a third time, finding any figures of speech used.** What metaphors, similes, or personification does the poem contain? Has the poet used overstatement or understatement? Are there any surprises hidden in the poem's language?

☑ **Finally, read the poem a fourth time, searching for any symbols concealed below its surface.** Are you certain of the poem's meaning, or do you need to look deeper?

After . . .

☑ **Reflect on the poem.** If you can, annotate it—circling the words that have the strongest impact, underlining the parts that you like best.

☑ **Discuss the poem.** Ask others to read it; then talk about how it works.

☑ **Write about the poem.** Reflect on the poem in a journal entry, or create a new poem inspired by the original.

Your Turn Use the process above to read and reflect on one or more of the poems on the next page.

Sample Poetry

The following poems represent a variety of forms. The first is a traditional haiku, with five syllables in the first line, seven in the next, and five in the last. "Fire and Ice" has an irregular meter but a regular rhyme scheme. The other examples include a sonnet and a free-verse poem.

For a lovely bowl
let us arrange these flowers . . .
since there is no rice

Basho
(trans. Peter Beilenson)

SONNET—TO SCIENCE

Science! true daughter of Old Time thou art!
Who alterest all things with thy peering eyes.
Why preyest thou thus upon the poet's heart,
Vulture, whose wings are dull realities?
How should he love thee? or how deem thee wise,
Who wouldst not leave him in his wandering
To seek for treasure in the jewelled skies,
Albeit he soared with an undaunted wing?
Hast thou not dragged Diana from her car?
And driven the Hamadryad from the wood
To seek a shelter in some happier star?
Hast thou not torn the Naiad from her flood,
The Elfin from the green grass, and from me
The summer dream beneath the tamarind tree?

—E. A. Poe

FIRE AND ICE

Some say the world will end in fire,
Some say in ice.
From what I've tasted of desire
I hold with those who favor fire.
But if it had to perish twice,
I think I know enough of hate
To say that for destruction ice
Is also great
And would suffice.

—Robert Frost

ONE'S-SELF I SING

One's-self I sing, a simple separate person,
Yet utter the word Democratic, the word *En-masse*.
Of physiology from top to toe I sing,
Not physiognomy alone nor brain alone is worthy for the Muse,
I say the Form complete is worthier far,
The Female equally with the Male I sing.
Of Life immense in passion, pulse, and power,
Cheerful, for freest action form'd under the laws divine,
The Modern Man I sing.

—Walt Whitman

Poetry Glossary

Accent is a stressed syllable or word (for example, the word *accent* has an accent on the first syllable).

Alliteration is the repetition of sounds at the beginnings of words (for example, *big-boned beasts*).

Antithesis is setting two statements in opposition (for example, *"To err is human, to forgive, divine"*—Alexander Pope).

Assonance is the repetition of vowel sounds in words (for example, *old rose thorns*).

Ballad is a form of narrative poem that recounts a folktale.

Blank verse is poetry with an iambic pentameter rhythm, but no end rhyme (for example, Shakespeare's plays).

Canto is a major division in a long poem.

Classicism refers to poetry that embodies Greek and Roman ideas of beauty: formality, simplicity, and reserve. Compare to *Romanticism*.

Consonance is the repetition of consonant sounds within words (for example, *hissing reception*).

Couplet refers to a pair of lines that are usually of the same length and exhibit end rhyme.

Elegy is a poem that memorializes someone or something that has passed away.

Enjambment is the continuation of a thought from one line into the next.

Epic poetry is a lengthy form that tells of the works of heroes, gods, and monsters.

Epigram refers to a very short poem that captures an idea in a witty way.

Figure of speech refers to a set of literary devices that include *analogy, antithesis, hyperbole, metaphor, metonymy, personification, simile,* and *understatement*.

Foot is a repeated pattern of stressed and unstressed syllables:
- **Anapest:** two unstressed, one stressed
- **Dactyl:** one stressed, two unstressed
- **Iamb:** one unstressed, one stressed
- **Pyrrhic:** two unstressed
- **Spondee:** two stressed
- **Trochee:** one stressed, one unstressed

Free verse is poetry that does not contain regular meter or rhyme.

Haiku is a short form of Japanese poetry with a line of five syllables, a line of seven, and a line of five.

Heroic couplet refers to two lines that rhyme and express one complete idea.

Idyll poems depict an idealized picture (rustic or pastoral) or capture heroic events from long ago.

Imagery refers to the sensory elements in a poem—visions, sounds, textures, flavors, and so on.

Limericks are short, humorous poems of five lines. The first, second, and fifth lines rhyme and have three stressed syllables each. The third and fourth lines also rhyme but have two stressed syllables each.

Line break refers to the end of a line in free-verse poetry—an important technique for introducing a pause or emphasizing a word.

Lyric is a short poem that focuses on the poet's feelings.

Metaphor is a comparison that equates two things, saying one is the other (for example, *her smile is a pearl*).

Meter refers to the pattern of stressed and unstressed syllables in a poem. See *rhythm*.

Metonymy refers to using one word in place of another with which it is associated (for example, saying *lend me your "ear"* instead of *give me your "attention"*).

Narrative poetry tells a story.

Near rhyme refers to words that don't actually rhyme but sound similar, often used for humorous effect (for example, *metaphor* and *better war*).

Ode is a classical lyric poem with a serious tone.

Onomatopoeia refers to words that sound like what they describe (for example, *crack, whip, shudder, roar*).

Pastoral is a poem that represents an idyllic scene.

Personification means giving human traits to nonhuman things (for example, *the sun glowered at the escapees*).

Quatrain is a four-line poem or stanza.

Refrain is the part of a poem that is repeated, often at the end of a stanza.

Repetition is the intentional repeating of a word or phrase for effect (for example, *she reclines on a green chair on a green lawn in her green world*).

Rhyme refers to words that sound the same (for example, *great* and *weight*).

Rhyme scheme is the way end rhymes line up (for example, if the first two lines rhyme and the next two lines rhyme, the rhyme scheme is *aabb*).

Rhythm is the pattern of stressed and unstressed syllables in a line of poetry. See *meter*.

Romanticism refers to a movement in poetry that favored emotion over reason, opposing the rigidity of classicism.

Scansion is an analysis of the meter of a poem—the pattern of stressed and unstressed syllables.

Simile is a comparison using *like* or *as* (for example, *his shoulder was like Gibraltar*).

Sonnet is a traditional form of rhymed poetry with 14 lines in iambic pentameter:
- **Elizabethan** sonnets have three quatrains followed by a couplet, with the rhyme scheme *abab, cdcd, efef, gg*.
- **Petrarchan** sonnets have an octave (eight lines) followed by a sestet (six lines), with the rhyme scheme *abbaabba, cdecde*.

Stanza refers to a group of lines:
- **Couplet** (two)
- **Triplet** (three)
- **Quatrain** (four)
- **Quintet** (five)
- **Sestet** (six)
- **Septet** (seven)
- **Octave** (eight)

Stress refers to a syllable or word that receives emphasis.

Synecdoche is using one part of something to represent the whole (for example, *ten "head" of cattle*).

Trope refers to the use of a poetic device or figure of speech.

Verse is a line of poetry with meter.
- **Monometer** (one foot)
- **Dimeter** (two feet)
- **Trimeter** (three feet)
- **Tetrameter** (four feet)
- **Pentameter** (five feet)
- **Hexameter** (six feet)
- **Heptameter** (seven feet)
- **Octometer** (eight feet)

Reading-to-Learn Activities

Note Taking

Note taking enhances learning by activating your kinesthetic and visual senses. Use the following activity to practice taking notes.

Your Turn Choose a location in your school, whether in a classroom, the library, the cafeteria, or even the hallway. Take notes about what you observe, writing down the key features of the scene before you. Try to find at least three things that you have not noticed in this location before. Reflect on how note taking affects your observational skills.

Annotating

Annotating a text helps you to dig through it and focus on its specific features. The following activity asks you to use annotation.

Your Turn Select and photocopy a text from one of your classes. Read through the material, annotating as you go. Then reread the text, adding more notes in the margins. Consider your annotations. How has marking the text helped you think more deeply about it?

Vocabulary for Reading

Knowing the specific vocabulary related to a type of writing can help you to understand and discuss an example text. By studying the vocabulary of nonfiction, fiction, or poetry, for example, you can better comprehend the features and intent of what you are reading.

Your Turn Turn to pages 148-149, 152-153, and 156-157. From each section, choose three words that are unfamiliar to you. Write down the words and their definitions. Then look for examples of these features in current reading assignments. Copy the examples you find and review the terms. Finally, make a point of using the terms as you discuss your reading.

Comparing the Readings

As you have experienced, different types of texts require different reading approaches. The activity below reviews recommendations for approaching different texts.

You Turn Turn to pages 146, 150, and 154. Compare and contrast the tips for before, during, and after each type of reading. How are reading nonfiction, fiction, and poetry similar? How are they different?

Chapter 11
Building Your Vocabulary

Much of what we do in life requires tools. At school you may use a wide array of tools—from pens and pencils to tablets and calculators, from microscopes and Bunsen burners to paint brushes and power saws. With the right tools, you can build your knowledge of the world, create art, make things you need, and mend what is broken. With the right tools, you can do just about anything and everything.

Your vocabulary is one of your most valuable tools, enabling you to read, think, write, and communicate. So expanding your vocabulary is important. The more words you know, the better you will be able to think, learn, and build new ideas. Strengthening your vocabulary will broaden your world. This chapter will show you how.

You will learn . . .

- Keeping a Vocabulary Notebook
- Using Context
- Using a Dictionary
- Using a Thesaurus
- Understanding Word Parts
- Prefixes, Roots, and Suffixes

Keeping a Vocabulary Notebook

For each subject in school, reserve part of your notebook or create a digital file for words, definitions, word parts, synonyms, and other information. Notes about new words help you remember them. Here are example vocabulary entries.

Example Entries

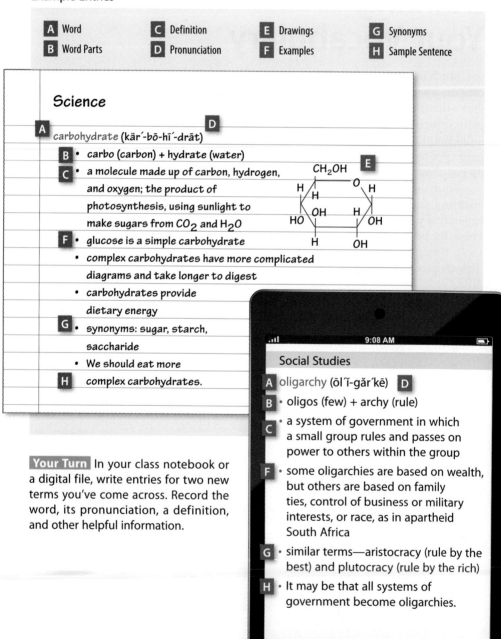

A Word   C Definition   E Drawings   G Synonyms
B Word Parts   D Pronunciation   F Examples   H Sample Sentence

Science

A carbohydrate (kär´-bō-hī´-drāt) D

B • carbo (carbon) + hydrate (water)
C • a molecule made up of carbon, hydrogen, and oxygen; the product of photosynthesis, using sunlight to make sugars from CO_2 and H_2O
F • glucose is a simple carbohydrate
 • complex carbohydrates have more complicated diagrams and take longer to digest
 • carbohydrates provide dietary energy
G • synonyms: sugar, starch, saccharide
 • We should eat more
H complex carbohydrates.

E CH_2OH

Your Turn In your class notebook or a digital file, write entries for two new terms you've come across. Record the word, its pronunciation, a definition, and other helpful information.

9:08 AM

Social Studies

A oligarchy (ōl´ĭ-gär´kē) D
B • oligos (few) + archy (rule)
C • a system of government in which a small group rules and passes on power to others within the group
F • some oligarchies are based on wealth, but others are based on family ties, control of business or military interests, or race, as in apartheid South Africa
G • similar terms—aristocracy (rule by the best) and plutocracy (rule by the rich)
H • It may be that all systems of government become oligarchies.

Using Context

When you come across a new word, try to understand it by studying how it is used as well as its context. In the text surrounding the word, look for **clues** like these:

Look for . . .

■ **Cause and Effect** (Robber-baron capitalism rapidly made a few wealthy.)	The transformation of Russia took place very rapidly and with little regulation, allowing *robber-baron capitalism* to sweep the nation, concentrating the wealth in only a few hands.
■ **Definitions** (A vector is a ray showing position and movement.)	A *vector* not only indicates the position of a ray in space but also its motion in time.
■ **Comparisons** (Phalanges are long on hands, short on feet.)	The *phalanges* on our hands are elongated compared to those of our feet, which have lost the ability to grasp.
■ **Series** (Intonation is a vocal quality.)	Pitch, duration, and *intonation* shape each note that a singer produces.
■ **Examples** (Saturn is a gas giant.)	*Gas giants* have a relatively low average density. Saturn's density is less than that of water.
■ **Synonyms** (A GED is a high school equivalency diploma.)	A person without a high school diploma can take an equivalency exam to earn a *GED*.
■ **Antonyms** (An ad hoc leader is the opposite of a duly elected leader.)	The transitional powers appointed an *ad hoc leader* until the country could select a duly elected leader.
■ **Tone** (Jim Crow was a discriminatory and hypocritical policy.)	*Jim Crow* discriminated against entire generations of African Americans, demonstrating the lie of "separate but equal."

Your Turn Read a few pages of a class text, writing down at least four words that are new to you. Use context clues to write a beginning definition for each word. Then check your definitions against a dictionary. How close were your definitions?

Using a Dictionary

The dictionary is your main source of information about new words. Either print or online versions can serve well, but be certain that the dictionary you consult is reputable and reliable. The best dictionaries provide these features:

A **Guide words** indicate the first and last words defined on a page. Refer to them to discover whether the term you are looking up is on that page.

B **Entry words** being defined appear in bold type and in alphabetical order.

C **Pronunciation guides** in parentheses show how vowels and consonants are pronounced and which syllables are accented.

D **Syllabication** shows the entry word divided into syllables.

E **Spelling and capitalization** of the entry word shows the conventional use of the term.

F **Part of speech abbreviations** tell how a word is used in a sentence. Many words are used as more than one part of speech.

G **Definitions** provide the denotative meaning of the term. Many terms have more than one definition, which are usually organized from the most common to the least common.

H **Etymology** indicates the language origins of the word, using abbreviations for different language families.

I **Illustrations,** either drawings or photographs, are given for some terms.

J **Variants** indicate other spellings of the word. If a variant is preceded by *or*, the variant is equally accepted. If the variant is preceded by *also*, the main form is preferred.

K **Inflected forms** are other forms of the word. For example, *swim* has the inflected forms *swam* and *swum*; the word taco has the inflected plural *tacos*; and *child*, the inflected plural *children*.

Other Dictionary Features

- **Labels** can indicate the subject a word refers to, such as *biology,* or to the status of the term, such as *nonstandard, slang, informal, offensive,* and so on.
- **Examples** show how the word is used in a sentence. Often, example sentences are taken from the work of well-known writers or historical figures.
- **Idioms** show how the word is used in a construction whose meaning, while familiar to a particular group, cannot be derived literally.

▶ **Online dictionaries and thesauruses** offer additional features, including audio pronunciation, word games like hangman, information about interesting word trends, forums, quotations, multimedia links, and spelling bees.

geoscience
geriatrician

ge·o·sci·ence (jē′ō-sī′əns) *n.* Any of the sciences, such as geology or geochemistry, that deals with the earth.

ge·o·sta·tion·ar·y (jē′ō-stā′shə-nĕr′ē) *adj.* **1.** Of, relating to, or being a satellite that travels above Earth's equator from west to east at an altitude of approx. 35,900 kilometers (22,300 miles) and at a speed matching that of Earth's rotation, thus remaining stationary in relation to Earth. **2.** Of, relating to, or being the orbit of such a satellite.

ge·o·strat·e·gy (jē′ō-străt′ə-jē) *n., pl.* **-gies 1.** The branch of geopolitics that deals with strategy. **2.** The geopolitical and strategic factors that characterize a certain geographic area. **3.** Governmental strategy based on geopolitics. —**ge′o·stra·te′gic** (-strə-tē′jĭk) *adj.* —**ge′o·strat′e·gist** *n.*

ge·o·stroph·ic (jē′ə-strŏf′ĭk) *adj.* Of or relating to the pseudo force caused by the earth's rotation. [GEO- + Gk. *strophē,* a turning; see STROPHE + –IC.] —**ge′o·stroph′i·cal·ly** *adv.*

ge·o·syn·chro·nous (jē′ō-sĭng′krə-nəs, -sĭn′-) *adj.* **1.** Of or relating to an orbit that has a period of one sidereal day. **2.** Geostationary. —**ge′o·syn′chro·nous·ly** *adv.*

ge·o·syn·cline (jē′ō-sĭn′klīn′) *n.* An extensive, usu. linear depression in the earth's crust. —**ge′o·syn·cli′nal** (-sĭn-klī′nəl) *adj.*

ge·o·tax·is (jē′ō-tăk′sĭs) *n.* Movement of a motile organism using the earth's gravity for orientation. —**ge′o·tac′tic** (-tĭk) *adj.* —**ge′o·tac′ti·cal·ly** *adv.*

ge·o·tec·ton·ic (jē′ō-tĕk-tŏn′ĭk) *adj.* Of or relating to the shape, structure, and arrangement of the rock masses resulting from structural deformation of the earth's crust.

ge·o·ther·mal (jē′ō-thûr′məl) also **ge·o·ther·mic** (-mĭk) *adj.* Of or relating to the internal heat of the earth.

ge·ot·ro·pism (jē-ŏt′rə-pĭz′əm) *n.* The growth of a living organism in response to gravity, as the downward growth of plant roots. —**ge′o·tro′pic** (jē′ə-trō′pĭk, -trŏp′ĭk) *adj.*

ger. *abbr.* gerund

Ger. *abbr.* **1.** German **2.** Germany

ge·rah (gîr′ə) *n.* An ancient Hebrew coin and unit of weight. [Heb. *gērâ,* grain, bean.]

ge·ra·ni·al (jə-rā′nē-əl) *n.* A structural isomer of citral obtained from the oxidation of geraniol. [GERANI(OL) + –AL³.]

ge·ra·ni·ol (jə-rā′nē-ôl′, -ōl′, -ōl′) *n.* A fragrant pale yellow liquid alcohol, C₉H₁₇COH, derived chiefly from the oils of geranium and citronella and used in cosmetics and flavorings.

ge·ra·ni·um (jə-rā′nē-əm) *n.* **1.** Any of various plants of the genus *Geranium,* having pink or purplish flowers. **2.** Any of various chiefly southern African plants of the genus *Pelargonium,* having showy clusters of red, pink, or white flowers. **3.** A strong to vivid red. [NLat. *Geranium,* genus name < Lat. *geranium,* cranesbill < Gk. *geranion,* dim. of *geranos,* crane.]

ge·rar·di·a (jə-rär′dē-ə) *n.* Any of various herbaceous, root-parasitizing, New World plants of the genus *Agalinus,* having large pink, purple, or white flowers. [NLat., after John *Gerard* (1545–1612), English botanist.]

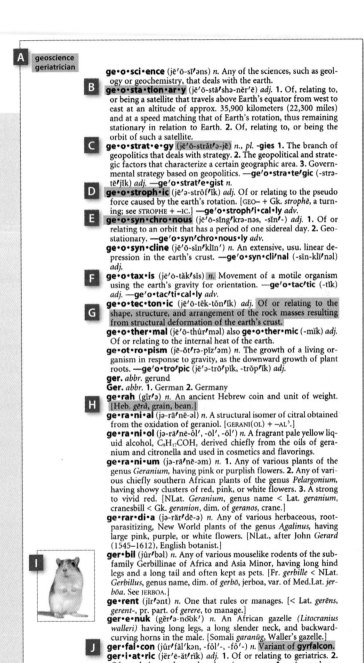

ger·bil (jûr′bəl) *n.* Any of various mouselike rodents of the subfamily Gerbillinae of Africa and Asia Minor, having long hind legs and a long tail and often kept as pets. [Fr. *gerbille* < NLat. *Gerbillus,* genus name, dim. of *gerbō,* jerboa, var. of Med.Lat. *jerbōa.* See JERBOA.]

ge·rent (jîr′ənt) *n.* One that rules or manages. [< Lat. *gerēns, gerent-,* pr. part. of *gerere,* to manage.]

ger·e·nuk (gĕr′ə-nook′) *n.* An African gazelle (*Litocranius walleri*) having long legs, a long slender neck, and backward-curving horns in the male. [Somali *garanūg,* Waller's gazelle.]

ger·fal·con (jûr′făl′kən, -fôl′-, -fô′-) *n.* Variant of gyrfalcon.

ger·i·at·ric (jĕr′ē-ăt′rĭk) *adj.* **1.** Of or relating to geriatrics. **2.** Of or relating to the aged or the aging process. ❖ *n.* An aged person. [Back-formation < GERIATRICS.]

ger·i·a·tri·cian (jĕr′ē-ə-trĭsh′ən) also **ger·i·a·trist** (-ăt′rĭst) *n.* A physician who specializes in geriatrics.

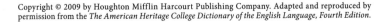

Using a Thesaurus

A thesaurus is a dictionary of synonyms and antonyms. It can help you build your vocabulary and is most useful when you want to replace a general word with a more specific synonym. For example, instead of using the word *red,* you might want to use *scarlet* or *crimson* or *vermilion.*

Some thesauruses organize words alphabetically, as a dictionary does. In more traditional thesauruses, you find a word by referring first to an index in the back of the book. Online thesauruses ask you to enter a search term and automatically return results.

Example Entry

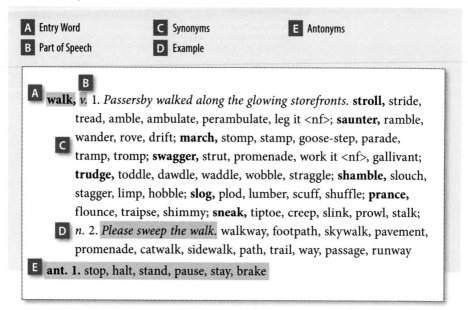

A Entry Word   **C** Synonyms   **E** Antonyms

B Part of Speech   **D** Example

A **walk,** **B** *v.* 1. *Passersby walked along the glowing storefronts.* **stroll,** stride, tread, amble, ambulate, perambulate, leg it <nf>; **saunter,** ramble, **C** wander, rove, drift; **march,** stomp, stamp, goose-step, parade, tramp, tromp; **swagger,** strut, promenade, work it <nf>, gallivant; **trudge,** toddle, dawdle, waddle, wobble, straggle; **shamble,** slouch, stagger, limp, hobble; **slog,** plod, lumber, scuff, shuffle; **prance,** flounce, traipse, shimmy; **sneak,** tiptoe, creep, slink, prowl, stalk;

D *n.* 2. *Please sweep the walk.* walkway, footpath, skywalk, pavement, promenade, catwalk, sidewalk, path, trail, way, passage, runway

E **ant. 1.** stop, halt, stand, pause, stay, brake

Dictionary Follow-Up

Make sure that you understand the meaning of any word you choose from a thesaurus. Don't replace common words with obscure words just to sound more impressive. Also recognize the connotation of your choice. For example, asking someone to *walk* to the store is completely different from asking the person to *shamble* to it.

Your Turn Use a print or online thesaurus to find synonyms for the word *build* in these phrases: *building* a reputation; *building* a computer; *building* expectation. Look up your choices in a dictionary to double-check their denotation (literal meaning) and connotation (implied meaning).

Understanding Word Parts

Often, words consist of prefixes, suffixes, and roots that come from Old English, French, Latin, or Greek. By learning the meaning of a root or base, you hold the key to understanding not just one word, but many. And being familiar with numerous word parts gives you a good chance of puzzling out the meanings of even the most unfamiliar words. (See pages 166–177 for common word parts and their meanings.)

Example Words and Parts

Tele·kinet·ic

Telekinetic combines
- the root *tele*, meaning "distant";
- a form of the root *kines*, meaning "movement"; and
- the suffix *ic*, meaning "pertaining to/having."

So *telekinetic* pertains to some sort of movement from a distance. (The dictionary definition of *telekinetic* is "having the ability to move objects without contact or other physical means.")

Zygo·morph·ic

Zygomorphic combines
- the root *zygo*, meaning "united/paired";
- the root *morph*, meaning "shape"; and
- the suffix *ic*, meaning "pertaining to/having."

So *zygomorphic* refers to having a paired or united shape of some sort. (In the world of botany, a zygomorphic flower is one whose parts are unequal in some way but can be divided through one plane into mirror-image halves.)

Your Turn Select one word from each content area and break it into word parts to figure out its basic meaning. Use the lists of word parts (pages 166-177) and a dictionary.

Social Studies:

| aristocracy | denomination | neoclassicism |

Science:

| hydrocarbon | protoplasm | polypeptide |

Math:

| heptameter | quadratic | polynomial |

English:

| conjunction | polyglot | linguistic |

Prefixes, Roots, and Suffixes

The following pages list common prefixes, roots, and suffixes. When you are not sure about the meaning of a new word, try to figure it out by studying its parts. Each word part can unlock dozens of new words for you. The listed prefixes, roots, and suffixes are boldfaced, followed by their meanings in parentheses, and then by example words.

- **Prefixes** come before root words and act as modifiers.
- **Roots** provide the main meaning of a word and can be connected to other roots, prefixes, and suffixes.
- **Suffixes** come after the root word and act as modifiers.

Prefixes

a(n) *(without, not, no)* amoral, anaerobic, anarchy, apathy, asymmetrical

ab *(from, away from, down from)* absent, absorb, abstract, abdomen

ad *(attached to, on, increase)* adhere, adductor, adrenal

ag *(together, gather)* aggregate, agora

ambi *(both, around)* ambidextrous, ambiguous, ambivalent

amphi *(both, in)* amphibian, amphitheater

ana *(again, backward)* analogy, anaphase, anabolic

ante *(in front of, before)* antebellum, antecedent, antechamber, anterior

ant(i) *(against)* antacid, antibody, antidote, antioxidant

auto *(self, same)* autograph, automatic, automobile, autonomous

be *(totally, overly)* belittle, bemoan, bemuse, beware

ben *(well, good)* benefit, benediction, benefactor

bi *(two)* bipedal, binary, binocular

cata *(down, against)* cataclysmic, catastrophic, catatonic

circum *(around)* circadian, circumference, circumstance, circus

co *(with, together)* coed, cohere, cooperate

com *(together)* compare, compete, compose, compromise

con *(with, together)* congregate, conjoin, connect, connote

contra *(opposed to)* contradict, contrary, contrapuntal

counter *(against, opposite)* counterargument, counterfeit, counterpart

de *(away, opposite)* degenerate, decommission, deodorize, detoxify

di *(two, apart)* diatomic, dichotomy, digress, divergent

dia *(through, across)* diagnosis, diagonal, diaphragm, diameter

dis *(undo, apart)* disconnect, dismiss, disrespect, dissolve

dys *(bad, ill)* dysfunctional, dystrophy, dyslexia

e(c) *(out of, exclude)* eccentric, elicit, elect, emit

en *(in, within)* enfold, engage, entangle, enter, enwrap

end(o) *(inside)* endocrine, endoskeleton, endothermic

epi *(over, on, attached)* epidemic, epidermis, epiphenomenon, episode

eu *(good)* euphony, eulogy, euphemism, euthanasia

ex *(from, former)* exit, excrete, ex-president, extinct

exo *(outside)* exoskeleton, exothermic

exter *(outside)* external, exterior, extrinsic

extra *(additional)* extracurricular, extraterrestrial, extraneous

fore *(preceding)* forecast, forehead, foreshadow, foreshorten

hemi *(half)* hemisphere, hemicycle, hemiplegia

hepta *(seven)* heptagonal, heptathlon

hexa *(six)* hexadecimal, hexagon, hexameter

hyper *(excessive, above)* hyperactive, hyperextension, hyperventilate

hypo *(less than, under)* hypochondria, hypodermic, hypoglycemia, hypothermia

im *(not)* immaculate, immediate, immature, immobile, impractical

in *(into, not, without)* incarnate, inception, incompetent

infer(i) *(below)* infer, inference, inferior, infernal

infra *(beneath)* infrared, infrastructure, infrasonic

inter *(among/between)* interact, Internet, interstate, interval

intra *(inside)* intramural, intrapersonal, intravenous

intro *(into, within)* introduction, introspection, introvert

iso *(equal)* isobar, isometric, isosceles, isotope

kilo *(thousand)* kilocalorie, kilogram, kilometer, kilowatt

mal *(bad)* maladapted, malevolent, malformed, malicious

micro *(minute, millionth)* microorganism, micrometer, microscope, microwave

mid *(middle)* midday, midnight, midpoint, midsummer

milli *(thousand, one-thousandth)* millennium, milliliter, millimeter, millipede

mini *(least, small)* miniature, minimize, minivan, minimal

mis *(bad)* misbehave, misconception, miscue, misdemeanor

mono *(single)* monochromatic, monogamy, monogram, monolith

mult(i) *(many)* multicellular, multilateral, multiple, multitude

nano *(one billionth)* nanometer, nanosecond, nanotechnology

neo *(new)* neoclassical, neophyte, neologism

non *(not)* noncompliant, nonconformist, nonfiction, nonsense

ob *(toward, against)* oblong, obstruct, obtrusive

oct(o) *(eight)* octave, octagon, octopus, October

omni *(all)* omnipotence, omnipresence, omniscience, omnivorous

over *(above, exceed)* overestimate, overpay, overwhelm

pan *(all)* panacea, pandemic, pantheism

para *(beside, beyond)* parabola, paramedic, paranoia, parasite

penta *(five)* pentad, pentagon, pentameter, pentadactyl, pentatonic

per *(through, completely)* perfuse, permeate, perspective

peri *(all around)* pericardium, perimeter, periodontal, periphery

poly *(many)* polygamy, polygon, polynomial, polypeptide

post *(after)* posterior, posthumous, postmodern, postpartum

pre *(before)* prepare, predict, preposition, preview

pro *(before)* proboscis, procure, prognosis, prologue, prophase

pro *(favoring, substituting for)* pro-choice, pro-life, protagonist, pronoun

prot(o) *(first)* protoplasm, prototype, protozoa

pseudo *(false)* pseudonym, pseudopod, pseudoscience

quadri *(four)* quadruped, quadrilateral, quadruplet, quatrain

quart *(four)* quart, quarter, quartet, quartile

quint *(five)* quintet, quintuplet, quintessence, quintessential

re *(back, again)* redo, regain, resound, retract, revise

retro *(backward)* retroactive, retrorocket, retrospect

semi *(partly)* semicircle, semipermeable, semipro, semisolid, semitrailer

sept *(seven)* septet, septuagenarian, septuple

sesqui *(one and a half)* sesquicentennial, sesquipedal, sesquipedalian

sex *(six)* sexpartite, sextet, sextant, sextuplet

sub *(under)* subcutaneous, submarine, subspecies, substance

super *(above)* superimpose, superior, superluminal, supernatural, supersonic

supra *(above)* supramolecular, supraorbital, supreme, supremacy

sym *(with, same)* symbol, symphony, symmetry, sympathy

syn *(together)* synapse, synergy, synthetic, syndicate, synchronous

ter *(three)* tertiary, tercet, tertian

tera *(trillion)* terabyte, teraflop, terahertz

tetra *(four)* tetrad, tetrameter, tetrahedron, Tetragrammaton

trans *(across)* transact, transfer, transmit, transport, transpose

tri *(three)* triangle, triceratops, tricuspid, triceps, triptych, trinity

ultra *(beyond)* ultraliberal, ultramarine, ultrasonic, ultraviolet

un *(not)* uncharted, unexamined, unwashed, unworthy

under *(below)* underage, underrated, underrepresented, understated

uni *(one)* unicorn, unilateral, unicycle, unisex, unit, unite

up *(above)* update, uphold, upscale, upstage, upturn

with *(together)* withhold, within, without, withstand

Roots

acet *(acid, vinegar)* acetic acid, acetyline

ac, acu *(bitter, sharp)* acrid, acumen, acute

acr(o) *(high, hill, top)* acrobat, acropolis

aer(o) *(air, gas)* aerobic, aerial, aerodynamic

agon *(struggle)* agony, protagonist, antagonist,

agr(o) *(fields, soil)* agriculture, agronomy

alb(u) *(white)* albino, albumin, albatross

alim *(digestion)* alimentary, alimony

allo *(other, different)* alloy, allocate

alter *(another)* alter ego, alternative

alt(o) *(high)* altitude, altimeter, alto

am *(love)* amateur, amoretto, amour propre

amb(ul) *(walk)* amble, ambulate, ambulance

ampli *(large, increase)* ample, amplify, amplitude

Roots (Cont.)

andr(o) *(male)* android, androgynous

angio *(vessel)* angiogram, angioplasty

anim *(soul, breath, spirit)* animal, animus, animate

anni, annu, enni *(year, segmented)* annual, anniversary, annuity, centennial

anth *(flower)* anther, acanthus, anthesis

anthrop *(human)* anthropology, anthropoid, philanthropy

antiq *(old)* antique, antiquated, antiquity

aper *(open)* aperture, apertif

apo *(detached, off)* apogee, apocalypse

append *(hang on, addition)* append, appendage, appendix

aqua *(water)* aquarium, aqueous, aquifer

arbor *(tree)* Arbor Day, arboreal, arboretum

arch(eo) *(beginning, primitive, ancient)* archaic, archeology, archive

arterio *(vessels leading from heart)* artery, arteriosclerosis

arthr(o) *(joint, jointed)* arthritis, arthropod

articul *(joint)* articulate, articulation

aster, astro *(star)* aster, asteroid, astronaut, astronomy

audi *(hear)* audio, audible, audition, auditorium, audience

avi(s) *(bird)* avian, aviary, aviator

axi *(axis, turn)* axis, axle

bar *(pressure, weight)* barometer, baritone

bas *(base)* base, basal, basis, bass

bib(lio) *(book)* bibliography, bibliophile

bio *(life)* biography, biology, biosphere, biopsy

boli *(ball, throw)* bolus, metabolism, parabola, parable,

bot *(plant)* botany, botanical, botanist

brachi *(arm)* brachia, embrace

brevi *(short)* abbreviate, brief, brevity

bronch *(trachea)* bronchia, bronchitis

bulla *(important)* bullet, bulletin

bursa *(purse, bodily pouch)* bursitis, disburse, reimburse

calc(i) *(lime, chalk, pebble to render)* calcium, calcify, calculate

calo(r) *(heat)* calorie, caloric, calorimeter

cand *(bright)* candle, candent, incandescent

capilli *(hair)* capillary, capillarity

capit *(head)* capital, decapitate, captain

carcin *(cancer)* carcinogen, carcinoma

cardi(o) *(heart)* cardiogram, cardiology

carn(i) *(flesh)* carnage, carnal, carnival, carnivore

carp *(wrist)* carpus, carpal-tunnel syndrome

caryo *(nucleus)* eukaryote, prokaryote

cath *(clean, pure)* catheter, catharsis

caus *(burn)* caustic, cauterize, holocaust

cav *(hollow)* cave, cavity, concave

caval *(horse)* cavalry, cavalier, chivalry,

cede, ceed *(go, yield)*, concede, precede, recede, secession, succeed

cereb *(brain)* cerebellum, cerebral, cerebrum

cervi *(neck)* cervical, cervix

chemo *(chemical)* chemical, chemotherapy

chlor(o) *(green, chlorine)* chlorine, chlorophyll, chloroplast

chol *(bile)* cholera, cholesterol

chondr *(cartilage, small)* hypochondriac, mitochondria

cell *(room)* cell, cellular

cens *(judge)* census, censor, consensus

cent *(hundred, one hundredth)* centigrade, century, centimeter, percent

centr *(center)* centrifugal, centrifuge, centripetal, eccentric, ethnocentric

cephal(o) *(head)* cephalic, cephalopod, hydrocephalus

ceps *(head)* biceps, forceps, triceps

cept *(take)* concept, interception, perception, reception

chrom(o) *(color)* chromatic, chromosome, chromoplast

chron(o) *(time)* anachronism, chronology, chronograph

cine *(movement)* cinema, cinematic, cinematography

cis(e) *(cut)* excise, incise, incisor, scissors

claim *(cry out)* exclaim, declaim, proclaim

class *(group)* class, class-action, classification

clast *(broken)* clastic, iconoclastic, pyroclastic

claust *(tight space)* claustrophobia, closet

clima *(region)* climate, climatic, climax

cline *(lean)* incline, recline

clude *(close)* conclude, exclude, include, seclude

cogni *(know)* cognition, cognitive, recognize, cognizant, incognito,

colo *(colon)* colon, colonoscopy, colitis

copia *(abundance)* copious, cornucopia

corn *(horn)* cornea, cornucopia, unicorn

corpus *(body)* corporation, corpse, corpuscle

cosm *(universe)* cosmos, cosmopolitan, microcosm

cracy *(rule)* autocracy, aristocracy, democracy, meritocracy

cran *(skull, brain)* cranium, craniology, craniosacral

crat *(supporter of, rule)* aristocrat, bureaucrat, democrat

cred *(to believe)* credible, credit, credence, incredulous

cruc(i) *(cross)* cruciform, excruciate, crucify, crusades

crusta *(shell)* crustacean, crusty

cry(o) *(extreme cold)* cryogenic, cryonics, cryophilic

crypt *(hidden)* crypt, cryptic, encrypt

cubo *(lie in)* incubate, incubator, incubus

culp *(fault)* culpable, culprit

cumu *(mound)* accumulate, cumulus, cumulative

curs *(run)* cursor, cursory, cursive, precursor

cusp *(point)* cusp, cuspid, bicuspid

cuti *(skin)* cuticle, subcutaneous

cyan(o) *(blue-green)* cyan, cyanide, cyanobacteria

cycl *(wheel)* cycle, cyclonic, encyclical, unicycle

cyt(o/e) *(hollow vessel)* cytology, cytoplasm, leukocyte, lymphocyte

dactyl *(finger, toe)* dactyl, polydactyl, pterodactyl

deca *(ten)* decade, December, dodecahedron

deci *(one tenth)* decibel, decimate, decimeter

dem *(people)* demagoguery, democratic, demographic, epidemic

dent, dont *(tooth)* dentist, dentin, orthodontist

derm *(skin)* dermis, epidermis, hypodermic, echinoderm

dextr *(right)* ambidextrous, dexterity, dextrose

dict *(speak)* diction, dictate, indict, predict, verdict

divi *(cut, apart)* divide, dividend, individual

dorm *(sleep)* dormant, dormitory

dox *(belief)* doxology, orthodoxy

drome *(race course, running)* hippodrome, syndrome, velodrome

duct *(carry)* abduct, aqueduct, conduct, product

dura *(hard)* durable, duration, endure, epidural

dyn(a) *(force, power)* dynamic, dynamo, dynasty

eco(s) *(house)* ecology, economy, ecosystem

ech *(sound)* echo, echocardiogram, echolocation

eff(u) *(pour out)* effluence, effulgent, effuse, effusive

ego *(self)* ego, egotistical, superego

elast *(regain shape)* elastic, elasticity

electr(o) *(electricity)* electric, electrocute, photoelectric

embryo *(swelling within)* embryo, embryonic, embryogenesis

entero *(intestine)* enteritis, gastroenterologist

epheme *(passing away)* ephemera, ephemeral

equ *(equal)* equate, equator, equilateral

erg(y) *(work)* energy, ergonomic, synergy

eso *(within)* esophagus, esoteric

esthesia *(feeling)* anesthetic, esthetic, kinesthetic

eth(i) *(character)* ethics, ethical

ethno *(race)* ethnic, ethnicity

faci, fact *(make)* facile, facilitate, facility, manufacture

feli *(happiness)* felicity, felicitous

fera *(wild)* feral, ferocity

fido *(faithful)* fidelity, fiduciary, hi-fi, infidelity

fin *(final)* finial, finish, finitude, infinite

fissi *(split)* fissile, fission, fissure

flect *(turn)* deflect, inflect, reflect

flex *(bend)* circumflex, flexible, flexor

flict *(strike)* afflict, conflict, inflict

flor *(flower)* flora, Florida, florist

flu(x) *(flow)* effluent, fluent, fluency, fluctuate, influence

fluor *(glow)* fluoresce, fluorescent, fluoroscope

foli(o) *(leaf)* defoliate, exfoliate, folio, foliage, foliate

form *(shape)* cruciform, formidable, formula

fort, forc *(strong)* enforce, forcible, fortify

fossa *(dig)* fossil, fossilize

fract *(broken)* fraction, fracture, infraction, refract

fragi *(delicate)* fragile, fragility, fragment

frat *(brother)* fraternal, fraternize, fratricide

fric *(rub, carve)* friction, fricative

frigi *(cold)* frigid, frigidity, frigorific, refrigerate

fruc *(fruit)* fructify, fructose, frugivorous

fug(e) *(drive out, flee)* centrifuge, fugitive, fugue, refugee

fuma *(smoke)* fumigate, fuming

fund *(bottom)* fund, funding, fundament, fundamental

fung *(mushroom)* fungus, fungicide

furi *(rave, insane)* furious, furor, fury, infuriate

fuse *(melt, combine)* confuse, fuse, fusion, infuse, transfuse

gala *(milk-white)* galaxy, galactose

gamet *(reproductive)* gamete, gametophore, gametophyte

gamy *(marriage)* bigamy, monogamy, polygamy

gangli *(knot, tumor)* ganglia, ganglion

gastr(o) *(digestive)* gastric, gastritis, gastrointestinal

gen *(origin)* gene, generation, genetics, oogenesis

gen(y) *(kind, tribe)* genealogy, genotype, homogeny, progeny

genus *(class, become)* gene, general, genus, genuine

ge(o) *(earth)* geocentric, geography, geology, geometry

geri *(old)* geriatrics, gerontology

germ *(sprout, seed)* germ, germicide, germinate

gesto *(carry)* egest, digest, gestate, ingest

giga *(giant, billion)* gigabyte, gigantic, gigahertz, gigawatt

gloss *(tongue)* gloss, glossary

glot *(tongue)* glottal, glottis, polyglot

Roots (Cont.)

gluc, glyc(o) *(sugar)* glucose, glycerin, hypoglycemia

gnos(is) *(knowledge)* agnostic, diagnostic, Gnostic, prognosis

gon *(angle)* octagon, pentagon, polygon

grad *(step)* centigrade, gradient, gradual, graduated

gram *(written record)* cardiogram, diagram, grammar, program, telegram

graph *(write, recording)* autobiography, autograph, cartography, cinematography, geography, graphic, photograph, polygraph, topographical

gregate *(gather)* aggregate, congregate, gregarious

gress *(walk, enter)* digress, egress, ingress, progress, transgress

gyn(ec) *(female)* androgyny, gynecology, gynecologist

gyro *(whirl)* autogyro, gyration, gyroscope

hab, habit *(live)* cohabitate, habitat, inhabit

hal *(salt)* halide, halite, halophile, halophyte

hallu *(wander mentally)* hallucinate, hallucinogenic

hect *(hundred)* hectare, hectogram, hectoliter, hectometer

hedron *(shape)* dodecahedron, heptahedron, polyhedron, tetrahedron

heli *(spiral)* helix, helicopter

helio *(sun)* heliocentric, heliograph, heliopause, heliostat

hem(o), hemat *(blood)* hematoma, hemoglobin, hemophilia, hemostat

hepat *(liver)* hepatic, hepatitis

herb(a) *(plant)* herbaceous, herbal, herbalist, herbivore

hereo *(cling)* adhere, adhesion, coherence, cohesive

herp *(reptile)* herpetology, herpetological

heter(o) *(other)* heterogenous, heterosexual

hibern *(winter)* hibernal, hibernate

hist(o) *(tissue)* histamine, histology, histogram

holo *(whole)* Holocene, holocaust, holograph

homeo *(same)* homeostasis, homeopathic

homi *(human)* homicide, hominid, hominoid

homo *(same)* homogenous, homosexual

hum *(earth)* exhume, humus, inhume, posthumous

hydr(o) *(water)* hydrate, hydrant, hydroelectric, hydrophobia, hydrothermal

hypn *(sleep)* hypnotic, hypnotism, hypnotherapy

icon *(image)* icon, iconic, iconoclastic, iconography

idi(o) *(individual, self)* idiom, idiosyncratic

ignis *(fire)* igneous, ignite, ignition

immune *(safe, exempt)* immunity, immunology, immunotherapy

incis *(cut into)* incision, incisor, incisive

ject *(throw)* eject, inject, project, reject, trajectory

jud(ic) *(judge)* judge, judicial, judiciary, injudicious

junct *(join)* adjunct, conjunction, junction, disjunct

juven *(youthful)* juvenile, rejuvenate

karyo *(nucleus)* eukaryote, prokaryote

kines(a) *(movement)* cytokinesis, kinesthetic, kinesiology, telekinesis

lacer *(slash, mangled)* lacerate, laceration

lact *(milk)* lactation, lactic, lactose

lamin *(layer)* laminar, laminate

langui *(faint)* languid, languish, languor

lapid *(stone)* dilapidate, lapidary

larva *(specter, mask)* larvae, larval, larvicide

laryng *(throat)* laryngitis, laryngoscope, larynx

laten *(hidden)* latency, latent

later(o) *(side)* lateral, bilateral, multilateral, unilateral

lati *(broad)* latitude, latitudinarian

lax *(loose)* laxative, laxity, relax

lega, legit *(bequeath, law)* legacy, legal, legitimate, illegitimate

leuk(o) *(white, clear)* leukocyte, leukemia

levat(a) *(raise)* levitate, levy, elevate

leve *(balance)* level, lever

lex *(speech, word, law)* dyslexia, lexicology, lexicon

liber *(free)* liberal, liberation, libertine

libra *(balance)* deliberate, equilibrium

liga *(to bind)* ligament, ligate, ligature

limbus *(edge)* limb, limbic, limbo

limin *(threshold)* eliminate, liminal, limit

linea *(line)* lineage, lineal, lineament

lingu *(tongue)* bilingual, lingo, lingual, linguistics,

linum *(flax)* linen, linnet, linoleum

lip *(fat)* lipase, lipid, lipoprotein, liposuction

liqua *(fluid)* liquid, liquidate, liquor

lith *(stone)* gastrolith, lithograph, monolith, Neolithic

lobe *(rounded)* lobe, lobotomy, lobular

loca *(place)* locale, locate, locus, locomotive

logo *(word)* apology, logic, eulogy, monologue

logy *(study of)* astrology, biology, ecology, zoology

lubri *(slippery)* lubricant, lubricate

luci *(light)* lucid, lucent, lucifer, luciferous

lud *(play)* allude, elude, ludicrous

lumb *(lower back)* lumbar, lumbago

lumen *(light)* bioluminescent, illumine, luminary, luminous

luna *(moon)* lunacy, lunar, lunation

lymph *(clear liquid)* lymph, lymphatic, lymphoma

lysis *(break up, dissolve)* analyze, dialysis, hydrolyze, lysosome

macro *(large)* macroscopic, macrophage, macronucleus

magn(i) *(great)* magnify, magnanimous, magnificent, magnitude

mal(i) *(bad)* malicious, malevolent, malformed, malignant

mall *(hammer)* malleable, mallet, malleus

mamm *(breast)* mammal, mammary, mammogram

mani, manu *(hand)* manipulate, manicure, manual, manufacture

mania *(insane desire)* manic, monomaniacal, kleptomaniac

mar *(sea)* marina, marine, mariner, maritime

masto *(breast)* mastectomy, mastitic, mastitis

materi *(matter)* material, materialism, immaterial

matic *(relating to)* automatic, mathematical, plasmatic, somatic

maxi *(most)* maximum, maximal, maximize

mea *(pass through)* permeate, permeability

mechani *(machine)* machine, mechanic, mechanize

medi *(middle)* median, mediate, medieval, mediocre

medic *(heal)* medicine, medical, medicate

mega *(million, great)* megabyte, megahertz, megaphone

megal(o) *(swollen)* megalomania, megalopolis

melan *(black)* melancholy, melanin, melanoma

memor *(mindful)* memory, memorial, memoir

ment *(mind)* dementia, mental, mentality, mention

mes(o)(i) *(middle)* Mesoamerica, Mesopotamia, mesosphere, Mesozoic

meta *(later, change)* metabolism, metamorphic, metaphase, metaphysics

meteor *(weather)* hydrometeorology, meteorology, meteorologist

meter, metr *(measurement)* centimeter, diameter, metronome, optometry

metr(o) *(mother)* metropolis, metropolitan

migra *(wander)* immigrant, migrant, migratory

mime *(mimic)* mimetic, mimicry, pantomime

minis *(assist)* administer, administrator, ministry

minu *(less)* minus, minute, minuet

mira *(wondrous)* miracle, miraculous, mirage

miso *(hate)* misogamy, misogyny, misanthropy

miss *(to send)* mission, missionary, missive

mit *(send)* admit, permit, submit, transmit

mito *(thread)* mitochondria, mitogen, mitosis

mobil *(movable)* automobile, immobile, mobilize

modus *(way, mode)* mode, moderate, module, modulate

mole *(mass)* mole, molecule, molecular

mollis *(soft)* mollify, mollusk

mor(t) *(death)* morgue, mortality, mortify, mortuary

morph *(shape)* endomorph, ectomorph, metamorphic, morphological

moto *(moving)* motif, motile, motive, motorcycle

mural *(wall)* intramural, mural

mut(a) *(change)* mutagen, mutate, mutation, mutable

mycin *(from fungus)* erythromycin, neomycin, streptomycin

narc *(sleep, torpor)* narcoleptic, narcosis, narcotic,

nat *(birth)* nationality, nativity, neonatal

naut *(ship, sailor)* astronaut, nautical, nausea

nebul *(fog, mist)* nebula, nebulous, nebulizer

necr(o) *(death, corpse)* necrotic, necromancy, necropolis

nema *(thread, round)* nematode, nematocyst

neur(o) *(nerve)* neurology, neuron, neurotransmitter

neutr(o) *(neutral)* neuter, neutron, neutrino

nictare *(wink)* nictitate, nictitating membrane

noct *(night)* nocturnal, nocturne, noctambulism

nod(o) *(knot)* nodular, nodule

nomen, nomin *(name)* nominal, nominate, nominee, nomenclature

nomy *(science of, name)* astronomy, economy, nominal

norm *(rule)* abnormal, normal, normative,

nota *(know)* notary, notation, notarize, notary, note

nova *(new)* Nova Scotia, novel, innovate, supernova

nox *(harm)* noxious, noxiousness, obnoxious

nucle *(kernel)* nuclear, nucleolus, nucleus

null *(none)* null, nullify

numer *(number)* enumerate, numeral, numerical, innumerable

nutri *(food)* nourish, nourishment, nutrient, nutrition

obver *(turn)* obverse, obversely

oculo *(eye)* binocular, monocle, ocular, oculist

odo *(way, path)* anode, cathode, odometer

odon *(tooth)* iguanodon, orthodontic, mastodon

offic *(duty)* office, officer, official, officious

oid *(resembling)* anthropoid, humanoid, mongoloid, ovoid

ol *(alcohol)* butanol, ethanol, methanol, propanol

olfact *(smell)* olfaction, olfactory

oligo *(few)* oligarch, oligarchy, Oligocene

oma *(swelling, tumor)* carcinoma, glaucoma, hematoma

ome *(biological entity)* biome, chromosome, cytosome, genome

Roots (Cont.)

onco *(cancer)* oncological, oncologist, oncology

onoma *(name)* onomatomania, onomatopoeia

onomy *(knowledge)* anatomy, astronomy, economy, taxonomy

onto *(existence)* ontological, ontology

onym *(name)* anonymous, acronym, pseudonym

oo *(egg)* oocyte, oologist, oospore

opera *(work)* opera, opus, operate, operant

ophthal *(eye)* ophthalmologist, ophthalmology, ophthalmia, ophthalmoscope

opia *(vision)* myopia, presbyopia

opin *(think)* opine, opinion

opsis *(appearance)* caryopsis, synopsis

opsy *(examination)* autopsy, biopsy

opt *(choice)* opt, option, optimism, optimum

opt(i/o) *(eye, vision)* optical, optician, optometrist

ora *(mouth)* oral, oracle, oration

orb *(circle)* orb, orbit, orbital

ordino *(arrange)* ordain, order, ordinal

ornith *(bird)* ornithology, ornithopod, ornithopter

orno *(adorn)* adorn, ornament, ornate

ortho *(straight)* orthodontic, orthodox, orthopedic, orthoscopic

oscill *(swing)* oscillate, oscillograph, oscilloscope

os, ossi, oste(o) *(bone)* osteoporosis, osteopath, ossify, ossification

osten *(exhibit)* ostensible, ostentation, ostentatious

ov(i) *(egg)* oval, ovary, ovoid, ovule

ox(y) *(oxygen)* oxygen, oxygenate, oxidization, deoxyribonucleic acid

pac, pax *(peace)* pacify, Pacific, pacifist

pachy *(thick)* pachyderm, pachytene

paleo *(ancient)* Paleocene, Paleolithic, paleontology

palpa *(touch, feel)* palpable, palpate, palpitation

pate *(shallow, pan)* pate, patella, paten, patent

pater, patr *(father)* paternal, paternity, paternoster

path(o) *(feeling, suffering, disease)* pathetic, pathological, pathogen, psychopath

pect *(chest)* expectorate, pectoral

ped *(child)* pediatrician, pediatric, pedagogy, pedigree

ped(i) *(foot)* bipedal, pedal, pedestrian, pedicle

pel *(drive)* expel, impel, propel, repel

pena *(punishment)* penal, penalize, penalty, penance, penitentiary

pend *(to hand)* append, dependent, impend

penetr *(insert)* penetrate, impenetrable

pept *(one)* peptide, peptize, polypeptide

period *(time)* periodic, periodical, periodically

pessimi *(worst)* pessimism, pessimist, pessimistic

phag *(eat)* esophagus, macrophage, phagocyte, sarcophagus

phal *(fingers/toes)* phalanges, phalanx

phan *(show, appear)* cellophane, diaphanous, phantom

pharmac *(drug)* pharmacy, pharmaceutical, pharmacological

pharyng *(throat)* pharyngeal, pharynx

phas *(speech)* aphasia, aphasic, dysphasia

phase *(stage)* anaphase, metaphase, prophase

pheno *(visible, show)* phenomenon, phenomenal, phenotype

philia *(attraction)* hemophilia, sophophilia

phil(o) *(love)* Philadelphia, philanthropy, philosophy

phleb *(vein)* phlebitis, phlebotomy

phob *(fear)* arachnophobia, claustrophobia, hydrophobia, phobia

phon(e) *(sound)* microphone, phonetic, symphony, telephone

phos *(light)* phosphor, phosphorescent, phosphorus

photo *(light)* photograph, photon, photosynthesis

phren *(brain)* phrenetic, phrenic, phrenology

phyl *(tribe, class)* phylogeny, phylum

phyll *(leaf)* chlorophyll, phyllode, phyllotaxy

physic *(nature)* physical, physician, physics

physis *(change, growth)* epiphysis, physical, physique

phyt(e) *(plant)* epiphyte, phytogenesis, phytoplankton

pinn *(feather)* pinna, pinion, pinnate

placeo *(pacify)* placate, placebo, placidity

plagia *(kidnapping)* plagiarism, plagiarist, plagiarize

plasm(a) *(fluid substance)* cytoplasm, ectoplasm, endoplasm, protoplasm

plast(y) *(particle)* chloroplast, euplastic, leucoplast

plat(y) *(flat)* plate, plateau, platform, platypus

plaud *(praise)* applaud, laud, plaudit

plect *(braid, weave)* complected, complex, complexion

plegia *(paralysis)* hemiplegia, paraplegia, quadriplegia

plete *(fill)* complete, deplete, replete

pleth *(excessive)* plethora, plethoric

pleur *(rib)* pleura, pleuropneumonia, pleurisy

plex *(interwoven, strike)* complex, perplex, solar plexus

plica *(fold)* pliant, compliant, complicate, replicate

plum *(feather)* plumage, plumate, plume

pne(a/um) *(lungs, breathe)* apnea, pneumonia, pneumatic

pod(a) *(foot)* arthropod, gastropod, pseudopod, podium, tripod

polar *(opposed)* dipolar, polarity, polarization, polarize, pole

polis *(city)* acropolis, metropolis, megalopolis, necropolis

pom *(knob, fruit)* pome, pomegranate, pommel

popu *(people)* populace, popular, populate, population

por *(hole)* osteoporosis, pore, porous, porosity

port *(carry)* export, import, portable, portfolio, transport

porta *(gate)* port, portal, portcullis

posi *(place)* deposit, imposition, position, positive

pota *(river, drink)* hippopotamus, potable, Mesopotamia

potent *(power)* impotent, omnipotent, potentate, potential

prehend *(seize)* apprehend, comprehend, prehensile

prim *(first)* primal, primary, primate, prime, primitive

proach *(near)* approach, rapprochement, reproach

propag *(multiply)* propaganda, propagate

propel *(drive)* propellant, propeller, propulsion

prox *(near)* approximate, proximal, proximity, proxy

psych *(mind)* psychic, psychology, psychopath, psychosomatic

pter *(wing, fly)* helicopter, ornithopter, pterodactyl

publi *(populace)* public, publicize, publish

pulmo *(lung)* pulmonary, pulmonology

pupa *(doll)* pupae, pupate, pupation

purg *(purify)* purge, purgative, purgatory

putr *(decay)* putrefaction, putrefy, putrescent, putrid

pyr(o) *(fire)* pyre, pyroclastic, pyromania, pyrometallurgy

qual *(characteristic)* qualify, qualitative, quality

quant *(amount)* quantify, quantity, quantum

quasi *(partly, so called)* quasi-intellectual, Quasimodo, quasar

quer, ques *(seek)* conquest, inquest, query, quest, question, request

quota *(amount)* quota, quotient, quotidian

radic *(root)* eradicate, radish

radio *(spoke)* radial, radiate, radioactive, radiometer

ranc *(stink)* rancid, rancor, rancorous

rapi *(plunder)* rapacious, rape, ravish

ras *(scrape)* abrasion, rasp, razor

rati(o) *(fixed, reason)* ratio, ration, rational, ratiocination

recidi *(backslide)* recidivism, recidivist

rect *(right, straight)* erect, direct, rectangle, rectify

reg *(rule)* regal, regent, regulate

relat *(carried back)* relate, relative, relativity, relation

relic *(leave, neglect)* relic, derelict, dereliction

render *(return)* rendering, rendition, surrender

repta *(creep)* reptile, reptilian

resid *(remain)* reside, residual, residue, residence

resona *(echo)* resonance, resonator, resound

reti *(web)* reticulate, retina, retinaculum

reve *(show)* reveal, revel, revelation

revi *(see again)* review, revise, revision

rhin(o) *(nose)* rhinoceros, rhinoplasty, rhinoscopy

rhiz(o) *(root)* rhizoid, rhizome, rhizosphere

rhod(o) *(red, rose)* rhodium, rhododendron, rhodolite

rig *(stiff)* rigid, rigor, rigorous

rogare *(ask)* rogation, interrogate, interrogative

rota *(wheel)* rotary, rotor, rotate, rotisserie

rrhea *(flow)* diarrhea, gonorrhea, menorrhea

rub *(red)* rubella, rubious, rubric, ruby

rupt *(break)* abrupt, disrupt, interruption, rupture

sacchar *(sugar)* polysaccharide, monosaccharide, saccharine

sacr *(holy)* sacred, sacrament, sacrifice, sacrum

sagac *(wisdom)* sage, sagacious, sagacity

sal *(salt)* saline, salary

saliv *(spit)* saliva, salivary, salivate, salivation

salu *(health)* salute, salubrious, salutary

salv *(safe)* salve, salvo, salvation, salvage

sanct *(holy)* sanctify, sanction, sanctity, sacrosanct, sanctuary

sangui *(blood)* sanguine, sanguinary, sanguineous

sanit *(health)* sanity, sanitary, sanitize, sanitation, sanitarium

sapien *(wise)* sapience, sapient, savant

sarc *(flesh)* sarcoma, sarcomere, sarcophagus, sarcosome

saur *(reptile)* dinosaur, Ichthyosaur, Tyrannosaurus

scala *(ladder)* scale, scalar, escalade, escalator

scene *(stage)* scenic, scenario, scenery

schizo *(split)* schist, schizoid, schizophrenia

scien *(know)* conscience, omniscience, science, scientist

sciss *(cut)* scission, scissor

sclera(o) *(hard)* arteriosclerosis, sclera, sclerotic, sclerosis,

scope, scopy *(see)* colonoscopy, microscope, oscilloscope, periscope, telescope

scrib, scrip *(write)* describe, inscribe, manuscript, prescribe, scribble

scrutia *(study)* inscrutable, scrutinize, scrutiny

Roots (Cont.)

sculp *(carve)* scalpel, sculpt, sculptor, sculpture

sect *(divide)* bisect, dissect, intersect, sect, section, transect

seism *(shake)* seismic, seismograph, seismology

sema *(sign)* semantics, semaphore, semiotic

semble *(similar)* assemble, dissemble, ensemble, resemble

seni *(old)* senile, senior, senescence

sens *(experience)* insensate, sense, sensation, sensible, sensual

seps *(infection)* asepsis, sepsis, septicemia

sequi *(follow)* consequence, sequel, sequence, sequential

sero *(body)* serology, serum

serpen *(crawling)* serpent, serpentarium, serpentine

serrat *(jagged)* serrate, serrations, Sierras

sert *(join)* assertive, desert, insertion

sessi *(sit, attached)* séance, sessile, session

sibilat *(hiss)* sibilant, sibilate, sibilance

sicc *(dry)* desiccant, desiccate, exsiccate

signum *(sign)* sign, signal, signet, signature, signify

similis *(alike)* facsimile, similar, simile, simulate, similar

sinu *(wind, bend)* insinuate, sinuate, sinuous

sipho *(tube)* siphon, siphonal, siphonophore

sist *(stop, stand)* assist, desist, insist, persist, resist

skeleton *(dried body)* cytoskeleton, exoskeleton, endoskeleton, skeletal

sol *(sun)* solar, solarium, solarimeter

solu, solv *(loosen)* absolve, dissolve, insoluble, solution, solve, solvent, resolve

soma(t), some *(body)* chromosome, lysosome, psychosomatic, somatic

som(e) *(body)* chromosome, lysosome, psychosomatic, somatic

somn(i) *(sleep)* insomnia, somnambulism, somniferous, somnolent

son(a) *(sound)* consonant, sonata, sonic, sonogram, sonorous

soph *(wise)* philosophy, sophist, sophisticated

sopor *(lethargy)* soporific, soporiferous

spasm *(draw, rend)* spastic, spasmodic, spasticity

spati *(empty)* space, spatial, spatiotemporal

speci *(type)* special, speciation, species, specific, specimen

spect *(see)* circumspect, inspect, prospect, respect, spectacle, spectator

spectro *(spectrum)* spectra, spectroscope, spectrometer

specul *(spy)* speculate, speculation, speculum

spend *(hang)* spend, expend, suspend

sphere *(ball)* atmosphere, ecosphere, hemisphere, spherical

spir(o) *(breathe)* aspire, expire, inspire, respire

spons *(promise)* response, responsible, sponsor, spouse

spont *(free)* spontaneous, spontaneity, spontaneously

squal *(foul)* squalid, squalor

stab *(firm, standing)* establish, stable, stabilize

stagn *(sill pool)* stanch, stagnate, stagnation

stalak *(drip)* stalactite, stalagmite

stasis, stat *(stationary, control)* homeostasis, static, statue, thermostat

stella *(star)* constellation, interstellar, stellar

stereo *(two)* stereomicroscope, stereophonic, stereoscopic

stigma *(stain)* astigmatism, stigmatic, stigmatize

still *(drip)* distill, instill, still

stoma(t) *(mouth)* stoma, stomata, stomach

strati *(layer)* stratus, stratum, stratify, stratosphere

stria *(groove)* striated, striation

strict *(bind)* constrict, restrict, strict, stricture

struct *(build up)* construct, destruct, obstruct, restructure, structure

stud *(diligent)* student, studio, studious, study

styl *(stem)* stylist, stylus, turnstile

suas *(to advise, agree)* assuasive, dissuade, persuade, suave

sublim *(lofty)* sublimate, sublime, subliminal

succu *(juice)* succubus, succulent, succulence

supin *(lying back)* supine, supinate, supination

suppos *(put under)* presuppose, suppose, supposition, suppository

surg *(rise)* insurgency, insurrection, surge

suspen *(hang)* suspend, suspense, suspension, suspender

syllab *(take together)* syllable, syllabic, syllabus

sylv *(forest)* sylph, sylvan, Pennsylvania

synthes *(put together)* photosynthesis, synthesis, synthesize, synthetic

symbio *(live together)* symbiotic, symbiosis, symbiote

sympto *(fall together)* asymptomatic, symptom, symptomatic

system *(stand together)* systemic, systematic, systematize

systol *(contract)* asystole, diastole, diastolic, systole, systolic

tabul *(board)* table, tabulate, tabloid, tableau

tachy *(rapid)* tachycardia, tachyon

tacit *(silent)* tacit, tacitly, taciturn

tact *(touch)* tactful, tactile, tactical

tag *(touch)* contagious, tag

tail *(cut)* curtail, detail, retail, tailor

tain *(hold)* ascertain, certain, detain, obtain, retain,

tang *(touch)* intangible, tangible, tangent

tard *(slow)* tardy, tarry

tars *(ankle)* metatarsal, tarsier, tarsus

taxi *(movement)* phototaxis, taxicab, taximeter, taxiway

taxo *(arrangement)* taxidermy, taximeter, taxonomy

techn *(skill)* technical, technician, technique, technology

tele *(distant)* telepathy, telephone, telescope, television

telo *(end)* teleology, telomere, telophase,

temp *(time, state)* temper, temporary, temperature

tempt *(touch)* attempt, contempt, temptation

ten *(grasp)* tenacity, tenant, tenet

tend, tens *(stretch, sinew)* extend, portend, pretend, tendon, tendril, tensile

tenebr *(dark)* Tenebrae, tenebrific, tenebrous

tens *(tight)* intense, tense, tensile

term *(boundary)* interminable, term, terminal, terminate

terra *(earth)* terrain, terrestrial, territory

terri *(frighten)* terrible, terrify, terror, terrorism

test *(witness)* attest, contest, detest, protest, testament

text *(weave)* context, text, textile, textual, texture

thalam *(inner chamber)* hypothalamus, thalamus, thalamic

thana *(death)* euthanasia, thanatology, Thanatos

the(o/a) *(God)* atheism, polytheism, theism, theology

therap *(treatment, examine)* therapy, therapist, therapeutic

therm *(heat)* geothermal, endothermic, exothermic, hydrothermal, hypothermic

thora(c/x) *(chest)* thoracic, thorax, cephalothorax

thromb *(clot)* thrombophlebitis, thromboplastic, thrombosis

tinct *(color)* tinct, tint, tincture

tinni *(ringing)* tingle, tintinnabulation, tinnitus

titan *(giant)* titan, titanic, Titanism, titanium

tom(e) *(part)* atom, epitome, diatom

tom(y) *(cut, slice)* appendectomy, tonsillectomy, tracheotomy

ton(ic/o) *(stretched)* hypertonic, isotonic, tonus

topo *(surface)* topic, topical, topographic, topology

torsi *(twist)* torque, torsion, tortellini, tortuous

tox(i) *(poison)* antitoxin, intoxicate, toxic, toxemia, toxicology

trache *(windpipe)* trachea, tracheal, tracheobronchial, tracheotomy

tract *(drag, draw)* attract, extract, protract, retract, tractor, traction

trapez *(four-footed)* trapeze, trapezium, trapezoid

trauma *(injury)* trauma, traumatic, traumatize

tribu *(press, tribe)* retribution, tribulation, tribunal, tribune

trit *(worn, frayed)* attrition, trite, triturate

trope *(turn toward)* geotropic, hydrotropic, phototropic

trophy *(feed, eat)* atrophy, autotrophy, dystrophy, hypertrophy

tropism *(movement or growth in)* geotropism, hydrotropism, phototropism

trud *(thrust)* extrude, intrude, protrude

trunc *(maim)* truncate, truncheon

tuber *(swelling)* tuber, tubercle, protuberant, tuberculosis

turb *(mob, muddled)* disturb, turbidity, turbulent

twi *(two)* twain, twice, twin, twilight

tympan(o) *(drum)* tympani, tympanic, tympanum

typ *(style, print)* atypical, prototypical, typical, typography

ule *(small)* granule, module, vestibular

ulti *(beyond)* ulterior, ultimate, ultimatum

ulul *(howl)* ululate, ululation

umbilic *(navel)* umbilical, umbilicus

umbra *(shadow)* penumbra, umbrage, umbrella

undu *(wave)* inundate, undulate, undulation

ungu *(hoof)* ungula, ungulate, unguis

urb *(city)* urban, urbane, urbanize, suburb

uro *(urine)* urethane, uric, urinal, urine, urology

usu *(use)* unusual, usual, usury, usurpation

uter *(womb)* intrauterine, uterine, uterus

uti *(use)* utensil, utilitarian, utilize, utility

vacan *(empty)* evacuate, vacant, vacate, vacation

vacu *(hole)* vacuum, vacuole, vacuous

vade *(go)* evade, invade, pervade

vaga *(wandering)* vagabond, vagary, vagrant, vague

vagin *(cup)* invaginate, vagina, vaginal

vain *(empty)* vainglorious, vanity, vanish

vale *(value, worth)* equivalent, evaluate, valence, valiant, valid

vario *(change, bent)* variation, varicose, variegated, various

vas(o) *(vessel)* vasectomy, vasodilation, vascular, vasculature

vec, veh *(carry)* convect, convey, vehement, vehicle, vector

velo *(swift)* velocity, velocipede, velociraptor

ven *(vein)* intravenous, vena cava, venous

venal *(sale)* venal, venality, vendor

vera *(true)* veracious, veracity, verdict, verification, very

verb *(word)* verbal, verbalize, verbose, verbatim

verd *(green)* verdant, verdigris, verdure

verg *(incline)* converge, diverge, verge

Roots (Cont.)

vermin *(worm)* vermicelli, vermin, vermiform

vers *(turn, direction)* converse, inverse, obverse, reverse, transverse, versatile, version

vert *(change, turn)* advertise, convert, divert, invert, revert, versatile, vertigo

vesic *(bladder)* vesicant, vesicle, vesicular

vest *(robe)* divest, invest, vestment, vestry

vestig *(trace)* investigate, vestige, vestigial

via *(road, through)* deviate, devious, Via Dolorosa, viaduct

vibr *(shake)* vibrant, vibrate, vibrato

vice *(in place of)* vicar, viceroy, vice president

vin *(grape)* vinegar, vineyard, vintage, vintner

vir *(slime, ooze)* virology, virulent, virus

vis, vid *(see)* advise, revise, video, visage, vision, visor

viscero *(guts)* eviscerate, viscera, viscus

vit(a) *(life)* revitalize, vital, vitality, vitamins

vitr(e) *(glass)* in vitro, vitreous, vitrify, vitriol

vivi *(alive)* revive, revivify, vivacious, vivid

voc *(call)* invoke, revoke, vocal, vocation, vociferate

voli, volo *(will)* malevolent, volitional, volunteer

volt *(turn)* revolt, volt, voluble

volv *(roll)* convolute, devolve, evolve, involve, revolve

vor(e) *(eat)* carnivore, herbivore, omnivore, voracious

vot *(vow)* devote, vote, votive, votary

vuln *(attack)* invulnerable, vulnerable, vulnerability

xen(o) *(stranger)* xenobiotic, xenophobe, xenophile

zo *(animal)* zoology, zoophyte, zoon, zoospore

zygo *(united, paired)* heterozygous, zygomorphic, zygote

Suffixes

able *(capable of, able)* inflammable, notable, reliable

ac *(pertaining to)* hypochondriac, maniac

acean *(class or order)* crustacean, cetacean

aceous *(of the nature of)* herbaceous, sebaceous

acious *(tending toward)* gracious, rapacious, spacious

acy *(state)* democracy, legacy, lunacy, normalcy

ad *(toward)* cycad, monad, triad

age *(state)* blockage, heritage, marriage, sewage

agogy *(leading)* demagogy, pedagogy

al *(pertaining to)* facial, mental, nominal, physical, spiritual

ality *(property of, condition of)* causality, personality, reality

an, ian *(belonging to, resembling)* arcadian, Canadian, Hadean, hydrozoan

ance *(the act of)* avoidance, dominance, substance

ane *(attribute)* arcane, humane, mundane, urbane

ant *(having, showing, or doing)* combatant, merchant, penchant, peasant

ar *(pertaining to)* cellular, molecular, polar, scholar

arch *(ruler)* patriarch, matriarch, monarch

archy *(rule, leadership)* anarchy, monarchy, oligarchy

arian *(age, sect, occupation)* grammarian, librarian, octogenarian, vegetarian

arium *(place for)* aquarium, sanitarium, terrarium

ary, ery, ory *(relating to)* aviary, boundary, bribery, dictionary, illusory, library, victory

ase *(enzyme)* lactase, lipase, sucrase

asis *(state of)* cirrhosis, metastasis, psoriasis

ate *(to cause, having)* enervate, laminate, oxygenate, pronation, supination

ate *(compound)* carbonate, hydrate, silicate

atic *(of the kind of)* asthmatic, democratic, emphatic, erratic, somatic

ation *(act of, condition of)* intimation, perspiration, recitation, specialization

atory *(characterized by, related to)* ambulatory, circulatory, laboratory, observatory

cian *(having a skill)* clinician, musician, technician

cide *(kill)* insecticide, herbicide, homicide, patricide, genocide, suicide

cy *(function, condition)* deficiency, pregnancy, relevancy

dom *(state, realm)* boredom, freedom, princedom, wisdom

ectomy *(cut out)* appendectomy, thyroidectomy, tonsillectomy, vasectomy

ee *(receiver of action)* employee, payee, trainee

emia *(blood issue)* anemia, hypoglycemia, leukemia, toxemia

en *(cause to be)* harden, lighten, spoken, stolen

ence *(process, state)* emergence, luminescence, science

er, or *(one who)* baker, builder, governor, pollster, ranger, rover, senator

escent *(becoming)* luminescent, phosphorescent

ess *(female)* actress, princess, waitress

fer *(carry)* aquifer, conifer, ferry, transfer

ferous *(bearing)* coniferous, crystalliferous, pestiferous, soporiferous

fic *(making)* beatific, horrific, malefic, scientific

ful *(full of)* colorful, grateful, hopeful, respectful

fy, ify *(make, cause to)* exemplify, purify, putrefy, simplify, stupefy

genic *(creating)* carcinogenic, eugenic, mutagenic, photogenic

hood *(order, condition)* brotherhood, falsehood, neighborhood, womanhood

ia *(condition)* anorexia, bulimia, hypochondria, hysteria

iac *(pertaining to)* hypochondria, maniac

ial *(relating to)* arterial, cranial, medial, pericardial

ian *(skilled in, resembling)* comedian, librarian, reptilian

iasis *(disease)* paralysis, psoriasis, elephantiasis

iatric *(treatment)* geriatric, pediatric, psychiatric

iatry *(treatment)* optometry, podiatry, psychiatry

ible *(capable of being)* credible, mobile, risible, terrible

ic *(pertaining to, having)* atomic, biotic, frenetic, manic, medic

ician *(specialist)* magician, musician, physician, technician

ics *(technology)* acoustics, mathematics, physics

id *(quality)* acid, gelid, limpid, tepid

ify *(become)* petrify, rectify, sanctify, stratify

ile *(relating to)* compile, docile, senile

ing *(act of)* cleaning, hunting, living, regretting

ion *(process of)* extinction, fusion, reversion

ior *(pertaining to)* junior, savior, senior

ious *(full of)* bilious, cautious, religious, rubiginous

ish *(of, somewhat)* smallish, yellowish

ism *(condition, belief)* alcoholism, communism, socialism

ist *(one who specializes in)* dermatologist, optimist, optometrist

istics *(science of)* ballistics, linguistics, statistics

ite *(nature of)* stromatolite, stalactite, trilobite

itis *(inflammation)* appendicitis, arthritis, bronchitis, hepatitis

ity *(state)* formality, parity, reality

ium *(element, chemical)* barium, calcium, potassium

ive *(tending toward)* disruptive, expressive, pensive

ization *(result of making)* de-Stalinization, industrialization, organization

ize *(cause to be)* idealize, ionize, metastasize, realize

less *(without)* hopeless, needless, timeless, worthless

ling *(smaller)* duckling, hatchling, sapling

ly *(manner)* chronologically, happily, publicly, quickly

ment *(act of, related to)* ailment, fragment, government, movement

ness *(quality)* correctness, helpfulness, wellness

ologist *(one who studies)* anthropologist, biologist, entomologist, psychologist

ology *(study of)* anthropology, biology, entomology, psychology

or, er *(one who)* accelerator, doctor, governor, orator, rector, renter

ory *(place)* dormitory, factory, laboratory

ose *(sugar ending)* fructose, glucose, lactose, ribose, lactose, sucrose

osis *(state, disease)* arterioslerosis, prognosis, thrombosis, neurosis, psychosis

otic *(affected with, producing)* antibiotic, neurotic, symbiotic

otomy *(incision)* lobotomy, tracheotomy

ous *(containing, pertaining to)* analogous, bulbous, dexterous, porous, rigorous

ship *(rank, quality)* courtship, readership, relationship, scholarship

sis *(state, process)* hypnosis, mitosis, psychosis, trichinosis

some *(like, leading to)* gruesome, lonesome, twosome

ster *(person associated with)* gangster, mobster, youngster

th *(ordinal number)* tenth, hundredth, thousandth, millionth

ty *(condition, state)* conformity, exclusivity, realty

ular *(resembling)* cellular, circular, singular

ure *(act, process)* erasure, procedure, legislature

vious *(characterized by)* envious, previous, obvious

ward *(in the direction of)* downward, inward, outward, upward

where *(location)* anywhere, everywhere, nowhere, somewhere

wise *(direction, regarding)* clockwise, otherwise

y *(inclined to)* cheery, curvy, grouchy

Vocabulary Activities

Noteworthy Words

One powerful way to increase your vocabulary is to keep a list of new words and their definitions for each subject you study.

Your Turn Use a section of your notebook or a digital file to create a vocabulary list. Whenever you hear or read an unfamiliar word, record its definition. List the word's parts. Give an example of the term. Use the word in a sentence. Draw a picture of what the word represents if possible.

Word Builders

You can learn many of the prefixes, roots, and suffixes on pages 166-177 by using them to build your own words.

Your Turn Use prefixes, suffixes, and roots to create new terms described here:

1. Miracle cure (for example, *eucardioize,* meaning "making the heart good")
2. Pop band (for example, *Macrosonics,* meaning "related to big sound")
3. Newly discovered dinosaur (for example, *Supersanguisaur,* meaning "really bloody reptile")
4. Surgical procedure (for example, *malomaotomy,* meaning "cutting out the bad lump")
5. College course (for example, *Neodoxometry,* meaning "the measurement of new beliefs")

Analyze the Parts

Most new words you encounter in school subjects will be built from the word parts on pages 166-177. This activity will help you parse the words.

Your Turn Write down four or five new words that you find browsing the Web. Circle any parts you think are roots. Underline any parts you think are prefixes. Double-underline any parts you think are suffixes. Then look up the parts and write down their meanings.

- eso—within
- phage—eat
- al—pertaining to

Pertaining to the passage for eating—the esophagus

Chapter 12
Writing to Learn

At one time, students were primarily consumers of information. They absorbed whatever their teachers and textbooks provided. Today, however, students are often expected to produce information, cultivating and growing new thoughts and ideas.

One powerful way to produce information is to write. Writing compels you to connect with the information you are learning. As you write, you think; and thinking deepens your understanding of the topics you study. This chapter focuses on strategies that you can use to improve your writing and learning in any subject.

You will learn . . .

- Writing to Learn
- Writing to Inquire
- Using the Writing Process
- Applying Basic Conventions
- Writing Glossary

Writing to Learn

Writing-to-learn activities help you think more deeply about whatever you are learning. Use the techniques on these two pages in any class.

▶ **Admit/exit slips** engage your brain at the beginning of a lesson and give you the opportunity to reflect on your learning at the end. You can write questions, comments, observations, or reflections about the material presented.

> Why isn't "logarithm" spelled "logarhythm"?

▶ **Brainstorming** is the process of writing down as many ideas as possible, as quickly as possible, without pausing to evaluate them. To brainstorm, pose a question and answer it in as many ways as possible. (See page 87.)

▶ **Class minutes** are notes that record what happens in a class as if it were a meeting. By keeping class minutes, you enhance your learning, produce a record of what was covered, acquire a study aid, and help students who are absent. (See page 91.)

▶ **Clustering** or **mind mapping** is a form of brainstorming in which you record a topic in the center of a piece of paper and make as many connections or associations around it as you can. This technique provides a visual of your thoughts on a topic. (See page 50.)

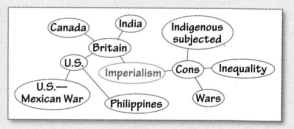

▶ **Correspondence** involves writing a letter or an email to a person connected to an event or topic you are studying. Examples include a letter to a Civil War general or one to Robert Oppenheimer, father of quantum mechanics.

▶ **Dialogues** are made-up conversations between yourself and another person (or two). Your written script of an interview with Mao Tse-tung or Madame Curie would be an example.

▶ **First thoughts** are your initial ideas about a topic. At the start of a new unit, write down your first thoughts in a paragraph. This will remind you of what you already know about the topic.

▶ **Freewriting** is writing nonstop for 5 to 10 minutes about a topic. The main point is to keep going without worrying about errors. If you can't think of anything else to write, write a phrase like "What's next?" or "I wonder" over and over until more ideas pour out. This activity helps you think through ideas. (See page 349.)

▶ **Learning logs** are journals in which you reflect on what you are learning. Keeping a learning log gives you the chance to explore and deepen your understanding of new concepts. (See pages 130-131.)

▶ **Listing** is simply writing items in a column, trying to remember each important detail. A list offers you a way to record many facts, steps in a process, and so on. A list can also evolve into an outline or a plan of action.

> Mitosis
> ----
> Prophase
> Metaphase
> Anaphase
> Telophase

▶ **Nutshelling** is writing the main idea of a lesson in a single sentence. This technique gets its name from the idiom "put it in a nutshell" (the smallest possible space).

> Terminal velocity is the point at which the "pull" of gravity equals the "push" of drag.

▶ **Predicting** is simply writing what you expect to happen next. When predicting, you must think carefully about what has already happened. Your expectations will either be met or not, but either way, you will have thought more deeply about the material.

> I predict that Huck and Jim will get caught and put on trial.

▶ **Question of the day** is a question that you either ask or answer in a given class session. If you write your own question, it will focus your attention on the material; if your instructor supplies a question for you to answer, you will listen and watch for crucial details.

▶ **Summarizing** means capturing the main point and key details in a form briefer than the original body of information.

Your Turn Use one of these strategies to think deeply about what you learned on these pages.

Graphic Organizers

Graphic organizers are visual tools that can spur your thinking about any topic. You can use them to either devise new ideas or to analyze existing ones. Using the following graphic organizers will deepen your thinking in different ways.

Branching Diagram

Branching diagrams trace complex relationships. You can use branching diagrams for genealogies, animal and plant groups, and related cultural developments.

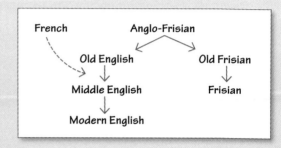

Cause-Effect Chart

Cause-effect charts trace the causes of a phenomenon, as well as its effects. Write the topic in a center circle; then list causes to the left and effects to the right.

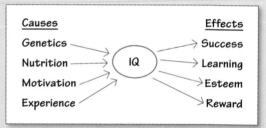

Cycle Diagram

Cycle diagrams provide a way to graph the series of steps or events in a typical process or cycle.

Your Turn Use one of the graphic organizers on this page to record the details about a subject you are currently studying.

5 W's and H Chart or Sensory Chart

A 5 W's and H chart answers the essential questions about a topic. You can use a similar chart for recording sensory details.

Who?	King John of England and the nobles in his court
What?	Signed the Magna Carta
Where?	Runnymede
When?	Signed June 15, 1215, but became law in 1225
Why?	To limit the power of the king and increase the power of the nobles
How?	By drafting a document that was a precursor to the American Constitution

T-Bar

T-bars are two-column tables used to consider pros and cons, causes and effects, problems and solutions, similarities and differences, or any other two-part structure.

Wind Power

Pros	Cons
Renewable	Unsightly windmills
Carbon neutral	Harm to birds
Available tech	Expensive start
Green jobs	Regional

Time Line

Time lines organize information chronologically. They work well for tracking events in history and literature, and they can also outline processes and give instructions.

Paleozoic Era (mya = million years ago)

```
              Cambrian
-500 mya --
              Ordovician

-400 mya -- Silurian-Devonian

              Carboniferous
-300 mya --
              Permian
```

Venn Diagram

Venn diagrams compare and contrast two topics. Similarities between the topics occupy the central space, and contrasts appear in the outer circle portions under each heading.

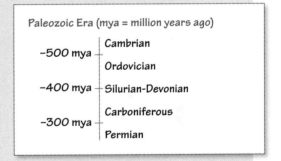

Earth — Venus

oceans, temperate, axial tilt, magnetic field, N, O_2 | mass, diameter, gravitation, atmosphere, volcanoes, close to sun, rocky | dry, broiling, no seasons, no magnetic field, CO_2

Your Turn Use one of the graphic organizers above to analyze a topic you are currently studying.

Writing to Inquire

Besides deepening your understanding of a topic, writing can assist at each stage of the inquiry process.

Questioning

Questions create voids that will be filled with answers. The following chart explains the types of questions you will write and answer during the inquiry process.

■ *Is and do* questions elicit *yes* or *no*.	**Are** the noble gases inert?
■ *Who, what, where,* and *when* questions need specific answers.	For **whom** is the element flerovium named?
■ *Why* and *how* questions ask for elaborate information.	**Why** is element 116 called livermorium?
■ **Socratic** questions probe thinking. (See page 107.)	What assumptions are we making about naming elements?
■ **SCAMPER** questions require innovation. (See page 41.)	How could we **adapt** element names to make them more memorable?
■ **Open-ended** questions require creative responses.	What would you name the next element?
■ **Counterfactual** questions require careful thought. (See page 38.)	If you had to eliminate one element, which would it be?
■ **Thought-experiment** questions explore concepts.	How can energy condense to form matter?
■ **Paradoxical** questions require metaphysical thinking.	Could a living thing be made of pure energy?

Bigger (arrow pointing down along left margin)

Your Turn Choose a topic you are currently studying. Write one example for each type of question above about the topic. Find answers to four or more of your questions.

Planning

Writing also serves well during the planning phase of inquiry. The planning sheet on page 361 directs you to write a goal and objectives (answering the five W's and H questions about a project) and to reflect on tasks, time, team, and tools.

Your Turn Set a goal in one of your classes. Then answer the 5 W's and H about the goal to come up with objectives. See the planning sheet on page 361 for an example.

Researching and Creating

The researching and creating stages of inquiry often involve various types of writing:

- **Taking notes** (resource information, details, interviews)
- **Reporting information** (essays, articles, stories)
- **Communicating with others** (text messages, invoices, subpoenas)
- **Recording data** (weather data sheets, double-elimination tournaments, medical charts)

Your Turn Think about the different ways you use writing throughout your day. When do you use it to report information, to communicate with others, to record data, to take notes? In what other ways do you use writing?

Improving

Writing is a key evaluation tool. For example, the rubric on page 417 offers space to assess how well the goal and objectives of a particular project have been met. Written evaluations can tell you what works and what doesn't, so you can make improvements.

Your Turn Using the goal and objectives you created on page 184, create a rubric (download a template from thoughtfullearning.com/h185). Keep it on hand to track your progress with your goal.

	Goal	Evaluation	Rating			Score
Goal	Create a public service announcement (P.S.A.) about the problem of child warriors.	We created a powerful P.S.A. with strong narration and images.	Beat 60	Met (40)	Didn't 20	40
	Objectives					
Who?	1. I will work on this with the other three students at my table.	Stephen and I did most of the work. We had some trouble with teamwork.	Beat 10	Met 6	Didn't (2)	2
What?	2. We will research child warriors and find resources to create a P.S.A.	We found creative photos and composed our own music.	Beat (10)	Met 6	Didn't 2	10
Where?	3. We'll work in class, in the library, and in the media center.	We worked at home, in the library, and in the media center.	Beat (10)	Met 6	Didn't 2	10
When?	4. The P.S.A. needs to be ready to present on 1/24.	We got our P.S.A. done the night before the deadline, so we're in good shape!	Beat 10	Met (6)	Didn't 2	6
Why?	5. We want viewers to help end the use of children in wars.	Our P.S.A. is pretty convincing.	Beat 10	Met (6)	Didn't 2	6
How?	6. We'll use the equipment in the media center.	We used the media center as well as our home computers.	Beat (10)	Met 6	Didn't 2	10
					Total:	84

Presenting

Writing often plays a role as you prepare to present your finished work. For example, you may need to make posters, write articles, print tickets and labels, design signs, compose captions, and so on.

Using the Writing Process

When you write specifically for publication, you will follow a version of inquiry called the writing process. Completing the steps in this process will take you from the blank page/screen to a polished, published draft.

Steps in the Writing Process

The writing process breaks a large task into small, manageable steps, each with a different purpose.

1. **Prewriting** involves exploring a subject, narrowing your focus to a specific topic, researching the topic, gathering details, and organizing them. (Corresponds to these inquiry stages: **Questioning, Planning,** and **Researching**)

   Prewriting

2. **Drafting** is creating a first written version or draft (beginning, middle, and ending). During this step, you work steadily to connect your ideas to form a first version of your writing. (Corresponds to this inquiry stage: **Creating**)

   Drafting

3. **Revising** is making large-scale changes, focusing on the ideas, organization, and voice of the writing. This step can involve both the writer's and a peer's evaluation of the work. (Corresponds to this inquiry stage: **Improving**)

   Revising

4. **Editing** is making small-scale changes to fine-tune the style and correctness of the writing. This step involves the use of style guides, dictionaries, checklists, and other supports. (Corresponds to this inquiry stage: **Improving**)

   Editing

5. **Publishing** is making your written work public, whether in person, in print, or online. Publishing involves choosing a medium and using an effective design to make the information accessible. (Corresponds to this inquiry stage: **Presenting**)

   Publishing

Your Turn Reflect on the writing process. Which step do you excel at? Which step is most challenging? Skim the following pages, noting the instructions and reminders offered for each step of the process. Which ideas do you think will be most helpful to you? Why?

Prewriting

Prewriting involves exploring a general subject, selecting a specific topic, creating a thesis statement, conducting research, and organizing the information.

▶ **Exploring the Subject:** Subjects are general areas of interest. The Dewey decimal categories below demonstrate how broad these areas of interest can be:

100 Philosophy/Psychology	600 Technology
200 Religion	700 The Arts
300 Social Sciences	800 Literature/Rhetoric
400 Language	900 Geography/History
500 Natural Science/Math	

▶ **Selecting a Topic:** Trying to cover all of philosophy, or language, or the arts, and so on, in a single written work is not possible. Doing some basic research can help you to narrow your subject to a particular topic. Look for a topic that you can discuss in a thorough manner in whatever form you are using.

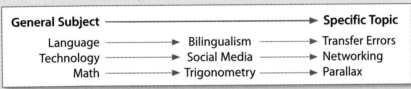

General Subject ⟶ **Specific Topic**

Language ⟶	Bilingualism ⟶	Transfer Errors
Technology ⟶	Social Media ⟶	Networking
Math ⟶	Trigonometry ⟶	Parallax

▶ **Forming a Thesis:** A thesis states the specific thought or feeling about the topic that you will explain and share in your written work. You can form your thesis using this formula:

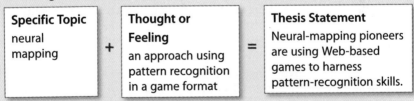

Specific Topic		**Thought or Feeling**		**Thesis Statement**
neural mapping	**+**	an approach using pattern recognition in a game format	**=**	Neural-mapping pioneers are using Web-based games to harness pattern-recognition skills.

▶ **Researching:** Continue to research your topic, gathering information and details that support and develop your thesis. Chapters 23 and 24 of this book provide an in-depth guide to conducting research.

▶ **Organizing:** While conducting your research, remember to keep track of the sources you consult. Also plan how you will order the information in order to present your ideas clearly.

Your Turn Think about a general subject you are currently studying; choose a particular part of the subject; then narrow that part to a specific topic that interests you. Finally, form a thesis statement that includes a specific thought or feeling about the topic.

Drafting

When you draft, you work steadily to put your ideas into an initial, rough form without stopping. Afterward you can rework this initial writing into a clear first draft, but do not worry about mechanical errors at this point. Your first draft ought to contain a beginning, a middle, and an ending.

▶ **Beginning:** The beginning does a number of important jobs.
  - **Grabs the reader's attention** with an interesting fact, question, or anecdote
  - **Provides necessary background**
  - **Establishes a voice** appropriate for the purpose of the writing
  - **States the thesis** of the piece

▶ **Middle:** The middle supports and develops the thesis, providing a variety of details and information:
  - **Facts and statistics** explain ideas.
  - **Definitions and examples** clarify ideas.
  - **Anecdotes and observations** connect the topic to real life.
  - **Quotations and citations** offer expert information.
  - **Experiments** supply scientific evidence.
  - **Logic and argumentation** persuade the reader.

The middle also organizes the supporting details according to a pattern. Here are a number of basic patterns of organization:
  - **Time:** Organizing details chronologically
  - **Location:** Organizing details spatially
  - **Logic:** Presenting statements according to correct reasoning
    - **Deduction:** Working from a general principle to specific details
    - **Induction:** Working from specific details to a general principle
  - **Conversion:** Taking a position, then arguing toward an opposite opinion
  - **Least to most:** Presenting details from least to most important
  - **Most to least:** Presenting details from most to least important
  - **Subject by subject:** Describing one subject completely; then the other
  - **Point by point:** Treating one point at a time
  - **Causes and effects:** Covering causes and then effects
  - **Similarities and differences:** Covering comparisons and then contrasts
  - **Pros and cons:** Covering benefits and then drawbacks

▶ **Ending:** The ending leaves an impression in one or more ways.
  - **Sums** up the thesis
  - **Emphasizes** a key point
  - **Connects** with the reader's life
  - **Calls** the reader to act
  - **Provides** a strong final thought
  - **Asks** a provocative question

Revising

After completing a solid first draft, take a break. The length of the break can vary depending upon the complexity of the writing, but it should be long enough for you to return to your work refreshed and ready to revise your draft.

Revising the Global Traits

The checklist below can help you revise your work, checking it for the "big" traits of effective writing: ideas, organization, and voice. Use this checklist to determine what is working and what is not working in your own or a classmate's writing.

Revising Checklist

Ideas

☑ 1. The writing focuses on one part of an interesting topic.
☑ 2. The thesis is clear, concise, and compelling.
☑ 3. A variety of details develops the thesis.
☑ 4. Each paragraph focuses on a main point.
☑ 5. The writing achieves its purpose (inform, persuade, entertain).

Organization

☑ 6. The beginning captures the reader's attention and provides the thesis.
☑ 7. The middle develops the thesis.
☑ 8. Details are arranged effectively (time, location, importance) and paragraphs appear in the best order.
☑ 9. The ending sums up the thesis and provides a final thought.

Voice

☑ 10. The voice is appropriate to the topic and purpose of the writing.
☑ 11. The voice connects with the reader.
☑ 12. The level of language is appropriate to the writing form.

Making Improvements

When you revise, you make four basic improvements: **(1) add** necessary information, **(2) remove** unnecessary details, **(3) reorder** disorganized material, and **(4) rework** unclear ideas.

Your Turn Use the checklist above to review the first draft of a paper that you have recently written. Whenever you need to revise a first draft or help another writer revise, return to this checklist. (Download a copy at thoughtfullearning.com/h189.)

Editing

Once you have completed the large-scale improvements and made a clean copy of your revised writing, it is time to edit your work. Editing involves fine-tuning the words, sentences, correctness, and design of the piece. The checklist below will help.

Editing Checklist

Words

☑ 1. Nouns are specific and verbs are active.
☑ 2. Modifiers are used sparingly and only to improve clarity.
☑ 3. Words show respect for gender, ethnicity, age, and ability.

Sentences

☑ 4. Sentences vary in length and begin in different ways.
☑ 5. Sentences flow smoothly.
☑ 6. Most sentences use active voice.
☑ 7. All sentences include a subject and a predicate and express a complete thought. (See pages 195-196.)

Correctness

☑ 8. All sentences end with correct punctuation.
☑ 9. Commas are used correctly. (See page 191.)
☑ 10. Subjects and verbs agree. (See page 194.)
☑ 11. Pronouns and antecedents agree. (See page 194.)
☑ 12. Spelling and capitalization are correct.

Design

☑ 13. The document follows the requirements of the assignment or form.
☑ 14. The typeface is easy to read.
☑ 15. White space (margins, blank lines) creates accessible blocks of text.
☑ 16. The overall design enhances the clarity of the piece.

Publishing

Publishing brings your work to the public so that others can learn from it, respond to it, and build upon it. In addition to traditional publications, online options allow you to share your ideas across the globe.

Your Turn Choose a piece of writing that you have recently completed. Use the checklist above to edit the document. (Download it at thoughtfullearning.com/h190.) Then find a publication form that fits your purpose and reaches the reader in the best way possible.

Applying Basic Conventions

Conventions include punctuation, usage, mechanics, and sentence rules. The following pages outline the most important conventions of English.

Punctuation Rules

1. **Use correct end punctuation.** End statements and mild commands with a period. End direct questions with a question mark. Use exclamation points sparingly, one at a time.	I arrived early. Why was everyone else late? I'm sick of it!
2. **Use commas after introductory words.** Set off a group of four or more introductory words.	Before the sun rose, we ate breakfast.
3. **Use commas to separate items in a series.** Include a comma before the last *and* or *or.*	We couldn't decide whether to have beans, rice, or corn.
4. **Place a comma between equal adjectives.** Two adjectives modify a noun equally if you can change their order and they still make sense.	I like spicy, hot chili. ("I like hot, spicy chili" works.)
5. **Use a comma and a coordinating conjunction to form compound sentences.** You can join two sentences (independent clauses) with a comma followed by a coordinating conjunction (*and, but, or, nor, for, so, yet*).	The pillow is hypoallergenic, **and** the sheets are freshly washed.
6. **Use a semicolon to form compound sentences.** You can join two closely related sentences (independent clauses) with a semicolon.	The pillow is hypoallergenic; the sheets are freshly washed.
7. **Place a colon before an example or list.** Write a complete sentence before the colons.	She needs one thing: respect. I need three things: lunch, a shower, and a nap.
8. **Use an apostrophe to show possession.** Add *'s* to most words, and an apostrophe to plurals ending in *s.* (The owner precedes the apostrophe.)	Friend's report (owned by one) Friends' report (owned by more than one)
9. **Use quotation marks around a speaker's exact words.** Periods or commas at the end of a quotation appear inside the quotation marks; colons or semicolons appear outside the quotation marks; question marks/exclamation points appear inside the marks if they belong to the quotation, outside if they end the sentence.	When did Lincoln say that the Civil War might continue "until every drop of blood drawn with the lash shall be paid by another drawn with the sword"?
10. **Set off titles of short works with quotation marks; use italics (underlining) for long works.** Short works are songs, short stories, articles, etc. Long works are albums, books, newspapers, etc.	The song "Fly by Night" is on the album *Fly by Night.*

Usage Rules

1. **Accept, except:** The verb *accept* means "receive." The preposition *except* means "other than"; the conjunction, "unless"; and the verb, "leave out." | I won't *accept* any answer *except* yes.

2. **Affect, effect:** *Affect* is a verb that means "influence." As a noun, *effect* means "result"; as a verb, *effect* means "bring about." | The situation doesn't *affect* me. I've realized no negative *effects*, so why should I *effect* a change?

3. **Among, between:** *Among* often refers to groups of more than two; *between* often refers to only two. | *Among* the possible candidates, I'll choose *between* these two.

4. **Amount, number:** *Amount* refers to things in bulk or mass; *number* refers to separate things that can be counted. | A *number* of glasses held the same *amount* of water.

Amount   Number

5. **Bad, badly:** *Bad* is an adjective, used before a noun or after a linking verb; *badly* is an adverb. | The report is *bad* (bad report); I look *bad* (bad appearance); I play *badly* (bad at playing).

6. **Choose, chose:** *Choose* means "select"; *chose* is the past tense of *choose*. | I *choose* today the same thing I *chose* yesterday.

7. **Farther, further:** *Farther* refers to physical distance; *further* refers to a greater extent or degree. | *Further* reflection tells us that we should walk *farther*.

8. **Fewer, less:** *Fewer* refers to separate items that can be counted; *less* refers to a quantity that can be measured but not counted. | I like using the "10 items or *fewer*" lane. It takes *less* time than the others.

9. **Good, well:** *Good* is an adjective, never an adverb. *Well* is an adjective that means "healthy," but it is most often used as an adverb. | Carl is a *good* athlete. He eats *well* (adverb) in order to stay *well* (adjective).

10. **Hole, whole:** *Hole* refers to an opening or gap; *whole* refers to completeness. | The *whole* day turned sour when I fell in the *hole*.

Your Turn Review the words on these two pages and choose three pairs that you have trouble keeping straight. For each word pair, write a sentence or two, using the words correctly.

11. **Imply, infer:** *Imply* means "suggest"; *infer* means "deduce."

Writers *imply*. Readers *infer*.

12. **It's, its:** *It's* is the contraction for "it is" or "it has"; *its* is a possessive pronoun.

It's possible that you can replace *its* missing case.

13. **Lay, lie:** *Lay* means "put" or "place" and is transitive (it must have a direct object). Its past tense is *laid*. *Lie* means "recline" or to "speak falsely" and is intransitive (it cannot have a direct object). Its past tense is *lay* (that's where the confusion comes in).

Since you don't feel well, just *lay* your cards on the table and go *lie* down.

Lay Lie

14. **Plain, plane:** *Plain* is a noun meaning "an area of level, treeless ground," or an adjective meaning "ordinary" or "easily understood." *Plane* is a noun meaning "a flat surface," "a tool for making something smooth," or "an airplane." *Plane* is also an adjective meaning "level."

The *plain* truth is that this *plane* cannot land on just any *plain*.

15. **Principal, principle:** *Principal* is a noun meaning "highest-ranking person" or "invested money." *Principal* is also an adjective meaning "primary." The noun *principle* means "guiding rule."

The *principal* of the school promotes the *principle* of respect.

16. **Real, very, really:** *Real* is usually an adjective meaning "authentic." It should not be used in place of the adverbs *very* or *really*.

These monetary gains are *real*, which is *really* encouraging.

17. **Than, then:** *Than* is a conjunction that creates a comparison; *then* is usually an adverb referring to time.

I showed that I was taller *than* my brother. *Then* he slugged me.

18. **To, too, two:** *To* is a preposition that indicates direction and is also the word used to form an infinitive. *Too* is an adverb that means "excessively." *Two* is the number 2.

We went *to* the upscale market *to* buy *two* zucchinis, though they were *too* expensive.

19. **Who's, whose:** *Who's* is the contraction of "who is" or "who has." *Whose* is a possessive pronoun.

Who's in charge here? *Whose* mess is that?

20. **You're, your:** *You're* is the contraction of "you are." *Your* is a possessive pronoun.

You're telling me that's *your* mess?

Mechanics Rules

1. **Capitalize proper nouns:** names of people, organizations, languages, religions, ethnic groups, months, days, trade names, geographical names, etc.	Thursday Asia Jennie Congress Jupiter
2. **In a title, capitalize first, last, and important middle words** (not articles, coordinating conjunctions, short prepositions, or *to* in an infinitive).	*Heart of Darkness* *Of Mice and Men* *Into the Woods*
3. **Form plurals correctly.** Add *s* to most words; *es* to words ending in *ch, s, sh, x,* or *z*; and *s* or *es* to the most important word in compounds. Watch for irregular plurals (child—children; medium—media).	tacks buildings foxes mothers-in-law switches
4. **Use words for numbers under 10.** Usually use numerals for numbers 10 and over. Combine numerals and words for very large numbers.	one seven 19 12 million 35 (thirty-five)
5. **Apply the silent *e* rule.** Keep the final silent *e* when adding a suffix that begins with a consonant. Drop the *e* when adding a suffix that begins with a vowel.	careful caring valueless valuable

Agreement Rules

1. **Subjects and verbs must agree in number.** Singular subjects take singular verbs, and plural subjects take plural verbs.	The stock **car zooms** down the track. The stock **cars zoom** down the track.
2. **Compound subjects joined by *and* are plural.** Two or more subjects joined by *and* take a plural verb.	**Teri and Lisa work** hard. A **file and notes are** ready.
3. **Some compound subjects are joined by *or*.** Match the verb to the last subject.	**The assistants or Lisa writes** the report.

4. **Pronouns must agree with their antecedents in person, number, and gender.**

	Singular			Plural		
	Subject	Object	Possessive	Subject	Object	Possessive
First person	I	me	my	we	us	our, ours
Second person	you	you	your, yours	you	you	your, yours
Third person	he, she, it	him, her, its	his, her, hers, its	they	them	their, theirs

Sentence Rules

1. **A sentence needs a subject and a predicate.** The subject is a noun, pronoun, or word group that functions as a noun. The predicate includes the verb and tells what the subject is doing or being.	**Subject** / *Predicate* **Cats** *play.* **To play** *is the cat's favorite activity.* **Whoever wants to see a funny sight** *should watch my cat play.*
2. **A command has an implied subject,** the pronoun *you.*	(You) Hand in your assignment. (You) Include your name, please.
3. **Questions and other constructions have inverted structure.** This means that the subject comes after the verb.	*Verb* / **Subject** *Are* **you** *participating?* (**You** *are participating.*) Where *is* my **equipment**? (My **equipment** *is* where.) There *are* three **reasons** for my decision. (Three **reasons** . . . *are* there.)
4. **A sentence must express a complete thought.** Subordinate clauses and relative clauses have subjects and verbs, but they do not express complete thoughts. They must be joined to independent clauses to make complete sentences.	**Subordinate clause:** After we clean **Complete sentence:** After we clean, we'll decorate. **Relative clause:** Who are strong **Complete sentence:** We need helpers who are strong to move the furniture.
5. **Compound sentences combine two independent clauses.** The clauses are joined with a semicolon or a coordinating conjunction *(and, but, or, nor, for, so, yet),* and a comma is used before the conjunction.	You can play the piano, **and** I will play the electric guitar. My amplifier is loud, **but** you've got a heavy hand on that keyboard.
6. **Complex sentences combine an independent clause with one or more dependent clauses (subordinate or relative).** Subordinate clauses begin with subordinating conjunctions *(after, because, although),* and relative clauses begin with relative pronouns *(who, which, that).*	*Although* the class hadn't started, my friend was already working. My friend, *who* is planning to be a teacher, is an excellent tutor.

Your Turn Write two simple sentences (rule 1). Combine them into a compound sentence (rule 5). Change one independent clause into a subordinate clause and create a complex sentence (rule 6).

Sentence Error Rules

1. **Fix sentence fragments.** Add whatever part the fragment is missing: the subject, the predicate, or both. If the fragment has a subject and predicate but does not express a complete thought, join the fragment to a complete sentence.

   Needs subject: is hot
   ↳ **The day** is hot.
   Needs predicate: All of us
   ↳ All of us **want to go swimming.**
   Needs both: in the afternoon
   ↳ **We will swim** in the afternoon.
   Not compete: When we swim
   ↳ When we swim, **we use sunscreen.**

2. **Avoid comma splices.** A comma splice combines two sentences with only a comma. To correct this error, add a coordinating conjunction after the comma, change the comma to a semicolon, or separate the independent clauses into two sentences.

   Incorrect: Information rules our lives, we can't live without it.
   Information rules our lives, **and** we can't live without it. (conjunction added)
   Information rules our lives; we can't live without it. (semicolon added)
   Information rules our lives. **We** can't live without it. (two sentences)

3. **Correct run-on sentences.** A run-on sentence combines two sentences without any punctuation or conjunction. (See rule 2 above.)

   Incorrect: Information rules our lives we can't live without it.
   Information rules our lives **because** we can't live without it. (conjunction added)

4. **Split up rambling sentences.** Rambling sentences include too many related ideas in a long sentence. Remove unimportant information and split the remaining pieces into individual sentences.

   Rambling: The Constitution guaranteed that all men are created equal but really meant only that white, landowning, adult males were created equal, which excluded all women and all people of color, which is totally unfair and something that had to be addressed through amendments to the Constitution over two hundred years to extend equality and its rights to all people.
   Corrected: The Constitution guaranteed that all men are created equal but really only meant white, landowning, adult males. Two hundred years of amendments to the Constitution finally extended equality and its rights to all people, including women and people of color.

5. **Use parallel constructions.** Connect items of similar structure when using coordinating conjunctions— all nouns, all adjectives, all phrases, all clauses.

   noun   noun   phrase   phrase
        and   **and**
   clause   clause   by the door in the room
        and   **and**

Writing Glossary

Active voice means that the subject of the sentence is doing the action of the verb.

Analysis writing breaks a subject into parts, explores each part, and shows how they connect.

Appeals are methods for persuading readers, including showing integrity (ethos), creating an argument (logos), and touching emotion (pathos).

Arguments are a series of logical statements that lead toward proving or supporting a specific point.

Audience refers to those who read writing—whether they are the intended or unintended readers.

Brainstorming is the process of rapidly gathering as many ideas as possible.

Cause-effect writing explores why something occurred and the results of its occurrence.

Chronological order is time order—first, next, then, later, and so on.

Citing sources means indicating where ideas in writing have come from.

Classification writing sorts a subject into groups and shows how the groups are distinct and related.

Clauses are groups of words that include a subject and verb; some clauses express a complete thought and can stand alone (independent), but others do not express a complete thought and cannot stand alone (dependent).

Coherence means that ideas "stick together"—they logically belong.

Comparatives show how one thing exceeds another, using *-er, better, worse, more,* or *less* (funnier, older, less spindly).

Compare-contrast writing focuses on two topics, showing how they are similar and how they are different.

Context refers to the situation in which a message is created, transmitted, and received.

Conventions of language are the rules for using words, sentences, and punctuation (grammar, usage, spelling).

Coordination refers to connecting equal ideas using a coordinating conjunction *(and, but, or, nor, for, so, yet).*

Deductive reasoning ensures its conclusion by beginning with a general principle and ending with a specific circumstance.

Definition writing explores the meaning of a term, including denotation, connotation, etymology, usage, synonyms, antonyms, and other such details.

Descriptive writing creates a mental picture of a person, place, or thing.

Design is the seventh trait of writing, referring to the use of headings, white space, lists, colors, and graphics to communicate ideas.

Details support the thesis or topic sentence in writing and should follow a clear order.

Writing Glossary (cont.)

Dialogue refers to the spoken words in narrative writing, usually set off with quotation marks; internal dialogue refers to the unspoken thoughts of a character.

Diary writing is a periodic personal reflection on the events in one's life.

Documentation indicates where ideas in writing have come from: a list of sources of information following a standard style.

Drafting is the step in the writing process in which the writer creates a beginning, middle, and ending, organizing ideas into a first draft.

Editing is fine-tuning a piece of writing, checking for errors in conventions.

Editorializing means expressing a personal opinion; this term is often used to describe bias in an article that is meant to be objective in nature.

Editorials are opinion pieces written by staff writers for newspapers, magazines, and blogs.

Essays are multiparagraph compositions that develop a thesis by using a variety of details.

Expository writing explains a topic or tells how to do something.

Fictional writing tells a story set in a specific place and time, with characters that must overcome some sort of conflict.

Five W's and H are the journalist's questions that focus on the key features of a situation: who, what, where, when, why, and how.

Form refers to the type of writing; for example, *editorial, article, report, proposal, business letter,* or *short story.*

Fragments are groups of words that lack a subject or verb or do not express a complete thought; fragments can't stand alone as sentences.

Freewriting is a prewriting technique that involves writing nonstop for a period of time about a given topic.

Graphic organizers visually represent ideas in the form of a T-bar, a Venn diagram, a time line, and so on; graphic organizers engage thinking during prewriting and aid analysis during reading.

How-to writing provides instructions for accomplishing a task or tells readers how something works.

Ideas, the first trait of writing, share the thesis, main points, and supporting details in a piece.

Idioms are casual expressions that cannot be understood by looking at the individual words (for example, "up in arms" means "upset").

Imperative sentences are commands with an implied subject (you) and a command verb.

Indicative statements express facts or ask questions.

Inductive reasoning begins with specific observations and ends with a general conclusion, or hypothesis, whose truth is not guaranteed.

Interrogative sentences are questions, often in an inverted order (verb before subject).

Intransitive verbs express a complete action without requiring a direct object.

Jargon is technical language used by a specific group but not easily understood by those outside the group.

Journals are personal reflective writing often connected to a specific experience or period in the writer's life.

Learning logs are personal reflective writing focused on what the writer is learning in a course of study.

Logic is using reasoning to examine a topic.

Logical fallacies are mistakes of reasoning that should be avoided in writing and identified in reading.

Medium is the form that communication takes.

Metaphorical thinking searches for connections between two ideas or topics, often through metaphors, similes, or symbolism.

Multimedia refers to a presentation that incorporates words, images, video, audio, and other forms of media.

Narration is writing that tells a story, whether real or imagined.

Nonfiction is writing that focuses on facts and true-life experiences.

Objections are disagreements that readers may have with a writer's position.

Objective writing shares information without adding personal feelings or opinions.

Opinion is a personally held belief that cannot be directly proven to be true but can be supported by evidence.

Opinion or position statements express an opinion in persuasive writing.

Organization refers to the overall structure (beginning, middle, ending) of writing as well as the arrangement of details by a pattern such as time order.

Outlines list the thesis, main points, and key support for a piece of writing.

Paragraphs are groups of sentences that relate to a single topic.

Parallel structure is using the same grammatical form for ideas that are connected with coordinating conjunctions.

Paraphrasing means expressing another's idea in one's own words.

Passive voice occurs when the subject of the sentence receives the action of the verb instead of doing the action of the verb.

Person indicates whether someone is speaking (first person—I, me), is spoken to (second person—you), or is spoken about (third person—he, she, they).

Personification is giving human traits to nonhuman things.

Persuasive writing supports an opinion in order to convince readers or call them to act.

Phrases are groups of words that function together as a part of speech (for example, prepositional phrases function as adjectives or adverbs).

Point of view is a writer's position; or, in fiction, **point of view** refers to who is telling the story, either a character within the tale (first person) or someone outside of it (third person).

Portfolios are collections of a writer's work over a period of time, often accompanied by reflection and analysis.

Writing Glossary (cont.)

Possessive words indicate ownership.

Predicate is the part of the sentence that contains the verb and tells what the subject is doing or being.

Prewriting refers to the thinking and research that a writer does prior to drafting.

Primary sources provide a researcher with first-hand information; for example, experiments, surveys, interviews, or events.

Problem-solution writing explains a problem and then advocates for a solution to fix the problem.

Process writing tells how to do something or explains how something works.

Proofreading means carefully checking a final draft for conventional errors.

Publishing is the process of making ideas public.

Purpose is the reason for writing; for example, to inform, persuade, entertain, or reflect.

Questions are sentences that request information.

Quotations are someone's exact words.

Reasoning is the use of logic to connect statements and arrive at a true conclusion.

References are sources used to create a piece of writing, often presented in a list.

Reflective writing looks back at an experience and thinks about its significance.

Reports provide detailed information about a topic.

Research is finding information and tracking sources of information.

Response to literature is writing that reflects on a work of literature.

Revising is making large-scale improvements to writing, focusing on ideas, organization, and voice.

Rhetoric is the use of language to persuade.

Rhetorical devices are special uses of language to make a point; for example, metaphor, understatement, or irony.

Rhetorical situation, or the communication situation, refers to the source, message, medium, receiver, and context.

Rubrics list goals and are used to score sets of desired traits.

Secondary sources provide secondhand information; for example, articles, books, or documentaries.

Semantics is the study of meaning.

Sentences are groups of words that include a subject and a verb and express a complete thought.

Series refers to a set of three or more items connected with commas or the conjunctions *and* or *or.*

Similes compare two things using *like* or *as.*

Source refers to the origin of information.

Story is a narrative with a specific setting, characters, and conflict, leading to a climactic situation.

Storyboards use graphic frames to plan an audio-visual presentation.

Style refers to a writer's individual way of writing.

Subject is the general topic for a piece of writing; or, in a sentence, the **subject** is the noun, pronoun, or noun form that names the topic.

Subjective writing shares information with personal feelings or opinions.

Subordination uses subordinating conjunctions (though, unless, because) to show that one idea depends upon another.

Superlatives compare one thing to two or more others, using *–est, best, worst, most,* or *least.*

Support is the details used to develop and explore a thesis.

Syntax is the way in which words are put together into sentences.

Synthesis is combining two or more things to make something new.

Tables present information in rows and columns.

Tense refers to the time (past, present, or future) of a verb's action.

Thesis refers to the specific main point of a piece of writing, indicating the topic and particular emphasis.

Thesis statements provide the main point in essays.

Titles name pieces of writing.

Tone refers to the writer's attitude toward the topic; for example, serious, whimsical, or annoyed.

Topic is the specific subject of a piece of writing.

Traits refer to the seven qualities of writing—ideas, organization, voice, words, sentences, conventions, and design.

Transitions are words or phrases that connect ideas in writing.

Transitive verbs require a direct object to express a complete action.

Unity occurs when all the ideas in a piece of writing relate to the topic and follow a logical order.

Usage refers to selecting the correct word from a pair of commonly misused words.

Verbs are words that express action or state of being.

Voice is a trait of writing that reflects the writer's personal interest in the topic/communication situation.

Word choice is a trait of writing that focuses on selecting the best words for a particular purpose.

Writing process refers to the series of steps that writers go through in order to go from the blank page/screen to a finished document.

Writing-to-Learn Activities

Read and Write

The graphic organizers on pages 182-183 can help you analyze others' writing as well as gather details for your own. This activity gives you practice in both uses.

Your Turn Think about the reading that you do for a particular class. From the list below, choose the type of material you are assigned. Use the suggested graphic organizer to analyze the reading.

> **Story:** Sensory Chart (page 183)
> **History:** Time Line (page 183) or Cause-Effect Chart (page 182)
> **Explanation:** Branching Diagram (page 182) or Cycle Diagram (page 182)
> **Report:** 5 W's Chart (page 183) or Cause-Effect Chart (page 182)
> **Editorial:** T-Bar Problem-Solution (page 183) or Pro-Con Chart (page 183)
> **Instructions:** Time Line (page 183)
> **Comparison:** Venn Diagram (page 183) or T-Bar Comparison-Contrast (page 183)

Now use the same type of graphic organizer to gather details for your own writing. Create a piece of writing in the style you read and analyzed above.

Processing Your Writing

Writing is a process that moves through a set of steps to reach a final product. The following activity will help you explore your own writing process.

Your Turn Pick out the most useful instruction/suggestion given for each of the following steps:

1. **Prewriting** (page 187)
2. **Drafting** (page 188)
3. **Revising** (page 189)
4. **Editing** (page 190)

Write one sentence for each idea, telling how you will use it to improve your writing.

Following Conventions

Conventions ensure the correctness of your writing. The following activity will help you improve your use of conventions.

Your Turn Pick out the rule you most need to practice in each of the following areas:

1. **Punctuation** (page 191)
2. **Usage** (pages 192-193)
3. **Mechanics** (page 194)
4. **Agreement** (page 194)
5. **Sentences** (pages 195-196)

Chapter 13
Taking Exit and Entrance Exams

A test is like a door. When you learn how to unlock it, you can pass through, heading into an ever widening world of knowledge and opportunity.

This chapter readies you for high school exit and college entrance exams. It reviews ways to prepare and explains the kinds of questions and writing tasks these tests contain. Besides keeping up with your daily schoolwork, using the insights in this chapter will help you to succeed on these tests . . . and be on your way.

You will learn . . .

- Preparing for Exams
- Understanding Question Types
- Answering Objective Questions
- Answering Comprehension Questions
- Answering Revision Questions
- Writing on Demand
- Responding to Documents

Preparing for Exams

Despite what you might think, cramming is the worst way to prepare for an exam. You can't cram a semester of learning into one evening of study. It leaves you exhausted and distressed. Worse, it forces information into short-term memory, where it will soon vanish. To succeed on exams and learn for the long term, follow these tips:

Keys to Exam Preparation

- **Keep up with your daily work.** Do the readings, complete the assignments, and focus your efforts on grasping the information. If you learn the material day by day, you will be better prepared to take an exam, whenever it comes.

- **Know the exam.** Find out what the test will cover, what kinds of questions you will face, how much time you will have, and how best to prepare.

- **Use multimodal study forms.** Read, then write, then discuss, then reflect. View visuals and videos. Conduct experiments. Participate in class projects. Get your senses involved to make the information vivid and memorable.

- **Study in different places.** If you study only at the kitchen table or at a desk in your room, you are telling your brain that the information is specific to one location. If you study in different locations, your brain will categorize the material as something that is needed in many places, including the test location.

- **Interweave topics.** Don't study one subject solidly for hours at a time. Doing so fails to create deep connections in your brain. Instead, study one subject for a while, and then shift to another subject. Interweaving subjects keeps your brain fresh, helps you form connections across disciplines, and teaches your brain that the information is needed in multiple contexts.

- **Study at different times.** Instead of cramming for four hours on the night before a big test, study for one hour a week for each week before the test. You're spending the same amount of time, but by spacing out your study, you train your brain to put the information into your long-term memory.

- **Get a good night's sleep before the exam.** Your brain works best when it is rested. Staying up all night to study makes you less sharp and less capable.

- **Eat breakfast.** Your brain needs glucose in order to function well, so going into an exam hungry limits your ability to think. Eat well, without stuffing yourself, which will make you sleepy and sluggish.

- **Calm yourself.** Panic is not your friend. Take deep breaths (but don't hyperventilate). Remind yourself that this is just an exam, and life is much bigger than exams.

- **Move, if you can, during the exam.** Stretch occasionally. Pivot and flex. Movement gets your blood flowing. Your brain needs 20 percent of the oxygen supply in your blood to function optimally.

Understanding Question Types

You use a ruler to measure the length of something, a thermometer to measure its temperature, a scale to measure its weight, and so on. An exam is also a measurement tool, designed to measure your knowledge and thinking in specific ways. The types of questions on an exam target different types of thinking. Here are the typical question types:

Question Types

Objective questions—multiple choice, true/false, fill in the blank, or matching—have specific correct answers. Exams that feature these types of questions often have you provide answers on a bubble sheet—a page with letters in circles that you need to darken.

16. What is ¼ of ¼?
    Ⓐ 1
    Ⓑ 1/2
    Ⓒ 1/8
    Ⓓ 1/16
    Ⓔ 1/32

Short-answer questions ask you to complete a sentence, write a sentence or two of your own, or supply a short answer. These questions may require a specific correct answer or ask you to reflect on your own experience.

32. Name the three multicellular life-form kingdoms.

    ＿Animalia, Plantae, Fungi＿＿＿＿＿

Essay questions require you to share your thoughts or knowledge about a specific topic, asking you to state a thesis and support it with details. You may be prompted to provide information, argue for a point, reflect on an idea, compare two concepts, tell about an experience, or respond to a piece of literature.

Writing Prompt

Think of a career that you would like to pursue. What qualities do you possess that make you well suited to this career? Where might you go for an intern experience? Write a letter to a business owner, convincing the person to offer you an internship.

Your Turn Reflect on the question types listed above. Which type do you prefer? Why? Which is your least favorite? Why? Now page forward in this chapter and look for a strategy that could help you improve your performance on the type of question that is most difficult for you.

Answering Objective Questions

Objective questions—multiple choice, true/false, fill in the blank, or matching—have specific correct answers. Read carefully to select the correct answer.

Multiple Choice

Multiple-choice questions start with a question or command and provide a number of optional answers. Read the entire question before selecting an answer, and follow these tips:

Comply with special instructions such as "select all" or "choose the best" when you make your answer.	32. Select all irrational numbers. (A) 3/4 (C) π (B) $\sqrt{2}$ (D) −6
Consider multiple answers such as "Both A and B" or "All of these" instead of automatically choosing just one.	21. Which calculation results in 12? (A) 15 − (+3) (C) 17 + −5 (B) 27 + −15 (D) All of these
Note negations such as "not" or "except," which can make the question mean the opposite of what you expect.	25. What number below is not rational? (A) 05 (C) π (B) 0.001 (D) 1.5
Move past distractor answers to find the correct response.	16. What is $\sqrt{-4}$? (A) −2 (C) −8 (B) 2 (D) None of these

True or False

True/false questions provide a statement that is either true or false. Carefully read the statement and follow these tips:

Beware words such as "all," "always," "none," and "never," which make a statement absolute and often false.	41. All fundamental particles have mass. True or False?
Carefully consider negatives such as "not," "except," or "without" to make sure you understand the statement's meaning.	22. Photons and gluons are particles without mass. True or False?

Your Turn Study a recent test that you took. Search for examples of negations, absolute words, and distractor answers. Did you answer these trickier questions correctly? Which reminders on this page will prove most helpful to you on future tests?

Fill in the Blank

Fill-in-the-blank questions provide sentences with blanks for missing words. You must provide the word or words that the test designer anticipates. As always, read carefully and follow these tips:

If "a" precedes a blank, write a singular word starting with a consonant sound. **If "an" precedes a blank,** write a singular word with a vowel sound.	16. To demand that a prisoner be released from unlawful detention, a lawyer can file a _writ of habeas corpus_ .
Use singular or plural words in the rest of the sentence to decide if the missing word is singular or plural.	54. The rights that are read to a person being arrested are called the _Miranda rights_ .
Write a response in each blank when multiple blanks are provided.	37. Lincoln pledged that "government _of the people_ , _by the people_ , and _for the people_ shall not perish from the earth."

Matching

Matching questions require you to match items in one column with items in another. Often, one column will contain words and the other column definitions or examples. Read both columns completely before matching any items. Then start with the column that holds the longer phrases (definitions or examples), and work to match those to the shorter terms in the other column. Follow these tips:

Deal with similar items with subtle differences at the same time to better ensure correct matches.	1. _c_ Thrombocytes 2. _b_ Leucocytes 3. _a_ Erythrocytes	**a.** Red blood cells **b.** White blood cells **c.** Platelets
Leave confusing items until the end, when a process of elimination can help in finding the correct match.	1. _b_ Smooth 2. _c_ Skeletal 3. _a_ Cardiac	**a.** heart muscle **b.** involuntary muscle **c.** voluntary muscle

Your Turn List unfamiliar terms from a class and use them to create test questions:

1. Create a set of fill-in the blank questions, focusing on the terms.
2. Create a matching exercise with terms and scrambled definitions.

Ask a classmate to complete the activities, and keep a copy of your "quiz" as a study aid for a unit exam.

Answering Comprehension Questions

Some tests present you with a reading selection and then ask you to answer questions about it. Often, these tests measure reading comprehension and the ability to draw inferences. Follow these tips to score well on reading-comprehension questions:

▶ **Think about time.** Read with pacing and focus—not so fast that you must do a lot of rereading, but not so slow that you can't get through the material.

▶ **Underline key points if possible.** If you can't write on the page, jot quick notes on another piece of paper.

▶ **At the end of each paragraph, mentally recap the point of the paragraph.**

▶ **In each question, look for references to paragraphs or lines.** If a question says, "In the second paragraph" or "in line 15," go to that spot to find your answer.

▶ **In multiple-choice questions, look for answers that paraphrase the text.** Often such answers are correct.

▶ **Eliminate obviously incorrect answers.** Then focus on the possible answers and seek evidence from the text to choose the best one.

▶ **Recognize the question types:**

- **Main-point questions** ask you to identify the main point. Consider the answers, and then check the first and last paragraphs to find the point.

- **Vocabulary questions** ask about the meaning of specific words. Find the word in the text and use context clues to guess the meaning. (See page 161.) Replace the word with answers to see which makes the most sense. Remember that a strict dictionary definition of the term may not match the way the term is being used in the reading example.

- **Evidence questions** ask you to find facts, statistics, examples, quotations, or other details that support a specific point. Return to the part of the reading that made that point and find the evidence used.

- **Inference questions** ask you to draw conclusions based on evidence. If you are asked to infer, do not select answers that are literally expressed. Instead, select those that are unstated in the reading but are supported by evidence.

- **Style questions** ask you about the specific way that the author expresses ideas. Think about the communication situation, with the writer as the sender of the message. What features of language give you clues as to who the writer is and what attitudes the writer has toward all aspects of the communication situation?

Your Turn Use the tips above as you carefully read the article excerpt at the top of the facing page and answer the reading-comprehension questions about it. (Check your answers by going to thoughtfullearning.com/h208.)

Our Dog-Help-Dog World

1   Some people see nature as all hungry mouths—a dog-eat-dog world driven by fierce competition for scarce resources. That's not the whole story, though. In fact, the most successful life forms place a premium on collaboration.

     Each cell in our bodies has two distinct types of DNA—nuclear and
5   mitochondrial. That's because the mitochondria in our cells are basically energy-generating bacteria that collaborate with the larger cell for mutual benefit. At the cellular level, each of us is a collaboration. And collaborative cells (eukaryotes) out-compete cells that work alone (prokaryotes).

     The trick of collaboration also works between cells. Some of the simplest
10   multicellular life forms are basically just tubes set up to bring food in one end and send waste out the other. By working together, individual cells benefit, and the collaborative as a whole out-competes cells that go solo.

     Higher organisms introduce a form of collaboration called specialization. A single fertilized egg divides and divides and divides, and the resultant cells take
15   on specific jobs to benefit the whole. They become the cells that make up hearts, lungs, brains, kidneys, and so on. Each of us is a collaboration of trillions of cells.

1. In line 1, what does the writer mean by "Some people see nature as all hungry mouths"?

    a. Domestic animals are fed by humans, but wild animals are naturally hungry.

    b. Some people see animals as a source of food.

    c. Some people assume that competition for food drives nature.

2. In the second paragraph, which type of cells are collaborations?

    a. Eukaryotes

    b. Prokaryotes

    c. Mitochondria

    d. Bacteria

3. In line 9, the word "trick" is best replaced by which word?

    a. magic

    b. strategy

    c. cheating

    d. equipment

4. All of the following answers except ____ could be inferred from the fourth paragraph.

    a. Specialization allows cells to collaborate by taking on different jobs.

    b. Highly successful people have more cells than people who are less successful.

    c. Specialized cells cannot survive without other cells that do other jobs.

Answering Revision Questions

Other reading tests ask you to find problems in a piece of writing and select the most effective revisions. Once again, you must carefully read the selection, noting any confusing or rough spots. Follow these tips:

▶ **Plan your time.** Read the passage before trying to answer questions. You need to understand the topic, focus, and purpose of the piece to select the best revisions.

▶ **Underline problem spots.** In your first read through, make note of any problems you find so that you will be aware of some of the issues before you are asked about them.

▶ **Read each question and watch for text references.** If the question directs you to the second paragraph or the sixth sentence, go to that spot to search for the problem that is mentioned. (You may have already underlined it.)

▶ **Imagine how you would fix the problem.** By first considering your own revision strategies, you'll be better equipped to select the right revision strategy from among those offered.

▶ **Read the multiple-choice answers and seek the best response.** Remember that sometimes more than one answer will be correct, and you will need to select "All are correct" or "Both a and b are correct."

▶ **If you are stumped by a question, write a question mark by it and move on.** Once you finish the other questions, you can return to any question marks. Sometimes after answering other questions, your brain will have worked out a solution to an earlier problem.

▶ **Recognize the different types of revision questions:**

■ **Error-identification questions** ask you to indicate which sentence has a specific type of error, or what type of error exists in a specific sentence.

■ **Error-correction questions** require you to select the best strategy or option for correcting an error or revising a sentence.

■ **Sentence-combining questions** require you to join two related sentences into one by choosing the best option for combining the ideas.

■ **Sentence-addition questions** require you to add a sentence to the existing material—often a thesis statement, topic sentence, or concluding sentence—by selecting from a set of options.

Your Turn Use the tips above as you carefully read the article excerpt at the top of the facing page and answer the revision questions about it. (Check your answers by going to thoughtfullearning.com/h210.)

Pathways to Learning

(1) In brain science, connections rule. (2) A thought that has a single neural pathway is an ephemeral idea it will flit away and be gone forever. (3) A thought that has multiple neural pathways has real staying power. (4) But how can we develop these complex neural pathways?

(5) One simple method is to start the neural pathways in different locations. (6) For example, when you read, a thought enters your brain through your eyes, which route the thought to the occipital lobe of your brain. (7) The impulse then shoots to the temporal lobe, which deciphers language, before going to the frontal lobe for logical analysis. (8) That's one path. (9) Then you can speak the idea aloud in your own words, and the path starts in the temporal lobe to formulate language and then shoots through the cerebellum, which controls the motor neurons that make your mouth form words, and then propagates through air to enter your ears, where it is decoded again and makes its way back to the logic centers of your brain. (10) That's another path.

(11) So by engaging an idea in multiple ways reading, speaking, listening, writing, thinking, reflecting, moving you trace many pathways through your brain and create a deep connection.

1. How can the run-on sentence in the first paragraph be fixed?
   a. It can be split into two separate sentences.
   b. It can be fixed with a comma and a coordinating conjunction.
   c. It can be fixed with a semicolon.
   d. The word "it" can become "that."
   e. All are correct ways to fix the run-on.

2. In the second paragraph, which is a rambling sentence?
   a. Sentence 6
   b. Sentence 7
   c. Sentence 8
   d. Sentence 9
   e. Sentence 10

3. How can you fix a rambling sentence?
   a. Connect it to other sentences.
   b. Break it into shorter sentences.
   c. Delete parts that aren't on topic.
   d. Both b and c
   e. None of these

4. In sentence 11, the words "reading, speaking, listening, writing, thinking, reflecting, moving" should be set off from the rest of the sentence. What punctuation mark should be used before and after this series?
   a. comma
   b. dash
   c. semicolon
   d. quotation mark

Writing on Demand

Often, exit and entrance exams include an on-demand writing component. Its purpose is to assess both your writing and thinking ability. This kind of writing task usually begins with a prompt that you must analyze and then respond to.

Analyzing Prompts

A writing prompt provides the writing situation. You can analyze a prompt by answering the **STRAP** questions.

> **Subject:** What should I write about? (Topic? Focus?)
> **Type:** What form should my writing take? (Essay? Letter? Editorial?)
> **Role:** What role do I have as writer? (Student? Citizen? College applicant?)
> **Audience:** Who will read my response? (Tester? Classmates? Administrators?)
> **Purpose:** What should this writing do? (Inform? Persuade? Reflect?)

Read the prompt carefully, watching for key words that answer the STRAP questions. Note that you will sometimes need to infer answers if a prompt does not address all five points.

Example Prompt and Analysis

A strong education may be the greatest single possession that a person can own. What makes a strong education so valuable? Is it more important than all other possessions? As a college applicant, write an essay that evaluates the importance of education and compares it to the other possessions you have.

> **Subject:** The value of a strong education
> **Type:** College entrance essay
> **Role:** College applicant
> **Audience:** College admissions board (implied)
> **Purpose:** To evaluate education's importance and compare it to other possessions

Your Turn Answer the STRAP questions to analyze the following prompt.

Some people believe travel provides the best education. How can travel teach you? How is learning by traveling better than or worse than learning by studying? In an editorial, compare book learning to learning on the road and tell which you as a student prefer and why.

Responding to Prompts

In the allotted time, you need to generate an appropriate response to the prompt, including the following parts:

- ☑ A **beginning** that gets the reader's attention, introduces the topic, and provides the thesis of the response
- ☑ A **middle** that develops the thesis using a variety of details in well-formed paragraphs
- ☑ An **ending** that revisits the thesis and leaves the reader with a strong final thought

Example Prompt and Response (Beginning)

Goals provide you direction. If you have a goal, even when you aren't actively moving toward it, you are passively drifting that direction. How do goals shape your life? What goals do you have? What steps are you taking to reach your goals? In an essay, reflect on the goals you have for the future.

Subject: my goals
Type: essay
Role: high school student
Audience: tester
Purpose: reflect on my goals for the future

The beginning gets the reader's attention and leads to the thesis statement.

Goals usually start small. Young kids aren't thinking as much about their careers as they are about the next recess or slumber party. Sometime in middle school, though, most students realize they've got to start making some plans. In middle school, I decided I wanted to be a veterinarian, a goal that defines me.

My dog Grover began my goal to be a veterinarian. He got a bad cut, and a vet saved his life. Standing in that examination room in seventh grade, I knew I had to become a vet. What I didn't know was how hard it would be. Volunteering at the Humane Society changed my understanding. There I worked with many animals that had been abandoned or neglected. I had to do a lot of cleaning up, but I worked hand in hand with vets. They told me that the hard part was only beginning.

The middle uses paragraphs to cover different main points.

I now understand what I need to do to reach my goal. Vets get their licenses after eight years of schooling. They start by taking a four-year undergraduate degree studying biology, chemistry, physics, nutrition, and animal science. The pre-vet courses are really rigorous, and graduates have to have top grades and connections to be able to move to veterinary schools. Vet school takes four more years, which includes learning to do surgery and run tests. Some vets specialize, but many have to learn to treat anything from a parakeet to a horse. After vet school comes a test, a license, and an internship.

Each paragraph has a topic sentence and supporting sentences.

When I discovered how much work went into becoming a vet, I realized I had to accomplish many short-term goals to reach my long-term goal. In high school, I'm focusing on biology, chemistry, and physics, and I'm targeting my college applications to outstanding undergraduate schools. I'm also consciously developing relationships with veterinarians and asking them for help in shaping my career. Already I have two recommendation letters from vets I've worked closely with. My experiences . . . .

Responding to Documents

Some timed writing exams, such as those for AP English courses, give you a set of documents—literature, poetry, articles, images—and ask you to construct a response. Your response should demonstrate a careful reading of the documents, include evidence drawn from them, and thoughtfully develop an idea. Here is an example literary prompt and response (page 215).

Sample Prompt

Read the following sonnets. The first was written by Oscar Wilde, a great poet. The second was written unintentionally by 14 different Twitter users who happened to tweet lines in iambic pentameter—lines later assembled by a computer program. Both poems seem to contain meaning. Use evidence from these poems to discuss what writers and readers bring to poetry.

Sonnet to Liberty
Oscar Wilde

Not that I love thy children, whose dull eyes
See nothing save their own unlovely woe,
Whose minds know nothing, nothing care to know,
But that the roar of thy Democracies,
Thy reigns of Terror, thy great Anarchies,
Mirror my wildest passions like the sea,—
And give my rage a brother—! Liberty!
For this sake only do thy dissonant cries
Delight my discreet soul, else might all kings
By bloody knout or treacherous cannonades
Rob nations of their rights inviolate
And I remain unmoved—and yet, and yet,
These Christs that die upon the barricades,
God knows it I am with them, in some things.

Sonnet to Twitter
Random tweeters via Milkmoon

I wouldn't mind a holiday again.
It's gonna be a awesome day today :)
Who doesn't love a weekend getaway?
Will Sharma get another over then?

Who watches television nowadays?
If happy ever after did exist
I really wanna make a bucket list :)
I never was a factor anyways.

Does Karlsson ever leave the ice? Unreal.
Tomorrow doesn't equal yesterday
I learned and realized a lot today
I'll rage and roar, whatever for a meal

I feel a separation coming on
Keep looking up c'mon c'mon c'mon

Your Turn Analyze the sample poems above by responding to the following prompt.

Read the sonnets above. The first sonnet refers to the "great Anarchies" of democratic movements as they oppose old tyrannies. The second sonnet embodies these great anarchies because it is constructed from random Twitter tweets. In what ways does the "Sonnet to Twitter" demonstrate the "dissonant cries" that delight Wilde's "discreet soul"? What would Wilde think of the "roar of [Twitter's] Democracies"? Use evidence from the poems to support your points.

Example Response

The following essay discusses what writers and readers bring to the experience of creating poetry.

The beginning provides background information and leads to the thesis.

The great Oscar Wilde wrote "Sonnet to Liberty" to comment on the ravages of populist movements during his time. Fourteen random tweeters (plus a computer program) wrote "Sonnet to Twitter" to comment on nothing at all. The opposite origins of these two poems provide an insight into the roles of writers and readers.

One paragraph closely analyzes the first sonnet.

Oscar Wilde's poem "Sonnet to Liberty" follows the 14-line sonnet form, with lines in iambic pentameter and a prescribed rhyme scheme. These are the first clues that this sonnet is carefully constructed by an author. The sonnet contains two long sentences stretched out over 14 lines. The two main thoughts of this poem find expression line to line through imagery like "dull eyes," word play like "love thy children" and "unlovely woe," and personification such as "give my rage a brother." Wilde creates parallels between the "roar of thy Democracies," the "reigns of Terror," and the "great Anarchies"—violent and "dissonant cries" that delight his soul only because they are better than the "treacherous cannonades" of kings who would "rob nations of their rights inviolate." The language is carefully crafted, and the poet makes his point clear—he would rather put up with the chaos of mass rule than the injustice of tyranny.

Another paragraph closely analyzes the second sonnet.

On the other hand, the randomly generated "Sonnet to Twitter" also follows the 14-line sonnet form, and perhaps the iambic pentameter and regular rhyme scheme trick our minds into believing that it is intentional. Unlike Wilde's poem, "Sonnet to Twitter" contains 13 sentences over 14 lines. Each sentence is the thought of a separate tweeter, except for "If happy ever after did exist / I really wanna make a bucket list :)." What's strange, though, is the way that our brains find similar patterns to those in Wilde's poem: imagery such as "rage and roar, whatever for a meal" and word play like "holiday," "getaway," "bucket list," and "a separation coming on." In fact, the more you read the poem, the more meaning you find. For example, a bucket list includes the things you wish you could do before you die, and the poem's wished-for holiday derives from the anguish that "happy ever after" doesn't exist. Then the reader remembers that this poem didn't have a single writer—but fourteen. The meaning within each line is intended, but the meaning across lines is completely inferred by the reader.

This paragraph draws inferences based on the textual evidence above.

We're used to believing that poets bring a world of meaning to their poems. "Sonnet to Liberty" demonstrates that fact. But "Sonnet to Twitter" demonstrates that readers bring their own world of meaning to a poem. Readers show up with everything they know and draw upon it to decode poems and discover meanings. A metaphor that resonates in one way for the poet may resonate in a completely different way for the reader. In fact, words never intended to be associated may create a profound pattern in the mind of a reader.

The ending provides the reader with a final thought.

In the end, a poem is a meeting place. The poet brings his or her world to that meeting, but so does the reader. One works to encode meaning, and the other to decode it. The poem's power isn't that the reader gets the same meaning as the poet, but that their minds meet for a discussion of ideas.

Exit-and-Entrance-Exam Activities

Rate Your Study Skills

Strong study skills will make you a strong student. Use the following activity to rate your study skills.

Your Turn Indicate the strength of your study habits by rating each item below. Then choose your two lowest scores and write down a strategy for improving each of those areas.

	Never		Sometimes		Always
1. I keep up with my class work.	1	2	3	4	5
2. I learn about the exam ahead of time.	1	2	3	4	5
3. I use many different senses when studying.	1	2	3	4	5
4. I study in different places.	1	2	3	4	5
5. I interweave topics when I study.	1	2	3	4	5
6. I study at different times.	1	2	3	4	5
7. I avoid cramming.	1	2	3	4	5
8. I am fed, rested, and calm before exams.	1	2	3	4	5

Know the Exam

Understanding what is expected of you on a given exam, before you take it, can improve your test performance. This activity will help.

Your Turn Answer these questions about an upcoming exam:

1. What subject(s) will be tested?
2. What abilities will be tested?
3. What types of questions will be included?
4. How many questions will be on the test?
5. How much time will you have to complete it?

Questioning Questions

Knowing strategies for handling different types of questions will help you perform well on tests. The following activity will help.

Your Turn Complete these tasks:

1. Write a tip for each question type: multiple choice, true/false, fill in the blank, matching.
2. Answer STRAP questions to analyze the first writing prompt on page 214.
3. Search online for practice SAT and ACT tests and complete them.

Chapter 14
Developing Visual Literacy

We are living in a culture awash in images, graphics, and videos. These visuals are not just for decoration or entertainment. Rather, they are powerful communication tools that carry both meaning and emotional intent. The most effective visuals present complex information in a form that is easy to understand.

This chapter can help you navigate the flood of visual messages you encounter daily. You'll find many tips and techniques for developing visual literacy, including how to communicate visually and how to analyze images critically.

You will learn . . .

- Introduction to Visual Literacy
- Viewing Actively
- Understanding the Elements of Visual Art
- Understanding the Principles of Design
- A Closer Look at Colors
- Understanding Symbols
- Understanding Page Design
- Understanding Information Graphics

Introduction to Visual Literacy

How powerful are images? Ninety percent of the information you take in from the world around you is visual rather than textual. Images express information and emotion all at once. In fact, studies indicate humans process visual information sixty thousand times faster than text. You can see how images often speak to us in more influential ways than words, and why understanding the language of visual information is important.

What Is Visual Literacy?

Visual literacy is the ability to understand and produce visual messages—to interpret images and graphic elements and use them to communicate more effectively. Today's digital tools and advanced technology make it easier than ever to represent information and ideas visually (see the "time-lapse" panorama below). Such tools also make it possible to alter reality in potentially persuasive ways. What you see is not always what you get, so developing a keen sense for visual manipulation can help you distinguish fact from fiction and reality from fantasy.

> "Visual images have the power to bring our senses together simultaneously and to impact our emotions."
>
> —Brian Kennedy, director of the Hood Museum of Art at Dartmouth College

Your Turn

1. What do you notice about the photo above? How would you describe it to a friend? What conclusions can you make from viewing the photograph? Discuss your answers with a classmate.

2. Compared to reading and writing, how much of your education has been devoted to visual literacy? Why do you think this is so? Write a paragraph that shares your answers to these questions.

3. Have you ever seen a photograph or image that was clearly distorted? What was the subject of the photograph? How could you tell it was distorted? Discuss your answer with a classmate.

Viewing Actively

The path toward visual literacy starts with active viewing. Active viewing involves understanding, interpreting, and evaluating what you see. Just as you can read and discern the meaning of a text, you can "read" and decode the meaning of a visual. The process for "reading" visual images is outlined below.

Understanding What You See

Before you can derive meaning from an image, you must understand it. Understanding involves a process of observation, inspection, description, questioning, relating, and interpreting. Each step will help you think more critically about what you are viewing.

1. Observe

   Observe the image as a whole. Where are your eyes drawn? What is the focus of the image? How does it make you feel?

2. Inspect

   Inspect all parts of the image. Look for any symbols, body language, lighting, or other clues about the meaning.

3. Describe

   Describe what you see by writing or speaking about it. Imagine describing the image to a friend at a party.

4. Question

   Question the image. Who made it? When was it made? What does it show? Where did it come from? Why was it placed here? What confuses you about it?

5. Relate

   Relate the image to what you already know—your life experiences and prior knowledge. Also consider any surrounding text or images.

6. Interpret

   Interpret the image's meaning. What is it meant to do, say, or show? (See page 220 for more on interpreting images.)

Your Turn Follow the first five steps explained on this page to decode the meaning of the image above. Afterward, summarize what you understand so far about the image.

Interpreting What You See

When you interpret an image, you attempt to explain its meaning. Although the creator of the image (the photographer, painter, graphic artist, and so on) may intend to communicate a certain meaning to the viewer, most images are open to various interpretations.

How can I make sense of an image?

Several factors influence the way you interpret a visual—some relate to how the image is delivered, and others are based on the personal perceptions you bring to the task (see "Perception Cloud" below). As you interpret an image, also remember to consider the elements of the communication situation (see page 68).

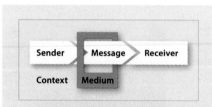

- **Sender:** Who created the image?

- **Message:** What is the subject of the image? How is the subject portrayed?

- **Medium:** What type of image is it (a painting, graphic, sculpture, photograph, and so on)?

- **Receiver:** Who is able to view this image?

- **Context:** How are you viewing this image (in person, in a magazine, on a Web site)? How might a different person interpret this image?

Perception Cloud

Our individuality, upbringing, and knowledge base filter our perception of visual messages. Your perception of an image may be different from someone else's based on your unique traits.

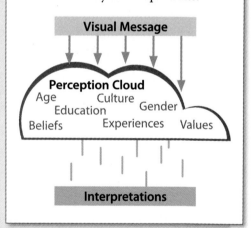

Your Turn

1. How many ways can you interpret the image on the previous page? Consider the image in the context of the communication situation and come to a final conclusion about it. Write a paragraph about your conclusions and share it with a classmate.

2. Imagine that you are someone else. Write down a different age, gender, culture, and education level from what you currently have. Now, with your new identity, interpret the image on the previous page. Summarize how this interpretation differs from your first interpretation of the visual.

Evaluating What You See

After you interpret the meaning of a photo or image in news media, you can assess its quality, truth, and value. The questions below will help you to make an educated judgment of any image's effectiveness.

Quality

Quality refers to an image's visual appeal and effectiveness.

Assess quality by asking these questions:

- ☑ Does the image clearly portray its intended subject?
- ☑ Is it visually appealing?
- ☑ Does it look professional?
- ☑ Is it memorable?
- ☑ Does the image achieve its intended purpose?

Truth

Truth measures the accuracy of an image's communication. Today's advanced image-editing software makes it possible to dramatically improve the quality of images, making them clearer and more visually appealing. However, those same tools can be used to distort reality or misrepresent the subject of the image.

Assess truth by asking these questions:

- ☑ Does the image look real?
- ☑ Is the lighting consistent?
- ☑ Does it represent factual information?
- ☑ Does it convey information without distortion?

Tip: You can critically view the photos of people featured in advertisements and magazines by looking for inconsistent lighting. Pay special attention to lighting around facial features. Inconsistent lighting is a common indicator of image alteration.

Value

Value measures an image's worth.

Assess value by asking these questions:

- ☑ Does the image say something important?
- ☑ Is it worth viewing?
- ☑ Does it appeal to me?

Your Turn

1. Choose an image from your favorite magazine and assess it for quality, truth, and value. Compare your evaluation to a classmate's and discuss.

2. Imagine that you needed to create a poster about yourself (see pages 530-531). Choose a favorite image to use. How would you want to alter the image to make a stronger point? What changes would you make, and how would they affect the quality, truth, and value of the visual?

Understanding the Elements of Visual Art

Developing an understanding of the elements of visual art will provide you with the vocabulary for analyzing and discussing images and graphics. Common elements of visual art are discussed here:

1. **Lines** create boundaries and influence meaning. Soft lines create a dreamlike effect and may indicate elegance and beauty. Sharp, heavy lines stand out and may create tension.

2. **Shapes** enclose two-dimensional spaces. They may be geometrical, like a circle or a square, or free flowing and irregular, like a leaf or a seashell.

3. **Value** in relation to visual art is the relative lightness and darkness of a visual. The contrast between light and dark creates meaning. Lighter images tend to appear closer to the viewer, while darker images appear farther away.

4. **Colors** work together in special ways to describe an object, convey emotion, and symbolize meaning. (See page 224 for a closer look at colors.)

5. **Space** creates depth and perspective. It includes the background, the middle ground, and the foreground.

6. **Texture** refers to the quality of a surface and appeals to our sense of touch. Texture may be real or implied.

Your Turn Find a painting or an illustration that interests you. In a paragraph, analyze the image's elements, which are discussed above.

Understanding the Principles of Design

The basic elements of visual art (line, color, texture, and so on) are mixed, like ingredients, into an image. However, drawing a line or creating space won't necessarily produce effective art. The elements must be arranged in a way that achieves the intended impact on the viewer. Thoughtful application of design principles produces an effective image. The principles include the following:

1. **Proportion** and **scale** relate to the size of elements in a visual. *Proportion* refers to the size relationship of one element to another and to the piece as a whole. The picture to the right compares the size of people to the size of the Gateway Arch. *Scale* refers to the size of an object in comparison to what is expected. The statue in the Lincoln Memorial depicts the president on a very large scale.

2. **Unity** is the principle of making the different elements of a visual function together to form a complete whole. Unity can be achieved through *contrast, alignment, repetition,* and *proximity.*

3. **Balance** refers to the visual weight and distribution of elements. When an image is balanced, its parts complement each other. An off-balance visual can create an uncomfortable effect, but one with symmetrical balance can feel static and uninteresting.

4. **Direction** refers to the visual flow of the composition—how the viewer's eye moves through the piece. Directional movement can be real or implied. Real direction is literal movement. Implied direction is when non-moving art uses visual techniques to suggest movement.

5. **Emphasis (focal point)** is the area of a composition that first attracts the viewer's attention, indicating importance.

6. **Contrast** is the juxtaposition of two elements in an image. Contrast can be created using colors, fonts, objects, or images.

Your Turn How does the painting *Ballet Rehearsal* by Edgar Degas (above) reflect the principles of design? Write your analysis, making sure you cover each principle.

A Closer Look at Colors

While you may know the colors of the rainbow—red, orange, yellow, green, blue, indigo, and violet—you may not have considered how the colors are related. The following color wheel illustrates this relationship.

Primary colors are red, yellow, and blue (in paint or other pigment). They are not a combination of other colors. (In light, the primary colors are red, green, and blue.)

Secondary colors are orange, green, and violet. They are a combination of the two primary colors next to them on the color wheel.

Tertiary colors are the many shades of brown and tan, a combination of three or more colors on the wheel. For that reason, realistic skin tones are difficult to produce on an artist's palette.

Complementary colors, such as red and green or blue and orange, appear opposite each other on the color wheel. The complementary color of a primary color is the combination of the other two primary colors. When complementary colors are next to each other, they create energy and intensity.

Related colors, such as red and violet or orange and yellow, appear close to each other on the color wheel. They tend to blend with each other, creating a sense of harmony.

Hot colors are red, orange, yellow, and any shades closely connected with them. They are bright, eye-catching colors that create energy.

Cool colors are green, blue, and violet. They are soothing and calming.

Your Turn Imagine that you have been given the assignment of choosing colors for the walls and furniture in the following locations. Choose three or four colors you would use in each setting and explain why:

1. a doctor's waiting room
2. a rock band's rehearsal space
3. the dining room in a fast-food restaurant

Understanding Symbols

From the time of Stone Age cave paintings to the present, symbols have served as a powerful means of communication. Symbols bring a lot to mind. They can represent ideas and beliefs; give commands and warnings; sell products and ideas; evoke thoughts and feelings. Visual symbols are all around us, and we are constantly interacting with and interpreting them.

Reading Symbols

Like reading words, you must "read" symbols in order to derive their meaning, both denotative and connotative. Denotative meaning is the more immediate surface meaning. For example, the American flag uses 50 stars to represent the 50 states and 13 stripes to represent the 13 original colonies.

But symbols also hold connotative, or secondary, meaning. This meaning stems from the personal associations you may have with a symbol, based on your unique experience, beliefs, and culture. For some people, the American flag may evoke thoughts of freedom, democracy, patriotism, and opportunity—ideas connotative of their particular experience.

When you encounter symbols, ask these questions:

- What does the symbol look like as a whole?
- What are the symbol's individual parts?
- What is the symbol's literal meaning? What does it represent?
- Does the symbol command you to do something? If so, what?
- How does the symbol make you feel?
- What other ideas do you associate with this symbol?
- How might someone with a different experience than yours "read" this symbol?

Your Turn Which of the symbols shown above are familiar to you? List their denotative meanings. Then choose one of the above symbols (or some other symbol) and analyze it by asking the questions given on this page. Report your findings in a paragraph or short essay.

Understanding Page Design

Effective design manages visual elements to clarify and enhance the message of the page rather than distract from it.

Page Design Elements

An effective combination of print, graphics, and white space will result in an inviting, balanced page design. The following graphic elements are often employed.

- **Bulleted or numbered lists** break up long sections of text. When the sequence of items is important, use numbered lists. Otherwise, use bullets. Lists also create **white space**, which can enhance the readability of a page.
- **Headings** introduce new concepts. Headings used for similar levels of content should be consistent in type style and size.
- **Tables and charts** display information; **graphs** represent data visually (see pages 228-231).
- **Photos and artwork** visually portray ideas on the page, while **diagrams** (see page 234) show the arrangement and relation of parts.

Typography

Type size and style affects the readability of a text and the impression it leaves.

- **Type size** is measured in *points*. A 10–12 point type is often used for body text, 14–16 point for subheadings, and 16–20 point for main headings.
- **Typefaces** are either *serif* or *sans serif*. In general, printed material (like this book) use serif typefaces for body text and sans-serif typefaces for headings.

Serif typefaces have short projections at the ends of letters.	The quick brown fox jumps over the lazy dog.
Sans-serif typefaces do not have end projections.	The quick brown fox jumps over the lazy dog.

- **Typeface styles** vary widely. A standard practice is to use one serif and one sans-serif typeface per document.

Document Type	Headings	Body Text
Print	Sans-serif fonts (Helvetica, Arial)	Serif fonts (Times Roman, Georgia)
Web	Serif fonts (Times Roman, Georgia)	Sans-serif fonts (Helvetica, Arial)

Your Turn Choose a page from your *Inquire* handbook and analyze its design. Which elements mentioned above were used? Could the design be improved? How so?

Principles of Page Design

The document below is attractive and easy to follow. It includes many design elements, such as headings, lists, and boldface type. In addition, it follows the four CARP principles of page design: contrast, alignment, repetition, and proximity.

Contrast deals with the differences between the components of a page. Parts that serve a particular purpose must stand out from other parts.

Example document: The headings feature a different type size and style than the body text uses.

Alignment deals with the position of page components.

Example document: All the headlines and body paragraphs line up on the left side of the page, and all the bulleted items are indented.

Repetition deals with consistency in style.

Example document: The subheadings use the same typeface and wording.

Proximity deals with the spacing between the components of a page.

Example document: Items that are related to each other are grouped together, while items different from each other are separated.

Example Document

One Word, Many Meanings: Counter

In our increasingly interconnected world, English plays a dramatic role in business. Consequently, it pays to recognize that many English words can serve as different parts of speech, often with very different meanings. One such example is the word *counter*.

As a noun . . .
counter is commonly used in the following ways (among others):
- a flat marker used in games
- a long, level surface where transactions are conducted (e.g., a display counter) or where food and drink are prepared or served (as opposed to a table, which is generally lower and not as long)
- a person or device that counts
- a stiffener around or within the heel area of the upper part of a shoe

As a verb . . .
counter is typically used in one of the following ways:
- to oppose (as in working against a current trend)
- to defend or react (as in a debate or in the game of chess)

As an adjective, adverb, or prefix . . .
counter conveys negation, opposition, or reverse action, as in these examples:
- The results were counter to expectations. (predicate adjective)
- Jeeves acted counter to my express wishes. (adverb)
- We added a counterbalance to even the scales. (prefix)

Your Turn

1. Print out a copy of one of your recent writing assignments. Consider its design in terms of the CARP principles discussed above: contrast, alignment, repetition, and proximity. How could you improve the design?

2. Make any improvements that occur to you and print out a new version. Finally, compare the two versions with a classmate. Discuss the benefits of the new version in terms of readability.

Understanding Information Graphics

Graphs and charts present facts and figures in concise visual ways, while diagrams offer a clear picture of objects and other structures, highlighting the parts of each and their relationship.

Knowing how to "read" different types of graphics will help you understand and evaluate the information they represent.

Line Graphs and Scatter Plots

Line graphs and scatter plots show changes in amounts over time. Generally an independent variable is represented as a horizontal line (x axis) and a dependent variable as a vertical line (y axis).

Line Graph

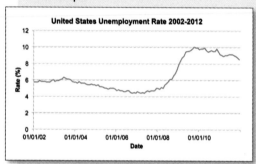

Source: U.S. Bureau of Labor Statistics

Scatter Plot

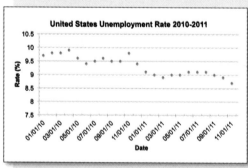

Source: U.S. Bureau of Labor Statistics

Reading Line Graphs and Scatter Plots

- Study the title and any information below it.

- Review the axes and their labels, especially any units of measure (percent, kilograms, and so on).

- Note the scale of each axis. (Consider the varying starting values of the y axes in the graphs to your left.)

- Check the horizontal and vertical axes for gaps and missing information.

- Note the direction of the line or scatter points. Also note any data points that look out of place.

- Consider what predications could be made about future data relating to the graph.

- Check the source of the data (if included).

Your Turn Go online and search for a line graph and a scatter plot related to a subject you are currently studying. Use the tips above to closely read these diagrams.

Bar Graphs

Bar graphs are effective for comparing amounts of something or the number of times something occurs. A basic bar graph uses columns to compare groups of data. A stacked bar graph divides each column to show further comparisons.

Bar graphs are common in business and financial reports and documents, because they simplify the relationships between complex data sets. Similar to reading line graphs, bar graph readers should pay special attention to information in the x and y axes. Below are some additional reading tips.

Bar Graph

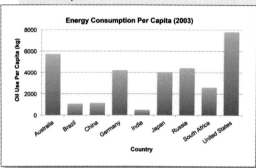

Source: World Resources Institute

Stacked Bar Graph

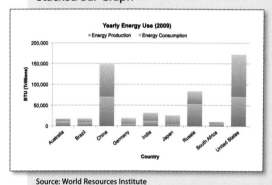

Source: World Resources Institute

Reading Bar Graphs

- Check the title and any information below it.

- Review the horizontal and vertical axes and their labels.

- Identify the information represented by each bar.

- In a stacked or double bar graph, examine the legend that distinguishes each bar from the next (usually by color).

- Note the scale of each axis. Does the dependent (y) axis start at zero? Are the numbers equally spaced? If the y axis doesn't start at zero or the numbers are not equally spaced, the information shown may be misleading.

- Check the axes for gaps and missing information.

- Note any trends or major disparities between the bars.

- Identify the source of the information (if available).

Your Turn Go online and search for a regular bar graph and a stacked bar graph related to a subject you are currently studying. Use the tips above to closely read them.

Pie Charts

A pie chart shows how something is divided or distributed at a given point in time. The entire pie, or circle, represents the whole sample, and the pie pieces, or sectors, represent its parts. The values of the parts added together must not exceed 100 percent, otherwise the sectors will not form a meaningful whole. The main purpose of a pie chart is to show part-whole relationships.

Pie Charts

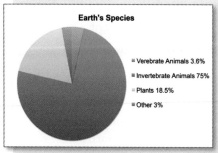

Source: Current Results Nexus

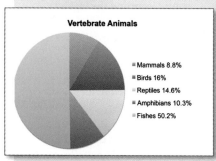

Source: Current Results Nexus

Note: Reading the relative size of pie sectors is more difficult than reading the relative length of the bars in a bar graph.

Reading Pie Charts

- Read the title and any information below it.

- Inspect the individual sectors and their relative sizes.

- Inspect the angle of each sector at the center of the chart.

- Examine the numeric data (often a percentage) represented in each sector.

- Make sure the values of the pieces add up to the correct total (usually 100 percent).

- Make sure the slices are mutually exclusive, meaning the information represented by each slice does not overlap.

- Consider what statements you can make about the sectors relative to each other and relative to the whole pie.

- Identify the source of the information (if available).

Your Turn

1. Which of the earth's species has the highest population? How is that information represented in the first pie graph above?

2. What inferences can you make about the mammal population compared to that of other vertebrate animals? Compared to the whole population of Earth's species?

Bubble Charts

A basic bubble chart uses bubbles, or circles, to represent data. The size (area) of the circles corresponds to their value.

Bubble Chart

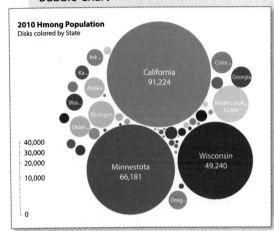

2010 Hmong Population
Disks colored by State

Source: 2010 U.S. Census Bureau

Reading Bubble Charts

- Read the title and any information below it.
- Study the legend or scale to see its relation to the data.
- Read the labels within bubbles.
- Consider how the size, shape, and color of the bubbles relate to the data.
- Note major size disparities between bubbles.

Your Turn In which states do most of the Hmong people who reside in the Unites States live? Why might those particular states attract the Hmong population?

Word Clouds

A word cloud is a graphic representation of the words used in a piece of writing. The most frequently used words appear in the largest type size.

Word Cloud

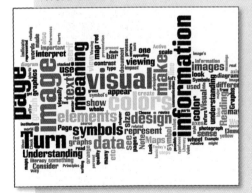

Generated by wordle.com

Reading Word Clouds

- Scan the cloud, noting the largest words.
- Look for words that appear in their singular and plural forms, because both forms of the word may appear in the same cloud.
- Evaluate the relationship between the largest words. Are they connected in any way?

Your Turn The word cloud above comes from the text of this chapter. Which words are used most often? How are they related? Create your own word cloud by copying and pasting a section of text into Wordle.com. Which words are largest?

Maps

Maps help you get to where you need to go and can display information about the world around you.

Online Maps

Online maps allow you to search for addresses, get directions, and view locations.

Map View

Source: Google Maps

Reading Online Maps

Familiarize yourself with the features of the map:

- The arrows allow you to move the map in any direction.
- The slider lets you zoom in (+) or zoom out (-).
- The scale helps you estimate the distance between points.
- Often you have options for viewing traffic patterns and satellite views.

Satellite View

Source: Google Maps

Your Turn Go online to find a street-view and satellite-view map of your local area. Trace your route to school. Then find maps of a place you would like to visit. Write a journal reflection about which view is most useful and why.

Public Transportation Maps (Tube Maps)

Transportation maps show public transportation routes.

Washington D.C. Metro Map

Source: Washington Metropolitan Area Transit Authority

Reading Transportation Maps

■ Find your current location on the map and your intended destination.

■ Use the map key to determine the colors, letters, and symbols that indicate routes and stops.

■ If you need to transfer routes, identify the closest transfer stations.

Information Maps

Information maps use colors or symbols to show geographic data.

Freedom of the Press Worldwide 2009

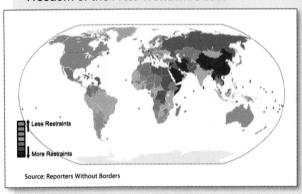

Less Restraints

More Restraints

Source: Reporters Without Borders

Reading Information Maps

■ Note the location of the map.

■ Study the map key for its relation to the data.

■ Consider how the information is separated (by shades of color, symbols, etc.).

■ Look for clustering of colors or symbols in specific regions.

Your Turn In your social studies textbook or online, find an information map. Use the notes above to carefully read and understand the map.

Diagrams

A picture diagram provides a clear picture of the parts of something and how they are arranged. A process diagram visually displays the steps in a process, while a cycle diagram does the same for the sequence of events in a cycle.

Reading Diagrams

When looking at diagrams, pay special attention to all *labels, colors, shapes, textures, symbols, scales, arrows,* and *numbers.*

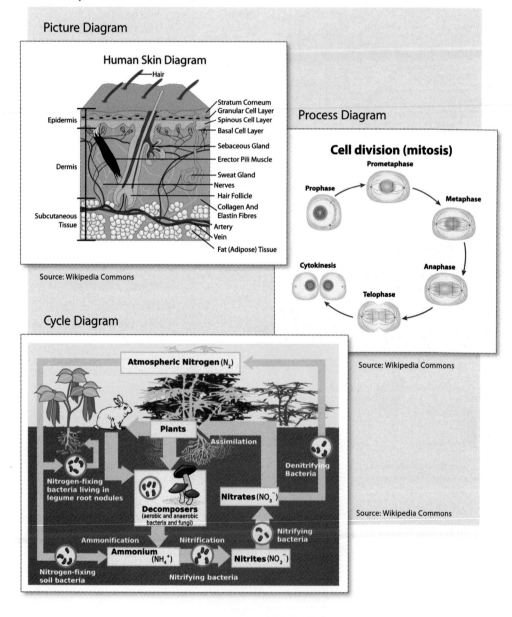

Picture Diagram

Source: Wikipedia Commons

Process Diagram

Source: Wikipedia Commons

Cycle Diagram

Source: Wikipedia Commons

Visual-Literacy Activities

Poster Presentation

You can apply many of the visual/design elements to a scientific poster presentation. A poster presentation offers a visual representation of a scientific abstract by combining text and graphics. Successful posters are visually appealing and present findings in a professional, easy-to-follow, and attractive manner. (You may be able to submit your poster to a contest or present it at a conference. Discuss this with your instructor.)

Your Turn

1. Choose a science topic for your poster presentation.
2. Carry out your research and experiments.
3. Plan how you will display your findings in poster form. Share and discuss ideas with a classmate or your teacher.
4. Prepare any graphs, charts, maps, or diagrams you will use to display your findings (see pages 487–506).
5. Create a 3 ft. x 5 ft. poster about your science topic, following your plan.
6. Follow the elements and principles of page design (pages 226–227) to strike a balance between text and graphics.
7. Submit, present, or display your poster for others to learn from and enjoy.

Front-Page Photos

Today's mainstream media are packed with visual components. Over the last two decades, the newspaper industry has cut space for text in favor of more pictures and graphics. The most dramatic photographs in newspapers are often displayed on the front page. At Newseum.org, you can view the daily front pages of all the major newspapers in America. Actively viewing these front-page photographs gives you a sense of the most important news of the day.

Your Turn

1. Visit "Today's Front Pages" on the Newseum Web site (http://www.newseum.org/todaysfrontpages/default.asp).
2. Browse the front pages, looking for a particularly eye-catching photograph.
3. Choose a photo that interests you, and analyze it in a short paragraph by applying the information provided in this chapter about active viewing: understanding (page 219), interpreting (page 220), and evaluating (page 221).
4. (a) Write a short paragraph about your analysis of the photograph. Share and discuss your ideas in a small group or with your class. (b) Or write a blog entry about your analysis of the photograph and continue the discussion online.
5. Bonus: Choose one newspaper. Analyze the photographs on its front page every day for two weeks. Write a research paper that evaluates the overall quality, truth, and value of the front page's photograph selection (see page 221).

Tuition Dollars and Sense

The vast amount of data and statistics available on the Web presents a unique challenge and an opportunity to practice your visual-literacy skills. Sites like Data.gov and UN Data (data.un.org) offer comprehensive catalogs of statistics relating to government agencies and global organizations. Knowing how to find data and represent it graphically can help you make sense of the important issues affecting the world around you. In this lesson you will access college tuition information and represent it graphically.

Your Turn

1. Visit the College Affordability and Transparency Center Web site by accessing http://www.collegecost.ed.gov/.
2. Think about what type of college, university, or vocational program you would be interested in attending.
3. Search the site, writing down the cost of tuition for least five institutions you wish to explore in your future.
4. Create a bar graph and pie chart comparing the tuition costs of the different institutions.
5. Bonus: Review Chapter 18, "Developing Financial Literacy," on pages 291–314. Create a budget plan (page 308) that will help you cover tuition at one of the institutions represented on your bar graph and pie chart.

Graphing Outside the Box

Graphs and charts, while perfect for displaying complex data sets and statistics, can also be used to tell stories and represent ideas graphically. For instance, the pie graph to the right shows a graphic representation of a famous saying from the Occupy Wall Street movement. Many popular Web sites like coolinfographics.org use creative infographics like the example to display interesting ideas and information.

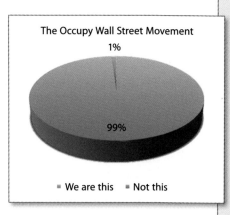

The Occupy Wall Street Movement

1%

99%

■ We are this   ■ Not this

Your Turn

1. Choose a current or historical event in government, business, sports, or pop culture.
2. Create a visual representation of the event using one of the forms explained in this chapter—graphs, charts, maps, or diagrams.
3. Bonus: Create a visual representation of a math, science, English, or social studies concept you are discussing in class.

Chapter 15

Improving Information and Media Literacy

Why is it important to understand media? To begin, media play a big role in informing us about the world we live in. For another, the media's commercial messages can influence how we think and act. These two factors alone dictate that we take a close look at the media, carefully evaluating the information and opinions they share.

The media include all channels of communication—from traditional forms like print newspapers to modern forms like digital-based Web sites. Especially considering the fast-paced nature of today's messaging, both producers and consumers of information must learn to assess media communications with a critical eye. This chapter provides you with strategies for doing so.

You will learn . . .

- Introduction to Media Literacy
- Definition of Media Literacy
- Key Concepts of Media Literacy
- Evaluating Media Messages
- Creating Your Own Media
- Media Literacy Glossary

Introduction to Media Literacy

In 2010, a television station in Los Angeles aired an "exclusive" three-part series called "The View from the Driver's Seat" during the evening news. The series focused on the "dramatic turnaround" of the Ford Motor Company, praising the automobile manufacturer for its perseverance and innovation in the face of a failing economy. At the end of the series, a disclaimer appeared on-screen. It said that Ford had paid a sponsorship fee to the station in connection with the series.

This story shows how the line between news and promotion can be blurred. Consider a viewer who missed the disclaimer at the end of the series. Would seeing the disclaimer change the viewer's opinion of the series? Did the television station deceive its audience? Was the series legitimate news or self-promotion? Was the series unethical? These are the types of questions you need to consider as consumers of today's media.

After all, media rely on advertising to stay in business. And advertisers are constantly innovating new ways to reach target audiences through news and entertainment media. Passive media consumers are vulnerable in this media-saturated environment, especially when an advertisement or a biased message is packaged cleverly, say as an "exclusive" report on the evening news. And when you contemplate the numerous new forms of media joining the marketplace, it is clear that developing media literacy skills has never been more important.

Media Literacy Defined

Media literacy is the ability to access, analyze, evaluate, and create communication in various media formats. Media-literate consumers have the following skills:

- Identifying the source and purpose of information
- Understanding how the medium creates meaning
- Understanding the context of the communication message
- Discovering what is "not said" in a message
- Identifying logical fallacies
- Understanding how different people perceive media
- Creating meaningful messages
- Accessing and navigating different media forms

Your Turn

1. Network officials at the Los Angeles television affiliate claimed there was no self-interest involved in airing "The View from the Driver's Seat" (see the introduction above). Do you believe them? Why or why not?

2. What problems may result when viewers cannot distinguish news stories from promotional material? Explain.

Key Concepts of Media Literacy

Media literacy is evolving, especially as savvy marketers find new ways to deliver messages. A knowledge of the following concepts will help you interact successfully with the media.

1. Media messages are constructed.

While they are meant to appear "real," media messages are crafted with a specific purpose in mind. As you begin to evaluate a message, remember that the 30-second video clip you see on TV is captured, edited, and packaged by a team of people. Throughout this process, "reality" may or may not be skewed.

2. Media messages share a point of view.

Some media broadcast overt points of view, such as a radio-show host who often takes a particular political stand on issues. At the same time, even media outlets that promote fairness and objectivity may be telling only part of the story. Every media message includes some details and omits others. Those decisions—what to cut, what to include, and so on—reflect the embedded values and viewpoints of the media makers.

3. Different media use special techniques.

Messages go beyond the words used. Lighting, music, camera angles, and body language, for example, convey their own messages. To carefully analyze communication, you must be aware of such influences (see pages 222–227 and 245 for visual-literacy techniques and pages 102–112 for methods of persuasion).

4. Different people interpret media differently.

Depending on your age, gender, education, values, upbringing, life experiences, and so on, you will interpret a media message in a unique way, not exactly as someone else would. This is important to consider when you create your own media messages as well.

5. Many people today can create media.

The digital age provides you with the tools to create media and influence mass audiences. For example, Justin Bieber launched his singing career by posting home videos on YouTube. Likewise, the concept of *citizen journalism* has evolved in recent years, as public citizens have gotten more involved in collecting, reporting, analyzing, and disseminating news and information through the use of cell phones, flip cameras, and blogging technologies. In fact, CNN launched an "iReport" feature on its Web site to allow everyday citizens to upload, share, and comment on breaking news as it happens.

Your Turn Why is it important to think of a media message as a "construction"? What are the implications of believing that all media messages are "real" and trustworthy? Discuss your answers with a partner or as a class.

Evaluating Media Messages

The fact that media messages are constructed means that they can also be deconstructed, or separated into parts. The checklist below relates to the five parts of the communication situation—sender, message, medium, receiver, and context (see page 68). Asking questions about a message in the context of these parts will help you to analyze and evaluate it. The pages that follow will delve deeper into each checklist question.

Media-Message Evaluation Checklist

Sender → Message → Receiver

Context   Medium

Sender

☑ 1. Who created the message? Is the source reliable? Was it by a news organization, a public citizen, or an advertiser? (See page 241.)

Message

☑ 2. What does the message say (subject, main point, support)? (See page 242.)

☑ 3. Is the information fair and logical? (See page 243.)

☑ 4. What points of view are shared in the message? Which ones are left out? (See page 244.)

☑ 5. What images or sounds catch my attention? (See page 245.)

Medium

☑ 6. What type of media is used to deliver the message? (See page 246.)

☑ 7. What are the strengths and weaknesses of the media format? (See page 247.)

Receiver

☑ 8. Who is the target of the message? (See page 248.)

☑ 9. How might people different from me interpret this message? (See page 249.)

Context

☑ 10. What is the purpose of the message? (See page 250.)

☑ 11. Who controls the transmission of this message? (See page 251.)

Your Turn Read and consider each question in the checklist above. Apply the questions to the next media message you encounter.

Sender: Who created the message?

As you encounter a media message, ask first about authorship. Did one person or a team of people author the message? Is this source reliable? What choices about content did the source make? Review the following source analyses of two media messages.

Source Analysis 1: An article from a scientific journal

- **Who created the message?**
  The writer's name appears in a byline. The article includes two photographs, so a photographer is also involved. A designer was responsible for the layout. A team of editors have fact-checked the article for accuracy, revised its wording, and proofread it.

- **Is the source reliable?**
  Scientific journals are peer reviewed and reputable, so you can assume that the writer they hired is knowledgeable about the topic.

- **What choices about content did the source make?**
  The magazine's editorial team decided to cover the particular topic. The writer made choices about which people to interview and about which information to include and exclude from the article. The designer chose photos and graphics to make the pages visually appealing.

Source Analysis 2: An online video advertising a popular snack brand

- **Who created the message?**
  An advertising agency made the ad, probably with a team of actors, scriptwriters, producers, camerapersons, and media arts specialists. However, the snack company is the actual source of the ad, because it hired the ad company and had the ultimate say on content.

- **Is the source reliable?**
  Because the message was paid for by a company for commercial purposes, its reliability is questionable.

- **What choices about content did the source make?**
  The snack company chose the agency that crafted the ad, approved the persuasive direction for the ad, and decided the production budget.

Your Turn Choose a media message and analyze its source by answering the three questions used in each analysis above.

Message: What does the message say?

Next, evaluate the content of the media message by asking these questions: What is the subject? What is the main point? How is the main point supported? Is the support strong or weak? Is the message accurate? These questions are particularly important when you are analyzing a persuasive message.

Identifying the Subject, Main Point, and Support

The subject of the message may be a person, a place, an event, a product, or so on; and the main point is the focus or central idea about that subject. Main points can be stated or implied.

How a message supports its main point depends on the format (see page 247) and purpose (see page 250) of the message. An online news article, for example, may use interviews, statistics, or graphics to support its main point, while a television infomercial may use demonstrations and testimonials to promote a product.

Checking for Accuracy

Besides double-checking facts and details, it is important to recognize flaws in logic (see the facing page). To do this, you must understand the difference between statements of fact, opinions, and claims.

Fact ■ A fact is a statement of truth that can be checked for accuracy. It is not debatable; it is either correct or incorrect. (See page 96.)

Thank Me Later is the debut studio album by recording artist Drake.

Opinion ■ An opinion is a personally held belief. It cannot be proven to be correct or incorrect, because it is a matter of personal feelings. (See page 96.)

Drake is my favorite rapper.

Claim ■ A claim is a debatable statement that can be supported with evidence and reason. (See page 104.)

With its self-aware yet playful lyrics and emotional appeal, Drake's *Thank Me Later* album redefines what it means to be "real" and pushed Drake into pop stardom.

Fact-Checking Resources
You'll find many fact-checking resources online, including encyclopedias and government databases. Also consult the media specialist at your school or local library for help.

Your Turn Identify a fact, an opinion, and a claim in a media message. Write them down and explain how they are different from one another.

Message: Is the information fair and logical?

Today's media messages, particularly the product and political ads, are littered with claims and rhetoric. Sometimes these claims include fuzzy, biased, or incomplete information, also known as logical fallacies. The following list highlights a number of fallacies often used in media. (See pages 108-112 for more examples of logical fallacies.)

Fallacy	Definition	Example
Bandwagoning (see page 112)	Implies that something must be true because a majority of people support it, ignoring the minority's point of view.	*Sixty-seven percent of residents support the new bill, so it will clearly benefit the state.*
Appeal to Popular Sentiment (see page 111)	Associates an idea, product, or person with something widely approved, such as family, patriotism, or apple pie. Also plays on emotions rather than employing reason and logic.	*Anyone who loves his or her country should buy only American-made automobiles.*
Argument from Authority (see page 111)	Uses a nonauthoritative person to testify in favor of a product, person, or idea.	A celebrity endorsement
Half-truth (see page 112)	Distorts an issue by telling only part of the story.	*The state lost 1.2 million jobs under Gov. Terry.* (The message did not mention that the state also experienced a net job gain.)
Threatening (see page 112)	Uses statements that intimidate those with opposing views.	*You better support this bill. Otherwise, our schools will fail, thanks to you.*
Broad Generalization (see page 108)	Uses scant evidence, offers no exceptions, and often includes intensifiers such as *all, every, never.*	*All vegetarians push a liberal agenda.*

Detecting Bias

A **biased statement** is characterized by partiality, preference, or prejudice. The following are indicators of biased information:

1. The language is extreme, characterized by all-or-nothing statements.
2. The message appeals to emotion rather than to reason and logic.
3. The message simplifies or generalizes information.
4. The message offers a one-sided or limited view on a topic (see page 244).

Your Turn Search the Internet for a political ad. Does it include any of the logical fallacies listed above? Can you detect any bias? Explain.

Message: What points of view are included? Which are left out?

All media messages reflect the values, lifestyles, and points of view of their creators while excluding others. A thorough analysis can tell you about the creators' values as well as uncover perspectives missing from the message.

Analyzing Values, Lifestyle, and Point of View

Consider a fictional ad for "Fresh Surf" scented men's deodorant and body wash. Its tagline reads, "Become Freshest Smelling Bro on Earth." Below are five critical questions you can ask to analyze its values, lifestyle, and point of view.

What values and lifestyle are represented in the ad?
- *Analysis:* Using this type of deodorant and body wash reflects confidence, masculinity, fun, adventure, fitness, attractiveness.

What point of view is represented?
- *Analysis:* Smelling good is manly; the "Fresh Surf" scent helps a man smell fresh.

What does the message imply about its creator?
- *Analysis:* The creator has a sense of humor and considers comedy, extravagance, physical fitness, charm, and confidence to be marketable.

Do the embedded values, lifestyle, and point of view reinforce present-day societal assumptions?
- *Analysis:* The advertisement shares a generalized view of masculinity: a man should be athletic, adventurous, strong, confident, and well kept.

What values, lifestyle, and point of view are omitted from the message?
- *Analysis:* The message ignores the fact that many men don't fit—and perhaps don't want to fit—this generalization about masculinity.

Your Turn Analyze the values, lifestyle, and point of view represented in your favorite TV show. How would the show be different if other values and lifestyles were also represented? How would the point of view change? Explain.

Message: What images or sounds catch my attention?

Beyond words, media messages create meaning through images and sound. The following elements and techniques can affect your interpretation of a message.

Visual Elements

Lighting ▪ Low lighting conveys gloom or fear, while bright lighting expresses happiness or joy. Soft lighting conveys beauty and romance.

Camera Angle ▪ A low-angle view makes people or things appear larger than they actually are, often indicating importance. Conversely, a high-angle view makes people or things appear smaller and less significant.

Composition ▪ The arrangement of visual elements in a picture or video affect the viewer's perception. Close-ups of a face convey tension or intimacy, while wider views showing people or things relative to their surroundings usually express something important about the setting (menacing, breathtaking, overbearing, and so on).

Body Language ▪ The words are often less revealing than the body language of the person expressing them.

For more information on visual elements, review Chapter 14, "Developing Visual Literacy," on pages 217–236.

Sound Techniques

Music ▪ The mood and intensity of a scene can be profoundly affected by music. Fast-paced pieces use rhythm and volume to heighten drama and often accompany fight scenes, car chases, and other action-packed scenes. Slower, softer, intentionally expressive compositions can create tension and foreboding, as in horror films.

Sound Effects ▪ Usually added after the filming, sound effects enhance a scene and make it seem very real, although the effects themselves are often artificially produced.

Narration (Voice-Over) ▪ Some films and television shows use a narrator, someone other than the characters in the story, to speak to the audience. For example, a newscaster acts as a narrator when he or she describes a video clip during a news show.

Your Turn Go online and find a scene from a movie that includes music. First watch it with the sound muted, and then with the sound on. What is the impact of silence on the scene? Of music?

Medium: What type of media is used to deliver the message?

Media types fall under two broad categories: traditional and new. The traditional media include the print and broadcast formats, while the new media include the ever-changing digital formats, such as blogs and podcasts.

Not so long ago there existed a clear distinction between the two categories. Today, they are evolving closer together. Traditional media have begun to embrace the interactive, adaptable, and social nature of new media, while new media are boosting their reputation as outlets for hard news. In fact, journalists often break new stories on Twitter before they appear on television or in a newspaper. As technology advances, traditional media and new media will resemble each other even further.

Explore the graphic below to better understand the types of media.

Types of Media

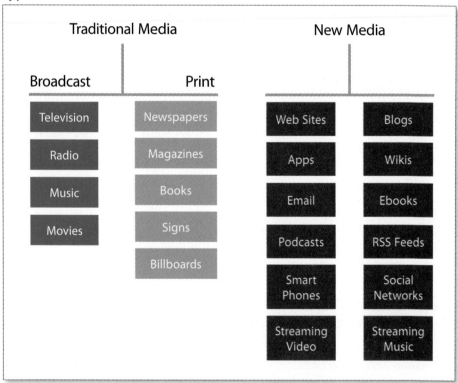

Your Turn

1. What types of media do you use most frequently? How are your media preferences similar or different from your parents' media preferences?

2. Twenty years ago, digital media didn't exist. How did people get their news back then? Consider the options for getting news today. Discuss with a classmate the relative strengths and weaknesses of news-delivery methods before and after the digital age.

Medium: What are the strengths and weaknesses of the media format?

Each media format has inherent strengths and weaknesses. Social media messages, for example, are quick and efficient but prone to inaccuracies. In general, newspapers provide depth and accuracy but lack the sensory appeal of television, the interactive feature of a blog, and the rapid delivery of radio.

Format	Strengths	Weaknesses
Web sites, blogs, microblogs	Accessible; interactive; diverse; immediate; inexpensive	Prone to inaccuracies; often biased and opinionated
Newspapers, magazines, books	Accurate; comprehensive; appeal to general public	Limited to text and pictures; slow delivery
Television, radio	Strong audio and visual appeal; current; local; friendly	Highly commercialized; highly persuasive; may be biased

Finally, consider the graphic below that compares various media by plotting the general reliability of the information against delivery speed.

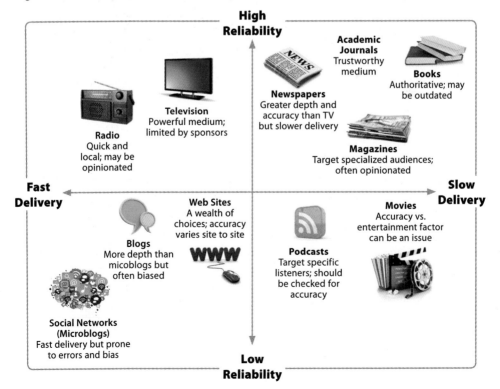

Receiver: Who is the target of the message?

When you take in a message, your values, life experience, and culture all play a role in how you perceive it. These factors could include your upbringing, education level, where you live, even your interests and aspirations. As you continue to evaluate messages, remember to consider those who are meant to receive the information

Target Audiences

In media, the target audience refers to the person or group for whom a message is created. Some messages, like personal email or thank-you notes, target just one person. Others are meant for larger audiences. Mainstream media producers in particular want to reach as many people as possible, because larger audiences are more attractive to advertisers (see below).

In fact, you can often determine the target audience of mainstream media by examining their commercial content. It is no coincidence that you see different types of commercials airing during professional football games than you do during an episode of *Gossip Girl*. Advertisers most often craft messages to suit specific audiences based on the characteristics shown in the checklist. Television shows and other forms of media also consider these factors when they decide when to air or distribute new content:

☑ Age ☑ Ethnicity ☑ Income level
☑ Gender ☑ Locale ☑ Habits and interests

Targeting Online Audiences

Have you ever wondered how advertisements on social networks seem to align with your interests and habits? All the information you share on social sites is stored as aggregate data, which is available to advertisers. The data could include information on your age, location, education, relationship status, and interests. Even titles of your favorite books, music, and movies may be available as data. Advertisers pay for this information and use it to filter selective messages to highly targeted audiences. Clearly, target audiences are big business.

You need to be selective with what information you post online. You also should understand when messages target you as opposed to someone else. When they do target someone else, consider how and why these others might react to the message, as you will learn on the next page.

Your Turn Examine the commercials aired during two television programs, preferably on different networks during different time slots. What types of products are advertised? Who uses these products? Considering this information, decide who the target audience of each program is. Explain your decision.

Receiver: How might people different from me interpret this message?

While media creators attempt to share an exact, clear message to a specific audience—using words, pictures, and/or sounds—the underlying meaning, or subtext, taken from a message varies from person to person.

Considering Different Perspectives

A variety of factors determine how we interpret media, including our age, gender, education level, experience, values, beliefs, family, and culture. Consider the film *Extremely Loud & Incredibly Close*, a fictitious story of a boy and his mother dealing with his father's death in the 9/11 attacks on the World Trade Center. Certainly, someone who lost a friend or family member during the same event would interpret this movie differently than someone who did not.

Analyzing the way different people perceive the same information builds awareness of diverse viewpoints and can redefine the way we think about a media message. The questions below will help as you evaluate a message in light of its audience.

1. How do I interpret the message?
2. Why do I interpret the message in this way?
3. How might someone from a different culture interpret this message? Someone of a different age, gender, education level, and so on?
4. Do those interpretations align with/differ from mine?
5. How does considering different people's perspectives affect my original perception of this message?

Your Turn Study the photograph to the right taken by Dorothea Lange entitled *Migrant Mother*. (A larger version can be found online at the Library of Congress Web site.) Write down a description of the photo and any conclusions you draw from it. Exchange your work with a partner who has completed the same activity. Look at the similarities and differences between your responses. Discuss how you came to your conclusions. Evaluate how much your own culture, values, and beliefs could have impacted your interpretation of the image. Bonus: Repeat the exercise with a different classmate.

Context: What is the purpose of the message?

Most media messages serve at least one of three purposes—to educate, to entertain, or to persuade—and some fulfill all three at once. A blog post, for example, may entertain its readers but also share some news or promote a cause or product. Always think about the purpose of a media message before taking it at face value. Also analyze purpose before sending your own media messages.

▶ To Educate or Inform

The news industry was built on society's interest in learning and keeping up with what is happening in the world. We read newspaper stories, magazine features, and news blogs; listen to radio broadcasts and podcasts; and watch and listen to television newscasts, documentaries, and online video tutorials. Media messages that are meant to educate or inform are typically more neutral and unbiased than messages meant solely to entertain or persuade. However, be aware of author or organizational bias that might accompany the message. (See page 243 for more on "Detecting Bias.")

Your Turn Read a print or online news article that is meant to educate or inform. Answer the questions about "Detecting Bias" at the bottom of page 243. Does the article you chose avoid bias?

▶ To Entertain

Some media messages are packaged to entertain. Music, movies, television sitcoms, sports broadcasts, and social networks are just a few examples of media that entertain. Popular entertainment media are especially appealing to advertisers because they are viewed by large audiences.

Your Turn Analyze your own media habits. How much of the media you consume is meant for entertainment purposes? How much of it is meant for education?

▶ To Persuade

As you learned at the beginning of this chapter, a key concept of media literacy is knowing all media messages share some point of view, even the ones that are meant to appear objective in tone. (See page 239.) While persuasive devices are easy to recognize in commercials and advertisements, they may be more subtle in other media messages. For example, a post on a political blog may influence you to think one way by covering only one side of a story. Media-literate individuals are able to detect bias and always consider objections or other sides of a story before making up their minds on an issue.

Your Turn Study at least three different messages from different media sources. Determine the main purpose of each message. Do any of the messages fulfill more than one of the purposes explained above? Share your work with the class.

Context: Who controls the transmission of this message?

Earlier in this chapter you evaluated a media message in terms of its creator, or sender (see page 241). The final critical question peels back another layer of authorship by considering the issue of media ownership and control. Here are the three main categories of media ownership.

▶ Corporations

In the United States and abroad, a few giant corporations control most of the media. These corporations are known as media conglomerates because they own assets across all media forms—television, radio, film, music, Web sites. Corporate-owned media are businesses motivated by commercial interests, which are gained through advertising. As a consumer of media, remember to ask if the message is serving *your* best interests, or the interests of the corporation.

▶ Governments

Also known as "state-owned media," some media are produced and funded by a government. State-sponsored media messages must be evaluated carefully for propaganda. Some nations do not allow freedom of the press and have even censored the Internet. The state-owned media in such nations may act as their government's mouthpiece and restrict independent voices.

▶ Individuals

Media that are free of corporate or government influence are known as independent media and are controlled by individuals. The Web and digital-based technologies have greatly benefited independent media voices. The practice of citizen journalism has gained momentum thanks to new media, affording everyday people the opportunity to report meaningful news to a widespread audience. Independent media sources were a big part of 2011's Arab Spring, where protestors turned to social media to spread information about uprisings.

Your Turn Search for three example messages—one transmitted by corporate-owned media, one by state-owned media, and one by an individual or individuals. Compare and contrast the messages using the questions on the "Media-Message Evaluation Checklist" on page 240. Discuss your findings with a partner or your class.

Creating Your Own Media

Not too long ago, mass communication was largely a one-way street. The tools for delivering information to large audiences were neither accessible nor affordable for the average person. But that has changed with the advent of the Internet and new digital technologies.

Today, these inexpensive, accessible, and efficient tools offer you a unique opportunity to create media messages for a global audience. Even taking a photograph on your smart phone and uploading it to a social-media site can result in a meaningful media message. Creating your own media messages is an important part of media literacy, as it will provide you with a new perspective on the news-making process. Here are some ways you can become a media maker. The projects in part three of *Inquire* will go into more depth on how to create different media forms.

How can I produce media?

- Start your own blog.
- Make a post on a social-media site (see page 272).
- Upload a video online (see pages 518–519).
- Create a Web site (see pages 592–595).
- Contribute to your school newspaper.
- Record a podcast (see pages 510–511).
- Respond to someone else's blog.
- Contribute to a wiki (see page 596–597).
- Take a photograph and post it online.
- Create a public-service announcement (see pages 520–521).
- Submit a short story (see page 454–456).
- Create an interesting visualization or infographic (see page 500–503).
- Design an online poster.
- Write a play or movie script.
- Write a movie or restaurant review.
- Create a digital story.
- Submit a letter to the editor of your local newspaper.
- Design a video game.
- Record a song.

Your Turn Create a meaningful media message in at least two different formats. Think of ways to deliver it to the largest possible audience.

How can I edit my media creations?

Part of media literacy is making responsible choices about your own media creations. For the best results, hold your own content to the same standards as you do to the other media messages you evaluated in this chapter. Always do your best to avoid publishing information that is false, inaccurate, or hurtful. Begin the editing process by applying the questions in the "Media-Message Evaluation Checklist" on page 240 to your work. In addition, consider the following tips.

▶ Give It Time

Unless you are working on a tight deadline, take a break before you begin editing. Being rested will make you more alert to your work's shortcomings.

▶ Know Your Audience

The way you speak to your close friends is different from the way you speak to your teacher or boss, so match your style and level of language to your target audience. Remember, too, that your audience may be wider than you think. This is especially true of work published online. Always be careful about what you say and how you say it. Take caution with humor and sarcasm. And consider the impact the message will have on its primary and secondary receivers.

▶ Consider All Sides

Look over your content and make sure you have considered all sides of the story. Ask yourself: Is my content fair and well supported? Is there another side to the story that I have ignored completely? Am I letting my emotions control my message?

▶ Check Your Text and Images

If your message includes text, correct all spelling, grammar, and usage errors (see pages 191–196). An error-free message keeps the audience focused on the content. If your message includes images or video, check the resolution and formatting.

▶ Give Credit

Mention the sources of any borrowed ideas, images, or words to avoid plagiarizing and exploiting the work of others. (See pages 392-395 for tips for avoiding plagiarism.)

▶ Get a Second Opinion

Your own evaluation of your work is vital, but always ask a trusted classmate or peer to review your work in order to identify issues you missed.

Your Turn Find a media message you recently published—a school paper, a blog entry, a social-media post, or so on. Critically analyze the work using the "Media Message Checklist" on page 240. What improvements, if any, would you like to make to the message?

Media Literacy Glossary

Media literacy involves a specialized language. The following list of definitions will help as you interact with the media.

Agenda-setting theory: A theory that the news media shape public opinion by controlling the transmission of stories

Audience: Anyone exposed to a media message, or anyone for whom a message is constructed

Bias: Partiality, preference, or prejudice for/against a person, thing, or idea

Branding: Creating an identity for a product or service based on a name, slogan, symbol, or feeling

Censorship: Controlling or suppressing any part of a media message or text

Connotation: Meaning added to a media message by the audience

Consumer: Any person who experiences or interacts with a media message

Convergence: Several separate media industries (newspapers, video, music) operating together through advances in technology (e.g., smart phones)

Demographics: Measurable characteristics of a particular group, such as age, gender, locale, and income level

Denotation: The literal meaning of a media message (what is seen, heard, etc.)

Digital media: Electronic media that use a digital code

Gatekeepers: Those within the news media who control the flow of information and spread of ideas (see also *agenda-setting theory*)

Mainstream media: Media that disseminate messages to the general public via the largest distribution channels

Mass media: Media that broadcast messages to large audiences (see also *mainstream media*)

Media: All channels of communication combined

Media literacy: The ability to access, analyze, evaluate, and create media in a variety of forms

Media specialist: Someone knowledgeable about accessing a range of information in a variety of media formats

Medium: Any single channel of communication (the singular form of "media")

Product placement: "Advertising" products by using them as props in television shows and movies

Propaganda: Information intended to influence an audience to adopt a certain point of view

Subtext: Indirect meaning contained in a media message

Target audience: The person or group that a media message is meant to reach

Text: Any media production (a newspaper article, song, music video, podcast, etc.)

Visual literacy: The ability to analyze, evaluate, and interpret visual elements

Information-and-Media-Literacy Activities

The Other Side of the Coin

How we view historical events is largely based on our experience, culture, and education. As an American student, your views on the Iraq War may not align with those of an Iraqi citizen the same age. It's important to consider all sides of the story to understand how history impacts different people from different regions of the world.

Your Turn

1. Read about a U.S. historical event in your classroom textbook or other reliable source.
2. Evaluate the values, lifestyle, and point of view demonstrated in the text.
3. Use other media sources about the event to gather as many alternative viewpoints as possible. Be especially attentive to how other cultures observe the event.
4. Create your own media message (text, graphic, image, or video) about the event that covers a wide spectrum of interpretations and viewpoints.
5. Bonus: Use social media to connect with a student from another country. Talk about a familiar event and compare how media in each country covers the event.

How Does It Rank?

In the United States, the Nielsen Ratings measure the size of a television show's audience. Each week, Nielsen releases a report of weekly television ratings that are used by networks to set advertising costs and by advertisers to determine how many people watch which shows and when.

Your Turn

1. Research the difference between "shares" and "ratings" in regard to TV viewership and the Nielsen Ratings.
2. Find the latest release of weekly Nielsen Ratings (go to http://tvbythenumbers.zap2it.com/).
3. Analyze the "Broadcast Top 25." What are the top-ranked shows? On which networks do the shows appear? How many people watched them?
4. Make at least three inferences based on the weekly ratings.
5. Bonus: Research how DVR (digital video recorder) viewership and online streaming affect television ratings.

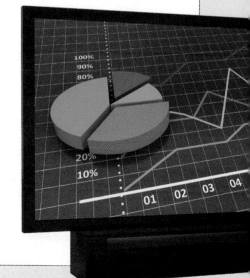

News Check

During election season, politicians will often cite statistics to support a main point. Sometimes the accuracy of those statistics is questionable. Luckily, you can double-check those statistics using one of many government databases found at usa.gov.

Your Turn

1. Research a news article that prominently uses statistics to support a main point.
2. Review online statistical resources (perhaps at usa.gov) to find data that confirms or refutes the main point of the article.
3. Has double-checking the statistics affected your opinion of the article? How so?
4. Bonus: Report your findings to your class.

Source Check

One criticism of mainstream media is that news producers do not use diverse sources. For example, a 40-month-long survey of the *Nightline* television show, published in 1989, revealed that 92 percent of the show's U.S. guests were white, and 89 percent were male. Since then, source diversity has improved, but by how much?

Your Turn

1. Choose an online news outlet.
2. For at least five days a week for four weeks, choose three or more of the most prominent stories on the Web site's homepage.
3. Read the stories and keep a tally of the gender of the sources used in each (see below).
4. When the four weeks are up, review your data. In total, what percent of sources were male? What percent were female?
5. What other observations can you make from your data?
6. Bonus: Report your findings in a research report (see pages 478–485). Submit the paper to an academic journal or present it at a research conference.

Date	Story Title	Total Sources	Male Sources	Female Sources
2/3/12	Two-star day cares face funding cuts	3	1	2

Chapter 16
Creating Internet Literacy

We live in an increasingly networked world. It's changing the way we read, view, talk, and even think. The Internet has given those who use it a world of information and a voice that can reach around the globe. So it is important to know what's "in the Net" and to understand its tools and how to put them to use.

Many of you may already feel comfortable with the online tools and technologies discussed in this chapter. But learning how they came about and considering best practices for using them will enhance your Internet skills and strengthen your connections in this information age.

You will learn . . .

- Understanding the Internet
- Understanding Web Browsing
- Communicating Effectively Online
- Using Internet Content Effectively

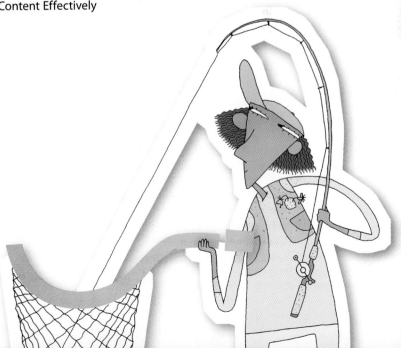

Understanding the Internet

The Internet is much more than the World Wide Web. It is a global network of computing devices connected in many different ways. To understand that, let's consider a few terms from the history of computing:

Mainframes and Terminals: The first electronic computers filled whole rooms. Programmers interacted with them by inserting "punch cards" that displayed holes in designated positions, and data was stored on large rolls of magnetic tape. As the technology advanced, computers could serve several operators at once. A mainframe computer would be connected to many user stations, called terminals, each with its own keyboard and screen.

Servers and Clients: When personal computers were developed, people began to connect them in a similar way. One PC would act as a server, and the others would connect to it as clients. Nowadays, a personal computer can act as a media server for other devices, such as your television. And a distant computer can act as a server to deliver a Web page to your personal computer, the client.

LANs, WANs, and WLANs: As more advanced computing devices were developed, home and office networks were established. LANs (Local Area Networks), which served a single office or home, and the larger WANs (Wide Area Networks) both used physical connections. Later, wireless technology allowed for WLANs (Wireless Local Area Networks). Your school or home may provide both LAN and WLAN connections.

Modems and Routers: Short for "*modulator-de*modulator," a *modem* is a device that can connect to the Internet. A *router* is a stand-alone device used to network multiple computing devices in one location, by Ethernet cable or wirelessly. Most often, a router is also connected to a modem to provide Internet connection to devices on its network.

ISPs: An ISP (Internet service provider) is a company that sells Internet access. Common connection types include the following:
- **Dial-Up** is a slow connection using a normal telephone line. While the computer is connected to the Internet, the line cannot be used for phone calls.
- **DSL** (digital subscriber line) uses a dedicated telephone line (or sometimes a pair) to provide a faster, always-on connection to the Internet. It works well for users within one mile of the service provider but weakens at greater distances.
- **Cable** uses heavy-gauge copper wires or even fiber-optic lines to deliver high-speed access over greater distances.
- **Satellite** provides Internet access from a satellite orbiting the earth to a receiving dish at the user's location. Download speeds (receiving data from the satellite) can be nearly as good as DSL or cable, but upload speeds (sending data to the satellite) are much slower.
- **T1** and above are high-speed connections typically offered only to businesses.

DNS: Every device on every network has its own unique numerical address. A router within a home network is often at 192.168.1.1, and it might assign 192.168.1.4 to one computer, 192.168.1.20 to another, and so on. Addresses on the Internet are assigned a similar numerical code. To make things easier for humans, these numbers are mapped in DNS (Domain Name System) servers to names like www.google.com or www.nasa.gov. When you send an email or access a Web page, a DNS server translates that address to its number code for computers to use.

Ethernet: Ethernet cables look like phone lines but are slightly larger. They are generally used for high-speed connection within a local network.

Bluetooth, Wi-Fi, and Mobile Telephony: These connection types use wireless modems to send and receive radio waves. Bluetooth is a short-range connection—about 10 meters (32 feet)—commonly used to connect a computer to peripherals like headphones, a keyboard, and a mouse. Wi-Fi (Wireless Fidelity) has a longer range—about 20 meters (65 feet)—and is the basis of WLAN networks (see previous page). Mobile telephony connects cell phones to towers wirelessly.

VOIP Telephony: VOIP (Voice Over Internet Protocol) is a technology for making free or low-cost phone calls over an Internet connection.

World Wide Web: The World Wide Web is a collection of files interconnected by clickable links and viewed as pages in a browser program. Those pages may contain text, images, and even audio or video files. Although many people use the terms Web, World Wide Web, Internet, and Net interchangeably, the Web is only part of the Net. (Also see "Deep Web" on page 391.)

The Cloud: As computing becomes increasingly portable and people use different devices to connect at work, at home, and elsewhere, the idea of storing files online in "the Cloud" has grown popular. This makes files accessible from anywhere with an Internet connection. Also, in "Cloud Computing," server computers do the more complex processing, allowing portable computers to run "thin client" software.

Example Home Network

This graphic shows how various devices might communicate within a home network, using technologies described above. This graphic shows how various devices might communicate within a home network, using technologies described above.

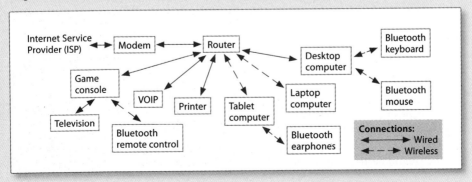

Understanding Web Browsing

In the early days of the Internet, there were no browser programs. Every page displayed black text on a gray background. Images, audio, and documents were downloaded as separate files and opened in separate programs. Nowadays, of course, most of the Internet is available through the Web. Browsers display text, photos, animations, and sound, with hyperlinks connecting one page to another. Hyperlinks can also connect to downloadable files, such as PDF documents and software. The diagram below shows common features of most Web browsers.

A Navigation buttons move to previous pages.

B Address (URL) of the current page

C Refreshes the current page

D Tabs to open other pages

E The status bar shows the actual address of links you point to. It also shows download progress of files.

F Often images are hyperlinked, too.

G A hyperlink to another page or file.

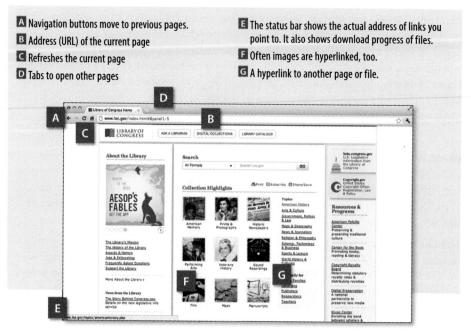

Web Code Terms

Understanding the basics of Web code can enhance your use of the Web.

■ **HTML** (hypertext markup language) sets the *content* and *structure* of a Web page.

This code, for example...	displays as this in a Web browser...
`<p>This is a paragraph with one <strong>bold</strong> word, one <em>italic</em> word, and one <a href="http://www.thoughtfullearning.com">link</a>.</p>`	This is a paragraph with one **bold** word, one *italic* word, and one <u>link</u>.

You should be able to predict where the link leads by looking at the code.

- **CSS** (cascading style sheets) is used for *formatting* and *styling* Web content.

This code, for example...	displays as this in a Web browser...
`<p>This paragraph has one <span style="font-color:red">tinted</span> word in it.</p>`	This paragraph has one tinted word in it.

Although CSS can be declared on a case-by-case basis as above, it's usually defined in a separate document. This is useful because if you need to change all red words to blue words, for example, you can change just one line of code, instead of having to search for and change each instance.

- **JavaScript** is a common programming language for adding *interaction* to a Web page. It operates on the "client side," meaning that it is included within the page's HTML code and uses the processing power of your computer. When you point your mouse cursor at a menu and it expands, or point it at an image and that image changes, chances are JavaScript is at work.

- **Server-Side Codes** are powerful programming languages used to interact with databases (see below). A server-side code allows a Web server to build exactly the page you need when you need it. For example, although the home page of a search site may be the same from day to day, each new search you make delivers a different page of results. You can often discover the server language of a Web site by checking the page extension in your browser's address bar. (An .htm or .html extension means a static HTML page.) Here are four common examples of dynamic server extensions:

.cgi	Common Gateway Interface, an older interface often written in Perl
.php	Originally Personal Home Page, now PHP: Hypertext Preprocessor, a very popular open-source script
.asp	Active Server Pages, a commercial script developed by Microsoft
.cfm	ColdFusion Markup language, a commercial script owned by Adobe

- **Cookies** are tiny text documents saved on your computer to help some servers remember who you are. Think of a cookie as a name tag or a license plate. If you tell your browser to save a password for a site, that is stored in a cookie.

- A **database** is a collection of tables organized for quick searching by special software. Databases are also designed to safely store personal information such as medical records and financial transactions.

- **Other Types of Web Code** include such things as Flash animations, embedded audio and video streams, Java (a language that shows up in everything from clocks to stoplights), and much more. The Internet and Web are constantly evolving pools of emerging technologies.

Communicating Effectively Online

The Internet allows many types of online communication, including text-based messaging like email, chat programs, and texting, as well as voice calls and video chat.

Emailing

Email has been around since the earliest days of the Internet. It has survived because it is so useful. To get the most out of email, it helps to understand the following:

- **Email addresses** take the form of *name@server.ext*—as in the example of *contact@thoughtfullearning.com*. If you have Internet service at home or on a phone, your ISP provides a preformatted email address for you. Unfortunately, if you change ISPs, you lose that email address. Another option is to create one of your own with a free service such as gmail.com, hotmail.com, yahoo.com, or such.

  Note: Try to create a professional-sounding address. In the future, you might want to use that account to apply for college or to communicate with a coworker. Also choose something that other people can easily remember. Ellis Toriello chose ellis.toriello@gmail.com, for example.

- **Email programs** may be online email providers such as gmail, hotmail, or yahoo mail, with a Web-based interface you can use from any computer. (Just remember to log out when done.) Most personal computers have their own email programs, which can download and save messages rather than leaving them online. The advantage to downloading is that you can read and respond to email even when not connected to the Internet.

- **Email formatting** may use HTML (see page 594), which allows styling and images, but some programs read only plain-text email. Text email can be safer than HTML, and it loads faster, which is better for portable devices.

- **Attachments:** Most email programs can send files attached to a message, but not everyone wants to receive attachments. For one reason, those files can take a long time to download. For another, email programs may have trouble recognizing a virus in an attachment. It's always best to ask before sending an attachment. Another option is to upload the file to online storage and provide a link inside your email message, so people can download it when they like.

- **Spam:** Bulk advertisements by ground mail require postage, but Internet spam costs little. Some unscrupulous people use bot software to spam every email address they can find. One way to fight this is to use an email service like gmail, hotmail, or yahoo mail. These companies maintain good spam blockers. Also, avoid posting your email address where spammers can find it.

Your Turn Discuss with classmates your experience with email. Brainstorm together a list of common problems and best practices. Share your list on a school Web page.

Elements of Human Communication

According to UCLA professor Albert Mehrabian, words convey only about 7 percent of our emotion in a communication. Tone of voice conveys another 38 percent, and body language (including facial expressions) reveals more than half—55 percent—of our feelings. As you use text, phone, and video chat, remember that the fewer the context cues, the more care you must take to ensure understanding.

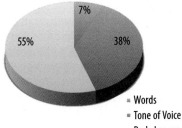

- Words
- Tone of Voice
- Body Language

Text Messaging

Text messaging, or texting, means sending messages in writing by Internet or phone service. Text messages are more immediate than email because devices can give an alert whenever a message arrives. A cell phone might play a special ring tone, or a laptop might show a pop-up window. The recipient can quickly review the message and decide whether to respond now or wait. Text messages also tend to be shorter than email, especially when sent from portable devices, where small screen size makes typing and viewing long messages tiresome. Long texts can also cost much more than short ones on phone-service plans.

Texting is handy for quickly letting a parent know, "Band practice is over. Can you pick me up?" or for saying to a friend, "Let's see Roobie Slipperz in concert this weekend."

- **Social Networking and Ambient Awareness:** Texting can be used to post messages to social-media sites like Twitter, Facebook, Google+, and such. (See "Using Social Media" on pages 269–290.) These messages become a mini blog (see "Blogging" on pages 598–601) where people can read an ongoing stream of messages from friends and colleagues. Viewers find out what is happening in the world around them, acquiring "ambient awareness."

- **The 140-Character Limit:** One popular social-media service, Twitter.com, limits messages to exactly 140 characters, including spaces, the length of this very sentence. Learning to compose such a short post is good writing practice.

- **Flash Events and Democratic Voices:** When we said earlier that online tools give us all a voice in our changing world, that wasn't hyperbole. Texting and social networking have allowed people to organize spontaneous crowds for performance art, dance, and peaceful demonstrations for a social cause.

Remember: Texting gives few context cues, so misunderstandings are common. Be cautious when composing a text message and forgiving when reading one.

Your Turn Create an account on a favorite social-media site. Use it as a research tool to communicate with people who share your interests. (See pages 269–290.)

Instant Messaging

Instant messaging (IM, sometimes called "text chat") is a real-time, text-based conversation. It's much like talking on a telephone but involves using a keyboard instead of speaking. Some IM programs can remain open on your computer while you do other work, and many social and game sites have their own built-in IM services.

Always remember to be polite when chatting. And work smart—if you're busy, turn off the program or set your status to "Away" so that you won't be interrupted.

Your Turn Discuss in class your experience with IM. How is it like other text messaging? How is it different? What are its strengths and weaknesses?

In Focus: Using Abbreviations and Emoticons

Email, text messaging, and instant messaging are often casual, using abbreviations like LOL for "laughing out loud." Emoticons—faces represented by punctuation, like this sideways "smiley," :) —are also used. Often, you can figure out abbreviations and emoticons from their context, or you can ask a friend or look them up online.

Note: Don't use emoticons and casual abbreviations in schoolwork or business writing.

Using VOIP

VOIP (Voice Over Internet Protocol) is a technology for making "phone calls" over an Internet connection. It is especially popular as a low-cost way to call long distance (even across oceans), using a computer with a microphone and speakers.

Bear in mind the following points when using VOIP:

- **Connection Costs:** With most VOIP services, a call from one computer to another is free. A call from a computer to a phone, however, is charged a fee. (Some cell phones can use VOIP when a Wi-Fi connection is available, saving you those minutes on your phone-service plan.)

- **Identity Display:** Free VOIP accounts usually do not have a telephone number. A person receiving a call by phone from a free VOIP account will not know who is calling.

- **Connection Quality:** The nature of the Internet means that connections may be routed through many hubs, over various lines (from fiber optics to copper wires to radio waves). As a result, VOIP sound quality can vary greatly. When making a VOIP call, let your listener know, and ask if the sound quality is okay. If it isn't, disconnect and try calling again.

Remember: While VOIP uses your voice, which offers five times the context words alone can offer, it still lacks the visual cues that carry more than half of your message. (See page 263.)

Your Turn To grasp the difficulties involved in technical communication, use VOIP (or the phone) to explain a technical subject (e.g., a computer program) to someone.

Using Video Chat

Video chat uses an Internet connection to conduct live video and audio communication between computers (or portable devices like smartphones). Each computer must have a camera (called a Webcam), a microphone, and speakers or headphones. In effect, video chat is like VOIP, plus the live image. When conducting a video chat, remember the following:

- **Connection Costs:** Like VOIP, computer-to-computer video chat is usually free. However, a video chat by smartphone, unless connected by Wi-Fi, will use up minutes on your phone service plan.

- **Connection Quality:** Video quality may vary considerably, depending upon the connection, the quality of the Webcam, and the computer settings. Before making a video call, refer to the "Help" section of your video chat program to set up the best picture and sound.

- **Camera Position:** Video chat programs typically include both a large image of the person you are speaking with and a smaller image of yourself. The smaller image allows you to see what the other person is seeing so that you can avoid being partly off camera.

- **Lighting and Movement:** Before making a video call, check your image on the screen to see if any lighting adjustments are needed. Your program may allow you to adjust brightness, contrast, and color, but the lighting itself can make a big difference. Also, the less movement you make on camera, the less chance there will be of your image breaking up, stuttering, or freezing.

Remember: Video chat combines your words, voice, and body language in full-spectrum communication that minimizes misunderstandings. (See page 263.)

Your Turn If possible, conduct an in-class video chat, interviewing an expert in one of the subjects you are currently studying.)

Understanding Webinars

A Webinar is an online seminar that combines many of the technologies in this chapter. Often, the video portion is a slide show rather than live video. However, the presenter speaks live via audio connection, and attendees can pose questions and comments in a group chat window. Sometimes it is also possible for the attendees to participate by audio connection.

Many businesses and educational organizations use Webinars to present information. Chances are at least one of your teachers has attended a Webinar related to education. Search online for "education Webinar" to find many examples.

Your Turn Search for a Webinar in a subject area of your choice. (NASA.gov provides many space-mission Webinars, for example.) Attend one. Then report to your class about what you learned and about the experience itself.

Using Internet Content Effectively

Multimedia is more than just a way of dressing up a project. It is a way of using multiple information channels to communicate very effectively. (See page 68.) The Internet provides you with many multimedia resources for your projects.

Online Clip Art

The term "clip art" comes from the previous century, when books full of general illustrations were published. These drawings were meant to be cut out and used wherever an illustration might be needed. Today, search engines allow you to use topic keywords to find clip-art graphics, in the same way that you search for information.

When using online clip art, remember the following:

- Many clip-art sites are businesses that charge for their drawings. Other sites are maintained by individuals who offer their content for free.

- Some free sites are paid for by pop-up advertisements that may infect your computer with spyware or a virus. Often, these use deceptive layouts and links to trick you into clicking. Be careful when using such sites.

- Free sites may not always observe copyright laws, *but you are still responsible for the ethical and legal matters concerning the images you use.* (See page 267.)

Tip: Some search engines allow you to upload an image and search the Web for others like it. This can help you find the original source or something similar.

Your Turn Practice searching for images online, using both keywords and images. Considering a recent or current project, how would each way of searching be helpful?

Online Photos and Videos

Sites like Wikimedia.org, Flickr.com, and YouTube.com can be good sources of photos and videos for your projects. Just be sure that what you borrow is from the "creative commons" area. (See page 267.)

Government sites like NASA.gov are also good sources of media. Media created by government organizations are in the "public domain" (see page 267), so you can use them for free, but be sure to credit the source. Some media on government sites may belong to a third party. Check for a copyright statement on the Web page.

Online photos and videos can help your projects in two distinct ways:

1. **Illustrate your reports, stories, and other works.** For example, a photo from NASA.gov could illustrate your report about a new space program.
2. **Inspire new projects.** Sometimes just browsing online photos can give you an idea for a poem, story, or other project.

Your Turn Make a how-to video. Brainstorm for a topic you know how to explain. Plan your demonstration, practice it, and record it. Then share your video on a public site or your school's Web site and spread the word via social media (see pages 269–290).

Using Internet Content Fairly

While much media on the Internet is freely accessible, most belongs to someone, and an owner's rights should be respected. Take care to pay for materials that are not free, and to give credit for everything you use, free or not. (See "Avoiding Plagiarism" on pages 392–395.) The following information will guide your use of Internet content.

- **Copyright** is legal ownership of a written work, a performance, a software program, a movie, and so on. It is automatically granted by law at the time a work is created. (For example, when you write a paper for school, you own the copyright to that paper.) Many publications include a formal declaration of copyright statement using the word "copyright" or a © symbol.

  Note: Copyright law protects works for a limited period of time. After copyright expires, a work enters the public domain, and anyone can use it for free. Visit Gutenberg.org and Librivox.org for examples of public-domain properties.

- A **trademark** is a legally recognized symbol, word, or phrase representing a brand, a property, or even an organization. Your favorite soft drink probably has a "registered trademark"—indicated by a ® character. A ™ indicates a trademark is not yet registered.

  Note: Although many companies prefer that you include a ® or ™ (whichever is appropriate) when referring to their brand names, this is not legally necessary. (See *The Chicago Manual of Style,* 16th edition, section 8.152.)

- A **patent** is a legal right to a unique idea, usually an invention. Patents in the United States are awarded by the U.S. Patent Office. Products granted patents must display their patent numbers to ensure protection. "Patent pending" means that a patent has been applied for but not yet awarded.

- An **open-source license** or a **creative-commons statement** is a declaration that material is free to use and distribute, as long as any copyright and license statement remains with that material. Some licenses also allow the material to be modified or added to. Often, an open-source license requires that adaptations remain free to the public.

Your Turn Notice how many copyright statements, trademarks, registered trademarks, patents, and open-source licenses you encounter in a day's time. Then research the topic of open-source licenses more fully online. Write a journal entry explaining your thoughts about what you noticed during the day and learned from your subsequent research.

Internet-Literacy Activities

A World of Support

The Internet gives us a global window. It lets human beings see one another, and interact and assist one another, in ways never before possible. From microlending to crowd funding to citizen journalism, we are offered an "ambient awareness" of the rest of the world and a chance to invest ourselves in its ongoing development.

Your Turn

1. Investigate the concepts of microlending and crowd funding.
2. Summarize in a journal entry how the two are alike and different.
3. Choose a microlending or crowd-funded project that you would like to support.
4. Prepare a presentation for your classmates to introduce your chosen project and suggest that they support it as well.
5. Use Internet resources for media to enhance your presentation.
6. Remember to credit your sources.
7. Make your presentation in class.
8. Consider posting your presentation online as well. (See pages 269–290.)
9. When the microlending or crowd-funded project ends, report back to your classmates about its success or failure.
10. Reflect on what you have learned from the experience.

When's the Webinar?

Countless experts (scientists, business leaders, political figures, and authors, among others) host webinars, either to spread information or to receive feedback about a project or policy. Usually these webinars are recorded and archived for later viewing by people who could not attend the live event. You can learn a lot both from the main part of a webinar and the question-and-answer session that most conclude with.

Your Turn

1. Choose a topic that you are studying in one of your classes or something else that you find interesting.
2. Search the Web for webinars on that topic.
3. Review the description of any archived webinars to focus on ones most likely to fill in your knowledge of your topic and to address any questions you may have.
4. Also schedule time to watch any upcoming webinars on the subject. *Follow the registration procedure to attend those webinars.*
5. Take notes during each webinar, and make a separate list of any questions you have.
6. If you are watching an archived webinar, listen during the Q&A period to see if your questions are answered.
7. In a live webinar, politely ask your question during the Q&A period.
8. Share with your classmates what you learned from your webinar experiences.

Chapter 17
Using Social Media

Chances are that you visit Facebook regularly, watch YouTube videos often, and use other social media as well. Why? Probably because you want to stay connected to the world around you. The popularity of social media is vast and growing larger by the day.

This chapter will inform you about the many social media options available. It focuses on how to use your social media to represent yourself and things important to you in the best way.

You will learn . . .

- Introduction to Social Media
- The Purpose of Social Media
- Evaluating Social-Media Messages
- Types of Social Media
- Creating a Positive Digital Footprint
- Networking on Social Media
- Building a Personal Learning Network (PLN)
- Using Social Media to Solve Problems
- Social-Media Etiquette: The Do's and Don'ts
- Staying Safe Online

Introduction to **Social Media**

Social media applications are great for personal status updates and celebrity gossip, of course. They can also alert you to events, topics, and products that you might find interesting. What's more, they are increasingly influential in world events.

Social Media and the Arab Spring

In late December 2010, citizens in the North African country of Tunisia gathered to protest the oppressive leadership, high unemployment rates, and political and social repression they had been enduring. The country's news media, which were tightly controlled by President Ben Ali, dismissed the protesters, and the unrest failed to attract the attention of the global mainstream media. The absence of media coverage presented the demonstrators with a serious problem: *How do we mobilize support within our country and raise awareness for our cause outside the nation?* They turned to social media, and the results were groundbreaking.

Demonstrators used Facebook to schedule protests, Twitter to coordinate protests and share real-time updates, and YouTube and TwitPic to visually broadcast their cause to the world. Support for the movement spread like wildfire through social-media communities. Similar protests began popping up in other countries throughout North Africa and the Middle East. The revolutions became known as the Arab Spring. To date, oppressive government regimes in Tunisia, Egypt, and Libya have been replaced with democratic leadership.

Evolution of Social Media

The story above exemplifies the evolution of social media from a new way to connect with friends into a vehicle for social change, business marketing, brand development, and much more. As social media continue to evolve, new ways to connect with and make an imprint on the world will emerge.

Your Turn What does this story reveal about social media? What lessons can you take from this story for your own social-media use?

The Purpose of Social Media

People are using social media for a variety of purposes. The four main uses of social media form the acronym **SLIM**: sharing, learning, interacting, and marketing.

Sharing —— With social media, you can share information and ideas in a variety of ways. Different outlets allow you to publish your own ideas in writing, with pictures, or through videos and voice recordings; and you can also hyperlink your audience to interesting articles, pictures, and videos. The information you share can be either private or public. For example, you can email a private message to one person and broadcast a video to a global audience via YouTube. Always consider your communication situation (see page 68) before sharing information.

Learning —— Social media can also serve as personal learning tools (see page 283). You can get updates about your friends and family, or learn about what's happening in your community and around the world. The immediacy of the information flow allows you to get the gist of the latest news almost as it happens. Today, breaking news is often broadcast via social media before traditional media like TV and newspapers are able to cover it in detail. Social media can also reveal public sentiment about the big issues of the day or, on a less urgent level, opinions about a new restaurant or movie.

Interacting —— Maybe the most powerful element of social media is their interactive nature. Social media break the traditional barriers of time and distance between people. With video chat technologies like Skype, you can talk to people face-to-face anywhere in the world. On Facebook and mobile devices, you can chat digitally and text with your friends and family. Twitter even allows you to interact with media members, public officials, professional athletes, and celebrities.

Marketing —— More and more, social media are being used for marketing purposes. Businesses use social media to promote themselves and their products. Nonprofit organizations raise funds and promote charity events. Individuals market themselves to prospective employers. And you can use social media to promote ideas and events that are important to you.

Your Turn Think about all the ways you use social media. Which categories above include your social-media habits? Have you used social media in any ways not covered above? Explain.

Evaluating Social-Media Messages

Social-media messages are typically fast paced and short. We digest one and move quickly on to the next. Sometimes, though, we need to slow down and think critically about the messages we produce and consume. After all, our social-media interactions reflect how we perceive others and affect how others perceive us.

Just as with traditional media forms (see page 246), you can use the communication situation to evaluate social-media messages. Review the evaluation checklist below.

Social Media Evaluation Checklist

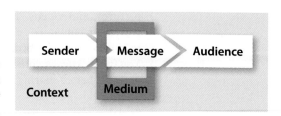

☑ **Sender:** Who created the message?

Discussion: What is your relationship with the source? You may perceive a message from a friend differently than you would one from your boss. Also consider the source's authority. A biologist talking about an invasive species has more authority than an accountant speaking on the same subject.

☑ **Message:** What does the message say (subject, main point, support)?

Discussion: Identify the main point and any supporting material. Is the main point supported by facts or by opinions? Follow links provided in the message to examine their information as well. Also analyze the message for fairness, logic, and accuracy. (See pages 240–251.)

☑ **Medium:** What type of media is used to deliver the message?

Discussion: Think about the medium's strengths and weaknesses. A microblog, for example, is quick and efficient but lacks depth. You wouldn't use a microblog service to send an important message. (See the graphic on the next page.)

☑ **Receiver:** Who is the target of the message?

Discussion: Social-media messages often spread far beyond their original intended audience. (Every Twitter message you write is even archived in the U.S. Library of Congress, for future generations to study!) Think about the various types of people your message may end up reaching. How might people of a different age group, culture, or nationality react to it? What responsibility might you have to those people? (See page 249.)

☑ **Context:** What is the purpose of the message?

Discussion: The purpose of a message may be to share, to inform, to interact, to persuade (market), or a combination of all four. (See page 250.) Are you using the best medium to achieve your message's purpose?

Types of Social Media

The world of social media is constantly evolving. Each year innovators are coming up with new ways to interact with people and share information online. The next several pages will discuss some of the more popular types of current social media, with tips and ideas for applying them in your school projects.

Before you dive into the types of social media in greater detail, examine the following graphic, which shows many of the current social-media communication platforms arranged by level of depth and formality—from very informal, personal messages to much more formal business emails.

Social-Media Communication

Media Types:	Formality:
Voice and video chats	Informal, personal
Texts	▪ quick
Microblogs	▪ conversational
Personal email	▪ short sentences
Message-board discussions	▪ occasional use of slang and abbreviations
Blogs	
Wikis	
Business emails	Formal, in-depth
	▪ carefully crafted
	▪ longer sentences and paragraphs
	▪ serious tone

Your Turn Which types of social media have you used? How would these forms compare in depth and formality to traditional communication forms like essays and personal letters? Share your ideas with a partner.

Email

Email may seem like an ancient form of communication to you. After all, it's been around since the earliest days of the Net. However, it is still a popular communication tool, especially in the workplace. In fact, both in school and on the job, the effective use of email is an essential skill.

Tips for Email Writing

- **Use a professional-sounding email address.** Instead of a using a nickname (T-Sm00th, J-Bow33, HoopsHero), use your real name in your email address. First initial and the last name is often a good choice. (See page 262 and visit thoughtfullearning.com/h274 for more information.)

- **Write clear and compelling subject lines.** The subject line should announce the main point of the message. This helps the receiver to decide what action to take with your email and helps in locating your message later, if necessary.

- **Start and finish your message with important points.** Begin by stating your purpose for writing, and end by noting any action you wish the reader to take.

- **Keep your messages simple and on target.** Receivers often put off reading long messages. If a message contains many different topics, readers may miss some or delay taking action.

- **Keep the message "cool" and respectful.** Strong emotion and offensive comments can derail messages and harm relationships.

- **Read every message before sending it.** Look for spelling, grammar, and usage errors. These can hurt your credibility with a reader.

Your Turn How often do you use email, and for what purposes? Discuss your experiences with classmates.

Chatting (Instant Messaging) and Texting

Two more forms of digital communication, chatting and texting, work well for quick and casual conversation. Unlike more formal types of writing, chatting and texting commonly use abbreviations and shorthand. As you chat and text, always consider who is on the receiving end of your message. Your level of language should suit your audience (see page 253).

Your Turn How often do you write text messages? How is the writing you do for a text message different from the writing you do for a school assignment? Explain.

Social Networks

Social networks allow you to connect and interact with a community of friends, family, and coworkers. You may already be a member of a social network like Facebook or Google+. If so, you know all about the ways you can interact and share slices of your life through messages, status updates, photos, games, recipes, music playlists, movie reviews, and so on. You can also interact with businesses and prominent figures by subscribing to fan pages and groups.

Tips for Social Networking

Here are some tips for making your social networking a positive experience:

- **Be friendly and social.** Maintaining a positive presence on a social network will help you make the most of the experience (see page 281).

- **Familiarize yourself with the privacy settings.** Remember that anything you say or do on a social site can be seen by anyone. You can protect yourself with privacy controls that restrict who sees what. However, the best way to protect yourself is to avoid posting information that could harm your reputation. Here is a good rule of thumb: Don't post anything you wouldn't want the public to see on a billboard.

- **Watch the clock.** There are so many things to do on social networks that it is easy to lose track of time. Don't let social networks control your life.

- **Avoid spam.** Spam and scams sometimes afflict social networks. Avoid clicking on links or apps that seem out of place or use baiting language like *OMG I can't believe this video* or *Check it out!* And always research an application before deciding to install it.

Using Social Networks for School Projects

Social networks enable you to work with others on group projects as well as promote things such as fund-raisers, band and theater performances, athletic events, and so on. Consider using the following features.

- **Group pages:** These pages allow for easy collaboration and communication between members of clubs, athletic teams, study groups, and so on.
- **Polling apps:** These applications allow you to create and distribute digital polls and surveys. Surveys can serve as primary sources of information for research projects, or they can be used for such simple things as polling the best date for a club meeting or noting who will bring what dish to a multicultural potluck.
- **Wall posts and messages:** These basic communication features are useful for posting project updates and instructions for group members or teammates.

Your Turn Which social-network sites do you prefer? How do you use them, and how often? Write a blog post or letter to the editor of your school newspaper, recommending one or more sites and offering best practices for its use.

Microblogs

A microblog is a short-form Web message. Microblogging is popular across social media, especially on sites like Twitter and Facebook. (Facebook "status updates" are examples of microblogs.) Though the messages are short, they can have a major impact and should be written carefully before posting and read carefully before responding. (See page 276.)

Tips for Microblogging

- **Strive for brevity.** Microblogs are meant for quick reading, so your message should be short, concise, and to the point. Character limits on sites like Twitter force you to produce brief notes.

- **Choose your words wisely.** Cut words that don't add value to the message, and replace dull, vague words with fresh, specific alternatives.

- **Know your audience.** Unless you are sending a message directly to a specific person, your post will be available for any of your followers to read, even if you are replying to someone else's message. Predict how others will react to the message, both positively and negatively. (See page 253.)

- **Time it right.** Schedule your post for a time you know your followers will be available to read it. (See thoughtfullearning.com/h276 for more information.)

- **Use hashtags thoughtfully.** Hashtags (see below) are a convenient way to categorize online conversations, engage readers, and make messages easy to find. But don't overuse them. Including too many hashtags in a message dilutes its impact and meaning.

> ### What is a **character**?
> Twitter sets a 140-character limit for Tweets. (See page 276.) Each letter, number, symbol, or space counts as one character. This sentence includes 37 characters.

Learning Twitter Terminology

Twitter is one of the most popular microblogging services. If you are unfamiliar with it, here are some key terms to understand.

- A **Tweet** is a microblog post on Twitter. (Be sure to capitalize "Tweet.")
- To **Retweet** is to share someone else's Tweet on your account, thereby spreading its audience.
- **Followers** are people who set their accounts to display your posts.
- **Following** someone means your account is set to display that person's posts.
- A **Hashtag** is a keyword with a # in front, like *#Chemistry* or *#World Series*. Hashtags help Twitter users to locate "conversations" about particular topics.
- **Trending** topics are those with lots of Tweets at the moment. By looking at a list of trending topics, you can get a snapshot of what is popular.

Your Turn Discuss with classmates strengths and weaknesses of microblogging.

Researching on a Microblog

A microblog like Twitter makes it possible to interact with people from all walks of life: journalists, scientists, public officials, educators, and athletes, just to name a few. As a learning tool, microblogs provide you with a great opportunity to interact with experts on a topic. Below are some steps you can take to search Twitter for authorities on subjects you are studying. Other microblogging services have similar tools.

Finding People of Interest

On Twitter, you can search for people by name, or choose the "#Discover" tab at the top of your Twitter page to browse accounts related to your interests.

1. **People searches:** If you know the name of the person you want to follow, simply enter his or her full name in the search box at the top of the page. Then review the list of people found in the search results.
2. **Topic searches:** If you want to connect with a professional or an expert in a particular subject but don't have someone specific in mind, complete a "browse categories" search to find accounts related to the subject. For instance, you can search for a specific topic like "cosmology" (see the example below), or enter a description like "professor of media studies."

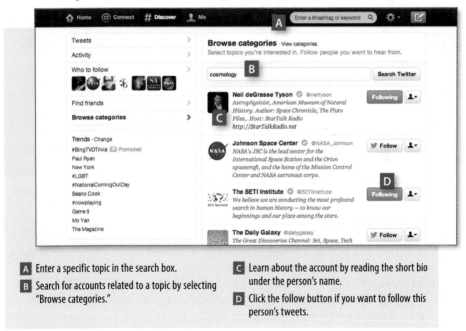

A Enter a specific topic in the search box.

B Search for accounts related to a topic by selecting "Browse categories."

C Learn about the account by reading the short bio under the person's name.

D Click the follow button if you want to follow this person's tweets.

Other Ways to Connect on Twitter

- **Join Twitter chats** to find people discussing subjects you care about. You can find a schedule of chats online. (Visit thoughtfullearning.com/h277 for more information.)
- **Follow professional groups** that are discussing topics related to your studies.

Blogs

A blog (short for Web log) is an online journal or electronic diary. Businesses use blogs to communicate with customers. Individuals use them to talk about topics important to them. (For more information about creating blogs, see pages 598–601, and visit thoughtfullearning.com/h278.)

Blogs can be an important source of news, entertainment, and opinions online. (Just be sure to consider the authority and credentials of the blogger.) Blogs are flexible, allowing dynamic integration of images, video, and sound. They are also interactive, allowing visitors to leave comments or questions about posts.

Message Boards and Internet Forums

A message board is similar to a blog, except that anyone can make posts. Typically, all conversations on a message board focus on one main topic, such as "Linux development" or "urban architecture." The different conversations within a message board are called "threads," which are monitored by a moderator who keeps discussions on track and respectful.

A Title of the message board

B Each new topic of discussion is a called a thread.

C The number of posts included in the thread

D The date, time, and author of the last post

A Mars Science Laboratory (MSL) News

Topic	Posts	Last Post
B Evidence of water on Mars	34	12/04/12 by SpaceMan
Images of the new drill bits	8	11/18/12 by john2837
MSL's first steps	**C** 12	10/12/12 by admin
First images from MSL are in	56	10/03/12 **D** by adam545
Touch Down!	66	10/03/12 by Mars8787
Landing event	71	10/02/12 by ApolloFan
New landing site picked	10	07/12/12 by adam545

Blog and Message-Board Comments

Comments on a blog or message board ought to be well crafted. Think about what you are going to say, and follow these guidelines.

- **Be polite.** Phrase any comments or questions politely, and be patient for a reply. Never make comments that attack the author or another contributor, even if you disagree with what he or she has to say.
- **Be clear.** The clearer and more concise a comment is, the more likely it is to be read and answered. Consider drafting your comments in a word processor before posting them online.
- **Be safe.** Never post personal information on blogs.

Your Turn Do you frequent any favorite blogs or message boards, or do you publish your own blog? Discuss your blogging experience with a classmate.

Collaborative Documents

Social media make it possible for you to collaborate on writing, research, and other projects. Two effective tools for collaborative projects are wikis and Google Docs.

Wikis

A wiki is a Web site that people build and edit together using a Web browser. Writers and editors around the globe have built many popular wikis. Wikipedia may be the best known, but many specialized wikis exist, including medical and science sites, as well as classroom wikis composed by teachers and students. Here are some tasks you can accomplish with a wiki.

- **Brainstorming ideas:** A wiki provides a space to gather ideas, along with links to images or information that support them.
- **Storing research:** A wiki offers a central location for saving your research for a project or paper.
- **Managing a group project:** A wiki can be used to conduct a group project, from planning and researching to improving and publishing.
- **Practicing collaborative writing:** Wikis are convenient for peer revising and editing.
- **Creating an electronic portfolio:** A wiki allows you to share an unfinished project with a group of people for feedback, and to publish the finished work.

(For more about wikis, see pages 596–597 and visit thoughtfullearning.com/h279.)

Google Docs

Google Docs is an online word processor, spreadsheet, and presentation editor that allows multiple users to create, revise, and edit the same document all at the same time. With Google Docs you can access your work from any computer at any time, and the chat feature allows you to discuss your work with others in real time. Here are some of the tasks you can accomplish with Google Docs.

- **Working together on group projects:** Collaborative tools allow you to work on a single document at the same time. You can even see others' changes as they happen. A chat feature allows you to discuss your work.
- **Making collaborative study guides:** On one document, you can share and discuss notes with your classmates.
- **Planning and tracking projects:** The document, spreadsheet, and drawing features allow you to plan and execute projects, keeping track of progress toward your goals. (See pages 355–362 and thoughtfullearning.com/h279.)
- **Sharing writing assignments:** Classmates can team up to review one another's writing and collaborate on group writing projects.

Your Turn Brainstorm with classmates about ways you could use a wiki or Google Doc for a group project on which you are currently working.

Social Bookmarking

Billions of pages fill the World Wide Web, and this wealth of knowledge can be difficult to keep track of. It's not uncommon to find a useful Web page one day, and completely forget its URL the next. Your browser's bookmark function can help, but a long bookmark list itself can be cumbersome to scan for a specific Web page.

Social bookmarking services like Delicious.com, Pinboard.in, Instapaper.com, and Evernote.com help solve this problem. With these services, you save Web page addresses to an online site, which means you can access your bookmarks with any device that connects to the Web. The greater benefit, however, is the ability to organize your bookmarked material into categories. Social bookmarking works like this:

1. Once you sign up for a social-bookmarking service (most are free), you can install its bookmark button on your browser. Then, anytime you want to add a new Web site to your list, you click the button.

2. Clicking that button opens a new window, where you can categorize the link with keyword tags ("Civil War," "Chemistry research paper," etc.). These keyword tags help you organize and find your bookmarks later.

3. As you bookmark more Web pages, those with similar tags become grouped together in your social-bookmarking service. That way you can go back and search for Web pages based on the tags you assigned, rather than combing through a never-ending list.

4. Finally, your library of bookmarked material can be made open to the public, so classmates can browse your bookmarked sites, and you can browse theirs, making collaboration easy.

Social News

Social-news sites like Reddit.com, Slashdot.org, and Digg.com are Web sites on which users submit and vote on news, stories, and media. These user-posted stories become ranked according to popularity on the social-news site, with the highest-rated ones appearing at the top of the list. Bloggers often submit their stories on social-news sites as a way to attract attention and gain exposure.

Social Multimedia

Social sites provide a platform for creating, editing, and sharing multimedia. The following user-generated multimedia sites are some of the most popular.

- **Music- and audio-sharing sites:** Pandora Radio, Spotify, and Last.fm
- **Photograph-sharing sites:** Flickr and Instagram
- **Presentation-sharing sites:** SlideShare and scribd
- **Video-sharing sites:** YouTube, Dailymotion, and Vimeo

Remember that although this material is easily accessible and free to view or play, it is still protected by copyright law. You cannot legally include it in your own projects without the creator's explicit permission. (See pages 266 and 267 for more about copyright, trademarks, patents, licences, and giving credit.)

Creating a **Positive Digital Footprint**

Digital citizenship requires some wisdom. As you know, you must protect your yourself and your computer from unscrupulous people. (See page 289.) But you must also protect your reputation. In an increasingly interconnected world, actions you take online today can affect you far into the future. Prospective colleges, employers, and even acquaintances may be able to view your past comments, photos, videos, and activities. As you move forward into adulthood, the choices you make also begin to establish an online personality—a personal "brand." Choose wisely, and you will make a positive digital footprint. Here are some ways to do just that.

Be diverse.

Being active on many different social-media platforms will spread your exposure. Beyond Twitter and Facebook, you could start your own blog (see page 278), contribute to a wiki (see page 279), or post videos and audio podcasts (see page 510) on sites like YouTube and Podomatic. (To help manage multiple presences, you can use a service like HootSuite or TweetDeck. Or you can choose one spot to focus your posts and use an app to crosspost to other locations. Facebook, Twitter, and WordPress all have apps for this purpose, for example.)

Be creative.

Social media allow you to showcase your creativity. Consider publishing schoolwork or other projects you are proud of. Create a digital résumé that features your talents and qualifications. Post a one-minute video along with your college application if the university allows it.

Be articulate.

The way you communicate on social media will establish your online reputation. Strive to write clear messages that avoid offensive or hurtful language and are free of embarrassing spelling and grammar errors. This is particularly important when you are addressing a public audience.

Be friendly and social.

Simply being nice can go a long way toward building a positive digital presence. Compliment your friends on social networks. Write constructive comments on other people's blogs and promote those people's efforts. Seek out groups that share your interests, and just be friendly in general.

Be yourself.

Artificial words and actions are easy to spot. Use social media to broadcast your true personality. People respond positively to genuineness.

Your Turn How would you describe your online brand? How could you improve it?

Networking on Social Media

Networking on a social-media site can feel like entering a room full of strangers. At first, you don't know whom to talk to, which voices to trust, and which to ignore. The situation can be awkward, and you may feel lost in the crowd, but here are some strategies that will help you break the ice and make a good impression.

Step 1: **Break the Ice**

On social media, you can connect with others either directly or indirectly. One direct approach is to simply ask someone a question and wait for an answer. This approach may feel a little abrupt, however, like a pushy salesperson at a mall. A less intrusive approach is to introduce yourself in one of the following ways:

- Share or Retweet (see page 276) one of the person's messages, along with a complimentary comment.

- Mention to your own followers how you respect or enjoy this person's ideas. Remember to include the person's social-media handle (name) in your "shout-out." That way, your mention will show up on his or her account.

Tips for Networking

As you network on social media, profile yourself in a respectable way with a picture and details that match your personality and interests (without exposing private information).

- Join a conversation by replying to one of the person's status updates or Tweets. Either add useful information, ask a good question, or show your genuine interest in the topic.

Step 2: **Advance the Conversation**

After you have engaged the person by focusing on his or her interests, you can advance the conversation by introducing yourself and asking any questions you may have. Twitter can prove to be a good source of school-related information. Remember to use a polite and friendly tone, and if the connection proves useful, you may be able to network beyond Twitter through avenues like email or Skype.

Your Turn Have you ever used social media to find help with your school projects? If so, discuss your experience; and if not, consider how you might use social media in your future projects.

Building a Personal Learning Network

A personal learning network (PLN) is a community of people who connect with each other to share knowledge, ideas, and resources. Social media offer an extraordinary environment for personal learning, allowing you to tap into a broad scope of people and knowledge. Cultivating a PLN helps you accomplish the following tasks:

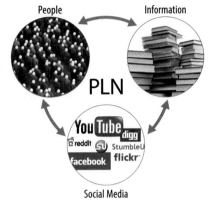

- **Seeking and storing information** about topics that are important to you
- **Fostering connections** with people from across the globe
- **Interacting with experts** in various fields
- **Gaining feedback and inspiration** from others' work
- **Sharing your knowledge** with others
- **Collaborating with others** to answer questions and complete projects

Using Social Media to Create a PLN

Use social networks (Twitter, Facebook, Google+, LinkedIn) to follow the people and organizations that share your common interests, even if you don't know them personally. Create separate PLNs for your personal and school-related interests, and follow these tips to establish strong learning networks:

Tips for Creating Strong Learning Networks

- **Begin the conversation.** Ask questions, make comments, and share relevant information on social networks.
- **Find relevant sites.** Bookmark or subscribe to blogs, Web sites, podcasts, or videos that offer content related to your interests or topic of study.
- **Organize material.** Use RSS feeds to syndicate your bookmarked material in one place.
- **Participate.** Discover and contribute to wikis or message boards related to your interests or topic of study.
- **Categorize messages.** Use (and search for) hashtags in microblogs that relate to your area of interest or topic of study.
- **Be helpful.** Offer constructive comments and questions on blogs and microblogs.

Your Turn Choose a topic, either school-related or personal, that especially interests you. Using social media, build a PLN and pursue your interest.

Using a PLN to Answer Project-Based Questions

You can use social media to answer questions about school projects. The next two pages explain how a group of students built a social-media-based personal learning network (PLN) to complete a science project.

Case Study: Project Biodiesel

Background: Students working on a science project are researching alternative fuel types, specifically biodiesel, which is diesel fuel made from processed vegetable oil. They want to learn as much as they can about the fuel type, including the viability of building a biodiesel processor in their school laboratory.

Questions: How can we build a basic biodiesel processor? What parts do we need? How can we obtain the parts for a reasonable cost?

Creating a Specialized PLN

The students used social media to find answers to their project-based questions.

▶ **Social Networks:** By creating a Twitter account for their project, the students began following a network of people and organizations that shared an interest in biodiesel fuel. They built this network by completing the following tasks.

- **Conducting a hashtag search:** With the hashtag #biodiesel, students found many current Tweets about their topic.
- **Following accounts:** Students followed the people and organizations that shared news and information about biodiesel.
- **Asking project-based questions:** Students directed their questions to people who shared a common interest in biodiesel.

Jenna Higgins Rose @Biodiesel_Voice
Jenna Higgins Rose specializes in biodiesel education & communications for the National Biodiesel Board and other organizations. She is founder of Rose Media.

Follow

Biodiesel Fuels @Biodiesels
Biodiesel market research, strategy and sales licensing.

Follow

Julene Dessie Houchins @JuleneDessieHouchens 22h
I understand that unlike coal and oil, biodiesel is renewable. But what about its carbon emissions? #biodiesel

Expand

▶ **Aggregators:** In the course of their research, a few news sites and blogs emerged as the students' favorites. Instead of checking each site daily for new content, the students saved time by subscribing to the sites' RSS feeds. Consequently, all the new content from each site automatically filtered into their Google Reader. (For more examples of aggregators, visit thoughtfullearning.com/h284.)

▶ **Wikis:** The students used the "Biodiesel" and "Biodiesel Production" wiki to do further research for their project.

▶ **Message Boards:** Using a search engine, the students found a message board titled "Biodiesel & SVO Discussion Forums." Two discussion threads on the message board caught their eye: "Making Biodiesel" and "Biodiesel Equipment." The students introduced themselves on each thread, explained their project idea, and asked and answered questions about it.

A The discussion threads are relevant to the project.

B The large number of posts shows the thread is popular.

C The date of the latest post shows the message board is active and up-to-date.

Topic	Posts	Last Post
Making Biodiesel **A**	**B** 1002	11/12/12 by Olive323 **C**
Biodiesel Quality	522	11/10/12 by Philip8493
Biodiesel Equipment	785	11/08/120

▶ **Social Bookmarking:** Discovering many different resources on biodiesel, the students realized they needed a way to keep track of them all. So each one signed up for a social bookmarking tool that allowed him or her to save the resources they came across to one place, creating a personalized digital library. By bookmarking, they could (1) have continual access to the material from any computer or digital device, (2) categorize the material with keyword tags for easy searching, and (3) share their entire bookmarked collection with other members in the group. (See page 280 for examples of social bookmarking tools.)

▶ **Online Video:** The students searched online for other high schools engaging in biodiesel projects. One video showed a high school's homemade biodiesel processor. The students contacted the video's creator and were able to contact the other high school group and learn about their experience building and maintaining a biodiesel processor in their school laboratory.

PLN Summary

The students' purpose for building a PLN was to answer pressing questions about a project. In doing so, they received a wide range of information about biodiesel processors, including how they are built and where to go for parts. In addition, students connected with others from another high school who had completed a successful biodiesel initiative in which they built a processor and donated the converted biodiesel to local farmers. The collaboration motivated the students to began creating, improving, and presenting their own biodiesel initiative.

Inquiry Timeline

The students created a PLN to answer questions about a project.	The students used their PLN as a planning and research tool for their project.	The students relied on their PLN as a resource for creating, improving, and presenting their project.

| Question | Plan | Research | Create | Improve | Present |

Using Social Media to Solve Problems

You can turn to social media to solve real-world problems, both big and small. In the example on this and the next page, you will read how students used social media to tackle a problem facing a local institution.

Case Study: Save Our Animal Shelter

Background: Every year, 11th graders at Wilmington South High School volunteer at their local animal shelter. The shelter receives no federal or state funding and relies on private donations from individuals, corporations, and foundations. For the last three years, private donations have steadily decreased, and the shelter is struggling to operate on a tight budget. There are even rumors that it may close.

Problem: How can students at the high school help the local animal shelter solve its budget crisis?

Solution: A group of five 11th graders decided to start a social-media campaign to support the animal shelter.

Research: The students used their study hall to research other animal shelters' social-media practices. They discovered that many of the country's largest shelters maintain a heavy social-media presence, from blogs to social-network pages to online videos. The students used Twitter to ask advice from the marketing director of their state-level Humane Society. That Twitter conversation eventually led to a Skype call between the students and the director, during which more questions were asked. The marketing director recommended some additional resources and provided the students with her email address for future contact.

Creating a Social Media Campaign

Having some good information and knowing where to look for more, the students at Wilmington South High School began their social-media campaign for the local animal shelter.

1. First, the students created a "WSHS for Animals" Facebook group, which included basic information about the cause. They took pictures of animals at the animal shelter and uploaded them to a photo gallery on the group's page. Then they invited all their friends to join the group and encouraged those friends to invite others. The group was made public so anyone could join.

2. Next, the students created an @WilmingtonAnimalShelter Twitter username for the campaign. Initially, they used their personal accounts to promote the campaign account. Soon it gained enough followers that they could use it to post updates, to share information about the shelter and its animals, and to announce a dance and other fund-raising ideas. They ended every Tweet with the #PuppyLoveDance hashtag and encouraged others to do so, which made it easy to search for any mention of their cause.

 WSHS for Animals @WilmingtonAnimalShelter
Who doesn't love puppies? #PuppyLoveDance

3. To boost appeal for their campaign, they created a digital video featuring interviews of staff members and volunteers from the animal shelter as well as footage of the animals themselves. The students uploaded this video to YouTube, embedded it on their Facebook group page, and shared a link to it on their Twitter account. In addition, they created a caption contest for a photo of two puppies. The person who delivered the most creative caption would win a #PuppyLoveDance T-shirt.

4. The students had already obtained school permission for their Puppy Love Dance. With the success of their social-media program, they brainstormed more ways to raise funds. They decided to approach local businesses about donating items for an auction at the dance and asked them to help advertise the event. Each new success was broadcast on Twitter and Facebook.

5. The dance and auction were huge successes. Staff members from the shelter showed up with animals, and photographers from the school newspaper and a local paper snapped photos. During the event, the emcee encouraged participants to Tweet live updates using the #PuppyLoveDance hashtag.

Social-Media Summary

Building on the success of the event, the animal shelter asked the students to help create an official, ongoing social-media presence for the society's local location. As more and more people in the community took notice of their cause, donations to the shelter increased, and the Puppy Love Dance became an annual event.

Inquiry Timeline

The students encountered a problem and inquired about how to solve it.	The students used social media to plan and research a solution to the problem	The students created a social media campaign to help solve the problem.

Question	Plan	Research	Create	Improve	Present

Social-Media Etiquette: The Do's and Don'ts

Day-to-day life has rules of etiquette. The challenges of online communication (see pages 262–265) mean that social media has an etiquette all its own, Below are 10 important rules to follow as you interact with others on all types of social media.

1. Do	read every message before clicking "Send."
2. Don't	click "Send" when you're tired or emotional. Especially avoid sending messages when you're angry. Once posted, a message is difficult or impossible to take back.
3. Do	introduce yourself whenever you "friend" someone, "follow" someone, or join a conversation.
4. Don't	post embarrassing or incriminating photos or video to social-media sites at any time. Again, once posted, they may be out of your control.
5. Do	comment on and promote other people's work.
6. Don't	bully or gang up on people.
7. Do	strive for honesty and transparency in your interactions.
8. Don't	feel obligated to "follow" or "friend" someone. Likewise, don't make others feel obligated to "follow" or "friend" you.
9. Do	consider your audience. Know the difference between a public and a private message.
10. Don't	post either your own or someone else's private information online (telephone number, home address, etc.).

Your Turn Brainstorm with classmates ways to recognize hazardous or difficult situations when communicating in social media. Discuss best practices for handling those situations.

Staying Safe Online

The World Wide Web is, any many ways, like the Wild, Wild West. It's full of exciting opportunities and emerging technologies like the various types of social media in this chapter. But it also has its share of hazards, including cyber bandits. To protect yourself, your family, and your computing device, you'll need to follow a few common-sense precautions.

▶ **Protect your identity.**

Don't reveal personal details to strangers online. Before making any information public, consider what it reveals about you, your home, and your family. That warning is especially true of photos and Web cam images.

▶ **Use trusted sites and services.**

Just as wandering down a dark alley in a city is unsafe, so is navigating an unusual Web site, chatting in an unfamiliar service, or opening a suspicious email. Stick to sites and services with a national or worldwide reputation to be safe.

▶ **Look before you click.**

Spammers disguise dangerous links with innocent names. (Your status bar may give you a clue.) Phishers send emails claiming to be from somewhere official, but with an infected attachment or a link to a fake Web site. If you aren't sure, don't click. If an email says you need to check your account, go directly to the actual Web site in your browser; avoid using links in emails.

▶ **Close the door.**

When finished using a personal account from a public computer—at school, at the library, or even at someone else's house—remember to log out, so the next person cannot access your account.

▶ **Don't download anything questionable.**

The surest way to get a computer virus is to download something you shouldn't. Unscrupulous people know how tempting a "free" album, movie, game, or book is, and they often offer infected files this way. Even legitimate programs are often packaged with lots of other software that can bog down your computer. Be sure you know *exactly* what you are installing before giving it access to your computer.

▶ **Make sure your computer has antivirus and antispam software.**

Many security companies offer free versions of programs that can help keep your computer safe from intrusion. Be sure to keep the program's virus definitions up to date, though. It is also a good idea to use an online scanner every six to twelve months to see if your antivirus program has missed anything.

Your Turn Check online for news reports of identity theft. Share in class what you discover, and discuss ways the victim could have avoided being taken advantage of.

Social-Media Activities

Use the following activities to improve your social-media skills.

Research a Topic

You can use social media to research interesting topics for yourself or for school projects. (See pages 275–287.)

Your Turn Follow the instructions below to research a topic of your choosing, using social media.

1. Select a topic that you are studying in school or that otherwise interests you.
2. Brainstorm a list of questions about the topic—things you want to know. Consider asking one or more friends to help generate this list.
3. Use a microblogging service or social-media site to search for information about your topic and to connect with experts on in that area. (See page 277.)
4. Start an account with a social bookmarking service, and explore any shared "tags" related to your topic. (See page 280.)
5. Don't settle just for text. Explore multimedia—graphics, audio recordings, video, animations, and webinars—related to the topic. (See page 280.)
6. Create a wiki or Google Doc to use as a research hub for taking notes, storing important links, and organizing your research.
7. Use your research hub to identify any gaps in your knowledge and to organize production of your project.

Start an Advocacy Campaign

As you have learned in this chapter, social media can provide a powerful platform for advocacy. In this activity, you will pick a cause or issue that is important to you and use social media to raise awareness and take action.

Your Turn Choose a cause or issue that you care about—something at school or in your community. The cause can be anything from encouraging volunteerism at a local institution to promoting a school club or organization.

1. Brainstorm with friends a list of causes you care about.
2. Select one cause to champion in a social-media campaign.
3. Brainstorm ways you could use social media to raise awareness for that cause.
4. Make a plan, identifying your goal, the steps to achieving it, the social-media tools available to you, roles for members of the group, and a target end date. (See pages 355–362.)
5. Put your plan into action.
6. Once the project is over, take time to review what you learned, including which social-media sites and strategies were effective.
7. Make notes of best practices for your next social-media project.
8. Share in class or in a blog post the story of your social-media project so that others can benefit from your experience.

Chapter 18

Developing Financial Literacy

You may have heard the phrase "drawing up a financial plan." It takes careful thought and good information. A well-drawn financial plan is much more than a doodle. After all, there's a lot to keeping track of money—earning, saving, buying, borrowing, investing, managing.

The truth is, all of us can use some help with financial literacy. Most likely, you'll need to work for your money, and with the right counsel, you can make your money work for you as well.

This chapter can help, but remember that Thoughtful Learning is not a licensed financial advisor or accounting institution. All your financial questions should be directed to professional financial-services individuals or companies.

You will learn . . .

- Developing Healthy Financial Habits
- Earning
- Saving
- Purchasing
- Borrowing
- Investing
- Managing
- Financial Glossary

Developing Healthy Financial Habits

Managing money is like managing your health—if you develop good habits, you won't have to constantly worry about money, or your health. If you develop bad habits, you'll struggle with both. A starting point is to understand financial terms. When you encounter terms you don't understand, turn to the financial glossary on pages 310–313 in this chapter. Also cultivate the following healthy financial habits:

1. **Know your income.** How much money do you make in a week? Being aware of your overall or gross pay per week (or hour) is important, but also note your take-home pay per week. If you work on a less regular basis, try to figure out your average take-home pay per week.

2. **Know your expenses.** How much money do you spend in a week? What do you buy every week? What do you buy occasionally? What are you hoping to eventually buy? Think about where your money goes.

3. **Make a budget.** Connect your income and expenses. Plan how to pay for everything you need. Save an amount of money each week for future purchases, unexpected or planned.

4. **Live within your means.** The surest way to avoid debt is to spend only what you earn. The only way to ensure you don't run out of money is to spend less than what you earn.

5. **Research your purchase options.** Which option is the least expensive? Which has the best features? Which has the best reviews? Which option is the most popular? Which fits what you actually need? Understand all the options before you buy anything.

6. **Think critically about choices.** Buying one thing means you won't have the money to spend on something else. Do you need the thing enough to spend your money for it? Are you buying it only because everyone else is or because the commercial for it is funny? Think about your purchases and avoid impulse buying.

7. **Plan for the future.** What do you want to be doing in 5 years? In 10? In 20? How much money will you need? What kind of job or career will provide that kind of money? Planning can help you realize the future you want instead of settling for whatever comes along.

8. **Save for the future.** Set aside a little money each time you get paid. By gradually building up your savings, you'll have the best chance of controlling your financial destiny.

Your Turn Rate your performance on the habits above. Choose two habits to improve upon and look for ways to do so by paging through the rest of this chapter.

Never	Occasionally	Usually	Always
1	2	3	4

Earning

Doing chores for your parents or neighbors and being paid for it might be the first job you'll have. The money you earn is handed to you, and that's that. Once you start working for a formal business, however, earning income gets a little more complicated.

W-4 Form

You'll start by filling out a W-4 form, which tells your employer how much of your pay to withhold for tax purposes. (The form includes worksheets to help you make these calculations.) "Allowances" in line 5 refers to the number of dependents (spouse and children) you have.

W-2 Form

At the end of each year, your employer will provide you with a W-2 form that shows how much you earned in the year. This is the amount reported to federal and state governments and by you on your tax forms. Earned income includes wages, salary, tips, commissions, and other compensation.

1099 Form

If you have income from royalties, interest, or dividends, the company or organization that pays you this will report it on a 1099 form. You'll have to include that income as well on your tax forms.

Your Turn Search for the W-4 form online at irs.gov, download a copy, and fill it out for practice.

Understanding Benefits

In addition to receiving money for your work, you might receive other benefits as well. These benefits are part of an overall compensation package—a way that employers compete for good employees. Sometimes the employer will pay the total cost of these benefits, but other times you may be required to pay part of the cost in the form of a deduction from your pay. Here are some types of benefits that may be offered.

- **Insurance:** If you work full-time (usually 30 or more hours a week), your employer may offer an insurance package that costs less than what you could purchase on your own. The package may include medical, dental, vision, disability, and life components. (See page 309.)

- **Retirement:** For full-time employees, many employers offer retirement-savings options such as 401(k)s, IRAs (individual retirement accounts), or pensions. Often these plans offer tax benefits. Talk to a financial advisor or tax accountant to learn more about the tax benefits.

- **Profit sharing:** Some employers reward employees by giving them a share of the business's profits. When the company benefits, the workers do as well.

- **Paid time off:** Full-time employees often receive paid time off for vacations, holidays, sick days, and bereavement (time off for a loss in the family).

- **Unpaid leave:** Full-time employees may also be allowed to take time off without pay.

- **Day care:** Some employers who want to retain employees with young children offer a child-care benefit or even on-site child care to help working parents.

- **Housing:** If you work at a remote location (such as a summer camp or an archaeological dig site), you may be provided with on-site housing so that you can do your job.

- **Meals:** If you work in a remote location (such as on a fishing boat or an Army base), or if your employer wants to encourage you to stay on-site during mealtime, you may be given meals.

Benefits like those explained above can make a lower wage more acceptable, but remember that employers can change the benefits they offer at any time. Consider all the factors of a job when making your choice—the work, pay, and benefits.

Your Turn Think of a job that you would like to do now or after you graduate. Search online to find out how much the job typically pays and what benefits come with it. Then search specific employers in that field and choose one that offers a strong compensation package. Write a journal reflection, imagining yourself working for the employer.

Paying Taxes

You've probably heard the old saying "Nothing is certain except death and taxes." To put a positive spin on it, if you're paying taxes, at least you're still alive. Your taxes pay for the many government services you receive, from paved roads to public education to firefighters to Social Security and national defense. Some taxes are deducted from your paycheck, while others are paid directly by you.

Deducted Taxes in the United States

- **Federal income tax:** Income tax provides the federal government with its largest source of funds—about 42 percent of total revenues.
- **State income tax:** Income tax provides the state government with its main source of revenue.
- **FICA:** This tax (Federal Insurance Contributions Act) is your payment into the Social Security system.
- **Medicare:** This tax supports the Medicare system, which currently provides medical insurance to U.S. citizens 65 years or older as well as to individuals receiving Social Security Disability Insurance.
- **Medicaid:** This tax supports the Medicaid program, which currently provides medical insurance for people who receive certain government benefits—including people who are over age 65 or are disabled and receive Supplemental Security Income (SSI) from Social Security.
- **Unemployment tax:** This tax pays into an insurance system for those who lose their jobs.

Other Taxes in the United States

- **Property tax:** Property tax is usually assessed by local governments to fund services such as schools and garbage collection. It is paid by anyone who owns real estate.
- **Sales tax:** This tax is usually assessed by states on most nonfood items purchased within the state.
- **Excise tax:** This tax is usually assessed by federal and state governments on specific products. "Sin taxes" on items such as tobacco and alcohol are meant to discourage their use. A "user fee," such as the tax on gasoline, is applied to some connected cost, in this case building and repairing roads.

Your Turn Go to thoughtfullearning.com/h295 for a link to activities on the IRS Web site. These activities will help you understand the taxes you pay to the federal government.

Saving

One key aspect of financial health is saving. If you spend everything you earn, you limit your financial flexibility. But if you save a little bit each week or month, over time, you will build a cushion. Your savings can help sustain you when unexpected issues arise or in moments when you are unable to earn, for whatever reason. You can save at a variety of institutions.

Comparing Institutions

When you decide to open an account, consider the type of institution you will use:
- **Banks** are for-profit financial institutions open to anyone. Accounts in banks are insured for up to $250,000 by the Federal Deposit Insurance Corporation (FDIC).
- **Credit unions** are not-for-profit financial institutions run to benefit a specific group of people (for example, teachers, health-care workers, or military families). Accounts in credit unions are insured for up to $250,000 by the National Credit Union Administration (NCUA).
- **Investment firms (and banks)** often offer bonds, CD's, and money-market investments as an alternative to a low-interest savings account. However, your money can be restricted from access for a period of time.

Comparing Accounts

Both banks and credit unions offer two basic types of accounts:
- **Savings accounts** are set up for saving money, so they typically offer a modest interest rate and may restrict access to funds.
- **Checking accounts** are set up to make money easily accessible through checks or debit cards, but they typically offer little or no interest and may charge a fee.

When you are shopping for the best account, think about the following issues:
- Is a **minimum balance** required to open and maintain the account?
- Are there any **fees** involved in maintaining the account?
- What **interest rate,** if any, does the account offer?
- What **restrictions** apply to accessing your money?
- What possible **penalties** are attached to the account?

Managing Accounts

Usually, you can manage your accounts online, on the phone, or in person. You can deposit funds into an account, withdraw funds from an account, transfer funds between accounts, and check the balance. It is important to track all transactions in an account register and check it once a month against the statement you receive by mail or online.

Your Turn Go online to investigate savings options. Write a journal reflection about the best savings options for you, and indicate why you chose as you did.

Using Checks

When you open a checking account, you'll be given a few checks, but you will need to order more if you plan on using them as your primary way to pay. When you write a check, you must have enough money in your account to cover it. The best way to be sure of this is to keep a check registry, listing all the checks you have written and all the deposits you have made. Here are the main features of a check:

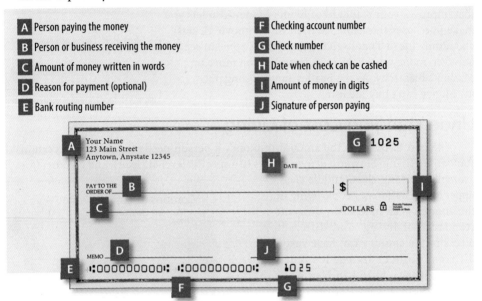

A Person paying the money

B Person or business receiving the money

C Amount of money written in words

D Reason for payment (optional)

E Bank routing number

F Checking account number

G Check number

H Date when check can be cashed

I Amount of money in digits

J Signature of person paying

Using ATM/Debit Cards

Most institutions today offer ATM or debit cards with their checking accounts. An ATM (automatic teller machine) card allows you to access your account at machines placed in businesses and throughout the community. Debit cards allow you to pay at most businesses with a direct withdrawal from your account.

Keeping a Register

Whether you write checks or use an ATM or debit card, you should keep track of your transactions. Whenever you make a payment or deposit, write the date, the recipient or source, the reason, and the amount. Then, whenever you need to find out how much you have in the account, you can subtract payments from deposits. You can also check this registry against the statement you receive from your financial institution.

Your Turn Go online to investigate banks near you to find out whether they offer checks, ATM cards, or debit cards. Write a journal reflection about which option you would prefer and why.

Purchasing

Of course, the reason to make money is to have purchasing power—the ability to buy the things you need or want. All of us have a common set of needs, as identified by Abraham Maslow. Money helps you get the water, food, clothing, and shelter you need to live, as well as the health care and property that improves your standard of living. Money also lets you make purchases that enhance friendships (movie tickets) and family life (a Thanksgiving turkey). As you can see, however, money slowly loses its power as you move up Maslow's hierarchy. As the Beatles' famous song puts it, "Money can't buy me love."

morality, creativity, problem solving

self-esteem, respect, achievement, confidence

friendship, family, acceptance

health, property, security, employment

air, water, food, clothing, shelter, sleep

Understanding Cost of Living

The cost of living is the amount of money a person needs to maintain a certain standard of living. *Standard of living* refers to a specific level of wealth and comfort (for example, working class, middle class, upper class). Different people living in the same city can have vastly different standards of living, and different places in the country can have vastly different costs of living. It's much more expensive to live in New York City than in a small rural town, for example. Both the cost and the standard of living can vary over time, depending on a variety of economic factors (jobs, income, property values, cost of goods, and so on).

Composite Cost of Living
1st Quarter 2012

Cost of Living Index Ranges
■ Greater than 115   ■ 105.1 - 115   ■ 95 - 105   ■ Less than 95

Consumer Price Index

One handy measure of the cost of living is the Consumer Price Index (CPI). The CPI measures the changes over time of the cost of goods and services in metropolitan areas. It takes the following items into account:

- **Food**—the cost of buying groceries
- **Merchandise**—the cost of clothing, furniture, cars, and so on
- **Housing**—the cost of purchasing or renting real estate
- **Energy**—the price of gasoline, heating oil, natural gas, electricity, and so on
- **Services**—the cost of haircuts, accountants, health services, and so on

Your Turn Go online to thoughtfullearning.com/h298. There you'll find a link for calculating the cost of living where you live and the cost of living somewhere else that you would like to live. Write a reflection about the differences.

Thinking Critically About Purchases

Have you ever bought something on a whim and regretted it later? Usually the regret is directly proportional to the amount of money you spent. Impulse buying might be fine for small items, but not for large purchases. Consider the following points before spending a significant amount of money:

- **Need or want:** Distinguish between what you truly need and what you only want. For example, if you need a car to get to work, you don't necessarily need a new muscle car. A used compact could work. By separating what you need from you want, you can make better decisions about what you buy.
- **Quality:** Purchase a product or service that is at least adequate in terms of meeting your need or want. For example, *needing* a car requires a vehicle that is safe, dependable, and affordable. *Wanting* a car may require one that is red and has a powerful engine.
- **Cost:** Think about how much money you must pay for the product or service. Know what the usual cost is and what you are willing to pay. If the cost is less, you may have found a deal. If it is more, be wary.
- **Alternatives:** Consider what other options you have for satisfying the need or want. It may be that you can buy something of higher quality for less money.
- **Opportunity cost:** Remember that by spending money on something, you no longer have that money to spend on other things. For example, if you finance a car, the down payment is spent, and the continued payments will come from your budget each month.

Researching Products and Services

In order to truly understand the alternatives available to you, you can create a comparison grid like the one below. In the left column, list alternative purchase possibilities. In the top row, list the features you want from the product or service. Then do your research and fill in the chart.

Used Cars	Age	Mileage	MPG (city/hwy)	Color	Price
Ford Focus	8 yrs	125,957	26/33	Red	$5,493
Chevy Cobalt	5 yrs	77,408	22/31	Blue	$6,896
Toyota Camry	9 yrs	81,140	23/32	Black	$8,990

Your Turn Imagine you are planning to buy a car to get to work or go to college. Think first about whether you actually need or just want a vehicle. Consider quality and cost (go to Kelley Blue Book at kbb.com). Then search online for cars for sale. Create a comparison grid to list the cars that most interest you. Which would you choose, and why?

Leasing and Buying

More-expensive items such as cars, apartments, and houses can be leased (rented) or owned. Each option has its own conditions.

Leasing

When you lease or rent something, you pay money on a routine basis for the use of someone else's property.

- **Lessee's responsibility:** The person paying rent is provided exclusive use of the property but must return the property in fair condition. Those who lease vehicles are often required to pay for maintenance as well.
- **Lessor's responsibility:** The person who owns the property must allow the lessee exclusive use of the property for the specified period. For real estate (apartments and houses), the owner usually performs routine maintenance.
- **Contract:** Renting involves a contract that grants the renter use of the vehicle or space for a specific purpose and period of time, with exact terms.
- **Security deposit:** Renting usually requires the renter to provide money up front to cover possible damage to the property. When checking into a hotel, for example, you have to provide a credit card up front. When renting an apartment, you often pay a deposit that will be refunded if you leave the property undamaged.
- **First month's rent:** Often the owner of the property will require you to pay the first month's rent before you move in.
- **Leasing with option to buy:** This arrangement, common with leased automobiles, asks the lessee to pay more money up front but less money per month than an outright purchase would require. At the end of a specified period, the lessee can opt to purchase the property.

Buying

When you buy something, ownership transfers from one person to another. The receipt you receive is a record of this transaction, showing what you paid and what you received. If you want to return something you bought, you need to bring the receipt to undo the transaction. Buying often includes other documents:

- A **guarantee** indicates that the item purchased is free of defects and is what the manufacturer purports it to be.
- A **warranty** indicates that the item purchased will work correctly for a specified period of time or be repaired or replaced by the seller.

Note: Always read the fine print of these documents so you know exactly what you are getting.

Your Turn Select one of the cars that you considered in your comparison grid on the previous page. Research any leasing options available for the vehicle. Examine the guarantee or warranty that is included with the vehicle's purchase. How would this information affect your decision to either lease or buy the car?

Understanding Payment Plans

Sellers want to make it easy for you to buy, so they often provide payment options:

- **Prepayment** allows you to reserve an in-demand item such as the latest novel by a popular author or the newest game release for a popular title. You can also prepay on a gift card or for cell-phone minutes.
- **Pay at purchase** refers to buying something online or at the checkout counter. You provide money and take possession of the product or service.
- **Layaway** means that you make a down payment on something, and the seller holds on to the item until you can pay the rest of the cost. There is often a charge for using a layaway service. If you don't make all of the payments, your money will be returned except for the initial charge.
- **Installments** allow you to pay for something in portions—perhaps a third down, a third the next month, and the final third the month after that. However, you can take the item with you after you sign the installment plan and make the first payment.
- **Rent to own** allows you to take the item and make regular rental payments on it, which slowly accumulate until you have paid a specified amount (usually much more than the regular price).
- **Billing** allows you to purchase a product or service and pay for it later when you get the bill. Most utilities work this way, as do services such as plumbing contractors or health-care providers.
- **Credit** purchases are paid for by a third party, whom you pay back. For more information about credit, see page 303.

Receiving and Paying Bills

If you are being billed for a product or service, you will receive a bill either in the mail or by email. The bill will indicate what product or service you received, the date of purchase, the total cost, the amount you have paid, the amount you owe, and the due date. By keeping up with your bills, you can avoid late fees and penalties.

Using Customer Service

If you have questions or concerns about a purchase, you can take the issue to the customer service department of the business involved. This service may be automated or person to person.

10/19/12

Bruisweist Automotive
2900 Preshing Dr
Oak Woods, IA 5065.
Phone (640) 555-918.
Fax (640) 555-812

SERVICE INVOICE

BILL TO:
John Harker
7752 Romayne Ave.
Oak Woods, IA 50652

Description	Parts	Labor	Cost
Oil Change	6 qrts 5W30	15 min	$24.25
Tire rotation		30 min	$40.00
		Subtotal	$64.2
Thank you		Tax	$3.21
for your		Total	$67.4(
patronage			

Due on receipt

Your Turn Go to a local store and show this page to a customer service representative. Ask the person which payment options explained above are offered by his or her store.

Borrowing

In a perfect world, we would all be debt free, but the world is not perfect. For instance, to get a job, you might need to have a car, but to get a car, you need to have a job. A car loan can help you get the car so that you can get the job. Understanding how to wisely and responsibly borrow money is important to financial success.

Note: Not all lenders are reputable, and some are even predatory—offering unfair, deceptive, fraudulent, or abusive loan terms. Beware of apparently "free money," variable interest rates, balloon payments, and offers that seem too good to be true. Deal only with reputable and fair organizations.

Developing a Credit Score

Your ability to borrow money is based on a variety of factors. One very important factor is your credit score. You are not born with a credit score. You must develop it by creating a credit history: borrowing and paying back small loans, gradually building up to larger loans. Here are some suggestions for developing credit:

1. **Consider a secured loan or a secured credit card.** If you're having trouble getting a loan, you can set one up by providing the collateral—money or a valuable object that you will give up if you default on the loan. Check with a loan officer at a bank (or with a credit card company) about getting a secured account. (Note that a secured bank loan is considered "closed-end credit," while a secured credit card is considered "open-end credit." Having both builds your credit score faster than having just one kind.)

2. **Find a cosigner.** You can also apply for a regular credit card with a cosigner who has an established credit rating. You must be the primary person on the account, however, or you won't be building your own credit score.

3. **Borrow up to 10 percent of your limit, and pay it back each month.** By borrowing only up to 10 percent, you make repayment manageable. Also, having a maxed-out credit card or loan hurts your credit rating.

4. **Make payments on time.** Your payment history is 35 percent of your overall credit score—the single biggest factor—so pay promptly each time.

5. **Apply for an unsecured credit card.** After six months of solid payments to secured loans or to a cosigned credit card, you should have enough credit to get a regular credit card. Often, unsecured cards offer lower interest rates and annual fees than secured cards do.

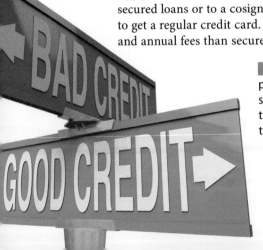

Your Turn With your parent's or guardian's permission, go online to search for options for secured loans, secured credit cards, and credit cards that allow cosigners. Which option would you prefer to use to establish your own credit? Why?

Understanding Credit

Credit comes in two basic varieties—closed-end credit and open-end credit. The next two pages discuss each type.

Closed-End Credit—Loans

Closed-end credit (sometimes called installment debt) refers to a specific amount of money lent for a specific purpose to be paid back in regular amounts at regular times. Car loans, student loans, and home mortgages are closed-end credit, and they usually involve much lower interest rates than open-end loans do. Here are some key terms to understand:

- **Secured loans** require collateral—money or valuable property that you offer to the lending institution in case you default on the loan (fail to make your monthly payments).
- **Unsecured loans** do not require collateral but often ask for a substantial down payment, money you pay up front, which you will lose if you default.
- **Principal** refers to the amount of money you are borrowing.
- **Interest** refers to the amount of additional money you pay the lender, based on an annual percentage rate.
- **Annual percentage rate (APR)** is the percentage of a debt that you pay in interest.
- **Prime lending rate** refers to the annual percentage rate offered to borrowers with excellent credit.
- **Points** refer to percentage points or tenths of a point added to the prime lending rate to borrowers with less than perfect credit ratings.
- **Fees** are charges for arranging and processing the loan. These can be paid up front or included in the loan.
- **Amortization** is the way that interest and principal are paid off over the lifetime of a loan. Most loans are structured so that you pay off more interest near the beginning of the loan and more principal near the end.
- **Penalties** are extra amounts that you must pay for making late payments or otherwise breaking the terms of the loan agreement.
- **Repossession** of property purchased by the loan (a car or a home, for example) occurs if you default on the loan (failing to make your monthly payments for a number of months in a row).

Your Turn Find an online amortization calculator. Calculate the total cost of a car purchase. Experiment by adjusting the following variables:
- price of the car (principal)
- annual interest rate
- down payment
- number of payments

When you find a combination that works for you, write it down. What price of car could you afford at what interest rate? How much money would you need for a down payment, and how many payments would you need to make?

Open-End Credit—Credit Cards

Open-end credit refers to an account with a specified credit limit that the person can draw upon at will, causing the principal and interest to fluctuate with purchases and payments. Open-end accounts such as credit cards usually charge much higher interest rates than closed-end loans do. In addition, interest is compounded daily or monthly, making the total interest rate even higher. When wisely managed, credit card accounts can help improve your credit rating. When poorly managed, however, credit cards can get you into financial trouble. Here are some key terms to understand:

- **Credit limit** refers to the amount that can be charged against a specific account—for example, $1,000. It is best not to charge more than you can fully pay off during each pay period.
- **Interest rates** refer to the percentage of interest charged on purchases using the credit card. There are different types of interest rates:
   - ▶ **Introductory interest rates** may be set as low as 0 percent for a certain period of time or for specific purchases, but these rates later shift to a standard interest rate.
   - ▶ **Standard APR** is usually set between 6 and 36 percent, depending on the credit risk of the cardholder.
   - ▶ **Penalty rates** that are even higher apply to late payments.
   - ▶ **Variable interest rates** change as the prime lending rate changes.
- **Minimum monthly payment** refers to the amount you are required to pay each month to avoid penalties. Usually, most of this payment is applied only to the interest you owe, so making only minimum monthly payments will not quickly reduce your debt.
- **Balance** refers to the amount you owe on the account, a combination of principal and interest, usually compounded daily.
- **Penalties** and penalty rates apply to late payments.

To avoid credit card pitfalls, follow these practices:
1. **Pay off the balance** each time if you can.
2. **Avoid paying only the minimum** monthly payment, which mostly covers accrued interest and only a small amount of principal.
3. **Pay on time** every time to avoid penalties and higher interest rates.
4. **Don't use credit card checks,** which simply encourage you to overspend.
5. **Be cautious of "reward" purchases,** since most credit cards require a lot of purchases to qualify for the reward.
6. **Avoid cards that offer perks but charge** high fees and service charges.

Your Turn Go online to search for other credit card pitfalls and how to avoid them. Write down a list of at least three. For each pitfall, write a suggestion for how to avoid it.

Applying for Loans

The only way to get a loan is to apply for one. The types of loans vary widely—from unsecured loans to car loans to mortgages. In each of these circumstances, you will work with a loan officer to complete a loan application.

Loan Applications

A loan application requires you to provide certain information about yourself and your financial status. Expect to provide the following information:

1. Your name, social security number, marital status, and contact information
2. Your employment information—current and sometimes past job information
3. A list of your assets (money and possessions) and your liabilities (debts)
4. Your monthly income and expenses

Note: The application also asks for the type of loan and the terms you seek, plus information about the lending agency, which is usually provided by the loan officer.

Credit Report

The application process will require your credit report as well. This report gives your credit score—a number ranging from 300 to 850 that indicates your likelihood of paying back a loan. Many loans use credit scores from Equifax, Transunion, or Experion. Mortgages use credit scores calculated by the Fair Isaac Corporation (FICO). Here is a listing of FICO-score levels and what each means.

760-850	**Excellent:** lowest interest rates and lowest down payments
700-759	**Great:** favorable conditions for credit and loan deals
660-699	**Good:** above-average terms
620-659	**Fair:** moderate rates and average terms
580-619	**Poor:** high interest, unfavorable terms, requiring proof of solvency
500-579	**Undesirable:** expensive credit, difficult to get approval
300-499	**Bad:** prohibitive to getting beneficial loan offers

Note: The figures shown here are guidelines. Values may vary from lender to lender.

Student Loans

Student loans can be acquired from individual institutions or directly from the federal government. In order to apply for student loans, you need to complete a Free Application for Federal Student Aid (FAFSA). (See page 124.)

Your Turn Go to fafsa.ed.gov, find the FAFSA, and complete it for practice.

Investing

Investing is putting money to work for you. Some investments involve little risk, for little reward. Other investments involve great risk, for great reward—or loss. Because of the rate of inflation, money that is not invested in some way actually loses value over time.

Planning Investments

You can use the inquiry process to set up investments. Here are the steps to follow when investing:

Questioning:
What do you want your money to do? Do you want it to be secure? Do you want it to earn as much as it can? Do you want quick returns, or are you investing for the long term? What options are available to you?

Question

Planning:
Think of the types of investment instruments you could use—savings, CDs, bonds, stocks, mutual funds, retirement accounts. Consider the strengths and weaknesses of each type.

Plan

Researching:
Discover which financial adviser has the best track record. Learn which stocks are performing best. Study markets. Investigate tax strategies.

Research

Creating:
Invest in an appropriate mix of different assets. With the help of a financial adviser, assemble a portfolio that matches your risk profile. Keep your records in a safe and easy-to-access location.

Create

Improving:
Monitor your investments. Note the instruments that deliver the dividends you want or the security you need. Adjust your investments to best match your goals.

Improve

Presenting:
Use the dividends from your investments as ready capital, or reinvest them to grow your wealth.

Present

Your Turn Begin your investment planning by writing answers to the questions listed above under "Questioning."

Understanding Investment Instruments

Investing starts with a simple savings account, which protects money and provides modest interest income. Other investment strategies offer less protection but can provide bigger returns. In that sense, investment strategies can be ranked in a continuum from secure, low-yield options to risky, high-yield options.

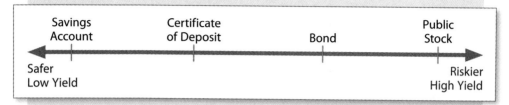

- **Savings accounts** at most banks and credit unions are federally insured for up to $250,000. The institution lends your money out to others and gives you a portion of the interest they make from the loans.

- **Retirement accounts** such as 401(k)s, IRAs, pensions, and profit-sharing accounts allow investors to set aside money with some tax advantages. The money is often professionally invested in a portfolio that represents the investor's individual strategy—from low-risk/low-yield instruments to high-risk/high-yield instruments, or a combination of the whole range.

- **Certificates of deposit** (CDs) are issued by banks and credit unions and indicate that the bearer has invested money for a specified period between three months and six years, to be repaid at an interest rate established at the time the CD is issued. Early withdrawal of the money can be subject to penalties. This federally insured instrument is low risk and low yield.

- **Bonds** are loans made by the bondholder for a specified period of time, during which the bondholder receives interest at intervals (monthly, semiannually, or annually). One way bonds differ from stocks is that a bondholder lends money while a stockholder buys shares of a business.

- **Stocks** are securities that establish ownership in a company and represent claims on part of the company's assets and earnings.
  - Holders of **common stock** usually can vote at shareholder meetings.
  - Holders of **preferred stock** generally cannot vote at shareholder meetings but receive a higher claim on assets and usually receive dividends before common stockholders.

- **Mutual funds** are professionally managed pools of money from a large group of investors. The money is invested in a variety of securities in an attempt to produce capital gains and income for the investors. Mutual funds are federally regulated.

Your Turn Which type of investment above would be most helpful to you right now? Why? Which type of investment will be most helpful to you in 10 years? In 50 years? Why?

Managing Your Money

Money management includes all the activities you've learned about so far—earning, saving, purchasing, borrowing, and investing. Successful money management creates a smooth and consistent cash flow rather than a cycle of feast or famine. The tool that brings all of these factors together is a budget.

Budgeting

A budget is a plan for balancing income and expenses. It is also a tool for assessing how well you are doing so that you can make adjustments. Some income and expenses are fixed—the amount you are always paid and the amount you always pay out. Other income and expenses vary. In the example budget below, the budget amounts were filled in before the month of June as a prediction, and the actual amounts were filled in afterward.

Example Budget

Budget for the month of June	Budget Amount	Actual Amount	Difference
Income			
Cashier at Whole Foods	$580	$610	$30
Lawn mowing	$80	$70	–$10
Odd jobs	$25	$38	$13
Other income (birthday money)		$35	$35
Total June Income	$685	$753	$68
Expenses			
Used Car Payment	$105	$105	$0
Car Insurance	$150	$150	$0
Trip to Six Flags	$150	$170	$20
Gas money	$100	$120	$20
Music downloads	$40	$28	–$12
Other expenses (bike repair)		$35	$35
Total June Expenses	$545	$608	$63
Savings			
Savings account deposit	$140	$145	$5

Your Turn Go to thoughtfullearning.com/h308 to download a budget template. Considering your own situation, fill in the first two columns for next month. Include both fixed and variable income and expenses. At the end of the month, fill in the last two columns of the budget. Were your predictions correct? Explain.

Managing Risk

As you have learned about investing, part of managing money is managing risk. Low-risk investments tend to have low-yield returns, while high-risk investments can have high-yield returns—or losses. Unexpected life events present another kind of risk.

The first defense against emergencies is to set up a savings account (see page 296). By putting aside a certain amount of money each paycheck, you'll eventually have the recommended three to six months of income stored up to support you.

However, some emergencies may require a great deal of money or may limit your earning ability. To prepare for such events, you need to have insurance.

Understanding Insurance

Insurance comes in various forms to help you manage risk in different areas of your life. Each insurance policy document outlines the terms of that particular policy, the premiums you must pay, and the benefits the insurance company will pay you under specific circumstances. Contact a professional insurance agent before you make any insurance decisions. Here are the basic types of insurance:

- **Auto insurance** protects you from liability in case of an auto accident that is your fault. Some policies also pay to repair or replace your vehicle and may also pay medical expenses.
- **Disability insurance** protects you in case you suffer an injury or illness that impacts your ability to work.
- **Health insurance** pays for specific medical expenses, from doctor visits and hospitalizations to medications and medical equipment such as wheelchairs.
- **Homeowner's insurance** pays you to repair or replace your home in case of fire or other property damage from specific causes. Often, flood insurance must be purchased separately.
- **Liability insurance** protects you in case another person sues you for injuries or loss caused by your negligence or improper actions.
- **Life insurance** protects beneficiaries (people that you name) from loss of your income by paying them money after your death.
- **Long-term care insurance** pays for custodial care in your home or in a nursing facility.
- **Renter's insurance** protects you from the loss of your property within a rental unit due to damages from fire, theft, or other named causes.

You, your employer, or both pay the premium that purchases an insurance policy. In addition, you may be required to make co-payments for services as well as pay a percentage of costs not fully covered by your policy.

Your Turn Which types of insurance do you currently have? Which type would you like to have? Investigate options for purchasing that type of insurance. What would the premiums be? What benefits would you receive?

Financial Glossary

Advertising: Media messages created to promote the purchase of a product or service

Amortization: The way interest and principal are paid off over the lifetime of a loan

Annual percentage rate (APR): The yearly percentage of a debt paid in interest and service fees; APR varies if installment payments are made

Annual percentage yield (APY): The percentage of an investment returned at the end of a year; APY varies if the amount is compounded over shorter terms

Asset: A valuable possession, such as personal property, business equipment, real estate, or stocks

Automated teller machine (ATM): A cash machine; a terminal that allows deposits, withdrawals, and other transactions with one's financial account

Balance: Amount of money in an account

Bank: For-profit financial institution that maintains accounts, offers loans, and provides other financial services

Bankruptcy: Legal release from some or all debts in exchange for losing some assets; personal bankruptcy is part of credit record for 10 years

Beneficiary: The person or group that receives assets after a person's death

Bond: An agreement to lend money to an organization (including a government) for repayment with interest at a certain time

Budget: A plan for maintaining cash flow; a record of income and expenses

Business plan: A company's mission, structure, staff, activities, and budget

Capital gain: Income from selling something for more than its purchase price

Capital loss: Loss from selling something for less than its purchase price

Career: A certain profession for which someone studies

Cash flow: The balance of income and expenses over a certain period of time

Certificate of deposit (CD): A financial instrument that allows you to invest money for a specific period and established return

Charitable gift: Money provided to support a cause

Closed-end credit: A loan for a specific purpose with an established interest

rate and repayment plan (for example, a mortgage or car loan)

Collateral: Assets a borrower offers to a lender in case of default

Collection agency: Business that secures payments from debtors in default

Comparison shopping: Seeking the best-quality products and services for the lowest price

Compensation: Money and benefits paid as wages or for an injury or loss suffered

Complaint: An expression of dissatisfaction with a product or service, including a request for a solution to the problem

Compounding: Adding earned interest to the principal amount before calculating more interest

Contract: A legal agreement that binds two or more parties

Credit: The use of another's money with an agreement to repay it with interest at a later time (easy-access, closed-end, and open-end)

Credit card: A card that accesses open-end credit, paying for goods or services in exchange for future repayment with interest

Credit counseling: Assistance with money and debt management

Credit report: A borrower's credit history, detailing debts, delinquencies, bankruptcies, and liens

Credit score: A rating of how likely a person is to pay back a loan

Credit union: A not-for-profit cooperative that functions much like a bank, providing financial services to member-owners

Debit card: A card allowing users to transfer money from their accounts at automated teller machines or for purchases

Debt: An amount of money owed

Deductible: An uninsured dollar amount, specified in an insurance policy, for a specific claim

Default: Not meeting an obligation or agreement to pay back a loan

Deflation: A general lowering of prices (See also *inflation*.)

Dependent: Someone who depends on someone else for the resources to live

Deposit: Money placed into an account

Disposable income: The income one receives after taxes

Diversification: Selecting a wide range of investments in order to reduce risk

Dividend: Money earned from corporate stock or credit-union share accounts

Down payment: Money paid up front for a loan

Earned income: Employment income, including tips and commissions

Easy-access credit: Short-term loans available regardless of credit history but at high interest rates (for example, payday and pawn-shop loans and rent-to-own)

Electronic funds transfer (EFT): Shifting funds from account to account electronically

Emergency fund: Money saved for unemployment or unexpected bills

Employee benefit: Compensation other than wages or salary (for example, insurance, memberships, and child care)

Employer-sponsored retirement savings plan: Tax-deferred retirement programs, such as 401(k) or 457 plans

Entrepreneur: A person who starts and runs a business

Equal Credit Opportunity Act: A federal law that forbids lending discrimination due to race, gender, age, religion, marital status, national origin, or need for public assistance

Equity: Common corporate stock

Estate: Financial assets and liabilities left after a person's death

Ethics: The moral principles that shape a person's actions

Expense: Money paid for goods and services (See also *fixed expenses* and *variable expenses*.)

FAFSA: Free Application for Federal Student Aid

Fair and Accurate Credit Transactions Act (FACT Act): A federal law that allows consumers one free credit report per year and helps victims of identity theft repair their credit scores

Fair Credit and Charge Card Disclosure Act: Part of the federal Truth in Lending Act, requiring credit-card companies to define APR, annual fees, penalty fees, and other key features on their application forms

Fair Credit Billing Act: A federal law that protects consumers during billing disputes with credit-card companies

Fair Credit Reporting Act: A federal law that grants consumers the right to review their credit reports, dispute inaccurate information, and have certain information removed after seven or ten years

Fair Debt Collection Practices Act: A federal law that protects consumers from abusive debt-collection practices

FICA: Federal Insurance Contributions Act—a federal act that funds Social Security

FICO: Fair Isaac Corporation—a group that calculates credit ratings

Finance charge: The amount of money paid in interest and service fees to obtain credit

Financial adviser: Someone who provides financial advice, such as a broker, an accountant, a bank employee, or a credit counselor

Financial goals: What a person wants to achieve financially

Financial literacy: Knowing how to manage financial resources

Financial plan: An outline of the financial goals and needs of a person, including earnings, savings, investments, insurance, and debt, often indicating net worth

Fixed expenses: Regular payments such as rent, mortgage, or car payments

Fraud: Intentional and illegal deception for financial gain

Garnishment: Part of a person's wage set aside by court order to pay a debt

Grace period: The time after a due date during which no interest or penalty is charged

Gross pay: Wages or salary before deductions for taxes and other purposes

Identity theft: Fraud committed by using someone else's name, identification numbers, or other personal information

Impulse buying: Buying something without thinking it through

Income: Money earned by working or investing

Individual retirement account (IRA): An account that allows the owner to save pretax dollars and pay taxes later when funds are withdrawn (See also *Roth IRA*.)

Inflation: A general rise in prices (See also *deflation*.)

Installment debt: Debt paid off in regular installments, such as a car loan or student loan, (See also *closed-end credit*.)

Insurance: A tool that manages risk

according to specific terms for premium payments described in a policy document (for example, auto, disability, health, homeowners, liability, or life insurance)

Interest: Money paid to get a loan, or money earned by lending

Investment: The purchase of stocks, bonds, or other securities to earn interest (at risk of loss)

IRA: See *individual retirement account.*

Job: Employment with duties and compensation (See also *career.*)

Lease: A contract that allows a person to use a resource for a specified payment and time period (for example, a car lease or a mineral-rights lease)

Liability: The amount of money a person owes or could owe in the future

Liquidity: The ability to be quickly converted into money without losing value (a bond is more liquid than real estate)

Living will: The written wishes of a person regarding medical care, enacted if the person is unable to make medical decisions

Loan shark: Someone who lends money at exorbitant interest rates

Medicaid: A state and federal program that pays health-care costs for those in need

Medicare: A federal program that pays health-care costs for seniors; managed by the Social Security Administration

Mortgage: A loan to buy real estate

Mutual fund: A pool of investor money invested in diverse securities

Net worth: The value of a person's assets minus his or her liabilities

Open-end credit: A line of credit that allows a person to borrow money up to a certain limit and requires the borrower to regularly repay portions of the debt with interest (for example, credit cards)

Opportunity cost: The cost of foregoing one opportunity to pursue another

Overdraft: Withdrawing more money than an account holds

Pawn shop: A business that provides short-term, high-interest loans secured by personal property such as jewelry

Payday loan: A high-interest loan based on the borrower's pay cycle (outlawed in some states)

Payment method: The way a payment is made (for example, cash, credit, debit)

Payroll deduction: Money withheld from a paycheck for taxes, insurance contributions, retirement-plan contributions, and so on

Penalty: Money charged for not following restrictions on an account or a loan

Pension Protection Act: A federal law that strengthens employees' retirement security

Personal finance: How a person acquires and manages income and assets

Philanthropy: Giving money to help others

Point of sale (POS): Where a transaction occurs

Points: Percentage points (or tenths of a point) added to the prime lending rate due to a low credit rating

Portfolio: Assorted securities (stocks, bonds, mutual funds, real estate) an investor owns

Prime lending rate: The annual percentage rate offered to borrowers with excellent credit

Principal: Money originally invested, originally borrowed, or the amount remaining to be paid (less interest and finance charges)

Privacy: The right to keep personal information from being released to the public

Probate court: A government body that handles the will and estate of a deceased person

Profit: The amount of money that exceeds the expenses

Prospectus: A legal document that describes investments offered for sale

Rate of return: The percentage of an investment's cost that the investment makes in a year (for example, a $30 share that makes a $3 dividend in a year has a 10 percent rate of return)

Record keeping: Accounting of personal finances

Rent: Regular payment made to use property

Rent to own: Renting a product over a period of time up to the final payment, at which point the renter owns the merchandise; total payments greatly exceed the purchase price

Repossession: The seller's recovery of merchandise due to default on a loan

Retirement account: An account, such as a 401(k) or IRA, used to save for retirement

Revolving credit: See *open-end credit.*

Risk: The uncertainty of an investment; the likelihood of loss

Risk management: Calculating risk and minimizing loss through insurance, diversification, or other means

Rotating credit: See *open-end credit.*

Roth IRA: An individual retirement account that takes after-tax contributions but permits tax-free withdrawals

Rule of 72: A tool to estimate roughly how long an investment at a certain interest rate will take to double: 72 ÷ annual rate of return = years to double

Salary: An annual payment sum for work, paid out weekly, biweekly, or monthly (See also *wage.*)

Saving: Keeping income for future spending

Savings account: An account that allows deposits and withdrawals and usually pays interest

Savings and loan association (S&L): A for-profit institution that pays dividends on deposits and issues mortgages

Savings bond: A loan made to the federal government for a specified term (a year or more), to be repaid with interest

Secured loan: A type of installment debt that requires collateral—money or valuable property offered to the lending institution in case of default

Securities and Exchange Commission (SEC): The federal body that oversees the buying and selling of securities

Security: A debt or equity obligation held by an organization (for example, stocks and bonds); a loan's collateral

Share: One of the equal parts into which the capital of an organization is divided

Simple interest: Interest on principal without compounding previous interest

Social Security: A federal program that benefits retirees, funded by an income deduction (labeled FICA for Federal Insurance Contributions Act)

Standard of living: How comfortable someone is in terms of the value of goods and services he or she uses

Statement: A record of actions (deposits, withdrawals, transfers) on an account

Stock: Ownership in the assets and earnings of a corporation

Stored-value card: Card allowing purchase up to a set limit

Take-home pay: Total payment received for work minus deductions (for example, taxes, insurance premiums, retirement savings)

Tax: Payment made to government based on income, assets, and transactions

Tax credit: An amount subtracted from tax owed when the payer meets certain criteria

Tax deduction: An amount subtracted from taxable income when the payer meets certain criteria

Tax deferral: Postponing taxation of principal and/or earnings on an investment until withdrawal (usually retirement)

Tax exemption: Income that is free from taxation (for example, interest from municipal bonds)

Tip: Money paid in gratitude for service well rendered (a gratuity)

Title loan: A short-term, high-cost loan using the borrower's car title as collateral

Transfer payment: Benefits paid by governments to citizens (for example, Social Security, welfare)

Trust: A contract that empowers a trustee to manage a trustor's assets and allocate them to beneficiaries

Truth in Lending Act: A federal law requiring disclosure of the terms and cost of credit (for example, annual percentage rate and finance charges)

Truth in Savings Act: A federal law requiring disclosure of the terms and costs of interest-earning accounts (for example, annual percentage yield)

Unearned income: Income that does not come from work (for example, royalties, investment returns)

Unsecured loan: A type of installment debt that does not require collateral but often requires a substantial down payment—money paid up front

Values: Beliefs about what is valuable, meaningful, or needed

Variable expenses: Payments that change over time (such as food, clothing, and entertainment)

Wage: Payments made for work done, calculated hourly, daily, or by the piece and paid weekly, biweekly, or monthly (See also *salary.*)

Warranty: A document defining the conditions under which a product will be replaced or repaired by a manufacturer

Wealth: A person's total assets, or positive net worth

Welfare: Assistance provided to the needy (often from the government)

Will: A document telling how a person's estate should be distributed after death

Withdrawal: Money removed from an account

Financial-Literacy Activities

Maximize Income

Most of us want to bring in as much money as we can. This activity will help you think of ways to maximize your income.

Your Turn Create a chart like the one below (go to thoughtfullearning.com/h314 to download a template). List your current monthly income sources and amounts, the amounts you could be making from each source, and how you might reach that full potential.

Monthly Income	Currently	Potentially	How to Get There
Wages	$225	$400	Work more hours.
Tips	$0	$200	Deliver pizzas.
Commissions	$0	$0	Don't want to be a salesperson.
Interest	$0	$?	Invest in bonds.
Dividends	$0	$?	Buy stocks.
Royalties	$0	$1,000	Finish smartphone application.

Minimize Expenses

Most of us would like to get what we need for less money. This activity will help you think of ways to minimize your expenses.

Your Turn Create a chart like the one below (go to thoughtfullearning.com/h314 to download a template). List your monthly expenses and the amounts you spend on them, the amounts you would rather spend, and how you might realize the decreased costs.

Monthly Expenses	Currently	Potentially	How to Get There
Gasoline	$110	$80	Start walking more.
Movies	$60	$10	Get DVDs instead of going to theater.
Music downloads	$30	$0	Listen to radio.
Going out	$45	$45	Don't want to cut back there.
Clothes	$50	$25	Buy during sales only.

Get Plenty of Excise

We all need to save. This activity will help you begin (or improve) this good habit.

Your Turn Think of something you often spend money on—like clothes or music or games. Collect an excise tax by saving one dollar for every ten you spend on the item. Keep records to see how this self-tax idea grows your savings account.

Chapter 19
Succeeding in the Workplace

By now you've spent quite a few years in school, and soon you'll be entering the adult workforce. How will you find your way there? And how will you fare once you arrive? Actually, the skills you use to succeed in school have already pointed you in the right direction. Continuing to hone those skills will smooth your transition into the workplace and ensure your success there.

In this chapter, you'll do some career planning and learn about finding work. You'll be coached to create the right résumé, ace the interview, and land the job. You'll also discover ways to thrive in the workplace or, as opportunity knocks, to create your own business.

You will learn . . .

- Connecting with Employers
- Career Planning
- Job Searching
- Acing the Interview
- Understanding Workplace Etiquette
- Gaining Entrepreneurial Skills

Connecting with Employers

Think about what both the employer and you want in an employment situation.

Knowing What Employers Want

A recent survey by the American Management Association found that employers first of all want someone who has the right skills and experience to do a given job. Beyond that, they value these abilities and traits in an employee:

- **Critical thinking**—researching, analyzing, evaluating, improving
- **Creative thinking**—innovating, problem solving, improvising
- **Communication**—listening, speaking, reading, and writing
- **Collaboration**—planning, cooperating, meeting, relating
- **Professionalism**—being confident, capable, ethical, committed, and loyal
- **Dependability**—working hard, keeping regular hours, meeting deadlines
- **Productivity**—managing time, producing results, meeting standards
- **Flexibility**—adapting, prioritizing, multitasking, learning, taking risks
- **Integrity**—being fair, telling the truth, giving credit, taking blame
- **Passion**—being positive, motivated, energetic, and self-starting
- **Technology literacy**—using computers, software, systems, and the Web
- **Leadership**—goal setting, planning, organizing, delegating, motivating

Your Turn Rate yourself for each trait above on a scale of 1 (none) to 5 (total). Which are your strongest traits? Pick two areas in which you would like to improve, and write down one way to do that for each.

Knowing What You Want

As an employee, you want to be paid for working; but beyond salary, there are several advantages and circumstances to consider when looking for a job.

- **Compensation**—being paid fairly, getting strong benefits, feeling valued
- **Security**—feeling safe, assured of continuing employment, belonging
- **Environment**—having a pleasant, healthful, efficient work space
- **Mission**—believing in the company's goals, sharing a common vision
- **Quality**—taking pride in the work, accomplishing great things
- **Challenge**—engaging, problem solving, achieving, overcoming
- **Learning**—growing, expanding, developing, improving, moving forward
- **Opportunity**—taking on new responsibilities, getting promotions
- **Collaboration**—working with others, being part of a team, contributing
- **Support**—getting help from colleagues, managers, and administrators
- **Flexibility**—being able to balance work and a personal life
- **Fun**—enjoying work, having friends in the workplace, being happy

Your Turn Rate each item above on a scale of 1 (unimportant) to 5 (vital). Which items are vital to you? Which are less important?

Career Planning

If you haven't thought much yet about a career, now is the time. Think of what you want to do with your life, and chose a career path you can have passion for. Also, be ready to have a backup plan in case your first idea doesn't work out. Start by considering the following list of existing careers.

Bureau of Labor Statistics Careers List

Accountant	Disc jockey	Physicist
Actor	Doctor	Pilot
Actuary	Drafter	Police officer
Agricultural and food scientist	Economist	Politician
Architect	Electrical engineer	Professional athlete
Artist	Electrician	Programmer
Automotive mechanic	Engineering technician	Psychologist
Bookkeeper	Environmental scientist	Real estate agent
Carpenter	Farmer	Recreation and fitness worker
Chemist	Financial analyst	Recreational therapist
Childcare worker	Firefighter	Reporter
Civil engineer	Graphic designer	Secretary
Coach	Human resources	Social worker
Computer hardware engineer	Judge	Statistician
Computer software engineer	Landscape architect	Surveyor
Computer support specialist	Lawyer	Systems analyst
Cost estimator	Librarian	Teacher
Court reporter	Loan officer	Urban planner
Dancer	Machinist	Veterinarian
Database administrator	Musician	Webmaster
Designer	Nurse	Web developer
	Paralegal	Writer
	Pharmacist	Zookeeper
	Photographer	

Your Turn What career would you find most fulfilling? Go to http://www.bls.gov/k12/azlist.htm to find a career list. By clicking on any of the career categories, you can read all about that career. Also think about careers that are not on the list as well as entrepreneurial opportunities that you can create for yourself.

Creating a Plan

A career plan is a document you create to explore a job you think you might like, consider the ways you are suited for it, and learn about the training and experience you need to prepare for it. Look over the following example career plan.

Career Plan

Page 1

Career Plan
Martha San Miguel
January 2013

The beginning states and explains the desired career.

Career: I want to be a medical assistant. In this job, I will provide administrative and clinical support to a doctor (or doctors). I will help the doctor's office run smoothly and serve as a go-between for the patients and their doctor.

The middle reflects on job skills, employers, and duties.

Interesting Job Skills: Three skills required in this career especially interest me.

- I like being around people, and this job will give me many opportunities to work with the public and the staff.
- I am detail oriented, which will help with scheduling, ordering, and filing.
- I want to help others, and recording medical histories, taking blood pressures, drawing blood, giving vision exams, and other duties will help patients maintain or improve their health.

Potential Employers: Many clinics and urgent-care centers hire medical assistants.

Potential Duties:

- Administrative responsibilities (schedule appointments, arrange lab services, fill out insurance forms, answer the phone, buy equipment, do bookkeeping, and keep files)
- Clinical responsibilities (take pulse and blood pressure, explain procedures, perform lab tests, sterilize instruments, draw blood, change dressings)

Listing job requirements helps the person get the right training.

Job Requirements:

- Graduate from a one-year medical-assistant program.
- Take courses in anatomy, medical terminology, typing, accounting, record keeping, and insurance processing.
- Be courteous, well groomed, and respectful.

Page 2

The next sections focus on the qualifications the person already has and those she needs.

Other Helpful Qualifications:
- American Association of Medical Assistants certificate
- Prior experience in health care (volunteer or paid)

Qualifications I Have:
- Biology, chemistry
- One year as hospital volunteer
- Summer job as a file clerk in a family practice office
- Member of Health Occupation Students of America

Qualifications I Need:
- High school diploma
- Tech school diploma
- GPAs of 3.0 or better
- AAMA certification
- Supervised practicum

Advisers/References
- Lindsey Crane, M.D., Potomac Clinic
- Camille Johnson, Biology Teacher, Farrugut High School
- David Kohl, Chemistry Teacher, Farrugut High School

The **ending** outlines specific action steps to help the person accomplish her goal.

Steps I Need to Take
- Apply to tech schools with strong medical-training programs.
- Take the right courses and keep grades up.
- Create a résumé and get letters of recommendation.
- Do my practicum.

Your Turn Create your own career plan with the headings that appear in the example above. (Download a template at thoughtfullearning.com/h319.)

Job Searching

Some people dread looking for a job. Instead, try to think of a job search as a chance to explore opportunities and create your future. Imagine yourself working in different places with different people.

Finding Opportunities

When you look for a job, make use of the following resources.

1. **Networking:** Ask family members, friends, neighbors, and teachers for recommendations of good places to work. Check with the guidance counselors at your school about job opportunities they may know of. Often, people you know will be aware of job openings and may even have inside information and connections that can help you.

2. **Career starters:** Think of places that provide entry-level experience in the career of your choice. For example, if you want to be a nurse or a doctor, look into jobs at hospitals or clinics that would bring you into contact with those professionals and their daily work experience. If you want to be a chef, find a job as a busperson or server at a restaurant, and so on.

3. **Chamber of commerce:** Check with your local chamber of commerce about businesses in your area of interest that have entry-level positions available.

4. **Want ads:** Check local newspapers to see which companies are advertising for help.

5. **Online search:** Go online to search for job possibilities in your area. Visit each company's official Web site to learn about the operation. Always find out if a business is reputable (not a scam) before applying. You can also consider using an employment Web site to find local job opportunities.

6. **Help-wanted signs:** Go window shopping for help-wanted advertisements. If you see such a sign, go inside and observe the working conditions. What are the workers doing? Do they seem happy? Are they helpful? What is the work environment like? If the situation looks promising, ask for a job application and fill it out. (See the facing page.)

7. **Community bulletin boards:** Check grocery store bulletin boards to find job advertisements from local businesses. Then visit the businesses that sound interesting and decide whether you'd like to apply there.

Your Turn Use one or more of the resources explained above to create a list of jobs that interest you. Then answer the following questions about your list. Which jobs would help you move along your career path? Which ones would best meet your present need for employment? Narrow the list to two or three jobs that you would like to consider more carefully.

Completing a Job Application

Many jobs require you to fill out an application form. You can pick up these forms at the place of employment or access them online.

Guidelines for Completing Applications

1. Discuss your job search plans with your parent or guardian before you apply for a job.

2. Photocopy the application so that you can fill in a rough copy first.

3. Gather the requested information.

4. Carefully read the directions and ask for help on any parts that are unclear.

5. Complete the whole application.

6. Write NA if a part does not apply to your situation.

7. Check your work.

8. Create a clean, legible final draft to hand in.

Your Turn Ask for a job application from a place where you would like to work. Follow the guidelines above as you complete the application form.

APPLICATION FOR EMPLOYMENT

PERSONAL INFORMATION

Name: Lakisha Jones

Address: 261 East Jefferson, Apt 16, Milwaukee, WI 53000   Social Security Number: 301-7

Phone: (414) 555-6351

Are you 18 or older? ☐ Yes ☒ N

EMPLOYMENT DESIRED

Position: Server or Busperson   Date you can start: 01/08/13   Salary desired: $8

Current employer: Frank's Hot Dog Haus

May we contact your employer? ☒ Y

EDUCATION

	Name and Location	Years	G
Grade School	Waller School, Elkhorn	2000-2006	Ye
Middle School	Lakeland School, Elkhorn	2006-2009	Ye
High School	Martin Luther King High, Milwaukee	2009-2013	in
College	NA		

EMPLOYMENT HISTORY (START WITH THE MOST RECENT)

Month / Year	Name / Location / Salary	Position	Why Le
From 2/12 To 1/13	Frank's Hot Dog Haus, Milwaukee $8.50/hour	Cashier	Want more opportunit
From 6/11 To 2/12	Downtown Media, Elkhorn $40 per week	Paper delivery person	Needed better pay

REFERENCES (NAME THREE NONRELATIVES YOU HAVE KNOWN AT LEAST 1 YE

Name	Address	Business	Y
1. Frank Niccoli	73115 S 27th, Milwaukee	Frank's Dogs	4
2. Sharissa Clark	351 N Harvey, Franklin	Frank's Dogs	3
3. Tonia Peters	2170 Weinstein, Milwaukee	Downtown Media	2

Creating a Résumé

Some jobs require a résumé instead of a job application. A résumé is a concise list of your experience in school, in the workplace, and your qualifications for a specific type of work. You should create a general résumé and then customize it for each position you apply for. The most successful résumés connect what you have to offer with what the employer needs. There are two types:

- **Chronological résumés** help you highlight your past work experience.
- **Functional résumés** help you highlight your skills and qualifications.

Chronological Résumé

Charlotte Anderson
73105 West State Street
Burlington, VT 05400
(802) 555-9678
charlander381@gmail.com

The **beginning** of the résumé states an employment objective.

Employment Objective:

Veterinary assistant position that includes daily feeding, exercising, and cleaning of animals as well as aiding the veterinarian with routine medical procedures

The **middle** lists work experience, skills and qualifications, and education.

Work Experience:

- Volunteer at the Burlington Humane Society, 2011-Present
- Owner of Charlotte's Rabbits breeding business, 2009-Present
- Farm worker on family farm, 2005-Present

Skills and Qualifications:

- Lifelong love of animals
- Experience caring for cats, dogs, rabbits, goats, cows, pigs, chickens
- Desire to pursue degree in veterinary science

Education:

- Senior at Burlington High School, 3.89 GPA
- Rabbit Care Certification through 4-H

Awards and Honors:

- Vermont State Fair Best in Show Rabbit Awards, 2011, 2012
- 4-H Young Agribusiness Award, 2012
- Women in Science Scholarship Winner
- National Merit Scholar

The **ending** adds awards and honors.

References available upon request.

Functional Résumé

Charlotte Anderson
73105 West State Street
Burlington, VT 05400
(802) 555-9678
charlander381@gmail.com

> The **beginning** of the résumé gives a job objective.

Job Objective:

Veterinary assistant position that includes daily feeding, exercising, and cleaning of animals as well as aiding the veterinarian with routine medical procedures

> The **middle** of the résumé focuses on the applicant's qualifications.

Qualifications:

Caring
- Experience caring for cows, pigs, chickens, cats, dogs, and rabbits
- Oldest of six children, with a lot of baby-sitting experience

Hardworking
- Milk cows before and after school
- Clean out cow stalls each day
- Maintain a strong GPA

Motivated
- Want to help heal animals
- Desire to pursue degree in veterinary science
- Determined to gain experience through hard work

Education
- Senior at Burlington High School, 3.89 GPA
- Rabbit Care Certification through 4-H

> The **ending** lists experience, starting with the most recent.

Experience:

2011-Present	Volunteer at the Burlington Humane Society
2009-Present	Owner of Charlotte's Rabbits breeding business
2005-Present	Farm worker on family farm

References available upon request.

Posting Online

Consider posting your résumé on an employment Web site. Include job-related keywords such as "veterinary," "assistant," "animal," and "care."

Your Turn Decide which résumé format would best highlight your qualifications for a particular job, and create the document. Remember to include keywords (search terms) that will help prospective employers find your résumé online.

Acing the Interview

After applying for a job or sending out a résumé, interested employers may ask you to interview for the position to find out more about you. You can prepare for an interview by anticipating the employer's questions and having answers ready. Here are common questions employers ask and the information they are seeking:

Question	Information Revealed
1. How did you find out about this job, and why did you apply?	1. Your expectations
2. How do your experience and education qualify you?	2. Your qualifications
3. What do you know about this organization?	3. Your understanding
4. How could you help this organization meet its mission?	4. Your contribution
5. Why did you leave your last position?	5. Your motivation
6. What compensation (pay) do you expect?	6. Your financial needs
7. If you and another employee had a conflict, what would you do?	7. Your problem solving
8. Do you have any questions about the position?	8. Your level of interest

Your Turn Imagine that you are interviewing for a job you would really like to have. Write an answer to each of the questions above.

Understanding the Questions

Use the following techniques to ensure that you understand what the interviewer is saying.

- **Politely ask for clarification** if an interviewer asks a question or makes a statement that you don't quite understand:

  Could you explain what you mean by "professional"?

- **Paraphrase what the interviewer has said** to check your understanding:

  So, you are asking what duties I performed at my uncle's shop, is that right?

- **Shift focus to job requirements** if the interviewer inappropriately asks you a question about your gender, religion, race, orientation, or personal life.

  If you are asking whether I would be available to work on Sundays, the answer is that my Sunday afternoons are free.

Your Turn For each interview question below, write a response, following the directions in parentheses.

1. Are you experienced with inventory management? (Politely ask for clarification.)
2. How much overtime do you expect? (Paraphrase the question to check understanding.)
3. What church do you belong to? (Shift focus from personal life to job requirements.)

Improving Nonverbal Components

Though your answers are important, remember that the interviewer is considering other attributes that tell a lot about you. These nonverbal signals that you give should be moderate in nature, neither over the top nor under the radar.

Guidelines for Nonverbal Components

1. **Promptness:** Arrive five minutes before the time set for your interview.
   Don't be even one minute late . . . or 30 minutes early.

2. **Professional appearance:** Arrive well dressed, well groomed, and clean.
   Don't wear street clothes . . . or a tuxedo.

3. **Eye contact:** Make eye contact with the interviewer.
   Don't look away the whole time . . . or engage in a staring contest.

4. **Facial expression:** Look happy to be there. Show your interest.
   Don't look sullen or bored . . . or fanatically thrilled.

5. **Handshake:** Shake the interviewer's hand confidently.
   Don't offer a limp handshake . . . or crush the person's hand.

6. **Posture:** Stand, walk, and sit in an upright and confident way.
   Don't slouch or lean . . . or be stiff and rigid.

7. **Clarity of speech:** Speak clearly and at a reasonable pace.
   Don't mumble at a snail's pace . . . or chatter incessantly.

8. **Tone of voice:** Sound sincere, honest, and direct.
   Don't be sarcastic . . . or pompous.

9. **Diction:** Be conversational but correct, using standard English.
   Don't use slang or street language . . . or sound pretentious.

10. **Energy:** Show an appropriate level of interest in the job.
    Don't yawn and drowse . . . or tremble with excitement.

11. **Confidence:** Show that you would do the job well.
    Don't be apologetic and self-deprecating . . . or be arrogant.

12. **Compatibility:** Demonstrate that you can get along with the interviewer.
    Don't be a lapdog . . . or a pit bull.

Your Turn Conduct a mock interview with a classmate, who will pretend to be a grocery-store owner who is seeking new cashiers. He or she will ask you the eight questions listed at the top of the previous page, and you will answer them. Afterward, ask the classmate to rate you for each of the 12 points above, using this scale:

Too Little ➡	**Just Right** ⬅	**Too Much**
1	2	3

A perfect total score would be 24. Scores below 20 may mean you need to ramp things up, while scores above 28 may mean you need to tone things down.

Understanding Workplace Etiquette

Succeeding at work is about doing your job while getting along with others who are doing theirs. Workplace etiquette boils down to a single word: respect.

Workplace Etiquette

Respect your . . .

- **organization or company,** understanding its mission, its current goals, and how you can help.
- **supervisor,** following her or his directions.
- **coworkers,** treating them well, communicating clearly, and collaborating effectively.
- **customers,** providing them with the best products and services possible.
- **self,** dressing appropriately and conducting yourself professionally.
- **job,** following the schedule, arriving on time, and working hard.
- **career,** providing your expertise and taking on new challenges.

Your Turn Think about a job that you currently hold, or consider school as your current workplace. Do you routinely show respect in all the ways discussed above? What changes can you make to become more respectful?

Resolving Conflicts

If you develop the gracious, helpful habits outlined above, you will probably face few conflicts with others. Sometimes, though, conflicts do arise. If you have a disagreement with someone, try the following listening exercise:

1. **Position 1 Statement:** The first person gets one to two minutes to calmly explain his or her point of view and to list the reasons why his or her suggested course of action would be best.
2. **Restatement of Position 1:** The second person then paraphrases the first person's thoughts aloud, starting with "I hear you saying . . ." and ending with "Am I understanding you correctly?"
3. **Clarification of Position 1:** If the answer is "no," the first person receives another 30 seconds to a minute to clarify his or her position.
4. **Position 2 Statement, Restatement, and Clarification:** Once the first person's position is clear, the second person takes one to two minutes to calmly explain his or her point of view, and the process starts over.
5. **Cooperation and Compromise:** Once both sides have been heard, both people should seek ways to cooperate and compromise on the matter.
6. **Mediation:** If the conflict still has not been resolved, it's time to get another person involved to mediate.

Your Turn Think about a conflict that you have had with another employee or with a person at school. How did you resolve the conflict? With a classmate, roleplay resolving the conflict with the process outlined above.

Receiving and Giving Instructions

When you are a new employee, you'll receive instructions for doing your job. After you're experienced, you'll occasionally need to give instructions to other workers. Follow these tips for both situations:

Receiving Instructions	Giving Instructions
1. **Listen carefully from start to finish** to make sure you understand everything.	1. **Provide an overview** of the process.
2. **Understand the purpose** of the instructions.	2. **Explain the purpose** of the procedure.
3. **Note the materials and steps,** mentally running through the process.	3. **List the materials needed, the steps involved, and any safety issues.** (Use visuals if appropriate.)
4. **Repeat the instructions aloud** to make sure you understand them.	4. **Review the instructions** clearly and completely.
5. **Ask questions** when you are unsure about something.	5. **Ask if there are any questions** and answer them.

Your Turn Think of a procedure that includes at least three steps. Give instructions to a partner concerning this process. Then switch roles, listening as you receive instructions for a different procedure from your partner. Use the tips above.

Receiving and Giving Criticism

When your performance on the job is unsatisfactory, you may receive constructive criticism to help you improve. Learning to take criticism well is a key life skill. As you become more experienced, you may be the one providing constructive criticism to others. Follow these tips for both situations:

Receiving Criticism	Giving Criticism
1. **Show a willingness to learn** and improve performance.	1. **Use a positive tone** so that the person knows you are trying to help.
2. **Listen calmly** and try not to take the criticism personally.	2. **Focus comments on the problem** rather than on the person.
3. **Think about the person's ideas,** including the suggested solution.	3. **Suggest a solution** that the listener can try.
4. **Offer any additional ideas** that occur to you.	4. **Invite input** from the listener.

Your Turn Imagine that you are a grocery store owner. Ask a partner to imagine being a cashier. Role-play giving criticism while your partner receives it. Then switch roles for a different owner-worker situation. Afterward, review the tips above and discuss which ones you used and which ones you wish you had used.

Innovating on the Job

As a new employee, your job is to follow instructions and learn the correct way to do the tasks required in your position. After you've done this and gained the trust of your coworkers and superiors, you can further contribute by looking for ways to solve problems that exist or occur on the job.

Don't be the problem person. Be the solution person. Often workers make the mistake of bringing problem after problem to their supervisors. Instead, bring solution after solution. Your supervisor will appreciate your initiative and will start to rely on you. Here's how to be the solution person:

Guidelines for Solving Workplace Problems

1. **Look for "pain points"**—situations that slow work, cause frustration, decrease productivity, cause conflict, reduce quality, or otherwise negatively impact the work that you do. Think about your company's mission and how your ideas can help accomplish the mission.

2. **Thoroughly examine the problem** to understand its causes and consequences.

3. **Brainstorm solutions** that eliminate the causes of the problem or reduce its negative effects.

4. **Consider the solutions and choose the best one** in terms of its cost and how well it will fix the problem and eliminate the negative consequences.

5. **Adjust the solution** until you are confident that it will work.

6. **Present the idea to your supervisor,** identifying the problem and suggesting your solution. Be humble. Make it clear that you are just trying to help.

7. **Do what your supervisor decides you should.** He or she may approve your idea, or decide against it. Either way, your supervisor will likely appreciate that you are aware and trying to make improvements in the workplace.

8. **If your solution is approved, put it into action** according to your supervisor's instructions.

9. **Monitor your solution's implementation** to make sure that it solves the original problem without causing others.

10. **Watch for other "pain points"** that require solutions. Carefully devise and suggest your ideas to be of service to your employer. Problem solvers are highly valued in the workplace.

Your Turn Think about problems you've noticed in your workplace or at school. Choose one and follow the guidelines above to devise a solution to the problem.

Gaining Entrepreneurial Skills

Entrepreneurs create business opportunities for themselves and for the people they will likely hire. By developing entrepreneurial skills, you may one day be able to create your own business and chart your own future.

Identifying a Need

Most businesses have the goal of solving a problem or filling a need that people have, and the natural result is that people buy the product or service that the business offers. The pyramid to the right, developed by Abraham Maslow, organizes the needs of people. Notice how McDonalds meets one of the most basic needs, State Farm meets a need on the next level up, Facebook one level above that, and so on.

morality,
creativity,
problem solving

self-esteem, respect,
achievement, confidence

friendship, family, acceptance

health, property, security, employment

air, water, food, clothing, shelter, sleep

Matching Needs to Your Skills and Passions

After identifying a need, consider what skills you have to meet the need. What are you passionate about that can help people? (Your passions connect to the highest level of the pyramid and tap into your problem-soving skills.) Then list the products you could make or the services you could offer to meet this need. In the following example, a student brainstormed products and services that related to the need for "health."

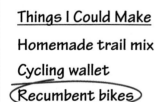

Things I Could Make

Homemade trail mix

Cycling wallet

Recumbent bikes

Things I Could Do

Start a bike club

Schedule a race

Repair bikes

Your Turn Choose one of the needs from the pyramid above. Then think about the skills and passions you have, and how they intersect with that need. Brainstorm a list of things you could make (products) and do (services) that would meet that need. Think of as many solutions as you can, even if some seem impractical. Finally, choose one or more of your ideas to consider as business ventures.

Planning a Product or Service

Once you have an idea for a product or service that would meet a need and that matches your skill, you can take your idea to the next level by filling out a planning sheet. (See pages 355–362 for more information.)

Recumbent Bike Business Planning Sheet

Goal: To build custom-made recumbent bikes and sell them locally and online

Objectives: *Who?* I will be the owner and employee of the business, but I'll ask Dad if I can use his welding equipment until I can afford my own.

What? I will build custom-made recumbent bikes to match people's body types and measurements.

Where? I will weld the frames and do all the other building in Mom's garage.

When? I'll build on evenings and weekends, and I'll advertise by riding one of my bikes around town with a sign.

Why? I love bikes, and I'm great at building stuff, so this business would be fun as well as profitable.

How? I'll use old bike parts to build inexpensive versions and will order new parts for customers who want high-end bikes.

Tasks: **Time:**
1. Plan and build my own bike and make a sign to advertise.   Today
2. Find/create plans for other models of recumbent bikes.   This week
3. Make a Web site to advertise the custom bike business.   Next week
4. Make and post posters around town.   By end of May
5. Build a second recumbent bike as a display piece.   Beginning of June
6. Start building customer orders.   Beginning of July

Team: I'll be the owner and mechanic. Mom will provide work and storage space in the garage. Dad will let me use his welding equipment. (Shipping?)

Tools:
Equipment: My tools and bench in the garage; Dad's welding equipment
Materials: Used and new parts, axle grease, oil, regular bike chains
Information: A Web site and posters
Resources: I'll study bike designs on the Web and look for a book of patterns.

Your Turn Fill out a planning sheet for your idea. (Go to thoughtfullearning.com/h330 to download a blank form.)

Pricing

Devon will need to decide how much to charge for his custom-built recumbent bikes. If his prices are too low, he won't be able to cover parts and labor. If his prices are too high, no one will buy the bikes. He must also consider the following factors:

- **Value:** What is a custom-built recumbent bike worth? Do people want inexpensive bikes built from old parts, or shiny new bikes at a premium cost?
- **Competition:** Who else in the area sells recumbent bikes? Who else builds custom bikes? What do competitors charge?
- **Market:** How much will people pay for a recumbent bike?
- **Return on investment:** What price will make it worth the effort?

Your Turn Consider the price you would set for your product or service. What value does this product or service hold for people? What does the competition charge? What will the market bear? Will you get a good return on your investment?

Budgeting

Part of operating a business is managing money. You need to start with an initial investment, perhaps money you have saved up from other work or money from a parent or guardian. The next step is setting up a budget, which is a list of the expected income and expenses for your business. Here is an example budget. (See chapter 18 for more information.)

Budget for the month of August	Budget Amount	Actual Amount	Difference
Income			
Henderson down payment	$100	$100	0
Blakely down payment	$100	$100	0
Stevens final payment	$150	$165	$15
Total August Income	$350	$365	$15
Expenses			
Henderson parts	$100	$75	-$25
Blakely parts	$100	$105	$5
Advertising	$20	$10	-$10
Web hosting	$6	$6	0
Total August Expenses	$226	$196	-$30

Your Turn Create a budget like the one above for your business idea. (See also page 308.) Write down how much money you expect to take in to your business. Then write down how much money you expect to pay out. As your business moves ahead, keep track of the money you take in and the money you spend. Then use that information to update your budget periodically.

Workplace-Skills Activities

Use these activities to practice your workplace skills.

Career Plans

Your first job may not be your dream job, but it will take you one step toward bigger and better things. Take a moment to brainstorm dream jobs that you would like to have and the paths that could lead you there.

Dream Jobs	First I Could ▶	Next I Could ▶	Finally I Could
Pilot	Get a private license	Get trained for commercial flights	Apply to major airlines
Engineer	Complete AP physics and calculus	Get into a strong engineering school	Apply to firms that need engineers

Your Turn Make a chart like the one above. List your dream jobs in the left column, and write the things you could do to finally land those jobs in the other columns.

Applying Yourself

Think about somewhere you would like to work that is near your home. Then do the following activity.

Your Turn Go to the place that you would like to work and see if they are hiring. If so, request a job application. Photocopy the application and practice filling it out. If you actually want to apply for the job, make a neat final copy on the original application and turn it in to the business. If that place isn't hiring, find another that is.

Respect in the Workplace

The key to succeeding in the workplace is showing respect. Use the following activity to think about important ways to show respect.

Your Turn Complete each sentence starter in this list:

Showing respect for my
  business means . . .
  boss means . . .
  coworkers means . . .
  customers means . . .
  self means . . .
  job means . . .
  career means . . .

Part II:
Using the Inquiry Process

Part II: Using the Inquiry Process

This section leads you through the steps in the inquiry process, from questioning to creating to presenting. As you learn about this process, you will apply many of the skills that you learned in Part I. You will also use the inquiry process to complete the great projects in Part III.

Chapters in This Section

Chapter 20
Understanding the Inquiry Process

Natural curiosity drives learning. We want to know why things happen as well as how, when, and where. You've probably heard of the famous scientist Isaac Newton, who saw an apple fall from a tree and asked why. Well, there are other questions to ask about apples: Why is this one sour and that one sweet? Why is this one green and that one red? And how did this worm get here?

The inquiry process is all about asking questions and following a series of steps to find the answers. Inquiry can help you manage everything from school projects to household chores. This chapter shows you how this process works.

You will learn . . .

- Understanding Inquiry
- Questioning
- Planning
- Researching
- Creating
- Improving
- Presenting
- Inquiry Process in Review

Understanding Inquiry

Inquiry is a process that starts with questions, which create a space for answers. You plan how you will find answers and then conduct research, making new discoveries along the way. Afterward you use what you discovered to create something new. Finally, you improve your creation and present it to others. This chapter provides an overview of this process, and the chapters that follow explain each step.

Questioning
You're just starting out, so now is the time to ask questions. Anything is possible. Ask creative questions, simple questions, deep questions. Imagine, wonder, dream, brainstorm, hope.

Question

Planning
Next, choose one possibility and plan how you will make it happen. Decide what you want to do, what your goals are, how much time you have, and what resources are available.

Plan

Researching
Then do the research. Follow your plan, use your resources well, and gather complete information and helpful details. This will involve working with media, technology, and people.

Research

Creating
As you create, use your discoveries to make something new and amazing. Build. Write. Design. Sculpt. Record. Don't worry about perfection at this point. Just get something out there.

Create

Improving
After creating something, you need to evaluate it. Does the end product meet your goals? Does it do what you want it to do? What works well? What could work better? How can you improve what you created?

Improve

Presenting
Once your work is ready, present it to your audience. Afterward, ask yourself if the work is everything you wanted it to be. What did you learn as you worked on this project?

Present

Your Turn How are the steps in the inquiry process related to each other? Why do you think they are ordered in this way?

1. Questioning

The process of inquiry is born out of curiosity. It begins with a question or an observation, which triggers more questions. As your questions become more pointed or specific, your thinking deepens. You seek a guiding question to drive your inquiry.

General

- How did our city get here?
- Who were the first settlers?
- Why did they come here?
- When did they arrive?
- Where did they live?
- What made them stay?
- What type of work did they find?
- Why did the city grow?
- What conflicts arose?
- What footprints from our early history are still here today?
- What lessons can our city learn from its past?
- Why does historical information about our city seem inaccessible?

Specific

- How can I help preserve our city's history?

Brainstorm

Once you arrive at a guiding question, consider how to answer it. Don't limit yourself, either, because at this point, all ideas are open for exploration. Brainstorming is one strategy for gathering ideas. Let your mind wander. If possible, invite others into the brainstorming process. The more minds the better.

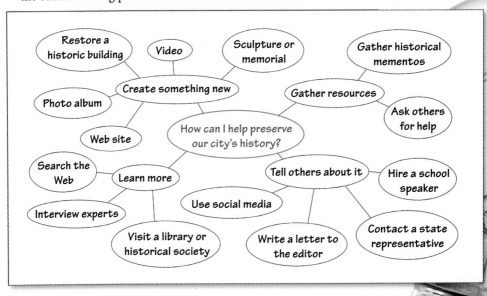

2. Planning

After considering the ideas you brainstormed, it's time to decide what you want to do and how to do it. Planning involves setting goals, listing tasks, scheduling time, and gathering a team and tools. A planning sheet can help.

Save the Miller House Planning Sheet

Goal: I want to help preserve the historic Miller House in northeast Bloomfield.

Objectives:

Who? I will lead, with help from students and community members.

What? Convince the Bloomfield Historic Commission to restore the historic Miller House; research possible grant money.

Where? In class, in the whole school, and in the community

When? Within the next six weeks

Why? The Miller House is a historic site in danger of demolition.

How? Through various campaigns to raise community awareness

Tasks: | **Time:**

Start... | Sept. 26

1. Find other people to help, and get an adviser. | Sept. 26

2. Research the Miller House, other restoration projects, and the grant application process. | Oct. 1

3. Decide on a multifaceted awareness campaign and divide up the work. | Oct. 5

4. Gather materials and start the campaign. | Oct. 8

5. Make pitch to the Bloomfield Historic Commission. | Oct. 22

6. Apply for the grant. | Nov. 2

Finish .... | Nov. 2

Team: I'll propose the idea to Andre, Cassie, and Harman, because we work well together.

Tools: We'll use the Internet and the local library to do our research on Bloomfield history and other historic restoration efforts. We'll also use the Internet to learn about any state- or national-level funding programs available for restoring historic sites. We may need to visit city hall at some point as well. We'll decide on tools and materials as we brainstorm the specific elements of our campaign.

Your Turn Go to thoughtfullearning.com/h338 to download your own planning sheet and complete it for a project you are working on. (Also see page 361.)

3. Researching

Doing research is vital to finding the answers you need. Depending on the project, you may use primary sources, secondary sources, or a combination of the two (see pages 376–391), but always use a reliable note-taking system to record the information you glean. Below you will find two examples of electronic note pages.

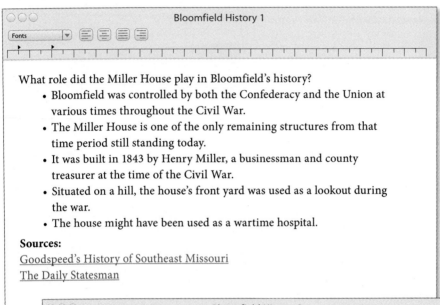

Bloomfield History 1

Fonts

What role did the Miller House play in Bloomfield's history?
- Bloomfield was controlled by both the Confederacy and the Union at various times throughout the Civil War.
- The Miller House is one of the only remaining structures from that time period still standing today.
- It was built in 1843 by Henry Miller, a businessman and county treasurer at the time of the Civil War.
- Situated on a hill, the house's front yard was used as a lookout during the war.
- The house might have been used as a wartime hospital.

Sources:
Goodspeed's History of Southeast Missouri
The Daily Statesman

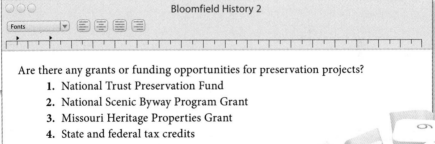

Bloomfield History 2

Fonts

Are there any grants or funding opportunities for preservation projects?
1. National Trust Preservation Fund
2. National Scenic Byway Program Grant
3. Missouri Heritage Properties Grant
4. State and federal tax credits

Your Turn Research specific questions related to a project. Take notes on note cards, in a notebook, or with an electronic note-taking system.

4. Creating

Having built a solid foundation of information about your topic, you are ready to carry out your project. Remember that turning an idea into a reality is both exciting and challenging. Some ideas will take more work than you had planned; other ideas may fizzle. That's okay. Learn from these experiences and move on. At this stage, you need to create just the first version of the project, not the final version.

Here's a video we shared on social media.

The Daily Statesmen
Attention: News Editor
378 Main St.
Dexter, MO 63841

Dear Editor:

A significant landmark in Bloomfield's history is at risk of bei̶ forever. The city is planning to tear down the Miller House at Shagbark Way. It is one of the only remaining structures in th survive the Civil War and should be a permanent fixture of Blo̶ history.

Built in 1843 by businessman and county treasurer Henry Miller, the house, which is situated at the top of a hill on the northeast side of the city, served as a lookout point for both Union and Confederate soldiers during the Civil War.

Today, it is the oldest house in Stoddard County, but it has remained uninhabited for nearly a decade and badly needs restoration. In fact, the city plans to tear it down if no money is allocated to its preservation. We must not let this happen.

A group of Bloomfield High School students wil̶ plan to the Bloomfield Historic Preservation Co̶ on Wednesday, October 20, at City Hall. Please̶ preservation of Bloomfield history.

Here's a letter to the editor we sent to a local newspaper.

Why preserve the Miller House?

- Historical Legacy
- City Beautification
- Architectural Landmark
- Potential Tourist Attraction (Historical Museum)

Our project doesn't meet the criteria for federal grants, but a restoration effort would make it eligible for tax credits.

Here's a slide we developed for our presentation.

5. Improving

After completing your project, you must properly evaluate it and make any necessary improvements. Leave enough time for this important step. Some improvements, especially those pertaining to accuracy or clarity, will come from critical thinking. Others will be more creative. An improvement plan like the one below can help.

Name: _Shantel Bailey_   Project: _Miller House Restoration (Slide Presentation)_

Critical Improvements

Cutting: What part or parts do not help me reach my goal or objectives? How can I make my work simpler, more concise, cleaner, or clearer?

> Problem: Some of the slides are messy and contain too much text. Also, I found out the grants are no longer federally funded, so those slides are mostly useless.

> Plan: I'll divide some slides into two and cut unnecessary text that may distract from the oral presentation. I'll also cut the information about defunct grant opportunities.

Rearranging: What part or parts are in the wrong place? How can I rearrange my work to make it more effective, efficient, and smooth?

> Problem: There isn't enough background—I should do a better job of setting the scene before making my final pitch.

> Plan: I will move the historical information and photographs closer to the beginning of the presentation in order to make my plea more persuasive.

Creative Improvements

Reworking: What part or parts need to work better? How can I rework them to achieve my goal?

> Problem: The photographs of the house in its present state are a bit fuzzy and not centered.

> Plan: I'll ask Andre to take some more pictures since he's a really good photographer.

Adding: What is missing from my work? How can I add just what is needed?

> Problem: The process for saving the Miller House seems like speculation. I need information about a similar historical restoration that succeeded.

> Plan: I'll do some research, find a similar project, and create a slide about it.

Your Turn Go to thoughtfullearning.com/h341 and download an improvement-plan template. Use it to brainstorm improvements to a project you are working on. (See also page 421.)

6. Presenting

After you've planned, researched, created, and improved your project, you are ready for the payoff: presenting your work to an audience. You could enter a design project in a contest or display it in your local library, a coffeehouse, or some other public place. You could present an audio-visual project on social media or in a subject-specific blog. And there are other possibilities, of course.

Shantel and his team sent a letter to the editor of their local newspaper. A week later, they appeared before their historical commission and delivered an oral presentation and slide show. All the while, they used social media to promote their ideas. These efforts made the community aware of the project and convinced the preservation commission to pursue funding options to restore the Miller House.

Inquiry Process in Review

You're using the inquiry process even when you don't realize it. Imagine that you want a healthy school lunch. You question what your options are in the cafeteria and in vending. You plan to check the lunch menu when you cut through the cafeteria after second hour and discover you don't like the foods offered. Research of vending options shows they aren't healthy enough. You ask a friend what he plans. He's picking up a veggie sandwich, so you give him money and an order, creating a solution. When the food arrives, you improve it with some mustard and present it to your mouth.

This example and the project discussed on the previous pages illustrate how the inquiry process applies to both big projects and everyday tasks. And at every step along the way, you are using 21st century skills to advance your plans and achieve your goals.

The Inquiry Process	21st Century Skills
■ question	■ creative thinking
■ plan	■ critical thinking
■ research	■ communicating
■ create	■ collaborating
■ improve	■ reading/studying
■ present	■ using technology

Your Turn Think of a time when you used the inquiry process, whether in or out of school. How did you use it? Was it effective? What step did you find most challenging?

Chapter 21
Questioning

You've been asking questions since you learned to talk. Perhaps, now that you are older, you're more hesitant to ask them. Don't be. Curiosity is essential to real learning. It can be said that if you don't ask, you'll never know.

In fact, poet Nancy Willard believes that "sometimes questions are more important than answers." In the context of the inquiry process, her statement rings true. Questions drive the process from start to finish. This chapter thoroughly explores those questions.

You will learn . . .

- Types of Questions
- Asking Creative Questions
- Asking Journalistic Questions
- Asking Deep Questions
- Asking Sensory Questions
- Asking Thought Questions
- Asking About Your Future
- Asking About the World
- Asking Survey Questions
- Using the SCAMPER Method
- Asking Socratic Questions

Types of Questions

Different types of questions trigger different types of responses. Before you dive into questioning, you should understand the strengths and weaknesses of closed-ended, open-ended, and theoretical questions.

Closed-Ended Questions

Closed-ended questions—which often start with *is, does, who, what, where,* or *when*—seek a limited response. They can be answered with a *yes,* a *no,* or a simple fact.

- *Strength:* Produce precise answers
- *Weakness:* Do not facilitate interpretation or deeper thinking

Example: Is Hungary part of the European Union? When did Hungary join the European Union?

Open-Ended Questions

Open-ended questions—which often begin with *how* or *why*—allow for wide-ranging responses and trigger ideas and discussion.

- *Strength:* Encourage critical and creative thinking and foster new ideas and connections
- *Weakness:* Produce complex answers that can be difficult to analyze

Example: How should I prepare for finals week? Why is so much emphasis placed on testing?

Theoretical Questions

Theoretical questions—which often begin with *will, would, should, could,* or *might*—seek hypotheses based on broad knowledge. They can be answered with educated guesses rather than definite information.

- *Strength:* Encourage critical and creative thinking; cultivate new understandings
- *Weakness:* Produce inconclusive answers that are difficult to assess

Example: Where might mass communication be headed next? How will media habits change in the future?

Your Turn Brainstorm a list of closed-ended, open-ended, and theoretical questions about a subject that interests you or a school project you are working on.

Asking Creative Questions

Creative questions open your mind to many possibilities, including unconventional ideas. Such questions can help you focus on your topic without limiting your horizons. Creative questions can lead you in interesting directions as you devise a school project. For example, consider the following creative question:

> "What would a universal language sound like?"

This question is open to many interpretations. It could inspire you to research the most widely spoken language in the world . . . or to look for a universally understood nonverbal language (no sound required). Your research may also uncover a few actual attempts to create a universal language, such as Esperanto, devised to be easily learned and understood by all nationalities.

Creative questions can open the door to fresh ideas for school projects. Here are some other examples:

What if Anne Frank had access to Twitter?

What was the most peaceful civilization?

How are grapes and grapefruits related?

Was the Korean War really "forgotten"?

Does space exploration still matter?

How do you become a genius?

Why is the stratosphere warmer than the troposphere?

What would happen if the U.S. Treasury phased out the penny?

Is the personal computer the future of musical instruments?

What is the origin of the phrase "knock on wood"?

Do Internet search engines make our brains lazy?

What is the ideal personality type for a president?

Is teleportation possible?

Do natural-born leaders exist?

How does laughter work?

Why don't we manufacture water?

How did Area 51 become associated with extraterrestrials?

Why does it feel good to stretch your muscles?

Your Turn Spend five minutes writing your own creative questions. Share them with a partner.

Asking Journalistic Questions

All journalists set out to find answers to the same essential questions: *Who* is involved? *What* is happening? *Where* is it happening? *When* is it happening? *Why* is it happening? *How* is it happening? These journalistic questions are also known as the 5 W's and H. Indeed, asking journalistic questions can help you assess most situations, whether you are planning a project, researching a topic, or evaluating finished work. The following chart shows the questions you could ask in each situation.

5 W's and H Chart

Journalistic Questions	Observing an Event or Situation	Researching a Topic	Planning a Project	Evaluating a Project
Who?	Who is involved?	Who caused this? Who is most affected by it?	Who is involved with this project? Who will benefit in the end?	Who created each part? Who provided the most help to others?
What?	What is happening?	What is the nature of this? What is the extent?	What goal do we have? What tasks should we complete?	What feature is strongest? What feature is weakest?
Where?	Where is it happening?	Where is this? Where else might it be?	Where will we work? Where will we present?	Where should we present this project?
When?	When is it happening?	When did this first appear? When will it cease?	When is the project due? When is each task due?	When was it due? When did we complete work?
Why?	Why is it happening?	Why is this important? Why does it impact our lives?	Why are we doing this project? Why will our project stand out?	Why did we choose this project? Why did it turn out as it did?
How?	How is it happening?	How is this useful now? How could it be used in the future?	How will we complete the work? How will others judge what we did?	How did our plan work? How did the team work together?

Your Turn Ask the journalistic questions about an event that just happened or about a new school project.

Asking Deep Questions

Questions can move you to deeper and deeper levels of thinking on Benjamin Bloom's taxonomy of thought. The chart below begins with questions that seek simple facts and ends with those that seek deep realities and possibilities.

Levels of Thinking

One Student's Questions

To remember, ask about facts.
- **Who** was involved?
- **What** happened?
- **Where** did it take place?
- **When** did it happen?

DNA Replication
Who/what is involved in DNA replication?
What is DNA replication?
Where does DNA replication occur?
When/how often does it occur?

To understand, ask about meaning.
- **Why** did it happen?
- **What** does it mean?
- **How** does it connect to other things?

DNA Sequencing
Why does DNA form a double helix?
What does DNA sequencing mean for biological inheritance?
How is DNA sequencing used in forensic science?

To apply, ask how to use ideas.
- **What** can I do with this idea?
- **How** can I use it?
- **When** should I use this?

Forensic Science
What DNA testing technique could I use to simulate a crime-scene investigation?
How can I simulate a crime-scene investigation using forensic DNA analysis?

To analyze, ask about the parts.
- **What** are the parts?
- **How** do they fit?
- **Why** do they work?
- **What** is their purpose?

Heredity
What are dominant and recessive genes?
How do dominant and recessive genes relate to heredity?
Why do dominant genes mask recessive genes?
What is the purpose of genes?

To evaluate, ask about quality.
- **What** is the value of this?
- **Will** it fulfill its purpose?
- **Could** it be made more effective?
- **Would** other ideas help?

Forensic Science
Of what value is DNA fingerprinting?
Will DNA fingerprinting solve more crimes?
Could it be improved?
Would other forensic techniques complement DNA fingerprinting?

To create, ask about making something.
- **Could** I make something new?
- **Should** these things combine?
- **How** can I use something in a new way?

DNA/Forensics/Heredity
What can I make with this information?
How can I combine/arrange it to produce a unique report/presentation/video/invention?

Asking Sensory Questions

Our senses help us take in the world. Asking sensory questions will help you to fully experience the people, places, and things around you.

What am I sensing?

Ask sensory questions to heighten your awareness of your surroundings, enliven your experiences, and mark your memories. Use descriptive words to record scenes in a sensory chart.

Sensory Chart

What do I . . .	
See?	North Michigan Ave., city landscape, stoplight stuck on red, blinking red hand, bustling black coats, block of skyscrapers, yellow fire hydrant, cars, buses, line of sparse green trees, hazy gray sky
Hear?	low rumble of engines, cars honking, shoe soles shushing, whistle of the wind, hushed conversations, crinkle of shopping bags
Smell?	exhaust, fresh pretzels, approaching rain
Taste?	grilled flatbread veggie sandwich, mustard
Touch?	chilly lamppost, rough pavement, steel bench, cool breeze, crinkly paper sandwich wrapper

Using Sensory Questions with Projects

Asking and answering sensory questions can provide you with a wealth of information about school projects, as shown below.

Assignment: Write a lab report for a chemistry experiment.

Possible sensory questions:
How can I describe what I am observing? What changes do I see over time? In color? In sound? In texture? Do I notice a specific odor? What does it smell like? Does it get stronger or weaker at any point?

Project: Design a scale model.

Possible sensory questions:
What specific parts do I see? What details stick out? What color are they? How does the object feel? Smooth? Rough? What materials will replicate the textures?

Project: Produce a digital story.

Possible sensory questions:
What do I want my viewer to see? Should the pictures be in color or black and white? Bright or dark? How can I use sound to convey emotion? Should I use background music?

Asking Thought Questions

To establish what you think about any topic, you can create a mind map or cluster. Write a question in the center, and cluster ideas around it, building connections.

Mind Map

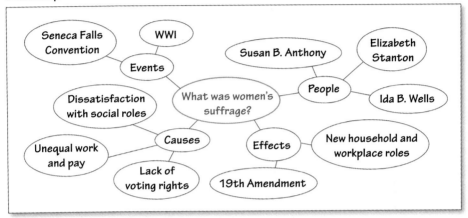

Your Turn Create your own mind map about a topic or project idea. Ask a question in the central oval, and write as many thoughts as you can to connect to it.

Freewriting

Freewriting is another brainstorming exercise. Start with a thoughtful question. Then write nonstop for 5 to 10 minutes, letting your answers and ideas flow. Don't worry about grammar or spelling. Just keep writing. Here is an example:

What do I know about the women's suffrage movement in the U.S.? Well, I know Elizabeth Stanton led a group of women at the Seneca Falls Convention to discuss women's roles in society and then outlined what needed to change. Women were fed up with their lack of voting rights and other inequalities. Part of it had to do with a backlash against the Victorian Era, when women were cast as homemakers. I would have been upset, too. I'm sure women of that time felt powerless and resentful toward a country that preached equality and justice for all but only afforded rights to white males, which leads me to think about the abolitionist movement that was going on at the same time. It must have been one of the more combustible times in American history, especially with the onset of World War I and the Great Depression right around the corner.

Your Turn Now write about another topic for five minutes without stopping. Let your mind wander through your ideas, but don't worry about getting everything "right."

Asking About Your Future

While it is important to take advantage of all that high school offers, it is not too early to pause and consider your future. After all, your experiences and education today shape your tomorrow. The questions below can help you kick-start your plans for the future.

What do I want to do after high school?

What skills do I possess?   Am I on track to graduate?

Which skills do I need to improve?

What is my dream job?   What do I want to do?

What steps do I need to take to get the job? Does it require further education?

Is college an option for me?

Public/private? Four-year/two-year?   Trade school/community college?

What type of institution should I attend? Where would I like to live?

What's most important to me?

Have I taken college entrance exams?

Urban setting? Rural setting? Warm climate? Cold climate?

How much does college cost?

How will I pay for college?

Family? Happiness? Career success? Wealth? Job satisfaction?

What is the cost of living?

Whom can I count on to support me?

What does success mean?

Where do I want to be in 10 years?

What do I love?   Friendship? Travel? Music? Sports?

What is my greatest strength?

What will I become?

Your Turn Read the questions above. Have you ever asked yourself questions like these? Answer the ones that are important to you.

Asking About the World

With all you've got going on—homework, after-school activities, work/chores, social life—it's easy to get wrapped up in your own world. However, every so often you should step outside of yourself and ask about the world around you, with its diverse people and ideas, complex problems, and amazing places. Considering your global citizenship provides perspective for your own triumphs and struggles.

People

- How am I similar to and different from someone else my age living in Europe, Africa, Asia, and so on?
- Who are the world's power brokers?
- How are women treated in different areas of the world?
- Where are the world's population centers?

Places

- Where do I wish I could live?
- Where would I love to visit?
- Which countries are most urbanized?
- Which areas of the earth are unexplored? What do we know about them?
- Which places have the greatest biodiversity? The least?

Cultures

- How are the Western world and the Eastern world different? How are they the same?
- How does food reflect culture?
- How is individual success defined in different cultures?
- What is the relationship between humans and nature in different areas of the world?
- What recreational games do different cultures play?

Customs

- What foreign custom or customs would I like to adopt?
- What are some unusual customs, and what are their origins?
- How are birthdays celebrated in other countries?
- How do marriage customs vary in different parts of the world?
- Which countries still have active monarchies? How much influence do these monarchs have?

Problems

- Is it possible to prevent international terrorism?
- What impact does climate change have on different places in the world?
- How can we protect endangered species?
- What factors contribute to poverty?
- What are the implications of the nuclear weapons race?

Solutions

- What can I do to contribute to a better world?
- How can the world supply more fresh water to poor countries?
- Is the United States responsible for feeding the world? Why or why not?
- What role can social media play in social change?

Your Turn Pick a question from above and share it with a classmate. Together, think about and discuss your answers and ideas.

Asking Survey Questions

Surveys help you gather information about people's behavior and attitudes about various topics. Here are tips for writing effective survey questions.

1. Analyze your communication situation.

Who is the survey's sender and receiver? What is the subject? Purpose? Context?

2. Choose the right question types.

- **Open-ended questions** allow responders to offer valuable information and opinions with no restrictions. However, they take time to complete, and the answers can be difficult to analyze.

    Example: Describe your music-listening habits.

- **Closed-ended questions** give responders a choice of answers (yes/no, true/false). While these questions produce only quick, simple answers, they are easily tallied. There are five types of closed-ended questions you can use:

    ▶ **Multiple-choice questions** ask responders to choose the best answer.
    On which medium do you most often listen to music?
    a) Internet radio   b) MP3   c) FM radio

    ▶ **Categorical questions** are used to classify participants according to age, gender, ethnicity, or other categories.
    Select your age range.
    a) < 20   b) 20–29   c) 30–39   d) 40–49   e) 50–59   f) 60+

    ▶ **Likert scale questions** provide choices on a scale.
    On a scale of 1 to 5, how important is it that musicians are compensated for the music you listen to? (choose one)

(Unimportant)			(Very important)	
1	2	3	4	5

    ▶ **Ordinal questions** ask responders to rank a list of choices.
    Rank the following activities from 1 (most likely) to 3 (least likely) according to the likelihood that you would listen to music while doing them. Write your ranking in the spaces provided.
    Doing schoolwork _____   Exercising _____   Working _____

    ▶ **Numerical questions** ask responders to choose a certain number.
    How many hours a day do you listen to music?
    a) Less than 1   b) 1–2   c) More than 2

3. Provide choices that are . . .

- **Mutually exclusive** (choices don't overlap)
- **Collectively exhaustive** (choices cover all possible alternatives)
- **Balanced** (an equal number of favorable and unfavorable choices)

Your Turn Create and implement a survey for a subject or project you are working on.

Using the SCAMPER Method

A researcher named Bob Eberle developed a set of questions for understanding any subject better. He used the acronym **SCAMPER** to identify the question sets that are described in the following chart.

Substitute — What can I use instead?
Who can be involved instead?
What other ingredients, materials, or power sources can I use?
Where else could I do this?

Combine — How could I put two or more things together?
How could I get two or more results from this?
How can I appeal to more people about this?

Adapt — What changes would improve this?
How could this better fit the situation?
What could I "copy" from the past?

Magnify — How can I make this bigger and more powerful?
How can I increase performance or appeal?
How can I slow it down or speed it up?

Put to
Other Uses — What else could I do with this?
Who else would be interested in this?
Where else could I apply this?

Eliminate — How can I make this smaller and more precise?
How can I decrease the cost?
How can I streamline this?

Rearrange — What other layout or order could I use?
How can I look at this from a completely different perspective?
How can I solve a different part of the problem?
How can I reverse cause and effect?

Your Turn Answer one question from each of the SCAMPER categories about a current project you are working on at home or in school. What new possibilities come to mind? (Download a SCAMPER sheet from thoughtfullearning.com/h353.)

Asking Socratic Questions

The ancient Greek philosopher Socrates is considered one of the most brilliant teachers in the history of the world, cultivating great minds such as Plato. Yet he never wrote down his wisdom or lectured his students. Instead, Socrates engaged them in discourse, asking questions to encourage discussion and deep thinking. Socratic questions will help you deepen your own and others' thinking.

Socratic Questions

Clarifying questions ask the person to say exactly what is meant.
- Could you rephrase that, please?
- Could you provide an example?

Assumption questions ask the person to explore underlying ideas.
- Are you assuming that _____?
- Could you explain why/how _____?

Reasoning questions ask the person to trace the logic of an idea.
- What is the main cause of _____?
- What evidence shows that _____?

Perspective questions ask the person to consider other points of view.
- How would another person see the issue?
- How is _____ like and different from _____?

Consequence questions ask the person to consider what might happen.
- What could result from that idea?
- What is the value of _____ and why?

Recursive questions ask the person to think about the original question.
- Why are you asking this question?
- Why do you think I am asking this?

Your Turn Choose a topic and practice Socratic questioning with a partner. One of you can play Socrates, asking questions from the list above, while the other answers. Then switch roles. Afterward, discuss whether this activity helped you come to a deeper understanding of your topic. Here is an example:
- **Clara:** I don't understand why some people think pizza is a junk food.
- **Sharissa:** Why do you think pizza isn't a junk food?
- **Clara:** Well, pizza has cheese, tomato, grains, and vegetables. They're healthy.
- **Sharissa:** Are you assuming these ingredients are in healthy proportions?
- **Clara:** That depends on how much the person eats.
- **Sharissa:** How does pizza compare to other fast foods?
- **Clara:** That's my point. Compared to a burger or hot dog, pizza isn't bad.
- **Sharissa:** Could you provide an example of the healthiest and least healthy pizza?

Chapter 22
Planning

Every project requires a plan. Like a recipe, a plan lays before you the particulars of the job—your goal, the tasks involved, available resources, and a schedule.

This chapter tells you how to make a good plan—from setting goals and objectives to gathering information and tools, from recruiting team members to setting deadlines. With the right mix of ingredients, your project will be off to a good start.

You will learn . . .

- Setting Goals, Objectives, and Tasks
- Scheduling Time
- Building Your Team
- Gathering Your Tools
- Creating a Planning Sheet
- Planning Throughout the Process

Setting Goals, Objectives, and Tasks

To begin planning, define your goal and objectives. Then devise a series of tasks to accomplish both.

Setting Your Goal

A goal begins with a desire. It may be spawned by curiosity; by an assignment at home, school, or work; or even by a basic need. In each case, a gap exists between the way things are and the way you want them to be. The more clearly you express the desire, the better you will be able to bridge the gap. One way to set a goal is to state the desire and then clarify it by applying the following set of **SMART** guidelines:

Specific —— A goal should aim for a specific target. It is not merely a general direction, but rather a particular location or achievement.

Meaningful —— A goal ought to require effort and accomplish something significant. Something that comes naturally doesn't need a goal.

Attainable —— On the other hand, a goal should be realistic. There is little point in setting a goal that clearly requires more resources than you have.

Relevant —— A goal should have a legitimate purpose and be relevant to a specific need.

Trackable —— Every goal needs a target date, including measurable achievements along the way.

Besides following the **SMART** guidelines, also remember to state your goal in positive rather than negative terms. Consider these examples:

My Desires	My Goals
I'm not very good at basketball, so I need to improve.	I will learn to shoot layups with both hands by the end of the month.
I wish I felt less tired all the time.	I will rearrange my schedule so I can get to bed sooner.
My French is really terrible, and I'll just have to change that.	I will read a short novel in French over the summer and submit a review, in French, to the school's foreign language blog.
I have to do a group project about rehabilitation of military veterans.	We will prepare a video interview of veterans and their caregivers and present it in class and online.

Defining Objectives

To more thoroughly understand your goal, define its related objectives by asking the 5 W's and H. Your answers will guide further planning.

Who?	Burton Raboin, Pamella Emard, Arminda Ferrar, Leif Semas, Felix Hofacker, and I will work together on the project.
What?	We will investigate the rehabilitation of military veterans, conduct interviews of veterans and their caregivers, and prepare a video presentation.
Where?	We'll do the initial investigation online, then record video interviews in person, or (if necessary) do audio interviews by phone.
When?	We have to finish the project by April 1.
Why?	We've read news stories that many military veterans are facing unique challenges in getting diagnosed and treated for post-traumatic stress disorder (PTSD) and similar conditions.
How?	We'll present ourselves as students of Brewster High to request stories from the veterans and their caregivers and use smartphone cameras to capture the interviews. Using our school's computer, we'll edit the footage into a final video.

Listing Tasks

Each project is accomplished with a unique set of tasks or steps. Establish these based on your goal, objectives, and resources.

"When it is obvious that the goals cannot be reached, don't adjust the goals; adjust the action steps."
—Confucius

What do we need to do?	What do we need to learn?
1. Research the subject. 2. Create a list of potential veterans and caregivers to interview in our area. 3. Request interviews. 4. Assign interview teams. 5. Conduct the interviews. 6. Evaluate the results. 7. Create a cohesive "story" for our video. 8. Edit the video. 9. Present the video in class and post it online.	We've read some reports about veterans being returned to combat with undiagnosed brain injuries, vets having trouble getting treatment, and vets ending up homeless after being discharged. We need to find out about (1) the resources available for the vets, (2) any success stories, and (3) the reasons behind vets not receiving the care they need.

Your Turn List your goal, objectives, and tasks for a current project or for one you would like to do. (Download templates at thoughtfullearning.com/h357.)

Scheduling Time

Schedule your project's tasks on a calendar. If the due date is fixed, begin with that date and work backward, dividing the available time between the various tasks. If, on the other hand, the project's due date is open, list the first task with an estimate of how long it will take, the second task with its estimate, and so on. There may be some overlap on the schedule, especially if team members work simultaneously on different tasks.

Using a Calendar

Use an actual calendar or simply list your tasks along with their dates. If possible, post tasks on a shared online calendar application. An online calendar allows you to display tasks in various views: by month, week, day (even hours), or as a dated agenda.

Month View

Sun	Mon	Tue	Wed	Thu	Fri	Sat
27	28 Begin research	1	2	3 Finish list	4 Send requests	5
6	7 Assign teams	8 Begin interviews	9	10	11	12
13	14	15	16	17	18	19
20	21 Finish interviews	22 Assess results	23	24 Create story	25	26
27	28 Start edit	29	30	31	1 Video due	2

Agenda View

Date	Task
Feb. 28	Research the subject.
Mar. 3	List veterans and caregivers in our area.
Mar. 4	Request interviews.
Mar. 7	Assign interview teams.
Mar. 8	Begin the interviews.
Mar. 21	Finish interviews.
Mar. 22	Evaluate the results.
Mar. 24	Create a cohesive "story" for our video.
Mar. 28	Edit the video.
Apr. 1	Present the video in class and post it online.

Making Adjustments

As your project unfolds, keep track of your progress with each task.

- **Speed up if you find that you are falling behind.** This may require either assigning more resources (perhaps asking for help) or reevaluating the task itself. Deadlines are important.
- **Slow down if you find that time permits.** This may allow you to go into more depth or to reassign resources. (For example, if you finish the background research in less time than anticipated, you could dig deeper or help a team member gather more data.)
- **Revise your schedule if necessary.** Due dates (deadlines) are sometimes extended if a strong case can be made. If problems arise, speak with your instructor early on.

Your Turn Use a calendar application to schedule your project's tasks, or plot them on a paper calendar. (See thoughtfullearning.com/h358 for a template and links.)

Building Your Team

When you consider the tasks you must accomplish, think of people who can help. Assign roles according to group members' skills, interests, and personalities.

Example Project-Role Sheet

Project: Video About Military Veteran Rehabilitation

Roles	Team Members	Responsibilities
Project Manager	Denice Sobiech	Project scheduling and troubleshooting
Interviewers	Burton Raboin, Pamella Emard, Arminda Ferrar	Arranging and conducting interviews
AV Recorders	Denice Sobiech, Leif Semas, Felix Hofacker	Record audio and/or video of interviews
Storyboarder	Burton Raboin	Review recordings and plan a final video script
AV Editor	Leif Semas	Create the final video
Web Person	Felix Hofacker	Build a Web page for the video, upload the file, and link it
Class Presenters	Entire Group	Introduce the video in class, describe the project process, and lead a Q&A session

Common Roles

The following list identifies a number of common roles necessary to the completion of various projects. Many of these are career oriented.

Accountant	Debater	Interviewer	Reporter
Actor	Designer	Leader	Salesperson
Advocate	Director	Manager	Scientist
Announcer	Disk jockey	Marketer	Screenwriter
Artist	Editor	Mechanic	Sculptor
Athlete	Engineer	Musician	Statistician
Builder	Entrepreneur	Novelist	Tailor
Caregiver	Explorer	Playwright	Teacher
Chef	Film editor	Poet	Technician
Comedian	Futurist	Politician	Welder
Composer	Game designer	Programmer	Writer
Counselor	Host	Promoter	Zoologist

Your Turn Working alone or in a team, make a list of roles for your own project, define responsibilities, and assign members to each role.

Gathering Your Tools

Every project requires tools—equipment, materials, information, resources—specific to its topic and purpose.

Example Tools Sheet

Equipment:

- 3 portable video cameras
- 3 voice recorders
- 1 phone recorder
- 2 computers
- storyboarding software
- video editing software
- Web design software
- video projector

Notes:

For this project we can use smart phones with cameras to record the video and audio.

We'll storyboard with an online app. Leif's home computer has video editing software installed. Felix says he can use the school computer lab for the Web part. We can connect the school video projector to my tablet computer for the live presentation.

Materials:

- 3 matching sport jackets, slacks, and ties for the interviewers
- 1 white dress shirt for Burton
- 2 white blouses for Pam and Arminda
- 3 yellow legal pads and black felt pens

Notes:

We'll need our interviewers to dress alike to connect the video visually.

The legal pads will contain the interview questions to prompt the interviewers. They can also be used to note correct spellings of names and terms.

Information:

- What is the standard process for evaluating veterans after combat duty?
- What resources are available for veterans who need rehabilitation?
- What appeal process exists for veterans who believe they need further help?
- What successes and problems do veterans and caregivers identify?

Notes:

We'll focus on the veterans' and caregivers' answers to these questions. If possible, we'll also arrange an interview with a legislator to learn what the government has to say about homeless vets.

Resources:

- Internet reports of veteran rehabilitation
- Regional veterans' hospital
- Local National Guard Armory staff
- Local VFW organization
- Local military recruiting offices
- Contact pages on state representatives' Web sites

Notes:

Our goal is to present a well-rounded report on both successes and problems with the current system. We need to accurately represent a multitude of viewpoints. (Maybe we could do a few "common person" interviews downtown to see how aware citizens are of the situation.)

Your Turn Create a list of equipment, materials, information, and resources for your own project. (Go to thoughtfullearning.com/h360 for a template.)

Creating a Planning Sheet

With a planning sheet, you can gather in one convenient place all of your thoughts and intentions for completing your project.

Example Planning Sheet

Veteran and Caregiver Interview Planning Sheet

Goal: Our team will prepare a video interview of veterans and their caregivers.

Objectives: *Who?* I will work with Pam, Burton, Arminda, Leif, and Felix.

     What? We'll make a video about rehabilitation of veterans.

     Where? We'll investigate online and interview in person and on the phone.

     When? We have to finish the project by April 1.

     Why? Veterans face challenges in diagnosis and treatment of PTSD.

     How? We'll use cameras, recorders, and computers.

Tasks:	**Time:**
Start.	Feb. 28
1. Research and prepare a list of veterans and caregivers.	Feb. 28-Mar. 3
2. Request interviews.	Mar. 4
3. Assign interview teams.	Mar. 7
4. Videotape interviews (interview by phone if necessary).	Mar. 8-21
5. Evaluate the results.	Mar. 22-23
6. Create a cohesive "story" for video presentation.	Mar. 24-25
7. Edit video.	Mar. 28-31
8. Present the video in class and post it online.	Apr. 1
Finish	Apr. 1

Team: Denice Sobiech (Project Manager); Burton Raboin, Pamella Emard, Arminda Ferrar (Interviewers); Denice Sobiech, Leif Semas, Felix Hofacker (AV Recorders); Burton (Story Boarder); Leif (AV Editor); Felix (Web)

Tools:

     Equipment: AV recorders, storyboarding, editing and Web-design software

     Materials: Matching clothes for the interviewers; legal pads and felt pens.

     Information: Evaluation process after combat tour, rehabilitation resources, appeal process, problems and successes

     Resources: Internet reports, veterans' hospital, local National Guard Armory, local VFW, local recruiting offices

Your Turn Create a planning sheet for your own project. (Download a template at thoughtfullearning.com/h361.)

Planning Throughout the Process

A planning sheet is important to any project, from preparing a video report to building a doghouse to arranging a camping trip. Your plan will guide you through the inquiry process and serve as an invaluable reference at each stage of a project.

Organizing

The planning sheet focuses your thoughts and orders the elements necessary for completing a project.

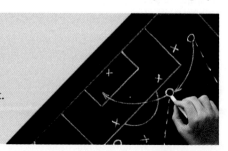

Gathering

The planning sheet guides you as you use resources to collect information and bring team members and tools together to complete tasks.

Developing

The planning sheet reminds you of your project's goal and objectives, governing your progress and keeping you on track.

Evaluating

The planning sheet provides the goal and objectives that you will use in your rubric sheet. (See pages 416–417.) In that way, your plan helps you evaluate and improve your project.

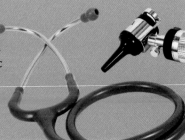

Chapter 23
Conducting Basic Research

What is basic research all about? Of course, it begins with a question. Then follows the searching and collecting. It's like filling a wheelbarrow with all the details, facts, statistics, anecdotes, thoughts, and ideas that you'll need to form an answer.

In this chapter, you'll learn how to get the most out of your research, from formulating a guiding question to using research tools to managing the load of information you collect.

You will learn . . .

- Asking Questions
- Finding Answers
- Searching with Keywords
- Using the Library
- Taking Notes
- Organizing Your Information

Asking Questions

Research begins with questions, but not all questions are created equal. Different types have different purposes.

- A **guiding question** (or **driving question**) directs your research.
- **Pointed questions** deepen and broaden your research.
- **Journalistic questions** gather details about a situation or an event.
- **Socratic questions** (see page 107) refine and evaluate your thinking.

Identifying Your Guiding Question

Whether you are doing an assignment or project or are exploring your own topic, your first task is to identify your guiding question.

Assignment:	Possible guiding questions:
Write a 3- to 5-page paper on the history of immigration in the U.S.	How has U.S. immigration policy changed over 230 years? Where have most U.S. immigrants come from and when? Where have U.S. immigrants settled and for what reasons?
Redecorating a room	What does the room need to function well and look good? What furniture suits this room, and where can I get it? What tools and supplies do I need to wallpaper the room?
Visiting another country	What country do I especially want to visit and why? How can I apply to programs for student travel? What preparations must I make to travel outside the U.S.?

Generating Pointed Questions

Once you have settled on a guiding question, generate a list of related questions about the topic.

Guiding question:	Pointed questions:
What preparations must I make to travel outside the U.S.?	What legal documents do I need? What medical records do I need? How much will the trip cost? What cultural differences will I face? How can I prepare for any language difference? What will I need to pack? What are my luggage limitations?

Your Turn Freewrite for five minutes about things you are curious about. Choose one of your topics and craft a guiding question about it. Then generate five to ten pointed questions to explore the topic further.

Using Journalistic Questions

Answering *who, what, when, where, why,* and *how* can provide important details about a subject. Asking these questions about the past creates analysis, and about the future creates prediction and persuasion. Questions about the present take either form.

	Past	Present	Future
Who?	Who was central to the event?	Who is involved in the situation?	Who will be affected by the situation?
What?	What happened, in detail?	What process is taking place?	What is predicted to happen?
When?	When did the event occur?	What time frame is involved?	How long will the situation last?
Where?	Where did the central events each happen?	Where is the situation unfolding?	Where will events likely occur?
Why?	Why did the situation happen as it did?	Why should we care about the event?	Why is the issue vital for the future?
How?	How did it occur?	How are we affected?	How will we cope?

Employing Socratic Questions

Socratic questions like the following help you think in new ways about your topic.

Questions of Clarification
- How can I state the main idea?
- Why do I believe that?
- Can I put the idea in different terms?
- What am I really saying?

Questions That Probe Assumptions
- What assumptions am I making?
- What am I implying?
- What alternatives are there?
- What might readers infer?

Questions That Probe Reasons and Evidence
- What evidence supports the idea?
- What evidence challenges it?
- How can I find out if the idea is true?
- What other information do I need?

Questions About Viewpoints or Perspectives
- What is my viewpoint?
- Why do I think that way?
- What other viewpoint may be valid?
- How would I respond to it?

Questions That Probe Implications and Consequences
- If this is true, what else is true?
- Would it always happen this way?
- How is this related to other effects?
- Should this apply in all cases?

Questions About the Question
- How can I find out?
- What does this question assume?
- How could I ask this differently?
- Why does this question matter?

Your Turn Ask journalistic and Socratic questions about your topic to uncover details.

Finding Answers

Answering your research questions will require you to use a variety of sources:

▶ **Direct observation** provides firsthand experience and includes everything from attending a concert to conducting a lab experiment. (See page 56.)

▶ **Electronic media** such as videos, audio files, and interactive programs supply information in an interesting way.

▶ **People** can be good sources of information, and experts are often interviewed on TV and radio. Consider conducting your own interview. (See page 385.) Teachers, parents, and other adults may be knowledgeable about your topic.

▶ **Print periodicals** (including **magazines, newspapers,** and **scholarly journals**) provide information on various topics. Search the *Readers' Guide to Periodical Literature* or a periodical database in your library to find what you need.

▶ **Reference books,** such as encyclopedias, atlases, almanacs, and dictionaries, can be good starting points for research. Check your library's reference section.

World Wide Web Research Tools

The World Wide Web provides access to a wealth of resources. Many can be reached from a home Internet connection, and your school or library system may be able to connect you to nonpublic sources.

- **Chat applications** allow you to talk in real time with other people around the world, whether by keyboard, microphone, or Webcam. More than a way to spend time with friends, chat can be used to interview an expert.
- **Email** allows scholars around the globe to communicate easily, one reason the Internet was invented. Today, you too can email questions to experts—everyone from authors to entrepreneurs to NASA scientists.
- **Forums** and **message boards** are special Web sites where people post questions and answers about various topics. Each site is devoted to a particular subject or interest. Often you can find leads in these message "threads" to information that is unavailable elsewhere.
- **Search sites,** or search engines, are decent starting points for research, especially if you compare results from more than one and also use their advanced search features. (See page 368.)
- **Scholarly databases** give access to articles across a wide spectrum of subjects.
- **Social media** can provide up-to-date insight into current events. They also allow for data mining and crowd-sourcing. (See pages 269–290 and 504.)
- **Wikis** represent a group effort to codify knowledge. While they can provide new insights about a topic, bear in mind that the information may be untested and even unreliable.

Your Turn Identify several likely sources of answers to your research questions (pages 364–365). Do initial research using those sources and write a one-page journal entry about what you learned.

Pursuing a Topic

The following tips will help you find the best answers in the shortest time.

▶ **Choose your starting point.** Consider your topic and decide where to begin, whether a reference book, a how-to video, or an email to an expert.

▶ **Note other sources.** Look for a bibliography or list of works cited, hyperlinks to other Web pages, people or events mentioned in interviews, and so on. Pay attention to footnotes and endnotes. (See pages 396–403.)

▶ **Use print-source features.** Check a book's back cover copy for an overview. Read the preface, introduction, and foreword. Use the table of contents to identify chapters and parts. Check the index for specific topics and page numbers. Follow cross-references to more information on a topic. Use a newspaper's front-page directory of sections and each section's contents list to locate specific stories and features.

Electronic Search Strategies

Early computer programmers used "GIGO" to mean "Garbage In, Garbage Out." In other words, the quality of your input determines the quality of your results. Here are some smart electronic search strategies:

- **Use more than one search site.** Different search engines use different algorithms to find and rank results. Some add a social element, adjusting results to match what other people have searched for, and all search engines adjust their algorithms regularly. Determine to go beyond your favorite search engine and compare the results from several sites.
- **Phrase questions and keywords carefully.** Try to predict which search words will bring the best results. The more accurately you phrase your search, the more efficiently the site will be able to locate good resources.
- **Notice suggested searches.** Many search sites begin suggesting common search phrases as you type yours in. These suggestions may give you new, useful ideas; either follow them or jot them down for later.
- **Read the result summaries.** Browse the list of results and the brief description of each entry. These summaries will help you to judge the source's potential and may give you new keywords to consider.
- **Go beyond the first page.** Sometimes your best search result shows up on a later page. Scan the first page of results and then keep clicking to the next and beyond, until you stop finding entries with potential.
- **Adapt your keywords** to include promising phrases in your result descriptions. Then search again, using those new keyword phrases.
- **Use advanced search strategies.** Most search programs have a link to an "Advanced Search" page. There you'll find instructions for using specific features, doing Boolean searches, and so on.

Your Turn Brainstorm a list of keywords for your guiding research question from page 364. Compare your list with a classmate's, and make suggestions to refine or expand each other's keywords.

Searching with Keywords

When you search a book's index for a particular topic, you have to think for a moment, predict which term or terms may be used to identify the topic, and then start looking. Doing a computer search involves a similar process. Follow these steps:

1. **Define your topic.** Precisely stated topics yield focused results.

   Too broad: Greek drama

   More Precise: Women in Greek drama; themes of Greek drama

   Note: Guiding research questions (see page 364) can serve as topics in a computer search. *Example:* What preparations must I make to travel outside the U.S.?

2. **Make a list of keywords.** Break your topic into parts or terms. Each term is a keyword or key phrase. Also list alternative words or phrases for your search.

   Examples: travel, preparations, outside the U.S.

   Alternatives: foreign travel, travel planning, visiting overseas, world travel

3. **Use Boolean operators.** Special operators such as the words *and, or,* and *not;* quotation marks; and +'s and –'s help a search site process your request. (Check advanced search options for operators.) Boolean operators work as follows:

Operator	Examples	Result	Graphic Representations
and or +	travel *and* foreign travel + foreign	Files with both "foreign" and "travel" separately	travel / foreign foreign / travel
not or –	travel *not* foreign travel – foreign	Files with "travel" but without "foreign"	travel / foreign foreign / travel
" "	"foreign travel"	Files with the exact phrase "foreign travel"	travel / foreign foreign / travel
or	travel *or* foreign	Files with "travel" or "foreign" or both	travel / foreign foreign / travel
* (or other "wild card")	travel*	Files with "travel" or "traveled" or "traveler" or "traveling" (and so on)	

4. **Evaluate your results.** If your keywords are well thought out and your search program has a complete database, you'll receive good results. If your results are disappointing, however, you'll need to either revise your keywords or use a different search program (or both) and try again.

Your Turn Review your list of keywords from page 368. Use Boolean operators to search with them.

Using the Library

Your local library is a "one-stop shop" for all kinds of resources.

Staff

Librarians, media specialists, technicians, and assistants can help you find what you need. Their duties may be divided among several desks.

- **Information desk:** Here you can ask questions about the library itself, its physical organization, hours of operation, contents, and policies.
- **Circulation desk:** Here you'll check out materials to be used outside the library.
- **Media services desk:** Here you'll get help with electronic media like videos, audio recordings, computer software, and devices for using these resources.
- **Reference desk:** Here you'll find access to encyclopedias, atlases, almanacs, periodical guides, and archives of periodicals on microfilm. Usually, reference materials cannot be removed from the library.

Resources

Explore your library to discover the location of the following resources:

- **Computer catalogs:** Every library keeps a catalog of its books and other media, identifying where to find each item. You can search by title, author, or subject.
- **Print books:** *Nonfiction* books are usually shelved according to the Dewey decimal system, which divides subjects into ten main classes:

000–099 General	**400–499** Languages	**800–899** Literature
100–199 Philosophy	**500–599** Sciences	**900–999** History,
200–299 Religion	**600–699** Technology	Travel, and Geography
300–399 Social Science	**700–799** Arts and Rec.	

  Fiction books are shelved separately, arranged alphabetically by the author's last name. *Biographies* are shelved separately, arranged alphabetically by the subject's last name.
- **Ebooks:** Your library may also lend ebooks and ebook devices.
- **Periodicals:** Libraries subscribe to many types of periodicals. You'll find recent newspapers, magazines, and scholarly journals as well as bound collections of old issues. Some may be stored on computer or microfilm.
- **Special collections:** Often, libraries house historical documents of local importance. You must ask for permission to view them.
- **Electronic media:** Videos, audio recordings, and computer programs, along with the equipment to use them, are usually available.
- **Personal computers:** Computer stations for public use, often with Internet access, are usually available. Ask your librarian how to sign up to use them.
- **Meeting rooms:** Your library may have rooms for discussions or study.

Your Turn Visit your school library and draw a map locating its service desks and resources. Do the same with a public library. How are the libraries similar and different?

Taking Notes

Note taking helps you grasp information, organize it, and document it for later use. Different situations call for different note-taking methods. Consider these factors:

- **The information source.** Interviewing someone calls for a different recording strategy than skimming a book for information.
- **The technology available.** You might handwrite notes or key them into a device. Cell phones and pocket media players can capture audio and video.
- **Your research purpose.** A quick product comparison might require just a Web-page printout. A multipage research paper requires more formal notes.
- **Your personal style.** Adapt note-taking methods to suit your own mental processes, and keep watching for new developments in note-taking technology.

What Information to Include

- **Your own words.** Wherever possible, summarize and paraphrase in order to understand and capture the ideas of a source.
- **Key words and phrases.** Jot down or underline key terms, especially if they are common jargon in the subject field.
- **Specific quotations.** Record exact quotations from a source when they best capture an idea. Well-chosen quotations, used sparingly, can add authority to your research project.
- **Source documentation.** Always note the source of ideas, whether you are quoting, using key phrases, or recasting information in your own words. Documentation keeps your work honest, adds authority, and helps your reader.

Types of Notes

▶ **Paper notebook.** The spiral notebook with pencil or pen is portable, durable, and adaptable—good for both sketching and writing. Try a two-column system: two-thirds of the page for main notes and one-third for headings and documentation.

A Key ideas	**C** Topic headings
B A quotation	**D** A source

A	• Most effective plane of World War II	**C**	DH Mosquito
	• Multiuse: reconnaissance, long-range bombing, fighter support of larger bombers	**D**	Bowman, Martin W.
	• All-wood design at a time of metal warplanes (Almost didn't get approved)		De Havilland Mosquito. Ramsbury: Crowood, 2005. Print.
B	"The Mosquito...gained such a...reputation for achieving the impossible that...the British press claimed that when one was shot down the Luftwaffe crew could count it as two victories." (page 9)		

▶ **Note cards.** Devote one card to each research-question answer along with its source. Then arrange them in the best order before writing your paper.

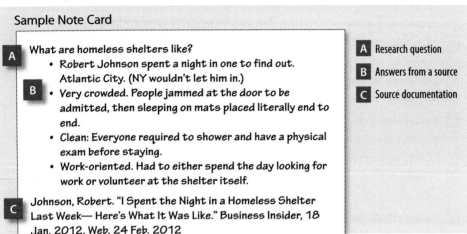

Sample Note Card

A What are homeless shelters like?
 • Robert Johnson spent a night in one to find out. Atlantic City. (NY wouldn't let him in.)
 B • Very crowded. People jammed at the door to be admitted, then sleeping on mats placed literally end to end.
 • Clean: Everyone required to shower and have a physical exam before staying.
 • Work-oriented. Had to either spend the day looking for work or volunteer at the shelter itself.

C Johnson, Robert. "I Spent the Night in a Homeless Shelter Last Week— Here's What It Was Like." Business Insider, 18 Jan. 2012. Web. 24 Feb. 2012

A Research question
B Answers from a source
C Source documentation

▶ **Electronic notes.** With a portable computer—or Internet access to a personal account—you can take notes with a word-processing program or note-taking application. The notes can be easily edited and reorganized, making them a good launching point for writing. With a touch screen, drawing pad, or mouse, you may be able to add simple sketches to your notes.

▶ **Printouts.** Printouts of Web pages, other Internet files, and microfilm documents can enhance your notes. You can write directly on printouts and save them in a folder. *Remember to write documentation details in the margins so you can credit the source.*

▶ **Photocopies.** Copying a few pages from a print source allows you to highlight important points and write your own thoughts in the margins. *Remember to jot down documentation information.*

▶ **Audio and video recordings.** Recordings are useful for interviews and other events. Portions of such recordings can be embedded in multimedia projects. Finally, a pocket voice recorder is handy for saving your ideas when pen and paper are not available.

▶ **Snapshots and OCR.** Digital cameras—including those on cell phones and on portable media devices and computers—can capture a printed page, a computer screen, a work of art, and so on. If your device has Internet access, you can upload the photos to a file-saving site, email them to yourself, or save them to a note-taking application. Optical-character-recognition (OCR) apps and services can even convert photographed text to a document you can edit.

Remember: When you use a public computer to access a personal account, sign out of the program when you finish so that the next user can't access your information.

Your Turn Try a number of the note-taking approaches mentioned above. Then write a journal entry explaining which ones you find most useful. Share your thoughts in class.

Organizing Your Information

After gathering information, you need to make sense of it. Organizing facts, data, and ideas is key to understanding. The following graphic organizers can help.

Graphic Organizers

A **5 W's and H chart:** Organizes answers to the six journalistic questions. (See page 346.)

B **Before-after chart:** Separates conditions before and after an event. Organize your details along the projecting lines.

C **Time line:** Shows a sequence of events. List each important event in order along the line.

D **Cause-effect chart:** Arranges the cause(s) and effect(s) of a subject. When a subject has multiple causes and effects, list them in a related order.

E **Line diagram:** Maps the relationship of a topic to its supporting details. For a deductive approach, place the main topic above (as shown). For inductive, place details above and the topic below.

F **Process diagram:** Maps a process by listing steps along a line.

G **Problem-solution chart:** Identifies a problem (as the subject), lists its causes, and offers possible solutions.

H **Venn diagram:** Compares and contrasts two subjects, with each circle as one subject. Lists similarities where the circles overlap and differences in the outer circles.

I **Cycle diagram:** Maps the steps in a recurring cycle along the perimeter of a circle.

Other graphic organizers: You may find these variations useful:

- sensory chart (page 348)
- pro-con chart (page 103)
- order of importance list (page 408)
- cluster (page 349)

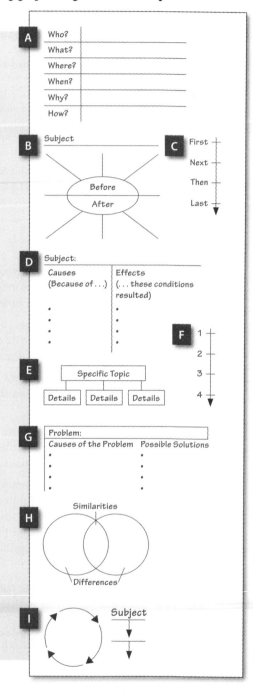

Mind Maps and Corkboards

The following organizers are handy for arranging the amounts and kinds of information gathered for a research paper.

Mind Map

A mind map resembles a cluster diagram (see page 349), with each bubble holding a key piece of research information. By connecting related concepts, you can see the big picture of your research results and cross out parts that don't fit.

▶ **Physical Mind Map**

Advantage: Drawing a mind map on poster paper or an erasable board is fast and convenient.

Disadvantage: Details cannot be moved easily. You can use lines to connect ideas that are across the map from each other, but the results can be messy.

▶ **Electronic Mind Map**

Advantages: Many computer programs and apps for mind mapping are available. You can easily edit and move details or zoom in or out to focus on parts. You can also paste text from your notes and export the map to your word processor.

Disadvantage: A computer or other electronic device is required.

Sample Electronic Mind Map

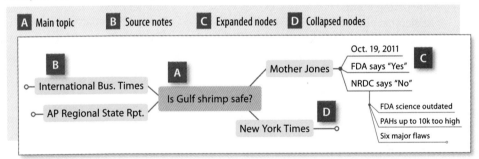

Corkboards

Like a mind map, a corkboard allows you to gather separate details (both text and images) and experiment with different arrangements, finding connections.

▶ **Physical Mind Map**

Advantage: You can tack note cards and pictures to your board and rearrange them as necessary.

Disadvantage: You may need a very large space for all your notes.

▶ **Electronic Mind Map**

Advantages: You can easily change the board and zoom in or out, and it doesn't take up a wall.

Disadvantage: It requires a computer, and the on-screen corkboard is small.

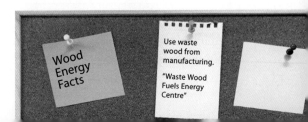

Outlines

Many writers use outlines, especially for longer, more complex works like research reports. The outline serves as an overview of your report, keeping you on track as you write. Don't be afraid to change your outline as new ideas occur to you.

Topic Outline

The topic outline lists your main ideas and supporting details, using words and phrases. As you write your report, you expand upon the outline, turning the words and phrases into complete sentences.

Topic Outline Guidelines

- List topics in the order they will appear in your report, labeled with Roman numerals (I., II., III.).
- Beneath each main idea, list supporting details labeled with capital letters (A., B., C.). If necessary, add an extra level of detail, labeled with Arabic numerals (1., 2., 3.), beneath the supporting points.
- Remember that each level of detail needs at least two points—a I. requires a II.; an A. requires a B., and so on.

Title: Understanding Research Basics
- I. Introduction
- II. Asking research questions
  - A. Guiding
  - B. Pointed
  - C. Journalistic
  - D. Socratic
- III. Finding answers
  - A. Direct observation
  - B. Electronic media
  - C. Interviews
  - D. Print materials
  - E. Internet

Sentence Outline

A sentence outline lists your main ideas and supporting details in complete sentences. Generally, your main ideas become the topic sentences of the paragraphs in your report. Turn your research questions into statements. Then use the guidelines for a topic outline. The following example covers the first two main ideas of a research report:

Thesis: Traveling outside the U.S. requires preparation.
- I. Vacationers leaving our borders must have legal travel documents.
  - A. They need passports.
    - 1. First-time applicants must apply in person.
    - 2. For some destinations, at least 30 days must remain on a passport.
  - B. Some trips require visas.
- II. These world travelers also need health documents.
  - A. Depending on the country, various immunizations are necessary.
  - B. Proof of health insurance is a must.

Your Turn Find answers to your research questions from page 364. Use a note-taking method that suits you (pages 370–371), and arrange your information using one or more of the organizational methods on pages 372–374.

Chapter 24
Conducting Advanced Research

"Curiosity killed the cat," they say. They also say, "A cat has nine lives." Now there's a contradiction worth wondering about. Just what is the history of these adages? If you're curious enough, research can uncover the answers for you.

In this chapter you'll go beyond research basics, dig deeper into sources, and learn about conducting your own experiments, surveys, and interviews. You'll also discover how to present your results in a scholarly fashion, crediting the sources you've used while displaying your unique vision in your own voice.

You will learn . . .

- Understanding Primary, Secondary, and Tertiary Sources
- Using Tertiary Sources
- Using Secondary Sources
- Using Primary Sources
- Researching on the Internet
- Avoiding Plagiarism
- Using a Citation Style
- Using Documentation Tools

Understanding Primary, Secondary, and **Tertiary Sources**

In the previous chapter, we discussed various sources of information—from personal interviews to audio-visual recordings, Web pages to print materials, and more. Sources can be labeled primary, secondary, or tertiary, depending on their distance from the information they share.

Primary Sources

Primary sources give firsthand information—original and unfiltered. Examples are eyewitness accounts, personal journals, interviews, surveys, experiments, historical documents, and artifacts. These sources have a close, direct connection to their subjects.

Example Project	Possible Primary Sources
Predicting your state's growth over the next decade	▪ Previous census reports ▪ Chamber of Commerce reports on business growth ▪ Interview with a state senator or similar official
Learning NASA's space-elevator plans	▪ Interview with NASA scientist ▪ Video of NASA Power Beaming Challenge events
Analyzing themes in *The Great Gatsby*	▪ The text of the novel ▪ Nonfiction essays by F. Scott Fitzgerald

Advantages: Primary sources directly address your topic and often provide information that is unavailable elsewhere. For example, the questions you compose for an interview or a survey will likely target your unique interest in the topic. Similarly, to test a particular hypothesis, you can design your own experiment.

Disadvantages: Some primary sources, such as eyewitness accounts, may be too close to the subject, lacking a critical distance. Others, such as interviews, surveys, and experiments, are time consuming to prepare, administer, and analyze. Finally, unless you have been trained in accepted methodologies, your own primary research in certain fields of study may not be recognized as valid.

Consider This

Whether a source is primary, secondary, or tertiary varies by topic. The letters from a Civil War soldier would be a primary source of information about his experiences. However, topics he might include about matters outside of his direct observation (other battle stories, news reported in the camp, etc.) would be considered either secondary or even tertiary information, depending on the situation.

Your Turn Imagine you are researching how the human brain is both like and unlike a computer. Where would you go for information? List two possible primary sources. Compare your ideas with a classmate's.

Secondary Sources

Secondary sources are one step removed from the topic. While they can be just as valuable as primary sources, you must remember that secondary information is filtered through someone else's perspective and may be biased.

Example Project	Possible Secondary Sources
Predicting your state's growth over the next decade	■ Scholarly article projecting future census numbers ■ Chamber of Commerce business forecast ■ State budget plan for the next decade
Learning NASA's space-elevator plans	■ Magazine article about space elevators ■ Television special about NASA's future
Analyzing themes in *The Great Gatsby*	■ Scholarly essays critiquing the novel ■ Film adaptations of the novel

Advantages: Secondary sources provide a variety of expert perspectives and insights. Also, peer review usually ensures the quality of sources such as scholarly articles. Finally, researching secondary sources is more efficient than planning, conducting, and analyzing certain primary forms of research.

Disadvantages: Because secondary sources are not necessarily focused on your specific topic, you may have to dig to find applicable information. Information may be colored by the researcher's own bias or faulty approach. Also, secondary sources can become outdated (in some fields more quickly than in others).

Tertiary Sources

Tertiary sources provide thirdhand information by reporting ideas and details from secondary sources. This does not mean that tertiary sources have no value, merely that they include the potential for an additional layer of bias.

Example Project	Possible Tertiary Sources
Predicting your state's growth over the next decade	■ Report by a lobbying group, citing secondary sources ■ Opinion-page essay in a newspaper ■ A student essay comparing scholarly forecasts
Learning NASA's space-elevator plans	■ Wikipedia.com article about space elevators ■ Web site of a private citizen who is a space enthusiast
Analyzing themes in *The Great Gatsby*	■ Summary booklet and study notes for the novel ■ Biography of F. Scott Fitzgerald

Advantages: They offer a quick, easy introduction to your topic. They may point to high-quality primary and secondary sources.

Disadvantages: Because of their distance, they may oversimplify or otherwise distort a topic. By rehashing secondary sources, they may miss new insights into a topic.

Using Tertiary Sources

For many topics, a tertiary source is a good starting point for your research. You will find topic overviews in encyclopedias and textbooks and on the Internet.

General References

Dictionaries, encyclopedias, almanacs, and other such references summarize topics, providing the most important facts and figures. They serve well as an overview but not for in-depth information.

Do . . .	Don't . . .
■ use them early in your research to find basic information. ■ use them to help formulate your research questions.	■ quote or paraphrase them in your writing. ■ include them in your list of citations.

Note: Information in general reference materials is almost always considered *common knowledge.* Unless you have a specific reason for citing such a source, avoid doing so.

Common Reference Works

- **Dictionaries** are alphabetical collections of words and their definitions.
- **Encyclopedias** are alphabetical collections of topics and their summaries. Some dictionaries and encyclopedias cover only a particular subject (for example, a medical dictionary or encyclopedia).
- **Atlases** provide maps and other information about geographical areas. Some are devoted to a specific region.
- **Almanacs** offer charts, graphs, and lists of facts about different topics.

Specific Reference Works

- *Bartlett's Familiar Quotations* contains thousands of quotations from ancient history to the present.
- *Current Biography,* published monthly and annually, focuses on interesting people.
- *Facts About the Presidents* is a reference book about U.S. presidents.
- *Famous First Facts* covers "firsts" in all areas of life.
- *Who's Who in America* provides short biographies of important people in the U.S., both past and present.

Crowd Sources

Wikipedia, YouTube, and countless online message boards allow everyday people to post information on any number of topics. So do social-media sites like Twitter and Facebook. Depending upon the topic and the source, you may find an encyclopedia-style entry, a video presentation, or a text-based debate. The reliability of that information varies.

Do . . .	Don't . . .
▪ use crowd sources as an introduction to current discussion on a topic. ▪ check them for clues to the latest details on a topic. ▪ check the credentials of the people posting. ▪ maintain a healthy skepticism about crowd-sourced information.	▪ rely upon crowd-sourced information alone for your understanding. ▪ cite such sources in your own writing (unless you are specifically discussing public opinion).

Note: When checking credentials, consider the authority of the organization behind a title. (Some well-known people called "Dr." are not actually doctors. And some may have bought their degrees from unaccredited online businesses.) Also remember that an expert in one field is not necessarily an authority in another.

Search Sites

We have become increasingly dependent upon search sites for our daily information about anything from products to current events to history to trivia. When using search sites, remember how the information is prepared.

Do . . .	Don't . . .
▪ understand that search results are ranked by complex algorithms that attempt to provide the most on-target information. ▪ note that some Web designers "game" the algorithms to move their sites up your search results. ▪ recognize that descriptive texts in search results are often written by Web-site owners, specifically to catch your attention. ▪ know that most search sites reserve space for paid results (advertised sites) at the top of each page and in a sidebar. ▪ realize that the results you get may change from day to day, reflect similar searches by other people, or be affected by your own search history. ▪ remember to use advanced search features for best results. (See page 368.)	▪ search without first considering the best search terms. (See page 368.) ▪ stop at the first or even the second page of results—helpful information may be found on the next pages. ▪ limit yourself to one search engine—other sites use different algorithms than can turn up different results. **Your Turn** Imagine researching a naval battle of the American Civil War. Which tertiary sources would give you a quick overview of the topic, and which would offer the most complete information?

Using Secondary Sources

Much of the research you do will involve finding and using high-quality secondary sources: nonfiction texts, video documentaries, multimedia reports, presentations by experts, and so on.

Understanding Nonfiction Books

Nonfiction books have a number of common elements, each of which provides a different type of information.

Common Parts of a Book

- A **title page** gives the full title of the book, the author's name, the publisher's name, and the city of publication.

- A **copyright page** comes right after the title page. It tells you the year when the copyright was issued. (If the copyright is too old, the information might be outdated.)

- A **preface**, a **foreword**, or an **introduction** usually follows. It explains the purpose of the book.

- The **table of contents** identifies the page numbers of major divisions of the book (units, chapters, and topics).

- The **body** or **main part** of the book contains the core information in the text.

- The **index** lists in alphabetical order the page location of specific topics covered in the book. It appears at the end of the book.

Additional Elements

- There may also be an **acknowledgment page**, listing people who helped with the book. (This information can also be combined with another page, as is shown in the example on the next page.)

- An **appendix** sometimes follows the main text, and it contains extra information such as graphics, maps, lists, and other special information.

- A **glossary**, if it is included, provides an alphabetical listing of special words and terms. Refer to this part if you are unsure of the meaning of a certain word.

- A **bibliography** lists sources that the author used and other sources on the topic.

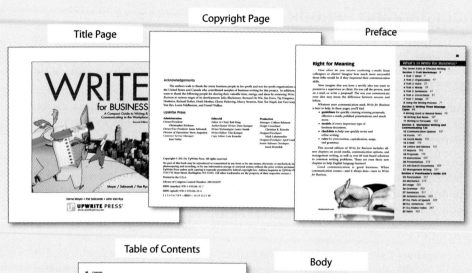

Title Page

Copyright Page

Preface

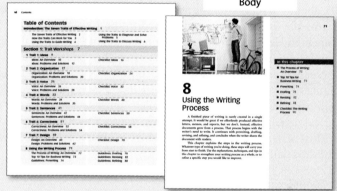

Table of Contents

Body

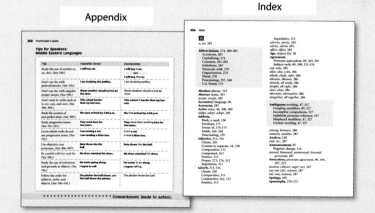

Appendix

Index

Your Turn Find the different parts in a nonfiction book of your choice. Pay careful attention to the type of information contained in each part, but remember that the book may not contain every part described here.

Understanding Periodicals

Periodicals are newspapers, magazines, and scholarly journals—all of which are published "periodically." Some periodicals are in print, some are electronic, and some use both formats (often with added information or a multimedia element in the electronic version).

Advantages of Periodicals: They publish recent, timely information from a variety of writers. Periodicals target a wide range of topics, and some are written for the general public, while others are meant for specific scholars.

Disadvantages of Periodicals: Rapid publication schedules can result in incomplete information, although updates and corrections are published later, especially in online versions. Editorial decisions can be biased by influential advertisers, powerful owners, or a particular subscribership.

Newspapers

Newspapers have a long history. The earliest true newspaper was published in Germany in 1605, about 150 years after the printing press was invented. In 1690, *Publick Occurrences* became the first newspaper published in the New World. By the 1830s, "Penny Press" papers in New York made news popular among the general population and developed modern journalistic practices, such as on-the-spot reporting.

Modern newspapers remain one of the best sources of local and regional news. In fact, public notices are required by law to appear in a "newspaper of record" before becoming official. Newspaper archives—often called "morgues"—are a great place to investigate historical details. Your library may have microfilm or microfiche copies of old newspapers. Most newspapers also keep an archive of old issues online. Newspapers are typically published daily or weekly.

Parts of a Newspaper

- **Front page:** The first page of a newspaper, showing its title, publication information, and index of sections, plus the most important headlines and articles
- **Folio:** Publication information under the paper's title, including date and price
- **Article:** An essay, often called a "story," about one news item
- **Feature:** An article on the front page or otherwise prominently displayed
- **Byline:** The name of the writer displayed below an article title
- **Editorial:** An opinion piece written by an editor of the paper
- **Editorial cartoon:** A cartoon expressing a political opinion
- **Letters to the editor:** Opinions from readers
- **Section:** A folded part of a newspaper, arranged by topic ("Business," "Sports," etc.)
- **Classified ads:** Pages of short advertisements arranged by category
- **Business:** A section devoted to business news
- **Entertainment:** A section devoted to entertainment news (or lifestyles)
- **Sports:** A section devoted to sports news and analysis
- **Obituaries:** Announcements of deaths, often noting memorials and funerals

Magazines and Journals

Unlike daily newspapers, magazines and journals may be published weekly, monthly, quarterly, annually, or at some other interval. Print editions also tend to use better paper and more color than newspapers do. The main difference between magazines and journals is their audience. Journals are written by scholars for scholars; magazines are produced by professional writers and editors for a general readership. Specific magazines and journals may be devoted to a particular topic or field of study. *Popular Mechanics,* for instance, is a magazine about developments in mechanical engineering, while the *Journal of Infectious Diseases* covers one aspect of medical study.

Note: Not all magazine or journal articles are secondary sources. Some are actually tertiary sources summarizing other secondary sources.

Parts of a Magazine or Journal

- **Cover:** Like a book cover, the front of a magazine or journal provides the title. Typically, it also shows volume, issue, and publication date and may list featured articles. *Issue:* Each new printing of a magazine or journal is an issue, which may be published weekly, monthly, quarterly, and so on. *Volume:* For some publications (especially scholarly works), a year's worth of issues is a volume.

- **Masthead:** Similar to the copyright page of a book, the masthead lists publication information (publisher, editors, directors, and office address).

- **Table of contents:** Like books, magazines and journals usually have a table of contents that lists the articles inside. Some have more than one list of contents: A "Features" page first, followed by a "Departments" page of other articles.

- **Editor's note:** Near the front, magazines and journals frequently include a letter or statement from the editor, revealing recent news about the periodical or providing background for articles in the issue.

- **Letters:** Reader responses to articles from earlier issues may be included near the front of a periodical. In an online publication, these responses may instead be published as comments directly following an article.

- **Body:** The body, or main part, of the magazine or journal contains the articles. *Pagination by issue:* Most magazines are paginated by issue. That is, each issue begins with page number 1. *Pagination by volume:* Journals are often paginated by volume. The first issue each year will begin with page 1, and subsequent issues will begin where the previous issue left off.

- **Advertisements:** Magazines often have nearly as many advertisements as articles. Somes advertisers try to make their ads look like articles, so it's important to distinguish the publication's articles from the advertisers'. Journals tend to have fewer ads, and those ads often promote other journals.

- **Indexes:** Some journals have indexes that identify authors and article titles. A volume often provides indexes for all of the issues included.

Your Turn Find a newspaper, a magazine, and a journal on a subject of your choice. Look for each part listed on these two pages.

Using Primary Sources

Depending upon your research purpose, primary sources may play a role.

Observing an Event or Exhibit

If you want to understand a Shakespeare play, you can read the script, but nothing compares to seeing it performed. Similarly, while you can read a book about Egyptian funerary items, nothing compares to seeing them in an exhibit. Such first-person experience adds a primary-source element to your research.

Tips for Observing

1. **Prepare** by learning what you can beforehand. The more you know before going into the event, the more aware you will be during it.

2. **Experience** the event fully while you are there. Pay close attention both to broad aspects and to details. If any handouts are available (such as programs, pamphlets, or menus), be sure to gather them as well. Besides providing additional detail, they can help you when documenting the event.

3. **Review** the event as soon as possible after the experience. Record everything you remember, including your own feelings and thoughts.

Viewing Historical Items

Historical documents, such as diaries, personal correspondence, maps, legal papers, and so on, can provide insights into many scholarly topics.

Library of Congress Web Site: The U.S. Library of Congress maintains a collection of documents, photos, sound recordings, and more. Much of this material is arranged into presentations by topic or period, and all of it is searchable. You will find the Library of Congress Web site at www.loc.gov.

Library Special Collections: Many libraries (especially college libraries) have special collections of original documents and other historical items. These may include rare books, personal journals, correspondence, maps, and so on. Items like these can give you a perspective on your topic that is not available elsewhere.

Typical Library Rules for Special Collections

- Material must be viewed in a special room and cannot be checked out.
- Backpacks, briefcases, coats, purses, and such must be left in lockers outside the reading room.
- No food or drinks may be taken into the special collections area.
- Only one item can be viewed at a time. A request slip must be filled out for each.
- No pencil marks may be added or erased, books must be laid flat on the reading table, gloves may be provided to protect pages, and so on.

Conducting Interviews

By interviewing an expert, you can ask questions and find answers you may have difficulty finding anywhere else. Carefully chosen quotations from an expert can also add authority to your research report.

Types of Interviews

- **Live:** Whether in person or by video conference, phone, or text chat, a live interview allows you to adapt questions and lines of inquiry as you go.
- **Correspondence:** An interview by mail or email is less spontaneous than a live interview, but it provides a record of questions and answers.

The Interview Process

Before the interview . . .

- ☑ **Do basic research.** Learn as much as possible about your topic. Don't waste the interviewee's time with basic questions.
- ☑ **Prepare a list of questions.** The better the questions, the better the answers. Write open-ended questions that invite extensive answers.
- ☑ **Identify possible experts.** Refer to your basic research to determine good candidates for an interview.
- ☑ **Arrange for an interview.** Contact one or more people from your list, identify yourself and your purpose, and politely ask for an interview. Schedule it at your interviewee's convenience.

During the interview . . .

- ☑ **Be polite.** Remember that the interviewee is doing you a favor. Experts are often very busy people, and taking time for an interview is a kindness.
- ☑ **Ask permission to record and quote.** While most interviewees won't mind, never assume that is the case. Always ask for permission.
- ☑ **Pay attention.** In a live interview, listen carefully and take notes. In a correspondence interview, carefully consider the person's answers. In either case, ask for clarification if needed.
- ☑ **Be prepared to reword a question** if the interviewee doesn't understand. Also ask follow-up questions if you need more information.
- ☑ **Review your notes before ending the interview.** Make sure that they are accurate and that you haven't forgotten anything.
- ☑ **Ask for recommendations** of other sources of good information.
- ☑ **Thank your interviewee** for his or her help.

After the interview . . .

- ☑ **Send a thank-you note** to the interviewee.
- ☑ **Review your notes and politely follow up** with any further questions.
- ☑ **Consider offering a copy of your finished work** to the interviewee.

Using Surveys

A survey is a detailed study used to gather data (statistics, opinions, or experiences) about a topic. The U.S. census conducted every 10 years is an example of a fact-finding survey. The Nielsen television ratings are based on another sort of survey. A public opinion poll held outside an election facility is yet another. You may also encounter surveys online, in a department store, or elsewhere. And you may conduct your own survey to gather information about your own research topic.

While the answers to some survey questions may be subjective ("What is your favorite fruit?" "How would you rate our customer service on a scale of 1 to 10?"), preparing a survey and compiling responses is serious business. Scientists and other scholars seek a statistically significant number of responders and calculate a margin of error in the results. To conduct your own survey, follow these steps:

Survey Guidelines

1. **Identify the purpose and audience for your survey:** What do you want to learn, and whom do you want to contact?

2. **Form the survey according to your purpose.**
   - Write questions that are clear and ask for the right type of information.
   - Word questions so they are easy to answer.
   - When possible, offer options to circle, underline, or click.

3. **Consider two types of questions.**
   - Closed-ended questions usually provide options and are easy to answer. (Yes-no, multiple choice, true-false, and fill-in-the-blank questions are examples.)
   - Open-ended questions ask survey takers to write out short answers.

4. **Arrange the information in a logical way.**
   - Start with a brief explanation of who you are or whom you represent, the purpose of the survey, and how to complete and return it.
   - Number and label all of the information that follows so the survey is easy to understand.
   - Provide enough space for readers to make their responses.

5. **Give it a test run.**
   - Have a few classmates or friends complete the survey.
   - Revise it as needed.

6. **Carry out the survey.**
   - Distribute it to the intended group.
   - Collect and evaluate the responses.

Sample Survey

This survey was prepared by student council members to gather information about students' lunchtime habits. The purpose is further explained in the survey itself.

Lunch Habits Survey

Background: As you know, for a trial period, Bernadine Ailts High School has adopted an open-campus policy for lunch. From now until the close of the school year, students can choose to either leave school grounds at lunchtime or stay on campus as before.

Purpose: The purpose of this survey is to better understand students' choices so that the student council can advise school administrators as they plan for the future.

Instructions: Please take a few moments to answer all the questions below; then fold your survey and drop it in the box outside the senior lounge by the end of school on Friday, April 20. All answers will remain anonymous. *Thank you for your help.*

1. What grade are you in? (Circle one.)

   Freshman   Sophomore   Junior   Senior

2. How often each week (on average) do you eat lunch in the school cafeteria? (Circle one.)

   1   2   3   4   5

3. How often each week (on average) do you eat lunch elsewhere on the school grounds? (Circle one.)

   1   2   3   4   5

4. Whether you eat in the cafeteria or elsewhere on campus, do you . . . (Mark one.)

   _____ **a.** buy food from the cafeteria?
   _____ **b.** buy food from school vending machines?
   _____ **c.** bring food from home?
   _____ **d.** buy food elsewhere?

5. How often each week (on average) do you leave school to eat lunch off campus? (Circle one.)

   1   2   3   4   5

6. How often each week (on average) do you leave school to eat lunch at home? (Circle one.)

   1   2   3   4   5

7. How often each week (on average) do you not eat lunch? (Circle one.)

   1   2   3   4   5

8. What advice do you have about a lunch policy for Bernadine Ailts High School?

   _____

   _____

Conducting Experiments

The scientific method is an inquiry strategy that can help you find the answers to research questions. Here are the steps involved:

The Scientific Method

1. Question Phenomena
2. Propose a Hypothesis
3. Research Experiments
6. Discuss Results and Draw a Conclusion
5. Analyze Results
4. Design and Conduct an Experiment

Recursiveness in the Scientific Method

As step 6 indicates, the scientific method is often recursive, with the results leading to more questions (step 1), new hypotheses (step 2), more research (step 3), and new experiments (steps 4–6).

Steps of the Scientific Method

1. **Question Phenomena** As you study any topic, questions naturally arise. Allow what you have been learning to spark curiosity about what you observe. Ask many questions and select the one that most interests you.

    Example: Is plant growth affected by music?

2. **Propose a Hypothesis** A hypothesis is a prediction of what you suspect may be true. Your experiment will test this hypothesis.

    Example: Soft, steady music promotes plant growth, while loud music with constant changes inhibits growth.

    Note: Disproving a hypothesis does not make your experiment a failure. Disproving a hypothesis can be as important as proving it. Both results advance knowledge.

3. **Research Experiments** Before designing and conducting an experiment, you should discover what work other people have already done on the subject. (This is why the *APA Style Manual* suggests that writers "describe relevant scholarship" in the introductions to their articles. See pages 398–399 for more about APA documentation style.)

    Example: Before conducting an experiment about the effect of music on plants, search for any previous studies and discussions of the topic. As it turns out, many people have written about the effects of music on living creatures, and several have experimented specifically with plants. Some suggest that music affects the human caretakers directly and the plants indirectly. Others have studied only specific musical tones.

4. **Design and Conduct an Experiment** A good experimental design controls as many variables as possible so that the results can be attributed to one specific variable or cause. (See the discussion of variables on pages 20–21 and 55.) This is why most experiments include a "control group." (In medical testing of a new drug treatment, for instance, one group of patients will receive the actual drug, while another otherwise identical group will receive a placebo.)

> *Example:* To test the possible effect of music on plants, our experiment will
> - focus on one specific plant type—indoor tomato plants;
> - start each plant from the same packet of seeds;
> - make sure each has the same environment of soil, water, light, and temperature;
> - expose each to a different type of music at different volumes 24 hours a day, using the same type of music player for each;
> - keep one plant in a quiet room, as a control;
> - let all plants grow until the fruit appears on each; and then
> - compare indications of health, including size, color, and number of tomatoes.

5. **Analyze the Results** Using your experimental design as a guide, keep careful records of data. For some experiments, this may mean recordings at specific intervals. For others, it may simply mean tracking end results. In any case, this data is necessary to prove, disprove, or revise your hypothesis, so accuracy is essential.

> *Example:* Our "effect of music on plants" experiment could measure growth each day, but we have chosen to use the end point "fruit appears."

6. **Discuss the Results and Draw a Conclusion** Like any other sort of research, while some experiments will offer a clear yes or no answer, most will raise new questions to explore or suggest design revisions of the same experiment.

> *Example:* Our "effect of music on plants" experiment might prove inconclusive for tomatoes, leaving us to wonder about other sorts of plants. Or one of the tomato seeds might not grow at all, encouraging us to redesign the experiment, including more than one plant in each music room to provide a larger, more accurate sampling.

Usually, "discuss the results and draw a conclusion" means writing a paper or an article about the experiment. In this way, you contribute to the background research that others can use in their own experiments about the topic.

Applications of the Scientific Method

This six-step process is useful beyond what you might think of as pure "science." Statisticians use the process to study Web-search patterns, for instance. Psychologists use it to study human behavior. Survey makers use it to draft and revise survey questions. You can apply it to nearly everything you're curious about.

Researching on the Internet

The Internet delivers *primary, secondary,* and *tertiary* sources. You can interact with experts in Webinars, social media, interactive Q&A pages, and so on—all primary sources. You can find high-quality secondary sources of information, too—articles, essays, or audio-visual materials. And you will encounter numerous tertiary sources within sites, pages, and postings. Judge Internet sources for their quality before using them in your research. Use your best reading and thinking skills and compare multiple sources to build a complete picture. (See pages 376–377.)

Tips for Navigation

- **Expect a long trip.** Finding the best information may take time.
- **Work smart.** Use keyword strategies (see page 368) and follow topic threads (see page 278) to ferret out answers.
- **Be creative.** Try multiple approaches to your Internet search. Allow time to pursue more than one path and see where each leads you.
- **Check all choices.** For most searches, you will have many options to review. Use a new browser tab or window to check each promising result while preserving your initial search in the original tab or window.
- **Take notes.** Research is all about learning, but you'll need to document your sources in any write-up, so take careful notes. (See pages 370–371.)
- **Stay on task.** It's easy to get distracted online, so maintain focus on your research topic. (Save unrelated links of interest by bookmark, email, or a special notes folder, and refer to them later.)

Special Research Sources

A general search engine isn't always the best place to start. Consider one of these gateways instead:

- The **Library of Congress** offers a wide variety of online texts, photos, and recordings, many of historical significance, that can serve as primary resources.
- **National** and **state governments** provide research sites to help you learn about a variety of topics. Examples include USA.gov (check its A-Z index of departments and agencies), NASA.gov, and CIA.gov (especially "The World Factbook").
- The **Internet Public Library** at ipl.org provides an entryway to information.
- Your **local library system** is another link to both area library resources and recommended Internet resources. (Check with your librarian or visit your library's Web site to see what is available.)
- **EBSCO, ProQuest,** and other such companies offer subscription-based access to searchable databases of periodical articles. For scholarly research of secondary sources, these databases are often the best starting point. Many school and public libraries have subscriptions to such services.
- **OverDrive, Amazon, Barnes & Noble** and others provide many books to library-lending programs. Check with your local librarian to learn more.

Surface Web and Deep Web

The Web is a virtual soup of different technologies, creating some special challenges for search engines. It means that not everything online is easily found. You can increase your chances of locating the best material in the shortest time by understanding the difference between the "surface Web" and the "deep Web" (often called the "invisible Web").

Surface Web

The "surface Web" is what's readily available to you, and everyone else, through search engines and advertised Web addresses. The only difficulty here is learning to separate high-quality resources from dubious ones. Think of the "surface Web" as the face of an ocean, readily visible in all directions.

Deep Web

The "deep Web" is material that has not been indexed by search engines, but is available to you—if you know where to look. Many community message boards, educational wikis, and government databases (such as a job-search site) fall into the "deep Web" category. Such material has not been indexed for various reasons: Often, pages on these sites don't actually exist until you request them, and they vanish afterward. In other instances, password authorization or CAPTCHA verification may block search-engine robots, or Web designers have inserted a "no robot" code. So while a search engine cannot index a site's information, you can visit the site and find the information yourself. Think of the "deep Web" as the ocean depths; if you know where to dive, you'll find treasure.

> ### Tips for Searching Within a Site
>
> - **Page search:** Most browsers provide a search tool to quickly find a word or phrase on a page. Check under "Edit" in your browser's menu for "Find."
> - **Search box:** Many Web sites have their own search boxes, so you can look within the site without searching the entire Web.
> - **Topics and threads:** Message boards arrange postings by topic, subtopics, and "threads." Browsing topics can help you zero in on information—when those topics are well titled. When they're not, you just have to click and see. A thread is a conversation following one idea. Some threads link to related threads or to information elsewhere online.
> - **Asking for help:** If a Web site or message board allows, you may post a question and ask for help finding answers. Keep the following in mind:
>   - ☑ **Stay safe online.** Don't post personal details about yourself or your family.
>   - ☑ **Don't expect others to do your work.** Do not ask questions you could find an answer to on your own.
>   - ☑ **Always be polite.** It's easy to mistake someone's tone online. Always be polite in your posts and forgiving of others'.

Avoiding Plagiarism

So far we've talked about research as the process of gathering information. But the flip side is organizing what you've learned and making it available to others. Research is actually a dialogue in which people build upon each other's work to advance the cause of knowledge for everyone. *Plagiarism*—which means using other people's ideas without crediting them—stifles that dialogue. *Citation* is a way of giving credit to your sources.

▶ Why Giving Credit Matters

There are three main reasons for giving credit to sources in your work.

1. **To serve your reader:** While reading your work, your reader may want to check your facts or learn more about a particular point. Citation allows that.

2. **To respect your sources:** Your sources deserve credit for the work they've done. Identifying them in your own writing helps to further their reputation.

3. **To support your work:** Giving credit adds authority to your writing. It shows that you are aware of the scholarly dialogue surrounding your topic, and that you understand how it applies to your own ideas.

Note: Other sources can lend authority to your work, but it needs to be *your work.* Don't present a series of quotations as a report. (See "Plunking" on the following page.)

▶ What Your Reader Needs to Know

When reading any sort of research—from a newspaper story to a scientific study to a business report—the reader needs to know two things.

1. **Where did this idea come from?** The reader will assume an idea comes from you, the writer, unless it is attributed to another source in a citation.

2. **How can I check the source myself?** This is the single most important point about documentation. Different disciplines have different ways of documenting sources (see pages 396–402). What they share in common, however, is this goal: *to make it possible for readers to find and check a source for themselves.* Keep this in mind.

▶ What Plagiarism Costs

Without a doubt, plagiarism hurts. Most importantly, it hurts those seeking knowledge, because it severs the tie between a reader and the origins of ideas and information. It also hurts those who created the material, robbing them of the credit they deserve for their ideas.

But plagiarism also hurts the plagiarist. It leads to lazy, shallow thinking and weakens the person's work. It frustrates the opportunity to root an argument or idea in a dialogue with other scholars. And it can destroy a person's reputation, earning a reprimand in school or dismissal from a college or a job.

Other Source Abuses

Plagiarism isn't the only way a source can be misused. Avoid these other source abuses.

▶ Misstating a Source

If you summarize an idea incorrectly, change or misspell words in a quotation, paraphrase inaccurately, or make an error in a statistic, you change the meaning of the borrowed material. This can hurt the reputation of the original author.

> *Example:* Mr. Eisler said, "My background makes me the **oblivious** candidate."

▶ Using a Source Out of Context

Another misapplication of source material is to take a statement out of its original context, making it seem to say something that was never intended.

> *Original:* Principal Bozzi argued, "If this disastrous budget is approved, there will be no room for music or arts in next year's class schedule."
>
> *Out of context:* Education should focus on core subjects and not frivolity. Principal Bozzi has said, "There will be no room for music or arts in next year's class schedule."

▶ Overusing Source Material

Your writing should present your own thoughts in your own voice, backed up by other sources. If it reads like a string of references, your ideas and voice are lost.

> *Example:* "The White House has already been accused of gagging the U.S. Environmental Protection Agency and NASA. . . . Now the U.S. Centers for Disease Control may have suffered the same fate" (*New Scientist*). Deceptions "occurred during the Nixon, Ford and Carter administrations, but their incidence increased dramatically when the Reagan team took over" (Sibbison 208). Of course, "even in the absence of deliberate abuse, scientific progress is stifled by secrecy" (Park 22).

▶ Relying Too Heavily on One Source

If your work relies too heavily on one source, readers may doubt the depth of your research and understanding. Be sure to incorporate a variety of sources into your writing.

▶ "Plunking" Quotations

Quotations should be used sparingly (to support a point or to encapsulate an idea), and they must be smoothly worked into your writing. Do not just "plunk" them into your text, expecting your reader to make the connection.

> *Plunked quotation:* Calling someone an enemy accomplishes little. "Nothing is easier than to denounce the evildoer; nothing is more difficult than to understand him" (Dostoevsky 9).

▶ Using "Blanket" Citations

When you incorporate a source, it must be clear to your reader where that citation begins and ends. For a quotation, that is usually obvious. For a longer paraphrase, however, signal both the beginning and end in your text.

What Plagiarism Looks Like

On these two pages, you'll find a brief article and ways the article could be plagiarized or abused. Use this as a guide to check your own work for these problems.

A **Copying Text** This type of plagiarism uses word-for-word sentences from the original without giving credit.

Humans have been using solar power for thousands of years. Even the ancient Romans focused the sun to heat water. Windmills and waterwheels have also been around for millennia, both using modified forms of solar power. Wind results from uneven distribution of sunlight on our planet. Rain is a result of solar evaporation of water, which rises, cools, and condenses to fall again. When that water lands at higher elevations, it flows toward the sea in streams and rivers, expending that solar power. In the past century, however, people have looked at new ways to harness the sun.

B **Neglecting Quotation Marks** This type of plagiarism identifies the source but fails to place quotation marks around sentences used word for word from the original.

Installing a solar array isn't easy. With a solar array correctly placed, however, a house may actually generate enough power to sell some to the utility company, especially when no one is home—during work hours, for instance (Sicurella). This means that a solar array can pay for itself not only in energy savings but in actual earnings.

C **Paraphrasing Ideas Without Crediting Them** This type of plagiarism paraphrases someone else's ideas but doesn't identify the source. The reader is left to assume that the ideas are the writer's.

Home solar power isn't a cure-all, however. It makes sense to consider other energy issues in your home before investing in a solar array. If your home is like a leaky boat, with gaps in insulation and full of drafts, it doesn't make sense to just bail harder. Fix those holes before installing solar panels or other green technology.

Additional Plagiarism Offenses

Self-Plagiarism The idea of plagiarizing oneself may seem paradoxical. However, when scholars publish their work, the publisher gains at least some rights to it. Scholars referring to their own work in later writing must credit the original source of publication. Similarly, when students submit a research paper in one class, that paper should not be submitted for an assignment in another class *unless both instructors give permission.*

Copyright Violation To protect creative works, governments make laws granting copyright and defining fair use. In general, it is illegal to use any part of a copyrighted work without the owner's permission. "Fair use" laws allow limited exceptions for educational purposes and reviews. Be sure you understand and follow copyright restrictions in your research. The *Chicago Manual of Style* provides an excellent discussion of this topic.

Note: Using a photograph or graphic without crediting its source is also plagiarism.

Own Your Own Solar System
Napoleon Sicurella

Would you like to have a solar system on your roof? Not a model of the sun and its planets, of course, but an array of panels to turn sunlight into electricity. According to Harry T. Roman in "Solar Electricity for Homes," published in *Tech Directions* magazine, a typical solar-panel array can save a home roughly half its usual utility bill.

Using solar power isn't a new idea, as Rex A. Ewing and Doug Pratt, authors of *Got Sun? Go Solar,* point out. Even the ancient Romans focused the sun to heat water. Windmills and waterwheels have also been around for millennia, both using modified forms of solar power. Wind results from uneven distribution of sunlight on our planet. Rain is a result of solar evaporation of water, which rises, cools, and condenses to fall again. When that water lands at higher elevations, it flows toward the sea in streams and rivers, expending that solar power.

Capturing solar power directly, in panels that generate electricity, is relatively new, however. Roman explains that these panels "are actually a large version of the little solar cells that power the calculators we use." Of course, the power needed for a calculator is small. Only in the past few decades have researchers devised materials to generate enough power for a building, and they continue to strive for higher energy efficiency.

With a solar array correctly placed, however, a house may actually generate enough power to sell some to the utility company, especially when no one is home—during work hours, for instance. Utility companies used to prevent this for safety reasons (to avoid power-line workers from being shocked during maintenance). However, Ewing and Pratt say that now this sellback, "called utility intertie, or simply grid-tie," is legal in every state. And Roman explains that modern solar arrays can detect when a power line has been shut off for maintenance so that they stop sending power.

Setting up a solar array requires considerable math. Roman explains that the panels have to be set at the best angle to catch the "solar window": the sun's arc across the sky in all seasons. Voltage output also has to be balanced against the size and costs of panels as well as a home's needs. (Price rises dramatically for smaller, more efficient panels.) Fortunately, the federal government provides a free PVWATTS calculator online to handle the trigonometry involved.

Before installing a solar system, it pays to consider other energy issues in your home. In "Energy Efficiency One Step at a Time" (*Qualified Remodeler*), New York contractor Joseph Malcarne offers the analogy of a leaky boat. Instead of getting a bigger bucket to bail faster, patch the holes first. Seal any gaps leaking air, improve the insulation, and then go for green technology like solar panels. Malcarne describes one local homeowner who followed this advice, cut his utility bills to less than a tenth, and—as a bonus—hosted a breakfast for his neighbors after a freak snowstorm downed power lines, but his home remained warm.

Using a Citation Style

Different fields of study format documents and cite sources in different ways, as shown on the next three pages. See pages 397–402 for details about formatting student papers.

MLA (Modern Language Association) Citation

MLA style is typically used for the humanities—languages, literature, philosophy, and so on—in which a source's age does not dictate its value. Within an essay, MLA identifies sources by author and page number. Full publication details are given at the essay's end in a list of works cited, alphabetized by author.

A typical citation ends with author and page in parentheses.

Through history's lens, any contradiction between free will and predestination evaporates. We see people make decisions freely even as we see the forces influencing them (Tolstoy 1007-1009).

A citation can open with author's name and close with page numbers, for clarity.

Tolstoy argues that history as a science reconciles any seeming contradiction between free will and predestination. In its moment, every decision seems arbitrary, but the more distant our view, the more forces we perceive influencing that choice (1007-1009).

Matching works-cited entry (book)

Tolstoy, Leo. *War and Peace.* New York: Random House, 1955. Print.

Common MLA Works-Cited Entries

List author by last name, then first. (Use normal order for any additional authors: "Smith, Jon, and Jo Jones.") "Medium of publication" may be "Print," "Web," "CD," and so on. "Pages" means the page range of the article. For Web resources, use "n.p." if no publisher can be identified, "n.d." for no date of creation.

Book:

Author(s). *Book Title.* City of publication: Publisher, year of publication. Medium of publication.

Magazine article:

Author(s). "Article Title." *Periodical Title* Day Month Year: pages. Medium of publication.

Article in a scholarly journal:

Author(s). "Article Title." *Journal Title* Volume.Issue (Year): pages. Medium of publication.

Web site:

Editor, author, or compiler name. *Site Name.* Site sponsor or publisher, date of creation. Medium of publication. Date of access.

Web page:

Author(s). "Page name." *Site Name.* Site sponsor or publisher, date of creation. Medium of publication. Date of access.

For more examples, see thoughtfullearning.com/h396.

MLA Student-Paper Format

A student paper in MLA format needs no title page. All pages have a one-inch margin on all sides, with a running head in the upper right corner listing the writer's last name and the page number. All text is double-spaced (except captions for graphics), and works-cited entries are formatted with a hanging indentation. (You can find more MLA details and view the full report at thoughtfullearning.com/h397.)

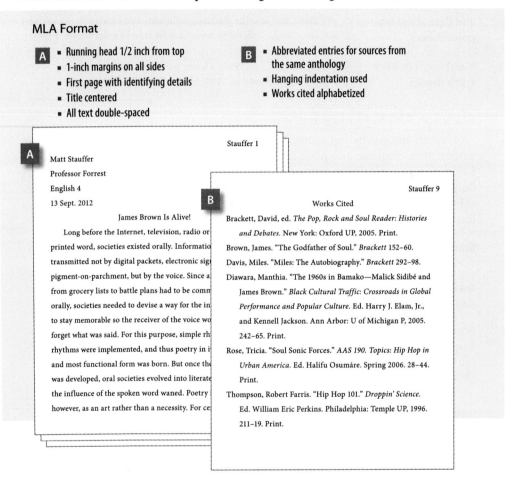

MLA Format

A
- Running head 1/2 inch from top
- 1-inch margins on all sides
- First page with identifying details
- Title centered
- All text double-spaced

B
- Abbreviated entries for sources from the same anthology
- Hanging indentation used
- Works cited alphabetized

A

Stauffer 1

Matt Stauffer

Professor Forrest

English 4

13 Sept. 2012

James Brown Is Alive!

Long before the Internet, television, radio or printed word, societies existed orally. Informatio transmitted not by digital packets, electronic sig pigment-on-parchment, but by the voice. Since a from grocery lists to battle plans had to be comm orally, societies needed to devise a way for the in to stay memorable so the receiver of the voice wo forget what was said. For this purpose, simple rh rhythms were implemented, and thus poetry in i and most functional form was born. But once the was developed, oral societies evolved into literate the influence of the spoken word waned. Poetry however, as an art rather than a necessity. For ce

B

Stauffer 9

Works Cited

Brackett, David, ed. *The Pop, Rock and Soul Reader: Histories and Debates.* New York: Oxford UP, 2005. Print.

Brown, James. "The Godfather of Soul." *Brackett* 152–60.

Davis, Miles. "Miles: The Autobiography." *Brackett* 292–98.

Diawara, Manthia. "The 1960s in Bamako—Malick Sidibé and James Brown." *Black Cultural Traffic: Crossroads in Global Performance and Popular Culture.* Ed. Harry J. Elam, Jr., and Kennell Jackson. Ann Arbor: U of Michigan P, 2005. 242–65. Print.

Rose, Tricia. "Soul Sonic Forces." *AAS 190. Topics: Hip Hop in Urban America.* Ed. Halífu Osumáre. Spring 2006. 28–44. Print.

Thompson, Robert Farris. "Hip Hop 101." *Droppin' Science.* Ed. William Eric Perkins. Philadelphia: Temple UP, 1996. 211–19. Print.

Journalistic Citation

Newspapers, popular magazines, and many books document their sources by working identifying information into the text itself, without a bibliography or list of references.

The source (a person) is identified within the text of the first sentence.	Adela Encinas, CEO of MagroCorp, argues that Congress must pass new tax laws to better sync with the global marketplace. "It makes no sense," she says, "to punish local businesses with taxes that local offices of international businesses are able to sidestep."

APA (American Psychological Association) Citation

APA style is most often used in the behavior and social sciences—psychology, anthropology, ecology, sociology, and so on—where timeliness of information is important. In an essay, APA identifies a source by author and date, matched to an alphabetized list of references.

A source's author and date are shown in parentheses.	Though it is difficult to show a statistical correlation between pollution and marine disease, pollutants are clearly stressors, and stressors make fish vulnerable to infection (Sindermann, 1996).
Matching reference entry (book)	Sindermann, C. J. (1996). *Ocean pollution: Effects on living resources and humans.* Boca Raton, FL: CRC Press.

Common APA Reference Entries

List all authors by last name, then first initial (and middle, if given). Separate authors with commas, and place an ampersand (&) before the last. Place the year of publication in parentheses, followed by a period. In book and article titles, capitalize only the first word (and any proper nouns). For location of publisher, list city and state abbreviation (or country for foreign publishers). For online articles, follow the print format with a "doi" (digital object identifier) if available or a "Retrieved from" note.

Book	Author, A. A., & Author, B. B. (Year of publication). *Title of work: Capital letter also for subtitle.* Location: Publisher.
Article in a journal paginated by issue	Author, A. A. (Year). Title of article. *Title of Periodical, volume number*(issue number), pages.
Article in a journal paginated by volume	Author, A. A. (Year). Title of article. *Title of Periodical, volume number,* pages.
Magazine article	Author, A. A. (Year, month day). Title of article. *Title of Periodical, volume number,* pages.
Online article with doi	Author, A. A. (Year). Title of article. *Title of Periodical, volume number*(issue number), pages. doi:0000000/000000000000
Online article, "Retrieved from"	Author, A. A. (Year). Title of article. *Title of Periodical, volume number*(issue number), pages. Retrieved from http://www.example.edu/path/page
Web page	Author, A. A. (Date of publication). Title of document. Retrieved from http://Web address

For more examples, see thoughtfullearning.com/h398.

APA Student-Paper Format

A student paper in APA format normally requires a title page and an abstract. All pages have a one-inch margin on all sides, with a shortened title as a running head in the upper left corner and a page number in the upper right. (On page 1—the title page—the running head is preceded by the phrase "Running head:") All text is double-spaced (as are any captions included with figures, unless your instructor allows single spacing), and reference entries are formatted with a hanging indentation. See the example pages that follow.

APA Format

A
- 1-inch margins on all sides
- Title, author, and school name centered, roughly one-third down the page

B
- Running head flush left, 1/4 inch from page top
- Page numbers flush right, 1/4 inch from page top
- "Abstract" title centered

C
- Paper title centered on first page

D
- "References" heading centered
- Entries alphabetized
- Formatted with hanging indentation

A Running head: HAVEN'T HEARD OF HEPATITIS C?

Haven't Heard of Hepatitis C?

You May Have It and Not Even Know

Amanjit (Amy) Sekhon

University of California Davis

B HAVEN'T HEARD OF HEPATITIS C?   3

Abstract

Over 30 million Americans and 170 million people worldwide are infected with Hepatitis C. Because they may be asymptomatic for years or mistake their symptoms for more common ailments, many are unaware of their ailment. This puts them at risk for permanent liver damage, leading to possible cirrhosis or cancer. It also puts people near them at risk of infection. As the number of incidences of the disease increase, we may need to more actively conduct blood tests for infection.

C HAVEN'T HEARD OF HEPATITIS C?   2

Haven't Heard of Hepatitis C?

You May Have It and Not Even Know

The recent news of Pamela Anderson publicly stating that she has been diagnosed with Hepatitis C has brought an otherwise unfamiliar disease into the limelight. Hepatitis (HCV) currently infects over 3 million Americans (Bren) and 170 million people worldwide (Drucker, 2001). Despite the enormous number of people infected, many infected the disease are not even aware that they have had the disease for many years because they are chronic carriers and are often asymptomatic for most of their lives. Thus, although disease is not life-threatening in every case, the real danger of this disease lies in the fact that it is often undiagnosed many years, allowing the virus to possibly cause severe health problems to the liver, such as cirrhosis or cancer.

The term hepatitis means inflammation of the liver. people are aware of the better-known Hepatitis A (HAV) Hepatitis B (HBV) but are relatively unaware that there is

---

D HAVEN'T HEARD OF HEPATITIS C?   14

References

Albrecht, J. H., Jensen, D. M., Peine, C. J., & Schiff, E. R. (1996, July 15). The danger of hepatitis C: Transfusions to tattoos. *Patient Care,* 112.

Bren, L. (2001, July). Hepatitis C (disease development and treatment side-effects). *FDA Consumer,* 24.

Cody, S. H., Nainan, O. V., Garfein, R. S.; Meyers, H., Bell, B. P., Shapiro, C. N., et. al. (2002, Feb. 11) Hepatitis C virus transmission from an anesthesiologist to a patient. *Archives of Internal Medicine,* 345.

Cowley, G. (2002, April 22). Hepatitis C: The insidious spread of a killer virus. *Newsweek,* 46.

Drucker, E., Alcabes, P. G, & Marx, P. A. (2001, Dec. 8). The

CMS (Chicago Manual of Style) Citation

CMS format can use either a numbered notation—common in the humanities—or an author-date notation—common in the sciences.

Author-Date Notation

Full publication details are given in a reference list.

In-text citation, open with author's name and end with the date in parentheses	Henig explains that while the dangerous side effects of ketamine make it too dangerous for antidepressant use, the motion-sickness drug scopolamine shows promise as a fast-acting solution (2012).
In-text citation, end with both author and date in parentheses.	The dangerous side effects of ketamine make it too dangerous for antidepressant use, but the motion-sickness drug scopolamine shows promise as a fast-acting solution (Henig 2012).
Matching reference-list entry	Henig, Robin Marantz. 2012. "Lifting the Black Cloud." *Scientific American* 306 (3): 66.

Common Author-Date Entries

CMS author-date documentation is similar to the style used for MLA bibliography entries. The significant differences are that (1) the year of publication is moved forward to just after the author's name, and (2) the page of entries is titled "References."

Book	Author's last name, first name. Publication year. *Book Title*. Publication city: Publisher.
Periodical	Author's last name, first name. Publication year. "Article Title." *Periodical Title* volume (issue no., month, or season): page number(s).
Online article with doi	Author's last name, first name. Publication year. "Article Title." *Periodical Title* volume (issue no., month, or season): page number(s). doi:0000000/000000000000.
Online article with URL	Author's last name, first name. Publication year. "Article Title." *Periodical Title* volume (issue no., month, or season): page number(s). http://www.example.edu/path/page.

For more examples, see thoughtfullearning.com/h400.

Numbered Notation

Superscript numbers point to notes. Full publication details are given *either* in those notes *or* in a separate alphabetized bibliography.

In-text citations —— Suzanne M. Bianchi notes that "the family system is more turbulent in the United States than elsewhere."[19] She says single parents now head a quarter of U.S. households with children.[20]

Matching footnote — 19. Bianchi bases this statement upon studies by Andrew
or endnote   Cherlin. See note 8.

Footnote or —— 20. This is true across the spectrum of social classes.
endnote with   Suzanne M. Bianchi, "Changing Families, Changing
publication details Workplaces," *Future of Children* 21, no. 2 (Fall 2011): 15-36.

Bibliography entry — Bianchi, Suzanne M. "Changing Families, Changing
(if not included in   Workplaces." *Future of Children* 21, no. 2 (Fall 2011): 15-36.
notes)

Common Numbered-Citation Entries

If you supply full publication details in your footnotes or endnotes, you will not need a bibliography. But if you must prepare a bibliography, notice that the treatment of the author's name and the punctuation of the publication details varies between a note and a bibliographic entry. Remember, too, to include specific page numbers in your notes for information you've quoted or paraphrased from a source.

Book in notes —— Note number. Author's first and last name, *Book Title* (Publication
                  city: Publisher, publication year), page number(s).

Book in —— Author's last name, first name. *Book Title*. Publication city:
bibliography   Publisher, publication year.

Periodical article —— Note number. Author's first and last name, "Article Title,"
in notes   *Periodical Title* volume, issue number (year): page number(s).

Periodical article —— Author's last name, first name. "Article Title." *Periodical Title*
in bibliography   volume, issue number (year): page number(s).

Online document —— Note number. Author's first and last name, "Document Title,"
in notes   *Site Title*, publication information [e.g., volume, posting
                      date], Internet address (access date).

Online document —— Author's last name, first name. "Document Title." *Site Title*,
in bibliography   publication information [e.g., volume, posting date].
                      Internet address (access date).

CMS Paper Format

In CMS format, either prepare a title page or include the title on the first page of text. (Follow your instructor's preference.) Leave a 1-inch to 1½-inch margin on all sides of a page. Place page numbers in the upper right corner, beginning with the first page of text, and double-space the body text. Single-space each note, bibliography entry, or reference entry, and double-space between them. Use hanging indentation for both bibliographies and reference lists. See the example pages below. (You can find more CMS details and view the full report in both numbered-note and author-date formats at thoughtfullearning.com/h402.)

CMS Format

A
- 1-inch to 1½-inch margins on all sides
- Title centered one-third down the page
- Writer, course, and date several lines below title

B
- Page numbers flush right, in upper margin, starting on first page of text
- Footnote identified by superscripted number
- Footnote indented, single-spaced*
  *Double-space between multiple notes.

C
- Individual entries are single-spaced, but double-space between them.

A

5

Johann Sebastian Bach and the Lutheran Chorale

Erinn Losness

Music 121: Topics in Music History

29 October 2012

B

In order to encourage group participation during worship services, Luther had to devise a musical genre that would be simple enough for lay people and yet still be able to communicate profound theological truths. Luther's solution lay in the development of German congregational hymns that are known as chorales. [3] Although each chorale contains its own unique characteristics, most chorales are identifiable by some similar musical and textual features. One of the most important of these features is the use of the vernacular language. In order to encourage the understanding and participation of the lay people, Luther replaced the tra[...] Latin liturgical language with German. This differe[...] significant for a number of reasons. It first and forem[...] allowed everyone in the congregation to participate, a[...] enabled less educated worshipers to understand the m[...] of the texts. Chorales, therefore, were the means for th[...] realization of Luther's desire that people not "merely [...]

---

3. The word "chorale" can apply to the melodic li[...] alone or to the combination of both the melody and h[...]

C

11

Bibliography

Ambrose, Z. Philip. *Texte zu den Kirchenkantaten von Johann Sebastian Bach.* Norwich: Thames Publishing, 1984.

Bach, Johann Sebastian. *The Passion of our Lord According to St. Matthew.* Trans. Rev. Dr. Troutbeck. London: Novello and Company, 1894.

Bischof, Walter F. *The Bach Cantatas: Original Texts (German).* http://www.cs.ualberta.ca/~wfb/bach.html (accessed February 22, 2003).

Blume, Friedrich. *Protestant Church Music: A History.* New York: W. W. Norton & Company, 1974.

Boyd, Malcolm, ed. *Oxford Composer Companion: J. S. Bach.* Oxford : Oxford University Press, 1999.

Butt, John. "Organ Chorale." In Boyd, *Oxford Composer Companions,* 344-347.

Halter, Carl, and Carl Schalk, ed. A *Handbook of Church Music.* St. Louis: Concordia Publishing House, 1978.

Using Documentation Tools

Many tools exist for formatting entries for a works-cited, reference, or bibliography page and for endnotes or footnotes. Bear two things in mind when using these tools:

1. **Automated tools are not perfect.** Often the quality of what is delivered depends upon the information you provide. It pays to be familiar with formats for basic entries. (See pages 397-402.)

2. **In-text entries are up to you.** No documentation tool can decide how to cite sources within your text. Use your best judgment about naming a source in the text or providing a parenthetical note instead.

Documentation Tools and Tips

Provided References Scholarly Web resources often include a "how to cite this" statement, usually at the bottom of the page. Always check that the format matches the citation style you are using.

Research Databases Research databases such as ProQuest and EBSCOhost provide a link to a citation for each resource in their collection. These citations are usually very accurate, and you can choose the format. Ask your librarian about access to these services.

Research Software For scholars who research and write a lot, computer applications such as EndNote, ProCite, Reference Manager, RefWorks, and BibTeX can build a bibliography automatically as the paper is written. Check with your instructor about the availability of such tools.

Web Forms Many Web sites offer free online forms to help students format bibliography entries. These can help with punctuation, capitalization, and order of elements. Unless you know what is and isn't needed in a particular citation, however, you may end up with incorrect results. Always check the final citation against a style guide (see below).

Style Guides and References

- Pages 376–389 of this book provide basic guides for the most common types of sources. You'll find more details online at thoughtfullearning.com/h403.
- We also recommend the Purdue Online Writing Lab (owl.english.purdue.edu), where you'll find quick links to MLA and APA styles. Use the search box on that site to locate other styles, such as CMS and CSE.
- For further details or specialized examples, check the various style guides themselves. Use each guide's table of contents and index to most quickly locate the answers you need and to develop a fuller understanding of the style's rationale.

Check with Your Instructor (or Publisher)

No style manual can cover every possibility, and different instructors (and publishers) may have different citation requirements. Always check with your instructor (or publisher) for specific format instructions before submitting an essay.

The Research Process as Inquiry

There is small "r" research (the third step in the inquiry process), and there is big "R" research—which encompasses the whole process. Scientists, archeologists, engineers, and entrepreneurs perform this kind of research, seeking new information to add to what is known. When you perform big "R" research, you are using a form of the inquiry process:

Research Process   Inquiry Process

Question   Question
You begin by questioning a person, place, thing, event, or idea. You settle on a guiding question, discover pointed questions, and use journalistic and Socratic questions to open up the space for information. (See page 354.)

Plan   Plan
Next, you decide how you will find answers to your questions, considering primary, secondary, and tertiary sources and deciding what you will search for in person, in print, and online. (See pages 376–391.)

Research   Research
Following your plan, you go to libraries and go online, conduct surveys and experiments, have experiences and make observations, and gather and organize your discoveries in notes, links, photos, recordings, and other media. (See pages 370–371.)

Create   Create
At a certain point, you put the pieces of your research together in a form that others can experience, whether a paper, video, speech, scale model, piece of legislation, composition, or whatever.

Improve   Improve
After the initial act of creation, you need to carefully evaluate what you have made, check its effectiveness, and make sure all research is correctly reported and all sources are cited. (See pages 392–403.)

Present   Present
At last, you are ready to present what you have found, adding your own work to that of other researchers—thinkers, writers, engineers, scientists, and artists.

Chapter 25
Creating

Creating is all about producing something of your own, taking an idea and making it a reality. The first Harley-Davidson motorcycle didn't appear until William Harley and Arthur Davidson took their idea to a machine shop and created an engine for a regular pedal bicycle. Sadly, they had to trash their first attempt because the motorbike couldn't even make it up a small hill. But they learned a lot, kept asking questions, and kept working until they succeeded.

Creating is very seldom a straight-line activity. This chapter will help you handle the curves and turn your ideas into something tangible—perhaps a convincing speech, a breathtaking movie, or a well-executed experiment.

You will learn . . .

- A Guide to Creating
- Creating a Basic Structure
- Using Informational Structures
- Creating Narrative Structure
- Creating Visual Structure
- Catching Attention
- 10 Tips for Getting Unstuck

A Guide to Creating

With your planning (pages 355–362) and research (pages 363–404) complete, you are ready to create something new. Expect a few twists and turns along the way, and don't worry about getting it right the first time.

Checking Your Readiness

If you're fully prepared for the task at hand, you'll be able to comfortably answer "yes" to these questions:

- Have I asked the right questions about my topic?
- Have I completed my planning and filled in a planning sheet?
- Have I carried out the necessary research?
- Do I understand my topic well?

Getting Started

Often, the hardest part of creating is beginning. Writers fear the blank screen; artists, the blank canvas. Here are a few tips for overcoming this natural anxiety:

- **Follow your schedule.** Use your planning sheet to guide your work. It will list your tasks, when they need to be completed, and who is responsible for what.
- **Be prepared.** Gather all the necessary equipment and materials before tackling each task.
- **Find a good spot to work.** Choose a quiet place without distractions. Turn off your cell phone.
- **Reserve plenty of time to complete each task.** Avoid the anxiety of deadline pressure by reserving blocks of time devoted solely to your work.
- **Make adjustments as needed.** Be adaptable, and change your schedule if certain tasks take longer than expected.
- **Start small.** The creation you envision may take a long time to complete. But just accomplishing part of it (to start) will put you in a creative mind-set.
- **Form a meaningful whole.** You goal is to develop a complete first draft or design so that you have something to work with and improve upon.

Your Turn Passion for your work helps ensure a quality end product. What are you passionate about? What could you create by tapping into that passion?

Creating a **Basic Structure**

Anything that is experienced over time has a three-part structure: a beginning, a middle, and an ending. This three-part structure is common in essays, oral presentations, stories, plays, videos, games, concerts, and other events.

▶ Beginning

The beginning orients the person who is having the experience, whether reader, viewer, fan, or participant. It catches the person's attention, provides background, and then identifies the goal or main point of the experience.

Your Turn Which beginning below does a better job of starting a podcast?

> **Host:** *Today we are speaking with Steve Redman. He knows a thing or two about fish and marine life.*

> **Host:** *Have you ever wondered how the shows on Animal Planet get all that amazing footage of life beneath the ocean's surface? Our guest today has answers for you and brings a unique perspective to the topic. Steve Redman is a marine biologist and deep-sea cameraman and is here to tell us about his experiences under the sea.*

▶ Middle

The middle provides the heart of the experience, whether the argument in an essay, the action of a story, the songs in concert, or the sites on a tour. The middle immerses the audience in the experience, leading them through details and events that are organized in a logical and meaningful way.

▶ Ending

The ending ties the experience together and brings it to a fitting close. It may reinforce the topic's importance, add a final thought, or include a call to action. A strong ending makes a lasting impression and rewards the audience's attention.

Your Turn Which ending below does a better job of wrapping up a persuasive essay?

> Dogfighting is violent and cruel and must be stopped. It treats dogs inhumanely and endangers communities. Education and awareness programs can sensitize youth and adults to animal cruelty. Citizens can help by speaking out against dog violence. Dogs—and our communities—deserve better.

> We need to do a better job of protecting our dogs. They are friendly and loyal companions to all and should not be subjected to the bad people running dogfighting rings. It's a tough problem to crack, but we can do better to end it.

Using Informational Structures

The way you organize information impacts how your audience receives it. The six informational structures on the next few pages will help you organize your information in a clear, easy-to-follow manner. Choose the pattern that best fits your project's purpose.

Importance

Use order of importance to rank details from least to most important, or from most to least important.

Most to Least Important	Least to Most Important
Detail 1	Detail 3
Detail 2	Detail 2
Detail 3	Detail 1

Note: Transitional words and phrases signal shifts in thought and are used to guide your audience through blocks of information.

Order-of-importance transitions: more important, most important, a more effective, most effective, good, better, best

First of all, a disclosure law will prevent corruption and the appearance of corruption. Currently, individuals and corporations can contribute no more than $2,500 per election to federal candidates. The main reason the Supreme Court upholds the limit's constitutionality is because large contributions can lead to actual or perceived corruption of those candidates. . . .

More important, passing a disclosure rule will at least hold super PACs and other political committees to some of the same campaign finance standards as candidates' official campaigns. For example, when a political candidate finances a political advertisement, he or she is required to approve the message. . . .

Transparency of information is the most important reason to support a disclosure law. Shouldn't voters have as much access to information as possible when deciding how to vote? Right now super PACs are beholden to leisurely disclosure policies. They need to report spending only on a monthly or quarterly basis. . . .

Chronological

Use chronological order (time order) to arrange details in a story or process in the order in which they happened.

Chronological Order
Start
Detail 1
Detail 2
Detail 3
Finish

Chronological-order transitions: first, next, then, before, after, later, second, finally, last

Problem-Solution

Use problem-solution order to explain a problem, outline a solution, or argue for or against a solution.

Solution-Focused
Introduce the problem.
Offer a solution.
Support the solution.

Problem-Focused
Introduce the problem.
Explain the severity of the problem.
Offer a solution.

Problem-solution terms:
at risk, a major problem, one symptom, should be saved, must not happen, to fix this, the best solution, please support

---

The Daily Statesmen
Attention: News Editor
378 Main St.
Dexter, MO 63841

Dear Editor:

A significant landmark in Bloomfield's history is at risk of being lost forever. The city is planning to tear down the Miller House at 1238 Shagbark Way. It is one of the only remaining structures in the city to survive the Civil War and should be a permanent fixture of Bloomfield history.

Today, it is the oldest house in Stoddard County, but it has remained uninhabited for nearly a decade and badly needs restoration. In fact, the city plans to tear it down if no money is allocated to its preservation. We must not let this happen.

A group of Bloomfield High School students will present a preservation plan to the Historic Preservation Commission at 7:00 p.m. on Monday, October 22, at City Hall. Please join us in supporting the preservation of Bloomfield history.

Sincerely,

Shantel Bailey
Junior, Bloomfield High School

Cause-Effect

Use cause-effect organization to show the relationship between events or conditions. You may focus on one cause and its many effects, many causes and their one effect, or many causes and many effects.

Cause-Centered	**Effect-Centered**
Cause	Cause
Cause	Effect
Cause	Effect
Effect	Effect

Cause-effect transitions:
as a result, because, consequently, since, therefore, due to the fact that

Infant Mortality Rate (U.S.)	Average Life Expectancy (U.S.)
1750-1850: 270 per 1,000 births	1850: 39 Years
1900: 165 per 1,000 births	1900: 47 years
1997: 7 per 1,000 births	1997: 76 years
2012: 5.98 per 1,000 births	2012: 78 years

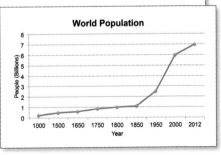

World Population

Comparison-Contrast

Use comparison-contrast organization to show the similarities and differences between two things.

Subject by Subject
Subject 1
Subject 2

Point by Point
Point 1
Subject 1   Subject 2
Point 2
Subject 1   Subject 2

Similarities and Differences
How Subjects 1 & 2 Are *Similar*
How Subjects 1 & 2 Are *Different*

Wind Power Versus Nuclear Power

Environmental Impact
☒ Wind   ☐ Nuclear

Cost Effectiveness
☒ Wind   ☐ Nuclear

Energy Output
☐ Wind   ☒ Nuclear

Comparison-contrast terms:
also, both, but, by contrast, even though, like, likewise, however, similarly

Classification

Use classification to break a subject into subgroups or categories. Then discuss the unique properties of each category.

Classification Structure
Subgroup 1
Point 1   Point 2
Subgroup 2
Point 1   Point 2
Subgroup 3
Point 1   Point 2

Types of Bones

- Flat
- Irregular
- Long
- Sesamoid
- Short

Classification terms:
another kind of, the first subgroup, a second category, a third variety, a final type, the most popular, a less popular, a common type, a rare kind of

Your Turn Search a class text to find examples of the structures on pages 408–410.

Creating Narrative Structure

The best stories display a common structure characterized by rising action that builds interest to a peak before falling again toward a satisfying resolution. This structure mirrors the shape of the most rewarding experiences in life, so it is not surprising that stories follow this structure.

The graph below plots narrative structure, using the x-axis to represent the story's beginning, middle, and ending and the y-axis to represent the audience's interest level. Employ narrative structure to develop a compelling story.

Narrative Plot Chart

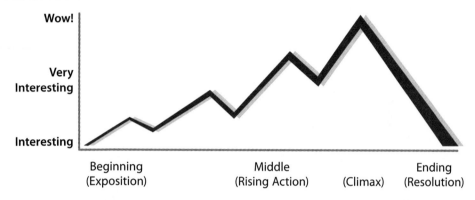

- **Exposition:** The beginning section of a story introduces the setting, the main characters, and the theme. It also presents the problem that the main character must face.

- **Rising Action:** The main character faces a series of conflicts that build toward a final confrontation with the main problem.

- **Climax:** Facing a turning point, the main character confronts the central struggle and either overcomes it or learns something important. This is the most intense moment in the story.

- **Resolution:** The problem is solved, and the story winds down to a satisfying conclusion.

Note: Use narrative structure whenever you want to tell a story: narratives (real or imagined), plays, movies, podcasts, digital stories, and the like.

Your Turn Think about the plot of one of your favorite books, television shows, or movies. Outline the key points in the beginning, middle, and ending of the story and see how the structure compares to the one shown above. What are the benefits of the narrative structure? What would happen if a plot exhibited falling action, but no rising action? How would this change the audience's experience?

Creating Visual Structure

Some creations are experienced all at once. Visual art—a painting, poster, sculpture, photograph, or drawing—often evokes immediate, powerful reactions. Such structures have common visual elements that work together to create this appeal.

- **Focus** is the main subject of the visual. Find it by observing the work in its full context (see pages 220–221).
- **Figures** are the people, objects, or things included in the visual.
- **Value**, being light or dark, offers the contrast that creates perspective. Light objects appear closer than dark objects.
- **Color** creates a mood. Contrasts in color convey energy and emotion.

By leon keer (Own work) [CC-BY-SA-3.0 (http://creativecommons. org/licenses/by-sa/3.0)], via Wikimedia Commons

- **Space**, the area occupied by the figures or existing between the figures, creates depth and perspective. Artists and photographers use a number of techniques to make a flat image look three-dimensional.
  - Overlap makes figures in front appear closer than those behind.
  - Diminishing size makes larger figures appear closer than smaller ones.
  - Vertical position makes lower figures appear closer than higher ones.
  - Linear perspective follows converging lines to a vanishing point.
  - Atmospheric perspective makes sharper figures look closer than hazy figures.
- **Proportion** describes a figure's size relative to its surroundings.
- **Perspective** is the way the work appears to the viewer. Point of view and angle affect the viewer's understanding. For the photo above, the photographer stands at the perfect angle to see the street painting. Those behind the painting have a completely distorted image to look at.
- **Emphasis** is the focal point of the work, the area that first attracts the viewer's attention.

Also consider typography in written work (see page 226). For more information about the elements of visual structure, see page 222.

Your Turn Analyze the visual elements in a favorite piece of art (painting, photograph, drawing, and so on). Comment on each of the elements listed above. How do these elements affect the work's overall impact?

Catching Attention

When you create something new, you want your work to stand out for all the right reasons—an interesting subject, appealing design, a creative vision. You also want it to generate buzz from your audience: *That looks awesome! Wow, this is interesting. I never thought of that. Where can I find out more about this?* Here are three strategies that will help you draw attention to your work.

▶ Make it visual.

Present information visually when possible. The old adage about a picture being worth 1,000 words is no exaggeration. Visual information serves two important functions: First, it draws the audience in, and second, it provides information in a format that is quickly understood and remembered.

Think of ways to make your creation visually appealing. Use photos and graphics in your written projects and accompany your oral presentations with visual aids. Make your Web content pop with well-placed images and videos. But make sure every visual serves your purpose.

▶ Make it original.

Think independently, and be unique, even unusual. You can draw attention to your creations by allowing your creative personality to shine through your work. Try these strategies:

- **Use an authentic voice** in writing and speaking. Sincere, conversational language goes a long way with an audience.
- **Go against the flow.** Tackle a problem in a completely new way.
- **Do something surprising.** Turn an essay into a song; use recyclables to build a sculpture; design your own experiment; write and film a short video about a math concept.
- **Write creative titles and headlines**. Successful bloggers will tell you that headlines offering something of value are more likely to attract and keep readers ("Get Rid of Your Test Jitters Once and for All").

▶ Make it useful.

Projects that prove worthwhile to your audience will garner attention. Art can appeal to viewers' emotions. Research reports can inform. Blueprints can demonstrate effective design strategy. Provide your audience with value, and they will return.

Your Turn List the qualities that make you unique. Then consider how you can reflect those qualities in your work.

10 Tips for **Getting Unstuck**

Creating does not always go smoothly. If you get stuck, here are some tips to get you going again.

1. **Step back.** You may be too close to your work. Close your eyes, clear your mind, and try again.

2. **Review your planning.** Look at your planning goals and schedule. Are you on track? If not, what steps can you take to get there?

3. **Define the hang-up.** Complete the following sentence: "I'm having trouble moving forward because . . ." Recognize and examine the problem.

4. **List ways around the problem.** Complete the following sentence: "I can solve my problem by . . ." List as many solutions as you can. Then choose the best one and carry it out.

5. **Think upside-down.** Instead of focusing on the problem, examine what you've done so far. Could you improve anything? Fine-tune the work you've finished, and then go back to the problem.

6. **Change your scenery.** Try working on your project somewhere else (outdoors, in a coffee shop, and so on). Sometimes the monotony of a room can suppress your creativity.

7. **Ask for a second opinion.** Get some outside help. Suggestions from other group members or peers may be just what you need to tackle your problem. Talk it out.

8. **Take small steps.** Divide the problem into chunks. Then solve it one step at a time. The projects that are most worth doing cannot be done all at once. They can, however, be done step by step.

9. **Work on a new part.** Skip ahead in your project. A solution to your present problem may present itself while you're thinking of other things. (That's your subconscious mind at work.)

10. **Get away.** If you're still stuck, stop what you're doing and get away. Do something completely different. Grab a bite to eat. Take a walk, jog, or run. Often, moving your major muscle groups untangles your thinking. Then you can return with a fresh mind.

Your Turn Have you found other effective strategies for getting unstuck? Share them with your classmates.

Chapter 26
Improving

Have you ever gone bowling? If not, you ought to give it a try. The goal is to knock down all 10 pins in two tries. You study the pins at the end of the lane, take four steps, roll the ball, and watch to see how many you knock over. Between frames, you naturally evaluate how you bowled, assessing what worked and what didn't. Then you make a plan and try again.

The inquiry process also involves evaluation. When you're working on a project, you consider how it's turning out. You ask yourself whether it's what you hoped for, and you often get a second opinion. Then you go about changing things and revising parts in order to reach your goal. This chapter discusses the important step of evaluating and improving your work.

You will learn . . .

- Evaluating
- Getting a Second Opinion
- Making Improvements
- Perfecting Your Work

Evaluating

During your project planning (see page 356), you set a goal—a target to aim for. Evaluation is about gauging how close you came to reaching your goal and its related objectives. One way of evaluating your projects is to create and use a rubric sheet like the one on page 417. Follow these guidelines:

1. **Fill in the goal and objectives for the project you are evaluating.** Copy this information from the planning sheet you created before starting the project. Remember, your objectives answer *who, what, where, when, why,* and *how.*

2. **Evaluate your goal and each objective.** Write a sentence or two describing how well you did for each one. Think about improvements that you could make to your project.

3. **Rate your project.** Assign a numerical rating for your overall goal and each objective. Circle the number score for each. The answers are explained here:
   - **Beat:** You accomplished more than you had planned.
   - **Met:** You accomplished what you planned.
   - **Didn't:** You fell short of what you had planned.

4. **Total your score.** Add up the points for your goal (60 points possible) and your six objectives (10 points possible for each). The resulting figure can serve as a percentage grade (above 100 percent would be an A+, above 90 percent an A, above 80 percent a B, and so on). Then compare the total to the following scale:

120	100	90	80	70	60	40
Amazing!	**Great**	**Strong**	**Good**	**Okay**	**Poor**	**Incomplete**

Your Turn Turn the planning sheet from your own project into a rubric. First download a template from thoughtfullearning.com/h416. Then fill in the goal and objectives. Finally, use the rubric to evaluate your project.

Rubric Sheet

The example rubric below evaluates a video project about veteran rehabilitation completed by Denice Sobiech and her team.

Example Rubric Sheet

Name: _Denice Sobiech_   **Project:** _Veteran Rehabilitation Video_

Goal:	Evaluation:	Rating			Score
Our team will prepare a video interview of veterans and their caregivers.	We produced a video that shares the veterans' story.	Beat 60	Met (40)	Didn't 20	40
Objectives:					
1. I will work with Pam, Burton, Arminda, Leif, and Felix.	The team worked very well together!	Beat (10)	Met 6	Didn't 2	10
2. We'll make a video about rehabilitation of veterans.	Although we wanted more interviews, the video looks great, and it definitely captures viewers' interest.	Beat (10)	Met 6	Didn't 2	10
3. We'll investigate online and interview in person and on the phone.	An interviewer and a recorder kept each appointment.	Beat 10	Met (6)	Didn't 2	6
4. We have to finish the project by April 1.	We barely made the deadline.	Beat 10	Met (6)	Didn't 2	6
5. Find veterans who face challenges in diagnosis and treatment of PTSD.	We had trouble finding people with PTSD to interview.	Beat 10	Met 6	Didn't (2)	2
6. We'll use cameras, recorders, and computers.	It was difficult to get good video, but Leif rescued the results in editing.	Beat 10	Met (6)	Didn't 2	6
				Total:	80

Your Turn Evaluate your own project using a rubric sheet (go to thoughtfullearning. com/h417). Review your goal and objectives, evaluate how well you achieved each, assign scores, and total them. Then rate your project using the scale on the previous page.

Getting a Second Opinion

Using a pair of satellites as sensors, a global positioning system (GPS) is able to "triangulate" the location of a navigation device. Each satellite perceives the device at a particular angle, and by plotting where those angles intersect, the GPS locates it.

In a similar way, a second opinion on your project can locate its strengths and any remaining weaknesses by looking at the work from a different angle or perspective.

Your Role

Ultimately, you are the person responsible for the project. You are the one with the best overall view of what it is intended to accomplish. The reviewer's response is intended only to help make a good thing better by pointing out parts that could be improved. To get the most out of that second opinion, use the following tips:

- **Introduce the project:** Explain briefly what you have created.
- **Outline your goal and objectives:** Give the reviewer a rubric sheet with the first column filled in. Make any necessary comments about the goal and objectives you have listed.
- **Focus the feedback:** Explain to the reviewer the kind of feedback you are hoping for. Depending on the type of project and where you are in the inquiry process, this may vary. For example, you may ask the person to focus on overall organization, on details that seem to be missing, on ideas for fine-tuning the end product, and so on.
- **Present your project:** Let your reviewer interact with your project, whether that means reading it, viewing it, listening to it, or using it.
- **Give the reviewer space:** Let the person fill out the evaluation sheet in private. When he or she is finished, discuss the evaluation together to make certain you understand the comments.
- **Thank your reviewer:** Critiquing another person's work requires effort. Be certain to let your reviewer know that the effort is appreciated.
- **Take time to read and consider the response:** Receiving a critique can be difficult. Give yourself time to get past any initial defensiveness. Also, a reviewer's comments may open your eyes to a deeper problem or a larger solution for your work.
- **Consider getting more opinions:** Some projects can benefit from several reviews, either by individuals or in a group.

Your Turn Present your project to one or more reviewers, giving each a rubric sheet that outlines your goal and objectives. Follow the tips above as you ask your reviewer(s) for help to improve the project.

The Reviewer's Role

A reviewer brings a new perspective to a project and is able to point out issues that the project creator cannot see. In this way, a good reviewer can help the creator recognize both strengths and weaknesses in the project so that the former can be accented and the latter eliminated. A poor reviewer, on the other hand, may offer no encouragement or helpful insights. To be a good reviewer, follow these tips:

- **Connect with the project creator:** Start with respect. Make sure the project creator knows you believe in her or him. Then focus attention away from personalities and onto the project itself.

- **Consider the goal and objectives:** Read the goal and objectives and restate them to the project creator. Understanding these foundational elements is key to giving an effective response to a project.

- **Focus first on the positive:** Show the project creator that you can see the effort that has gone into the project thus far and recognize the aspects that are working well.

- **State the negative in positive terms:** When you deal with a weak point, compare it to the stronger elements of the project. Show that improving the weak area will bring it to the same level as the rest of the work. Focus on positive outcomes.

- **Suggest options:** Follow any problem statements with one or more possible solutions. This can encourage the creator to remain positive as he or she begins to consider ways to improve the work.

- **Step back:** Once you have given your opinions and suggestions, step back. The creator must take responsibility for the project and go about fixing problems in his or her own way. You can help by respecting that fact.

Your Turn Help another person with his or her project by acting as a good reviewer. Follow the tips above as you learn about the project, review its goal and objectives, and carefully consider the work.

Making Improvements

After evaluating your work and receiving a second opinion, you are ready to begin making improvements, using both critical and creative thinking in the process.

Critical Improvements

These fixes involve the overall structure of your project and may include cutting and rearranging.

▶ Cutting

Ask yourself the following questions before deciding which elements of the project should be cut.

- Which part or parts do not help me accomplish the objectives and reach my goal?
- How can I make the project simpler, leaner, and more to the point?

Note: Just because you cut something doesn't mean it's useless. You may find that the material fits perfectly in another project.

▶ Rearranging

Ask yourself the following questions before deciding to rearrange any elements.

- Which part or parts seem to be in the wrong place?
- How can I rearrange my work to make it more effective, efficient, and smooth?

Note: Don't be afraid to try rearranging in more than one way. Keep working until the best arrangement presents itself.

Creative Improvements

These fixes involve reworking parts and adding new elements to your project.

▶ Reworking

Ask yourself the following questions before deciding which parts to rework.

- Which part or parts are confusing?
- How can I rework these parts so that the project better achieves my goal?

Note: Continue to rework parts of your project until the ideas are plain and the goal has been met.

▶ Adding

Ask yourself the following questions before adding new elements.

- What seems to be missing from my project?
- What additions might make my project stronger?

Note: Don't be afraid to experiment with possible solutions—adding various details or ideas until the project forms a satisfactory whole and leaves no obvious questions in the mind of the audience.

Using an Improvement Plan

The following example improvement plan was created by Denice Sobiech and her team for their video about veteran rehabilitation. (Go to thoughtfullearning.com/h421 to download an improvement plan form of your own.)

Name: _Denice Sobiech_   **Project:** _Veteran Rehabilitation Video_

Critical Improvements

Cutting: Which part or parts do not help me reach my goal and objectives? How can I make the project simpler, leaner, and more to the point?

The introduction runs long. Also, we have more interviews with caregivers than with veterans, which seems unbalanced.

Plan: _Trim down the introduction, and cut any caregiver interviews that don't add new information or surprising insights._

Rearranging: Which part or parts seem to be in the wrong place? How can I rearrange my work to make it more effective, efficient, and smooth?

Our initial plan of presenting all the veteran interviews first, then all the caregiver interviews, seems sort of artificial now.

Plan: _We should intersperse the interviews, using veterans as much as possible to introduce the situations and caregivers to add further detail. This will give us an effective problem-solution arrangement._

Creative Improvements

Reworking: Which part or parts are confusing? How can I rework these parts so that the project better achieves my goal?

Some of the video jerks around a lot. It distracts from what's being said.

Plan: _We can use the best moments of video and intersperse a number of still photos. This should preserve an illusion of movement while eliminating the distraction of shaky footage._

Adding: What seems to be missing from my project? What additions might make my project stronger?

It is likely that not every viewer is aware of the number of homeless veterans.

Plan: _Just after the introduction, we should work in a few news stories about the issue of homelessness among veterans and its negative effect on their rehabilitation efforts._

Your Turn Answer the improvement/revision questions about your own project before completing an improvement plan like the one above. (Download a template at thoughtfullearning.com/h421.)

Perfecting Your Work

A sculptor working in marble starts with a block of stone and a vision. With an assortment of tools, the artist chisels away the material until a rough image takes shape. Discovering the marble's veining, the sculptor may revise his or her original vision to use the stone in the best way possible. Finally, after the shape is established, the artist finishes the surface, leaving the piece highly polished, chisel marked, or something in between, depending on the goal or message of the sculpture.

This final step is important to every project, although the level of polishing necessary is dependent on the project's purpose. If the purpose is casual, polish your work until it is *clean, clear,* and *correct.* If the purpose is semiformal, add *effective, efficient,* and *enjoyable* to the mix. And if the purpose is formal, work until your project boasts the first six attributes plus *precise, powerful,* and *polished.* However, even with these levels of formality in mind, remember that it is always important to perfect your work, for yourself and for those with whom you will share it.

	Casual	Semiformal	Formal
Clean	✘	✘	✘
Clear	✘	✘	✘
Correct	✘	✘	✘
Effective		✘	✘
Efficient		✘	✘
Enjoyable		✘	✘
Precise			✘
Powerful			✘
Polished			✘

Your Turn Think about a project you are currently working on and ready to finish. Is the project casual, semiformal, or formal in its purpose? Depending upon that answer, how can you get your work to be clean, clear, and correct? Effective, efficient, and enjoyable? Precise, powerful, and polished?

Chapter 27
Presenting

Presenting, the final step in the inquiry process, is the culmination of all your hard work. You've done the questioning, the planning, the researching. You've created something new; you've fine-tuned it. Now it's time to share it.

You may feel uneasy about going public with your work. But if you have carefully followed each step in the inquiry process, you can feel confident that your project is the best that it can be. Presenting is just the cherry on top of the sundae.

You will learn . . .

- Understanding the Situation
- Presenting in Person
- Presenting on the Web
- Promoting Your Project

Understanding the Situation

Now that your project is complete, it's time to present it. Before going public, you should evaluate the situation using the 5 W's and H. Here is an example situation analysis from an anatomy and physiology student who prepared an oral report and poster presentation of a human skeleton fixed in motion. One-half of the poster shows a basketball player jumping for a rebound. The other half shows the player's skeletal structure while doing so.

Situation Analysis

Name: _Kooper Henderson_   Project: _Skeleton Project_

1. **Who** will interact with your work?
   Classmates and faculty at my school and anyone who visits our classroom blog. I'll also share the poster on my social networks so my friends and followers can see it.

2. **What** do you want the audience to get from this experience?
   I want people to see how remarkable the human body is, and I want them to learn about the human skeleton, which gives us our unique structure and mobility.

3. **Where** will you present your work?
   Though my oral presentation will take place in the classroom, my poster will appear on the wall of our school's auditorium. A picture of it will also appear online on our classroom blog and on my social networks.

4. **When** will you present your work?
   My oral presentation is scheduled for Tuesday, March 6. I'll post pictures of the poster afterward.

5. **Why** do you want to present your work?
   I want my audience to learn something from it. I hope my project reflects the effort I put into it.

6. **How** will your work be presented?
   I will give an oral report to my classmates and teacher, using a poster of the skeleton that I have drawn and labeled by hand.

Your Turn When you are ready to present, answer the questions above about your own work. (Download a blank template from thoughtfullearning.com/h424.)

Presenting in Person

Making oral presentations is a common activity in school and in the workplace, although some people feel more comfortable than others with speaking in front of groups. If public speaking makes you nervous, you can reduce your anxiety by being fully prepared. Here are some ways to prepare for an oral presentation.

Note Cards

Many presenters use note cards to keep themselves on track. Note cards are an unobtrusive way to record what you want to say. Write out a complete introduction and closing on the first and last cards, and list your main points on the middle cards. Remember to number each card and arrange them in order. (See page 78.)

Outlines

An outline is another common presentation format. Use it to organize your key points, and refer to it as necessary during your presentation. (See page 374.)

Slide Shows

Slide shows, such as PowerPoint presentations, can guide your delivery by correctly ordering the information you want to share. Use bulleted lists for main points; but unlike with note cards, do not include a word-for-word introduction and closing. As part of your oral presentation, prepare slides that augment but do not distract from your own words, and avoid reading slides word-for-word. (See pages 77-79.)

Sample Slide Show Slide

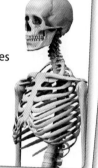

Functions of the Skeletal System

- Support for tissue and muscles
- Protection for vital organs
- Movement through attached bones and muscles
- Storage of minerals

Manuscripts

A manuscript provides a full transcript of your presentation, written out word for word. While a manuscript gives you the confidence of knowing exactly what to say, it may also keep you from making eye contact with your audience. Practice enough to be able to look up from the paper frequently. Follow these tips:

- Use large type (14 point or more) so that you can read without leaning forward or squinting.
- Set main ideas in bold so that you can easily pick them out.
- Use bolded brackets to set off directions for slides or props.
- See pages 77–79 for more help with oral presentations.

Your Turn Create note cards, an outline, a slide show, or a manuscript for an oral presentation of an upcoming project.

Presenting on the Web

The Web offers you the opportunity to present your work to a vast audience. To use the Web to best advantage, consider the following information:

Purpose

Why are you posting your work online? Do you just want others to see it, or do you have a larger purpose in mind? Here are some common reasons to post:

- **To Inform:** Did you create something others can learn from? Essays, articles, reviews, instructional videos, or podcasts can share important or new information with your audience.

- **To Entertain:** Is your creation entertaining? Other people with similar interests may find your work enjoyable.

- **To Persuade:** Do you want to argue for or against a decision or convince others to support a cause? Persuasive editorials, protest songs, promotional videos, petitions, and so on can be posted online.

- **To Invite:** Do you intend to share a topic or issue with a community of like-minded people? You can contribute your work to a sharing site or community message board.

Place

The Web holds a variety of sites. Some give users ultimate control over what is published and who can see it. Others are open to the entire public and allow users to submit, experience, and share all of a site's content. The table below lists the pros and cons of different types of sites:

Location	Pros	Cons
Personal Site	- Total control over the content - Complete ownership	- Hard to attract traffic - Perhaps not special-media friendly
Classroom Site (Blog or Wiki)	- Safe site - Student work fits with site's larger theme - Easily accessed by friends, family, and classmates	- Limited audience - Work eventually "taken down" - Limited room for displaying work
Public Site	- Broad audience - Professional presentation of material	- Give up some rights - Privacy concerns - Spam and advertisements

Timing

Time on the Web is a fickle thing. Nothing ever really goes away, so something you posted a long time ago may attract attention weeks, months, or even years later. Still, posting your work at premeditated times, depending on what you want to accomplish, can yield beneficial results.

If the post is time sensitive or your project is simply finished . . .	Post as soon as you've completed all the necessary steps of the inquiry process. Then use social media or other communication measures to promote your work through hyperlinks and direct messages to friends and family.
If you know your audience's general online habits . . .	Post at the time of day your audience is most likely to be present online.
If you normally post items at a certain time, or on a certain day . . .	Post your project to fit that schedule. For example, if you publish a blog entry every Tuesday afternoon, wait until then to post your project for a "waiting" audience.
If you need to draw an audience . . .	Connect your post to a special event, holiday, or contest.

Procedure

Because sites vary, check that your work is compatible with the one you've chosen to use. Before posting, study the site's rules and specifications for file size, file types, content, and so on. If you must sign a digital agreement, as many public sites ask you to do, read it carefully. The agreement may require you to give up certain rights to your material. If so, consider again whether the site is the best choice for presenting your work.

Once you fully understand the compatibility and property considerations, follow the instructions for uploading your work. Many sites will allow you to preview your uploaded material before you publish it.

Your Turn Before presenting your next project online, review the material on the last two pages. Post your work only after you are comfortable with your answers to the following four questions: *Why* am I posting? *Where* am I posting? *When* am I posting? And *how* am I posting?

Functions of the **Skeletal System**

• Support for tissue and muscles
• Protection for vital organs
• Movement through attached bones and muscles
• Storage of minerals

Promoting Your Project

You've worked hard on your project, and you're ready to present it. But how can you ensure that it will create a buzz? Here are some options for promoting your work.

Go Local

If you want your school or your local community to know about your work, consider the following ideas:
- Create fliers, posters, brochures, and so on.
- Distribute promotional materials at school.
- Send promotions in an email blast to friends.
- Ask local businesses to display posters in their windows or offices.
- Deliver brochures to your library and city hall.
- Write a letter to the editor or a press release for your local newspaper or television station.
- Publish an advertisement in a local paper or newsletter.
- Promote your project on the community calendar at a local civic center, either on-site or online.

Your Turn Create special promotional materials for your project. Then go out and spread the word.

Go Social

Social media sites may be your best marketing choice. They are free and interactive, and they reach a wide audience. Here are some ways you can promote your work using social media:
- Share a link to your project on your social network.
- Upload your project to a social network or personal blog.
- Create a group or event on Facebook. Then invite others to join.
- Send an email or direct message to friends and family.
- Write microblogs containing updates about your project.
- Comment on someone else's blog post about a subject related to your project.
- Post a comment on a message board related to your project's topic.

Your Turn Start a social media campaign to promote your project using one or more of the suggestions listed above.

Functions of the Skeletal System

Want to know more about our amazing skeletal system? Watch our online presentation! Topics covered include the following:

- Support for tissue and muscles
- Protection for vital organs
- Movement through attached bones and muscles
- Storage of minerals

Part III:
Developing Projects

Part III: Developing Projects

This section is overflowing with project ideas using the inquiry process. There are writing projects, graphic projects, Web projects, building projects, and much more. Each specific project includes guidelines, visuals, and examples. Listed below are the types of projects covered in Part III. Remember that these are just starting points. Let inquiry lead you to make these projects your own.

Chapters in This Section

Chapter 28

Basic Writing Projects

Communication skills are essential for success in today's world, and writing is a key to effective communication. In fact, business recruiters consistently rank writing among the required skills for today's employees.

The projects covered in this chapter include those you will be asked to complete in school and in the workplace. Practicing these writing forms will prepare you for the more advanced writing projects you'll encounter down the road.

You will learn . . .

- Writing Paragraphs
- Writing Summaries
- Writing Professional Emails
- Writing Business Letters
- Creating Instructions
- Writing Proposals
- Writing Poems
- Writing Informative Essays
- Writing Narratives

Project Overview

Here is a quick overview of the basic writing projects in this chapter.

A Paragraph

Paragraphs are the backbone of longer pieces of writing. Paragraph structure includes a topic sentence that shares the paragraph's main idea, and body sentences that provide details. You'll learn more about these parts and how to arrange them effectively. (See pages 434–435.)

B Summary

Summarizing new ideas helps you to understand them. You'll learn how to report the most important points of an academic reading selection in a summary paragraph. (See pages 436–437.)

C Professional Email

Email is a popular form of business and school correspondence. Here you'll find guidelines for writing effective professional emails. (See pages 438–439.)

D Business Letter

A business letter is a more formal type of communication used in the workplace. You'll learn about correct letter format and how to write letters to promote a cause and apply for a job. (See pages 440–443.)

E Instruction and Proposal

Instructions provide a series of steps for completing a task. (See pages 444–445.) Proposals present a plan of action and request permission to carry it out. (See pages 446–447.)

F Poem

A poem provides a unique creative expression of your ideas. The examples on these pages show the power of the right word. (See pages 448–449.)

G Informative Essay

An essay is one of the longer forms of writing and allows the writer to examine an idea in great detail. You'll learn how to construct an informative essay. (See pages 450–452.)

H Narrative

A narrative is a story. You'll learn how to write a personal narrative, which is an essay that shares a significant event from the writer's life. (See pages 454–456.)

A

In John Adams's Defense

The courage and conviction that would later mark John Adams's presidency was fully displayed in his defense of British soldiers involved in the Boston Massacre. After British soldiers shot and killed five Americans in Boston on March 5, 1770, the soldiers and their captain, Thomas Preston, were detained and left without legal representation. Several Boston lawyers, fearing criticism from fellow Americans and anxious for the safety of their families, declined to defend the soldiers. Adams was 34 at

B

Student Summary

In "When a Crystal Becomes Nobel Worthy," Ishmael Crowder explains the unique composition of quasicrystals and how their discovery was deemed controversial. Chemist Dan Shechtman first discovered a quasicrystal in 1982, but many of his colleagues in the science community were skeptical because it did not exhibit the traditional atomic makeup of crystals. Instead of displaying a regular and repeated atomic pattern, quasicrystals display a regular but nonrepeated structure based on pentagonal symmetry. Along with pentagonal atomic shapes, quasicrystals include glue atoms that fill in spaces left by the pentagonal patte . echtma discovery helped him win the 2011 l P addition, it proved that scie laws of nature are not set i

C

jobrien@Obrienhomes.com

Student Shadow Opportunity   Send

Dear Mr. O'Brien:

I am an eleventh-grade student at Grafton High School. Being interested in green energy projects, I discovered that your company has a history with innovative green home solutions. I would love the opportunity to spend a day shadowing you or one of your team members at an ongoing construction site.

One of my semester-long assignments is to research ways to make our school building more energy efficient. I'm specifically interested in strategies for . . .
- reducing energy waste,
- conserving water, and
- improving indoor air quality.

D

Aquinas High School
11300 Montgomery Drive
Fort Collins, CO 80525
March 14, 2012

Mrs. Kimberly Schaffer
Office Administrator
Campus Computer CSU
155 N. College Avenue, Suite 112
Fort Collins, CO 80524

Dear Mrs. Schaffer:

Do you have any used or malfunctioning electronics to dispose of? The Aquinas High School Student Council, in partnership with Asset Recyclers, will accept electronics for recycling from 9:00 a.m.–1:00 p.m. on Saturday, April 7, at the Aquinas gymnasium. The event is part Reality Project.

E

Date: March 12, 2012
To: Mr. Todd Willems
From: Eric Stevenson
Topic: Haitian School Design Project

Project: For a rural community in Haiti, we will design an affordable school that maximizes limited space. Our project will include a blueprint, site map, budget proposal, and a scale model of the school.

Group members: Keema Gray, Shaun Gill, and Eric Stevenson

Project questions: What are the needs of rural Haitians? How large is the proposed school's building site? What is the budget?

Materials:
- Articles and documentaries on Haitian culture and educ
- Scale model materials: open-cell foam, cardboard, see-th plastic, colored paper, scissors, tape, and glue

F

Store-Bought Fruit

Store-bought tomatoes taste too much like wax.
They're picked too green, and "ripened" with some gas.
They're tough enough to be cut with an axe.
Don't offer one to me. No thanks. I'll pass.

And store-bought peaches, that's another crime.
Biting a peach should never yield a crunch.
Unless a peach is soft and juicy, I'm
Not interested in having one for lunch.

Store-bought strawberries, too, are way too tough.
Those things   ainlv pith, s   nding air.
I ate one once   ugh.
I wouldn't

G

A New Age of Robots

In a poignant scene in the 2004 science fiction movie *I, Robot*, Sonny, a robot, asks Will Smith's character why humans wink at each other. Smith tells the robot: "It's a sign of trust. It's a human thing. You wouldn't understand." Smith's terse response reflects what many people think of robotic technology: Sure, robots can perform some tasks like a human, but they certainly cannot think like a human. Such a sentiment is evolving into a myth. Today's computer scientists and robotic engineers are creating robots capable of advanced human thinking.

One robot showing signs of artificial intelligence (AI) is called RuBot II. RuBot II is nicknamed the "Cubinator" because it can solve Rubik's Cube puzzles in record times. How does it work? After a human scrambles the cube, RuBot II picks it up, raises it to eye camera level, and scans all sides of the puzzle. In less than a second, RuBot II computes a solution to the puzzle using an algorithm. Next, RuBot II's hands deftly solve the puzzle in less than 20 moves. As computer scientist Aaron Sloman told *New Scientist* magazine, "Human brains

H

Like a Freight Train Coming

The familiar scream of the tornado sirens was startling but not entirely unexpected. "A severe storm system is moving quickly southeast into our northeastern viewing area, producing hail, severe thunderstorms, and wind gusts exceeding 100 mph. Several funnels have been spotted near Montgomery and Labette counties," cautioned a meteorologist from channel 7 not more than a half hour ago.

It's not like these warnings were uncommon. After all, this is Oklahoma, the heart of Tornado Alley. It wasn't the first time we'd heard tornado sirens, and it surely wouldn't be the last.

A few years ago a mild twister passed through our city. We waited it out in our basement. It sounded no different than one of many severe storms passing through our area in mid-July—hissing winds, the patter of hail pelting windows, like a steady stream of paint balls. When the storm subsided, we peered outside to see uprooted trees, displaced branches, and a few shattered car windshields.

Today felt like just another storm. It was dark, windy, and rainy, to be sure. Thunder cracked interminably, but it was nothing out of the ordinary, though our Jack Russell terrier, Bucky, whined and paced

Inquire To Write a Paragraph

1. Question the communication situation.
- **Subject:** What specific topic will you write about?
- **Purpose:** Why are you writing—to explain, to narrate, to persuade?
- **Audience:** Who will read this paragraph?

2. Plan your paragraph.
- **Identify your topic.** Make it specific enough to cover in one paragraph.

3. Research your topic.
- **Searching:** Consult primary and secondary sources as needed to learn about your topic. (See pages 376–391.)
- **Focusing:** Decide on a focus—the part of the topic that you want to emphasize in your paragraph.

  Topic: *East Africa*   **Focus:** *is facing a food crisis*

  State the focus in a topic sentence.

  Topic sentence: *Drought, high food prices, and extreme poverty are contributing to a severe food crisis in East Africa.*

- **Shaping:** List important details that support or explain your topic. Arrange the details in the most logical order.

4. Create the first draft.
- **Start** with a topic sentence that focuses the paragraph.
- **Follow** with a variety of details that support the topic sentence.
- **Organize** the middle sentence in an effective pattern. (See page 188)
- **End** with a sentence that ties the ideas in the paragraph together.

5. Improve your first draft.
- **Evaluate** your first draft.

  Purpose: Does the paragraph effectively fulfill your purpose?

  Audience: Will the paragraph hold the reader's interest?

- **Revise** your writing.

  Rewrite sentences that are confusing or unclear.

  Add details to explain your topic more fully.

  Reorder sentences that are out of place.

- **Edit** your revised writing.

  Replace general nouns and verbs with specific ones.

  Check your writing for accuracy.

6. Present the final copy of your paragraph to your classmates or upload it to your blog.

Paragraph

Here is an example paragraph created by a student for his history class. The student has included a clear topic sentence, body sentences that offer strong supporting details in an effective order, and a closing sentence that sums up the main idea.

In John Adams's Defense

The **topic sentence** (underlined) tells the reader what the paragraph is about.

<u>The courage and conviction that would later mark John Adams's presidency was fully displayed in his defense of British soldiers involved in the Boston Massacre.</u> After British soldiers shot and killed five Americans in Boston on March 5, 1770, the soldiers and their captain, Thomas Preston, were detained and left without legal representation.

The **body sentences** provide support for the topic sentence.

Several Boston lawyers, fearing criticism from fellow Americans and anxious for the safety of their families, declined to defend the soldiers. Adams was 34 at the time and faced similar fears. Yet he believed so deeply that everyone should be afforded a fair trial that he took the case without hesitation. An outsider might declare Adams's decision to be unpatriotic, but to Adams, it was the very definition of patriotism. He would later say his defense of the British soldiers was "one of the most gallant, generous, manly, and disinterested actions of my whole life, and one of the best pieces of service I ever rendered my country." At a moment of crisis and in the face of public scrutiny, Adams stood up for a core American value—that every person has the right to defense in a court of law.

The **closing sentence** refers again to the main idea and offers a final thought.

He was 34 at the time, but John Adams was already showing signs of becoming a great leader.

Inquire To Write a Summary

1. **Question** the communication situation.
   - **Subject:** What specific topic does the reading selection address?
   - **Purpose:** What is the goal of the selection—to inform, to persuade, to tell a story? What is the goal of the summary?
   - **Audience:** Who is most likely to read such material?

2. **Plan** your summary.
   - **Identify** the main point of the writing.
   - **Annotate** the original, noting key details (see page 145).

3. **Research** your topic.
   - **Searching:** Reread the selection and write down the key points—names, dates, times, and places.
   - **Focusing:** Find the focus of your summary—the selection's main idea.
     > **Topic:** *"Insects Have Personalities, Too" by Gerald Perkins*

     State the focus in a topic sentence.
     > **Topic sentence:** *In "Insects Have Personalities, Too," Gerald Perkins explains how a new study concludes that some honeybees' brain activity is linked to thrill seeking.*
   - **Shaping:** List the key points of the article in your own words.

4. **Create** the first draft.
   - **Start** with your topic sentence.
   - **Follow** with key supporting details. Use your own words to recount the selection's most important points. Leave out what is unimportant.
   - **End** with a sentence that restates the main point of the selection.

5. **Improve** your first draft.
   - **Evaluate** your first draft.
     > **Purpose:** Does your paragraph effectively sum up the selection?

     > **Audience:** Would a reader of the summary understand what the original selection is about?
   - **Revise** your writing.
     > **Add** details to summarize the selection more fully.

     > **Cut** unnecessary details.
   - **Edit** your revised writing.
     > **Check** your writing for accuracy.

6. **Present** the final copy of your summary to your teacher or post it on your classroom blog or wiki.

Article and Summary

A summary highlights the most important parts of a reading selection. The science article below is followed by a student's summary. The summary includes a topic sentence, body sentences, and a closing sentence.

When a Crystal Becomes Nobel Worthy
By Ishmael Crowder

When Israeli scientist Dan Shechtman discovered quasicrystals, some in the chemistry community might have thought of him as a "quasi chemist." After all, his finding was so controversial that his boss asked him to leave the lab. What Shechtman viewed under his microscope in 1982 defied the laws of nature: a crystal with an atomic structure based on pentagonal symmetry.

For years Shechtam's discovery was deemed blasphemous in the scientific community, but in 2011 it earned him the Nobel Prize in Chemistry.

Quasicrystals, as Shechtman showed, are a type of material whose atoms display a regular but nonrepeated pattern. An irregular atomic makeup was once thought impossible in crystals. It was believed that all crystals were composed of a three-dimensional or four-dimensional arrangement of atoms that always repeat in an orderly pattern.

However, quasicrystals' five-dimensional atomic pattern never repeats precisely but continuously fills all available space through the inclusion of glue atoms. Glue atoms are other atomic shapes that fill in the gaps left by the pentagonal pattern.

The irregular but snug atomic properties make quasicrystals an interesting material for practical uses. One particularly strong quasicrystal has been found effective in razor blades and surgical instruments. Their irregular atomic nature also makes them poor conductors of heat, so scientists are experimenting with using quasicrystals for insulators.

Student Summary

The **topic sentence** introduces the title, author, and main point.

In "When a Crystal Becomes Nobel Worthy," Ishmael Crowder explains the unique composition of quasicrystals and how their discovery was deemed controversial. Chemist Dan Shechtman first discovered a quasicrystal in 1982, but many of his colleagues in the science community were skeptical because it did not exhibit the traditional atomic makeup of crystals. Instead of displaying a

The **body sentences** give the details.

regular and repeated atomic pattern, quasicrystals display a regular but nonrepeated structure based on pentagonal symmetry. Along with pentagonal atomic shapes, quasicrystals include glue atoms that fill in spaces left by the pentagonal pattern. Shechtman's discovery

The **closing sentence** completes the summary.

helped him win the 2011 Nobel Prize in Chemistry. In addition, it proved that science is always evolving and that even the laws of nature are not set in stone.

Inquire To Write a Professional Email

1. **Question** the communication situation.
   - **Subject:** What is the specific topic of your email message?
   - **Purpose:** Why are you choosing to write an email? What response do you hope to get?
   - **Audience:** Who will read your email—a teacher, a business representative, a college adviser?

2. **Plan** your email.
   - **Be clear** about the purpose of your message.
   - **Decide** when you will draft and send the message.

3. **Research** your topic.
   - **Searching:** Identify the correct email address of the receiver.
   - **Focusing:** Decide on your focus—the topic and reason for writing the email.

     Topic: *College visit*   **Reason:** *to set up an appointment*

     Focus: *I am interested in visiting the campus on May 5. Can I set up an appointment with a tour guide?*
   - **Shaping:** List other important details, including any follow-up action or information you require.

4. **Create** the first draft of your email.
   - **Complete the email header.** Create a clear subject line that tells the reader what the message is about.

     Unclear: *College Visit*   **Clear:** *Confirmation for May 5 Campus Visit*
   - **Greet the reader** and give your reason for writing.
   - **Follow with other necessary details.**
   - **End the message.** Request any follow-up action or information you need. Then provide a polite closing and your name.

5. **Improve** your first draft.
   - **Evaluate** your first draft.

     Purpose: Does the email fulfill your purpose for writing?

     Audience: Is the language clear and appropriate for the reader?
   - **Revise** your email.

     Cut careless or unnecessary comments.

     Break up lengthy passages into short paragraphs with lists and headings.

     Double-space between paragraphs.
   - **Edit** your revised email.

     Check your message for spelling and punctuation errors.

6. **Present** the email by sending it to the receiver.

Professional Email

Take special care when writing email for school or work. Generally, professional email requires a higher level of formality than personal email does. Review the following example written by a student and sent to a local business owner. For more tips on writing email, see page 274.

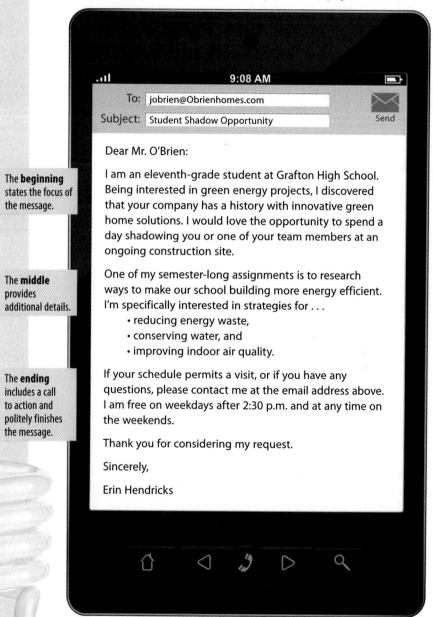

The **beginning** states the focus of the message.

The **middle** provides additional details.

The **ending** includes a call to action and politely finishes the message.

9:08 AM

To: jobrien@Obrienhomes.com

Subject: Student Shadow Opportunity

Send

Dear Mr. O'Brien:

I am an eleventh-grade student at Grafton High School. Being interested in green energy projects, I discovered that your company has a history with innovative green home solutions. I would love the opportunity to spend a day shadowing you or one of your team members at an ongoing construction site.

One of my semester-long assignments is to research ways to make our school building more energy efficient. I'm specifically interested in strategies for . . .
- reducing energy waste,
- conserving water, and
- improving indoor air quality.

If your schedule permits a visit, or if you have any questions, please contact me at the email address above. I am free on weekdays after 2:30 p.m. and at any time on the weekends.

Thank you for considering my request.

Sincerely,

Erin Hendricks

Inquire To Write a Business Letter

1. **Question** the communication situation.
   - **Subject:** What topic will you address in the business letter?
   - **Purpose:** Why are you writing a letter? What result do you want?
   - **Audience:** Who will read the letter? How will the person respond?

2. **Plan** your letter.
   - **Review** your topic and reason for writing the letter.
   - **Learn** the receiver's name, title, and address.

3. **Research** your topic.
   - **Searching:** Gather details that you need to include in your letter.
   - **Focusing:** Write down what you specifically want to accomplish.

4. **Create** the first draft of your letter.
   - **Start with the heading, inside address, and salutation.**
   - **Write the body**—the beginning, middle, and ending parts.
     Beginning: Introduce your topic and provide your reason for writing.
     Middle: Present important details in brief, effective paragraphs. Organize these details for clarity.
     Ending: Explain what action you would like the receiver to take.
   - **End with a complimentary closing and signature.**

5. **Improve** your first draft.
   - **Evaluate** your letter.
     Purpose: Does it achieve your goal?
     Audience: Does it give the reader all the necessary information?
   - **Revise** your writing.
     Rewrite sentences that are confusing or unclear.
     Add details to explain your topic more fully.
     Cut parts that are unnecessary.
     Reorder sentences to clarify the message.
   - **Edit** your revised writing.
     Replace general nouns and verbs with specific ones.
     Check your writing for accuracy using page 242 as a guide.

6. **Present** the final copy of your letter by mailing it to the intended receiver.

Letter Promoting a Cause

This letter follows the full-block letter format.

Aquinas High School
11300 Montgomery Drive
Fort Collins, CO 80525
March 14, 2012

Mrs. Kimberly Schaffer
Office Administrator
Campus Computer CSU
155 N. College Avenue, Suite 112
Fort Collins, CO 80524

Dear Mrs. Schaffer:

The **beginning** identifies the cause and the reason for writing.

Do you have any used or malfunctioning electronics to dispose of? The Aquinas High School Student Council, in partnership with Asset Recyclers, will accept electronics for recycling from 9:00 a.m.–1:00 p.m. on Saturday, April 7, at the Aquinas gymnasium. The event is part of the Earth and Reality Project.

The **middle** gives important information.

We will offer a free hard-drive wipe and data destruction for the items you donate. The cost of computer monitor disposal is $5, but all other items will be recycled for free. The following list includes the electronics we can accept. (Ask us, however, if you need to dispose of an unlisted item.)

- Desktop computers
- Laptops
- Printers
- Cell phones
- CD and DVD players
- Cameras

The **ending** states the next step and encourages action.

If you have any questions or need more information, please contact the Aquinas Student Council at the above address or via email at studentcouncil@aquinasstthom.edu. We hope you will join us in protecting our environment!

Sincerely,

Michelle Rodriguez

Michelle Rodriguez
Student Council President

Letter Applying for Work

4773 Shortridge Drive
Arlington, VA 22202
May 8, 2012

Maria DeGroot
Casey Trees
3030 12th Street
Washington, DC 20017

Dear Ms. DeGroot:

The beginning identifies the position of interest.

I am interested in applying for the Casey Trees' Summer Crew program. I am currently finishing my junior year at Arlington North High School and would love the opportunity to take care of the trees in Washington, DC, this summer.

The middle explains the writer's qualifications.

I have previous landscaping experience as an employee of Rustic Road Landscaping Service in Baltimore, Maryland, for the last two summers. My responsibilities at Rustic Road included the following:
- lawn mowing and weed pulling;
- planting, mulching, and watering flowers and trees;
- carrying and transporting equipment and supplies.

Please don't hesitate to talk to my former boss, Neil Avercamp, at Rustic Road. I have attached his contact information with my list of references. He can attest that I am a dedicated and hardworking employee. I have no trouble working in all weather conditions. In school, I am on the honor roll and participate in football and the Performing Arts Club.

The ending asks for an interview and provides contact information.

May I call you at 3:30 p.m. on Friday, May 11, to set up a time for an interview? If another time is more convenient for you, please contact me any day after 3:00 p.m. at (410) 555-8849 or jbiel22@gabbalink.com.

Sincerely,

Jordan Biel

Jordan Biel

Parts of a Business Letter

A business letter includes the *heading, inside address, salutation, body, complimentary closing,* and *signature.* (It may also include the word "Enclosure" or the abbreviation "Encl." at the bottom of the letter if any additional pages are included.)

A The **heading** includes the writer's address and the date of the letter. It is placed about an inch from the top of the first page.

B The **inside address** includes the name and address of the person or group you are writing to. Identify the title of the person after his or her name. (If the title is brief, place it after the name, separated by a comma. If the title is long, place it on the next line.) Place the inside address usually four to seven spaces beneath the heading.

C The **salutation** politely addresses the receiver of the letter. Use *Dear* followed by *Mr., Mrs., Ms,* or *Miss;* the person's last name; and a colon. If you don't know the person's name, use *Dear Sir* or *Madam, Dear EMT Director, Dear Edinburgh Technical School,* followed by a colon. Place the salutation two spaces beneath the inside address.

D The **body** is the main part of the letter and should consist of brief paragraphs that get right to the point. (Remember to create beginning, middle, and ending parts.) Single-space each individual paragraph, but double-space between the paragraphs.

E The **complimentary closing** announces the end of the main part of the letter with *Sincerely, Very truly,* or *Yours truly,* followed by a comma. Double-space after the last body paragraph for the closing.

F The **signature** gives the letter writer's name (in type) four spaces after the closing. The writer adds her or his written signature above the typed name.

Note: These letters follow full-block style, which means all of the information is placed at the left-hand margin. For tips on "Folding Business Letters" and "Addressing Business Letters," go to thoughtfullearning.com/h443.

Inquire To Create Instructions

1. **Question** the situation for your instructions.
   - **Subject:** What specific topic will your instructions cover?
   - **Purpose:** Why are you writing these instructions?
   - **Audience:** Who will read your instructions? How much do they know about the subject?

2. **Plan** your instructions by creating a list of steps.

3. **Research** your topic.
   - **Searching:** Consult primary and secondary sources to learn all about your subject. (See pages 376–391.)
   - **Focusing:** Decide on a focus—your topic and main reason for writing the instructions.

     Topic: *College application* **Importance:** *to get accepted*

     Topic sentence: *The college application process may seem lengthy and complicated, but if you follow these simple steps, you'll maximize your chances to get accepted.*
   - **Shaping:** List the steps of the instructions in the correct order. Also list any materials or tools required to complete the task.

4. **Create** the first draft of your instructions.
   - **Start** by introducing the process, explaining its importance, and stating its goal. Then, if necessary, list any materials needed.
   - **Follow** by writing numbered, step-by-step instructions. If possible, include well-marked visual aids.
   - **End** with a brief description of the final outcome.

5. **Improve** the first draft.
   - **Evaluate** your first draft.

     Audience: Are your instructions clear and helpful?
   - Revise your writing.

     Rewrite steps that are confusing or unclear.

     Add steps or visual aids as necessary.

     Cut steps that don't belong.

     Reorder steps that are out of place.
   - **Edit** your revised writing.

     Replace passive verbs with command verbs (*place* instead of *should be placed*).

     Check your writing for accuracy.

6. **Present** your project by printing a copy and posting it where the instructions will be most helpful.

Instructions

The following instructions provide the step-by-step procedure for closing off a cash register drawer—an important task to ensure that money is not mishandled and cashiers are not left liable.

The **beginning** identifies the task by using a clear title and providing the purpose of the instructions. Materials are listed.

Instructions for Closing Off the Cash Register

Follow the steps below in order to (1) close off the cash register and (2) account for the day's receipts.

Materials needed: Daily Account Form, deposit bag, adding machine, pen, and paper.

Steps

In the **middle**, steps appear in chronological order, and command verbs make each step clear.

1. **MAKE SURE THE STORE'S DOORS ARE LOCKED.** Then take the cash tray out of the register drawer and place the tray on the counter. (Leave the empty drawer open to deter thieves.)

2. Turn the cash-register key to the X setting and press the X key. The machine will print the X reading: the total amount of receipts for the day.

3. Turn the key to the Z setting and press the Z key. The machine will print the Z reading: itemized, department-by-department subtotals.

WARNINGS appear in boldface and caps; **cautions** in boldface only.

4. Count out $200.00 and place the bills in the envelope marked "FLOAT"; currency amounts are shown on the envelope. (The float is the $200.00 of cash placed in each cash register when the store opens.) The remaining cash, checks, and credit-card slips make up the day's receipts.
   Do not place the float back in the drawer.

5. Total the day's receipts using an adding machine, and check the total against the X reading. If the totals differ, count the receipts a second time and a third time if necessary. Write a note indicating any difference and attach the note to the receipts.

Closely related actions appear in a single step.

6. Fill out the Daily Account Form by entering the X reading total and the Z reading total and then the totals of the day's receipts. Place the day's receipts in the deposit bag.

7. Lock the following in the safe: (1) the deposit bag, (2) the Daily Account Form, (3) the X and Z printouts, and (4) the envelope marked "FLOAT."

The **ending** reviews a key point.

DOUBLE-CHECK THE SAFE DOOR TO MAKE SURE IT'S LOCKED.

Inquire To Write a Proposal

1. Question the communication situation.
- **Subject:** What topic does your proposal address?
- **Purpose:** Why are you writing—to explain, to suggest, to plan?
- **Audience:** Who will read the proposal? What do they need to know?

2. Plan your proposal.
- **Identify** your specific topic and goal.
- **Learn** about the form. Review the example proposal (page 447).

3. Research the topic.
- **Searching:** Learn as much as you can about your topic. Consult primary and secondary sources. (See pages 376–391.)
- **Focusing:** Identify the key features of your writing—project questions, materials, steps, and due dates.
- **Shaping:** Arrange the key features as shown on page 447 or according to your instructor's requirements.

4. Create the first draft of your proposal.
- **Introduce** the topic.
- **Follow** with the supporting details (materials, steps, and timeline) that explain your proposal.
- **End** with an explanation of your proposal's expected outcome.

5. Improve your first draft.
- **Evaluate** your first draft.
    - **Purpose:** Is the proposal clear and convincing?
    - **Audience:** Does it provide enough information for the reader to act?
- **Revise** your writing.
    - **Rewrite** parts that are confusing or unclear.
    - **Add** details to explain your proposal more fully.
    - **Cut** parts that don't support your topic and goal.
    - **Reorder** sentences, if necessary, to make your proposal plain.
- **Edit** your revised writing.
    - **Replace** words that are too general.
    - **Check** your writing for accuracy using page 242 as a guide.
    - **Follow** an accepted format.

6. Present the final copy of your proposal or submit it to a competition.

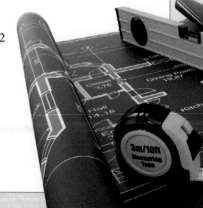

Proposal for a Project

Date: March 12, 2012
To: Mr. Todd Willems
From: Eric Stevenson
Topic: Haitian School Design Project

The **beginning** introduces the project.

Project: For a rural community in Haiti, we will design an affordable school that maximizes limited space. Our project will include a blueprint, site map, budget proposal, and a scale model of the school.

Group members: Keema Gray, Shaun Gill, and Eric Stevenson

Project questions: What are the needs of rural Haitians? How large is the proposed school's building site? What is the budget?

The **middle** part identifies the questions, materials, steps, and due dates.

Materials:
- Articles and documentaries on Haitian culture and education
- Scale model materials: open-cell foam, cardboard, see-through plastic, colored paper, scissors, tape, and glue
- Blueprint: Graphing paper, rulers, calculators, projectors
- Site map: SmartDraw computer program
- Budget estimate: Microsoft Excel

Description: The site map will show the school in relation to its immediate surroundings. The blueprint, or floor plan, will feature a drawing of the inside of the school, including its dimensions, while the scale model will show the relative proportions of the main classroom in the school. Finally, the budget proposal will provide a cost estimate of the project on a spreadsheet and will include at least two graphs.

Steps and due dates:
- April 1-7: Complete research on rural Haitian culture and education.
- April 8-14: Plan and create the site map using SmartDraw.
- April 15-21: Plan and draw the blueprint on graphing paper.
- April 22-28: Plan and build the scale model.
- May 8: Present the project.

The **ending** states the value of the project and asks for approval.

Outcome: Our project will offer a realistic design proposal for building a cost-effective and space-efficient school in Haiti.

Please let me know if this proposal is acceptable. I am willing to answer any questions and make necessary changes.

Inquire To Write a Poem

1. **Question** the situation and your goal for writing a poem.
   - **Subject:** What will the poem be about?
   - **Purpose:** Why are you writing the poem?
   - **Audience:** Who will read the poem?

2. **Plan** to use free-verse or traditional form in your poem.
   - **Free-verse poetry** doesn't have a strict rhythm or rhyme scheme.
   - **Traditional poetry** has a specific rhythm and rhyme scheme.

3. **Research** your topic.
   - **Gathering:** Brainstorm details about your topic. List descriptive details and feelings associated with your topic.
   - **Researching:** Study poetic forms and techniques. Use a rhyming dictionary to collect possible rhyme words for your poem—even free verse can use rhyme or near rhymes within its lines. (To learn much more, go to thoughtfullearning.com/h448.)

4. **Create** the first draft of your poem.
   - **Focus** first on ideas and imagery.
   - **Experiment** with rhythm, rhyme, and enjambment (carrying sentences from line to line and ending them inside a line).
   - **Create** similes (comparing two things using *like* or *as*), metaphors (saying one thing is another), and personification (giving objects or animals human characteristics) if appropriate for your poem.
   - **Shape** your ideas into the form you planned to use—free-verse or traditional.

5. **Improve** the first draft.
   - **Evaluate** your first draft. Does the poem present your topic in a fresh way? Does it achieve your purpose and connect to your audience? Does every word and line work toward the poem's success?
   - **Revise** your poem.
       Add sensory details to make your topic clearer.
       Cut parts of the poem that are not needed.
       Rearrange parts that are out of order. In a free-verse poem, experiment with different line breaks to affect overall flow and the emphasis of different words.
       Rewrite material that isn't working well.
   - **Edit** your poem to make it read smoothly. Add or remove punctuation and capitalization to best engage the reader.

6. **Present** your poem during a poetry reading or post it online for others to read. Gather many poems together (a group of your own, or together with friends) to create a collection, and publish it online, as an ebook, or through a print-on-demand service.

Poems

These student examples were all submissions to a call for gardening poems.

Shakespearean Sonnet

A Shakespearean sonnet (often called an "English sonnet") has an *abab cdcd efef gg* rhyme scheme. In a Shakespearean sonnet, each quatrain (four-line stanza) addresses the same central topic, though from a slightly different point of view.

Store-Bought Fruit

Store-bought tomatoes taste too much like wax.
They're picked too green, and "ripened" with some gas.
They're tough enough to be cut with an axe.
Don't offer one to me. No thanks. I'll pass.

And store-bought peaches, that's another crime.
Biting a peach should never yield a crunch.
Unless a peach is soft and juicy, I'm
Not interested in having one for lunch.

Store-bought strawberries, too, are way too tough.
Those things are mainly pith, surrounding air.
I ate one once, and once was quite enough.
I wouldn't eat another on a dare.

So don't ask me to dinner if you're rude
And hope to serve up such factory food.

—Joellen Romine

Canning with Gran

My gran said it was time to can green beans.
She wanted me to learn. That night we snapped
four bushels-full to pieces, rinsed them, scrapped
the stems, boiled jars and lids and seals (routine
for Gran, though new to me, not yet a teen),
filled jars with beans and boiling water, capped
them, listened for each seal to pop, then wrapped
a boxful just for me. She held the screen
door open as I left. Three years ago
that was. Now Gran is gone. That final scene
would be our last together, and my elbow
brushing hers our final touch. But echoes
of things that we discussed, her voice, serene,
are stored for me in Gran's canning mementos.

—Joaquin Manjarres

Petrarchan Sonnet

The *abbaabba* rhyme scheme of the octave (eight-line stanza) identifies this as a Petrarchan sonnet (often called an "Italian sonnet"). In a Petrarchan sonnet, the octave raises a topic, and the sestet (six-line ending stanza) responds. The rhyme scheme of a Petrarchan sonnet's sestet is often *cdecde* but may take many other variations.

plantings

why all these squared plots	the straight lines bending to suit a river's curve	squared plots and straight lines
and straight lines	or	are for stiff
and all these fences	the slope of a steep	
ever see farmland from the sky	steep hill	—Sherril Sovern

Free-Verse Poem

Free-verse poetry doesn't have a strict rhythm or rhyme scheme.

Inquire To Write an Informative Essay

1. **Question** the communication situation.
   - **Subject:** What specific topic will you write about?
   - **Purpose:** Why are you writing—to explain, to describe?
   - **Audience:** Who will read this essay? What does the audience already know about the topic? What do they need to know?

2. **Plan** your essay.
   - **Narrow** your topic so that you can cover it in a single essay.
   - **Study** similar essays so that you understand the structure.

3. **Research** your topic.
   - **Searching:** Consult primary and secondary sources as needed to learn about your topic. (See pages 376–391.)
   - **Focusing:** Form a thesis statement, expressing a specific thought about the topic of your essay.

      Topic: *Mayan math*   **Thought:** *used a unique counting system*

      Thesis statement: *As a foundation for their astronomical and calendar calculations, ancient Mayans relied on a unique counting system based on three symbols.*

4. **Create** the first draft of your essay.
   - **Open** with a paragraph that introduces your topic, grabs your reader's attention, and states your thesis.
   - **Follow** with middle paragraphs that support your thesis with appropriate details.
   - **Organize** the details in an effective order (see page 188).
   - **Close** with a paragraph that revisits your thesis.

5. **Improve** your first draft.
   - **Evaluate** your first draft.

      Purpose: Does the essay effectively fulfill your purpose?

      Audience: Will the essay hold the reader's interest?
   - **Revise** your writing.

      Rewrite sentences that are confusing or unclear.

      Add connecting words or transitions.

      Cut parts that are off the topic or do not further your thesis.

6. **Present** the final copy of your essay on a personal blog or a classroom wiki.

Informative Essay

An informative essay is also known as an expository essay. This type of writing explains an idea or demonstrates how something works. It is often assigned during high school and in college courses.

The beginning introduces the topic in an interesting way and includes a thesis statement (underlined).

Each **middle** paragraph focuses on a different supporting example.

A New Age of Robots

In a poignant scene in the 2004 science fiction movie *I, Robot*, Sonny, a robot, asks Will Smith's character why humans wink at each other. Smith tells the robot: "It's a sign of trust. It's a human thing. You wouldn't understand." Smith's terse response reflects what many people think of robotic technology: Sure, robots can perform some tasks like a human, but they certainly cannot think like a human. Such a sentiment is evolving into a myth. <u>Today's computer scientists and robotic engineers are creating robots capable of advanced human thinking.</u>

One robot showing signs of artificial intelligence (AI) is called RuBot II. RuBot II is nicknamed the "Cubinator" because it can solve Rubik's Cube puzzles in record times. How does it work? After a human scrambles the cube, RuBot II picks it up, raises it to eye camera level, and scans all sides of the cube. In less than a second, RuBot II computes a solution to the puzzle using an algorithm. Next, RuBot II's hands deftly solve the puzzle in less than 20 moves. As computer scientist Aaron Sloman told *New Scientist* magazine, "Human brains don't work by magic, so whatever it is they do should be doable in suitably designed machines."

Another robotic innovation is able to predict the intentions of its human partner. European researchers at JAST have built a robot capable of observation and anticipation. In JAST experiments, the robot and its human partner interact to build basic model airplanes. The JAST robot's computerized brain already knows the task, but it observes the partner's behavior, maps it against the task, and eventually learns to anticipate the partner's actions and spot errors when the partner does not follow the correct or expected procedure. For example, by observing how its human partner holds a tool or model part, the robot is able to predict how the partner intends to use it. The JAST project is groundbreaking because it demonstrates tangible progress in creating a robot that is proactive in its interaction with humans.

Maybe the most advanced robot in the world is Ecci, a C3PO look-alike with synthetic muscles, tendons, and bones. Ecci also has the visual capability of humans and the brain

> "Ecci also has the visual capability of humans and the brain capacity to correct its own mistakes."

capacity to correct its own mistakes. Researchers at the University of Zurich built a computer into Ecci's brain that allows it to study and analyze its own behavior. If, for example, Ecci moves in a way that causes it to stumble or drop something, the computer is able to evaluate the behavior and correct it so that it does not happen again. Ecci's unique engineering and correction capacity point to a future where robots could function in an unstructured human environment.

The **ending** revisits the thesis and discusses its future implications.

However, even though today's robots can imitate some specific aspects of human intelligence, they are still not capable of the artificial intelligence displayed by Sonny in *I, Robot*. Computer programming and algorithmic methods give robots limited ability to solve problems, interact with humans, and learn. But the technological advances necessary to give them the capacity to reason, to form new ideas, and to think critically confound today's scientists and engineers. Why? Natural intelligence is still largely an enigma—we simply do not understand how it works. At the same time, continued advancements in robotics indicate that a world where humans and robots interact on a daily basis is no longer a matter of pure science fiction.

▶ ## Organizing Expository Essays

Topic		
Point 1	Point 2	Point 3
Supporting Details	Supporting Details	Supporting Details

Building Essays

Essays provide a forum to advance your ideas, and, in turn, advance your thinking. An essay has a clear beginning, middle, and ending. The following chart compares the working parts of paragraphs and essays. The chart below examines the parts of essays in greater detail.

Paragraph	Essay
Topic sentence ⟶	Beginning paragraph (with thesis statement)
Body ⟶	Middle paragraphs
Closing sentence ⟶	Ending paragraph

Basic Structure of Essays

Beginning

1. **Build the reader's interest.** Introduce your topic in an interesting way. You can build interest in one of these ways:
   - Asking an engaging question
   - Telling a short anecdotal story
   - Offering a surprising fact or statistic
   - Posing a thought-provoking quotation
2. **Find a direction.** Briefly explain why the topic matters.
3. **State your focus.** Write a thesis statement.
   - Interesting topic + specific claim = compelling thesis

Middle

4. **Support your thesis.** Supply background information and include important main points. Supporting details may include any of the following:
   - Facts and statistics
   - Examples
   - Quotations and testimonials
   - Definitions
   - Comparisons
   - Descriptions
   - Stories
5. **Structure your paragraphs.** Start each paragraph with a separate main point.
6. **Add details.** Clarify each main point with supporting details (see above).

Ending

7. **Restate the focus.** Remind the reader of the essay's purpose and rephrase the thesis statement.
8. **Speak to the reader.** Sum up the essay with a final point that speaks directly to the reader.

Inquire | To Write a Narrative

1. **Question** the communication situation.
   - **Subject:** Who is the story's real or imagined main character (it may be you)? What other characters are involved?
   - **Purpose:** Why are you writing this narrative? To reflect on an event? To share a story? To examine what a character learns?
   - **Audience:** Who will read the narrative?

2. **Plan** your narrative.
   - What conflict or situation will the main character encounter?
   - What are the key plot points? How will the narrative begin, develop, and end? (See page 411 for the classic narrative structure.)

3. **Research** the topic.
   - **Searching:** Consult primary and secondary sources as needed to learn about the location, setting, and other information that will make your narrative feel authentic and vivid.
   - **Focusing:** Decide on the tenor, or mood, for your narrative—tense, uneasy, fearful, happy, humorous, and so on.
   - **Shaping:** Consider the climax or outcome of the central conflict, during which the main character faces a great challenge and either succeeds or fails.

4. **Create** the first draft.
   - **Start** by grabbing the reader's attention, introducing the main character, setting the scene (location and time), and introducing conflict.
   - **Follow** with rising action that unfolds and builds the conflict.
   - **Lead** up to the climax, the most exciting part, where the main character confronts the situation head-on.
   - **End** with the resolution, showing how the character is changed by the events in the narrative.

5. **Improve** your first draft.
   - **Evaluate** your first draft.
     - **Subject:** Is the main character memorable?
     - **Purpose:** Is the conflict interesting? Is the resolution revealing?
   - **Revise** your writing.
     - **Rewrite** dialogue and action that does not fit the characters.
     - **Add** missing details or background information.
   - **Edit** your revised writing.
     - **Replace** general nouns and verbs with specific ones.
     - **Check** your writing for accuracy.

6. **Present** the final copy online or submit it to a contest.

Personal Narrative

In this personal narrative, a student tells about what it was like to live through a tornado.

Like a Freight Train Coming

The **beginning** draws the reader in by starting in the middle of the action.

The familiar scream of the tornado sirens was startling but not entirely unexpected. "A severe storm system is moving quickly southeast into our northeastern viewing area, producing hail, severe thunderstorms, and wind gusts exceeding 100 mph. Several funnels have been spotted near Montgomery and Labette counties," cautioned a meteorologist from channel 7 not more than a half hour ago.

It's not like these warnings were uncommon. After all, this is Oklahoma, the heart of Tornado Alley. It wasn't the first time we'd heard tornado sirens, and it surely wouldn't be the last.

The writer provides context by sharing a flashback.

A few years ago a mild twister passed through our city. We waited it out in our basement. It sounded no different than one of many severe storms passing through our area in mid-July—hissing winds, the patter of hail pelting windows, like a steady stream of paint balls. When the storm subsided, we peered outside to see uprooted trees, displaced branches, and a few shattered car windshields.

Today felt like just another storm. It was dark, windy, and rainy, to be sure. Thunder cracked interminably, but it was nothing out of the ordinary, though our Jack Russell terrier, Bucky, whined and paced more feverishly than usual.

The **middle** paragraphs begin to build suspense.

I was sitting across from my dad at our kitchen table, methodically seizing control of Africa in an intense game of Risk, when we first heard the emergency sirens. Mom turned up the volume on the television to get the latest update when the lights began to flicker.

"Better grab the flashlights and head downstairs," Dad said.

"But what about our game? I was about to conquer the world!" I protested to no avail.

On our way to the staircase, I caught a glimpse outside. The sky had turned from dark gray to dark black to dark green, and rain whipped sideways.

Mom, Dad, Bucky, and I quickened our pace down the stairs, trotted through our carpeted television and game room—my favorite room in the house—and into our windowless concrete storeroom.

Tension increases, leading the reader toward the climax.

Shortly after we closed and locked the door, we lost power, and the room went black. Above us I could hear what sounded like a train in the distance.

"It's a twister," Dad said calmly. Mom nodded in agreement, though she didn't look so calm in the dim beam of the flashlight. The sound began to intensify, like the train was rolling closer. It grew louder and louder, and the ceiling began to shake. This was nothing like my first tornado experience.

The narrative reaches its climax.

Now I was officially scared, and I gripped a squirming Bucky tightly. Mom and Dad huddled next to me, as the sound turned more and more deafening, louder than any freight train I'd ever heard. For the next minute, it felt as if the whole world were shaking. I closed my eyes. My mind was numb.

Then everything stopped. Silence blanketed the room.

The next paragraphs offer the resolution.

"Is everyone okay?" my dad finally asked, his voice barely recognizable. I'd never heard him so rattled.

We all responded, "Yes."

After a few minutes of mostly stunned silence, we made our way back up the stairs. Most of the picture frames had fallen off the walls. Tiny red and blue Risk soldiers were scattered across the kitchen floor, accompanied by remnants of broken white dishes. Some drawers were half open, some cupboard doors were completely unhinged.

Outside, our yard was a mess. Black shingles from our roof covered the lawn along with fallen branches and a mixture of splintered wood and trash. The trees that still stood were completely barren, a skeleton of themselves.

Across the street we saw more devastation—homes with roofs ripped off, cars overturned. Our house certainly didn't get the worst of it.

The **ending** reflects on the experience and shares lessons learned.

The tornado was rated an F-3, one capable of twisting and deforming skyscrapers. Luckily, no one in our city suffered severe injuries. People had been careful. They had sought shelter. Before this experience, I never fully realized the immense power of the weather and our earth. It made me feel small and helpless. Yet I also felt more grateful for my health, my family, and my community. During the weeks after the tornado, generous people throughout our city and state pitched in with the cleanup efforts and provided shelter and support to those who had lost their homes. I feel proud to be part of this great community and humbled by the earth we live on.

Chapter 29
Advanced Writing Projects

As you advance in school, you advance in thinking. You connect concepts, evaluate information, and communicate complex thoughts. One of the best ways to express such ideas is through writing. Thinking and writing go hand in glove.

In this chapter, you will be asked to support ideas with sound evidence, build persuasive arguments, and research questions and procedures. You'll find guidelines and examples, but your own thinking is essential for completing each project. Use these advanced writing forms to take ownership of your learning.

You will learn . . .

- Writing Comparison-Contrast Essays
- Writing Cause-Effect Essays
- Writing Lab Reports
- Writing Argument Essays
- Writing Problem-Solution Essays
- Writing Literary Analyses
- Writing College Admissions Essays
- Writing Research Papers
- Using Transitions

Project Overview

Here is a quick overview of the advanced writing projects in this chapter.

A Comparison-Contrast Essay

A comparison-contrast essay explores the similarities and differences between two or more topics. (See pages 460–462.)

B Cause-Effect Essay

A cause-effect essay analyzes and explains the causes, the effects, or both the causes and effects of a particular event, occurrence, or situation. (See pages 463–465.)

C Lab Report

A lab report documents an experiment, from the beginning question and hypothesis to the conclusion. (See pages 466–469.)

D Argument Essay

An argument essay discusses a debatable issue, taking a particular stand or position. It supports the position with strong evidence and reliable logic. (See pages 470–471.)

E Problem-Solution Essay

A problem-solution essay identifies an unresolved problem and offers a solution or solutions to address it. (See pages 472–473.)

F Literary Analysis

A literary analysis examines the elements—theme, style, tone, etc.—in a piece of literature. The example analysis in this chapter analyzes a poem's theme. (See pages 474–475.)

G College Admissions Essay

Many colleges ask prospective students to submit an essay or personal statement with their applications. A college admissions essay usually shares a story or lesson from the writer's life. (See pages 476–477.)

H Research Paper

A research paper, formed from an in-depth study of a variety of sources, presents the writer's ideas and understanding of a topic or an issue. (See pages 478–485.)

A

Nuclear Versus Wind Power

Human beings have spent thousands of years burning [...] make energy, but that strategy needs to change. Fossil fuel su[...] limited, they're becoming increasingly expensive, and burnin[...] is harmful to the environment. Two energy systems have eme[...] potential replacements for fossil fuels—nuclear power and wi[...] Which is preferabl[...]ns, en[...] envi[...] disagree. While nu[...]er is th[...]syste[...] power is the cleane[...]e cost[...]ive.

In terms of th[...]enta[...]d an[...] energy are cle[...]

B

Unwelcome Visitors

Many departments of natural resources (DNRs) are working feverishly to enforce regulations that prohibit the import of firewood into their states. It is now commonplace to find bright "Don't Move Firewood" alerts alongside highways throughout states on the East Coast and in the Midwest. These efforts are aimed at halting the transport of a dangerous and invasive critter with a body size less than the width of a penny. The emerald ash borer's presence in North America is wreaking havoc on an entire tree species, harming economies, and threatening the stability of ecosystems.

[...]e emerald ash borer is an exotic, [...]e wood-boring beetle that makes [...]

C

Modern Galileo Experiment

Question: What is the relationship between velocity an[...] How does gravity provide uniform deceleration and a[...]

Hypothesis: Just as Galileo observed, the acceleration[...] should be constant.

Background:
Gravity = −9.81 meters/second²
Acceleration = a = $\Delta v / \Delta t$ = (vfinal − vinitial) / (tfinal −[...]
    a = acceleration (meters/second²)
    v = final velocity (meters/second)
    u = initial velocity (meters/second)
    t = time (second)

Materials: Cart, motion detector, graphing calculator

D

Support Disclosure Laws

The world of campaign finance has always had a shadowy history. No event better illustrates the secretive nature of money transfers than the Watergate scandal, when undisclosed piles of corporate cash were funneled to political candidates in paper bags. The scandal influenced Congress to pass a law in 1974 requiring the disclosure of political contributions to candidates and political committees (Hasen). Now corporations and wealthy donors [...] loopholes in the law to ar[...] upposedly indep[...] unds to buy p[...] ore [...]

E

Fighting Dogfighting

In 2007, NFL quarterback Michael Vick was charged for[...] an illegal dogfighting ring. On Vick's property, pit bull dogs w[...] housed and trained to fight each other, sometimes to the death[...] least eight dogs were executed for poor training. This grisly pic[...] exposed a major problem gripping both urban and rural Ameri[...] Dogfighting is a widespread problem that must be solved throu[...] education and awareness measures in schools and communities[...] Dogfighting is an illegal blood sport that pits two dogs aga[...] each other. Owners and spectators gamble high stakes on the [...] outcomes. Thou[...] the practice is illegal in all 50 states, an esti[...] 40,0[...]d in dogfighting. The Humane Societ[...] [...]her 100,000 people are involve[...] [...]ts. While mo[...] [...]nding the s[...] [...]come d[...]

F

Grieving for the Lost Captain

Grief is a common theme in literature, especially in poetry. Poets express their personal grief for lost lovers, mothers, fathers, and children. Grief can also be expressed on a larger stage. In "O Captain! My Captain!" Walt Whitman does just that by lamenting the loss of President Lincoln after his assassination by John Wilkes Booth. Experts say there are seven stages of grief. In "O Captain! My Captain!" Whitman displays three of the initial stages.

The first stage of grief is shock and denial. In the opening lines of his poem, Whitman declares "O Captain! my Captain! our fearful trip is done, / The ship has weather'd every rack, the prize we sought is won." He is praising Lincoln, his captain, for leading the United States [...] bells I [...]te the [...]nial.

[...]s this [...]ding

G

Lessons from Bully High

All those nightly news specials about bullying cou[...] filmed at my high school. You saw it in the hallways an[...] rooms and on the gym floor and behind computer scre[...] bullied girls, boys bullied boys, and vice versa. How do[...] school culture where bullying is the norm?

I didn't always stand up for those who were bullie[...] incident during my junior year changed things. In the [...] after health and fitness class, a friend of mine was taur[...] classmate for no reason in particular. When the classm[...] my friend, a big and muscular guy, slammed him again[...] repeatedly. Everybody just stood around watching. Aft[...] couldn't take it any more and stepped in between them.[...]

Later that day I confronted my friend. I told him h[...] too far. "I thought you had my back. I guess you punke[...] responded. In the weeks following the altercation, I los[...] that group of friends. It was a bit of a lonely time, but I[...] confident in myself and met people who are some of m[...] today.

During this period, I became more aware of the b[...] around me. I stopped being a silent bystander and star[...]

H

Beth Wadsworth

Mr. Dan Meadow

American Studies

17 April 2012

Understanding Hmong Americans

In the melting pot of cultures in the United States, Hmong Americans are among the most misunderstood and enigmatic ethnic groups. Hailing from mountainous regions in southern China, Thailand, Laos, and Vietnam, the Hmong population in America is concentrated mostly in three states—California, Minnesota, and Wisconsin. Such isolation has contributed to outsiders' misconceptions about these people. Besides the isolation, unfamiliarity with Hmong history, including the people's pro-American involvement in the Vietnam War, has contributed to this misunderstanding. Hmong Americans are a proud yet evolving culture wrestling with old-world tradition and new-world Americanism.

Inquire To Write a Comparison-Contrast Essay

1. Question the situation.
- **Subject:** What topics will you compare and contrast?
- **Purpose:** Why are you comparing these topics? What is your goal?
- **Audience:** Who will read this essay? What do they need to know?

2. Plan your essay.
- **Identify** two specific topics to compare and contrast.
- **List** your prior knowledge about these topics.
- **Project** what you'd like to find out about each topic.

3. Research your topics.
- **Searching:** Consult primary and secondary sources. (See pages 376–389.) Consider using a T-chart to organize details about the two subjects.
- **Focusing:** Decide on a focus and write the thesis statement, naming the two topics and summing up how they are similar and different.
- **Shaping:** List key similarities and differences. Consider using a Venn diagram.

4. Create the first draft of your essay.
- **Begin** by introducing the topics and stating your thesis about their similarities or differences.
- **Follow** with middle paragraphs that explain how the topics are similar or different.
- **Organize** each paragraph using a point-by-point, subject-by-subject, or similarities-and-differences pattern (see page 462).
- **End** with a paragraph that summarizes the comparison and contrast.

5. Improve your first draft.
- **Evaluate** your first draft.
    Subject: Are the two topics given equal attention? Does the comparison make sense and have worth?
    Purpose: Does the essay achieve your goal?
- **Revise** your writing.
    Rewrite parts that are confusing or unclear.
    Add details to explain the comparison more fully.
    Cut unnecessary details.
- **Edit** your writing.
    Check your writing for accuracy using pages 190–195 as a guide.

6. Present the final copy of your essay to your instructor or post it on a relevant blog or wiki.

Comparison-Contrast Essay

In the following comparison-contrast essay, a student uses a point-by-point comparison to explore nuclear power and wind power.

Nuclear Versus Wind Power

The beginning introduces the two topics of comparison and includes a thesis statement (underlined).

Human beings have spent thousands of years burning things to make energy, but that strategy needs to change. Fossil fuel supplies are limited, they're becoming increasingly expensive, and burning them is harmful to the environment. Two energy systems have emerged as potential replacements for fossil fuels—nuclear power and wind power. Which is preferable? Politicians, energy experts, and environmentalists disagree. While nuclear power is the more efficient system, wind power is the cleaner and more cost-effective alternative.

The middle paragraphs focus on different points of comparison.

In terms of the environmental impact, both wind and nuclear energy are cleaner options than fossil fuels. Neither wind nor nuclear energy emits harmful greenhouse gases that trap sunlight. As a result, they both benefit the atmosphere by reducing the danger of climate change, compared with fossil fuels. But wind power is cleaner than nuclear power because it uses a completely natural resource and has low environmental impact. (It harms some bird populations.) Conversely, nuclear power produces radioactive waste that must be contained in massive concrete structures or stored far underground. Nuclear disasters such as the one at Fukushima cause great environmental harm (Keeley).

Wind power is also more cost-effective than nuclear power. In 2011 the Energy Information Administration published an inflation-adjusted cost comparison for building and operating different types of energy plants over their life cycles. The report concluded that a state-of-the-art nuclear plant would cost $113.90 per MW-h (unit of energy equal to 1,000 kilowatt hours), while an onshore wind farm would cost $97 per MW-h. According to this report, wind energy is 15 percent cheaper than nuclear energy. For one thing, the upfront cost for building a nuclear plant with the appropriate emergency and containment systems is higher than the upfront cost for building a wind farm. For another, it costs 46 cents per MW-h to fuel a nuclear power plant, while the wind used to "fuel" a wind farm costs nothing (Koyama).

However, while wind is cleaner and cheaper than nuclear power, nuclear power production is more efficient, consistent, and flexible— better able to meet sudden jumps in energy demands. This is not surprising, as wind turbines spin only when the wind is blowing. And it is difficult to predict when the wind will blow and at what force. Even in the United States, which has greater wind potential than most places, wind turbines operate at about 33 percent capacity. Meanwhile, nuclear plants operate at 90 percent capacity at least. On average then, a wind farm takes two to three times longer to produce the same amount of energy that a nuclear power plant of the same capacity can produce (Koyama).

The ending paragraph summarizes the comparison.

Nuclear power and wind power are both environmentally friendly energy alternatives to fossil fuels, but they are substantially different from one another. While wind power is the cleaner, more cost-effective energy source, it is inconsistent in its efficiency and energy output. While nuclear power is more efficient and produces the greater volume of energy within a certain time frame, it comes with the additional safety concerns of radioactive waste and nuclear meltdowns. These differences have made it difficult for those concerned with energy production to agree on how to move away from fossil fuels . . . and still meet the general public's energy needs.

▶ Organizing Comparison-Contrast Essays

Point by Point		Similarities and Differences
Point 1		How Subjects 1 & 2
Subject 1	Subject 2	Are *Similar*
Point 2		How Subjects 1 & 2
Subject 1	Subject 2	Are *Different*

Subject by Subject

Subject 1
Subject 2

Inquire To Write a Cause-Effect Essay

1. Question the situation.
- **Subject:** What specific topic will you write about?
- **Purpose:** What cause-effect relationship are you trying to show?
- **Audience:** Who will read this essay? How would you like them to react?

2. Plan your essay.
- **Choose** a specific topic that has a clear cause-effect relationship.
- **Create** a cause-effect chart to explore your prior knowledge about the topic.
- **Think** about whether you want to focus on causes, effects, or both.

3. Research your topic.
- **Searching:** Consult primary and secondary sources to learn about your topic. (See pages 376–389.)
- **Focusing:** Form a thesis statement, establishing a clear cause-effect relationship.

  Topic: *The Renaissance*   **Thought:** *led to the discovery of the Americas*

  Thesis statement: *The scientific advancements and increased trade brought on by the Renaissance led to the discovery of the Americas.*

4. Create the first draft of your essay.
- **Begin** with an opening paragraph that introduces your topic in an interesting way and includes a thesis that points to a cause-effect relationship.
- **Follow** with middle paragraphs that discuss the causes and effects.
- **Organize** middle paragraphs with topic sentences and a variety of details that analyze the causes and effects.
- **End** with a closing paragraph that summarizes the cause-effect relationship.

5. Improve your first draft.
- **Evaluate** your first draft.

  Purpose: Does the essay effectively fulfill your purpose?

  Audience: Will the reader understand the cause-effect relationship?
- **Revise** your writing.

  Rewrite any sentences that are confusing or unclear.

  Add connecting words or transitions.
- **Edit** your revised writing.

  Check your writing for accuracy using pages 190–195 as a guide.

6. Present the final copy of your essay on a blog or read it out loud to your classmates.

Cause-Effect Essay

In this cause-effect essay, a student analyzes the effects of an invasive species on emerald ash trees.

Unwelcome Visitors

The beginning introduces the cause-effect relationship and leads to the thesis statement (underlined).

Many departments of natural resources (DNRs) are working feverishly to enforce regulations that prohibit the import of firewood into their states. It is now commonplace to find bright "Don't Move Firewood" alerts alongside highways throughout states on the East Coast and in the Midwest. These efforts are aimed at halting the transport of a dangerous and invasive critter with a body size less than the width of a penny. <u>The emerald ash borer's presence in North America is wreaking havoc on an entire tree species, harming economies, and threatening the stability of ecosystems.</u>

The first middle paragraph provides background information and discusses the cause.

The emerald ash borer is an exotic, invasive wood-boring beetle that makes its home in ash trees. The borer larvae are capable of infesting and killing entire landscapes of ash plantings by feeding on phloem and xylem tissue under a tree's bark. The voracious eaters disrupt the flow of carbohydrates and water between a tree's canopy and its roots,

Source: Forest Service, United States Department of Agriculture

eventually killing the tree (Herms). Natives of eastern Asia, the beetles were not discovered in North America until 2002, when large numbers of ash trees began dying in southeast Michigan. Biologists theorize that the borers had infested wooden boxes and pallets imported into areas of Michigan, Ohio, and Ontario.

Once inside the states, the invasive species caused much devastation to ash tree populations. In both southeast Michigan and northwest Ohio, the emerald ash borer has killed millions of ash trees. Through transport, they have crept their way into a half dozen other states east of the Mississippi. In total, the ash borer is believed to have killed approximately 50 million trees, though the destruction has been mostly isolated to Michigan and Ohio. Both states have suffered economically and ecologically, while surrounding states have doubled their efforts to prevent the same damage.

The emerald ash borer's effects have damaged Michigan's and Ohio's wood industries. In Ohio, a substantial tree-nursery economy lost millions. Before emerald ash borers arrived, the wholesale value of

The other middle paragraphs discuss the effects.

ash trees sold annually at local nurseries was $2 million (Herms). Now that number is zero. Meanwhile, the cost of removing dead and dying ash trees has squeezed already tight municipal budgets in both Great Lakes neighbors. Homeowners pay up to $1,000 dollars for tree removal, and counties must factor in annual costs for insecticide treatments. The negative economic impact also extends to sawmills and firewood dealers in both states. Over the next 10 years, economists conservatively estimate that the economic impact of ash borers will reach $20 billion (Gleason).

Potentially more damaging is the emerald ash borer's effect on forest ecosystems. Ash species grow ubiquitously in forests in the eastern half of the United States. The spread of emerald ash borers into those forests could essentially kill off all ash species, which have not yet developed a defense mechanism against the beetles. Were this die-off to occur, entire forest ecosystems would be affected, because ash trees provide essential thermal cover and protection for various wildlife species and

Source: Steven Katovich, USDA Forest Service

plant seeds, from small mammals to insects to different plant species (Knight).

The ending paragraph revisits the essay's beginning ideas and sums up the cause-effect relationship.

In an attempt to counter the spread of emerald ash borers, the U.S. Department of Agriculture researched and harvested a wasp parasite found in Asia that kills the emerald ash borer larvae. The parasite has been released in many states affected by borers. Additionally, state DNRs have implemented fines and advertising campaigns aimed at eliminating the transport of wood between state lines. Each attempt costs time and money but is necessary to protect local economies and ecosystems from the wrath of a tiny, yet perilous beetle.

▶ Organizing Cause-Effect Essays

Cause-Centered	Effect-Centered
Cause	Cause
Cause	Effect
Cause	Effect
Effect	Effect

Inquire To Write a Lab Report

1. Question the situation.
- **Subject:** What is the topic of the experiment that you will report on?
- **Purpose:** What is the purpose of the experiment? Are you writing to provide a procedure to replicate, to provide raw data, to interpret results, or all three?
- **Audience:** Who will read the report? What do they need to know?

2. Plan your report.
- **Identify your topic,** the scientific question that you will explore and test.
  Topic: *Decomposition*   **Thought:** *How efficient are decomposers?*
  Hypothesis: *Different types of decomposers draw different nutrients from decaying material, so a suite of different types will be most efficient.*
- **Become familiar with the appropriate form** for a lab report, one provided by your teacher or the one on pages 467–468.

3. Research your topic.
- **Searching:** Conduct your experiment using the scientific method (see pages 54–57). Take thorough notes.
- **Focusing:** Use observations and results to draw conclusions.
  Observation: *Fruits decomposed by fly larvae and fungi were reduced much more rapidly and completely than those decomposed only by fungi.*
- **Shaping:** Arrange the details of your report.

4. Create the first draft of your report.
- **Begin** with your scientific question and hypothesis.
- **Follow** with the materials, step-by-step procedure, and observations.
- **End** with the conclusions based on your findings.

5. Improve your first draft.
- **Evaluate** your first draft.
  Purpose: Does the report effectively explain or describe the experiment and results as you planned?
  Audience: Will the reader be able to follow your report?
- **Revise** your writing.
  Rewrite parts that are confusing or unclear.
  Add details as needed.
  Cut parts that don't relate to the topic.
  Reorder sentences or parts that are out of order.
- **Edit** your revised writing.
  Replace general nouns and verbs with specific ones.
  Check your writing for accuracy using pages 190–195 as a guide.

6. Present the final copy of your lab report to a classroom blog or use it to lead classmates through the same procedure.

Lab Report

The following lab report comes from Eli King, a high school student at Burlington High School in Burlington, Wisconsin. In his lab report, Eli discusses the outcomes of a modern Galileo experiment, exploring the relationship between gravity, velocity, and acceleration.

The **beginning** includes a title, a question, and a hypothesis about the question.

Modern Galileo Experiment

Question: What is the relationship between velocity and acceleration? How does gravity provide uniform deceleration and acceleration?

Hypothesis: Just as Galileo observed, the acceleration of the cart should be constant.

The **middle** includes a background section that defines the variables that will be measured and used for calculations.

Background:

Gravity = −9.81 meters/second²

Acceleration = $a = \Delta v / \Delta t = (v\text{final} - v\text{initial}) / (t\text{final} - t\text{initial})$

a = acceleration (meters/second²)

v = final velocity (meters/second)

u = initial velocity (meters/second)

t = time (second)

The materials and procedure sections outline what other people would need to replicate the experiment.

Materials: Cart, motion detector, graphing calculator

Procedure:

1. Set up a motion detector at the top of an incline.
2. Release a cart. Let it roll freely down the incline.
3. Record data from the motion detector. Observe the increase in speed and the constant acceleration.
4. Repeat procedure, this time pushing the cart up the ramp and letting it freely roll back down.
5. Observe the quadratic qualities of velocity, time, and acceleration.
6. Calculate the average acceleration.

The raw data appears in a table.

Data:

Table (Initial Test)

Data Point	Time(s)	Speed (m/s)	Change in speed (m/s)
8	1.65	0.337m/s	0.046m/s
9	1.7	0.383m/s	0.045m/s
10	1.75	0.429m/s	0.046m/s
Slope	0.8984m/s/s		
Average acceleration	7 m/s²		

Observations:

Despite a few values at the beginning, change in speed (acceleration) is almost perfectly constant. Our own calculation of acceleration was very close to the projected slope from the motion sensor.

Conclusions:

Hypothesis

We wanted to examine the relationship between velocity and acceleration, as well as the effect of a constant acceleration (gravity). We successfully graphed the motion of our cart as it traveled along the ramp. Our findings revealed a mathematical relationship between acceleration, speed, and position.

Evidence

Our data confirms Galileo's hypothesis—acceleration is constant. (Ours was nearly constant.) We observed an exponential increase in speed as the cart traveled down the ramp. The journey back down mirrored the trip up, revealing a mirror quadratic relationship between the up and down journeys. This demonstrates that acceleration is constant.

Reliability

This experiment was set up in a way that yielded little human error. We used machines to graph points and observe relationships, harnessing pure data. The only interferences may have occurred during the different cart releases. Perhaps different amounts of force were applied on the cart during different releases. However, even these slight interferences didn't affect the data as a whole.

Application

This type of knowledge applies to many different real-world scenarios. For instance, throwing a ball straight up in the air and observing its descent exemplifies this idea. It also works in engineering, such as roller coaster design. By examining velocity, acceleration, and angles, roller coaster engineers can design effective and safe rides. These ideas also help calculate the stopping distance of a car. The technical aspects of velocity and acceleration are everywhere, and we often take them for granted.

This observation provides a general inference drawn from data.

The conclusions section reviews the experiment, showing how the evidence supported the hypothesis.

A reliability section discusses the precautions taken to avoid experimental error.

The **ending** discusses applying the results of the experiment to life.

Inquire To Write an Argument Essay

1. **Question** the situation.
   - **Subject:** What specific debatable issue will you write about?
   - **Purpose:** Why are you writing? What are you arguing for?
   - **Audience:** Who will read this essay? What do they need to know?

2. **Plan** your essay.
   - **Identify a topic.** Choose a timely, interesting issue.
   - **Learn about forming a strong argument.** (See pages 95–114.)

3. **Research** your topic.
   - **Searching:** Consult primary and secondary sources. (See pages 376–389.) Take notes during your research.
   - **Focusing:** Decide on a focus and state it in a thesis statement.
   - **Shaping:** List key points that support or explain your thesis. Also identify important opposing arguments. You will need to counter these opposing positions in your essay.

4. **Create** the first draft of your essay.
   - **Begin** by introducing your topic and identifying your stand or position in a thesis statement.
   - **Follow** with supporting points in separate paragraphs. Also mention and counter any important opposing arguments.
   - **End** with a paragraph that stresses the importance of your thesis.

5. **Improve** your first draft.
   - **Evaluate** your first draft.
        Subject: Is the topic and argument compelling?
        Purpose: Does the essay achieve your goal?
        Audience: Will the reader be able to follow your argument?
   - **Revise** your writing.
        Rewrite parts that are confusing or unclear.
        Reorder ideas that are out of place.
   - **Edit** your writing.
        Cite sources correctly. (See pages 396–402.)
        Check your writing for accuracy using pages 190–195 as a guide.

6. **Present** the final copy of your essay on an appropriate social or blogging site or read and discuss it with your classmates.

Argument Essay

In this essay of argumentation, a student offers a stance on campaign-finance laws.

Support Disclosure Laws

The world of campaign finance has always had a shadowy history. No event better illustrates the secretive nature of money transfers than the Watergate scandal, when undisclosed piles of corporate cash were funneled to political candidates in paper bags. The scandal influenced Congress to pass a law in 1974 requiring the disclosure of political contributions to candidates and political committees (Hasen). Now corporations and wealthy donors are taking advantage of loopholes in the law to anonymously contribute huge sums of money to supposedly independent political action committees (PACs) that use the funds to buy political advertising to support or attack certain candidates. Such ads can swing elections—and candidates. There needs to be more transparency in campaign-related expenditures. Congress should pass a law requiring timely disclosure of donors to super PACs and disclosure of where the money is spent.

First of all, a disclosure law will prevent corruption and the appearance of corruption. Currently, individuals and corporations can contribute no more than $2,500 per election to federal candidates. The main reason the Supreme Court upholds the limit's constitutionality is because large contributions can lead to actual or perceived corruption of those candidates. For instance, if a candidate received an unusually large contribution from a donor, he or she might feel gratitude and distort policies in the donor's favor. Super PACs need to be held to the same standard. Currently, donors can contribute unlimited sums to PACs, and those funds can be used in support of, or opposition to, federal candidates, as long as the PAC doesn't "officially" align with the candidate's campaign. The case for corruption, real or perceived, is strong. Disclosing to the public who contributes what to a super PAC would be the first step in deterring real corruption. A candidate may be less likely to skew a decision in a donor's favor if the American public were informed of the donor-candidate relationship. At the same time, disclosure would help donors who give without ulterior motives, freeing them of perceived corruption.

Similarly, passing a disclosure rule will at least hold super PACs and other political committees to some of the same campaign finance standards as candidates are held to. For example, when a political candidate finances a political advertisement, he or she is required to approve the ad's message. The approval tells the public that the message is coming from and is funded by the candidate. Super PACs are not required to declare an approval in their messages. In the 2012 elections, super PACs spent millions of dollars on political advertisements, many attacking candidates they did not support (Stein). Mandating that PACs approve political advertisements just like candidates do is a fair and necessary step to keeping the public informed. Additionally, disclosing a PAC's top five donors during the advertisement (through at crawl at the bottom of the screen) would be another effective way to keep the public in the know.

The argument builds to this paragraph, which provides the most important reason.

Transparency is the most important reason to support a disclosure law. Voters ought to have as much access to information as possible in order to make wise choices. Right now, super PACs are held to leisurely disclosure policies. They need to report spending only on a monthly or quarterly basis. During primary season, PACs may fund special political advertisements in states and not disclose the spending until after votes have been collected, making the information useless to citizens. A more timely disclosure policy needs to be in place. With the immediacy of the Internet, it would not be unreasonable to require super PACs to report their spending and reveal their donors every 24 or 48 hours. Voters should not be kept in the dark.

A main opposing argument is discussed and countered.

Critics will argue that disclosure laws are unreasonable and may chill participation in politics or even violate first amendment rights. However, campaign finance laws have not curbed the number of people who can spend money, only how much money they can spend. The goal is to level the playing field. And to call disclosure laws unreasonable is, well, unreasonable. After all, disclosure laws for the PACs will not place limits on spending; they will only require disclosure of who is doing the spending and on what. The anonymity of donors is less important than preventing corruption and providing the electorate with complete information about political campaigns.

The **ending** paragraph stresses the importance of the thesis and adds perspective.

The political climate of the United States is already rife with distrust and skepticism. Allowing super PACs and wealthy super PAC donors to influence elections under the veil of anonymity only adds to the public's suspicion. Laws should require lobbyists to disclose their campaign contributions to PACs, should force corporations to tell shareholders about their campaign contributions, and should mandate that super PACs offer a timely disclosure of how they spend their money. These provisions are not only reasonable; they are necessary to prevent corruption and to keep the American public informed. As Supreme Court Justice Antonin Scalia once wrote, "Requiring people to stand up in public for their political acts fosters civic courage, without which democracy is doomed."

Inquire To Write a Problem-Solution Essay

1. Question the situation.
- **Subject:** What specific problem would you like to solve?
- **Purpose:** Why are you writing—to change a policy, to reveal a problem, to propose an effective solution?
- **Audience:** Who will read this essay? What action do you want them to take?

2. Plan your essay.
- **Choose** a problem to tackle in your essay.
- **Complete** a problem-solution chart to explore your prior knowledge.

3. Research your topic.
- **Searching:** Investigate to learn as much as you can about the problem.
- **Examining:** Consider many possible solutions to the problem.
- **Focusing:** Form a thesis statement about the problem and solution.

    Topic: *Child warriors*   **Thought:** *International intervention is needed*

    Thesis statement: *Warlords who force children to fight as soldiers will not be stopped until the international community intervenes.*
- **Shaping:** Arrange details about the problem and solution in an outline or other graphic organizer.

4. Create the first draft of your essay.
- **Begin** with an opening paragraph that introduces the problem and offers a solution in a thesis statement.
- **Follow** with middle paragraphs that offer supporting details to explain or defend the solution.
- **End** with a closing paragraph that revisits the problem and tells why your solution is important and will work.

5. Improve your first draft.
- **Evaluate** your first draft.

    Purpose: Does the essay effectively fulfill your purpose?

    Audience: Will the essay hold the reader's interest?
- **Revise** your writing.

    Rewrite any passages that sound too emotional. Use a knowledgeable and firm voice.

    Add connecting words or transitions.
- **Edit** your revised writing.

    Check your writing for accuracy.

6. Present the final copy of your essay to a classroom blog.

Problem-Solution Essay

The **beginning** grabs the reader's attention and leads to the thesis statement (underlined).

This **middle** paragraph analyzes the problem.

The remaining middle paragraphs outline three solutions to the problem.

The **ending** paragraph recaps the problem and solutions and promotes action.

Fighting Dogfighting

In 2007, NFL quarterback Michael Vick was charged for running an illegal dogfighting ring. On Vick's property, pit bull dogs were housed and trained to fight each other, sometimes to the death. At least eight dogs were executed for poor training. This grisly picture exposed a major problem gripping both urban and rural America. <u>Dogfighting is a widespread problem that must be solved through education and awareness measures in schools and communities.</u>

Dogfighting is an illegal blood sport that pits two dogs against each other. Owners and spectators gamble high stakes on the outcomes. Though the practice is illegal in all 50 states, an estimated 40,000 people are involved in dogfighting. The Humane Society of the United States estimates that another 100,000 people are involved in "streetfighting," or informal dogfights. While most outsiders can see the moral and ethical problems surrounding the sport, participants and spectators see dollar signs. They become desensitized to the violence, and such callousness spreads beyond the ring into schools and communities.

Prevention of dogfighting begins with education and awareness. Schools and youth centers ought to implement programs that discuss the horrors of dogfighting and teach participants how to treat dogs humanely. One program that could serve as a model is a nonprofit organization called Knock Out Dog Fighting. Knock Out reaches out to community centers, schools, and juvenile detention centers in California to raise awareness about dogfighting and provide healthy alternatives for dealing with aggression.

Another way to raise awareness of dogfighting is to produce Public Service Announcements (PSAs). Communities can urge local radio stations to air anti-dogfighting PSAs like the ones offered for free at the Humane Society Web site. Concerned citizens can also create their own PSAs and publish them through social media. Spreading important anti-dogfighting messages on local radio programs and through social media would get the word out to many people and build empathy for animals.

Lastly, people need to report any signs of dogfighting to their local police departments. It is imperative that we do not ignore dogfighting in our own neighborhoods. Anyone fearful of retribution for speaking out can report anonymously. Doing so can save dogs' lives.

Dogfighting is violent and cruel and must be stopped. It treats dogs inhumanely and endangers communities. Education and awareness programs can sensitize youth and adults to animal cruelty. Citizens can help by speaking out against dog violence. Dogs—and our communities—deserve better.

Inquire To Write a Literary Analysis

1. **Question** the situation.
   - **Subject:** What piece of literature will you analyze?
   - **Purpose:** What are you trying to accomplish in your literary analysis?
   - **Audience:** Who will read your analysis? How familiar will the reader be with this piece of literature?

2. **Plan** your analysis.
   - **Choose** a topic you are familiar with and interested in.
   - **Develop** an approach for analyzing the piece of literature—for example, using the KWL strategy (see page 143) or annotating the text (see page 145).

3. **Research** your topic.
   - **Searching:** Read the piece once without stopping. Then read it again more carefully, looking closely at its content and structure.
   - **Focusing:** Narrow your focus by concentrating on a specific literary element—theme, structure, context, and so on.

     Topic: The Lord of the Rings   **Thought:** *Tolkien's life traumas*

     Thesis statement: *In* The Lord of the Rings, *J. R. R. Tolkien depicts such life traumas as his childhood kidnapping in South Africa, the industrial ravaging of his home city of Birmingham, and his near death from illness contracted during the Battle of the Somme.*

4. **Create** the first draft of your analysis.
   - **Begin** by naming the author and title and expressing your thesis statement.
   - **Follow** with middle paragraphs that support the thesis by including evidence from the original work.
   - **End** with a paragraph that brings all your points together and demonstrates the significance of your analysis.

5. **Improve** your first draft.
   - **Evaluate** your first draft.

     Purpose: Does the analysis fulfill your purpose?

     Audience: Will the reader understand your point?
   - **Revise** your writing.

     Rewrite parts that are confusing or unclear.

     Add details to explain or make your point more convincing.

     Cut parts that don't support your analysis.
   - **Edit** your writing.

     Check your writing for accuracy using pages 190–195 as a guide.

6. **Present** your analysis to your class or on a literary wiki.

Literary Analysis

Grieving for the Lost Captain

Grief is a common theme in literature, especially in poetry. Poets express their personal grief for lost lovers, mothers, fathers, and children. Grief can also be expressed on a larger stage. In "O Captain! My Captain!" Walt Whitman does just that by lamenting the loss of President Lincoln after his assassination by John Wilkes Booth. Experts say there are seven stages of grief. <u>In "O Captain! My Captain!" Whitman displays three of the initial stages.</u>

The first stage of grief is shock and denial. In the opening lines of his poem, Whitman declares "O Captain! my Captain! our fearful trip is done, / The ship has weather'd every rack, the prize we sought is won." He is praising Lincoln, his captain, for leading the United States to victory in the Civil War. He continues, "The port is near, the bells I hear, the people are exulting." Loyal citizens are ready to celebrate the victory won by their great leader. Here, Whitman is clearly in denial.

In the second stage, after the initial shock, the griever acknowledges his loss and expresses his suffering. Whitman does this at the end of stanza one: "But O heart! heart! heart! / O the bleeding drops of red, / Where on the deck my Captain lies, / Fallen cold and dead." Stating that Lincoln has "fallen cold and dead" is a stark reminder that the captain has passed on and there will be no rejoicing.

Grieving is not a linear process. At the beginning of the second stanza, Whitman regresses to denial: "O Captain! my Captain! rise up and hear the bells; / Rise up—for you the flag is flung—for you the bugle trills." Then in the last two lines of this stanza, Whitman wonders if what has happened is just part of a bad dream: "It is some dream that on the deck, / You've fallen cold and dead." Then reality intrudes.

In the beginning of the final stanza, Whitman states, "My Captain does not answer, his lips are pale and still; / My father does not feel my arm, he has no pulse nor will." Whitman is facing the finality of the assassination. At this point, some people express anger (stage three), but Whitman skips to depression (stage four). Those on shore may exult, "But I, with mournful tread, / Walk the deck my Captain lies, / Fallen cold and dead." His depression will soon strike the whole nation.

The remaining stages of grief include a period of adjustment (stage five), a time for seeking solutions (stage six), and, finally, an acceptance of a different life (stage seven). In "O Captain! My Captain!" Walt Whitman clearly struggles with the initial stages of grief, but he has a long way to go—perhaps in additional poems—to find a new way forward while still accepting the intense pain of losing his president.

Inquire To Write a College Admissions Essay

1. **Question** the situation.
   - **Subject:** What specific topic will you write about? What prompt has the college provided for you to respond to?
   - **Purpose:** What are you trying to accomplish? How can you create a narrative that will reflect positively on your achievements and character?
   - **Audience:** How will you attract the attention of the admissions officer? What details about your life show you as a valuable addition to the college?

2. **Plan** your admissions essay.
   - **Reflect** on your life, your academic achievements, and your goals.
   - **Analyze** the prompt that you have been provided, making sure you understand what admissions officers seek in your response.
   - **Schedule** your submission, making sure to achieve the due date.

3. **Research** your topic.
   - **Search:** Collect details for your story, listing key events and people.
   - **Focusing:** Identify elements from your story that put you in the best light—likable, honest, hardworking, and so on.
   - **Shaping:** Plan to lead the reader to an important realization about you.

4. **Create** the first draft of the essay.
   - **Begin** your essay in a surprising or interesting way.
   - **Follow** with important details of your narrative.
   - **Build** the narrative toward the important realization about you.
   - **End** with the last detail or a closing statement about yourself.

5. **Improve** your first draft.
   - **Evaluate** your first draft.
      Purpose: Does the essay achieve its purpose?
      Audience: Will the essay hold an admissions officer's attention?
   - **Revise** your writing.
      Rewrite sentences that are confusing, unclear, or too long.
      Add details that will help you make your point.
      Cut unnecessary words or parts. Strive to be concise.
   - **Edit** your revised writing.
      Replace general nouns and verbs with specific and active ones.
      Check your writing for accuracy using pages 190–195 as a guide.

6. **Present** the final copy by submitting it with your application.

College Admissions Essay

Below is a sample college admissions essay. Most colleges ask for admissions essays of 500 words or less, so it is important to choose your words carefully.

Lessons from Bully High

The beginning relates the writer's experience to a pressing current issue.

All those nightly news specials about bullying could have been filmed at my high school. You saw it in the hallways and in the locker rooms and on the gym floor and behind computer screens. Girls bullied girls, boys bullied boys, and vice versa. How do you change a school culture where bullying is the norm?

I didn't always stand up for those who were bullied. However, one incident during my junior year changed things. In the locker room after health and fitness class, a friend of mine was taunting another classmate for no reason in particular. When the classmate fought back, my friend, a big and muscular guy, slammed him against a locker repeatedly. Everybody just stood around watching. After a while, I couldn't take it anymore and stepped in between them.

Later that day I confronted my friend. I told him he took it too far. "I thought you had my back. I guess you punked out," he responded. In the weeks following the altercation, I lost favor with that group of friends. It was a bit of a lonely time, but I also grew more confident in myself and met people who are some of my best friends today.

The middle shares lessons learned and exemplifies the writer's good character.

During this period, I became more aware of the bullying going on around me. I stopped being a silent bystander and started acting as a mediator. My actions garnered ridicule from my old friends but also respect from other students. One lesson I took from the experience is that bullies are actually a minority at my school, but other students are reluctant to speak out against them.

This silent majority offered an opportunity for change. I joined a group of students and teachers in a "Not in Our School" campaign aimed at curbing bullying and hateful speech. For the first month of the new school year, we implemented activities and classroom discussions to engage students in conversation and action against intolerance and bullying. The campaign was successful, and the prevalence of bullying dropped (though not completely). My hope is that the lessons from the campaign will carry over in years to come and that the culture of bullying will eventually cease to exist.

The ending ties the story to the writer's future goals and aspirations.

My high school experience is one of the main reasons for my interest in the field of social work. I've gone from being an observer of social problems to being an advocate for solving them. Working with others to solve conflicts has helped me grow as a person, and I hope to continue to learn and grow in college.

Inquire To Write a Research Paper

1. **Question** the situation for your research paper.
   - **Subject:** What specific topic will you research and write about? Is the topic engaging? Is it narrow enough to make it manageable for in-depth research?
   - **Purpose:** Why are you researching this topic? What do you hope to discover about it? Why are you writing—to share your discovery? To persuade your reader to do something or think a certain way?
   - **Audience:** Who will read this paper? What does the audience already know about the topic? What do they need to know?

2. **Plan** your paper.
   - **Identify your topic.** Be sure it interests you and you can find enough information about it.
   - **Narrow your topic.** Make sure it is neither so general that it makes research unmanageable nor so specific that there is not enough information about it.
   - **Establish a work schedule.** (See pages 355–362.)

3. **Research** your topic.
   - **Searching:** Consult primary and secondary sources to learn about your topic. (See pages 376–389.) Take notes and track sources. (See pages 370–371.)
   - **Focusing:** Develop a working thesis. A working thesis requires explanation.
     Limited topic + debatable claim/statement = working thesis
   - **Shaping:** Determine the best order of supporting details for your thesis.

4. **Create** the first draft of your research paper.
   - **Start strong.** Get the reader's attention and state your thesis.
   - **Support your thesis.** Use your organizing plan as a guide.
   - **Cite your sources.** Identify where ideas come from (see pages 396–402).
   - **End strong.** Tie everything together and restate your thesis.

5. **Improve** your first draft.
   - **Evaluate** the first draft of your research paper.
       Purpose: Does the paper achieve your goal?
       Audience: Will the paper engage and enlighten readers?
   - **Revise** your writing.
       Rewrite parts that are confusing or unclear.
       Add more details to explain your topic more fully.
       Cut parts that don't support your thesis.
       Reorder parts that could be more effectively arranged.
   - **Edit** your revised writing.
       Review your documentation. (See pages 396–402.)
       Check your writing for accuracy using pages 190–195 as a guide.

6. **Present** the final copy of your research paper.

MLA Research Paper

The following research paper on Hmong Americans follows MLA style. (See pages 396–397 for different documentation styles.)

Beth Wadsworth

Mr. Dan Meadow

American Studies

17 April 2012

Understanding Hmong Americans

The beginning introduces the topic and leads to the thesis statement (underlined.)

In the melting pot of cultures in the United States, Hmong Americans are among the most misunderstood and enigmatic ethnic groups. Hailing from mountainous regions in southern China, Thailand, Laos, and Vietnam, the Hmong population in America is concentrated mostly in three states—California, Minnesota, and Wisconsin. Such isolation has contributed to outsiders' misconceptions about these people. Besides the isolation, unfamiliarity with Hmong history, including the people's pro-American involvement in the Vietnam War, has contributed to this misunderstanding. Hmong Americans are a proud yet evolving culture wrestling with old-world tradition and new-world Americanism.

Each middle paragraph begins with a topic sentence and uses numerous details to support it.

To begin to understand the American Hmong population, one must consider where they came from and how they got here. Throughout history, Hmong people have never had a nation of their own but have always been motivated by autonomy. When the eighteenth-century Hmong population living and farming in the highlands of southern China feared for their independence, they fled south into Laos, Thailand, and Vietnam. When Laos experienced civil war in the 1950s and 1960s, the Hmong sided with the government, fearing a communist regime would disrupt their independence (Bankston). During this period of unrest, the United States sent elite soldiers to train the Hmong people to oppose Vietnamese and Laotian

communists. This partnership would later become an integral part

of the Secret War in which the United States CIA recruited Hmong

tribesmen to block North Vietnam's access to the Ho Chi Minh Trail

supply corridor in Laos (Her and Buley-Meissner 79).

    The war decimated the Hmong adult population. When Laos fell

to the communists and Americans fled Vietnam, the Hmong were

left to fend for themselves as the Pathet Lao communists and North

Vietnamese threatened to wipe them out. More than 100,000 Hmong

fled Laos to Thai refugee camps, and many were killed along the way.

Chang Yang was a refugee who survived a perilous swim across the

Mekong River in Laos to the shores of Thailand:

> We had a lot of people get shot while crossing the river. We used
>
> the moon for light. Babies were crying. People were drowning. And
>
> enemy soldiers [had] a boat that they used to circle around looking
>
> for these people. Whoever they [saw], they [shot] or pulled them
>
> off and took them back to Laos. ("Bridging the Shores")

An estimated 30,000 Hmong were killed in the war in Laos, a

devastating loss for an already small population ("The Secret War").

    The period after the Vietnam War marked the first wave of Hmong

migration to the United States, but a much larger migration occurred in

the mid-1980s when the United States passed the Refugee Act of 1980

(Lai and Arguelles). The Act permitted family members of the Hmong

Secret Army from the Vietnam War to immigrate to the United States.

By the 1990s, a bitter debate raged about what to do with the thousands

of Hmong who remained in refugee camps in Thailand. At the time, the

Thai government threatened to forcibly send Hmong refugees back to

Laos, where they expected to be met with discrimination and violence

(George and Mai). While Congress and the United Nations debated

An excerpt is indented to set it off from the text.

Wadsworth 3

what to do with the Thai-based Hmong, many refugees fled to other parts of Thailand, while others hid in the forests of Laos. Finally, in 2004, the United States granted immigration rights to 15,000 Hmong from one of the last major refugee camps in Thailand. Though many Hmong were reunited with family members, the unrest in South East Asia still weighs heavily on the Hmong people living in the United States (George and Mai).

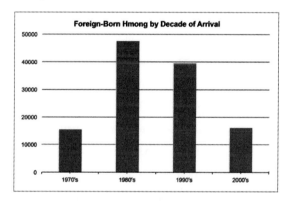

During the first wave of Hmong migration shortly after the Vietnam War, American resettlement agencies dispersed Hmong immigrants to major cities throughout the country. The first Hmong encountered racism from Americans who did not know about the integral role the Hmong had played in fighting communism during America's Secret War ("Bridging the Shores").

When the second, much larger wave of Hmong immigrants reached America in the mid-1980s, most of the Hmong population had reassembled in small northern California farming towns. And in the 1990s, many Hmong settled in Minnesota and Wisconsin. Today, of the 260,073 Hmong living in America, 91,000 reside in California, 66,181 in Minnesota, and 49,240 in Wisconsin ("2010 Census").

The population's concentration in a select few states is attributed

Statistics make the report informative.

At the top right of each page appears the writer's last name and the page number.

to two main factors. First, fertile soil in California and the Midwest attracted Hmong farmers, the most prevalent occupation in their homeland. Second, Hmong culture reveres family interdependence. Hmong family ties are extensive and loyal. They tend to live together with grandparents, children, grandchildren, and cousins all under one roof (Lai and Arguelles). Such a living arrangement stems from a clan mentality of self-governance and self-reliance dating back to the Hmong's time in ancient China. In fact, clan membership still plays a major role in the organization of Hmong populations. Hmong Americans are organized into 19 different clans. Membership is passed along through birth, and Hmong within the same clan are not allowed to marry ("The Secret War").

Early Hmong immigrants struggled to assimilate in American culture. Beyond bouts with racism, Hmong customs clashed with American culture and with U.S. laws. For example, in traditional Hmong culture, girls marry between the ages of 14 and 16, which conflicts with marriage laws in the United States. Second, extended Hmong families preferred to live in crowded households that often exceeded housing regulations. Last, language barriers put the entire Hmong family structure in flux. In Laos, the father was the most respected figure in the family. He made the decisions, and they were final. In America, elders relied on their children and grandchildren as translators. Translations between the youth and elders were not always correct, and household misunderstandings resulted (Fass 1).

Finding jobs proved particularly difficult for early Hmong immigrants. In 1990, almost two-thirds of Hmong Americans lived below the poverty line (Bankston). The Hmong's agrarian background meant the vast majority of immigrants could neither read nor write and had no experience with industrial jobs. Farming in the United States

Wadsworth 5

required large plots of land and expensive equipment, neither of which were affordable for Hmong immigrants. Further contributing to the Hmong's financial struggles were the large households. In 1990, Hmong households averaged 6.38 individuals compared to 3.73 in the average Asian American family, 3.48 in the average black family, and 3.06 in the average white American family (Bankston). Producing a small income for large households resulted in more than half of Hmong families relying on federal welfare programs to stay afloat (Her and Buley-Meissner 121).

As the economy improved in the late 1990s, so did Hmong employment. Census data reflects upward socioeconomic movement, though the Hmong's poverty rate is still among the highest in the country (Lai and Arguelles). Increasingly, Hmong adults, including women, have taken jobs outside of the home. Some Hmong have opened their own small businesses, and Hmong farmers have profited from the local farm-to-table food movement (Bankston). As more Hmong receive formal education, socioeconomic conditions are expected to improve.

In terms of education, 61 percent of Hmong Americans have graduated from high school, a number that is expected to rise as more American-born Hmong reach their teens. However, many Hmong struggle with the English language, and there are not enough bilingual Hmong teachers available (Vang 3). Language deficiency and poor socioeconomic conditions are the greatest barriers to academic achievement, and the Hmong Americans' academic advancement lags in comparison to that of the general public, especially at the post-secondary level (5).

Today, Hmong youth are more Americanized than the previous generation, which is a point of conflict between Hmong elders and youth. In fact, about 60 percent of the 260,073 Hmong living in the

The writer's discussion reaches the present day.

United States were born here. American-born Hmong are less bound by traditional Hmong customs than first-generation immigrants are ("Bridging the Shores"). But the elders, who endured bloodshed and poverty to make it to America, worry that the Hmong culture will soon be washed away. Addison Lee told Wisconsin Public Radio, "The gap between the youth and the elderly is broad, whether it is religion, weddings, or how you deal with certain issues" ("Bridging the Shores"). Young Hmong Americans are campaigning for women's rights and speaking out against domestic abuse, as well as rejecting some traditional customs such as teenage brides (Lai and Arguelles). Still, second-generation Hmong are not completely rejecting old traditions. The first-born daughter in a family is still responsible for taking care of the household when the mother is at work, marriage dowries are still commonplace, and Hmong Americans still celebrate Hmong holidays.

What the future holds for Hmong Americans is unknown. The Hmong are still one of the newest ethnic groups in America. While economic and educational opportunities are rising, workplace and academic achievements lag. Moving forward without diminishing their unique culture will remain a challenge. Hmong elders worry that Americanized youth will forget the sacrifices they made to preserve their culture in this country. Such sacrifices deserve to be commemorated by both Hmong and non-Hmong Americans, for thousands of Hmong gave up their lives to support the United States' fight against communism. The next chapter in the Hmong American experience is still unwritten, but the Hmong, as they always have, will write it together.

Wadsworth 7

Works Cited

Bankston III, Carl L. "Hmong Americans." *Countries and Their*

Cultures. 14 March 2012. Web.

"Bridging the Shores: The Hmong-American Experience." Wisconsin

Public Radio. WERN, Madison, 2008. Radio.

Fass, Simon M. "The Hmong in Wisconsin." *The Wisconsin Policy*

Research Institute Report 4.2 (1991): 1. Print.

George, William Lloyd, and Chiang Mai. "Hmong Refugees Live in Fear

in Laos and Thailand." *Time* 24 July 2010. Web.

Her, Vincent K., and Mary Louise Buley-Meissner. *Hmong and*

American: From Refugees to Citizens. Minneapolis: Minnesota

Historical Society Press, 2012. Print.

Lai, Eric, and Dennis Arguelles. *The New Face of Asian Pacific America:*

Numbers, Diversity, and Change in the 21st Century. Los Angeles:

UCLA Asian American Studies Center Press, 1998. Web.

"The Secret War." *The Hmong: An Introduction to Their History and*

Culture. The Cultural Orientation Project. 28 July 2004. 14 March

2012. Web.

"2010 Census Hmong Populations by State." Hmong American

Partnership 2010. 20 March 2012. Web.

Vang, Christopher T. "Hmong-American K-12 Students and the

Academic Skills Needed for a College Education: A Review of the

Existing Literature and Suggestions for Future Research." *Hmong*

Studies Journal 5 (2004): 1-31. Web.

Entries appear alphabetically, with runover lines indented.

Quotation marks surround titles of short works. Italics set off long works.

Designations such as "Print" and "Web" indicate the delivery method of sources.

Using Transitions

Transitions are useful in all types of writing. In paragraphs, transitions connect sentences and ideas. In longer writing, transitions can connect one paragraph to the next. Here are some effective transitions to use in your writing.

To Show Location

about	amid	beside	in front of	on top of
above	among	between	inside	outside
across	around	beyond	into	over
against	behind	by	near	throughout
along	below	from	now	to the right
alongside	beneath	in back of	next to	under

To Show Time

about	at	finally	next	tomorrow
after	before	first	meanwhile	to start
afterward	during	in the end	since	when
as soon as	every time	later	today	yesterday

To Compare

also	a type of	in kind	likewise	one way
analogously	as	in like manner	much as	similarly
another way	both	like	much like	so too

To Contrast

alternatively	by contrast	even though	on one hand	still
although	differently	however	on the other	though
but	despite	not	otherwise	yet

To Show Cause and Effect

a cause	at the start	consequently	in regard to	resultingly
accordingly	because	due to	on account of	therefore
after	by means of	finally	one solution	since
as a result	considering	from that	owing to	whenever

To Add Information

additionally	also	as well	for example	in addition
again	and	besides	for instance	moreover
along with	another	finally	furthermore	next

To Show Logical Connection

all in all	finally	for instance	in other words	therefore
as a result	for example	in conclusion	that is	to sum up

Chapter 30:

Data and Graphing Projects

Living in the information age, you have instant access to news, facts, and details of all kinds. At times, the flood of information can be overwhelming.

Fortunately, graphs can present a great deal of information in a form that makes it easy to understand and reference. Graphic tools can help you get your point across. With graphs, tables, time lines, and charts, you can distill the essential facts and data and present them in an accessible, concise form. This chapter discusses several of these tools and how to put them to good use.

You will learn . . .

- Creating Pie, Line, and Bar Graphs
- Creating Tables
- Creating Diagrams, Time Lines, and Flowcharts
- Creating Infographics
- Mining Data

Project Overview

Here is a quick overview of several ways to present information graphically.

A Pie Graph

A pie graph shows how a whole amount is split up into different segments. Each segment represents a specific part of the total. (See page 491.)

B Line Graph

A line graph shows changes in quantity over time. The horizontal axis measures time, and the vertical axis measures quantity. Multiple lines can be used to compare changes in different elements. (See page 492.)

C Bar Graph

A bar graph compares amounts. The horizontal axis measures time or groups, and the vertical axis measures quantities. Quantities of different items can be grouped for side-by-side comparison. (See page 493.)

D Table

A table arranges information in rows (horizontal) and columns (vertical) for quick comprehension. Often, subjects are listed down the left-hand side, and traits are listed across the top. (See page 495.)

E Diagram

A diagram illustrates an object and labels its parts. The diagram may be a photo, a painting, a drawing, or a cutaway, as shown here. (See page 497.)

F Time Line

A time line shows events in the order they occurred. (See page 498.)

G Flowchart

A flowchart outlines a process. Ovals indicate start and end points, diamonds show decision points, rectangles indicate steps, and arrows direct the flow. (See page 499.)

H Infographic

An infographic is a creative arrangement of graphic elements to communicate and dramatize information. Some online infographics include interactive elements and multimedia. (See page 501.)

I Data Mining

Data mining uses computer programs to analyze large bodies of information and identify predictive patterns. In a similar way, you can use spreadsheets and graphics to analyze the data you collect. (See page 505.)

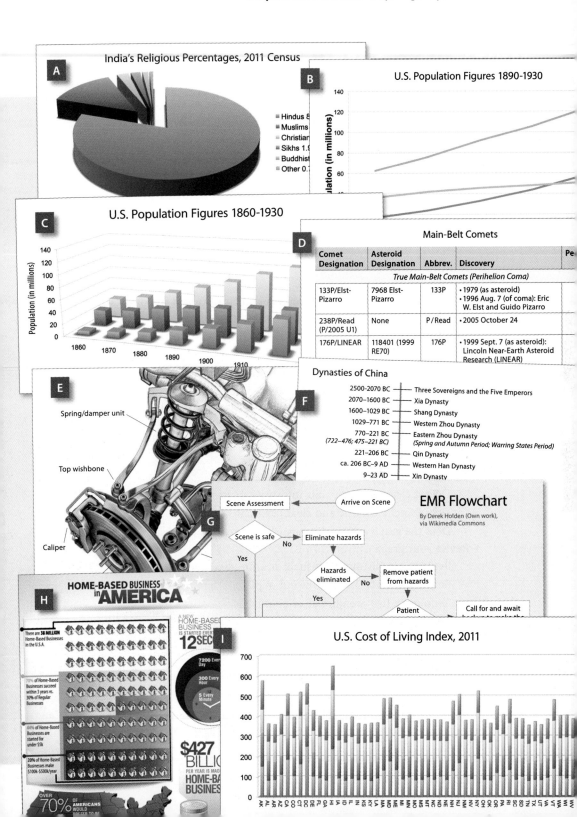

Inquire To Create a Pie, Line, or Bar Graph

1. **Question** the overall situation for the graph.
   - **Subject:** What information do I want to present?
   - **Purpose:** Why am I creating the graph? To show parts of a whole (pie graph)? To show changes over time (line graph)? To compare amounts (bar graph)?
   - **Audience:** Who will read the graph? What do they need to know?

2. **Plan** your graph, deciding whether you will use a spreadsheet or word-processing program or will create your pie graph, line graph, or bar graph by hand. Gather supplies (graph paper, ruler, compass, protractor) if you are creating a handmade graph.

3. **Research** your topic.
   - **Gather** data and information from experiments, surveys, reports, tables.
   - **Consider** mining data from public sites online (see pages 504–506).
   - **Organize** the information for your graph.

4. **Create** your graph.
   - **Pie graphs** show the parts of a whole. See page 491 for tips on creating pie graphs.
   - **Line graphs** show changes over time. See page 492 for tips on creating line graphs.
   - **Bar graphs** compare amounts. See page 493 for tips on creating bar graphs.

5. **Improve** your graph.
   - **Evaluate** your graph.
     - Does it clearly present your information? Is it accurate? Is it attractive?
     - Does it include a title and clear labeling?
     - Does the graph achieve its purpose? Do readers understand it?
   - **Revise** your graph.
     - **Remove** any distracting visuals or unnecessary words.
     - **Rearrange** parts that may be out of place.
     - **Redo** parts that are unclear or confusing.
     - **Add** any missing information or labels.
   - **Perfect** your graph, making it clean and correct.
     - **Use ink** to draw the lines in a handmade graph.
     - **Color** the parts effectively or shade them with appropriate black-and-white techniques.

6. **Present** your graph online, in a report, or during a presentation. (Go to thoughtfullearning.com/h490 for more help creating graphs.)

Example Pie Graph

The following pie graph displays the percentages of the population claiming affiliation with various religious faiths in India. This "exploded" pie graph shows segments separated for easier reading.

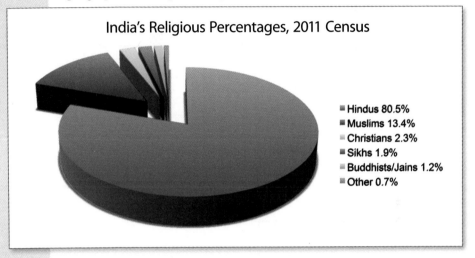

India's Religious Percentages, 2011 Census

- Hindus 80.5%
- Muslims 13.4%
- Christians 2.3%
- Sikhs 1.9%
- Buddhists/Jains 1.2%
- Other 0.7%

Tips for Pie Graphs

Use a pie chart to show the parts that together make up a whole.
- **Include no more than six sections.** The impact is lost if the graph contains too many pieces. Combine smaller amounts in "other."
- **Start at the twelve o'clock position** with the largest section and move clockwise in order of descending size.
- **Label each section,** either within the slice itself (if possible) or in a key to the side (as in the example above). Include percentages or other values as a frame of reference for the viewer.
- **Use a spreadsheet or word processing program** to create your chart. Enter the values for each pie section into the proper cells; then select a pie-chart display from the software's menu.

Drawing Pie Graphs by Hand

To draw a pie graph by hand, use the equation below to calculate the degrees for each section, then use a protractor to plot those angles.
1. Portion ÷ Whole × 100 = Percentage
2. Percentage × 3.6 = Degrees

Example:
1. 828,000,000 (Hindus) ÷ 1,029,000,000 (total population) × 100 = 80.5 percent
2. 80.5 × 3.6 = 290 degrees

Example Line Graph

The following line graph records four U.S. population trends from the years 1890 to 1930. Each line tracks changes for a particular segment of the population. A legend beneath the graph explains the use of colors.

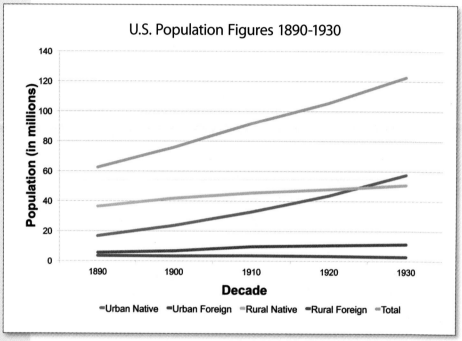

Source: United States Census Bureau

Tips for Line Graphs

Create a line graph to track changes in quantity over time. Either draw your graph by hand or use spreadsheet or word-processing software.

- **Plot time horizontally.** Mark units of time on the *x* axis (horizontal). This axis also often tracks the independent variable.
- **Plot quantity vertically.** Mark units of quantity on the *y* axis (vertical). This axis also often tracks the dependent variable.
- **Label the axes** for clarity. When possible, position words and numbers horizontally for easy reading.
- **Mark a dot** for each data point (where quantity and time intersect).
- **Draw lines** to connect the dots for each category being tracked.
- **Create a legend** if your graph includes more than one line.
- **Identify the various lines** with different colors or patterns.
- **Give the graph a clear title** that includes key terms so that the viewer can grasp its purpose.

Example Bar Graphs

These bar graphs allow readers to quickly compare population figures.

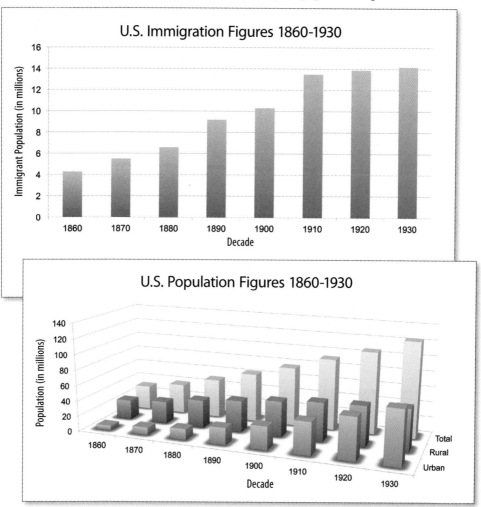

Tips for Bar Graphs

Use a bar graph to compare quantities. Either draw your graph by hand or use spreadsheet or word-processing software.

- **Mark points of time or other categories** on the x axis (horizontal).
- **Mark quantity units** on the y axis (vertical).
- **Give the graph a title and label the axes** for clarity.
- **Present your data accurately.** Don't exaggerate or minimize differences.
- **Create bars consistent in all measurements** except for height.
- **Use color or patterns** to distinguish categories.
- **Use a legend** to identify any categories displayed.

Inquire | To Create a Table

1. **Question** the overall situation for the table.
   - **Subject:** What topic am I dealing with? Which examples, traits, or other data do I want to share?
   - **Purpose:** Why am I creating the table? How will it be used?
   - **Audience:** Who will read the table? What information is most important to them? How should I arrange the information for ease of use?

2. **Plan** your table, exploring the table-making features of your spreadsheet or word-processing program.
   - **Decide** what data you need to find.
   - **Think** about what subjects you will place in rows and what traits you will place in columns.
   - **Plan** to place one type of data in each cell.
   - **Use** numerical data in cells that need to be involved in calculation.

3. **Research** your topic.
   - **Gather** the data that you will present in a table.
   - **Consider** mining data from public Web sites (see pages 504–506).
   - **Organize** your information according to subjects/examples and traits.

4. **Create** your table. (See also "Tips for Tables" on page 495.)
   - **Choose** the number of traits you'll deal with and list these across the top of the table.
   - **Choose** the subjects/examples you'll examine and list these down the left-hand side.
   - **Fill in the cells** of the table with data about each subject/example.
   - **Provide** a title that clearly identifies the table's content.

5. **Improve** your table.
   - **Evaluate** the table.

     Is each column and each row clearly labeled? Is the information in each cell accurate? Does the table include units of measure as needed?
   - **Revise** your table.

     Remove any nonessential information.

     Rearrange columns or rows if this will make the information clearer or more accessible.

     Redo any part of the table that is unclear or confusing.

     Add missing information as needed.
   - **Perfect** your table, making it clean, clear, and accurate.

6. **Present** your table online, in a report, or during a presentation.

Example Table

The following table displays information about "Main-Belt Comets," icy bodies whose orbits lie within our solar system's asteroid belt.

Main-Belt Comets

Comet Designation	Asteroid Designation	Abbrev.	Discovery	Perihelion (AU)
True Main-Belt Comets (Perihelion Coma)				
133P/Elst-Pizarro	7968 Elst-Pizarro	133P	• 1979 (as asteroid) • 1996 Aug. 7 (of coma): Eric W. Elst and Guido Pizarro	2.64
238P/Read (P/2005 U1)	None	P/Read	• 2005 October 24	2.36
176P/LINEAR	118401 (1999 RE70)	176P	• 1999 Sept. 7 (as asteroid): Lincoln Near-Earth Asteroid Research (LINEAR) • 2005 Nov. 26 (of coma): Henry Hsieh and David Jewitt	2.57
P/2008 R1 (Garradd)	None	P/ Garradd	• 2008 Sept. 24: G. J. Garradd, Siding Spring Survey	1.79
P/2010 R2 (La Sagra)	None	P/La Sagra	• 2010 Sept. 14	2.62
P/2006 VW139	300163 (2006 VW139)		• 2006 Nov. 15: Spacewatch at Kitt Peak	2.44
Disrupted Asteroids (Impact Coma)				
P/2010 A2 (LINEAR)	None		• 2010 Jan. 6: Lincoln Near-Earth Asteroid Research (LINEAR)	2.00
None	596 Scheila		• 1906 Feb. 21 (as asteroid): August Kopff, Heidelberg • 2010 Dec. 11 (of coma): Steve Larson, Catalina Sky Survey	2.44

Tips for Tables

Use a table to compare lists of data or other information.

- **List subjects in rows and traits in columns.**
- **Fill in the cells.** Reading across a row provides details about a specific subject; reading down a column compares details about a given trait for each of the subjects.
- **Provide units of measure** at the top of the column.
- **Give the table a title** that clearly identifies the topic. If necessary, add subtitles to separate sections, as in the example table above.

 **To Create a Diagram, Time Line, or Flowchart**

1. **Question** the overall situation for the graphic.
   - **Subject:** What is the topic of the graphic? What information am I trying to convey?
   - **Purpose:** Why am I creating the graphic? To show the parts of something (diagram)? To show a sequence of events (time line)? To show the steps in a process (flowchart)?
   - **Audience:** Who will read the graphic? What information do they need?

2. **Plan** your graphic, deciding whether you will use software or will create your diagram, time line, or flowchart by hand. (Go to thoughtfullearning.com/h496 for assistance.)

3. **Research** your topic.
   - **Consult** resources to gather the information you will need.
   - **List** the parts of the object, the steps of the process, or the events in the time line.

4. **Create** your graphic.
   - **Diagrams** illustrate an object and label its parts. Find or create a picture of the object you want to explain and label the important parts. Include a title. See "Tips for Diagrams" on page 497.
   - **Time lines** list a sequence of events in the order they occurred. See "Tips for Time Lines" on page 498.
   - **Flowcharts** show the steps in a process. Use ovals for start and end points, diamonds for decision points, rectangles for steps, and arrows to connect them in the right order. See "Tips for Flowcharts" on page 499.

5. **Improve** your graphic.
   - **Evaluate** the graphic.
     Does it achieve its purpose by presenting the topic clearly? Is it accurate and attractive? Does it include an informative title and clear labels? Do readers understand it?
   - **Revise** your graphic.
     Remove any parts that are off the topic or unnecessary.
     Rearrange parts that are out of order.
     Redo parts that are confusing.
     Add any missing information.
   - **Perfect** your graphic, making it clean and correct.

6. **Present** your graphic in the best context—online, in a report, or during a presentation.

Example Diagram

The following diagram shows the parts of a brake and suspension assembly. Words and images combine to present information.

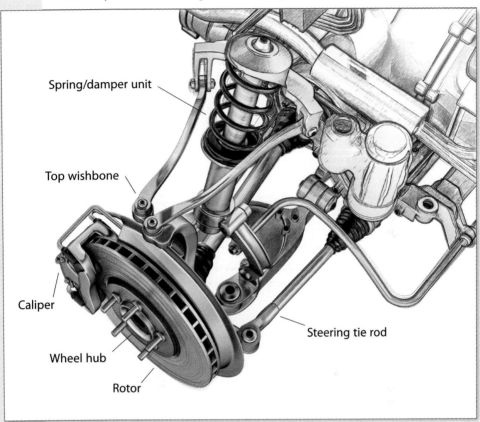

Spring/damper unit

Top wishbone

Caliper

Wheel hub

Rotor

Steering tie rod

Tips for Diagrams

Use a diagram to illustrate an object and label its parts. Diagrams are especially useful for explaining complex or unfamiliar subjects.

- **Choose the best type of image** for your subject: a simple illustration, a cutaway view (shown above), an "exploded view" (in which parts are pulled away from one another to be seen individually), or a photograph.
- **Draw, photograph, or find the image** you want to present. (Remember to respect intellectual property and copyright laws. See page 267.)
- **Clearly label the parts of the object,** using pointer lines where helpful.
- **Provide a descriptive title** for the diagram.

Example Time Line

The following time line traces China's major ruling families/groups.

Dynasties of China

2500–2070 BC	Three Sovereigns and the Five Emperors
2070–1600 BC	Xia Dynasty
1600–1029 BC	Shang Dynasty
1029–771 BC	Western Zhou Dynasty
770–221 BC (722–476; 475–221 BC)	Eastern Zhou Dynasty (Spring and Autumn Period; Warring States Period)
221–206 BC	Qin Dynasty
ca. 206 BC–9 AD	Western Han Dynasty
9–23 AD	Xin Dynasty
23–25 AD	Western Han Dynasty
25–220 AD	Eastern Han Dynasty
220–265 or 280 AD	Three Kingdoms
265–317 AD	Western Jin Dynasty
317–420 AD	Eastern Jin Dynasty
386 or 420–589 AD	Southern and Northern Dynasties
589–618 AD	Sui Dynasty
618–907 AD	Tang Dynasty
907–960 AD	Five Dynasties and Ten Kingdoms
960–1127 AD	Northern Song Dynasty
1127–1279 AD	Southern Song Dynasty
907 or 916–1125 AD	Liao Dynasty
1115–1234 AD	Jin Dynasty
1038–1227 AD	Western Xia
1271–1368 AD	Yuan Dynasty
1368–1644 or 1662 AD	Ming Dynasty
1636 or 1644–1911 AD	Qing Dynasty
1912–1949 AD	Republic of China
1949 AD–Present	People's Republic of China; Republic of China, Taiwan

Tips for Time Lines

Use a time line to list a sequence of events.

- **Choose the right scale**—hour by hour, day by day, and so on.
- **Size your project** so that it fits easily on one page or screen.
- **Record your data.** List significant events in correct order by date/time.
- **Give the time line a title** so viewers perceive the subject quickly.

Example Flowchart

This flowchart shows how emergency medical responders make decisions at the scene of an accident.

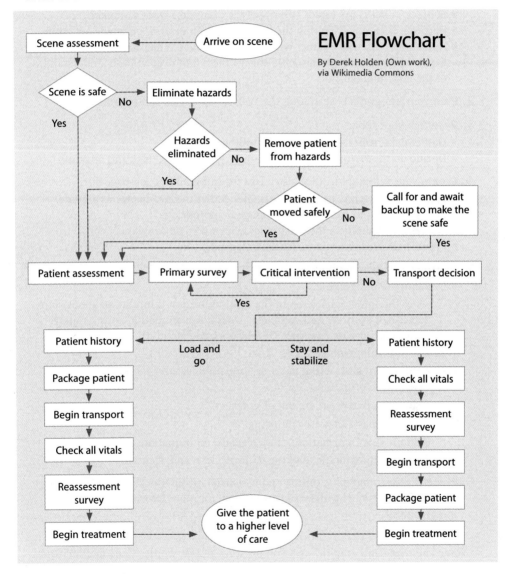

Tips for Flowcharts

Use a flowchart to outline a process.
- **Use ovals** to indicate the start and end points.
- **Use diamonds** to indicate decision points.
- **Use rectangles** to indicate steps in the process.
- **Use arrows** to connect the steps in order. Label the arrows where needed.

Inquire | To Create an Infographic

1. **Question** the overall situation for the infographic.
   - **Subject:** What is my topic? What specific point do I want to make?
   - **Purpose:** Why am I creating the infographic? To inform, persuade, or both?
   - **Audience:** Who will interact with the infographic? What does this audience expect? How can my infographic engage them and deepen their understanding of the information?

2. **Plan** your infographic, searching the Web for examples and options.

3. **Research** your topic.
   - **Gather** data from reliable print and online sources.
   - **Decide** on the format you will use—map, graph, table, diagram, or other.

4. **Create** your infographic. (See also "Tips for Infographics" on page 501.)
   - **Prepare** the graphic, using the examples earlier in this chapter as a guide.
   - **Add** animation to convey your message if appropriate.
   - **Give** the infographic a title that quickly identifies its contents.
   - **Provide** any necessary keys, labels, or legends.

5. **Improve** your infographic.
   - **Evaluate** the infographic.

     Does the infographic present the most important information about your topic? Is it accurate and complete? Does it use animation appropriately? Does it achieve its purpose? Do readers understand it?
   - **Revise** your infographic.

     Remove any distracting parts or animation features that do not provide essential information.

     Rearrange parts that are out of order.

     Redo any parts that are confusing.

     Add missing information, titles, legends, or animations.
   - **Perfect** your infographic, making it clean, clear, and accurate.

6. **Present** your infographic online and use social media (see chapter 17) to attract readers. (Go to thoughtfullearning.com/h500 for more information about infographics.)

Note: The term "infographic" is a combination of two words: "information" and "graphic." Technically, every graphic discussed in this chapter is an infographic, but the term most commonly refers to a graphic display that communicates in a dramatic or unusual way. Many infographics are designed like posters—positioning charts, graphs, time lines, and illustrations in revealing arrangements. Some online infographics also include animation or interactive features. In each case, the purpose is to communicate a body of data quickly and effectively.

Example Infographic

The following infographic focuses on the growth of home-based businesses in the United States.

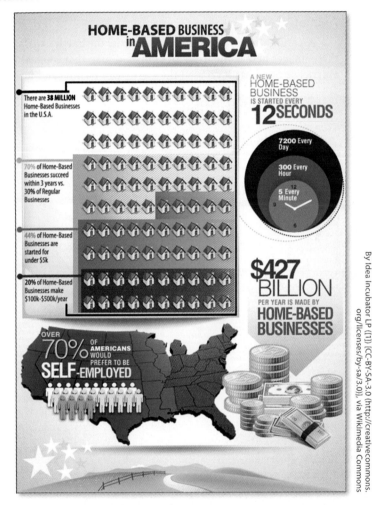

Tips for Infographics

Use infographics to convey information succinctly and dramatically.

- **Gather your data** and analyze its implications.
- **Consider the purpose** of your graphic. Are you comparing data? Illustrating changes? Dramatizing related facts?
- **Choose or create** a graphic approach that achieves your purpose.
- **Arrange your data** for special effect.
- **Provide a title** that attracts attention and reveals the topic.
- **Use subheadings, lines, and graphic devices** to connect ideas.

Additional Example Infographics

This page and the next provide several other examples of infographics. New types are being invented daily.

Animated Map

An animated map shows changes across the Earth's surface over time. The three images here come from an animated map that tracked the movement of Hurricane Sandy as it crossed the Caribbean Islands and headed for the U.S.

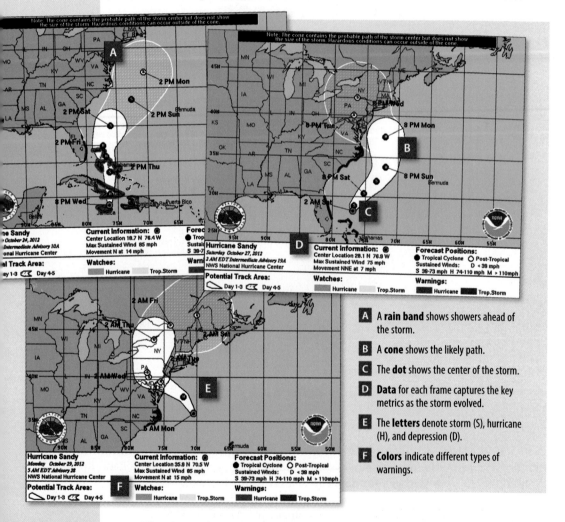

A A **rain band** shows showers ahead of the storm.

B A **cone** shows the likely path.

C The **dot** shows the center of the storm.

D **Data** for each frame captures the key metrics as the storm evolved.

E The **letters** denote storm (S), hurricane (H), and depression (D).

F **Colors** indicate different types of warnings.

The National Oceanographic and Atmospheric Administration (NOAA), like most federal agencies, provides images like this for public use. Check the use clause on a given agency's Web site to make sure that you can use images from that agency. (Check out www.noaa.gov.)

Illustrated Graphs

Illustrated graphs use symbols to quickly communicate abstract concepts. In the graphic below, the housing bubble of 2006 is demonstrated using house icons and bubbles to represent median home prices.

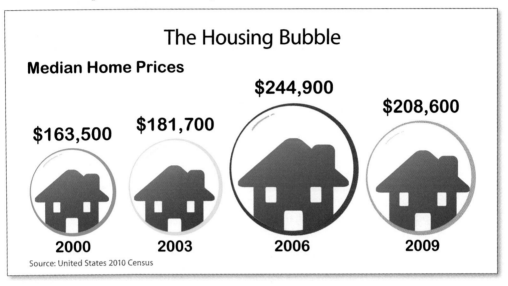

Word Clouds

A word cloud is a cluster of terms used frequently in a piece of writing. The size of each term reveals how often it is used in the writing, indicating its importance. Word clouds are often found on blogs, where they quickly tell what that blog is about.

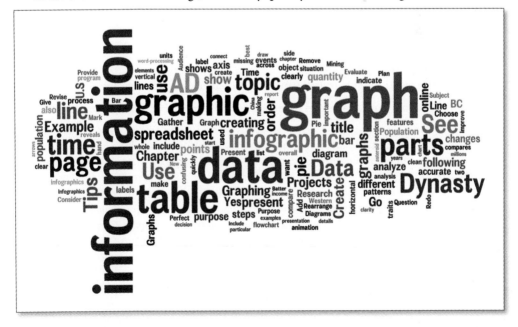

Inquire To Mine Data

1. **Question** the overall situation for data mining.
   - **Subject:** What topics am I dealing with? What traits or quantities do I want to analyze? Where can I find data to gather about this topic?
   - **Purpose:** Why am I analyzing the topic? Which data is most important?
   - **Audience:** Who besides me could benefit from this data analysis? What do they need to know?

2. **Plan** your approach, using the table-making features of your spreadsheet or word-processing program. (Go to thoughtfullearning.com/h504 for assistance.)

3. **Research** your topic.
   - **Gather** information about the topic from reliable sources.
   - **Use** analytics built into your own Web applications to find and graph data.
   - **Organize** your collected data in a table or spreadsheet.

4. **Create** your graphic or graphics. (See also "Tips for Data Mining" on page 506.)
   - **Choose** the data you will analyze.
   - **Insert** that data into a spreadsheet or table.
   - **Select** the best graphic (pie chart, bar graph, line graph, and so on) from your spreadsheet or the best arrangement for your table.
   - **Include** any necessary labels and keys.

5. **Improve** your understanding.
   - **Evaluate** the data you've presented.
     What patterns can you see? Do they accurately predict results from other data?
   - **Revise** your graphic or table.
     Remove nonessential information.
     Rearrange elements that are out of order.
     Redo any part that is unclear or confusing.
     Add missing information.
   - **Perfect** your graphic or table, making it clean, clear, and accurate.

6. **Present** your data analysis to others online, in a report, or during a presentation.

Note: Graphs and tables are often used to present information, but they can also be used to *gather and analyze* information—a simple type of "data mining." True data mining employs computer programs to analyze patterns in large databases. For example, a spam blocker searches for similarities between spam emails in order to filter new spam messages; an online shop analyzes customer purchases in order to suggest other products based on what you've put in your shopping cart. You can use data-mining techniques to deepen your understanding of a topic by gathering information into a spreadsheet or table, creating graphics that present the data, and analyzing the results.

Data-Mining Example

In the example below, a student reports information gleaned from mining data from a number of reports released by the United States Bureau of Labor Statistics. The information appears both in text and graphic form.

In D.C., Life Ain't Cheap

The **beginning** captures the reader's attention with an interesting title and a catchy opening.

It should come as no surprise that it takes a lot more money to get by in Washington, D.C., than in small-town America. Economists measure this difference by tracking a number of statistics, for example, the consumer price index, the cost of housing (renting or buying), the cost of groceries, and access to other necessities of life.

The **middle** provides data both in words and in images.

The following graph presents a cost-of-living index for each of four basic expenses. Note that, in some places such as California, New York, and the District of Columbia, housing costs far exceed those in other places, while other costs may be the same or slightly lower. For example, though a typical apartment in New York City is astronomically expensive, a typical restaurant meal isn't. It's one reason wait staff have a tough time living off low wages and tips. In Michigan, though, the same server would be able to afford better lodgings. . . .

This stacked bar graph emphasizes the overall cost of living in each location.

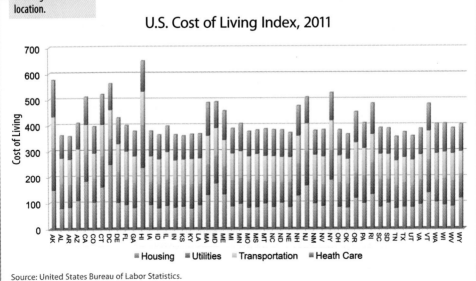

U.S. Cost of Living Index, 2011

Source: United States Bureau of Labor Statistics.

Features Table

Another data-mining technique uses a features table, which allows a side-by-side analysis of details for two or more subjects. In the following table, a high school student compares three possible career-training paths.

Emergency Medical Training Possibilities

	Junior College	College	Army
Degree	Emergency Medical Technician	BA Emergency Medical Technology	68W - Health Care Specialist (Combat Medic)
Training Length	4.5 months	62 course hours (about 4 to 5 semesters)	16 weeks (8 years duty, min. 2 years active)
Education Cost	$4,500	$14,500	None
Annual Salary After Degree	$27,000-$30,000	$34,000-$39,000	$33,500 in Army; per EMT as civilian
Entry Requirements	• 18 years of age • High school diploma or GED • Current CPR card or equivalent • C or better in English 101 • State police criminal background check	• State residency • Proficiency in English and math • Additional screening for limited-enrollment degree	• Age 18-35 • Citizenship or Green Card • Fewer than two dependents; not a single parent • Good credit • High school diploma • No criminal history • Meet height and weight standards

Tips for Data Mining

Use data-mining techniques to analyze data and search for patterns.

- **Gather your data.**
- **Consider your purpose.** What questions are you hoping to answer? What other questions are suggested by the data you have gathered?
- **Create a spreadsheet** or table that accommodates your data.
- **Arrange your data clearly.** Try different organizations and graphics.
- **Look for patterns.** What does the data suggest?
- **Test your patterns** by applying them to new data sets.
- **Write an analysis** of your graphic, explaining what it reveals.
- **Give your graphic a title** that reveals its scope and purpose.
- **Use subtitles and keys** to clarify parts.

Chapter 31
Audio-Visual Projects

To realize the massive appeal of video, look no further than YouTube. Millions of people visit that video-sharing site daily to watch one or more of its four billion user-generated videos. So move over, Hollywood. Your studios no longer control video production and distribution. Today, many of us can find the tools to create and distribute audio and visual projects of our own to a wide audience.

The projects in this chapter generate plenty of excitement. They mix technology with creative ideas. Use them as an outlet to entertain, to share knowledge, and to learn.

You will learn . . .

- Creating Podcasts
- Creating Slide Shows
- Creating a Pecha Kucha Presentation
- Creating Documentaries
- Creating Public Service Announcement Videos
- Creating How-To Videos
- A Basic Guide to Video Editing

Project Overview

Here is a quick overview of the projects in this chapter. Go to thoughtfullearning.com/h508 for additional help with your audio-visual projects.

A Podcast

A podcast is an audio or audio-video feature made available on the Internet. Podcasts can cover any topic and most commonly share an interview, present information, or provide entertainment. (See pages 510–511.)

B Slide Show

A slide show uses words and images to communicate information. Some slide shows accompany a speech or an oral presentation, while others include a sound track and can stand alone. (See pages 512–513.)

C Pecha Kucha Presentation

A Pecha Kucha is a special type of oral presentation and slide show. It lasts for 6 minutes and 40 seconds and includes 20 different slides, each of which is shown for exactly 20 seconds. (See pages 514–517.)

D Documentary

A documentary film focuses on an important nonfiction slice of reality. It educates and informs viewers on a relevant and interesting topic and often combines raw footage with interviews. (See pages 518–519.)

E Public Service Announcement

A public service announcement (PSA) encourages or persuades people to do something that will help them or their community. Although it is presented like a commercial, a PSA's purpose is to help others rather than to sell something. (See pages 520–521.)

F How-To Video

A how-to video demonstrates how to do or make something. As with the other video projects in this chapter, creating a how-to video is a process that involves scriptwriting, directing, storyboarding, acting, filming, and editing. (See pages 522–526.)

A

Two Guys in a Lab: Episode 28, Week 32

Krunal: Hey, everyone. Gill and I are back for another episode
Guys in a Lab. Have you ever wondered how shows on the Anima
Planet get all that amazing footage of life deep within the ocean?
guest today brings a unique perspective on the topic. Everett Red
is a mar   biologist and deep-sea cameraman and is here to tell
about his exper   ces under the sea. Mr. Redman, thanks for joi
us!

Mr. Redman: Glad to   here with you guys.

          d I w   talking about this last night . . . you've
          oles   jobs out there. Tell us how you became

          ays been fascinated by oceans and mari
          gy in college, and after I graduated I wa
          ortunity to help one of my professors film

B

Grow**ing** U**p**

How Urban Agriculture Is Changing
the Way Cities Feed Themselves

By: James Engelmann

■   year-round crop production
■ Offers new employment opportunities

2050
World population = 9.8 billi
70-80%

C

Thinking like a Social Entrepreneur

(Slide 1) My name is Kelly Dwyer, and I ate a
child. When I was eight, I used the leftover stic
for my dolls. It had a roof, a chimney, and win
Then I had an epiphany. My neighborhood didn't
park nearby, so I planned to collect everyone's Po
a huge playhouse for all the neighborhood kids to

Of course, I soon realized this plan was ridi
so sure. It was a logistical nightmare, yes, but my
on. I   olve a big neighborhood problem
I   ll should begin thinking like so
(Slide   urship is the process of
soci   em and   m-solving skills a
se   make the problem
          drew Youn thought big   Acr
          ld solve poverty and hun
b at a Fortune 5   velo
     er F   rs. (Sl   he One

D

Concussions in High School w

EXT: WILDCAT FOOTBALL FIELD—EARLY MORNING

The camera pans the vacant football field, cuts to B-roll footage of a
collision of helmets and pads, and returns to vacant field for narration.

> **NARRATOR:** If baseball is America's pastime, football is
> America's passion. The game's popularity has reached new heights
> across all levels of competition—from professional down to high
> school and Pop Warner. It's a fast, powerful, and hard-hitting
> sport. The gladiatorial hits entice viewers but also may be
> undoing. Concussions and brain trauma associated wi
> have taken on public scrutiny. In light of new dama
> what precautions, if any, are high schools takin
> players from concussions?

B-roll footage shows the outside of Darlington Sou

         arlington South, football
         von the district champio   aso
         championships i   10   n st
     d, however, Darl

E

Talk to Your Parents About Organ Donation

EXT: LAKE--AFTERNOON

A teenage girl sits on a pier next to her father, wh
reel. Their legs dangle in the water.

Girl 1

Hey, Dad. I've been thinking about something I h
It's about organ donation.

CUT TO: INT: KITCHEN

                   a slice of pizza. His mom
into a pot.

Boy 1

          Americans out there wait

** BORHOOD**

          ng a sidewalk with her m

Girl 2

     g will ever happen to me, b

** : LAKE**

F

How to Calculate a Monthly Car Payment

INT: CLASSROOM: The narrator stands in front of a whiteboard that
displays a picture of a sports car drawn with a blue dry-erase marker.

> **NARRATOR:** If you're like me, you have a dream car you hope to
> own one day. You may be curious to know how much a loan for
> that car would cost per month, or you may just want to find a car
> and a payment plan that fits your monthly budget.

She erases the drawing of the car.

> Today, I'm going to show you how to calculate m
> payments before you ever walk into a dealershi
> need a basic scientific calculator and a knowle
> and order of operations. Because most of us ca
> front, we usually have to take out a car loan, w
> it off in monthly installments.

She writes this equation on the board: $P(r/12)/($

> Here is the equation we'll be working with.
> the monthly price of any car payment as lo
> three variables; P, the price of the car; r, th

Inquire To Create a Podcast (Audio)

1. Question the communication situation.
- **Subject:** What will the podcast be about?
- **Purpose:** Is the subject meant to entertain, inform, persuade, or narrate?
- **Audience:** Who should listen to your podcast? What audience does it target?

2. Plan your podcast on a planning sheet.
- **Tools:** Find podcast-supporting software and equipment as well as Web sites that will post it. Then practice using the software.
- **Team:** Who will be involved in recording your podcast? You may need scriptwriters, audio engineers, and on-air personalities.

3. Research your topic and technical requirements.
- **Topic:** Learn as much as you can about the subject before you begin recording. If you are interviewing a guest, research about him or her.
- **Equipment:** Practice with the equipment so that you know how to use it.

4. Create your podcast using one of these approaches.
- **Scripted:** Create a script with beginning, middle, and ending parts. Then record it, and rerecord as needed.
- **Mixed:** Script some parts (opening, interview questions, main points, closing) but allow on-air personalities to improvise the rest. Repeat takes and edit the dialogue as needed.
- **Improvised:** Let the on-air personalities improvise dialogue as if they were having a real conversation. This approach may involve heavy editing.

5. Improve the rough cut.
- **Evaluate** the podcast against your goal and situation.
    Goal: Did you meet it? How could you improve your work?
    Situation: Did you cover the subject? Did you achieve your purpose? Are you reaching your audience?
- **Revise** your podcast as necessary.
    Cut parts that do not help you reach your goal.
    Reorder parts to create a better flow.
    Rerecord weak parts.
    Add new commentary to fill gaps.
- **Perfect** the podcast to meet the best possible audio standards.

6. Present the podcast by uploading it online.

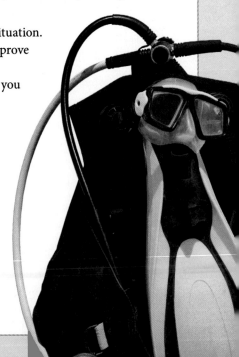

Podcast

Here is the first page of a transcript from two students' weekly podcast called Two Guys in a Lab. In this episode, the students interview an ocean videographer.

Two Guys in a Lab: Episode 28, Week 32

The **beginning** identifies the podcasters, the topic, and the interviewee.

Krunal: Hey, everyone. Gill and I are back for another episode of Two Guys in a Lab. Have you ever wondered how the shows on Animal Planet get all that amazing footage of life deep within the ocean? Our guest today brings a unique perspective on the topic. Everett Redman is a marine biologist and deep-sea cameraman and is here to tell us about his experiences under the sea. Mr. Redman, thanks for joining us!

Mr. Redman: Glad to be here with you guys.

Gill: So Krunal and I were talking about this last night . . . you've got to have one of the coolest jobs out there. Tell us how you became an underwater cameraman.

The **middle** includes a series of questions and answers between the podcasters and the interviewee.

Mr. Redman: Well, I've always been fascinated by oceans and marine life. I studied marine biology in college, and after I graduated I was given this incredible opportunity to help one of my professors film green sea turtles for her project. I fell in love with underwater filming and pursued it as a career.

Krunal: Awesome. I imagine it took some time to get the hang of filming underwater. Obviously, you're not exactly on stable ground.

Mr. Redman: You could say that. (*laughs*) The camera work definitely took some getting used to. You have to have steady hands and the ability to adjust to changing currents and water surges. If you expect to get good shots underwater, you have to be comfortable diving in a variety of environments; otherwise, you won't be able to concentrate on important cinematography aspects like composition and focus.

The **ending** (not included) thanks the interviewee and gives details about the next scheduled podcast.

Gill: Does your background in marine biology help with the job?

Mr. Redman: I think it helps tremendously. Understanding different types of marine life helps me anticipate behavior. . . .

Inquire To Create a Slide Show

1. **Question** the communication situation.
   - **Subject:** What is the topic of your slide show? What is the specific focus?
   - **Purpose:** Are you trying to inform, persuade, or narrate?
   - **Audience:** Who will see your slide show? Will it stand on its own, or will you present it in person?

2. **Plan** your slide show on a planning sheet. (See page 361.)

3. **Research** your topic and technical requirements.
   - **Write** research questions about your topic.
   - **Conduct** the necessary research, taking notes and tracking sources.
   - **Gather** pictures, images, or graphics related to your topic.
   - **Organize** the information in a reasonable way (see the informational structures on pages 408–412).
   - **Review** the features of various slide-show programs.

4. **Create** your slide show, using software such as the PowerPoint program.
   - **Beginning:** Provide an opening slide with the title of the presentation, your name, and an engaging visual. Use the next few slides to introduce the topic and offer a thesis.
   - **Middle:** Use your middle slides to support your thesis. Make use of numbered and bulleted lists. If possible, use visual aids to accompany your supporting evidence.
   - **Ending:** Sum up your topic on the final slide by leaving the reader with a strong closing point. If your slide show is meant to persuade, include a call to action.

5. **Improve** your slide show.
   - **Evaluate** your slide show against your goal and situation.
     - **Goal:** Did you meet your goal?
     - **Situation:** Did you thoroughly cover your subject? Did you fulfill your purpose? How will the audience respond?
   - **Revise** your slide show as necessary.
     - **Cut** slides that do not move you toward your goal.
     - **Reorder** slides for a better flow.
     - **Redo** slides that are overcrowded or ineffective.
     - **Add** slides to improve support.
   - **Perfect** your slide show, polishing and proofreading it.
     - **Check** grammar, usage, punctuation, and spelling (see pages 191–196).
     - **Practice** delivering your presentation.

6. **Present** your slide show in person or on the Web.

Slide Show

Here are some slides from a presentation about the urban agriculture movement. Note how the student balances text and visuals to get the point across.

The **beginning** slide includes the title, the student's name, and an image.

Grow**ing Up**

How Urban Agriculture Is Changing
the Way Cities Feed Themselves

By James Engelmann

This **middle** slide uses a bulleted list to offer supporting evidence.

Advantages of
Vertical Farming

- Creates sustainable environments for urban centers
- Reduces fossil fuel use
- Yields year-round crop production
- Offers new employment opportunities

The **ending** slide makes a strong concluding point.

Feeding Tomorrow

2012
World population = 6.8 billion
51% of people live in urban areas

2050
World population = 9.8 billion
70-80% of people will live in urban areas

 Inquire To Create a Pecha Kucha Presentation

1. **Question** the situation. A Pecha Kucha is specific presentation format involving an oral speech and a slide show. The slide show must include 20 slides shown for 20 seconds each. The special challenge is synchronizing the two components.
   - **Subject:** What is your topic and focus? Pecha Kucha presentations often share stories, tell about lessons learned, or present creative projects. Choose a topic you truly care about.
   - **Purpose:** What is your purpose? To entertain, to inform, to persuade?
   - **Audience:** How can you engage your audience?

2. **Plan** your slide show on a planning sheet. (See page 361.)

3. **Research** your topic and the format requirements.
   - **Learn** the rules of Pecha Kucha:
     - Each presentation is exactly 6 minutes and 40 seconds long.
     - The slide show must include 20 slides.
     - Each slide is displayed for exactly 20 seconds.
   - **Study** examples of other Pecha Kucha presentations.
   - **Read** about your topic, taking notes and tracking sources.
   - **Outline** the sequence of your oral presentation.
   - **Find** engaging images and quality graphics for your slide show.

4. **Create** your slide show and oral presentation. (See page 425.)
   - **Beginning:** Provide an engaging opening slide, including an image, the title of the presentation, and your name. Large images are preferable to small images.
   - **Middle:** Create middle slides that tell your story or support your thesis through images and graphics. Limit text to main points and labels.
   - **Ending:** Use your last slide to sum up your presentation and leave the audience with a strong final thought.

5. **Improve** your Pecha Kucha.
   - **Evaluate** your presentation after practicing it three or four times. Does the timing work? Do the slides enhance the oral part of the presentation, and vice versa? Do you display true interest in topic? Does the presentation achieve its purpose? Will it engage your audience?
   - **Revise** your presentation. Rework weak parts; remove unnecessary parts. Add stories, quotations, or other support as needed.
   - **Perfect** the slides and oral component of your presentation, making sure both are clear and correct.

6. **Present** your Pecha Kucha. (See more tips on page 517.)

Pecha Kucha Script

The following is a portion of the script for a Pecha Kucha presentation prepared by a student for her economics class. The next page displays some of the slides that accompany the presentation.

Thinking Like a Social Entrepreneur

The **beginning** introduces the speaker and engages the audience with a unique story that leads them to the thesis.

(Slide 1) My name is Kelly Dwyer, and I ate a lot of Popsicles as a child. When I was eight, I used the leftover sticks to build a guesthouse for my dolls. It had a roof, a chimney, and windows. It was awesome. Then I had an epiphany. My neighborhood didn't have a playground or park nearby, so I planned to collect everyone's Popsicle sticks and build a huge playhouse for all the neighborhood kids to use. (Slide 2)

Of course, I soon realized this plan was ridiculous. Today, I'm not so sure. It was a logistical nightmare, yes, but my intentions were spot on. I wanted to solve a big neighborhood problem.

The **parenthetical** notes indicate each slide change.

I believe we all should begin thinking like social entrepreneurs. (Slide 3) Social entrepreneurship is the process of identifying a pressing social problem and using problem-solving skills and a keen business sense to make the problem go away.

The **middle** slides share examples that support the topic and thesis.

Andrew Youn thought big with his One Acre Fund. He believed he could solve poverty and hunger in Rwanda and Kenya, so he quit his job at a Fortune 500 company and developed a business to empower East African farmers. (Slide 4) The One Acre Fund connects African farmers, educates them on farming techniques, provides up-front capital for supplies and materials, and helps farmers negotiate with export markets. The One Acre Fund now serves 75,000 farmers, each of whom has seen profits soar by an average of 100 percent ("Performance Reports").

(Slide 5) Social entrepreneurship has also visited Medellin, Colombia. Medellin is a crowded city situated in a large mountain valley. Living on the hillsides are some of the city's poorest residents, isolated from the jobs and markets of the central city. But in 2004, an idea to connect the hillside communities to downtown turned into a unique public transportation system. (Slide 6) The city implemented a ski-lift-like cable car between the hills and downtown. Travel time to the city's center went from hours to minutes. Adults had better access to jobs, children better access to libraries and parks. Crime rates plummeted (Chu).

The **ending** (not included) leaves the audience with a memorable last thought.

Pecha Kucha Slides

Slide 1: The first slide includes the title and author of the presentation.

Slide 2

Slide 3: The middle slides show compelling images with limited text.

Slide 4

Pecha Kucha Tips

Pecha Kucha presentations are fast paced and timed, which separates them from other slide shows and speeches. They are also more casual than other presentation formats. A Pecha Kucha presentation is like an open-mic night at a coffeehouse. The presenter needs to engage and hold the audience. As you begin to work on your own presentation, remember these additional tips:

- **Simplify your content.** You don't have time to share every detail. Stick to a general theme and present only the most important points.

- **Practice your timing.** Once you have an idea of what you want to say or have memorized your manuscript, practice presenting the material while changing the slides to get the timing right.

- **Allow yourself time to breathe.** Because of time restrictions, you may find yourself rushing. To avoid this, build in pauses between your slides and ideas.

- **Provide a buffer period between slides.** Synchronizing your slides with an exact word or phrase is too difficult, so give yourself some leeway by matching the slides to general ideas rather than to specific points.

- **Use powerful images.** Find bold, relevant images and limit the text on each slide.

- **Know the room setup.** Ask your instructor or the event organizer how the room will be set up on the day of your presentation. Find out where you can stand in relation to the screen and projector. Then practice with a similar setup.

- **Practice. Practice again. And practice some more.** The more you practice, the more comfortable you will become, and the smoother your presentation will go.

Your Turn Prepare a Pecha Kucha presentation following the tips above and the guidelines on the previous pages.

Inquire To Create a Documentary

1. **Question** the communication situation.
   - **Subject:** What issue or situation do you want to discuss or report in your documentary?
   - **Purpose:** Why is the subject important? What do you want people to learn?
   - **Audience:** Who will be interested in this subject? How do you want your viewers to respond?

2. **Plan** your video on a planning sheet. (See page 361.)
   - **Tools:** Decide what camera, computer, software, and lights you need.
   - **Team:** Decide who will do which tasks to make the documentary.

3. **Research** your topic and the technical requirements.
   - **Topic:** Research your topic. Find experts and other people to interview. Look for existing footage you can use.
   - **Equipment:** Practice with the equipment so that you know how to use it.

4. **Create** your video, following these tips.
   - **Write** a script including interview questions and a film location schedule.
   - **Film scenes more than once.** Try different takes and choose the best one when you edit.
   - **Give directions.** Use a confident, considerate voice to direct team members.
   - **Edit.** Use video-editing software to create a rough cut of your video, including transitions and background music. (See pages 524–526 for video-editing tips.)

5. **Improve** your rough cut.
   - **Evaluate** your video against your goal and situation.
       Goal: Did you meet it? How could you improve your documentary?
       Situation: Does the documentary tell a compelling story? Will the audience learn something from it?
   - **Revise** your video as necessary.
       Cut parts that aren't working. When in doubt, leave it out.
       Add B-roll (supplemental footage) to transition smoothly between scenes (see page 525).
       Reorder parts that are confusing or interrupt the flow of the narrative.
       Reshoot or digitally alter parts that have problems.
   - **Perfect** your video, polishing it to professional standards.

6. **Present** your documentary on a file-sharing site or at a local film festival.

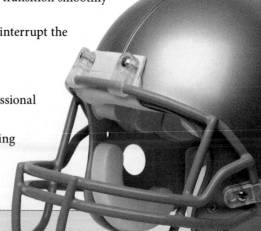

Documentary (Video)

This page provides a portion of the script from a documentary about concussions in football.

The beginning sets the scene and introduces the topic.

The middle tackles the issue at hand through interviews and expert testimony.

The ending (not included) brings the story to a close and suggests where the issue is headed.

Concussions in Football

EXT: WILDCAT FOOTBALL FIELD--EARLY MORNING

The camera pans the vacant football field, cuts to B-roll footage of a collision of helmets and pads, and returns to vacant field for narration.

NARRATOR

If baseball is America's pastime, football is America's passion. The game's popularity has reached new heights across all levels of competition—from professional down to high school and Pop Warner. But recently, concussions and brain trauma from football have drawn public scrutiny. What precautions are high schools taking to protect players from concussions?

B-roll footage shows the outside of Darlington South High School.

NARRATOR

The Darlington South football team won the district championship last season and has won three state championships in the last 10 years. In spite of their winning record, however, Darlington South's football team is not immune to concussions.

CUT TO:

INT: LOCKERROOM--DAY

The camera is set up in front of the red lockers. Sitting down is GAVIN HOLMEN, a junior football player.

GAVIN

I didn't see him coming. Then WHAM! He hit me right on the side of my head. When I got up, I felt woozy, like I was waking up from a nightmare. I wasn't quite sure what was going on.

CUT TO:

INT: COACH'S OFFICE--DAY

Sitting at his desk is STEVE WILDMAN, head football coach.

COACH WILDMAN

When I saw Gavin stumbling, I nodded to our trainer, and we jogged out to check on him. It was a big hit, and he was rattled. . . .

Inquire To Create a Public Service Announcement (PSA) Video

1. **Question** the communication situation.
   - **Subject:** What idea are you presenting in your public service announcement? Why is this topic important?
   - **Purpose:** What do you want your audience to do after viewing the PSA?
   - **Audience:** Who are the people targeted by your PSA? Why should the message matter to them?

2. **Plan** your PSA on a planning sheet. (See page 361.)
   - **Team:** Decide who will do what tasks to put your PSA together.
   - **Tools:** Find recording and editing software.

3. **Research** your topic and technical requirements.
   - **Topic:** Research your topic and write the script.
     Topic ideas: *overconsumption of energy drinks; texting and driving; bullying*
   - **Equipment:** Create props, costumes, and backdrops if needed.
   - **Practice:** Rehearse your PSA with your actors and the recording crew.

4. **Create** your PSA.
   - **Beginning:** Grab attention in a clever way—a startling image or statistic, an interesting anecdote, and so on. Provide a catchy title or memorable slogan.
   - **Middle:** Appeal to the needs of your audience.
   - **Ending:** Call the viewers to action.

5. **Improve** your PSA.
   - **Evaluate** your PSA against your goal and situation.
     Goal: Did you meet it? How could you improve your work?
     Situation: Does the message cover a relevant topic? Does it appeal to your audience? Will it influence your audience to take action?
   - **Revise** your PSA as necessary.
     Cut unnecessary parts.
     Reorder parts to grab attention up front and make a call to action at the end.
     Redo parts that need improvement.
     Add information that supports your goal.
   - **Perfect** your PSA, polishing the video to professional standards.

6. **Present** your PSA.
   - **Share** the video with classmates and post it online to a classroom blog or social media site.

Public Service Announcement Video

The following is a 30-second public service announcement script about organ donation.

Talk to Your Parents About Organ Donation

EXT: LAKE--AFTERNOON

A teenage girl sits on a pier next to her father, who is holding a fishing reel. Their legs dangle in the water.

The script identifies the setting, gives directions, and provides dialogue.

GIRL 1

Hey, Dad, I've been thinking about saving somebody's life.

CUT TO:

*The **beginning** introduces the topic and provides a surprising statistic.*

INT: KITCHEN--EVENING

A teenage boy is eating pizza. His mom is putting flowers into a pot.

BOY

There are over 100,000 Americans waiting for life-saving organs.

CUT TO:

EXT: NEIGHBORHOOD--MORNING

A teenage girl walks along a sidewalk with her mom.

GIRL 2

I don't expect anything will ever happen to me, but just in case . . .

CUT TO:

*The **middle** appeals to viewers' emotions.*

EXT: LAKE--AFTERNOON

GIRL 1

I want you to know that I'd like to register as an organ donor.

CUT TO:

INT: KITCHEN--EVENING

BOY

I could save eight lives and improve dozens more. Can we talk?

CUT TO:

EXT: NEIGHBORHOOD--MORNING

*The **ending** calls the viewer to act.*

GIRL 2

(Looks at camera) Have you talked to your parents about organ donation? Learn more about donating life at organdonor.gov or visit the Donate Life page on Facebook.

Inquire To Create a How-To Video

1. **Question** the communication situation.
   - **Subject:** What will the video show how to do or make?
   - **Purpose:** Why would a viewer want to learn how to do or make this thing?
   - **Audience:** Who will watch the video? What type of person does this subject appeal to?

2. **Plan** your how-to video on a planning sheet. (See page 361.)
   - **Tools:** Find out what tools, equipment, or supplies are needed for the demonstration and for making the video.
   - **Team:** Decide who will perform which tasks in putting the video together.

3. **Research** your topic and technical requirements.
   - **Topic:** Research the subject of your demonstration and develop a basic script.
     Topic ideas: *How to perform a difficult dance move; how to build a canoe; how to cook empanadas; how to play a card game*

4. **Create** your how-to video.
   - **Beginning:** Introduce the subject of your demonstration, its outcome, and its value for the viewer.
     Sample: *Do you wish you could design your own prom dress? Here's how.*
   - **Middle:** Describe steps in the demonstration process.
   - **Ending:** Display/discuss the outcome and provide a closing point.

5. **Improve** your how-to video.
   - **Evaluate** your video against your goal and situation.
     Goal: Does the video accomplish your goal?
     Situation: Does it explain the process clearly? Will a viewer know how to complete the process after watching the video?
   - **Revise** your how-to video.
     Cut parts that don't belong.
     Reorder steps that are out of place.
     Redo weak parts to make them stronger.
     Add materials and steps as needed.
   - **Perfect** your video, polishing it to professional standards. (See video-editing tips on pages 524–526.)

6. **Present** your how-to video by posting it online.

How-To Video

Here is the script for a how-to video for calculating a monthly car payment. For more on loans and financial literacy, see pages 300–305.

see pages 300–305.

The **opening** identifies the setting and provides an interesting anecdote.

The **middle** leads the viewer step-by-step through the process.

The script indicates both what the narrator says and what the viewer sees.

The **ending** connects the process to everyday life.

How to Calculate a Monthly Car Payment

INT: CLASSROOM: The narrator stands in front of a whiteboard.

> **NARRATOR:** If you're like me, you are curious to know how much it would cost to own your dream car, or you may just want to find a car and a payment plan that fits your monthly budget. Online calculators can help, but I'm going to show you how to calculate a monthly car payment on your own. After all, it's important to check your math, especially when money is involved.

CUT TO: WHITEBOARD: A definition of an amortized loan appears: *A loan where the periodic payments include both principal and interest.*

> To do this, you'll need a basic scientific calculator and a knowledge of fractions and order of operations. Because most of us can't pay for a car up front, you'll need to take out a car loan, with interest, and pay it off in monthly installments.

She writes two equations on the board and points to the variables:

$$M = P \times [J/(1 - (1 + J)^{-N})] \text{ and } J = I/(12 \times 100)$$

> We'll work with two equations and five variables: *P*, principal; *I*, annual interest rate; *L*, length of amortized loan; *J*, monthly interest rate in decimal form; and *N*, the length, in months, of the loan.

CUT TO: WHITEBOARD: The first equation now reads

$$M = 28{,}498 \times [J/(1 - (1 + J)^{-36}] \text{ and the second equation is } J = 7/1{,}200.$$

> Say my dream car costs $28,498, which is variable *P*. To pay for it, I'll use a 3-year, or 36-month, loan (*N*). In doing research, I learn my loan payment will come with a 7 percent monthly interest (*J*). I can solve my second equation to discover variable *J*.

CUT TO: CALCULATOR SCREEN: She shows how to enter and solve the second equation. The number 0.005833 appears.

> Now that I discovered my *J* variable, I can solve my first equation.

CUT TO: WHITEBOARD: $M = 28{,}498 \times [0.005833/(1 - (1 + .005833)^{-36}]$

CUT TO: CALCULATOR SCREEN: She shows how to enter and solve the first equation. The number $879.94 appears.

> So my monthly payment for the next 36 months is $879.94. Ouch, that's pricey! In fact, if I multiply those numbers, I learn the car costs $31,677.68, meaning I'll pay $3,179.68 above the sticker price due to interest. From now on, I'll use these equations before financing a car. And so can you.

A Basic Guide to Video Editing

Today anyone can create an engaging, professional-quality video, thanks to the video-editing software available on most personal computers. Below are the basic steps needed to create, edit, and publish a quality video. To get started, you'll need a video-recording device (camcorder, smart phone, tablet, and so on) and a computer with video-editing software.

▶ Step 1: Filming

Before you begin filming, plan and research your production using a planning sheet (see page 361). If you have a tripod available, use it. It will greatly improve the quality and focus of your shot. Then begin filming. Here are some tips:

- **Film different types of shots**—wide shots, medium shots, and close-ups—as well as filming from different angles.
- **Shoot different versions of the same shot.** You can pick the best one later.
- **Use framing techniques.** Look for horizontal and vertical lines in the frame. The horizontal lines should be level, while the vertical lines should be straight up and down.

▶ Step 2: Capturing your video on your computer

After you are done filming, move your footage from your camera onto your computer. To do so, you will need a USB cable or other connecting technology. Refer to help guides on the Web for assistance.

▶ Step 3: Selecting the right shots

Once your footage is on your computer, open your video-editing program and select specific shots to include in your video. Use the program to cut and edit your shots to your desired length. For example, you may wish to include only the best 8 seconds of a 45-second clip.

▶ Step 4: Arranging your shots

After you have some shots in mind, drag them onto the timeline feature of your editing software and arrange them in your desired sequence. The timeline is where you will spend most of your time polishing your video. You can add, delete, and edit video footage as well as audio within your timeline.

▶ Step 5: Adding transitions, background music, or narration

At this point you should be ready to smooth out the transition between shots within your timeline. There are a number of common transitional effects to choose from.

- A **cut** switches instantly from one shot to another with no special effect.
- A **fade** is a gradual transition from one shot to a solid color or blank screen (white or black). A shot may fade in or fade out.
- A **dissolve** is a gradual transition from one shot to the next, with the two shots overlapping for the duration of the effect.
- A **wipe** occurs when a new shot physically moves onto the frame and pushes out the old one.
- **B-roll** is secondary footage that can be used to intercut main shots. It is often shown during an audio voiceover (narration) or to introduce a new scene.

▶ Step 6: Background Music

Just as with your video footage, you can import music into your video-editing software and then drop it into the timeline, editing and arranging it as you wish.

▶ Step 7: Polishing your video

Once you are satisfied with all the elements of your video, preview it, making sure all the elements work together to create a pleasing whole.

▶ Step 8: Publishing your video

Present your video for others to see by uploading it online or burning it onto a DVD.

Glossary of Video-Making Terms

- **Close-up (CU):** A shot taken from a close distance, focusing on the subject
- **Depth of field:** Describes the depth of the shot, how the foreground, middle-ground, and background interact spatially
- **Establishing shot:** A wide shot that establishes the surroundings in which the video will occur
- **Framing:** The manner in which the subject of the shot is shown in relation to the surroundings
- **Long shot (LS):** A shot from far away, making the subject appear small in relation to the surroundings
- **Medium shot (MS):** A conventional shot, somewhere in between a close-up and long shot
- **Pan:** A panoramic shot in which the frame moves horizontally while the camera pivots from a fixed position, showing a wide scene
- **Point-of-view shot (POV):** A shot made from the perspective of one of the characters, as if the viewer is looking through the character's eyes
- **Shot:** A specific subject filmed from a specific angle

Storyboarding

After writing a video script, you can storyboard it. A storyboard is a series of pictures that previews a video shot by shot. It helps the director of the video communicate to others what he or she is thinking for each shot in the video. Here is the beginning of a storyboard for the PSA on page 521.

Shot 1

Shot 2

Shot 3

Chapter 32
Design Projects

We encounter a world of different objects every day—everything from the clothes we wear to the furniture we sit on to the tools and machines we use to do work. All of these items bear one thing in common: They all went through a design process.

In this chapter, you will learn about that process firsthand as you design and create a variety of your own items, including scale models, T-shirts, posters, and more.

You will learn . . .

- Creating Print Designs
- Creating Fashion Designs
- Creating Game Designs
- Creating Blueprints and Prototypes
- Designing Tools and Machines

Project Overview

Here is a quick overview of the design projects in this chapter.

A Print Designs

Posters, T-shirts, book covers, and brochures all use graphic concepts of *contrast, alignment, repetition,* and *proximity* to create an eye-catching design that also conveys information. See pages 531–533 for examples.

B Fashion Designs

Besides creating clothing, fashion design can involve costumes and jewelry for special occasions or events. See pages 534–535 to learn more about fashion design.

C Game Designs

Play is an important part of development for all mammals, humans included. Games not only entertain but also give us opportunities to problem solve and socialize in a safe environment. Designing a game that challenges even as it entertains is its own sort of test. See pages 536–539 to learn more about game designs.

D Creating Blueprints and Prototypes

Blueprints and prototypes allow designers to show a concept for a building or device before the actual thing is constructed. Blueprints are carefully drawn to scale, and prototypes are often scale models, as well. See pages 540–545 to learn more.

E Tool and Machine Designs

Tools are simple devices that help with a physical task. Machines are more complex tools with multiple moving parts. You can devise your own tool or machine to solve a problem or meet a need. See pages 546–548 to discover how.

A Volunteer! Learn Health Care Skills

Orientation at the Earlean Moench Health Center
7:30 p.m. to 9 p.m. Friday, September 13

BAND O'LEAR

B

C

51	52	53	54	55	56	57	58
50	15 Marriage (female)	16 Political Apprentice (male)	17 Army Duty /Childbirth	18 Marriage (female)	19	20 Marriage (female)	59
40	14	13	12	11 School	10 School	21 Marriage (female)	60
48	1 Year	2	3	4	9 School	22 Marriage (male)	61
47	6 Months	START	1st Trimester	5	8	23	62
46	Birth!	3rd Trimester	2nd Trimester	6	7 School	24 Marriage (male)	63
45	30	29 Marriage (female)	28	27 Marriage (female)	26 Marriage (male)	25 Marriage (female)	64
44	31	32	33	34	35	36	65
43 2nd Marriage	42 2nd Marriage	41 2nd Marriage	40	39 2nd Marriage	38 2nd Marriage	37 2nd Marriage	66
BONUS ROLL!	73	72	71	70	69	68	67

D

E

Stuck Window

Rubber Pad

Rubber Pad

Inquire To Create Print Designs

1. **Question** the overall situation for the print design.
   - **Subject:** What message or mood do I want to convey?
   - **Purpose:** Is the project intended to amuse, inform, or persuade?
   - **Audience:** Who will view the design? What do they need from it?
   - **Medium:** Is the design intended for a poster, a T-shirt, a book cover, a pamphlet, or something else? What constraints might the materials impose?
   - **Context:** Where will the design be encountered? How might this affect my design decisions?

2. **Plan** your print design by sketching general possibilities.

3. **Research** your subject.
   - **Gather** needed images and information.
   - **Organize** the elements of your sketch, using these CARP design principles:

     Contrast adds visual excitement and distinguishes significantly different elements by employing varying colors, sizes, textures, and fonts.

     Alignment avoids a scattershot appearance, arranging separate elements along invisible lines horizontally and vertically to satisfy the viewer's eye.

     Repetition builds unity and identifies related elements by employing similar colors, sizes, textures, and fonts.

     Proximity groups related elements for quick viewing and comprehension.

4. **Create** your print design.
   - **Posters** advertise an idea at a distance and provide details up close. See the next page for tips on creating posters.
   - **T-shirts** are intended to be viewed in passing and understood quickly. See the nest page for tips on creating T-shirts.
   - **Book covers** grab attention and communicate the essence of their contents. See page 532 for tips on creating book covers.
   - **Brochures** inform and promote. See page 533 for tips on creating brochures.

5. **Improve** your print design.
   - **Evaluate** your design.

     Is it attractive? Does it include all necessary information?

     Does the design achieve its purpose? Do viewers respond well to it?
   - **Revise** your print design.

     Remove or **redo** any distracting parts.

     Rearrange parts that may be out of place.

     Add any missing information.
   - **Perfect** your print design, making it clean and correct.

6. **Publish** your print design through a local or online print company. (Go to thoughtfullearning.com/h530 for more help creating print designs.)

Poster

This poster asking for student volunteers is designed to draw attention at a distance and then deliver detailed information up close.

Contrast in colors and a dramatic image draw attention.

Left and center text **alignment** adds visual continuity.

Repetition of colors creates unity.

Proximity of the final two lines identifies them as a single unit.

Volunteer! Learn
Health Care Skills

Orientation at the Earlean Moench Health Center
7:30 p.m. to 9 p.m. Friday, September 13

T-Shirt

This T-shirt design advertises an Irish band with an unusual name.

Contrast between the white lettering and traditional Irish green color pleases the eye.

Diagonal alignment of the text lines and the line of Irish knots creates continuity.

Repetition of the knot-work pattern and the Irish font creates unity.

Proximity of the text (even separated by the band) makes its meaning and word play clear.

Book Cover

The front cover of a book must catch the viewer's eye. The back must provide more detailed information (summary, price, publisher, and so on). The first image below shows the finished cover of a student-designed book for publication. The second image shows the same cover with its original guides superimposed. Dashed blue lines indicate intended spine folds and edge cuts, tan areas show possible variance, and the yellow box marks space needed for the publisher's bar code.

Finished Cover, Ready for Publication

Left **alignment** of text lines adds visual continuity.

Contrast between light and dark in the photo background adds interest, as does the choice of font styles and text sizes and colors.

Alignment of various text elements pleases the viewer's eye while also making clear the differing functions of different text blocks.

Repetition of one font style for title text on front, spine, and back creates a sense of unity. Similar repetition of a separate font for subtitle, author, and other text continues that feeling.

Proximity is used wisely to make discreet units of text on front, back, and spine.

Brochure

A brochure's front cover is much like a book's. But interior pages may carry more illustrations, like a magazine. The back is often used for a FAQ list and contact details.

Notice how the CARP principles are used—especially the *repetition* of font choices inside and the use of page divisions to create a *proximity* of information by topic.

Back Cover   **Front Cover**

Frequently Asked Questions

Q. Must I supply my own terrain and miniatures?
A. No. Members are free to use materials owned by the club, as well as their own.

Q. Are board games allowed?
A. Yes. The club encourages all types of historical games, miniatures, board games, card games, and computer simulations.

Q. Is food allowed at the meetings?
A. Yes. Snacks and soft drinks are available for purchase, or members can bring their own. (Please take care not to spill on the games.)

Meeting Time and Place

Where? Shyla Tyson library, Meeting Room B.
When? The second and fourth Thursday of each month.

We look forward to seeing you there!

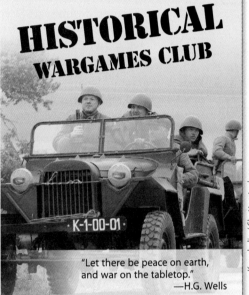

HISTORICAL WARGAMES CLUB

"Let there be peace on earth, and war on the tabletop."
—H.G. Wells

Sergey Kamshylin / Shutterstock.com

Page 1, Inside   **Page 2, Inside**

Our Mission

- The Historical Wargames Club promotes historical knowledge through games.

- In doing so, we also promote a discussion of alternatives to human conflict.

- Further, we foster a sense of community among our members.

Our Members

- The club is sponsored and managed by staff members of Wilford Mickell High School.

- All District 21 students are welcome to take part, regardless of grade level.

- Parents of students are also encouraged to join the club and attend its events.

Inquire To Create Fashion Designs

1. **Question** the overall situation for the design.
   - **Subject:** What context is the design intended for? A play or other sort of performance? A formal occasion? An office or other work environment? Home? The beach?
   - **Purpose:** What purpose will the item serve? Formal dress? A uniform? A costume? Exercise? Swimwear? Sleepwear?
   - **Audience:** Who will wear the design? What will they expect from it? How may it be tailored to suit them? Who will view the design in use? What trends in fashion may influence your design?

2. **Plan** your graphic design by making sketches. Use a computer design program or a sketch pad and pencils. For clothing, experiment by draping and pinning fabric on a tailors' dummy. For jewelry, mock up your design with cheap, disposable materials.

3. **Research** your design.
   - **Gather** information about the materials to be used in your design and the tools for working with those materials.
   - **Organize** your materials and tools.

4. **Create** your item.
   - **Costumes** work with stage design to create an overall impression while also conveying details about their actors.
   - **Clothing** both covers and adorns us. It serves a functional purpose as well as a decorative one.
   - **Jewelry** enhances clothing.

5. **Improve** your fashion design.
   - **Evaluate** your product.
     Does it serve its purpose well? Is it comfortable, durable, and attractive?
     Does it look good from all sides?
   - **Revise** your fashion design.
     Remove any distracting elements.
     Rearrange parts that look out of place.
     Redo parts that do not fit well or are otherwise unsuitable.
     Add any needed elements to strengthen the design visually or physically.
   - **Perfect** your design.
     Smooth any troublesome spots.
     Finish any last touches for polish and durability.

6. **Present** your fashion design, arranged in an attractive package, displayed in a fashion show, or worn yourself.

Costumes

At first glance, this Raggedy-Ann-style costume appears to be a haphazard collection of rags. Closer inspection reveals a careful design.

Note the repeated pattern of pink and gray patches diagonally across the bottom half and the gray sleeve above. Note as well how the three brown sections (in different shades) work with the tan section containing dark gray circles.

Also note the three shades of pink, including the patterned section that makes up much of the top.

Clothing

This knit cap is both functional and eye-catching, combining several colors of brown yarn in a progressive pattern, and adorned by yarn tassels simulating an owl's ears. The eyes and beak are felt patches stitched to the yarn. Felt was used because its soft surface matches the soft appearance of the yarn itself.

Jewelry

This bracelet was constructed from an assortment of old beads. Notice how the warmth of the long wooden beads adds a welcome contrast to the colorfulness of the plastic beads. Note also how the metal charms draw attention to the smaller metal beads, lending the collection a sense of whimsy and character.

Inquire To Create Game Designs

1. **Question** the overall situation for the game.
   - **Subject:** What is the topic or genre? What information will the game draw on?
   - **Purpose:** What should the game accomplish? Is it intended to train? Test? Entertain? Recruit?
   - **Audience:** Who will play the game? What will they expect from it? What difficulty will they be prepared for? What level of instruction will they need?

2. **Plan** your game by contemplating the bigger picture. Make a note of design goals—including story, mood, game mechanics, victory conditions, and so on.

3. **Research** your topic.
   - **Gather** information about the subject being simulated. Familiarize yourself with other games in that field.
   - **Understand** the odds of any randomizers. (Two standard dice create a bell curve, with a 1 in 36 chance of a rolling a 2, and a 1 in 6 chance of rolling a 7.)

4. **Create** your game. Design a prototype for play-testing.
   - **Board and card games** involve one or more players and may be competitive or cooperative. See the next page for tips on creating board and card games.
   - **Computer game levels** are often fan-created add-ons to existing products. See page 538 for tips on creating computer game levels.
   - **Role-playing games** let players describe their characters' actions in a fictional adventure led by a game host. See page 539 for tips about role-playing games.

5. **Improve** your game.
   - **Evaluate** your game.

     Is it fun and engaging? Do people want to play again?

     Is it understandable? Can people play without you present to explain rules?

     Are people happier, more skilled, or more knowledgable after having played?
   - **Revise** your game.

     Remove any distracting or boring parts.

     Rearrange rules or parts that may be out of place.

     Redo ideas or game text that is unclear or confusing.

     Add any missing rules, explanations, or background about the topic.
   - **Perfect** your game, making it clean, clear, and attractive.

6. **Present** your game to the public, publishing it online or having it manufactured. (Go to thoughtfullearning.com/h536 for more help publishing games.)

About Educational Designs: Nearly all types of games can be used to teach. When designing an educational game, be sure the learning suits the context. Don't make "chocolate-covered broccoli," in which a task like multiplying numbers is disguised as a game like "Climb the Mountain!" Instead, use the mountain as a setting for plotting a climb (calculating trajectories, time required, food and oxygen needed, and so on).

Board Game

Board games range from abstract (such as Checkers or Go) to simulations (such as Risk or Life). Most are some mix of those two. Chess, for example, is abstract, but pieces simulate kings, queens, and so on.

In this board game, a student simulates life expectancy in Ancient Rome. The spiralling game track represents higher mortality rates in early years. Romans who survived early hazards were statistically more likely to reach old age. For added interest, other details not specifically related to survival are included.

THE ANCIENT ROME LIFE EXPECTANCY GAME

Game Rules

- Begin by placing your marker at START.
- Roll a six-sided die each turn and move ahead that many spaces.
- If you pass over a space, you have survived that event.
- If you land on a colored space, see the Key below and apply its effects.
- **The winner is the player who attains the greatest age!**

Key

If you land on "3rd Trimester" or "BIRTH!" on your first roll, you are a commoner or slave, without access to regular food and water. *Subtract 1 from future die rolls.*

If you land on "1 Year" on your first roll, you are of the ruling class, with access to regular food and water, as well as medical care. *Add 1 to future die rolls.*

If you land on a gray space by exact count, you have died at this age.

If you land on the "BONUS ROLL!" space by exact count, roll again and add the result to 73 to determine your final age at death.

51	52	53	54	55	56	57	58
50	15 Marriage (female)	16 Political Apprentice (male)	17 Army Duty /Childbirth	18 Marriage (female)	19	20 Marriage (female)	59
40	14	13	12	11 School	10 School	21 Marriage (female)	60
48	1 Year	2	3	4	9 School	22 Marriage (male)	61
47	6 Months	START	1st Trimester	5	8	23	62
46	Birth!	3rd Trimester	2nd Trimester	6	7 School	24 Marriage (male)	63
45	30	29 Marriage (female)	28	27 Marriage (female)	26 Marriage (male)	25 Marriage (female)	64
44	31	32	33	34	35	36	65
43 2nd Marriage	42 2nd Marriage	41 2nd Marriage	40	39 2nd Marriage	38 2nd Marriage	37 2nd Marriage	66
BONUS ROLL!	73	72	71	70	69	68	67

Card Game

Rules for common games can be adapted to your own purposes. A Cribbage game with the "Show" portion of scoring removed can simulate a fencing match of foils or epees. Or you might create a simulation of 19th century mining, using the spades suit as digging tools, hearts as miners, diamonds as ore, and clubs as guards.

Electronic Game

There are many opportunities for you to create electronic games or game levels. Here are a few things to bear in mind:

- **Consider the Mood:** Images, text, and any audio should work together to maintain an appropriate feeling.
- **Consider the Mission:** Players should know what they need to do to win, whether it is surviving for a set period, traveling to an end point, solving a puzzle, or gathering a list of items.
- **Consider the Map:** Watch a few people play your game or level. If many of them fail at a particular point, revise that area. On the other hand, if most of them easily complete the game, adjust the difficulty.

▶ Navigation Games

Many computer games mainly involve moving from point A to point B while avoiding traps and solving puzzles. One of the first examples to include a level editor was Atari's *Lode Runner*. A more current example is *Little Big Planet*, which includes a drag-and-drop interface for building levels players can share online.

▶ Real-Time Strategy Games

Some real-time strategy games are simple "tower defense" games, involving careful use of materials and personnel to defend against invaders. Others involve managing resources to capture new territory. Many of the most popular—*Command and Conquer, World of Warcraft, Civilization,* and so on—combine both requirements. These last three also include map editors so that you can create your own missions. For an open-source alternative, see www.zero-k.info.

▶ Point-and-Click Games

Using an HTML editor, you can create your own which-way or pick-a-path adventure games, mixing text and images on each page. Or you can use image mapping code to hyperlink parts of an image, allowing players to click on different areas for different results. With the addition of javascript coding, you can even simulate dice rolls and keep track of character equipment and statistics.

▶ Hidden-Object Games

Hidden-object games present the player with a complex image and ask that specific items be found within it. As each item is clicked, it disappears from the screen. You can create your own simple hidden-object game for free at hidenseek.viquagames.com, or build an HTML document with images in clickable layers.

Role-Playing Game

Role-playing games (RPGs) ask players to imagine themselves as characters in a fictional setting.

- **Tabletop role-playing** involves rule books and randomizers such as dice or cards. Players describe or narrate their characters' actions, and a "game master" (GM) represents the world around them.
- **Mystery parties** and live-action role-playing (LARP) are more theatrical examples, with players portraying their characters' actions, often in costume.
- **Electronic role-playing games** may be text-based chat sessions with few if any rules. Or they may be either single-player computer games or massively multiplayer online role-playing games (MMORPGs), both focused on quests and character enhancement rather than collaborative storytelling.

Role-playing is also often used as a training or testing technique, particularly for healthcare workers, emergency staff, and military personnel.

A Simple Example

For a very easy role-playing party game, find the rules for "Werewolf" online. You can assign character roles using several cards from a standard deck: a king for the moderator, two queens for the werewolves, a jack for the seer, and one number card for each of the villagers.

Werewolves
Moderator   Seer
Villagers

Designing a Role-Playing Game Adventure

Most role-playing design involves preparing adventures, rather than inventing rules. Use the following steps to prepare and run your own adventure.

1. **Choose a genre and rules.** Do you intend to run a fantasy, science fiction, or historical adventure? Do you prefer simple, cinematic rules or more complex, realistic ones? Once you have chosen a set of rules, familiarize yourself with them so that you can handle questions during play.
2. **Decide on a scope for your adventure.** An adventure to be played in one evening must be simpler than one intended to stretch over multiple weekly sessions.
3. **Invent adversaries.** Unlike fiction, in which the author controls all characters, role-playing is collaborative storytelling. The game master's role is to invent one or more villains and their goals. The players' characters will try to thwart those adversaries.
4. **Devise a plot.** With the adversaries' goals in mind, sketch a plot of events. Imagine when and where the players' characters might encounter those events, and prepare scene descriptions, henchmen to overcome, bystanders to save, rewards for success, penalties for failure, and so on.
5. **Run your adventure.** Host a group of friends to play your adventure. Adapt your story to their characters' actions. Make sure everyone has a good time.

 **To Create Blueprints and Prototypes**

1. **Question** the overall situation for the design.
   - **Subject:** What information should the blueprint or prototype convey?
   - **Purpose:** What is the goal of the design? What function will the object serve?
   - **Audience:** Who will view my blueprint, prototype, or final design? What will they expect of it?

2. **Plan** your blueprint or prototype. Explore materials and tools you will use to create it. Make a basic sketch of your intention.

3. **Research** your design by investigating the topic and studying similar examples.
   - **Gather** information about the subject.
   - **Collect** your materials and tools.
   - **Organize** your workspace to have everything you need at hand.

4. **Create** your blueprint or prototype.
   - **Blueprints** illustrate on paper the layout and features of a structure. They are portable and easily changed or replaced.
   - **Scale models** provide a more realistic, 3D view of a structure or device in smaller scale. They add visual impact to a proposal.
   - **Dioramas** show a scene featuring many figures within their habitat or context. Often labels provide additional information about the scene or figures.

5. **Improve** your blueprint or prototype.
   - **Evaluate** your design.
       Are all features clear and visible? Is the scale accurate? Is it interesting and informative?
   - **Revise** your design.
       Remove any distracting elements.
       Rearrange parts that may be out of place.
       Redo parts that are incorrect or unclear.
       Add any missing parts and labels.
   - **Perfect** your design, making it clean and correct.
       Clean any messy lines on a blueprint or smudges on a prototype.

6. **Present** your blueprint or prototype in class or elsewhere. (Go to thoughtfullearning.com/h540 for more help creating blueprints and prototypes.)

Blueprint

Here are sample blueprints showing the floor plan, front elevation, and architectural rendering of a fishing cottage. A student created them using the Trimble Sketchup computer-aided design program.

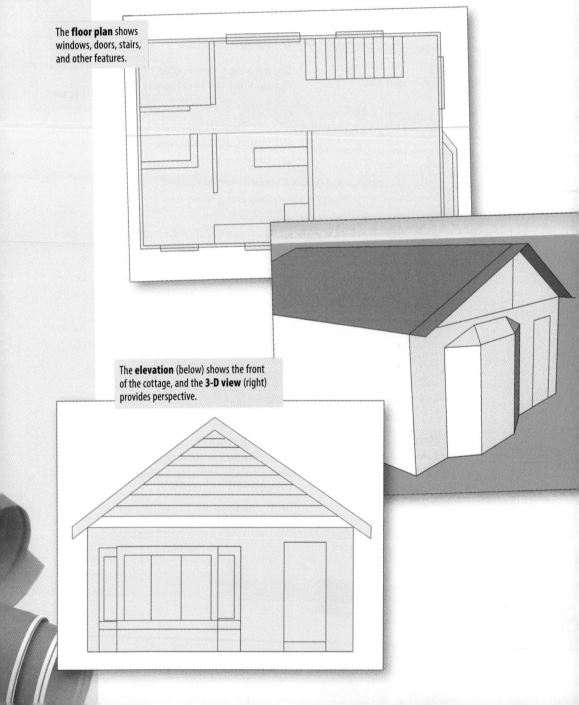

The **floor plan** shows windows, doors, stairs, and other features.

The **elevation** (below) shows the front of the cottage, and the **3-D view** (right) provides perspective.

Parts of a Blueprint

A blueprint is a drawing that shows the plan for a building, a vehicle, or an object. A blueprint needs to be correctly proportioned. That means each part of the subject is the right size when compared to the other parts. The key is to use a scale.

▶ **Scale**

The scale is the ratio between the drawn size and the actual size.

Drawn Size: 1 inch **Actual Size:** 12 inches	$= \dfrac{1}{12}$ scale
Drawn Size: 1 centimeter **Actual Size:** 100 centimeters	$= \dfrac{1}{100}$ scale

Your Turn Choose a scale that will work for your blueprint. Use measurements that will be easy to use for both drawn size and actual size.

▶ **Drafting Tools**

You can create a blueprint by hand, using these tools:

- **Table:** For best results, use a table with ninety-degree edges.
- **Drafting paper:** Drafting paper can be unlined or graphed.
- **T-square:** A T-square is used to orient the drafting paper on the table, to draw horizontal lines, and to accommodate various-shaped triangles.
- **Triangles:** A triangle with points at 30, 60, and 90 degrees combines with another with points at 45 and 90 degrees to make angles.
- **Protractor:** A protractor calculates all other needed angles.
- **Drafting pencils:** Sharp pencils make clean lines.

Many people nowadays use drafting software. These CAD (computer-aided design) programs make it easy to create floor plans, elevations, and three-dimensional structures. They also allow you to add material types to plans—from wood to cement to shingles.

Your Turn Gather drafting tools or download a free CAD program. (For CAD programs, go to thoughtfullearning.com/h542.) Experiment with the tools until you are comfortable using them.

▶ Views

Because a blueprint uses a flat picture to show a three-dimensional structure, multiple views will offer the best overall vision. Here are different options:

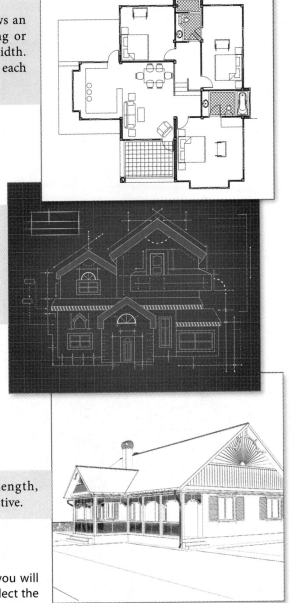

Floor Plan: This basic view shows an overhead image of the building or object, indicating length and width. Blueprints include a floor plan of each level of a building or an item.

Elevation: This view shows the side of the building or object, indicating height and length. Blueprints often include an elevation of each side of the item.

Note: Advanced building projects also have special views to show plans for plumbing, electricity, and other systems.

3-D View: This view shows length, width, and height, using perspective.

Your Turn Decide which views you will draw for your blueprint project. Select the best tools for creating your plan.

Scale Models

Using the concept of scale (see page 542), architects may build models to allow a true 3D view of a building, as in this photo.

This model shows exact dimensions and precise architectural details.

Scale models can also show the details of other sorts of prototypes, such as vehicle designs, as in the photos below.

These prototypes show how large-scale vehicles would be built.

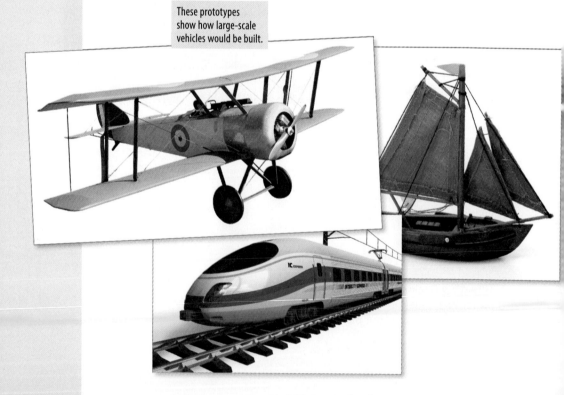

Dioramas

Museums often expand the concept of scale models to create an entire scene, as in the photos below.

Dioramas can depict past places and events or propose future places and events.

Each **scene** captures a specific action with props and the position of the characters.

A meticulous **attention to detail** creates a sense of realism.

Songquan Deng / Shutterstock.com

Inquire To Design Tools and Machines

1. **Question** the overall situation for the tool or machine.
   - **Subject:** What problem or need will your tool or machine address?
   - **Purpose:** What will your tool or machine accomplish?
   - **Audience:** Who will use this tool or machine? What will they need to know about it?

2. **Plan** your tool or machine by sketching a diagram or making a mock-up with scrap materials.

3. **Research** your topic.
   - **Gather** information about materials to be used and previous approaches to the problem or need.
   - **Organize** your materials and equipment to fabricate your tool or construct your machine.

4. **Create** your tool or machine.
   - **Tools** are held items that help perform a physical operation.
   - **Machines** are more complex constructions, consisting of multiple moving parts that work together.
   - **Rube Goldberg machines** are humorous contraptions that employ fanciful elements to accomplish a mundane task. See page 548.

5. **Improve** your tool or machine.
   - **Evaluate** your tool or machine.
      Does it clearly solve the problem or meet the need? Is it easy and safe to use? If it is a Rube Goldberg machine, is it fanciful and fun?
   - **Revise** your tool or machine.
      Remove any troublesome or unnecessary parts.
      Rearrange parts that may be out of place.
      Redo parts that don't work effectively.
      Add any features or parts that will improve the function.
   - **Perfect** your tool or machine.
      Smooth any rough edges.
      Cover any moving parts to protect them, the user, and so on.
      Paint parts both to preserve the materials and to make the device more appealing to users. Consider naming the tool or machine and painting that on as well.

6. **Present** your tool or machine as a diagram or image online, in a report, or in a presentation. (Go to thoughtfullearning.com/h546 for more help creating tools and machines.)

Tool

A tool is a held item that helps perform a physical operation. (Humans are not the only tool-using creatures. Many animals use tools, as well.) A student designed the tool below to lever up windows that stick.

The curved end fits under the handle or into the handle slot. Once the window begins to open, the end fits under the window itself.

The rubber padding protects the window frame and ledge from pressure marks.

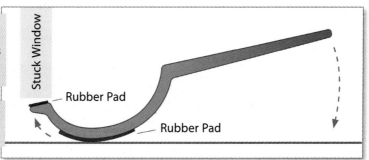

Machine

A machine is a more complex tool, consisting of multiple moving parts. A student designed this machine to open the Venetian window blinds without getting out of bed.

1. A dry cell battery supplies the power.

2. A two-pole knife switch turns the power on, off, or reverse.

3. The electric motor from a toy car converts that stored energy to mechanical energy.

4. A wheel from the toy car, large rubber band, and large paper spool convert the motor's high-speed revolutions to a lower rate.

5. The rod to the window blinds is affixed to the center of the spool.

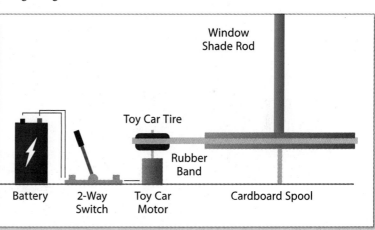

With the knife switch flipped one way, the device turns the rod counterclockwise and opens the blinds. With the knife switch flipped the other way, the device turns the rod clockwise and closes the blinds.

Rube Goldberg Machines

The following photos show Rube Goldberg machines entered into various competitions. Note the diverse use of materials, each capturing potential energy and releasing it as kinetic energy. Also note the themes of the machines. The drawing below comes from Arnold Zucker's burglar alarm patent.

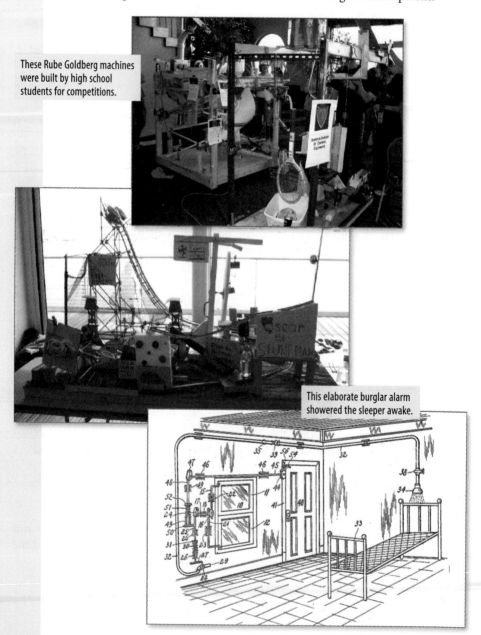

These Rube Goldberg machines were built by high school students for competitions.

This elaborate burglar alarm showered the sleeper awake.

Chapter 33
Performing Projects

A performing project, which is ultimately about presenting your work in front of an audience, requires careful preparation and practice. No matter whether you are giving a speech, participating in a debate, or presenting a play, "winging it" will not give you the result you hope for. But "plugging into" a solid plan, including preparation and practice, will.

This chapter features a wide variety of performing projects, from speeches and interviews to debates, dramatic interpretations, and simulations. Proper preparation means you will be able to focus on your message and relate well to your audience.

You will learn . . .
- Preparing Speeches
- Conducting/Giving Interviews
- Debating an Issue
- Holding Simulations
- Staging Plays

Project Overview

Here is an overview of the performing projects in this chapter.

A Speeches

Speeches are formal presentation in front of an audience. They often are accompanied by a slideshow and other visuals. (See pages 552–555.)

B Demonstration Speeches

Demonstration speeches show how to do something or how something works. (See pages 556–557.)

C Interviews

Interviews are carefully planned conversations conducted in front of an audience or for broadcast. Conducting and giving interviews are key performance skills. (See pages 558–559.)

D Debates

Debates are formal discussions about important topics. They follow a format in which one side is in favor of a resolution and the other side opposes it. (See pages 560–563.)

E Character Debates

Character debates pit two historical or literary figures against each other in a discussion of opposing points of view. A character debate with multiple participants is a round-table. (See page 562.)

F Simulations

Simulations are acted-out games that allow you to explore situations, re-enact historical events, or practice for emergencies. Simulations range from trials of historical figures to MMORPGs—Massively Multiplayer Online Roleplaying Games. (See pages 564–565.)

G Plays

Plays are formal dramatic presentations that involve actors and scripts and often include elements of stagecraft such as costumes, props, sets, and lighting design. (See page 566–568.)

A

Education Reform: What Google Taught Me

Hello, everybody. My name is Jason Carter, and I've got an [idea?] for making things better for high school students here and nation[wide?].

I'm going to show you a pair of photos, and I want you to stud[y?]

them for a few [seconds?]. [On] the left [was?] [a?] [factory?] in China. Th[e] [one] [on?] [the right?] [was?] [a?] [ch?]

B

How to Use the Quadratic Formula

If you have taken algebra, you've run up against the quadratic equation. It looks like this: a times x squared plus b times x plus c equals zero. Often you can solve this equation using the FOIL method, but when you have fractions, decimals, or radicals, it might be easier to use the quadratic formula to solve the [problem].

[The] quad[ratic] [formula] [is:]
[b] [plus] [or] [minus] [the]
[square] [root] [...] [a]
[...] [by] [2] [...] [st]
[...] [the] [...] [m]
[...] [and] [...] [calculations. Note, however,]

Quadratic Equation

$$ax^2 + bx + c = 0$$

Quadratic Formula

$$x = \frac{-b \pm \sqrt{b^2 - 4ac}}{2a}$$

C

Interview with Keri Johnson

Darius: Hey, everybody, this is Darius for another installment [of] the Dare We Ask podcast. Today, I'm talking to physics teacher [and] exoplanet enthusiast Keri Johnson. Thank you for joining me.

Mrs. Johnson: It's a pleasure to be here.

Darius: So, the big question "dare we ask" is how soon human be[ings] will be living on exoplanets.

Mrs. Johnson: I wish I could say, "tomorrow," or even "within a [few] hundred years," but it's going to be closer to a thousand.

Darius: A thousand! But you said that scientists have found near[ly a] thousand exoplanets, and some are earthlike and in the habitable [zone.] What's the holdup?

Mrs. Johnson: Well, it comes down to a few factors. The first ear[thlike] planet proven to be in the habitable zone of its star was Kepler 22[b.]

D

Wind Power: Cure or Curse for the Planet

Moderator: Welcome to today's debate, which focuses on the following topic: "Resolved: The state should budget $10 million to develop a wind farm in Gannet Valley." The team to my right will begin our debate with five minutes of opening remarks in favor of this resolution.

Latrisha Evans: Thank you, Mr. Kao. Our world faces an energy crisis. Growing populations and growing demand means we will need more energy in the future, not less. Most experts agree that we have reached "peak oil," and that the fossil fuels yet to be tapped are more difficult to get, such as oil-sand deposits in Canada and oil reserves beneath the melting Arctic ice sheet. And let's think about that melting ice sheet and other environmental damage caused by the burning of [fossil fuel]s. Carbon-neutral, clean, and renewable energy sources offer [solutions to these pr]oblems. A wind farm in

E

Abraham Lincoln and Muammar Gaddafi Debate

Gaddafi: Mr. Lincoln, when your countrymen chose to reb[el against] you, you attacked them with the full force of your military. I [did the] same thing. You are considered a saint, and I am considered a [villain.]

Lincoln: Mr. Gaddafi, let us consider the reasons for the two [...] rebellions. The southern states rebelled because they feared th[at I?] would abolish slavery. The National Transitional Council rebe[lled] because of your repressive 40-year regime enslaving an entire [...] population.

Gaddafi: My regime made Libya a wealthy nation.

Lincoln: Your regime made Libya a state sponsor of terror an[d a rogue] nation.

Gaddafi: You are talking of events in the 1980s. By the 1990s [...] made amends for our sponsorship of terrorism and had dism[antled] our weapons of mass destruction. After 9/11, I was an [ally of the] United States in its war on terror.

Lincoln: But when the NTC rebelled, you attacked [...] populations.

Gaddafi: What do you call the Siege of Vicksburg, M[r. Lincoln?] you cannot argue that you fought to free the slaves. T[...] fought to preserve the union at all cost. You said that [if you could save] the union without freeing any slaves, you would do it[...] trying to preserve your own power, just as I was.

Lincoln: Not my own power, sir, but the power of a d[emocratic] government. The South seceded even before I took th[e office.] And f[...] [I] would have handed ov[er power] to a s[uccessor...]

Ga[ddafi:]
tru[...]
the[...]
yo[...]
hu[...]
res[...]
int[...]

F

Social-Process Roleplaying

Peer-Pressure Scenario
Bullying Confrontation
Persuading a Parent
Customer-Service Issue
Job Interview
Employee Evaluation
Apologizing to a Friend

Evacuation Drill
First-Aid Application
Hostage Negotiation
Escape Scenario
Pandemic Scenario

Tactical Simulations

Miniatures Combat
Civil-War Reenactment
Pencil and Paper Roleplaying
Capture the Flag
Laser Tag/Paint Ball
MMORP Games
War-Room Briefing

Constitutional Convention
Session of Congress
United Nations Session
Stock Exchange

G

Einstein's Letter
By Terrance Young

ALBERT EINSTEIN, a genius
LEO SZILARD, a genius
FRANKLIN DELANO ROOSEVELT, president of the United States

ACT I, SCENE 1

SETTING: The porch of a seaside cabin on Long Island, July 12, 1939.

(SZILARD, well-dressed in a suit, approaches the door of a screened-in porch and knocks. EINSTEIN emerges from the cabin, wearing a T-shirt and pants rolled up at the ankles.)

EINSTEIN: Leo, so glad you could come.

SZILARD: My friend. Thank you so much for meeting with me.

EINSTEIN: *(Opening porch door)* Come inside. Let's sit on the porch. There's a nice breeze off the Atlantic. *(The men move to sit in chairs beside a coffee table.)*

SZILARD: *(Jittery)* The matter weighs heavily on me.

EINSTEIN: As on me, my friend. It's quite a request to ask a pacifist to encourage the president of the United States to build the most destructive weapon man has ever known.

SZILARD: It is either the president of the United States builds it, or Hitler builds it. Which would you choose?

EINSTEIN: [I would choose that neither one have such power...]

Inquire To Prepare a Speech

1. **Question** the situation for your speech.
   - **Subject:** What should I talk about? What should my focus be?
   - **Purpose:** What should my speech do? Inform? Persuade? Memorialize?
   - **Audience:** Who will hear this speech? What does the audience know about the subject? What do they need to know?

2. **Plan** your work by completing a planning sheet. (See page 361.)

3. **Research** your topic.
   - **Topic:** Gather information about your topic and prepare any necessary handouts for the audience. Also gather props or demonstration materials.

4. **Create** your speech.
   - **Beginning:** Get the audience's attention and present your main idea.
   - **Middle:** Provide details that support or explain your main idea.
   - **Ending:** Return to your main point and leave the audience with a strong final thought.
   - **Visuals:** Present visuals through a slide show, during a demonstration, or with handouts.

5. **Improve** your speech.
   - **Evaluate** the speech after practicing it three or four times.
       Does the speech have a clear focus and position on the topic?
       Does it achieve the purpose?
       Do test audiences get the point? Are they interested?
   - **Revise** your speech.
       Remove extra words or unneeded parts.
       Rearrange details that appear out of order.
       Rework parts (beginning, middle, ending) that don't work well.
       Add stories, statistics, quotations, or other support as needed.
   - **Perfect** your speech, making sure it is clear and correct.

6. **Present** your speech in person or record it for later use.
   Follow these tips for a successful presentation.
   (See also pages 77–79.)
   - **Take** a deep breath before you begin.
   - **Greet** your audience politely and get their attention.
   - **Speak** slowly and loudly.
   - **Look up** frequently and make eye contact with your audience.

Persuasive Speech

In the following speech from an all-school convocation, a speaker presents the value of student-centered education.

Education Reform: What Google Taught Me

The **beginning** gets the audience's attention and introduces the topic.

Hello, everybody. My name is Jason Carter, and I've got an idea for making things better for high school students here and nationwide.

I'm going to show you a pair of photos, and I want you to study them for a few moments. The photo on the left shows a modern factory

in China. The photo on the right shows a typical school in the U.S. Do you notice how these two places follow the same model?

In a recent *Forbes* article entitled "The Single Best Idea for Reforming K-12 Education," Steve Denning writes, "To my mind, the biggest problem is a preoccupation with, and the application of, the factory model of management to education, where everything is arranged for the scalability and efficiency of 'the system,' to which the students, the teachers, the parents and the administrators have to adjust. 'The system' grinds forward, at ever increasing cost and declining efficiency, dispiriting students, teachers, and parents alike." All around us, the world is transforming from an industrial economy to an information and innovation economy. It's time for education to catch up.

The **middle** develops the main idea, using words and images to persuade the audience.

Here, by the way, is a shot from inside the UK office of one of the most innovative companies in the world: Google.

In the school photo, everyone was doing the same thing—probably taking a standardized test. In this photo, everybody is doing something different: writing code, playing a game, watching a film, contributing to a schedule. In the previous picture, everyone was sitting in rows of identical, bland furniture. In the Google photo, some people are sitting, some are standing, some are reclining. The furniture comes in all shapes and sizes and colors. It invites you. The school photo has no technology in it. Even cellphones are prohibited. The Google shot shows all kinds of technology, both native to the room and brought in by the users. The school photo raises my blood pressure just to look at it. The last one makes me feel, "I want to be there."

Shouldn't schools aspire to be places that students want to be? If students are engaged at school, they will focus and work and contribute and learn. If they aren't engaged, education is an uphill battle.

So what can schools learn from companies like Google and Apple? These companies focus on being useful and providing a great user experience. Once again, shouldn't schools want first and foremost to provide an enriching education—one that clearly helps every student rather than one that begs the question, "Why do I need to know this?"

A slide summarizes the spoken points, helping the audience to focus.

Here are some suggestions for creating a positive educational experience for students:

Suggestions for Creating a Useful Educational Experience
- Make us welcome.
- Make us active.
- Let us use tech.
- Let us solve problems.
- Let us innovate.

- Make us welcome in the classroom, not just bodies taking up desks.
- Make us active in the classroom, searching for information rather than just passively receiving it.
- Let us use a variety of technologies to find answers to our questions, not a single textbook.
- Let us work on real problems along with other students instead of slaving away on bubble sheets by ourselves.
- Let us innovate and create rather than just fill in the blanks.

The **ending** sums up the student's argument.

Many of the factory jobs like those we saw in the first photo have shifted overseas, so I need to be ready for a different kind of workplace. I need to be prepared to think, innovate, interact, and take responsibility for my own progress. The changes I'm suggesting would help me and my whole generation do so.

Your Turn Think about ways your school is changing or evolving. Then think about other changes that might improve your school experience. Write these thoughts down and share them with a classmate.

Other Speech Formats

The speech on the previous pages is written out word for word in manuscript form. This format works well when every word has to be right. For other situations, try one of the following speech formats.

Outline

An outline provides an organized listing of the main points to be covered in a speech. Here is the speech from the previous page in a simplified outline format. (Also see page 374.)

Convocation Speech

1. Beginning: Greet audience.
   A. Show two factory model photos.
   B. Show photo of Google office.
2. Middle: Introduce idea of learning from Google
   A. Discuss differences:
      - All doing same test vs. each working individually
      - All in strict rows in uniform furniture vs. standing, sitting, lying
      - No technology vs. many forms
      - No one wants to be there vs. everyone wants to be there
   B. Create a school that provides an enriching education and great user experience.
   C. Outline how:
      - Make us welcome.
      - Make us active.
      - Let us use tech.
      - Let us solve problems.
      - Let us innovate.
3. Conclusion: Call for a change from factory model.
      - Let us think, innovate, interact, and take responsibility.

List

For simpler, shorter speeches, you can create a simple list of main points.

Your Turn Create an outline, a list, or a manuscript for a speech of your own.

Convocation Speech

1. Greet audience.
2. Show photos.
3. Discuss differences.
4. Introduce idea of learning from Google.
5. Outline how.
6. Call for a change from factory model.

Demonstration Speech

In a demonstration speech, you show how to do something or how something works. The following speech explains how to use the quadratic formula to solve quadratic equations.

The beginning introduces the topic and provides the first visual.

The middle provides the formula and gives step-by-step instructions for using it.

The presenter runs through an example.

How to Use the Quadratic Formula

If you have taken algebra, you've run up against the quadratic equation. It looks like this: a times x squared plus b times x plus c equals zero. Often you can solve this equation using the FOIL method, but when you have fractions, decimals, or radicals, it might be easier to use the quadratic formula to solve the problem.

Quadratic Equation

$$ax^2 + bx + c = 0$$

The quadratic formula looks like this: x equals negative b plus or minus the square root of b squared minus 4 times a times c divided by 2 times a. I know, that sounds really complicated, but it's just a matter of plugging in the terms from the quadratic equation and doing your calculations. Note, however, that the plus or minus sign before the radical means that you need to calculate the formula twice to get two different answers.

Quadratic Formula

$$x = \frac{-b \pm \sqrt{b^2 - 4ac}}{2a}$$

Example Problem

Imagine that we have the following quadratic equation that we need to solve: 2 times x squared minus 3 times x minus 5 equals zero. In our original quadratic equation, there were no minus signs. That means our b and c variables are negative. So our variables are a equals 2, b equals minus 3, and c equals minus 5.

Quadratic Equation

$$2x^2 - 3x - 5 = 0$$
$$a = 2, b = -3, c = -5$$

Step 1: We start by plugging these variables into our quadratic formula. Remember that negative b is the opposite of b, so in this case, negative negative 3 will be positive three.

Quadratic Formula

$$x = \frac{3 \pm \sqrt{-3^2 - 4(2)(-5)}}{2(2)}$$

Steps are numbered
to help the audience
follow along.

Step 2: Next, we need to run our calculations. Remember your order of operations! We have to start by figuring out the value of the radical. First, we square negative 3 to get 9. Then we multiply negative five times negative two times four to get negative 40. So 9 minus negative 40 equals 49. Also, 2 times 2 equals 4 (and as we said, negative negative 3 is just 3).

Quadratic Formula

$$x = \frac{3 \pm \sqrt{49}}{4}$$

Step 3: Now, we have to run calculations twice, one with the plus sign and once with the minus sign. The square root of 49 is 7, so 3 plus 7 is ten divided by 4, which gives us 2.5. That's one answer for x. The other is 3 minus 7, which is negative 4 divided by 4, which is −1.

$$x = 2.5$$
$$x = -1$$

A graph helps
viewers understand
the purpose of
quadratic equations.

Step 4: Finally, we can graph the equation as a parabola that crosses the *x* axis at points 2.5 and −1.

Because the quadratic equation creates a parabola, we can use it to predict the arcs of moving objects, from cannon balls to comets. This equation also helps aeronautical engineers predict how air will move over a plane's wing. Think about that next time you see one hanging in the sky!

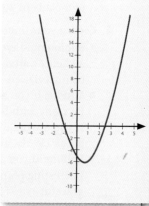

The **ending**
wraps up the
demonstration and
encourages the
audience to try the
process.

Conclusion

At first glance, the quadratic formula might look too daunting to be useful. But as you can see, it makes calculating quadratic equations just a matter of plugging and chugging.

Inquire To Conduct/Give an Interview

1. **Question** the situation for your interview.
   - **Subject:** Who will you interview? Who will interview you? What will you talk about? What should you focus on?
   - **Purpose:** Why are you holding this interview? What do you want to result from this interview? How can you achieve your purpose?
   - **Audience:** Who will watch or listen to the interview? Is there a specific audience or a general one? How much does the audience know and need to know?

2. **Plan** your work by completing a planning sheet. (See page 361.)

3. **Research** your topic.
   - **Topic:** Read, write, view, think, and discuss before you have the interview.
   - **Questions:** If you are the interviewer, prepare a list of questions, focusing on those that require more than a yes or no or single response.
   - **Answers:** If you are the interviewee, think of the questions you might be asked, and write responses.
   - **Practice:** Rehearse the interview with another person playing the other part.
   - **Visuals:** Gather books, props, film clips, or other visuals that you might want to include in your interview.

4. **Create** your interview.
   - **Beginning:** If you are the interviewer, create a beginning that catches the audience's attention, introduces the topic, and introduces the person who will be interviewed.
   - **Middle:** If you are the interviewer, ask the questions that you have prepared. Be ready with follow-up questions to help the interviewee elaborate on ideas. If you are the interviewee, listen to each question and provide your response. Speak clearly, and connect with the interviewer and the audience.
   - **Ending:** If you are the interviewer, wrap up the discussion by focusing on an interesting point. Remind the audience who the interviewee is, and make a graceful exit. Thank the interviewee for his or her time.

5. **Improve** your interview.
   - **Evaluate:** View a recording of your interview, thinking about the ideas exchanged, the emotional connection between the participants and the audience, the voice and body language of the participants, and overall effectiveness. Think of at least two improvements you could make in future interviews.

6. **Present** your interview by posting excerpts on your Web site or on YouTube. (See also pages 423–428.)

Interview Transcript

The following transcript comes from an interview with a high school physics professor about the search for exoplanets.

Interview with Keri Johnson

The **beginning** introduces the podcast, the interviewer, and the interviewee.

Darius: Hey, everybody, this is Darius for another installment of the Dare We Ask podcast. Today, I'm talking to physics teacher and exoplanet enthusiast Keri Johnson. Thank you for joining me.

Mrs. Johnson: It's a pleasure to be here.

Darius: So, the big question—"dare we ask"—is how soon human beings will be living on exoplanets.

The **middle** includes prepared questions, the interviewee's responses, and the interviewer's reactions.

Mrs. Johnson: I wish I could say "tomorrow" or even "within a hundred years," but it's going to be closer to a thousand.

Darius: A thousand! But you said that scientists have found nearly a thousand exoplanets, and some are earthlike and in the habitable zone. What's the holdup?

Mrs. Johnson: Well, it comes down to a few factors. The first earthlike planet proven to be in the habitable zone of its star was Kepler 22b. It's about twice Earth's diameter but probably about 40 Earth masses. That means it would have about 70 Gs of gravity on the surface. Your weight times 70.

Darius: You'd be crushed flat.

Instead of dominating the conversation, the interviewer allows the interviewee to speak.

Mrs. Johnson: Right, unless you could be in a water ocean. Our bodies are 70 percent water, so if we were in the ocean, we could stand the tremendous gravity. But this planet is nearly 700 light years away. Even traveling at the speed of light, which is impossible, it would take 700 years to get there.

Darius: So I can give up hope of going where no man has gone before?

Mrs. Johnson: Not entirely. The problem is human bodies. We're perfectly suited to life here on Earth. But human-made machines, and the computers in them, can happily live elsewhere. The Mars Rovers that were supposed to survive just a few months lasted years. And the Voyager probes sent out in 1977 are now outside the reach of the sun's charged particles and are heading into interstellar space.

Darius: Are you saying that, while human bodies can't live easily off our planets, our minds—at least in the form of human-built machines—can live out there happily forever?

The **ending** wraps up the conversation and thanks the interviewee.

Mrs. Johnson: If we design machines to do so, they may be carrying on the torch of human civilization into the future.

Darius: Thanks so much for your time, Mrs. Johnson. That's it for another episode of Dare We Ask!

Inquire To Debate an Issue

1. **Question** the situation for your debate. (Often a debate centers around a proposition, with one team arguing for it and one team arguing against it.)
   - **Subject:** What is the topic (issue) that will be debated?
   - **Purpose:** Why are you putting on the debate? What is the goal of the experience?
   - **Audience:** Who will witness the debate? Will the audience have an opportunity to ask questions? Will they choose the winning team?

2. **Plan** your debate by creating a resolution, forming two teams, and giving team members specific roles:

   > **Resolved:** To address a funding shortfall, Rockland High School should raise its annual textbook fee by $100 per student.

3. **Research** the issue.
   - **Topic:** Learn as much as you can about the topic so that you know all sides.
   - **Support:** Fill out a pro-con chart, listing reasons for and against your position.
   - **Discussion:** Rigorously discuss the issue with your team, seeking to explore it fully before building your arguments.

4. **Create** your side of the debate.
   - **Beginning:** Decide who will present opening remarks, and what those remarks will be.
   - **Middle:** Lay out the main arguments for your position. Anticipate objections and decide how to answer them. Imagine the main arguments for the other position and prepare rebuttals. Assign group members to present the different types of material.
   - **Ending:** Decide the key points you will want to provide to sum up, but be prepared to adjust your closing arguments depending on how the debate goes.
   - **Visuals:** Think of any visuals you might want to use to make your point.

5. **Improve** your team's performance.
   - **Evaluate** the team's main arguments.
       Are they strong?
       Do you effectively answer objections?
       Have you anticipated opposing arguments and prepared rebuttals?
   - **Improve** your presentations as needed:
       Add new evidence or lines of reason where needed.
       Remove any weak arguments.
       Rearrange details that may not be in the best order.
       Rework parts that aren't clear.

6. **Present** the debate. Answer the rebuttals of the opposition. Listen carefully to the points of your opposition and determine which rebuttals to use.

Debate

The transcript below shows excerpts from the beginning of a typical debate—with a moderator's comments and the opening remarks of the first two speakers.

Wind Power: Cure or Curse for the Planet

Moderator: Welcome to today's debate, which focuses on the following topic: "Resolved: The state should budget $10 million to develop a wind farm in Gannet Valley." The team to my right will begin our debate with five minutes of opening remarks in favor of this resolution.

Latrisha Evans: Thank you, Mr. Kao. Our world faces an energy crisis. Growing populations and growing demand mean we will need more energy in the future, not less. Most experts agree that we have reached "peak oil," and that the fossil fuels yet to be tapped are more difficult to get, such as oil-sand deposits in Canada and oil reserves beneath the melting Arctic ice sheet. And let's think about that melting ice sheet and other environmental damage caused by the burning of fossil fuels. Carbon-neutral, clean, and renewable energy sources offer a compelling solution to many of these problems. A wind farm in Gannet Valley would be one way for our state to move into the future.

Let's consider the proposed site. . . . *(She continues.)*

Moderator: Your five minutes are up for opening remarks, and now we turn to the opposing team for two minutes of rebuttal.

Wesley Keonig: Thank you, Mr. Kao, and thank you, Latrisha, for your opening comments. Though I agree with many of the problems that Latrisha pointed out, I disagree that an expensive wind farm in Gannet Valley is the best answer for our state. To start with, the notion that a wind farm is an environmentally friendly alternative is ignoring the impact of windmills on bird populations. Take, for example, the Maple Ridge facility in New York, which killed an estimated 2,000 to 4,000 birds and bats during a five-month period. That much damage was done by 120 turbines. The proposed wind farm in Gannet Valley would have a similar number.

Then, let's consider the fact that Gannet Valley is part of a state park system. The wind farm would be visible for 10 miles around from the peaks of the two mountains on either side. . . . *(He continues.)*

Moderator: Thank you for your two-minute rebuttal. Now we turn to another member of the opposing team for five minutes of opening remarks, which will be followed by a rebuttal from the team in favor. . . .

Character Debate

In a character debate, the participants play the parts of historical or literary figures. The following transcript shows part of a debate between "Abraham Lincoln" and "Muammar Gaddafi" about what makes a just war.

Abraham Lincoln and Muammar Gaddafi Debate

Each person in the debate plays the role of an important figure.

Gaddafi: Mr. Lincoln, when your countrymen chose to rebel against you, you attacked them with the full force of your military. I did the same thing. You are considered a saint, and I am considered a monster.

Lincoln: Mr. Gaddafi, let us consider the reasons for the two rebellions. The southern states rebelled because they feared that I would abolish slavery. The National Transitional Council rebelled because of your repressive 40-year regime enslaving an entire population.

The participants must thoroughly research both characters to be able to carry on a meaningful debate.

Gaddafi: My regime made Libya a wealthy nation.

Lincoln: Your regime made Libya a state sponsor of terror and a rogue nation.

Gaddafi: You are talking of events in the 1980s. By the 1990s, I had made amends for our sponsorship of terrorism and had dismantled our weapons of mass destruction. After 9/11, I was an ally of the United States in its war on terror.

The characters discuss a controversial topic that they each would have strong feelings about.

Lincoln: But when the NTC rebelled, you attacked civilian populations.

Gaddafi: What do you call the Siege of Vicksburg, Mr. Lincoln? And you cannot argue that you fought to free the slaves. To start, you fought to preserve the union at all cost. You said that if you could save the union without freeing any slaves, you would do it. You were only trying to preserve your own power, just as I was.

Lincoln: Not my own power, sir, but the power of a democratic form of government. The South seceded even before I took the oath of office. And four years later, I would have handed over the reins of government to a successor if the people had chosen someone else.

The conversation promotes deep thinking about both characters and the topic.

Gaddafi: Let's compare my supposed "scorched earth" policies with true scorched earth—Sherman's burning of Atlanta on his march to the sea. If an International Criminal Court had existed in your time, you and Grant and Lee would have been charged with crimes against humanity.

Lincoln: A kind of ICC did exist in my time. Britain, France, and the rest of Europe watched the Civil War closely and were contemplating intervention on behalf of the South. But when I made the Emancipation Proclamation, changing the focus of the war from Union to abolition, the international community decided it would not come in on the side of slavery. . . .

Round Table

A round-table discussion involves multiple characters from history, science, or literature. Here, Physics Club members portray scientists discussing string theory.

Quantum Physics Round Table

Stephen Hawking: The center of a black hole is a singularity, with a mass many times that of our sun squeezed into a space smaller than an atom. There, the laws of the very small (quantum physics) and those of the very large (general relativity) must meet. String theory provides a mathematical model that allows such a meeting.

Isaac Newton: But string theory is pure mathematics. It cannot be tested, and so it cannot be disproved, and so it is not scientific.

Hawking: Mathematics is the language of the universe. If it can combine quantum physics and general relativity—two theories supported by galaxies of evidence—I will take the mathematics.

Galileo Galilei: String theory works only if many additional dimensions exist on the quantum scale, dimensions that are so tightly "rolled up" that they can never be observed.

Hawking: And yet the math describes what we see.

Galileo: In my day, astronomers predicted the movements of the planets using elaborate mathematical models that included cycles and epicycles. The elaborate math did describe the phenomena really well, but the math was wrong because it was based on a geocentric universe. Once we moved the sun to the center of the solar system and allowed planets to follow elliptical orbits, all those complex epicycles vanished, and the math became simple.

Hawking: So, are you saying that even though the math describes what we are seeing, it may not capture the basic reality of what is going on?

Newton: That's exactly right. And I think we have the same problem with quantum physics itself. The Heisenberg Uncertainty Principle and Schrödinger's Cat describe the quantum fuzziness that we see experimentally. We see that our observations of the quantum world change that world, but there's no explanation how our intentionality would do so.

Hawking: Are you suggesting that quantum physics has been off track for the last hundred years?

Newton: I'm suggesting that, when we have an explanation that describes observations but has some hidden mechanism or can't be tested, the theory doesn't get at root causes.

Galileo: It may just be prolonging a mistaken assumption, such as the idea that the Earth is the center of the universe. . . .

Sidebar notes:

Each participant must know a great deal about the person he or she is portraying.

Each participant must also be well-versed in the topic.

The discussion that results isn't a simple pro or con debate, but rather is a wide-ranging discussion that explores an important idea.

Inquire To Hold a Simulation

1. **Question** the situation that you are simulating.
   - **Subject:** What are you simulating? What roles do different people play within the situation? What goals do people in the situation have? What rules are they bound by?
   - **Purpose:** Why are you simulating the situation? Do you wish to reenact events? Explore ideas? Predict outcomes? Model complex systems?
   - **Audience:** Who will participate in the simulation? Who will view the simulation? What should the group get out of the experience? Should the simulation be somehow recorded and shared to a wider audience?

2. **Plan** your simulation by completing a planning sheet. (See page 361.)
   - **Goal and objectives:** Write your goal, and then unpack it by answering the 5 W's and H about it.
   - **Tasks, time, team, and tools:** Consider the work that needs to go into creating the simulation; the people involved; and the resources, equipment, and information that the group needs.

3. **Research** your topic and the roles different people will play.
   - **Topic:** Find out as much as you can about the topic.
   - **Roles:** Determine what roles different simulators will play. (For example, an interview needs an interviewer and an interviewee; a trial needs a judge, a prosecution, a defender, a defendant, witnesses, and a jury.)
   - **Rules:** Decide how the different people involved will interact. (For example, in a trial, each counsel needs to give an opening statement, present evidence, call and question witnesses, cross-examine witnesses, and give a closing statement.)

4. **Create** your simulation.
   - **Assign** roles to participants.
   - **Ask** some participants/observers to document the event in writing, photos, videos, and/or play-by-play commentary.
   - **Explain** the rules.

5. **Improve** your experience by reflecting on what happened.
   - **Review** what happened and how the events made people feel.
     Ask participants and observers what they learned.
   - **Connect** the simulation to the real world.
     Ask "what if" and "what now" questions.
     Document the debriefing with more writing, photos, and/or video.

6. **Present** the simulation by posting your documents in a format that allows others to share the experience.

Example Simulations

Below, you'll see simulation games you can run to explore many different scenarios.

Social-Process Roleplaying

Peer-Pressure Scenario
Bullying Confrontation
Persuading a Parent
Customer Service Issue
Job Interview
Employee Evaluation
Apologizing to a Friend

Tactical Simulations

Miniatures Combat
Civil War Reenactment
Pencil and Paper Roleplaying
Capture the Flag
Laser Tag/Paint Ball
MMORP Games
War-Room Briefing

Crisis Simulation

Evacuation Drill
First Aid Application
Hostage Negotiation
Escape Scenario
Pandemic Scenario
CPR Practice
Pool Rescue

Political/Economic Game

Constitutional Convention
Session of Congress
United Nations Session
Stock Exchange
Treaty Convention
Propaganda Office
World Peace Game

Trial Simulation

Trial of Historical Figure
Trial of Literary Character
Trial of Mythological Figure
Trial of Scientific Theory
Trial of Political Theory

System Simulation

Resource Management Games
City Building Games
Biome Simulations
Flight Simulator
Business Games

Inquire To Stage a Play

See pages 567–568 for tips on writing a play.

1. **Question** the situation for the play.
   - **Subject:** What is the subject of the play? Is it a comedy? A tragedy? A mystery? Is it a new play or a classic?
   - **Purpose:** Why are you putting on the play? What effect should it have? What mood do you want to create?
   - **Audience:** Who will see this play? How can you connect with the audience?

2. **Plan** your play by completing a planning sheet. (See page 361.)

3. **Research** the play.
   - **Actors:** Cast actors. (Conduct tryouts if necessary.) Get copies of the play for all of those with speaking parts and read through it.
   - **Technical crews:** Enlist others to help design and build sets, create costumes, work backstage, run lights and sound, provide publicity, create a program, and handle ticket sales.

4. **Create** your production of the play.
   - **Read** through the script together.
   - **Block** scenes by deciding where actors enter, stand, move, and exit.
   - **Run** scenes to help actors learn lines and blocking.
   - **Practice music** first offstage. Then add music to the practice runs.
   - **Rehearse** with the whole cast, but require actors to memorize lines on their own time.

5. **Improve** your performance by evaluating and revising it.
   - **Evaluate** your play.

     Does the performance suit the goal of the project?

     Do the performers get the ideas across? Do they create the right emotional impact? Does the audience respond appropriately?
   - **Tighten** the performance.

     Remove awkward pauses and unnecessary actions.

     Rearrange blocking so that speakers can be seen and heard.

     Rework scenes that aren't functioning well.

     Add subtle reactions to lines and actions.
   - **Perfect** your performance.

6. **Present** your performance. Listen to the audience's response; then continue to refine your work to improve your next performance.

Play Script

This page shows the first part of a play script, which includes all the main features of a script.

Title

Cast

Act / Scene

Setting

Stage Direction

Dialogue

Einstein's Letter
By Terrance Young

ALBERT EINSTEIN, a genius
LEO SZILARD, a genius
FRANKLIN DELANO ROOSEVELT, president of the United States

ACT I, SCENE 1

SETTING: The porch of a seaside cabin on Long Island, July 12, 1939.

(SZILARD, well-dressed in a suit, approaches the door of a screened-in porch and knocks. EINSTEIN emerges from the cabin, wearing a T-shirt and pants rolled up at the ankles.)

EINSTEIN: Leo, so glad you could come.

SZILARD: My friend. Thank you so much for meeting with me.

EINSTEIN: *(Opening porch door)* Come inside. Let's sit on the porch. There's a nice breeze off the Atlantic. *(The men move to sit in chairs beside a coffee table.)*

SZILARD: *(Jittery)* The matter weighs heavily on me.

EINSTEIN: As on me, my friend. It's quite a request to ask a pacifist to encourage the president of the United States to build the most destructive weapon man has ever known.

SZILARD: It is either the president of the United States builds it, or Hitler builds it. Which would you choose?

EINSTEIN: I would choose that neither one have such power.

SZILARD: One will.

EINSTEIN: Yes.

SZILARD: *(Pause)* He has taken the Sudetenland. . . .

EINSTEIN: *(Grave)* Perhaps it will be enough.

SZILARD: It has only whetted his appetite. With an atomic bomb, think how far he will go. He is already mining uranium. He is looking for sources of deuterium. He is bent on making a bomb.

EINSTEIN: Bent. It is a very telling word. Hitler is bent, and now we must be bent as well.

SZILARD: It is a terrible circumstance.

EINSTEIN: You have written to the president. What was his response?

SZILARD: None. But he will listen to the great Albert Einstein.

EINSTEIN: That's exactly what I fear. . . .

Types of Plays

The Western world has created many types of plays over the last three thousand years, though most fit into the following broad categories.

▶ Drama

Drama refers to a serious play that depicts real-life situations and addresses important themes. Dramas tend to explore human relationships, historical events, and the human condition. (The term *drama* also sometimes refers to theatre in general, encompassing both comedy and tragedy.)

▶ Comedy

Comedy refers to a play in which the main character is redeemed, often despite his or her faults. Here are four common types of comedy:

- **Farce** uses fast-paced and ludicrous situations, accidents, misunderstandings, mistaken identities, physical humor, and racy material to get a laugh. Examples include *Pseudolus* and *Lend Me a Tenor.*
- **Romantic comedy** follows the struggle of two or more people who are falling in love. Examples include *A Midsummer Night's Dream* and *Guys and Dolls.*
- **Satire** pokes fun at human vice and folly, often depicting public figures and institutions as absurd. Examples include *The Wasps* and *Candide.*
- **Comedy of manners/ideas** focuses on sophisticated characters, witty dialogue, and philosophical ideas. Examples include *Helen* and *Man and Superman.*

▶ Tragedy

Tragedy refers to a play in which the main character is destroyed, often because of his or her faults. Here are three versions of tragedy:

- **Aristotelian tragedy** depicts the downfall of an essentially good person due to his or her own faults. The play evokes fear and pity from the audience. Examples include *King Lear* and *Death of a Salesman.*
- **Hegelian tragedy** depicts the fatal conflict between two good causes in opposition—for example, Albert Einstein the pacifist having to suggest an atomic bomb to Roosevelt. In this type of tragedy, good itself is the victim. Examples include *Antigone* and *Miss Saigon.*
- **Revenge tragedy** depicts a wronged hero who seeks revenge on the perpetrator of his or her misery and is destroyed by the act of revenge. Examples include *Hamlet* and *Sweeney Todd.*

Chapter 34
Community Projects

Groups and communities flourish when the individuals within them work together to achieve a common purpose like cleaning up a neglected park or school yard. Accomplishing such a purpose requires that group members cooperate and assume responsibility for their given tasks.

The projects in this chapter are too big for one person to take on. But a team of workers in which each member fulfills a defined role can accomplish big things. Together, a team can organize fund-raisers, service projects, and much more. The guidelines that follow show the way.

You will learn . . .

- Organizing Fund-Raisers
- Organizing Service Projects
- Organizing Flash Events
- Running Contests
- Running Campaigns
- Creating Clubs

Project Overview

Here is a quick overview of the community projects in this chapter.

A Fund-Raisers

A fund-raiser is an event that raises money for a special cause. Organizing a fund-raiser takes careful planning, including a consideration of budget and division of labor. (See pages 572–575.)

B Service Projects

A service project is a volunteer-driven event focused on addressing a need of a community or organization. Some examples of service projects include community clean-ups, food drives, neighborhood restoration projects, and visits to senior homes. (See pages 576–577.)

C Flash Events

A flash event is a carefully organized public performance in which a large group of seemingly indifferent people assemble in a public area and carry out a synchronized display—a dance, song, and so on. Many flash events are meant to create a buzz about a particular issue. They are commonly organized through social media. It is necessary to get permission from property owners before carrying out such an event. (See pages 578–579.)

D Contests

Contests are a great way to drum up excitement for a particular cause or event. They can also be used as a creative outlet for visual and verbal expression. Running one takes careful planning and organization. (See pages 580–581.)

E Campaigns

Running a campaign means promoting an idea or cause on a large scale. Targeting a campaign, publicizing it, and creating campaign materials are important elements of campaigning. Campaigns work best through a variety of publicity, including social media. (See pages 582–585.)

F Clubs

Joining or creating a club is a fun way to interact with people who share your interests. Clubs can empower you to improve your school and community. (See pages 586–588.)

A

Save Our Animal Shelter Planning Sheet

Goal: Host a fund-raising dance to support the local animal shelter.

Objectives: *Who?* Eleventh-grade students, faculty, and animal shelter
employees will organize the event. We'll ask local business
to sponsor the dance.

What? To run a successful dance we'll need a DJ, decorations, chair
tables, refreshments, and event T-shirts.

Where? The school gymnasium.

When? Saturday, September 22 from 8:00 p.m. - 10:30 p.m.

How? We'll divide the tasks among interested 11th-grade studen

B

Tasks:	Time:
Start.....................................	Sept. 4
1. Host dance kick-off meeting in the activity center.	Sept. 4
2. Plan the budget. Research music options.	Sept. 4
3. Reserve the gymnasium and disc jockey.	Sept. 9
4. Create publicity materials (posters, fliers, T-shirts).	Sept. 4 - Sept. 22
5. Visit local businesses; make a pitch for sponsorships.	Sept. 9 - Sept. 22
6. Reserve tables and chairs. Purchase decorations.	Sept. 17
7. Set up and decorate the gymnasium.	Sept. 21
8. Host the dance!	Sept. 22
9. Clean up and return equipment and materials.	Sept. 23

C

I'm Attending

Maybe

No

Veteran's Day Festival Flash Event

When: Sunday November 11, 2012

Time: Secret!

Description: Help us salute our troops in style! We're
organizing a flash event dance for the
annual Veteran's Day Festival at Byer Park.

What exactly is a flash event? It's an organized public
performance that is made to look spontaneous. We've
gotten permission from the city council to perform a
fun dance/song combo to honor our troops. It's a simple
routine but will only work if many of people participate.
If you're interested, please join our event page or follow
us on Twitter at @VetDayGroove. More details will follow.

D

Presented by the Literary Club and
Barrington Public Library

Verse to First

BHS Poetry Contest

Interested in poetry? Want to win great prizes?
Enter the "Verse to First" poetry contest. This
year's theme is **"Lost and Found."**

Submit your work to Mr. Connelly in Room 312.
Submission deadline is Friday, March 17.

Rules
✓ Must be an original work
✓ Maximum of three entries per person
✓ No poem longer than one page

Prizes
1st Place: $250 scholarship
Best "Lost" entry: $25 Amazon.com gift card
Best "Found" entry: $25 Amazon.com gift card

E

Live Better 2013

Do you ever feel like you're sleepwalking through the day?
Does getting out of bed feel like a chore of epic proportions? Are
you nodding off in class more than you'd like? Forget gas prices,
high schoolers these days are enduring an energy crisis of our
own. More and more, we turn to quick, carbonated pick-me-ups
and ignore the real energy solution: wellness.

The "Live Better 2013" campa
minds and bodies—and to provide
boost we need to stay focused in th
the field. Each week we'll post a ne
and locker rooms. To get started, h
better in 2013:

- Drink more water.
- Exercise for at least 30 minu
- Eat at least one serving of fr

Help make our school a health
2013" campaign and get busy livin

Have you had enough water today?

LIVE BETTER 2

F

9:08 AM

Physics Club

Home | About Us | Projects | Photos | Contact

What we do

Mission Statement: The Oak Ridge South Physics Club is a
club for high school juniors and seniors interested in learning
more about physics.

We meet monthly to learn new concepts,
discuss ideas, observe field work, and
design and test new experiments.

Some topics we're interested in include:
- Energy
- Kinematics
- Momentum
- Waves

Who can join

Physics Club is open to any junior and senior who has
completed Physics 1 and maintains at least a 2.5 GPA.

When we meet

We meet after school on the third Thursday of the month at
3:30 p.m. in Room 104. Meetings last between 30 minutes
and 1 hour.

Who we are

President
Camila Ortiz

Faculty Advisor
Mr. Adams (kwadams@nhhseduc8or.edu)

Inquire To Organize a Fund-Raiser

1. **Question** the situation for the event.
   - **Subject:** What will the fund-raiser be about? Will it have a theme? How will you raise money? Is it a one-time event, or is it one that happens often?
   - **Purpose:** Why are you putting on the event? How much money do you wish to raise? Why should people participate?
   - **Audience:** Who will attend the event? What do they expect? What response do you want from them?

2. **Plan** the event by completing a planning sheet. (See page 573.)
   - **Fund-raiser ideas:** Raffle, car wash, battle of the bands, dance marathon, beach clean-up, walk-a-thon, chili cookoff, youth-mentorship program
   - **Organize:** Recruit a team of people to plan and carry out the event.
   - **Materials:** List materials you will need and plan how to obtain them.
   - **Budget:** Fill out a budget sheet. (See page 574.)

3. **Research** the event.
   - **Arrange** to use the location you need for your event. Assign team members to reserve the space. Then decide how the space will be set up for the event.
   - **Publicize** the event using posters, fliers, social media, and other creative forms of publicity (see page 428).

4. **Create** the event, considering the following roles for team members.
   - **Budget committee** to keep track of expenditures, ticket sales, and donations
   - **Publicity team** in charge of creating publicity materials and building awareness for the event
   - **Host** to guide the group through the event
   - **Entertainers** for the event (DJs, actors, and so on)
   - **Cooks/servers/dishwashers** for food events
   - **Refreshment** people to provide and sell refreshments
   - **Runners** in charge of retrieving new materials and doing other odd jobs during the event

5. **Improve** your event.
   - **Evaluate** the event.

     Did the event fulfill its goals and objectives?

     Did it focus on an appropriate idea or activity? How much money did it raise? Did enough people attend or give money? How could it be improved next time?
   - **Improve** the event by adding value, removing inefficiency, rearranging the sequence, and reworking parts to make them more effective.

6. **Present** the results of the fund-raising event, including earnings generated, in a newsletter, school calendar, social media post, blog, or school newspaper article.

Event Planning Sheet: Fund-Raiser

A planning sheet lays out the most important details for planning an event, including goal, objectives, tasks, time, team members, and tools. The following example is a fund-raising idea that came from the "Save Our Animal Shelter" campaign (pages 286–287).

Save Our Animal Shelter Planning Sheet

Goal: Host a fund-raising dance to support the local animal shelter.

Objectives:

Who? Eleventh-grade students, faculty, and animal shelter employees will organize the event. We'll ask local businesses to sponsor the dance.

What? To run a successful dance we'll need a DJ, decorations, chairs, tables, refreshments, and event T-shirts.

Where? The school gymnasium.

When? Saturday, September 22, from 8:00 p.m. - 10:30 p.m.

How? We'll divide the tasks among interested 11th-grade students.

Tasks:	Time:
Start..	Sept. 4
1. Host dance kick-off meeting in the activity center.	Sept. 4
2. Plan the budget. Research music options.	Sept. 4
3. Reserve the gymnasium and disc jockey.	Sept. 9
4. Create publicity materials (posters, fliers, T-shirts).	Sept. 4 - Sept. 22
5. Visit local businesses; make a pitch for sponsorships.	Sept. 9 - Sept. 22
6. Reserve tables and chairs. Purchase decorations.	Sept. 17
7. Set up and decorate the gymnasium.	Sept. 21
8. Host the dance!	Sept. 22
9. Clean up and return equipment and materials.	Sept. 23
10. Present earnings to the animal shelter	Sept. 25
Finish..	Sept. 25

Team: Students—Jamie Pollin (host), Tyrone Long, Selena Gelhart, Tameka Dubay, Josh Muller, and Neva Patel. Faculty—Mr. Meadow, Mr. Kaufmann, and Mrs. Kresken. animal shelter employees—Nicole Sullivan and Rodrigo Flores

Tools:

Equipment: DJ equipment and microphone

Food and drink: Fresh fruit, veggies, water, and punch

Materials: T-shirts, decorations, tables, chairs, cups, and plates

Event Budget Sheet: Fund-Raiser

When an event involves money management, a budget sheet will help you plan where and how to spend your money.

Benefit-Dance Budget Sheet

Expense	Estimated Cost	Actual Cost
Entertainment		
DJ	$450	$400
Publicity		
Posters/Fliers/Tickets	$50	$52
Social Media	Free	Free
Venue		
Panther Pavilion	Free	Free
Equipment		
Microphone/ lighting	Free	Free
Materials		
Custom T-shirts	$400	$427
Decorations	$60	$54
Tables/chairs	Free	Free
Cups/plates/napkins	$35	$38.52
Food/ Drink		
Snacks/drinks	$40	Free (donated)
Total Expenses	$1,035.00 (Budget)	$971.52
Business Sponsorships		$625
Total expenses after sponsorships		$346.52
Ticket sales ($ per)		$888 (111 sold)
T-shirt sales ($12 per)		$576 (48 sold)
Total profit		$1,117.48

Your Turn Go to thoughtfullearning.com/h574 to download a budget sheet. Create a rough budget for an event you are planning or would like to plan.

Event Work Roster: Fund-Raiser

Running a successful event is a group effort. Each volunteer needs to know what her or his responsibilities are and when to do them. Creating a work roster helps define each person's roles and responsibilities.

Benefit-Dance Work Roster

Job	Arrive By	Volunteers
Decorations Set up tables, chairs, and ticket booth; decorate gym	5:00 p.m.	**Students:** Jamie Pollin, Tyrone Long, Selena Gelhart, Tameka Dubay, and Neva Patel
Entertainment • **Music:** Set up and sound check • **Dog Meet-N-Greet:** Supervise	7:30 p.m.	**Students:** Tyrone Long **Adults:** Chris Crary (DJ)
	8:00 p.m.	**Students:** Selena Gelhart **Adults:** Nicole Sullivan and Rodrigo Flores
Food and refreshments Prepare veggie and fruit trays	7:45 p.m.	**Students:** Neva Patel **Faculty:** Mrs. Kresken
	9:30 p.m.	**Students:** Tameka Dubay **Faculty:** Mr. Meadow
Tickets Supervise ticket sales and cash box	7:45 p.m.	**Students:** Jamie Pollin **Faculty:** Mr. Kaufmann
T-shirts Take T-shirt orders and collect money	7:45 p.m. 9:00 p.m.	**Students:** Josh Muller and Tyrone Long
Supervisor Supervise inside and outside of the gym	7:45 p.m. 9:30 p.m.	**Faculty:** Mr. Barton **Adults:** Two local police officers
Runners Assisting, getting supplies	8:00 p.m.	**Students:** Selena Gelhart

Your Turn Create a work roster for an event you are planning. (Download a template at thoughtfullearning.com/h575.)

Inquire To Organize a Service Project

1. **Question** the situation for the service project.
   - **Subject:** What community issue will you address? How can you help? What will the project entail?
   - **Purpose:** Why are you choosing to address this issue? Why is it important?
   - **Audience:** How many people will the event involve? Who can help you coordinate the event?

2. **Plan** the event by completing a planning sheet. (See page 361.)
   - **Service-project ideas:** Park, highway, or beach clean-up; charitable food drive; soup kitchen or thrift store work; adult or children's reading programs; tutoring or mentorship programs

3. **Research** the event.
   - **Gather** information about the agency or organization you are interested in helping. Contact the agency's supervisor or volunteer coordinator for more information—ask about the organization's needs and secure a date and time for the event. Then ask people to help you plan and execute the event.
   - **Arrange** transportation to and from the event. Determine what materials or equipment you will need to complete the service project.
   - **Publicize** the event, using a variety of print (posters, fliers), digital (social media), and other media options (television, radio).

4. **Create** the event, considering the following roles.
   - **Project coordinator:** This person is in charge of setting up ground rules and supervising the event as it happens.
   - **Team leaders:** These people lead teams of volunteers to complete different aspects of the project.
   - **Volunteers:** These workers do the various jobs.

5. **Improve** your event.
   - **Evaluate** the event. Did the service project fulfill its goals and objectives? Did it achieve its purpose? How many people attended? Did they enjoy it? How were you received by the group or agency? How could a similar project be improved next time?
   - **Improve** the event by fixing any inefficiencies, adding additional parts, and reworking parts to make them more effective.

6. **Present** the results of the project through social media, in a local or school newspaper, in a newsletter, on a school Web site, or in other media. If the service project happens more than once, publicize the next event.

Service Project

Here are photos from a various high school service projects. Each project improves communities in a different way.

In this repeated service project, teams of students volunteer at a local after-school youth program, administering games and activities, helping with homework, and acting as mentors.

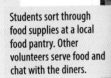

Students sort through food supplies at a local food pantry. Other volunteers serve food and chat with the diners.

Students beautify a community center by painting a mural on an interior wall.

During a park restoration project, students plant flowers and trees. Other volunteers pick up trash and debris.

Inquire To Organize a Flash Event

1. **Question** the situation for the flash event.
   - **Subject:** What will you do for your flash event? How will you set it up? Where will you perform?
   - **Purpose:** Why are you choosing to do a flash event? How do you want it received?
   - **Audience:** Who will be involved? How will you recruit participants? Who will see it?

2. **Plan** the flash event by completing a planning sheet. (See page 361.)
   - **Background:** Study other flash events. Compare ideas. Find out how they recruited participants and set up rehearsals.
   - **Location:** Discover a place to carry out the event. Ideally, you will want it to occur in a public place where lots of people are gathered.

3. **Research** the flash event.
   - **Obtain permission** from property owners, the town board, and parents before moving forward with the event.
   - **Arrange** a rehearsal or create instructions for practicing the event so that participants know what to do, where to do it, and when to do it. Also, decide if any costumes and props are needed.
   - **Publicize** your event using digital resources to recruit participants. Use social media, text messages, and email chains to provide details and updates about the event.

4. **Create** the flash event.
   - **Send** clear instructions about what, where, when, and how your event will take place. Participants must know when the performance is to begin and end.
   - **Begin** the performance by gathering in the desired location, as if your group is just going about their day. Then, at the scheduled time, begin your performance.
   - **Continue** with the main part of the performance, until all of the performers have joined in.
   - **Finish** the event by walking away as if nothing happened.

5. **Improve** the flash event.
   - **Evaluate** the flash event. Did it fulfill its purpose? Did enough people participate? Was the audience's reaction what you expected? What went right? What improvements could you make next time?
   - **Improve** your performance by taking notes of any changes you would make for the next time you want to organize a flash event.

6. **Present** a video of the event online, at your school, through social media, or perhaps on a local news station.

Flash Event

A flash event needs many participants to make an impact. You can use social media to recruit and communicate with your team. The examples below show how a student took advantage of a variety of social media to encourage participation in a flash event in her community.

Social Networks

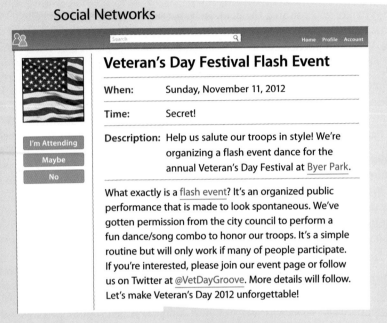

Veteran's Day Festival Flash Event

I'm Attending
Maybe
No

When:	Sunday, November 11, 2012
Time:	Secret!

Description: Help us salute our troops in style! We're organizing a flash event dance for the annual Veteran's Day Festival at Byer Park.

What exactly is a flash event? It's an organized public performance that is made to look spontaneous. We've gotten permission from the city council to perform a fun dance/song combo to honor our troops. It's a simple routine but will only work if many of people participate. If you're interested, please join our event page or follow us on Twitter at @VetDayGroove. More details will follow. Let's make Veteran's Day 2012 unforgettable!

Microblogs

 Veteran's Day Festival Flash Event @VetDayGroove
October 24
We've scheduled a rehearsal for Friday, Nov. 2, at 7 p.m. on the football field. Tell your friends! #VetDayGroove #SupportTheTroops

Text Messages

To: Veteran's Day Flash Event Participants

The dance will start at exactly 2:30 p.m. at the Byer Park Terrace. Wear yellow. And . . . shh! Don't tell anyone what's about to go down!

 Veteran's Day Festival Flash Event @VetDayGroove
October 26
Yellow is the official awareness color for supporting the troops. Plan on wearing a yellow top on Nov. 11. #VetDayGroove #SupportTheTroops

 Veteran's Day Festival Flash Event @VetDayGroove
November 06
Go crazy! The big dance just 5 days away. Remember to check your phones Sunday a.m. for the exact time and location of the dance.

Inquire To Run a Contest

1. **Question** the situation for the contest.
   - **Subject:** What sort of contest is it? What is the focus? What do you want out of it? Will there be a prize? How will you pick the winner? Where will the contest take place?
   - **Purpose:** Why are you running the contest? What value will the contest offer to its participants?
   - **Audience:** Who will participate? How will you convince people to take part? How will people learn about it?

2. **Plan** the contest by completing a planning sheet. (See page 361.)
   - **Contest ideas:** Art competitions, engineering competitions, design contests, photo contests, essay or short story contests, code-breaking competition, film-festivals, battles of the bands

3. **Research** the contest.
   - **Gather** information and ideas for contests. Compare your idea to other contests. What has made them successful or unsuccessful? What sort of prize will generate interest?
   - **Obtain permission** from teachers, parents, or other necessary parties before moving forward with the contest.

4. **Create** the contest.
   - **Introduction:** Briefly explain what the contest is about. Entice the reader to participate.
   - **Rules:** Make the rules clear and easy to follow. Generally, you should strive for no more than three to five rules per contest.
   - **Notes:** Explain any special rules or considerations that will make the entry acceptable or unacceptable.
   - **Media:** Decide which media you will use to publicize the event—posters, fliers, social network pages, and so on.
   - **Announcements:** Periodically remind participants of deadlines for submission.

5. **Improve** the contest.
   - **Evaluate:** Does the contest fulfill its purpose? Does the contest offer value to the participants? Will they find it enjoyable? How could it be improved?
   - **Revise:** Add any rules that answer the readers' key questions. Delete any rules that make the contest too complicated.
   - **Edit:** Check all print and digital materials for correct spelling and grammar.

6. **Present** the contest by announcing the winners through social media, in a local or school newspaper, in a newsletter, on a school Web site, or through other media. Publicize your next contest if you have one planned.

Contest Flier

The following flier promotes a poetry contest. It includes rules and information about prizes.

Presented by the Literary Club and
Barrington Public Library

Verse to First
BHS Poetry Contest

Interested in poetry? Want to win great prizes?
Enter the "Verse to First" poetry contest. This
year's theme is "**Lost and Found**."

Submit your work to Mr. Connelly in Room 312.
Submission deadline is Friday, March 17.

Rules
✓ Must be an original work
✓ Maximum of three entries per person
✓ No poem longer than one page

Prizes
1st Place: $250 scholarship
Best "Lost" entry: $25 Amazon.com gift card
Best "Found" entry: $25 Amazon.com gift card

Notes: Each poem should include a cover letter with your name, the title of the poem, and email
address. Do not include your name on the poem itself. Entries will be judged by the BHS
English faculty, Principal Connelly, and librarians at the Barrington Public Library.

Inquire To Run a Campaign

1. **Question** the situation for the campaign.
   - **Subject:** What does the campaign promote? What candidate or cause does it support?
   - **Purpose:** Why am I running this campaign? To raise awareness? To support a cause? To support a candidate?
   - **Audience:** Who is the target audience of this campaign? What does the audience want and need? How can I reach them?

2. **Plan** your campaign by completing a planning sheet. (See page 361.)
   - **Profile:** Learn about your target audience, including their wants and needs, interests and habits, and likes and dislikes.
   - **Connection:** Brainstorm ways your campaign can reach your audience.

3. **Research** your campaign.
   - **Develop** a platform, plank, or slogan that meets the basic needs of your audience (see page 584).
   - **Enlist** others to assist in your campaign.

4. **Create** your campaign, considering the following publicity components:
   - **Posters:** Provide an attention-grabbing image, catchy slogan, and important details. Post online and in print.
   - **Fliers:** Create a paper-sized (or smaller) slip to distribute at school or in your community. Include a catchy headline and striking image or graphic.
   - **Campaign wear:** Create campaign buttons, wrist bands, or T-shirts (see pages 584–585).
   - **Speeches:** Write and deliver a speech in favor of the candidate or cause. (See pages 583.)
   - **School media:** Write an article promoting your cause in the opinion section of your school newspaper.
   - **Social media:** Use a variety of social media outlets to post information, video, and hyperlinks in support of the candidate or cause.
   - **Personal Touch:** Introduce yourself and your campaign to others. Shake hands, be enthusiastic, and encourage others to get involved.

5. **Improve** your campaign.
   - **Evaluate:** Does each part of the campaign achieve its goal and objectives? How has the audience received the campaign? How can it be improved?
   - **Revise:** Remove parts that are not needed. Rework parts that don't work well. Add new ways of reaching your audience.
   - **Perfect** each part, making sure it is bold and persuasive.

6. **Present** the campaign through posters, fliers, campaign wear, speeches, or social media. If possible, arrange a public debate with the opponent in an election campaign.

Campaign Speech and Poster

The following campaign speech and posters were built in support of a student wellness campaign.

Campaign Speech

Live Better 2013

The **beginning** engages the audience.

Do you ever feel like you're sleepwalking through the day? Does getting out of bed feel like a chore of epic proportions? Are you nodding off in class more than you'd like? Forget gas prices; high schoolers these days are enduring an energy crisis of our own. More and more, we turn to quick, carbonated pick-me-ups and ignore the real energy solution: wellness.

The **middle** explains the campaign and lists ways to get involved.

The "Live Better 2013" campaign is out to improve our minds and bodies—and to provide us with the natural energy boost we need to stay focused in the classroom, on stage, and on the field. Each week we'll post a new wellness tip in the cafeteria and locker rooms. To get started, here are some easy ways to live better in 2013:

- Drink more water.
- Exercise for at least 30 minutes a day.
- Eat at least one serving of fruit with your breakfast.

The **ending** calls the listener to act.

Help make our school a healthier place. Join the "Live Better 2013" campaign and get busy living!

Campaign Posters

Have you had your servings of fruit today? LIVE BETTER

Have you had enough water today? LIVE BETTER 2013

Have you exercised today? LIVE BETTER 2013

Targeting Your Campaign

A campaign should target real needs in order to generate support and make a maximum impact. Before beginning your campaign, check if it addresses one or more of the needs on Abraham Maslow's pyramid. The pyramid identifies a hierarchy of needs, starting with the most essential and working up toward those that help us reach our fullest potential. What needs does your cause or campaign address?

Your Turn Write down the needs you will address. For example, the campaign on the previous page addresses water, food, sleep, health, achievement, and confidence.

morality, creativity, problem solving

self-esteem, respect, achievement, confidence

friendship, family, acceptance

health, property, security, employment

air, water, food, clothing, shelter, sleep

Planks

A plank is a statement that addresses a core idea connected to the audience's needs. Political campaigns will often focus on a series of planks, which, when put together, make up the candidate's platform. Effective planks target the needs of the audience.

Your Turn Write a series of planks for your campaign. Start by listing the needs. Then, for each need, complete the sentence "We believe that . . ." by stating an idea that meets the need. Here's an example from the wellness campaign:

Audience Need	Plank of Campaign
Water and food	We believe that eating and drinking right provides the energy needed to seize the day.
Health	We believe that wellness improves your physical and emotional health.
Achievement	We believe that wellness improves performance in school, in athletics, and in the workplace.
Confidence	We believe that wellness makes you feel good about yourself.

Slogan

Every campaign needs a catchy slogan to generate interest and stick in people's minds. Slogans should begin with command words.

Your Turn Write a slogan beginning with a command word and telling the reader what to do.

Get Busy Living!
Say "yes" to the wellness challenge.

LIVE BETTER 2013

Publicity

Of course, a necessary component of any campaign is getting the word out and persuading others to join. There are many ways to promote a campaign:

- **Posters and fliers** provide eye-catching visuals and can be placed strategically to reach your target audience. Both posters and fliers should include an attractive and memorable headline or slogan, an engaging visual, and details about actions the viewer should take. Consider distributing them in print and online. (See sample posters and fliers on pages 428 and 531.)

- **An event** is a great way to gather people in support of a cause, but events require careful planning and execution. (See pages 572–575.) Events include rallies, demonstrations, fund-raisers, flash events, speeches, and debates.

- **A speech** can stir up support for your campaign. There are different approaches to writing and delivering speeches (see pages 552–557), though all speeches in support of a candidate or cause should be lively and engaging. Beyond words, the speaker can use tone of voice, facial expressions, and body language to demonstrate passion for the campaign.

- **A debate** is like a speech but also includes an opponent. In a debate, you argue in favor of your candidate or cause and in opposition to your opponent's position. Debates help define an issue through argumentation and an exchange of ideas, but they should never resort to personal attacks. (See pages 560–563.)

- **The "personal touch"** means getting yourself out there and connecting on a personal level with your audience. This means speaking earnestly with people one-on-one, shaking hands, explaining what your campaign is trying to do, and offering ways to help. Remember to extend the "personal touch" beyond your immediate group of friends and family.

- **Passing out campaign gear,** such as buttons, T-shirts, and wrist bands, can help you break the ice with potential supporters. Make sure your campaign materials fall within your budget.

- **Social media** allow you to deliver your message to anyone in the world in a timely manner, making it a powerful and efficient avenue for publicity. The best social media campaigns take advantage of diverse social forms, including short messages, Web links, or audio and visual media. (For more on using social media to support a campaign, see pages 286–287.)

Your Turn Decide which types of publicity you will use to promote your campaign.

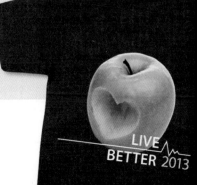

Inquire To Create a Club

1. **Question** the situation for your club.
   - **Subject:** What is the focus? What will the members have in common? What will the members do?
   - **Purpose:** Why do you want to create this club? Why will people join? What will members get out of being involved?
   - **Audience:** Who will be a part of this club? Why would someone want to join? Do you need a faculty advisor?

2. **Plan** your club by completing a planning sheet. (See page 361.)
   - **Survey:** Study similar clubs. Find out what works and what doesn't.
   - **Plan:** Identify activities your club might enjoy or want to be involved in.

3. **Research** the best way to set up your club.
   - **Discover** as much information as you can about the focus of the club and the people who might want to join.
   - **Organize** your club, writing a mission statement that explains who is in charge, how decisions are made, and how to become a member.
   - **Find** a place to hold the meetings and decide on a meeting time. For school clubs, find a faculty advisor.

4. **Create** your club.
   - **Publicize** the club.
   - **Invite** people to come to the meeting.
   - **Hold** your first meeting and explain the purpose of the club.
   - **Ask** for ideas and input.
   - **Plan** activities for your next meeting and decide how you will elect a president and club officers.
   - **Encourage** others to return for the next meeting, giving a time and place.

5. **Improve** your club.
   - **Evaluate** the meetings.
     Do they achieve your goals for the club? What activities worked well? What could be improved? What other activities might people enjoy?
   - **Refine** your meetings.
     Remove activities or parts that are uninteresting or off topic.
     Add new activities that members will enjoy.
     Rework the club charter as necessary.

6. **Present** your club, creating a Web page for it. (See pages 592–595 for instructions.) Then publicize it online through social media and in your school through newsletters, posters, and fliers.

Club Web Page

A club Web site lets people know what the club is about and how to join. Here is a sample Web page.

Physics Club

Home | **About Us** | Projects | Photos | Contact

What we do

Mission Statement: The Oak Ridge South Physics Club is a club for high school juniors and seniors interested in learning more about physics.

We meet monthly to learn new concepts, discuss ideas, observe field work, and design and test new experiments.

Some topics we're interested in include:
- Energy
- Kinematics
- Momentum
- Waves

Who can join

Physics Club is open to any junior or senior who has completed Physics 1 and maintains at least a 2.5 GPA.

When we meet

We meet after school on the third Thursday of the month at 3:30 p.m. in Room 104.

Who we are

President
Camila Ortiz

Faculty Advisor
Mr. Adams (kwadams@nhhseduc8or.edu)

Types of Clubs

Are you unsure what type of club you would like to create? Here is an overview of some general types.

▶ **Social**

Social clubs serve as a place for members to meet and discuss whatever is on their minds. You might create a social club to socialize and have fun. Unlike most other clubs, the main focus is the people within a club.

▶ **Honors**

An honors club connects people who excel in similar subject areas. Members are recognized for their achievement, and they work together to further their skills. Honor societies, in particular, celebrate academic achievement and involvement in the classroom.

▶ **Interest-Based**

Other clubs focus on a common interest and attract people who share that interest. Some examples include chess, math, fashion, art, or shop work. Sometimes club members team up to enter state or national competitions related to the club's focus.

▶ **Cause-Based**

A cause-based club brings together people who share a passion for a particular cause. These clubs launch campaigns to fight bullying, feed the hungry, save the environment, and rally for human rights.

▶ **Service-Based**

Similarly, service-based clubs, like Key Club, are set up for members to serve the needs of their communities through volunteer work. Members share an interest in community and helping others. They might volunteer at local festivals, visit senior homes, or help out at a thrift store or soup kitchen.

▶ **Event-Based**

Event-based clubs meet for specific events. A fan club might meet to cheer on their favorite team or watch their favorite TV show. A breakfast club might meet before school every Friday to eat at a local restaurant.

Your Turn Pick three types of clubs from above. Then, for each type, identify a focus of a club you might join or create.

Chapter 35
Web Projects

The desire to communicate and connect with others certainly predates the Web. Long ago, our ancestors made cave paintings, and since that time, we have progressed through many other forms, such as storytelling, the printed word, radio, and photography before reaching the Internet. The new Web technologies have given more and more people the opportunity to publish their ideas and social concerns far and wide.

In this chapter, you'll learn about setting up a Web site, contributing to a wiki, and posting to a blog. You'll also peek behind the curtain and learn some basic Web-related technologies.

You will learn . . .

- Creating Web Projects
- Building a Wiki
- Creating a Blog Post
- Understanding the Basics of CSS
- Understanding the Basics of JavaScript
- Understanding the Basics of PHP

Project Overview

Here is a quick overview of the Web projects in this chapter.

A Web Site Diagram

A Web site diagram organizes information into main topics and subtopics and shows how the pages will be linked. It also gives a visual overview of the site, so changes can be made before the writing, designing, and coding begins. (See pages 592–593.)

B HTML Structure

HTML code provides the content and structure of Web pages. It outputs text, defines hierarchies of headings, creates hyperlinks, and embeds multimedia files. HTML can be coded by hand or generated by software. (See pages 594–595.)

C Wiki

A wiki is a quick way for teams of people to create a Web site. Team members can take on separate assignments, leave one another notes, edit one another's work, and choose when to make each page public. (See pages 596–597.)

D Blog Post and Blogging Software

A blog (short for Web log) is another easy way to build a Web site. Blog posts are added to the site over time, and visitors can often leave comments. Blogging software simplifies the process of setting up and managing the blog. (See pages 598–601.)

E CSS, JavaScript, and PHP

HTML is used to build basic Web pages and sites. Cascacading Style Sheets (CSS), JavaScript, and PHP are used to add more advanced functionality to Web sites. The basics of each are explained in the final few pages of this chapter. (See pages 602–606.)

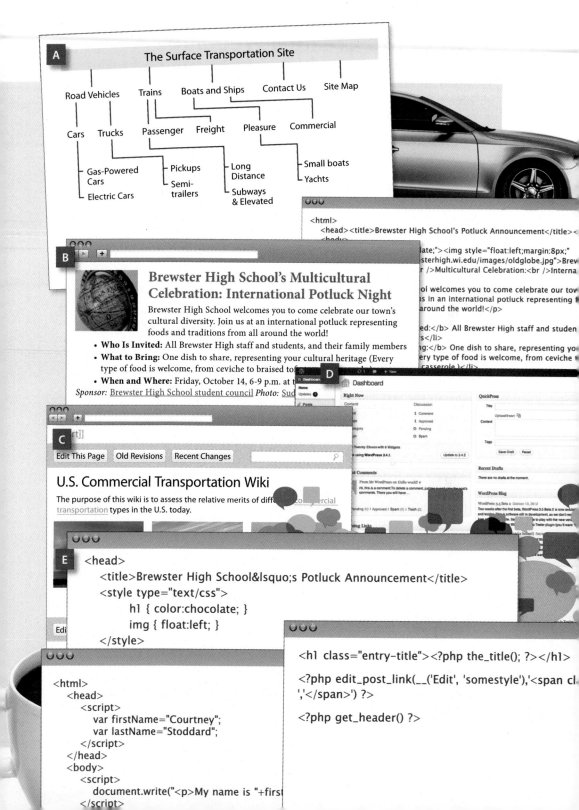

A

The Surface Transportation Site

Road Vehicles   Trains   Boats and Ships   Contact Us   Site Map

Cars   Trucks   Passenger   Freight   Pleasure   Commercial

— Gas-Powered   — Pickups   — Long   — Small boats
Cars   Distance   — Yachts
— Electric Cars   — Semi-   — Subways
                   trailers   & Elevated

```
<html>
    <head><title>Brewster High School's Potluck Announcement</title><
```

ate;"><img style="float:left;margin:8px;"
sterhigh.wi.edu/images/oldglobe.jpg">Brew
r />Multicultural Celebration:
Interna

ol welcomes you to come celebrate our tov
is in an international potluck representing
around the world!</p>

ed:</b> All Brewster High staff and studen
s</li>
ng:</b> One dish to share, representing you
ery type of food is welcome, from ceviche
casserole)</li>

B

Brewster High School's Multicultural Celebration: International Potluck Night

Brewster High School welcomes you to come celebrate our town's cultural diversity. Join us at an international potluck representing foods and traditions from all around the world!

- **Who Is Invited:** All Brewster High staff and students, and their family members
- **What to Bring:** One dish to share, representing your cultural heritage (Every type of food is welcome, from ceviche to braised tof
- **When and Where:** Friday, October 14, 6-9 p.m. at t

Sponsor: Brewster High School student council *Photo:* Sud

D

Dashboard

C

rt]]

Edit This Page   Old Revisions   Recent Changes

U.S. Commercial Transportation Wiki

The purpose of this wiki is to assess the relative merits of diff   comercial transportation types in the U.S. today.

E

```
<head>
    <title>Brewster High School&lsquo;s Potluck Announcement</title>
    <style type="text/css">
        h1 { color:chocolate; }
        img { float:left; }
    </style>
```

```html
<h1 class="entry-title"><?php the_title(); ?></h1>

<?php edit_post_link(__('Edit', 'somestyle'),'<span cl
','</span>') ?>

<?php get_header() ?>
```

```html
<html>
    <head>
        <script>
            var firstName="Courtney";
            var lastName="Stoddard";
        </script>
    </head>
    <body>
        <script>
            document.write("<p>My name is "+first
        </script>
```

Inquire To Create a Web Site

1. **Question** the situation.
   - **Subject:** What will the Web site's content be about?
   - **Purpose:** Is the Web site meant to entertain, inform, persuade, or narrate?
   - **Audience:** Who should view your site? What needs and expectations will they have?

2. **Plan** your Web site project on a planning sheet. (See page 361.)
   - **Tools:** Depending upon the scope and type of site, you may need different skills, software, and online hosting services, as well as offline equipment and software.
   - **Team:** Who will be involved in building your Web site? You may need writers, editors, artists, designers, and coders.

3. **Research** your topic and technical requirements.
   - **Topic:** Know your topic well so that you can best plan your Web site. Although Web text and images are easy to change, revising the architecture of a Web site is more difficult, and changes are likely to frustrate your visitors.

4. **Create** your Web site.
   - **Organize the information:** Create a Web site diagram, listing the site's topics and subtopics.
   - **Generate the text:** For a formal site, write and arrange all your text before posting it online. A less formal site can be created one page at a time, as you go, and can be expanded indefinitely.
   - **Prepare the multimedia:** Gather and edit any images, video, and audio to be included in your Web site.
   - **Generate the code:** Depending on the situation, you may wish to create the code by hand or by using software. (For more information on using software to create Web sites, visit thoughtfullearning.com/h592.)

5. **Improve** the Web site.
   - **Evaluate** your Web site. Does it adequately cover its **subject**? Does it achieve its **purpose**? Does it satisfy the **audience**'s needs?
   - **Revise** your Web site as necessary.
      Cut sections and media that do not help you reach your goal.
      Reorder material as needed.
      Redo weak parts.
      Add missing information.
   - **Perfect** the Web site.

6. **Present** your Web site by promoting it through social media (see pages 269–290) and among your contacts offline.

Example Web Site Diagram

The first step in creating a Web site is organizing the information you want to present using a diagram. Here is an example Web site diagram for a multi-page site about modern surface transportation:

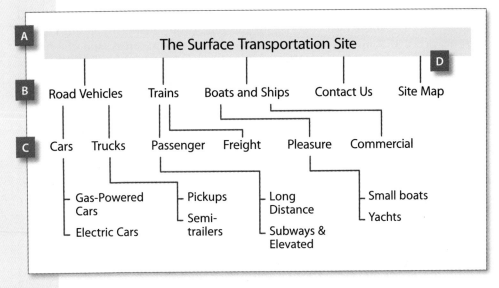

A The **home page** introduces visitors to the site and provides a menu of its contents. Home pages should be clearly organized so visitors can easily understand the Web site's purpose and where to find more information about each topic.

B Each **main topic** introduces a section of the site. For example, an author's site might have several sections—a list of published works, a blog, a schedule of appearances, a bio or press sheet, and so on.

C Each **subtopic** explores part of a main topic. An author's list of published works, for instance, may devote a page to each book, describing it and linking the visitor to a purchase site.

D A **site map** usually offers a list of pages on the site, each item being a clickable link to its own page. Site maps are a useful way for visitors to quickly locate the information they want.

Making a Web Page with HTML

Most pages on the World Wide Web are created using HTML (Hypertext Markup Language). There are many software programs that generate the HTML code for you, but it helps to be familiar with some basic HTML tags.

1. HTML tags are indicated by angle brackets: <html>, for example.
2. Most HTML tags come in pairs, such as <b>**bold text**</b>, to signal where their effect begins and ends. (The / marks the closing tag.)
3. Some tags are single—such as <br /> for line break, and <hr /> for horizontal rule. (Beginning and ending are in the same tag.)

Common HTML Tags

- <html> tags tell browsers that this is a Web page.
- <head> tags indicate hidden code such as page title, page description, JavaScript functions (see pages 604–605), and other such information.
- <title> tags set the text of the title bar in the browser.
- <body> tags hold the part of the page displayed in the browser.
- <h1> tags set a level-one heading. Heading tags range from <h1>, the largest, to <h6>, the smallest.
- <img src=""/> places an image. (The location of the image is placed between the quotation marks.)
-
 inserts a line break.
- <p> tags enclose a paragraph.
- <ol> tags start and end an ordered list. (The order is numbered by default, but letters and other options are also possible.)
- <ul> tags start and end an unordered (bulleted) list.
- <li> tags set a bulleted or numbered list item, depending on list type.
- <b> tags indicate bold text.
- <i> tags indicate italic text.
- <em> tags mean "emphasis" and typically display as italic.
- <strong> tags mean "strong emphasis" and typically display as bold.
- <pre> tags mean "preformatted." Text between these tags keeps its line breaks, spacing, and indentation.
- <a href=""> tags set a link (or anchor). The href defines the destination.
- <script> tags in the head section of a page allow insertion of JavaScript and other client-side (see pages 604–605) programming code.
- <meta> tags in the page head hold keywords and descriptions for search engines.
- <style> tags in the page head hold CSS code. (See pages 602–603.)
- <span> tags are used to style a section of content with CSS.
- <div> tags can be used to assign CSS style or apply JavaScript behaviors.

Your Turn Use the information on this page and the next to code your own Web page. Remember to credit any media you use. (See pages 392–403.)

Example Web Page

○ ○ ○   Brewster High School's Potluck Announcement

◄ ► [+]

 # Brewster High School's Multicultural Celebration: International Potluck Night

Brewster High School welcomes you to come celebrate our town's cultural diversity. Join us at an international potluck representing foods and traditions from all around the world!

- **Who Is Invited:** All Brewster High staff and students, and their family members
- **What to Bring:** One dish to share, representing your cultural heritage (Every type of food is welcome, from ceviche to braised tofu to tuna casserole.)
- **When and Where:** Friday, October 14, 6-9 p.m. at the High School Cafeteria

Sponsor: <u>Brewster High School student council</u> *Photo:* <u>Sudhamshu</u>

Example Page Code

A The \<h1\> tags set the level-one heading text. (Note that the heading image and text are styled using "inline CSS," explained on page 602.)

B The \<ul\> and \<li\> tags set the unordered (bulleted) list.

C The \<a href=""\> tags set the hypertext link.

○ ○ ○

```
<html>
    <head><title>Brewster High School's Potluck Announcement</title></head>
    <body>
```
A
```
        <h1 style="color:chocolate;"><img style="float:left;margin:8px;"
        src="http://brewsterroosterhigh.wi.edu/images/oldglobe.jpg">Brewster
        High School&rsquo;s<br />Multicultural Celebration:<br />International
        Potluck Night</h1>
        <p>Brewster High School welcomes you to come celebrate our town's
        cultural diversity. Join us in an international potluck representing foods
        and traditions from all around the world!</p>
        <ul>
```
B
```
            <li><b>Who Is Invited:</b> All Brewster High staff and students, and
            their family members</li>
            <li><b>What to Bring:</b> One dish to share, representing your
            cultural heritage (Every type of food is welcome, from ceviche to
            braised tofu to tuna casserole.)</li>
            <li><b>When and Where:</b> Friday, October 14, 6-9 p.m. at the High
            School Cafeteria</li>
        </ul>
        <p><i>Sponsor:</i> <a href="http://brewsterroosterhigh.wi.edu/
        studentcouncil.htm">Brewster High School student council</a> <i>Photo:</i>
```
C
```
        <a href="http://www.flickr.com/photos/sudhamshu/">Sudhamshu</a></p>
    </body>
</html>
```

Building a Wiki

A wiki is a Web site that many people build together using a Web browser. Wikis provide editing tools to contributors who are signed in, and then display the finished pages to the public afterward. You've probably heard of the Wikipedia site, an online encyclopedia edited by volunteers around the world. The Web has other specialized wikis, from medical dictionaries to recipe collections to game sites. You might use a wiki to brainstorm ideas (with links to related information), assemble a group report, publish a Web site, compose an instruction manual, and so on.

Example Class Project Wiki Pages

A This is the first page of a wiki.

B Click to edit the page.

C These are embedded images.

D Green words are clickable links.

E Red words are links to planned pages that don't yet exist.

A [[start]]

B Edit This Page | Old Revisions | Recent Changes

U.S. Commercial Transportation Wiki

The purpose of this wiki is to assess the relative merits of different commercial transportation types in the U.S. today.

C

D Ground Transport | **E** Water Transport | Air Transport

Edit This Page | Old Revisions | Recent Changes | Back | Log Out

Your Turn In a small group, choose a topic suitable for a 6- to 12-page wiki. Build your wiki and then write a group report detailing what was learned from the process. What advice or "best practices" can you share with other wiki builders? Add the report to your wiki as an "About This Project" page.

Example Class Project Wiki Pages (cont.)

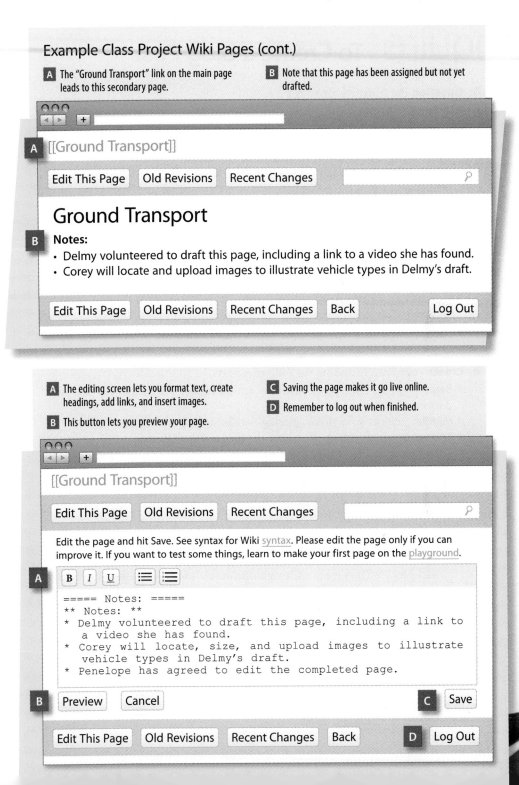

A The "Ground Transport" link on the main page leads to this secondary page.

B Note that this page has been assigned but not yet drafted.

A [[Ground Transport]]

| Edit This Page | Old Revisions | Recent Changes | 🔍 |

Ground Transport

B **Notes:**
- Delmy volunteered to draft this page, including a link to a video she has found.
- Corey will locate and upload images to illustrate vehicle types in Delmy's draft.

| Edit This Page | Old Revisions | Recent Changes | Back | Log Out |

A The editing screen lets you format text, create headings, add links, and insert images.

B This button lets you preview your page.

C Saving the page makes it go live online.

D Remember to log out when finished.

[[Ground Transport]]

| Edit This Page | Old Revisions | Recent Changes | 🔍 |

Edit the page and hit Save. See syntax for Wiki syntax. Please edit the page only if you can improve it. If you want to test some things, learn to make your first page on the playground.

A **B** *I* U ☰ ☰

```
===== Notes: =====
** Notes: **
* Delmy volunteered to draft this page, including a link to
  a video she has found.
* Corey will locate, size, and upload images to illustrate
  vehicle types in Delmy's draft.
* Penelope has agreed to edit the completed page.
```

B | Preview | Cancel | **C** | Save |

| Edit This Page | Old Revisions | Recent Changes | Back | **D** | Log Out |

Inquire | To Create a Blog Post

1. **Question** the situation for your post.
   - **Subject:** What do you want to write about? What specific focus will you have? What main point do you want to express?
   - **Purpose:** Why are you making a post? Are you explaining, persuading, entertaining? How do you want readers to respond?
   - **Audience:** Who will read the post? What will readers gain? What do you want readers to do with the information?

2. **Plan** your blog post by brainstorming, clustering, or using other prewriting activities.
   - **Site:** Will you be posting on your own blog? Will you post on a classroom blog? What other social media could help promote the posting?

3. **Research** your topic.
   - **Gather** information about your topic, watching for links you can provide to other articles or videos.
   - **Focus** your ideas about the topic with a thesis statement.
   - **Organize** the details with a quick list.

4. **Create** your post, including the following parts.
   - **Beginning:** Get the reader's attention and introduce your topic. Provide your thesis up front, or build to it.
   - **Middle:** Support your thesis, placing details in the best order.
   - **Ending:** Wrap up your post, giving the reader a final thought.
   - **Title:** Create an interesting title that will work well on Twitter, Facebook, and other social media. (You can use these services to promote your post.)
   - **Visuals:** Include an attention-getting image.
   - **Links:** Include links to related articles, videos, or pages in the blog.

5. **Improve** your post.
   - **Evaluate** the post.
      Does the post fulfill your purpose? Does it have an interesting topic and clear focus? Does it have the right impact? Will readers respond well to it?
   - **Revise** your post.
      Remove ideas and details that aren't needed.
      Rearrange ideas so that they are in the best order.
      Rework parts (beginning, middle, or ending) that don't work.
      Add new details that help you achieve your goal.
   - **Perfect** your post, checking it for errors.

6. **Present** your post and send the link via other social media. Respond to readers who leave comments on the post.

Sample Blog Post

The following blog post on the Thoughtful Learning Web site deals with two different types of mindsets and their impact on learning.

This blog post is one of a series on a company Web site.

The title addresses the audience (teachers) and uses key words to identify the contents.

Graphics and tables help to express ideas clearly.

Links connect to other articles and resources.

A table sorts information, making it accessible.

9:08 AM

Thoughtful Learning

Home | Our Story | Blog | Store

Thoughtful Learning Blog >

Creating a Growth Mindset in Your Students

▶ Submitted by King on Tue, 2012-03-27 00:00   Click to Print

Belief that you can become smarter and more talented opens the doorways to success. That's what twenty years of research has shown Carol Dweck of Stanford University. She has identified two opposing beliefs about intelligence and talent, beliefs that strongly impact our ability to learn.

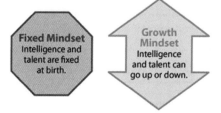

Fixed Mindset Intelligence and talent are fixed at birth.

Growth Mindset Intelligence and talent can go up or down.

Though the fixed mindset has traditionally held sway, many recent studies show that the growth mindset better represents our abilities. Our brains are much more elastic than previously thought, constantly growing new connections. IQ and talent are not fixed, but are mutable based on experience and attitude.

In her book *Mindset*, Dweck outlines the dramatic effect that these opposing beliefs have on learners:

Fixed Mindset	Growth Mindset
Wants to **prove** intelligence or talent.	Wants to **improve** intelligence or talent.
Avoids challenges for fear of failure.	Engages challenges to improve.
Gives up in the face of tough obstacles.	Persists in overcoming obstacles.
Avoids hard labor.	Sees labor as the path to success.
Treats criticism as an attack.	Treats criticism as an opportunity.
Feels threatened by others' success.	Feels inspired by others' success.

Using Blogging Software

A blog (short for *Web log*) was originally a type of personal journal shared online. Nowadays, blog applications are often used as content-management systems (CMS), as are wiki applications. One popular open-source blog application is WordPress. You can build a blog for free at WordPress.com or install WordPress on your own space, if your Web host allows. (Check with your Internet service provider or do a search for "domain hosting.")

The Blog Dashboard

The WordPress administrator screen, shown in a photo on the next page, is called the dashboard. Other blog applications have similar screens. Each term in the left-hand column links to another page of the dashboard where you can control features of the blog. These terms are defined here:

- **Home:** Home is the main screen of the dashboard.
- **Updates:** This link allows you to install updates and "plugins" (see below) to the blog application.
- **Posts:** Blogs are designed to list posts one after another on a Web page. The newest post appears at the top, and others follow in reverse time order. Posts are often tagged by category to help visitors navigate the site.
- **Media:** This accesses a control panel for images, audio, and video you may add to the blog.
- **Links:** Most blogs provide a sidebar that lists other recommended sites. WordPress "Links" lets you edit the list of links your visitors will see.
- **Pages:** This link is a control panel for pages containing copy that doesn't change often, like an "About Me" page.
- **Comments:** Many blogs allow visitors to post comments. The "Comments" control panel lets you approve, delete, or edit these.
- **Appearance:** This link is a style control panel. From here you can install graphic "themes," select sidebar "widgets," and even edit the CSS.
- **Plugins:** These are add-on bits of code you install to add functions to your blog—live chat pages, for example.
- **Users:** The administrator of a blog has full control-panel access. Other people can be given levels of control: editor, author, or contributor.
- **Tools:** These are special maintenance features for your site.
- **Settings:** The "Settings" link offers separate panels for controlling everything from the date and time display to the size of your entry space.

In the **middle column**, you will find an overview of your blog's contents, including the number of posts, pages, categories, the current theme installed, and so on.

At the top of the **right column** is a box for quickly creating a new blog post. Below that you will find a list of unpublished drafts and then a block of stats to help you determine the most visited and popular parts of your site.

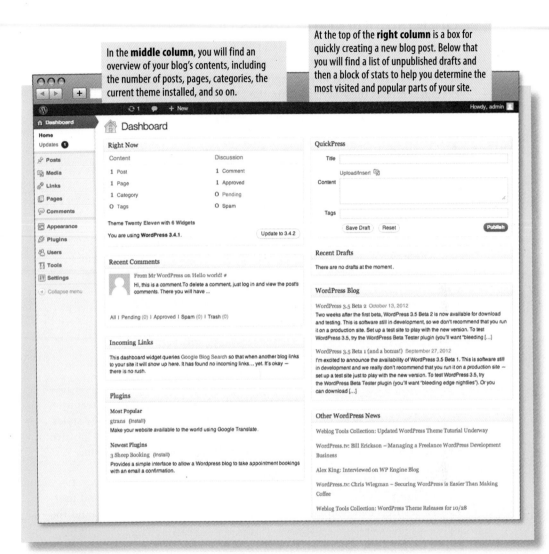

Your Turn Using what you have learned so far about Web-page design, site planning, and blogs, build your own blog. Use it to post reviews of books, films, music, and games.

Other Open-Source Blog Applications

Besides the WordPress application, consider using Serendipity (available from s9y. org) and Simple PHP Blog (from sourceforge.net/projects/sphpblog/). Both are free open-source programs. The last has the added advantage of saving to a text file, or "flat database," instead of requiring a database server. You will also find other free blog *hosts* online, including LiveJournal.com, Blogger.com, Blogster. com, Tumblr.com, and Yahoo 360.

Understanding the Basics of CSS

On page 595, the HTML embeds CSS (Cascading Style Sheets) commands into h1 and img tags to indicate heading style (style="color:chocolate;" and style="float:left;"). This way of applying styles is called "inline" CSS. The next example embeds these styles within the HTML document head:

```
<head>
   <title>Brewster High School&lsquo;s Potluck Announcement</title>
   <style type="text/css">
        h1 { color:chocolate; }
        img { float:left; }
   </style>
</head>
```

These two examples use a separate document called from the head:

```
<head>                                  <head>
   <link rel="stylesheet" type="text/      <style type="text/css">
   css" href="http://some.url/folder/         @import url(http://some.url/
   file.css">                                 folder/file.css);
</head>                                     </style>
                                        </head>
```

In CSS, *cascading* means your browser checks any *external* style sheet first, then styles in the head of the current document, and then any *inline* styles. If styles contradict, inline styles override styles in the head, which in turn override external styles. (See thoughtfullearning.com/h602 to learn more.)

▶ CSS and HTML Measurements

Differences in screen size, screen resolution, browser behavior, and user-chosen settings can complicate on-screen layout. It helps to understand the following measurement types used in CSS and HTML code.

- **px:** Short for "pixels," the glowing dots in a video screen. Each pixel has three components—red, green, and blue.
- **dpi:** Short for "dots per inch," or the number of pixels in one inch. Most computer monitors have a resolution of 72 dpi; some have 96 dpi.
- **in, cm, mm:** Short for "inches," "centimeters," and "millimeters" respectively. (**Note:** They seldom display accurately on-screen.)
- **pt, pc:** Typographical abbreviations for "points" and "picas." An inch holds 72 points or 6 picas. (Again, on-screen display may vary.)
- **em, ex:** Typographical abbreviations for changes to the "em-height" and "x-height" of the current font family. (See page 603.)
- **%:** Used with fonts to show a percentage change from the base font. If p { font:10pt; }, then h1 { font:120%; } would make the h1 size 12pt.

▶ Height and Width

As some Web pages load, the text jumps around to make room for images as they appear. You can avoid this on your pages by setting a *height* and *width* for images and other "block-level elements" such as p, h1 through h6, and div.

▶ Padding and Margin

Padding adds space *to* an object; *margin* adds room *around* it. Browsers apply both in "top, right, bottom, left" order, so padding:10px,5px,10px,5px; adds 10 pixels of space above and below, with 5 pixels on right and left. (Abbreviating to padding:10px,5px; sets top *and* bottom to 10, left *and* right to 5, while margin:10px; sets all four margins to 10.)

▶ Font Characteristics

Font is a typographical term for a collection of letters, numbers, and symbols in a particular style, such as *Apple Chancery*, Bookman Old Style, Courier, and so on. In CSS, font styles can be assigned to nearly any HTML tags that can surround text, including body, p, h1 and other header tags, a, span, and div.

- **Font-family** can be specific (like "Comic Sans") or generic (serif, sans-serif, or monospace). Not all computers support all fonts, so you'll often see a declaration like font-family { "Times New Roman", Times, Serif; }, allowing those without the first to default to another. (*Note:* Font names with spaces must use quotation marks.)
- **Font-style** sets normal, italic, or oblique (a leaning, pseudo-italic style).
- **Font-size** determines the size in any of several different measurements.
- **Font-variant** is used to set "small-caps."
- **Font-weight** can make a font "bold," "bolder," or "lighter" or can be set to any of nine values from "100" (lightest) to "900" (boldest).
- **Font** is the catchall declaration, allowing any or all of these to be set at once (e.g., font { "Times New Roman", Times, Serif; 24pt; small–caps; bold; }).

▶ Classes (.) and IDs (#)

In CSS, *classes* and *ids* make coding easier.

- **Classes** group similar items: .left { float:left; padding:5px,20px,5px,5px; } and .right { float:right; padding:5px,5px,5px,20px; } in the page head would let us use <img class="left" src="some.url"> and <img class="right" src="some.url"> on the page.
- **IDs** are for individual items. You could set all images right with img { float:right; } in the head, then add #firstimg { float:left; } in the head to define an exception, and use <img id="firstimg" src="some.url"> to apply that exception in the body.

Your Turn Using what you've learned about HTML and CSS, experiment with the sample code from page 595, changing content and layout. As an added challenge, can you replace the image?

Understanding the Basics of JavaScript

JavaScript is one of the more popular programming languages on the Web. It is an "object-oriented" language, applying *actions* (such as functions) to *objects* (such as images, paragraphs, and forms).

```
<html>
  <body>
    <script>
      document.write("<p>My name is Courtney Stoddard.</p>");
    </script>
  </body>
</html>
```

Example 1: In this case, "document" (the HTML page) is the object, and "write()" is the action.

```
<html>
  <head>
    <script>
      var firstName="Courtney";
      var lastName="Stoddard";
    </script>
  </head>
  <body>
    <script>
      document.write("<p>My name is "+firstName+" "+lastName+".</p>");
    </script>
  </body>
</html>
```

Example 2: JavaScript often uses variables to assign values to a statement.

Save each of the above code examples as HTML files and open them with your web browser. The output is the same: My name is Courtney Stoddard.

```
<html>
  <head>
    <script>
      function popUpName() {
        var firstName=document.nameForm.myFirstName.value;
        var lastName=document.nameForm.myLastName.value;
        alert("My name is "+firstName+" "+lastName+".");
      }
    </script>
  </head>
  <body>
    <form name="nameForm">
      <p>First name: <input type="text" name="myFirstName"></p>
      <p>Last name: <input type="text" name="myLastName"></p>
      <p><input type="submit" onClick="popUpName();"></p>
    </form>
  </body>
</html>
```

Example 3: Variables are most useful when the person viewing the page can set the value, using a form. Here, the onClick action calls the popUpName(); function, which inserts the current values of firstName and lastName into an alert() message.

JavaScript Syntax

Viewing the sample code on the previous page, you'll notice a few important features of JavaScript syntax:

- <script> </script> tags surround JavaScript code in most cases. (Like CSS, a few JavaScript statements can be included inline.) Generally, JavaScript is placed in the page head (to load into the browser before the page displays).
- A **semicolon** signals the end of a JavaScript declaration.
- **Identifiers** are functions, variables, and label names (e.g., popUpName(), firstName, and myFirstName on the previous page).
- New **functions** and **variables** must be specifically declared and defined. (Some functions, such as write() and alert() are prebuilt into JavaScript.)
- **Case sensitivity** means that myName and myname and MyName are all different entities. Common practice is to begin with a lowercase letter and capitalize the first letter of embedded words (e.g., myLastName).
- **Curly braces** {} surround the content of new functions.
- **Straight quotation marks** indicate text "strings." These may be single (') or double (").
- Some **keywords** (such as if, else, true, and false) are reserved for special use.
- Many **operators** have predefined roles in JavaScript. (On the previous page, + is used to "concatenate," or link together, strings and variables. A . can also concatenate, while a + can add numbers, a - subtract them, a / divide them, a * multiply them, and so on.)

Common Uses of JavaScript

The main purpose of client-side JavaScript is to reduce the number of times a browser must connect to a server. This reduces Web traffic while improving the user's experience. JavaScript is also commonly used to complete the following actions:

- **Deliver specific formatting.** JavaScript is often employed to read your browser and computer and choose the most suitable format, such as for a smartphone.
- **Check form elements,** ensuring that nothing essential is left blank, making calculations, and so on.
- **Swap images** in menus, buttons, and games. If you point your mouse cursor at an image, and that image changes, chances are JavaScript did the work.
- **Autocomplete** search boxes, making suggestions for keywords as you type.

Your Turn Starting with the code at the bottom of page 604, create a page with an alert message that includes both name and age. You'll need to add a third <input> tag to the form, declare a third variable to read it, and add new text in the function's alert box.

Understanding the Basics of PHP

Just as JavaScript is one of the most popular client-side programming languages, PHP is one of the most popular server-side languages. As open-source software, it is used in countless Web applications, including blogging applications like WordPress. If you log into WordPress as administrator and select "Appearance," then "Editor," and then "Page template" (page.php), you'll notice a few significant details about PHP:

- **.php** in the file name tells the server to process the file as PHP code rather than straight HTML.
- <?php indicates the beginning of a section of PHP code in a file.
- ?> indicates the end of a section of PHP code in a file.

▶ You'll also notice that sometimes PHP is used to insert information within an HTML tag:	`<h1 class="entry-title"><?php the_title(); ?></h1>`
▶ Sometimes it outputs an HTML tag, as in the case of this span tag:	`<?php edit_post_link(__('Edit', 'somestyle'),'<span class="edit-link">','</span>') ?>`
▶ And sometimes it imports another document entirely:	`<?php get_header() ?>`

PHP for Templates

Server-side code is often used to create a new HTML document from separate files on the spot. Rather than save every blog page as an individual file, PHP can draw a post from a database—with author name, creation date, and so on—and output it all within an HTML template. Shopping sites do a similar thing with products' names, descriptions, images, and current prices.

PHP for Security

Because its work is done on the server, PHP code is not visible to the end user. This helps to safeguard information such as details of database access, visitor addresses, credit card numbers, and so on. To discover just how different a PHP file is from the code it delivers to the browser, visit any page on your blog, choose "View Source" from the browser menu bar, and compare what you see there with what you see as administrator in the blog dashboard.

Your Turn

1. In your WordPress blog (or other PHP application), choose a place in the footer to insert a current-year copyright statement: Copyright © <?php echo date("Y")?> Explain what each part of that code does.

2. Choose blog elements that you wish to hide (perhaps the RSS block or the archives section) and use PHP comment tags to do so (<?php /* to start hiding and */ ?> to end). Visit your blog with your browser to check the results.

Index